EQUAL JUSTICE UNDER LAW

BY EVAN THOMAS

First: Sandra Day O'Connor

Being Nixon

Ike's Bluff

The War Lovers

Sea of Thunder

John Paul Jones

Robert Kennedy

The Very Best Men

The Man to See

The Wise Men (WITH WALTER ISAACSON)

FIRST

FIRST

SANDRA DAY O'CONNOR

EVAN THOMAS

RANDOM HOUSE
New York

Published in the United States by Random House, an imprint and
division of Penguin Random House LLC, New York.

RANDOM HOUSE and the HOUSE colophon are registered trademarks
of Penguin Random House LLC.

LIBRARY OF CONGRESS CATALOGING-IN-PUBLICATION DATA
Names: Thomas, Evan, author.
Title: First : Sandra Day O'Connor / Evan Thomas.
Description: New York : Random House, 2019. | Includes
bibliographical references and index.
Identifiers: LCCN 2018040502| ISBN 9780399589287 (hardback) |
ISBN 9780399589294 (ebook)
Subjects: LCSH: O'Connor, Sandra Day, 1930– | Women judges—
United States—Biography. | United States. Supreme Court—Officials
and employees—Biography. | BISAC: BIOGRAPHY &
AUTOBIOGRAPHY / Women. | LAW / Legal History. | HISTORY /
United States / 20th Century.
Classification: LCC KF8745.025 T46 2019 | DDC 347.73/2634 [B] —dc23
LC record available at https://lccn.loc.gov/2018040502

Printed in the United States of America on acid-free paper

randomhousebooks.com

2 4 6 8 9 7 5 3 1

FIRST EDITION

ENDPAPERS: © iStock/AdamParent

Book design by Simon M. Sullivan

To our granddaughter, Joanna

CONTENTS

Prologue · xi

CHAPTER ONE
LAZY B · *3*

CHAPTER TWO
STANFORD · *25*

CHAPTER THREE
THE GOLDEN COUPLE · *47*

CHAPTER FOUR
MAJORITY LEADER · *71*

CHAPTER FIVE
ARIZONA JUDGE · *101*

CHAPTER SIX
THE PRESIDENT CALLS · *121*

CHAPTER SEVEN
INSIDE THE MARBLE PALACE · *147*

CHAPTER EIGHT
SCRUTINY · *175*

CHAPTER NINE
FWOTSC · 197

CHAPTER TEN
CANCER · 227

CHAPTER ELEVEN
A WOMAN'S ROLE · 253

CHAPTER TWELVE
CIVIC RELIGION · 283

CHAPTER THIRTEEN
BUSH V. GORE · 307

CHAPTER FOURTEEN
AFFIRMATIVE ACTION · 335

CHAPTER FIFTEEN
END GAME · 359

CHAPTER SIXTEEN
LABOR OF LOVE · 385

Acknowledgments · 407
Notes · 413
Bibliography · 445
Illustration List and Credits · 449
Index · 453

PROLOGUE

On horseback at the Lazy B. Sandra learned to brand a calf and fire a rifle before she was ten, and to drive a truck as soon as she could see over the dashboard.

I N 1981, WHEN Ronald Reagan nominated Sandra Day O'Connor to become the first female justice on the Supreme Court, the bulletin led every TV news broadcast and major newspaper in the country and many abroad. The cover of *Time* magazine read simply JUSTICE—AT LAST.

O'Connor's confirmation hearing that September quickly became a huge media event. There were more requests for press credentials than there had been for the Senate Watergate Committee hearings in 1973. A new media institution—cable TV—carried the hearings live, a first for a judicial nomination. Tens of millions of people saw and heard a composed, radiant, hazel-eyed woman with a broad gap-toothed smile and unusually large hands testify for three days before middle-aged men who seemed not quite sure whether to interrogate her or open the door for her. The vote to confirm her was unanimous.[1]

Nearly sixteen years before Madeleine Albright became secretary of state, a dozen years before Ruth Bader Ginsburg joined O'Connor on the bench, two years before Sally Ride flew in space, Sandra O'Connor entered the proverbial "room where it happens." No woman had ever sat in one of the nine chairs at the mahogany table in the oak-paneled conference room where the justices of the United States Supreme Court meet to rule on the law of the land. By the 1980s, women had begun to break through gender barriers in the professions, as well as in the academy and the military, but none had achieved such a position of eminence and public power. The law had been an especially male domain. When she graduated from Stanford Law School in 1952, established law firms were not hiring woman lawyers, even if, like O'Connor, they had graduated near the top of their class.

O'Connor did not regard herself as a revolutionary. Her success was owed in no small part to her ability to marry ambition to restraint. She was "a person for all seasons," said Ronald Reagan when he nominated her for the Court. She saw herself as a bridge between an era where women were protected and submissive toward an era of true equality between the sexes. At the same time, she saw that women might have to work twice as hard to get ahead; that men might be threatened or at the very least unsure about the new order; and that there was no use fretting about it. She understood that she was being closely watched. "It's good to be first," she liked to say to her law clerks. "But you don't want to be the last."

IN HER CHAMBERS at the Supreme Court that autumn of 1981, the mail poured in by the truckload—tens of thousands of letters, many supportive, some not. A few were from angry men who sent naked pictures of themselves. O'Connor was taken aback by this ugly, primitive protest against the presence of a woman on the Court, but she had learned how to shrug off insults, snubs, and innuendo and focus on the job at hand.

At the traditional opening of the Court term, on the first Monday in October, O'Connor took her place at the end of the long mahogany bench above where the lawyers would argue. As the first case was presented, the other justices immediately began firing questions at the lawyer standing at the lectern ten feet away. For thirty minutes, as the legal arguments and questions flew back and forth in a complex case involving oil leasing, she remained silent. "Shall I ask my first question?" O'Connor wondered. "I know the press is waiting—All are poised to hear me," she wrote later that day, re-creating the scene in her journal. From her seat on the high bench, she began to ask a question, but almost immediately the lawyer talked over her. "He is loud and harsh," O'Connor wrote, "and says he wants to finish what he is saying. I feel 'put down.'"

She would not feel that way for long. She was, in a word, tough. She could be emotional; she laughed easily and was not ashamed to cry in private, though never over embarrassment or small slights. But she refused to brood and instead forged ahead. She knew she was smarter than most (sometimes all) of the men she worked with, but she never felt the need to show it.

"The Court is large, solemn. I get lost at first," she wrote in her journal on September 28, 1981. "It is hard to get used to the title of 'Justice.'" A few of the other justices seemed "genuinely glad to have me there," she wrote. Others seemed guarded, not only around her but even around each other. At the regularly scheduled lunch in the justices' formal dining room that week, only four of her colleagues—Chief Justice Burger and Justices Stevens, Brennan, and Blackmun—showed up. "The room is cold," O'Connor wrote.

O'Connor soon set about warming it up. The justices, she was surprised to discover, rarely spoke to one another; they preferred to communicate by memo. So she made it her custom to cajole her brethren into attending the weekly lunches, sometimes just sitting in their offices until they agreed to come along. She had long appreciated the simple truth that if people get to know each other in a relaxed setting, they are more likely to find common ground. As the first female majority leader of a state senate, in Arizona during the early 1970s, she had from time to time gathered her colleagues from both political parties around her swimming pool and plied them with Mexican food (and "beer, plenty of beer," she recalled). She needed to know them and how they thought. She needed them to vote for her bills.

As the Court's newest justice, she wanted to show her colleagues that she belonged. In late October, three weeks after the term began, Justice Lewis Powell wrote his children that O'Connor was "off to an impressive start. It is quite evident that she is intellectually up to the work of the Court." Slowly, a little uncertainly, the other justices came to embrace her. In January, O'Connor attended the president's State of the Union address to Congress and to a national TV audience. Along with the other justices, she sat in the first row. To avoid appearing partisan, the justices had decided not to applaud when the audience did. When President Reagan extolled from the podium his appointment of the first woman to the Supreme Court, Sandra wrote in her journal, "As he spoke he looked at me and smiled—with pride. I wanted to hug him but—kept quiet. Some senator behind me tapped me on the shoulder and said, 'You can clap at that!'—and my colleagues on the Court did!"

That March, at the annual Gridiron Dinner, a Washington rite attended by top journalists, politicians, and policy makers, the revelers sang a song about her—"I'm one of the girls who's one of the boys." The advice columnist Ann Landers told the new justice to shorten her skirts or lengthen her robe, asking if it was true that she still wore her robe from the Arizona Court of Appeals. "'Indeed it was,' I said, gleefully," O'Connor wrote in her journal. "She was a little shocked! I explained I couldn't bear to throw out old clothes."

Talking to one of her law clerks in the mid-1990s, O'Connor remarked that when Ruth Bader Ginsburg joined her on the Supreme Court in 1993, she was glad to have another woman because then the press could stop commenting on her clothes when she went out at night. O'Connor's remark was a light aside. In another age, she might have complained more fiercely about double standards, about how women could be trivialized, about how the media never obsessed about what *men* wore.

But that was not her way. She would walk away from fights she deemed unnecessary, while never shying away from the important ones. She knew when to tease, when to flatter, and when to punch the bully in the nose. She wanted to set an example for her young law clerks, the twentysomethings hired from the top of their law school classes to work for a year in the justices' chambers, about how to carry yourself and how to help others. She made sure half of her clerks were women. She wanted them to become judges, top-level lawyers, and professors, and they did.[2]

O'CONNOR WAS THE most powerful Supreme Court justice of her time. For most of her twenty-four-plus years on the Court, from October 1981 to January 2006, she was the controlling vote on many of the great societal issues, including abortion, affirmative action, and religious freedom, so much so that the press came to call it the O'Connor Court. She was a global ambassador for the rule of law, and a role model for a generation of young women who saw her break the glass ceiling and were inspired to believe they could do the same.

In many speeches, O'Connor read from an old poem about a man on a pilgrimage who successfully journeys through a canyon, then returns to build a bridge over it.

> *"Old man," said a fellow pilgrim near,*
> *"You are wasting strength with building here;*
> *Your journey will end with the ending day;*
> *You never again must pass this way;*
> *You have crossed the chasm, deep and wide—*
> *Why build you the bridge at the eventide?"*

So others may cross, the old man replied. That was O'Connor's answer, too. She was never absolutist in the cause of women's rights—or any other cause—in part because she was always practical. She knew she could do more good by her own acts and case by case, by laying a foundation for others to build on. She understood that the justices do not always have the last word, that they should more often set flexible standards than dictate hard-and-fast rules. She saw the three branches of government as necessary partners in a great civic conversation. About her civic duty, she was adamant. She cherished the system of government that gave us the rule of law, and she devoted her life to supporting and preserving it.

Confident but humble, and a born politician, she effectively controlled the Court because she was a moderate who believed in compromise. Also, she liked power and knew how to use it. At an awards ceremony in 2016, I watched her as she worked a room of 150 people, charming them one by one. None knew that she had been diagnosed with dementia, probably Alzheimer's. She was, then as before, embracing, exuberant, and warm.

"Never complain, never explain" might have been her motto. She was not one for looking back, but in a sense, she never left the Lazy B ranch, the place from which she had come. Although she lived most of her life in the city, she remained close to nature. "When in doubt, go out," she would say, as she headed off to play golf in the rain or ski in a blizzard. Every year, she dragooned her overworked clerks to walk down the National Mall with her to see the cherry blossoms blooming near the Jefferson Memorial. She knew, for that moment, they would be overwhelmed by the delicate beauty of nature in a setting of reverent grandeur. Then it was back to work.

The wide-open Southwest of her girlhood stayed with her always. As an old woman, driving with a friend through the dense Virginia countryside, she said, "I don't like it." She felt hemmed in by the tall trees lining the road. Deep in her heart, she longed for the vistas of the ranch where she had grown up.[3] She imagined the big sky and remembered the hard-earned truths of the Lazy B, where, in the unforgiving vastness of the high desert, she had learned to be at once selfless and self-reliant.

FIRST

LAZY B

"You need to expect anything out here."

Young Sandra, at about eleven, with her mother, Ada Mae, and her siblings, Alan and Ann. When she was only six, she was sent away to school in El Paso, where she lived with her grandmother. She always longed for the Lazy B.

I T TAKES A cowhand on horseback a full day to ride from one end of the Lazy B ranch to the other, across rock-strewn hills and through cactus-filled draws, over land primeval in its stony wildness. The ranch, which occupies about 250 square miles along the Arizona–New Mexico border, has its own mountain, a perfect cone visible from the chaise longue in her parents' bedroom, where Sandra Day liked to curl up to read. As a girl, Sandra would climb Round Mountain with her father, careful to avoid the rattlesnakes. The future justice could stand at the peak and see and feel the vastness and ancientness, as well as the forbidding desolation and living wonder, of her family's domain. "We thought of it as our own country," Sandra Day O'Connor recalled of the ranch that had been in the Day family for more than a century.[1]

Far-distant mountain ranges ring a swelling and undulating mesa. If the rains come in the winter, the land blooms with yellow and purple wildflowers in the spring. In the summer, a searing sun scorches the precious grass in the pastures. Volcanic hills are littered with boulders, "angry black and dark red," as O'Connor vividly described in her memoir of the Lazy B—molten lava suddenly cooled as it burst forth from earth's core. In the flatlands to the east, yucca plants stand as "sentinels" that are "weirdly beautiful." Their stalks, when dry, "make good cattle prods, or fine lances for children's war games." No river runs through the Lazy B, but the Gila River, a tepid stream most of the year, a torrent in storms, skirts the northern edge. Canyons with chalky cliffs and cottonwood trees shelter fine picnic grounds. As a girl, Sandra would climb into the dark caves of prehistoric Indians or, hair flying, gallop her horse across the open range. On clear nights, she would stand with her family "in silent awe," looking at the glittering constellations, past the sweep of the diaphanous Milky Way, into the universe beyond. Returning home from an all-day roundup in the pitch black of a moonless, cloudy night, she was guided by the tiny sparks, struck by horseshoe on rock, thrown off by the rider ahead.[2]

SANDRA DAY WAS born on March 26, 1930, in the city of El Paso, Texas, the only city close enough—four hours by train—to have a proper hospital. The Arizona ranch house to which she was brought a couple of weeks later, after the two-hundred-mile trip, was a square, four-room adobe structure. Known as Headquarters, it stood eight miles from the main road. Visitors were announced by the cloud of dust they raised. The house had no running water, indoor plumbing, or electricity. Coal gas lamps lit the rooms; the bathroom was a wooden privy 75 yards downwind from the house. Harry and Ada Mae Day and their baby daughter, Sandra, slept in the house; the ranch's four or five cowboys slept on the screened porch. Flies were everywhere. On still summer nights, when it was too hot to sleep, Sandra's parents soaked her bedsheets in cool water. "It was no country for sissies," O'Connor recalled. "We saw a lot of life and death there."[3]

Until she was nine years old, Sandra grew up as an only child. She had no neighboring playmates but also no shortage of fascinating and fearsome living creatures—animals, insects, and birds, including antelopes, javelinas, coyotes, bobcats, snakes, Gila monsters, desert tortoises, scorpions, and all manner of spiders. Most of them had teeth, horns, or poison, but Sandra tried to make some of them into pets. Until she was about four years old, Sandra liked to play with a bobcat named Bob, who would arch his back and growl around fresh meat but was otherwise reasonably domesticated, until he disappeared one night after raiding the chicken coop.*

Over the years, Sandra collected various critters, including a sparrow hawk named Sylvester, who perched watchfully in the eaves and would splatter hawk droppings in her hair, and a desert tortoise that

---

* "When I was a child, I had as a pet a cat," recalled Judge J. Harvie Wilkinson III of the Fourth Circuit Court of Appeals. "When Sandra was a child she had as a pet a *bobcat*."[4]

learned to wait by the icebox for food. "We tried keeping a baby coyote as a pet but learned that what the cowboys said was true: you cannot make a pet of a coyote," Sandra recalled.[5]

Aside from the cattle, the animals that mattered most were the horses. The cowboys gave them colorful names: Hysterectomy ("a great horse. She would carry a cowboy all day," Sandra remembered), Scarhead, Swastika, Idiot, Hemorrhoid ("After riding him all day, you felt tired and bruised"), and Hell Bitch, who turned out to be a gentle horse, once broken. Sandra's favorite was Chico. Unlike most horses, Chico would not run away after his rider was thrown or fell off, but rather wait patiently for Sandra to climb back on. In *Lazy B*, Sandra described what it was like to ride Chico as a young girl:

> We moved together. I felt the horse's every move. I was aware of his breath, his sweat. When he stopped to pee, the strong smell of urine enveloped us, and drops of liquid splattered my boots. When he expelled gas, I heard and felt it. I often talked to my horse while riding.[6]

Often, during the heat of the day, Sandra would lie on the chaise in her parents' bedroom, a book in her hands. Reading was the Day family pastime. Hungry for news of the world beyond his domain, Harry Day pored over week-old copies of the *Los Angeles Times, Time, U.S. News & World Report, Fortune*. His wife, Ada Mae, read *Vogue, The New Yorker, House Beautiful, The Saturday Evening Post*. Copies of *National Geographic* were stacked in piles in the corner or stuffed under the beds. As a girl, Sandra read *The Book of Knowledge, Black Beauty, Mary Poppins*. Her favorite books were the Nancy Drew series, about a girl detective who wore skirts, was confident and curious, and adored her powerful lawyer father.[7]

One day, while she was reading a Nancy Drew mystery, her father interrupted her, saying, "Sandra, you'd better get your nose out of that book and come with me. I want to show you something."

Sandra grumbled, but she dutifully put aside the book and climbed into her father's Chevy pickup. They drove down a dirt road, to a place where vultures were circling. A small calf lay in the road, bleeding and groaning. Its rear end had been mostly chewed off by a coyote. "Let's help it," said Sandra, who was about ten years old at the time. "We can't help this calf," replied her father. He took the rifle off the gun rack behind the pickup's front seat. "Oh, don't shoot it," protested Sandra. Her father aimed between the calf's eyes and fired. The calf's head jerked and he was still.

"DA, how could you?" Sandra asked. She called her father DA, pronounced *Dee-Ay*, like the letters. "It was the only kind thing we could do," her father replied. "The calf was too far gone to live. Now we have to send Rastus out to find the mother cow."

Rastus, whose real name was Rafael Estrada, was one of the Lazy B's cowboys. An illegal immigrant from Mexico, he had arrived on the ranch as a chore boy and never left. He was small and crippled, he could not read or write, and he had no wife. But he was good at what he did—handling horses and livestock—and he had high standards. If you met them, you had his respect.[8]

The next day, Rastus rode out to the pasture, took out his pocketknife, and sliced off most of the hide of the young dead calf. The mother cow was nearby, bawling for her dead calf, her udder swelling with unused milk. Rastus drove the cow back to headquarters and into the corral.

There he found a young calf, a "dogie," who had lost its own mother. Rastus tied the dead calf's hide over the dogie's back and put the dogie into a holding pen along with the cow with the bursting udder. The calf bawled and tried to suckle the cow. The cow kicked the calf away—but then sniffed at it, recognizing the familiar smell of her own calf. After about an hour, the cow was suckling the calf. He had found a new mother. Sandra, watching, had learned another lesson about death, renewal, and moving on.[9]

"DA" was a patient teacher. He always spoke to Sandra as an adult. He took his daughter everywhere around the ranch. He taught her how to brand a calf and how to fire a rifle (before she was ten). He taught her how to drive a truck as soon as she could see over the dashboard. He taught her how to paint a screen door. He was exacting—he always made her redo slipshod work—but, with Sandra at least, he was gentle.[10]

. . .

WITH OTHERS, HE could be harsh. If the Lazy B was its own country, Harry Day was the absolute ruler. A tall, fit, handsome man with a straight nose and thin mustache, he covered his bald head under an ever-present, sweat-stained Stetson hat. He smoked Lucky Strikes, pulling them out of his shirt pocket and fitting them into a well-worn silver and black cigarette holder, like President Roosevelt, or a Hollywood tycoon. His hands were rough and scarred, but he used his long fingers to perform delicate tasks. He could set a broken leg on a cow and clean out an infected eye. He expected his cowboys to know what to do without ever asking, but when it came to fixing something difficult and urgent—like a broken well pump during a drought—he always insisted on doing the work himself. He would listen, but he was never wrong.[11]

The cowboys called him Mr. Day. Like his own children, they revered him as the largest and most successful rancher around. Most of them spent their whole lives on the ranch. If the cowhands arrived illiterate and alcoholic, they left that way, too. Injury was common on the ranch, doctors far away. A longtime hand named Jim Brister was a great horseman and sometime rodeo star. He had broken both arms, both legs, his collarbone, and several fingers—and rarely missed a day of work. In *Lazy B,* Sandra and her younger brother and coauthor, Alan, describe Jim giving himself a root canal with a piece of glowing hot barbed wire: "We listened to the sizzle and watched smoke come out of his mouth. Jim sat there without a word and never flinched."[12]

When it came to the moral lives of his men, and of men generally, Harry Day was live-and-let-live. It was expected that Bug Quinn, the cook, would vanish into one of two saloons in town, the Bonnie Heather, where drunken cowboys left toothmarks in the bar, or the Snakepit, and wind up in jail until he dried out.[13] From time to time, Harry would stop in and see a homesteader named Jim Black, whose land was adjacent to the Lazy B. One time Sandra, who was about thirteen years old, went with him and noticed that the man's wife's face was black and blue. "DA," asked Sandra, "what happened to Jim's wife?" DA responded, "I don't know." Sandra pressed: "Yes, you do. Did she have an accident?" DA: "I suspect Jim was drinking and probably hit her too hard." Sandra asked, "Can't you do something about it, DA?" DA: "No, Sandra, I don't think I can." Sandra: "Well, I think we ought to tell the sheriff." DA: "I think we'd better leave well enough alone, Sandra."

ON SUMMER DAYS, DA would gaze, broodingly, at massive thunderheads boiling up over the mountains to the south, fed by the hot, moist air pushed north by the Mexican monsoons. DA could fix a windmill, but he could not control the weather. A cattle rancher is dependent on rain to grow the grass to feed the cows. The Lazy B got about ten inches a year, barely enough, and in some years not that. On some days, the lightning flickered, the distant thunder rumbled, and filmy gray sheets descended—but miles away, too far away to help succor the Lazy B's scorched and dying grass. DA could just stare and make bitter jokes that "it never rains in God's country."[14]

Decades later, when Sandra Day O'Connor was eighty-six years old and recalling her childhood at the Lazy B, she leaned forward in her wheelchair and exclaimed, "Rain! Rain! Rain was *everything*."[15] In her memoir of the ranch, she described the precise moment on a day of deliverance:

> a sudden stillness—the earth silent and waiting for the momentous event. Then the crack of lightning touching something on earth with all the electric fury of the universe. Seconds later the incredible sound of the thunder, the sound produced by the lightning bolt rolling through the clouds above. And then— wonder of wonders—the first few big wet drops of rain. . . . Joy. Wonder. Incredible gift from above. Our salvation. *Rain.*

The parched land of the Lazy B, dulled by drought, awakened. The birds chirped frantically, rabbits peeked from the burrows. The gray-green greasewood bushes released a powerful perfume as the water struck their dense, oily leaves. In her memoir, O'Connor continued:

> Everything stirring and excited from the rain, and no one more excited than my father. We were saved again—saved from the

ever present threat of drought, of starving cattle, of anxious creditors. We would survive a while longer.

And as proof we would look in wonder at the rainbow that had formed in the sky at the end of the rain.

As Sandra and her father watched, they began a sweetly giddy ritual of renewal. "You know what the old-timers say?" DA would ask. "No, what?" Sandra would say. "They say there is a pot of gold at the end of the rainbow." "No, really?" "That's what they say." "Do you believe them?" "Of course, why not?" "Have you ever seen it yourself?" "No, not really." "Well, let's go, Daddy. Let's go find it. It is right over there. Don't you see?"

And off they would go, careering along in DA's pickup truck, skidding and jolting along the muddy road, as Sandra egged on her father, "Oh, let's keep going—let's get there and find the gold."

After a while, DA would end the folly, saying that her mom would be worried, and that the rain may have made the canyon road impassable. Sometimes the road became a river, and DA would stop the truck, scoop up Sandra (and, in later years, her little brother and sister), and wade across the flood. They would walk the rest of the way home.

"Well, Ada Mae, how about a Cuba Libre to celebrate?" DA would call out when he walked in the door to his waiting wife. He would pour some rum and Coca-Cola into two glasses. His hazel eyes would be alert and bright, and he would begin to talk—and talk. "DA was a good listener," recalled Sandra, "and even a better talker."

In bed that night, Sandra would listen for the toads emerging from their holes beneath the backyard dirt tank, which was a man-made pond, now newly filled with water. The desert spadefoot toad buries itself in the soil beneath dried-up ponds. It can remain in hibernation for several years if necessary. When the pond fills, the male toads peek out and begin to croak for sexual partners. "Our most contented nights in the summer were the nights after we had enough rain to fill the tank behind the house," O'Connor recalled, "and we could hear the toads all night long."

In the dark, Sandra lay awake. The night amplified the ranch sounds, and a coyote's howl would make her draw up her covers.

When the wind blew, which was often, she could hear the creak of a loose gate, or the deep thrum of the windmills, the tall wooden towers standing over the bleak terrain. She listened for the clank of the sucker rods as they drew water from deep underground to fill the dirt tanks for the cattle. The Lazy B had thirty-five wells by the home and in the pastures, some several hundred feet deep. When the wind blew, the high galvanized steel blades turned, and the sucker rods drew out the water, ever so slowly, a thin stream that produced only four gallons a minute. When the wind died or the mill broke or the single-cylinder engine that powered some of the windmills conked out, it was a serious matter. There might be only a couple of days before thirsty cows began to die.[16]

On those nights when a well was broken, the ranch turned out—DA and the cowboys could spend all night trying to repair or replace a broken sucker rod. All around the Lazy B there were what looked like junk piles: broken windmills, dysfunctional motors, gears, shafts, pump rods. Harry Day was thrifty to an extreme, and there was no repairman to summon. Scouring the junk pile closest to the broken well, he would fish around for the right cast-off part and set to fixing the problem. The cowboys handed him tools. Sandra stood by, sometimes reading a book, other times chatting with the cowboys, observing.[17]

Sandra began to read when she was four years old, a joyful occasion for her doting and already proud parents. That same year, 1934, the rains did not come in the winter, and they did not come in the summer. Slowly, inexorably, the grass died. Normally, the 160,000 acres of the Lazy B could support about two thousand cows, bulls, and calves (about half of them were sold off each year), but Harry Day could not afford to buy feed. He had to begin winnowing his herd. It was the height of the Great Depression, and the bottom had dropped out of the cattle market. DA took eight hundred thin, sad cows and tried to sell them priced at one and a half cents a pound. He could not find a buyer.

He was depressed. He was worried about his wife and child and fearful that he would have to sell the ranch—if he could find anyone to take it off his hands.

The federal government came to the rescue, but with a heavy hand. As part of a New Deal program to support agriculture, the feds offered to pay ranchers caught in the squeeze $12 for every cow they killed. The rancher had to kill and bury the cows while a government official looked on. For Harry Day, who had worked so hard to nurture his beef cattle, the sight of cows and calves being shot and dumped into big pits was almost "unbearable," Sandra recalled. Later, the government bought some more cows, at $18 apiece, to feed people who were going hungry in the hard times.[18]

In the fall, the rains finally came, the grass grew, and the Lazy B survived. But Harry Day, in the way of many ranchers dependent on federal largesse, did not grow fonder of the government. The Day family owned outright only about eight thousand acres; the rest of the land—the vast majority—was leased, mostly from the feds, some from the states of Arizona and New Mexico.

Day remained a lifelong anti–New Deal, anti–Big Government conservative, even after the Rural Electrification Administration brought a steady supply of electricity to the ranch. Sandra and her brother, Alan, vividly recalled DA's tirades against Franklin Delano Roosevelt. "Why, that son of a bitch even tells me when to get up in the morning and go to bed at night," he railed when FDR instituted Daylight Saving Time at the beginning of World War II.[19]

HARRY DAY WAS strong, but he was not silent. He did not hide his passions. He was not shy about complaining, and he was prone to moodiness and sometimes depression. He shouldered his burdens manfully, but not quietly.

He had never meant to be a rancher. He had grown up in a comfortable home in Pasadena, California, where he was a champion high school swimmer looking forward to going to college at Stanford. But his father died, leaving the ranch in the hands of a partner. The man made a poor job of it. After Harry was discharged from a short stint in the army at the end of World War I, the lawyers for the family estate sent him out to the Lazy B to see what could be salvaged from the ranch investment. Harry wrote his sister Eleanor about the miseries of living on dried salt pork and sleeping on frozen ground. He concluded: "This certainly is a terrible place to live and I hate it here."[20]

But he stuck it out, forsaking college. Moved by duty or sheer cussedness, he slowly made himself into a rancher. Not a cowboy—he always wore khaki-colored cotton or wool pants, not Levi's jeans like the hands—but a ranch boss who scrimped and saved, who fought the elements and bad luck, and never took the easy way.[21]

Lonely and frustrated during those early years, he was spared from self-absorbed grimness by falling in love. Harry had first noticed Ada Mae Wilkey, the daughter of a local businessman, on a trip to Arizona as a teenager. One night over dinner at the Wilkey house in El Paso in June 1927, he met her again—she was now twenty-three—and was smitten. Their love letters, saved by Sandra to show her own children, brim with wanting and need.

"The poignant longing, the ache, the desire to be with you is more than I can stand. I think I am losing my mind," Harry wrote Ada Mae in August 1927. He insisted he was not worthy of her. "Here are the facts. I am no more intelligent than the law allows. My education is not what it should be. My social position is nil. I am the personification of poverty. Prospects for the future bum. . . . Disposition terrible—selfish, cruel, stubborn, lazy. My one redeeming feature is that I am healthy." Ada Mae returned the ardor: "Oh, how I miss you my beloved—I love you until it hurts—and I am so lonesome for you!" In touching fashion, she gave him the reassurance and boosting he craved: "You are the personification of all that is perfect in a man," she declared. "Harry, I want to give you laughter and courage, ambition and fulfillment, and in that way, I shall find my own."[22]

They became engaged. But Ada Mae's mother, Mamie, disapproved of the match, worried that her daughter would face a harsh life in the desert with Harry. So Harry and Ada Mae eloped to Las Cruces, New Mexico. "Ada Mae, don't ever learn to milk the cow," Mamie warned her daughter.[23]

Ada Mae did not allow ranch life to harden her. All her life in the ranch house, she wore stockings and perfume, even as she carried around a flyswatter. She kept her skin out of the sun and seldom rode a horse. She was fashionable, buying linen dresses from designers she read about in *Vogue*. She read all the magazines that arrived "cover to cover," Sandra recalled. Although she would never live in a beautiful house, she saved the pictures from the house and garden magazines. In the early years, she had to take her bath in a tub filled with water heated on a wood-burning stove. When she was done, the cowboys took turns bathing in the increasingly murky water. Every week, even after the house had hot water, she drove thirty-one miles into Lordsburg, New Mexico, for an appointment at a beauty salon.[24]

DA and MO (also pronounced like the letters), as they were called by their children, had a sturdy, if slightly shockworn, marriage. In *Lazy B,* Sandra and her brother wrote, "The strong physical attraction MO and DA had for each other overcame many of the difficulties of ranch life." But it was not an easy relationship. Harry Day could be caustic. He never tired of second-guessing Ada Mae's cooking—necessarily, many variations on beef—though, as Sandra noted, he never tired of eating her meals. The Day family played at cards and other indoor games with a competitive zeal that Sandra carried on in later life, to the amusement and occasional pique of her friends. Losing must be borne, but winning was to be celebrated. When he won at bridge or gin rummy, Harry would rub it in a little too gleefully.[25]

After a drink or two, Harry could become bombastic or petulant, especially in later years. "There were two Harry Days, a Daytime Harry and a Nighttime Harry," recalled Alan, who, as the only son and ranch heir apparent, sometimes bore the brunt of his father's scorn. When Harry badgered or railed, Ada Mae would often grow quiet. But she did not let her husband's verbal taunts or crankiness upset her, or, if she did, she concealed her hurt. When others were around, she remained resolutely warm and gracious, refusing to be provoked. "She made a hard life look easy," Sandra recalled, referring, though not explicitly, to life married to Harry Day as well as to life lived on a desert ranch. Only on rare occasions would Ada Mae even acknowledge that Harry could be mean. Alan, who was especially close to their mother, recalled her saying, "I married him for better or for worse, and sometimes it's worse."[26]

In *Lazy B,* Sandra and Alan note that they inherited from their father an unfortunate need to have the last word.[27] Among her friends in later life, Sandra was famous, or infamous, for her bossiness, a word she used to describe herself. But as a girl, she learned something else by watching her mother. She learned how to not let bullying or passive-aggressive males get under her skin. She learned not to take the bait. That may have been the most valuable lesson.

. . .

THROUGHOUT HER LIFE, Sandra Day O'Connor's eyes would brighten at the mention of the Lazy B. "It was the *best* life," she liked to say.[28] When the family decided to begin selling off the ranch in the early 1990s, she could not conceal her disappointment and sadness. For years, sitting in her chambers in the U.S. Supreme Court in Washington, she would look at the national weather map in the newspaper, hoping to see signs of rainstorms over the Lazy B.[29] Unlike other members of her family, she never went back to visit the ranch under its new owners. She could not bear to.

The depth of her feeling—her extreme, unquestioning devotion to the ranch—was owed partly to a longing, an absence that made her heart grow fonder. After the age of six, Sandra was away from her parents and the Lazy B from September to June, except for holidays and vacations.

As SANDRA GREW from toddler to little girl, the Lazy B's remoteness created a dilemma for the Days. For a year, Ada Mae tried to home-school little Sandra, but she and Harry decided their precocious daughter needed to go to a proper school, where she could be with other children.

The nearest schools—in Lordsburg, New Mexico, and Duncan, Arizona—were each about an hour away and of poor quality. So, in the fall of 1936, after some anguished discussion, Harry and Ada Mae decided to send Sandra to school in El Paso, four hours away. She would live with Ada Mae's mother and father.

There was never any serious talk of Harry and Ada Mae's relocating. Some ranching families moved to El Paso altogether and let foremen run their ranches. This was unthinkable to Harry, who recalled that absentee ownership had almost ruined the Lazy B in his father's generation. In other families, just the mother moved to the city for the school year. This, too, was unacceptable to Harry. He wanted Ada Mae with him at the Lazy B. Early in their marriage, Ada Mae went to El Paso for a month to see her parents. With an almost desperate neediness, Harry wrote her: "I wonder continually what you are doing, where you are, who you are with. I wonder what you will be like when I see you again. Will you be changed? Somehow I am afraid you will be different."[30]

Every September, the Days would put their young daughter on a train headed east toward Texas. Harry would tip the conductor to keep an eye on Sandra, by now old enough to make the trip alone, and warn her not to talk to soldiers and other strangers. Sandra would wave bravely, if forlornly, out the window at her parents and be on her way to a woman she would refer to, in a tone more matter-of-fact than affectionate, as "my second mother."[31]

Mamie Scott Wilkey, Ada Mae's mother, was headstrong and formidable. As a girl, she had traveled to Texas in a covered wagon, chased from Mexico across the Sierra Madre by the bandit insurrectionary Pancho Villa. Alan Day recalled that Mamie was "loyal and double tough"—high praise coming from a cowboy—but, he added, "she could not be close to anyone. She had your back, but she would never pat you on the back."[32] Sandra recalled Grandmother Wilkey's almost eccentric pridefulness on trips to the shopping district of Juárez, Mexico, just across the border from El Paso. Unable or unwilling to parallel park, Grandma Wilkey would leave the car in the middle of the road while she went off to shop, leaving little Sandra to contend with the police. "Just tell them who we are," Grandma Wilkey instructed.[33]

In later life, Sandra Day O'Connor described her grandmother as a "bossy old lady who told me what to do. She talked nonstop. If her eyes were open, her lips were moving." Indeed, Justice O'Connor's extraordinary ability to focus on work and tune out distractions she attributed to her grandmother's incessant chattering while Sandra did her homework at the dining room table. Every once in a while, Sandra would sigh and say, "Yes, Grandmother" or "No, Grandmother."[34]

At the same time, Sandra felt supported by Grandmother Wilkey, and she heeded one particular lesson that she heard over and over again: the importance of striving for success, in life and in one's career.[35] "She loved success stories," O'Connor recalled. "She would focus on anybody that she thought had made a success of their lives, and she'd want them to tell her their life story so she could somehow figure it out." Sandra's grandmother did not distinguish between men and women: The important thing was to be a *success*. "Go be the best!" Grandmother Wilkey commanded. "It didn't matter if you were a female or not—you could still make something of your life," said O'Connor. Mamie Wilkey was not exactly a protofeminist, but she had learned from painful experience that women needed to be able to look out for themselves.[36]

Shortly after Sandra arrived in El Paso in 1936, Sandra's grandfather, W. W. Wilkey, unexpectedly died. A cattle broker who had made and lost a fortune, he left Mamie with nothing but debt ("I think she never forgave him," recalled O'Connor). His widow was forced to take in boarders. Aghast that little Sandra might be sharing a bathroom with itinerant oil engineers, Harry Day dipped into his own savings to buy Mamie a small house.[37]

The bungalow was comfortable, furnished with oriental rugs, but it paled next to the grand houses of some of the ranching families who made El Paso their winter home. Invited over by her classmates, Sandra remembered feeling awkward amid the maids bustling about and the gardeners tending to the lawns and flowers. After Sandra had finished fourth grade in the local public school, Harry Day further loosened his purse strings to send Sandra to the Radford School for Girls, a proper finishing school, where the students studied Latin and Greek, ballet and piano, and, if their parents were ambitious for them, went on to colleges like Smith and Wellesley.[38]

The girls at Miss Radford's ate lunch on white tablecloths and used silver napkin rings. They learned elocution and enunciation from Miss Fireovid, a stern, flame-haired dramatic arts teacher. "These were frightening and painful experiences, but her insistence on proper and clear enunciation of the words and looking at the audience have stayed with me ever since," Sandra recalled.[39] (In later years, Supreme Court clerks would vie to perform the best imitation of Justice O'Connor exclaiming "We-e-ll! My *good*-ness!" in her emphatic, deliberate diction.) The all-girls school brought in inspiring guest speakers, including Helen Keller and Eleanor Roosevelt. Sandra particularly recalled the First Lady—"homely, but charismatic"—alighting from her limousine wearing a slouch hat and a fur stole made of a fox biting its tail, and addressing the school in her aristocratic accent. Harry Day may have denounced FDR as a Big Government usurper, but Sandra would remember Mrs. Roosevelt as her first role model of a woman in public service. "I didn't dare tell my parents," she recalled.[40]

Sandra did well academically—so well that she skipped a grade and became a year young for her class. But she was uneasy. In a group photo taken when she was about ten years old, the other girls are smiling and poised. Some sport colorful bows in their hair. Sandra, her dark hair unkempt, her expression dour, looks scraggly and glum. She missed home. In 1980 she told an interviewer, "I dislike El Paso to this day, largely because I was homesick."[41]

A six-year-old child has a hard time understanding why her parents would send her to live apart. She adapted her thinking; if the Lazy B was to be far, far away, then it must be a magical kingdom. In El Paso and at Miss Radford's, she felt like an outsider, despite making some friends (a few visited her at the ranch and became lifelong pals). By necessity, perhaps, she developed a tough hide—in her later steeliness she may have become more like her grandmother than she would care to let on. Yet even after she had lived in El Paso for a number of years, there were moments of insecurity. When Sandra was eleven, one of her school friends told her she knew a secret about Sandra and her mother. What was it? demanded Sandra. "Well, my mother says your mother was married to somebody else, not Harry Day." "I don't believe you!" shouted Sandra.

But her mind filled with doubt. "I was shocked and frightened," she recalled. "Had I been adopted? Is that why MO and DA sent me off to school in El Paso?" Back at the bungalow, she confronted Grandmother Wilkey. Gingerly, her grandmother informed Sandra that her mother had been married, briefly, to another man. (The marriage lasted only a couple of months.) "We don't talk about that," said Grandmother Wilkey. At home that summer, Sandra worked up the courage to ask MO. "I never think about it," said MO. "DA is my husband and you are my daughter."[42] Do not look back, do not regret, take life as it comes and make the most of it. That was Ada Mae's way, and in time it would be her daughter's way, too.

But as a girl, Sandra saw herself as shy and unconfident.[43] Beverly Timberlake, a classmate at Miss Radford's, recalled liking Sandra right away but being puzzled that Sandra's family did not live in town like the other ranch families. Sandra, she observed, did not fit in easily with her more frivolous peers. "There were Junior League tea dances on Sunday," Beverly recalled. "She hated it. She would rather be on a horse at the ranch." Beverly's father owned hotels and banks as well as a ranch. One night, when Sandra was staying as a guest at the Timberlake home, he told Beverly and Sandra, "I think both of you need to go to law school, so you can handle your family business." Sandra solemnly replied, "Yes, Mr. Timberlake." Beverly recalled thinking, "My daddy's crazy. I'm going to get a convertible and feel the wind in my hair."[44]

Sandra cheered up when her favorite cousin, Flournoy, who was a year older but in the same class after Sandra skipped a grade, came to live with Grandmother Wilkey. Charming, vivacious, raised by her mother, Evelyn (Ada Mae's sister), to be socially accomplished, Flournoy reached out to the shy Sandra.[45] She "was like a loving older sister," Sandra recalled, "creative and fun loving, joyful and affectionate." In the summers, Sandra brought Flournoy out to the Lazy B, where they would tear along on their horses playing Indian girls, or, avoiding the heat, slouch on the couches and read.[46]

In *Lazy B*, Sandra recalls going swimming with Flournoy on a hundred-degree day. About two hundred yards from the Headquarters house stood a steel-rimmed water tank, six feet high, fifty feet across. Built to water the livestock, the tank doubled as the ranch swimming pool. Small clumps of algae drifted on the surface, but the water was deliciously cool. Flournoy and Sandra floated in some old inner tubes.

Harry Day appeared to roust them out. "Sandra, Flournoy! It's time to go! We need to leave," he said. Sandra protested, "No, DA, we want to stay." Harry said, "Girls, get out *now*. We have to leave." More protests.

Harry went to the barn and returned with a rope. "Come on out, girls, or I'll pull you out," he said. He formed a loop in his lariat and circled it over his head. The girls ducked underwater, but when Flournoy surfaced, "Thump. The rope was around Flournoy's neck," Sandra recalled in *Lazy B*. Harry pulled on the rope. "Okay, DA, I'll get out, let me go. The rope hurts!" said Flournoy. "Now Sandra," said DA. He lassoed his daughter. "Ouch, DA, that hurts!" she cried.

"Our necks were a bit red, and our egos too. We learned we couldn't always have our way," wrote Sandra. As she told the story in *Lazy B*, Harry had pulled them out of the pool in order to take a trip into Lordsburg to go shopping.[47] To an interviewer for *People* magazine, Harry Day told the same story, but with a different ending. He recalled that he was hauling the girls out of the water to put them on the train back to El Paso—to begin another school year away from home.[48]

AFTER SANDRA WAS born in 1930, Harry and Ada Mae were unable to conceive for years. But then, in 1938, to their surprise, Ada Mae became pregnant and bore another daughter, Ann. A year and a half later, they had Alan. Headquarters stirred with new life; DA added on new bedrooms, a bathroom, and a bunkhouse for the cowboys.

In El Paso, Sandra, still homesick, was jealous. In the summer of 1942, as the day approached when she would have to glumly board the train back to El Paso and Grandmother Wilkey, Sandra began to pester her parents, "Why can't I stay home and go to school? I'll ride the school bus in. It will be all right. You'll see." MO and DA had "misgivings," Sandra recalled, but they relented.

Each school day, Sandra would rise before dawn. Her mother or father would drive her down the eight-mile dirt road to Highway 70, where she would wait for a school bus. The trip to Lordsburg, with many stops along the way, took more than an hour. She felt isolated in eighth grade among the children of Mexican laborers, who lived nearer the school and were already friends. The teachers were unmemorable. By the time she returned home to the Lazy B, it was dark.

At the end of the school year, Sandra decided to go back to El Paso, not to Miss Radford's, but to the coeducational public school, Austin High. Her parents were pleased, but the choice, she insisted during an interview more than seven decades later, was hers. "*I* decided," she recalled, eyes flashing.[49]

ON A CATTLE ranch, the true test of a cowhand is the roundup. On the Lazy B, they happened twice a year, in midspring and midfall, when the cowhands branded the new calves and culled out the yearlings for sale. On the Lazy B, the hands could work about ten square miles a day, which, on a ranch of more than 250 square miles, meant the roundup would go on for more than a month—day in and day out, from before sunrise until after dark. The pastures were scattered, and the cows sometimes ranged up into the mountains and down into the draws. The work was demanding and sometimes grisly. In addition to branding the calves with the Lazy B—a B lying on its side—the cowboys sliced off the tips of their ears. They also gouged out any horns forming in the calves' heads and castrated the bull calves.[50]

If a man, woman, or child could do this work efficiently and without complaint, he (or she) earned the respect of the cowhands. If not, "they ignored you. You didn't count. They mentally left you behind," recalled Alan Day. Sandra's younger brother spoke almost reverentially about "making a hand." "It was my biggest goal in life," Alan recalled. He rode on his first roundup at the age of five.[51]

Because she went away to school, Sandra never rode a full, month-long roundup. But she did ride on roundup at least for several days during her eighth-grade year at Lordsburg and on other occasions when she was home from El Paso or back from college. She had always been comfortable with the cowboys, who had been her "tobacco-chewing, unshaven, unbathed" babysitters when she was tiny. Riding for ten hours at a time in unforgiving terrain, with only a couple of breaks for water or the rare chance to squat behind a cactus, changed her relationship with Rastus, Jim Brister, and the other hands. The roundup at the Day ranch "had been an all-male domain," she recalled in *Lazy B*. "Changing it to accommodate a female was probably my first initiation into joining an all-men's club, something I did more than once in my life." She went on: "After the cowboys understood that a girl could hold up her end, it was much easier for my sister, my niece, and the other girls and young women who followed to be accepted in that rough-and-tumble world." After she was appointed to the Supreme Court, a magazine reporter asked one of the Lazy B cowboys how she had done as a cowgirl. He replied, "She worked well with us in the canyons. She held her own."[52]

IN JULY 1945, the summer before Sandra began her senior year in high school (she was only fifteen but had skipped another grade), she was home helping with a mini-roundup. Harry Day was worried that his men had missed a few calves up in the rugged hills around Antelope Well during the earlier spring roundup, so he took the crew back out into the blazing heat to find the rest.

Sandra's job that day was to bring the ten-man crew lunch (Bug Quinn, the regular trail cook, was off fighting forest fires). This was no small undertaking. With MO, she cooked a pot roast, heavily seasoned with chili peppers, overnight. Rising as the cowboys were heading out at dawn, she finished preparations for the meal, including an applesauce cake, and loaded the chuck wagon box on the pickup. A little after seven she headed out on the twisting dirt roads that were barely tracks across the rocky soil. An hour into the drive, the truck began to lurch and slew. Sandra put on the brakes and got out to find a flat tire. She knew that no one would be coming along to help. She found two large rocks, braced the front tires, got out the jack, and began cranking up the rear of the truck. When she tried to unscrew the lug nuts, she discovered she had no purchase on the nut. She lowered the truck back down so the tire touched the ground. Gathering her slender frame, Sandra stood on the lug wrench and jumped on it to create force. Finally there was a bit of movement. One by one, she pried off the other nuts, jacked the truck back up, pulled off the tire, pushed on the spare, tightened the bolts, and lowered the truck.

She knew she was late. Changing the tire had taken more than an hour. Her father had told her that the herd would get to Antelope Well sometime between 9:30 and 11:30. She knew that the cowboys liked to eat before they began the rough work of searing flesh with hot brands and slicing off ear tips and testicles.

It was just before eleven when she pulled up to Antelope Well. She could see through the clouds of dust—and hear from the bawling of the calves and their mothers—that the cowboys had already begun to brand and cut. The smell of burning hair and hide filled her nostrils.

Standing off with the cowboys was DA. He did not acknowledge his daughter. She began to build a cook fire to heat the beef and coffee.

It was after one thirty when the cowboys came over to the truck for lunch. No one was joking or even talking. "You're late," said DA. "I know," said Sandra. "I had a flat tire the other side of Robbs' Well and had to change it."

"You should have started earlier," said DA, no longer the gentle father.

"Sorry, DA, I didn't expect a flat. I'm lucky to be here at all," she responded.

"You need to expect anything out here," DA said.[53]*

JUSTICE O'CONNOR TOLD that story about the flat tire to generations of her law clerks, and to her many friends and acquaintances, and she often worked it into question-and-answer sessions following her speeches, sometimes with no apparent relevance to the question.[55] The description of Sandra's ardor and DA's cold response made some wince. "I always thought it was a sad story about a daughter trying desperately to please her father," said Ruth McGregor, Justice O'Connor's first law clerk on the Supreme Court in 1981 and her close friend thereafter.[56] To most of her law clerks, the message was obvious: No excuses. Get the job done. In public, O'Connor rarely spelled out a moral to the story, but she was probably sending several messages, said RonNell Andersen Jones, another former law clerk who became a close friend and drafted many of O'Connor's speeches. One was simply that life on the ranch—like any worthy undertaking— could be unforgiving. "Getting lunch to everybody on time was priority. Feeling good was not," said Jones. Another was an implicit recognition that hard work—which O'Connor revered with almost sacramental devotion—did not always produce the desired results. O'Connor could be direct and blunt, but often she delivered difficult messages through stories, sometimes meandering, sometimes pointed.

* A couple of days after the tire-changing incident—on July 16, 1945—Sandra wanted to ride with DA to gather some cattle from a big pasture near headquarters. At about five thirty in the morning, father and daughter were rinsing off dishes, looking out the kitchen window toward the northeast. There was a little light in the sky as dawn approached. Suddenly they saw an intense flash. There was no sound, but a mushroom cloud rose in the sky. The Days looked at each other. What had they just seen? About a month later, when the news of the bombing of Hiroshima arrived through the weekly mail, they read about the test at Alamogordo, New Mexico, 180 miles distant, and realized they had seen the first blast of an atomic bomb.[54]

When Alan and Sandra were writing *Lazy B* in 1999, Sandra toned down or cut most of Alan's criticisms of his father. But she wanted to let the reader know that her beloved DA "wasn't always a nice guy," said RonNell Andersen Jones. She also wanted to tell a story about ingenuity, believing that the reader could appreciate it, even if DA could not.[57]

SANDRA DAY ENTERTAINS was the headline in the El Paso newspaper society pages. "The home of Mrs. W. W. Wilkey, elaborately flower-decorated, was the pretty setting for the party at which 150 guests were received." Ada Mae, who on occasion would take the long train ride to visit her daughter and mother, was the cohostess for the reception for the proper young women of El Paso society. Tall, slender, pretty, darkly tanned, Sandra is shown standing with seven smiling, laughing friends.[58] Still, Sandra was not entirely happy at Austin High School. She was near the top of her class in grades, but she was "not one of the gang," and she felt pressure to disguise her intelligence to get on socially. "It didn't enhance your popularity to have good grades. That just kind of set you apart as being a little strange," she remembered. "So you wanted to have good grades, but you didn't want to have anybody know about it." She missed the personal attention of the teachers at Miss Radford's.[59]

Her father's ambition, and hence her own, was for her to go to Stanford, the college he had once dreamed of. Austin High School "forgot to tell me when the college exams were given, because the kids there didn't take them," O'Connor recalled. The principal had to wangle a provisional acceptance for Sandra, conditioned on her passing some tests when she arrived on campus.[60]

During World War II, beef prices had risen, and Harry could afford to buy a new car. In September 1946, Harry and Ada Mae drove their daughter to Palo Alto, California, where a new world awaited.

STANFORD

"How well do you type?"

Ready to go to Stanford

Entering as a sixteen-year-old freshman, Sandra finished Stanford and Stanford Law School in just six years. She was proposed to four times, was formally engaged twice, and graduated near the top of her class—but couldn't find a job at a law firm.

FOR TWO DAYS, they drove west across the Arizona desert, through the Sierra Nevada, then north up California's great central valley, across the peninsula south of San Francisco to the grounds of Stanford University. On a blue-sky morning in mid-September, Harry Day turned his new Chrysler up the mile-long Palm Drive into the eight-thousand-acre campus. The long straight rows of Canary Island palm trees gave way to a sunken oval fronting a vast Mission Revival–style quadrangle. All the way up Palm Drive, Sandra could glimpse from the back seat a series of arches opening to a Romanesque church adorned with a huge golden mosaic. She was "overcome," she would later recall, "with the beauty of the place."

Before the turn of the twentieth century, the railroad tycoon Leland Stanford had commissioned the Boston architect H. H. Richardson and the landscape designer Frederick Law Olmsted, the creator of Central Park in New York, to imagine a campus that would rival or outdo the older, more established East Coast universities. In archways and arcades, cloisters and courtyards, the architects had blended the styles of ancient Rome, medieval Europe, and imperial Spain into a grand tableau, set on a broad plain backing toward softly rounded hills. On sunny California days, the yellow sandstone walls and red tile roofs are suffused with warm light. For years afterward, Sandra would recall the golden autumn afternoons and the fresh green of spring after the rains had come.[1]

The Stanford Quad in September 1946 was "full of smiling men in bomber jackets," recalled one of Sandra's freshman classmates, Diane Porter Cooley. The end of World War II was, Philip Roth wrote in *American Pastoral*, "the greatest moment of collective inebriation in history." He was describing the outburst of celebration, relief, and optimism that erupted across the country, but he could have been describing the sheer joy of the young men who arrived at Stanford that autumn.[2] Well over half of them were veterans, thrilled to be home, happy to be in pursuit of a prosperous future, and in want of a wife.

On Stanford's bursting campus, swollen by the returning vets, the women undergraduates were outnumbered by more than three to one. The university administration made some effort to protect the women—mostly from one another. Sororities, blamed for a suicide, had been abolished, and the *Regulations for Women Students,* a printed brochure mailed to each new female student, prohibited in its Code of Student Conduct "excessive expenditures and other excesses on the part of students," as well as "the development of exclusive or undemocratic castes." (Fraternities were apparently exempt from this rule.) At the same time, "for teas" and "dancing in San Francisco," the Suggestions for Clothes Appropriate for Stanford recommended "one or two silk dresses" as well as "one or two formals" for "more dressy campus dances." An "evening wrap" was deemed "not essential."[3]

At Branner Hall, her freshman women's dormitory, Sandra Day was "one of the last to show up," recalled Diane Porter Cooley, who lived in the room across the hall. "We were standing around sizing each other up, and she came swishing in. She had a put-together outfit. A tailored dress and pumps. No bobby sox and saddle shoes for her." Nina van Rensselaer, who had arrived from a fancy girls' school in New York, recalled that Sandra was wearing a "smart Scottish print," a "lunch-at-the-Plaza dress," as Cooley remembered it.

But when Sandra opened her mouth, she "sounded like the Dust Bowl," recalled Cooley. The ranch girl from Arizona spoke slowly, with a flat twang. She seemed shy but very deliberate. She had dark, short, wispy hair—"baby curls," recalled van Rensselaer. "We thought her hair looked pretty good but she seemed to think it was a problem." (Sandra suffered from a medical condition that inhibited hair growth and later consulted a Palo Alto doctor; only after she began having babies years later did hormonal changes thicken her hair.)[4]

The girls of Branner Hall were not quite sure what to make of the newest arrival. She was only sixteen years old, about two years younger than most freshman girls. With a gap-toothed smile and a thin, sharp face and gangly figure, she looked waiflike. But she was stylishly dressed and, they soon learned, purposeful. On the first Saturday night, the girls went together to an informal campus dance known as a jolly-up. At first, standing at the edge of the dance floor in the Women's Gym, she seemed reticent, unsure. "Sandra didn't know what to do," recalled Martica Ruhm Sawin, another Branner girl. "So her eyes lit on a tall, good-looking boy, and she asked him to dance."[5]

The boy's name was Andy Campbell. He was twenty-four—eight years older than Sandra. He had been a naval antisubmarine warfare officer in the fleet preparing for the invasion of Japan. Trained to operate sonar devices at Caltech, he had come to Stanford to get his engineering degree after the war. He drove a wine-red convertible with a V-8 engine and white sidewalls, a conveyance that evoked admiring comment from the girls of Branner when Campbell delivered Sandra back to the dorm after the last dance at the jolly-up.

Campbell was smitten by his dance partner and, sixty years later, spoke rapturously of her. "Was she self-confident?" he asked, rhetorically. "Yes, she was! She was a very pretty woman and self-possessed. I liked to dance. She liked to dance. I was a pretty good dancer. We went to a lot of dances. We tried tango, swing, twirling her. But I liked to fox-trot—I got to hold her." Andy took Sandra dancing at the Kappa Sig house and at the Saint Francis Hotel in San Francisco. They went to the opera and to art-house French movies that were "out of her experience. Mine, too," Campbell recalled. In his wine-red roadster, they went on picnics to Half Moon Bay, where they built a bonfire and Andy played "Ain't She Sweet" and "It Had to Be You" on his banjo. "She wanted to do things, see things. Go for drives." Campbell played the trombone in the university marching band but gave it up to sit with Sandra at football games. Mindful of her youth, he did not ask to "pin" her. "There didn't seem to be anyone else, but there was no arrangement," he recalled. "But she invited me to the ranch at the end of the first year, which I thought was a pretty good sign."

All his life, Campbell would keep a color photo of Sandra, looking fetching in a short-sleeved white piqué dress as she climbed up on a wooden windmill at the Lazy B. ("I never saw her in Levi's," he said.) To get to the ranch in southeastern Arizona, Campbell had driven for two days in his convertible, sleeping in the desert at night with a shotgun and a rifle by his side.

Sandra had warned her suitor about her father. "Before I went to the ranch, she told me that Harry did not like tenderfeet, or show-offs, or people who talked too much," Campbell recalled.

The Lazy B was, as usual, suffering from a drought that summer. On Campbell's second day at the ranch, "the wind stopped blowing." Each windmill had a backup engine, and one had conked out. So Mr. Day summoned Andy to drive out with him to look at it. "Can you fix it?" he asked. Andy replied, a little tentatively, that he had some experience with outboards, single-cylinder, two-stroke motors somewhat similar to this one. He began to examine the busted engine, and when he looked up, Harry's truck was pulling away. "He just waved at me!" Andy recalled. Taking a breath, Campbell went to work. After a while, he managed to tweak the motor back into operation. "It was hot and dusty," he recalled, and there was no sign of Mr. Day or his truck. Campbell lay down and took a nap. "After a few hours Harry came back and picked me up. I realized it was a test."[6]

REMINISCING MANY YEARS later about his courtship of Sandra Day, Andy Campbell said, "That first summer, I asked her what she liked. She answered 'Western Civ.' She just loved that." In retrospect, and even at the time, it occurred to Campbell that Sandra loved "Western Civ" more than she did him.

Late in her own life, looking back on History of Western Civilization, the Plato-to-the-present-day survey course required of all Stanford freshmen of her era, Sandra O'Connor said, "I loved it. I thought it was wonderful. Something registered with me." Week by week, the freshmen of Western Civ were marched through tyranny and plutocracy, into revolution and repression, past absolute monarchy and the ghastly choices of fascism and communism, until they arrived, with newfound appreciation, at the liberal democracy of the United States at the end of World War II. Western Civ was an ode to reason and the Enlightenment, to the rule of law, to the separation of powers, to the balance of individual liberty and democratic rule. These would remain O'Connor's guiding lights; in later life, long after Western Civ had been banished by the academy as "patriarchal" and "hegemonic," O'Connor would wish that all schoolchildren be required to learn civics, so they could have some idea of what she had learned about the foundations of government in Western Civ.[7]

At year's end, in the last lecture ("Whither Civilization?"), the Western Civ students were asked, "In what ways has the study of the history of Western Civilization changed your philosophy of life?" O'Connor had arrived at Stanford "without any particular philosophy of life," she recalled.[8] She devoted hours in the Western Civ reading room on the Quad to studying cardboard-backed mimeographed copies of Great Books. "It was pretty dismal," recalled Martica Ruhm Sawin, but Sandra disagreed. One Sunday night, Sandra's Branner friend, Beth Harrelson Growden, invited her to the home of Beth's uncle, Professor Harry Rathbun. In a stucco house filled with Mexican antiques, the two girls, as well as other fortunate students, would sit week after week on oriental rugs, listen to classical music, discuss philosophy, and quietly reflect. "Sandra was mesmerized," recalled Growden.[9]

At the Lazy B, Sandra had once asked her father, "Why don't we go to church on Sunday?" Harry Day had responded that church was too far away, that the preachers were no good, and that in any case, "church is all around us."[10] Looking up at the stars at night, "so close you could reach up and pluck them," Sandra felt awed, humbled that she was but a small speck. But not a random one: She believed—or, under Professor Rathbun's tutelage, wished to believe—that she lived in an ordered universe, with a reason and purpose for everything and everyone, even if God did not always provide enough rain.

At his Sunday night salons, Professor Rathbun taught Sandra and the other reverential students that they were part of a grand design. Everyone, declared Rathbun, had a religion, though they might not know it. Rathbun had studied under a University of Chicago professor who had tried to apply scientific inquiry to the Bible. Like Thomas Jefferson with his razor, Rathbun had removed the Gospels' improbable miracles to expose ethical meaning. The most important lesson from God was that one individual, however insignificant he or she may seem, could make a difference in the world.[11]

In later years, after he got involved in Banning the Bomb and experiments with LSD, Rathbun would be regarded as something of a New Age shaman, if not slightly kooky.[12] Even in his day he was seen as "a bit cultish," recalled Sandra's hallmate Diane Cooley. But Rathbun was a wildly popular professor; his annual term-end lecture on "the meaning of life" filled the seventeen-hundred-seat Memorial Church. To a girl who had not yet turned eighteen, Rathbun represented enlightenment. "I was pretty much of a sponge," O'Connor recalled. She absorbed his earnest lessons, including one that was ahead of its time in 1947. "If the world's crisis is to be met successfully, the need is that woman shall be given, and shall take, her proper place, that place male domination has heretofore denied her," Rathbun intoned, a little pompously, but meaningfully to Sandra. "In achieving this equality, not only must woman claim her place, but the male must make sure this is accorded her. Together, they can make a new world."[13]

Sandra was no longer the forlorn high school girl hiding her good grades. She gushed about her new life in letters home. "College just gets better and better. I think it is the Utopia that the philosophers we studied about in history dreamed of. It just couldn't be better," she wrote her parents in the spring of her freshman year. "People are different here than in high school. They actually like to talk about such things as politics and religion."[14]

She was, generally speaking, more serious than most girls. "She could be cute, coquettish, but she wasn't going to marry the fullback," Cooley recalled. "She was going to save the world." At Austin High, she had been overlooked for any special honors or positions. Determined to be a "good citizen" at Stanford, she served on a committee indoctrinating freshmen into the Honor Code and as president of her dorm her last year.[15] At times in college, she was overwhelmed by the older students, particularly the veterans. In her creative writing course, taught by Wallace Stegner (who later became a great novelist of the West and whose writing style she would emulate in *Lazy B*), Sandra felt her homey stories about life on the ranch could not live up to the raw war stories of men back from the front. ("I got a B minus," she recalled.)[16] As a freshman, she could be a little lonely and a little fey. Beth Harrelson recalled Sandra wandering the halls of Branner singing "Beautiful, Beautiful, Beautiful Brown Eyes," a sad country song about a pretty woman married to a drunk and abusive man. In letters home, she worried, unnecessarily, about her grades while showing her silly side. "Andy and I went to a Kappa Sig party, all this old time music [a Dixieland jazz band] where you hop around and it was real crazy and real fun," she wrote "Mother and Daddy" at the end of freshman year.[17]

Sandra majored in economics, and her father was not happy when she came home spouting the deficit spending theories of John Maynard Keynes. Harry Day was strictly a pay-as-you-go man. "Do you mean to tell me I am spending my hard earned money to send you to a school where they are teaching you that garbage?" he fulminated. But his fearsomeness could not disguise his pride. Watching Sandra and her father argue at the dining table, her little brother, Alan, thought they seemed like "twins."[18]

By Sandra's junior year, Andy Campbell had graduated and gone to work as an engineer building a dam in Oregon. But he continued to woo Sandra, coming down for a football game in the fall of 1948 and inviting her to visit him in Oregon. Over Thanksgiving, she traveled to his muddy rural town in the Oregon woods and had a "nice time," she reported to her parents. (Sandra stayed in a motel; to chaperone the couple, Andy's mother had driven all the way from Pasadena, sleeping at night in the back of her station wagon.) "Andy wants to come down next weekend," Sandra wrote her parents in the winter of 1949, but she went on to confide:

> I really think I'd better tell him that I don't think I'm in love with him. I don't believe, sincerely, that things would work out. I've decided love is only self-hypnosis anyway, mostly, and I am not ready to get married, and I may change so much that we wouldn't get along at all later on. And it wouldn't be fair to Andy to let him think I feel in a way I don't about him. This has been coming on a long time I think. I have always liked Andy and had a nice time with him and he is such a wonderful person and you all like him. But, after all, there must be something else needed for it to be perfect and there are many other boys in the world.[19]

Andy did come down to Stanford and took Sandra for a ride in his roadster. He proposed marriage. "She didn't say anything," Campbell recalled many years later. "We were young and stupid," he added, with some anguish. He persisted in his courtship, driving back down to the Lazy B. In the kitchen, Ada Mae cornered Andy by the sink in the kitchen and asked, "You don't intend to marry Sandra, do you?"

"I didn't know what to say," Andy recalled. "She just kept talking, and the next day I slunk back to my job in Oregon." He continued to pine for his lost love, but he tried to understand her. Life as an engineer's wife in the woods of Oregon "would have been a waste," he said, years later. "Her mother could see it. Sandra wanted to have a profession as a woman."

EARLIER THAT YEAR, in between joining the annual Spring Sing and her induction into Cap and Gown, Stanford's honor society, Sandra wrote her parents, "My score on the law school test was very good. In the upper 15 percent, so I will undoubtedly get in. Isn't that nice?"[20] Sandra was a junior, and still only nineteen years old, but she was eligible to start law school the next year. Qualified Stanford students—about a third of her entering class in the law school—could get both their undergraduate and law degrees in six years instead of the usual seven. For the veterans, it was a chance to make up for lost time in their careers.

Sandra later said that she was inspired by the example of Professor Rathbun, who seemed to use his own legal training to sharpen his powers of persuasion. Sandra's father was willing to pay the $600 law school tuition (about $6,300 in 2018 dollars). The younger Sandra and her friend from Miss Radford's, Beverly Timberlake, had once imagined owning side-by-side ranches. Like Beverly's father, Harry did not seem to have thought that his daughter could help manage the family ranch, but he did think that Sandra could be useful to the Lazy B as a lawyer. Harry had taken charge of the Lazy B when it was mired in a ten-year lawsuit over his father's estate, and he would bitterly complain that lawyers had made off with most of the money.[21]

Sandra decided to try law school for a year and see if she liked it. She had an additional reason to stay on campus, one that she never spoke about. "In our day, a woman who graduated from Stanford without a husband, even if she was the valedictorian, was destined for the secretarial pool. There were no other jobs for women," said Diane

Cooley. In America in 1950, the average age of a new bride was twenty. Only about one in twenty women graduated from college; the tired joke was that women went to college for an "MRS" degree. Sandra's classmates never thought of her as a "ring-by-spring" husband hunter, but they believed that she was sensitive to the pressure they all felt to find a mate.[22]

Whatever Sandra was thinking—and her letters home suggest some inner turmoil—the fact is that during her six years at Stanford, she was proposed to four times, formally engaged to be married twice, and "loosely engaged" another time.[23]

DURING HER FIRST year of law school, with Andy Campbell now out of the running, Sandra accepted the marriage proposal of John Hamilton, a senior whose father ran the Chamber of Commerce in Honolulu and who planned on becoming an academic studying labor relations. He was not the man for Sandra that Harry and Ada Mae—or Grandmother Wilkey—had in mind. They were hoping for someone closer to home and with more elevated prospects. The Days had even scouted out the scion of a well-off Houston family as a more eligible candidate for Sandra's hand.

Sandra's letters home were at once pleading and defiant. In January, she informed her parents that she planned to wear Hamilton's ring and had picked out a suitably elegant place in San Francisco to hold an engagement party. ("Mother," she wrote, "the Marie Antoinette is very lovely inside with real antiques—marble topped tables, etc.") At the same time, she ruefully referred to her fiancé as "the disapproved of boy" and squabbled with her parents, who wanted her to delay wearing the ring and announcing her engagement until she had met the more suitable boy from Houston. That made no sense, scoffed Sandra. "After all, if my mind is made up I would hardly be receptive to the boy you have picked out in Houston anyway, would I—with or without a ring?"

She went on to mount a vigorous argument for her freedom to chart her own course. Her letter brims with a determined, if not stubborn, will to live a good and meaningful life:

It is my life and tho' I love you dearly I would be unable to live with you all my life anyway. It is impossible to tell someone what will make them happy. I want to lead an interesting life—I want to study, practice law, and experiment with all such things. Rather than hinder me, marriage would help—John is interested in the same kind of things and would keep me in the atmosphere I want. I would be very happy to be associated with a University or intellectual group—in fact, I can't think of anything nicer. Please be tolerant of my ideas and simply because I want something different from you don't think it is wrong, or wrong for me.

To Grandmother Wilkey, she wrote a systematic brief, with numbered paragraphs and lettered subsections. Knowing her audience, she stressed status and success: "John has a future. . . . His I.Q. is very high. . . . His father has introduced him to very influential people in the City who will help in the future . . ." She tried to rebut Grandmother Wilkey's poor first impressions of her intended: "John is not exuberant in personality (probably the reason you were not impressed) which suits my personality, for a) I am not exuberant; b) I am fond of books, education, and so is he." She ardently summed up: "He wants a) to be materially well off in the sense of a comfortable, pretty home; b) to be well dressed at all times; c) to be HAPPY; d) to do something worthwhile."[24]

The engagement broke off, as did many impending nuptials in those days of hurried and distantly formal courtships. Sandra had by then become best friends with her housemate Beatrice ("Beatsie") Challis Laws, one of four other women in Sandra's entering law school class of about 150 students (always referred to as "the men" or "the boys" by the faculty). Laws recalled that John Hamilton (possibly sensing the opposition from Sandra's family)* wrote Sandra to say

---

* Asked about John Hamilton's courtship of Sandra for a family oral history in the late 1970s, Sandra's parents were laconic. "She had him out here and we just didn't think that was a good deal," said Harry. "Wasn't made for her," said Ada Mae. "He was nice enough."[25]

that he had fallen for another girl. "Sandra was devastated," Beatsie recalled. "For about two weeks."[26]

Then she got on with studying law. Stanford Law School in 1950 was not yet the powerhouse rival of Harvard and Yale. During the war, it had shrunk to about thirty students. Even in the postwar boom, the school accepted about half its applicants, including some college boys cruising on their gentleman's C's. The school did not start a law review, the traditional showcase for fledgling legal brains, until 1948. In January 1950, Sandra's first year, the law school moved to the front of the Outer Quad. Out went the stained-glass windows and the marble stairway, lamented *The Stanford Daily;* in went the "modern" linoleum floors and fluorescent lighting. Most students were studying to become commercial lawyers; little attention was paid to the policy questions posed by constitutional law.[27]

A professor accused Sandra's classmate Beatsie, "You took a place in the school that could have been for a man who is now not able to get in. You're just going to work for a couple of years and then leave to get married." But Sandra had no memory of resentment or hostility from her male classmates or the faculty. In May of her first year, she and four other Stanford students (two men and two women, including her pal Diane Porter Cooley) challenged five professors to a TV-style quiz show (the ticket sales went to charity).[28] She did not speak up much in class, but when she did, in her deliberate but incisive way, her classmates listened.[29] She flourished in the classroom, in moot court, and as one of the top scholars on the new law review.* She later remembered her late-night hours at the law review, editing dense legal arguments with other brainy young students, as an intellectual awakening. "We had the sense that law would be our life," she recalled.[30]

The top student in the class of 1952, by all accounts, was a lanky midwesterner with a flattop haircut named William Rehnquist. A fellow student recalled that in the classroom the professors would torture students with the so-called Socratic method for a while, leading

---

* In later years, it was widely reported that Sandra Day O'Connor stood third in her class at graduation. In fact, Stanford did not keep class rank, leaving her classmates at reunions to don T-shirts all proclaiming I'M NUMBER TWO.

them down logical blind alleys and tripping up their false assump-
tions. Then they would turn to Bill Rehnquist for the answer.

Rehnquist was jovial, quirky, and opinionated. He enjoyed provok-
ing arguments so he could win them. The son of a Wisconsin sales-
man, he had served in the war as an army weatherman in North Africa;
he liked the warm, dry desert climate so much that he vowed to live in
the American West or Southwest when he returned home. Influenced
by Friedrich Hayek's 1944 antisocialist manifesto, *The Road to Serfdom,*
he developed a strong libertarian streak—and saw the American West
as its natural expression. Earning a B.A. at Stanford on the GI Bill, he
spent a year at Harvard, studying politics and reinforcing his suspi-
cion of East Coast know-it-alls and dislike of northern winters. The
professors, he believed, were "liberal blatherers" who condescended
to the rubes from the provinces.[31]

Back at Stanford for law school in the fall of 1949, Rehnquist began
sitting next to Sandra Day in class. They shared their equally meticulous notes. By the end of spring term, as Sandra was moving beyond
John Hamilton, she and Rehnquist were going out on dates to the
movies and picnics at Half Moon Bay. Rehnquist would remember his
time with Sandra in the spring of 1950 as "idyllic."[32] Sandra was less
swept away, but she did invite him home to meet her parents. In the
late summer of 1950, Rehnquist made the long trek to the Lazy B to
woo Sandra under the watchful eyes of Harry and Ada Mae.

The trip did not go well. Harry greeted his daughter's latest suitor
by cooking a bull's testicle over the branding fire and offering it to
Rehnquist to eat. He gamely choked down the so-called "mountain
oyster," but he failed to impress MO or DA. He made the mistake of
referring to Harry Day as "the old cattle baron," and, at least according to family legend, he offended Ada Mae with his table manners.[33]

In later years, Rehnquist himself had little to say about the trip to
the Lazy B or his courtship of Sandra, except to tell an interviewer for
the Stanford Law alumni magazine, "I visited her at her family's ranch
that summer. We dated some in the second year, and then we kind of
went different ways." Actually, they were a steady couple until December 1950, well into their second year. Then Sandra told Rehnquist
she wanted to break up. Stung by Sandra's rejection, Rehnquist later
blamed himself for being presumptuous and inattentive. Beatsie

Challis Laws recalled, "He was enthusiastic about her. She liked him, but she was less enthusiastic." Diane Porter Cooley thought that Rehnquist was "just a study buddy." By the late fall of 1950, Sandra's eye may have wandered to another boy.[34]

In romance, Sandra was accustomed to being the pursued, not the pursuer. Although she had been jilted by John Hamilton, she had regarded him as an innocent mistake (without crediting her parents for warning her). But in the winter term of 1951, she fell for a fellow law student named Richard Knight, who broke her heart. This time, she was so shaken that she considered abandoning her ambitions in the law. In an anguished letter to her parents, she told the story:

> *Dear Mother and Daddy,*
>
> *Well, I've just never seen things turn out so terribly. I thought I had at least made up my mind as to what and who I wanted and had finally found the perfect boy—Richard. As so often happens, I communicated my feelings for a while, thought them fully reciprocated. But yesterday he told me it was all over. I'm sure I'll live over it, but I am certainly wondering—for what? I just can't hold an interest in the law forever, nor do I want to. It is indeed a cold empty comfort. I am nothing but a girl law student—and believe me, it is my greatest liability, and I do wish I had never begun it. I am resigning from the law review after completing my recent assignment of a note on California water pollution. I don't know why my "love affairs" have never turned out to be mutual.*[35]

Self-pity was uncharacteristic of Sandra, and she did not brood for long. To be a woman unafraid to demonstrate her intelligence may have been her "biggest liability" in the male-dominated world of the early 1950s, but she rallied from rejection. She did not quit the law review. She was consoled by her friend Beatsie and her other pals living in Cubberley House, a women's residence just behind the president's house at Stanford, where she played charades and began dating other boys. Sandra was not a comfortable public speaker—her knees shook and her throat went dry, she recalled—but she entered the moot court competition with Bill Rehnquist that spring, finishing as runner-up to a former B-24 pilot named Alan Fink. ("It was nothing compared to being shot at," Fink later told the alumni magazine.)[36]

Before the competition, "I was worried about Sandra because she was so shy," recalled Beatsie. "I knew it would be particularly hard for her. She managed just fine."

IN LATE JANUARY 1952, her final year of law school, Sandra wrote her parents that "Bill Rehnquist left Tues. for Washington, and it does not seem the same school without him. We all truly hated to see him leave, in spite of, perhaps even because of, all the funny things he does. He certainly has a brilliant career ahead." Graduating a semester early, the future chief justice was off to serve as a law clerk to Justice Robert Jackson at the U.S. Supreme Court. Sandra went on to tell her parents that she was going out with a couple of other boys, including Richard Knight (now just a friend), and "a new friend, John O'Connor (law school and San Francisco)."[37]

In a private memoir written in the late 1990s, John O'Connor, by then Sandra's husband of more than forty years, recalled a January day in 1952 when he got a note in his mailbox at the law review telling him that he was to cite-check and proofread an article. He was paired with a third-year member of the review (and the only woman on the law review from her class), Sandra Day. He called Sandra and proposed meeting at the library at seven the following evening.

"When we started talking the next night, I liked her immediately," John wrote in his memoir. "I thought she was attractive, smart, and fun. I tried to be charming and funny as we checked the citations. As we were finishing the cite checking, I said, 'How about doing the proof reading over a beer at Dinah's Shack?'"

The genial fraternity man with a broad smile and the slender, bright-eyed ingenue with a gap-toothed grin drove in Sandra's car, a green Plymouth, over to the college town roadhouse ten minutes away and "just talked," O'Connor recalled. "We talked for a long time. By the end of our visit, it was clear that we liked each other. She drove me to my dorm. I asked her if we could do something the next night. She said that would be fine."

John O'Connor was charming and funny. He was a proud achiever; in his memoir, written largely for his three sons, he recorded that he had been Head Yell Leader and president of the debate club at St.

Ignatius High, and at Stanford he was honored to be one of fifteen students in his class of 150 to make the law review. The son of a successful doctor and a socially ambitious mother, young John was status conscious from an early age. He dutifully recorded that his undergrad fraternity, DU, ranked "seventh or eighth" out of Stanford's twenty-seven frats. But he had a relaxed, humorous manner. "He walked easy, and he talked easy," recalled a fraternity brother, Jim Watkinson.[38]

John and Sandra went out again the next night and the night after that. Finally, after going out night after night for a week or two, John asked, "How about the next five nights?" and Sandra said yes. They eventually went out forty-one nights in a row, until John pleaded exhaustion; he had started sleeping through his first class in the morning and had to borrow Sandra's notes from the year before.[39]

As a boy growing up in San Francisco, John had been sent by his mother to take dancing lessons (the better to shine at a debutante cotillion). Sandra loved to spin around the dance floor with him, following his lead, not missing a step or a beat. At a dance party in San Francisco, the crowd stopped to watch the couple show their moves.[40]

John led, but he did not dominate. He had a light touch. "Other guys were solid and purposeful," recalled Diane Porter Cooley. "But John was lighthearted and fun." He seemed to delight in Sandra. He gently mocked her deliberate speaking style and her sometimes abrupt or bossy manner, but he never seemed annoyed. Most important, to Sandra, he was not threatened by her intellectual power. Stanford was far more sophisticated than Austin High, but in the early 1950s, women everywhere were expected to be submissive. "If you were smart, the boys didn't like you. Being self-assured and smart were turnoffs to the men," said Cooley. "They were the ones who were permitted to be smart and self-assured. You wanted to keep it under wraps." While Sandra knew how to placate or steer around bumptious males, she did not wish to hide her intelligence.

John was different from Sandra's other suitors—at once less assertive and less in awe. He was also different from her father. Born and raised in a city that regarded itself as a bastion of refinement against the crude West, John was a smooth city slicker, not a hard-riding, tough-talking cowboy; he would not have "made a hand," the standard of excellence at the Lazy B. He would have been lost at a cattle roundup. Still, to a young woman feeling her way toward independence from a father who was overbearing as well as adoring, the contrast between the two men may have been, at some level, welcome. John was graceful, debonair, and far more diplomatic than Harry. He was not engaged in a survival struggle with the weather or government regulators. Nor was he freighted with Harry's at times tortured ambivalence toward the ones he loved.

Harry Day was inconsistently hot and cold; John O'Connor was reliably warm. Sandra's father could be gruff or downright heartless about teaching Sandra the harsh lessons of life on a ranch, even as he venerated his daughter's precocious mind. (When Beatsie Challis Laws first visited the Lazy B in the spring of 1951, Harry Day said to her, "Sandra is really smart." Beatsie nodded in agreement, and Harry said again, "No, Sandra is *really* smart.") Beatsie could see that John equally appreciated Sandra's natural gifts, but did not confuse the issue by feeling a need to show off his male superiority. "John was just so proud of Sandra," she said. From the very beginning of their relationship, John O'Connor seemed content, at times eager, to bask in Sandra's brilliance. "It was great the way he took a back seat. He would not assert himself. He was not pushy," Beatsie recalled. Sandra, in turn, lit up at John's puns and wit—and showed her pleasure in ways that made him feel fulfilled. Notwithstanding her precise Miss Radford diction, Sandra could be goofy and earthy. "She laughed at his jokes," Beatsie recalled—not a titter or smirk, but a deep, sometimes raucous belly laugh. "He was buoyed up by it."[41]

BY SPRING, SANDRA was telling her family more about the new man in her life. Sandra's sister, Ann, age twelve, wrote with characteristic Day directness: "The whole family wants to know something about him. Answer these questions: 1. Is he handsome? 2. Does he have a car? 3. Does he have money. 4. Is he smart in Law School. 5. Where is his home." She decorated the card with the shapes of hearts and wrote "Sandra Day—courtship. John O'Conner [sp]—Friendship."[42]

Sandra was, by then, more than friendly with John. She was smitten. At the same time, she was—guardedly—corresponding with Bill Rehnquist, who had rediscovered his feelings for her.

Back in January, just before he left for Washington for his clerkship with Justice Jackson, Rehnquist had taken Sandra on a last date and blurted out that he was in love with her and had been for the last two years.* Now, lonely in his new city and new job, he was pining for her. He had gone out on a few dates with other women, but he teasingly confessed, "Maybe you spoiled me, with your demure manner and sweet smile (cloaking a ruthless impulse to dominate, of course!)." He suggested that she join him in Albuquerque, New Mexico, that summer, to study for the bar exam. (He planned to settle in New Mexico after his Supreme Court clerkship.) "Maybe we could review our notes together! Wouldn't that be exciting!"

On March 11—just about the time Sandra and John O'Connor were going out on their fortieth straight date—Rehnquist wrote to "Dearest Sandy" in a tone that turned more serious. He invited her to come to Washington that summer. "I would like to speak to you of important things." He alluded to some inner turmoil: "I can't live without you, but I'm just not sure I can live with you."

In a letter on March 29, he became confessional and imploring. He painfully tried to sort through their breakup in December 1950. He blamed himself for "taking things too much for granted. But whatever the case may be, I know I can never be happy without you," he wrote. Then he popped the question: "To be specific, Sandy, will you marry me this summer?"

Sandra temporized. She did not say no, and she did not tell her old beau that she was now seeing someone else. On April 11, Rehnquist wrote Sandra, "I, too, was sorry that you couldn't 'say yes and come running.' But I appreciate your feeling that you would like some time to make the decision." He began making plans to come visit her in California in August.[44]

Was Sandra cruelly stringing along a besotted old boyfriend? In later life, Sandra would be known for her directness—for being almost too brusque. But from an early age, possibly from watching her mother handle her father, she had picked up a knack for avoidance, for

* In November 1951, in his notebook for his class on wills, Rehnquist doodled, inside a heart shape, a sketch of a pretty girl who may have been Sandra.[43]

maneuvering around emotional flare-ups. She seemed to have a feel for which fires would flame out on their own.

Her own future was very much up in the air. For all his persistence at Dinah's Shack, John O'Connor had not yet asked her to marry him, and she had reason not to get her hopes up again: She had already been jilted twice before. She was also preoccupied by her own career prospects. As law school ended, Sandra was consumed with a frustrating search to find a job as a lawyer.

After graduation, she did not want to be a small-town attorney. In the summers, she had worked as a part-time secretary for a solo practitioner in Lordsburg, New Mexico, who represented everyone from the local banker to the town prostitute. While the experience was an "eye opener" about life in a rural community, she was hoping for something grander.[45] On the bulletin board at Stanford Law School were posted notices from all the big-city law firms in San Francisco and Los Angeles: Third-year students with a B average or better were invited to apply. Sandra was Order of the Coif, top 10 percent of her class. "I applied to every firm on the bulletin board," she later recalled. "Not a single one would give me an interview." Some did not bother to respond; others explained they were not hiring women lawyers.

An undergraduate friend had a father who was a partner at Gibson, Dunn & Crutcher, a top L.A. firm. Sandra traveled to Los Angeles to see him. "You have a fine résumé, Miss Day," the partner explained. "Fine. But, Miss Day, this firm has never hired a woman lawyer. I don't see that it will. Our clients won't stand for it."

Then, as Sandra liked to tell the story, the Gibson Dunn partner asked, "Well, how well do you type?" She answered, "So-so." He said, "Well, if you type well enough, we might be able to get you a job as a legal secretary."

Sandra responded, "That isn't the job I want to find."[46]

Sixty years later, asked how she felt about this rebuff, she responded, "It was a total shock. It shouldn't have been. I should have known better. I should have followed what was going on, but I hadn't, and it just came as a real shock, because I had done well in law school, and it never entered my mind that I couldn't even get an interview. . . . I was quite downhearted by what I experienced."[47]

She struggled to explain how she could have been surprised by discrimination that was, in that time and place, routine. "I was quite naïve," she told the author. "But I felt capable. I felt more competent than the others. Why wouldn't I be able to get a job? I felt it in my heart."[48] Getting a job was not out of the question. There were law jobs for women in the public sector, clerking for a judge or working for a government agency. A woman could get a law job in a private law firm—but only if she knew the right person. Because of her father's connections, Beatsie Challis Laws was offered a job with a firm specializing in oil and gas cases in San Francisco. But she turned the job down when she learned she was being offered a lower starting salary than the men. (Thanks to an old boyfriend, she got a job clerking for the chief justice of the California Supreme Court.)

Years later, Beatsie puzzled over her friend's shock at being turned away by the law firms. "I was surprised that she was surprised," she said. By her last year at Stanford, Sandra had become accustomed to getting her way in most things, if not in romance. After her father gave her a car, a 1951 Plymouth, she took a bucket of paint, went to a campus parking lot, and painted in a reserved parking space for herself. Perhaps, in a way, Stanford had been too comfortable for Sandra. At Harvard Law, the few women students of the era endured something called Ladies' Day, when they were grilled in class to the derisive amusement of their professors and male classmates. But at Stanford, "the professors all liked Sandra. She was smart and fun. She wasn't just there to fool around," said Laws.[49] O'Connor appreciated all of her professors, O'Connor later recalled, except for her professor in constitutional law, the one course (ironically, given later events) that left her cold. She felt free to visit the teachers in their offices and ask any legal question. But no professor took her aside to explain that she might graduate with high honors from law school and still be unemployable at a law firm.[50]

IN MID-JUNE, AFTER graduation, Sandra drove John O'Connor to Lake Tahoe to meet her parents, who were picking up their daughter on the way to a cruise to Alaska. "I knew they knew about me; so, it was a momentous meeting," John recalled in his private memoir. John found Ada Mae to be "very attractive, always dressed perfectly, kind, warm, and friendly. She made me feel comfortable right away. Sandra's father," wrote John, "was a different matter." While "perfectly polite," he was "far from ebullient" to meet John. "You had to prove to Harry Day that you were the right kind of person before he would really open up. In addition, it was clear that Sandra was his treasure."[51]

On the cruise up the Canadian coast, Sandra made it obvious to her parents how she felt about John. Amid fishing and looking at the scenery, she darned some socks for him. On June 21, she wrote from a "quiet little cove in British Columbia," "Am busy ruining my eyes on your socks. And thinking and talking of you most constantly. No Eskimos for me. I love you, Sandra."[52]

Meanwhile, Bill Rehnquist was busy making plans to meet up with Sandra in August. "I will be in the Bay Area for about ten days, and of course the main purpose of the visit is to see YOU. . . . I am looking forward more than I can say to seeing you," he wrote on June 25.

Finally, at the end of July, Sandra wrote him, special delivery, to tell him she was seeing John. Rehnquist disguised his hurt beneath some huffiness: "Sandy, you are 22 years of age, and it is about time you realized that you've got to put some rein on your impulses as a gesture of decency."

But despite his upset, he recovered and regained his equanimity and geniality. He did see Sandra in San Francisco and even visited Yosemite with her. Hiking in the woods, they found a way to move beyond romantic illusions and back to teasing warmth and mutual respect—a friendship that would last the rest of their lives. On August 26, Rehnquist wrote, "Dear Sandy—Was most happy to find your letter awaiting when I arrived in Milwaukee. I, too, enjoyed our time together tremendously, and often think back over some of the good times we had."[53] It may have helped that Rehnquist was already in touch with the woman he would marry a year later. (He had met Nan Cornell at Stanford in 1951; just before he died in 2005, Rehnquist told a close friend that Nan was the only woman he had ever really loved.)[54]

Back in Palo Alto, John was having dinner with Sandra and Beatsie every night in a little rented cottage on Princeton Street. John recalled in his memoir, "One night, when Beatsie was not at their house, I proposed to SOC, who promptly accepted my proposal."*

Writing some years later, John recorded that "my feelings about her had been, to say the least, very strong for very long." But he had hesitated to propose to Sandra. He was only twenty-two, he explained in his memoir, and still had a year to finish law school and pass the bar. He "didn't even have a car," and "had no funds." The Korean War was dragging on, and he knew he would have to go in the service. There was another reason, which O'Connor did not state in his memoirs, though he hinted at it. Earlier in the summer, he had asked his mother if he could bring Sandra to dinner at their house in San Francisco. She said yes, but John was "very nervous about this meeting. My mother was very, very picky. I prayed that she would make things easy and relaxed. I was so nervous about my mother that, just before we walked into our home, I asked SOC if her fingernails were clean. She couldn't believe I asked that, but I knew my mother."[55]

---

* In his private writings, John usually referred to Sandra by her married initials.

CHAPTER THREE

THE
GOLDEN COUPLE

"Oh, for God's sake, Sandra, do you always have to overachieve?"

Sandra and John O'Connor share a loving cup at their wedding at the Lazy B in 1952. John went to work at a top law firm in Phoenix, Sandra hung out a shingle in a strip mall, and they had three babies. The O'Connors were soon the toast of the town.

S ANDRA CALLED HER parents on Monday, September 1, to say she was engaged to John and wanted to marry him over Christmas at the ranch. Unwilling to risk no for an answer, John had avoided formally asking Harry for his daughter's hand in advance. Instead, by long distance telephone, John and Sandra sought Harry and Ada Mae's blessing and approval. The Days were supportive, though less than enthusiastic. A week later, Ada Mae wrote her prospective son-in-law, "the announcement was received with mingled feelings, as you realize." Still, she went on, "we have enough confidence in Sandra's judgment to feel that if you are the one she has chosen to love and cherish then you must have the qualities necessary to be worthy of her love. We are happy to welcome you as a member of our family, John. Please don't think that my delay in writing you has been a reflection of our liking you, or otherwise." She fretted about money. "You and Sandra are brave to undertake marriage without more financial security. . . . Sandra has said all along that she wants to utilize her education so it is perfectly all right for her to work for a while. She will enjoy it, I am sure," wrote Ada Mae, measuring her words—and signaling, by carefully underscoring the words "a while," her assumption that Sandra would get down to raising a family soon enough.[1]

If Ada Mae's warmth for John was tepid (and mostly a matter of taking Sandra's word), Harry remained cool toward his prospective son-in-law. Some years later, asked how he had received John, Harry answered with a double negative: "I didn't indicate I didn't like him."[2] But the Days, unlike John's mother, Sally, did not try to stand in the way of the marriage.

In her letter of September 8, Ada Mae wrote that she planned to drive over to Tucson to meet Sally, who was there visiting friends. The two proud mothers faced off. "My mother got a little haughty about how terrific I was," recalled John O'Connor. She questioned whether Sandra was good enough for her son.[3]

"Mrs. O'Connor wanted John to marry into Society, with a capital S," recalled Diane Porter Cooley. "Not to a girl from Postage Stamp, Arizona. She didn't send her son to Stanford to marry a ranch girl." Sally O'Connor had been grooming John to be a perfect gentleman all his life. As a little boy, he had been taught by his mother to bow at the waist to adults. John's father had attended the University of California, Berkeley, but the family made clear that John was to attend Stanford, which had slightly more social cachet than the public university across the bay. Though John's father was a doctor, the Depression years made finances tight, and the O'Connors did not belong to any of the several exclusive clubs that counted in San Francisco's social hierarchy.[4] "In San Francisco, there is always a higher rung," said Cooley. Sally O'Connor wanted her son to keep climbing.

After the uncomfortable meeting between the two mothers in Tucson, Ada Mae wrote Sandra that Mrs. O'Connor had found Sandra to be "inappropriate" for her son. "I didn't fit the bill," Sandra recalled many years later. She worried that John would have second thoughts about the engagement. "For John to buck his mother was difficult," recalled Beatsie Challis Laws.[5]

But John stood by Sandra. He was supported by his father, Dr. Jay O'Connor, who did his best to play peacemaker. A relieved Sandra wrote her parents that she felt "uneasy and insecure" about John's mother, but that in time, "I think these things will be all right."[6]

Navigating the moods of their parents—sometimes by simply ignoring them—helped bring Sandra and John closer. "It was good to hear that your parents are in such a fine mood," Sandra wrote John. "One never knows." Her father, she reported, "is still in a bad mood. Honestly, I hope you stomp on me the minute I'm getting ready to be in a bad mood."[7]

In October, Sandra took the California bar exam, the demanding hurdle for a license to practice law in the state. The results were published three months later. Unable to find her name on the list of students who had passed, a group of Stanford law professors anxiously gathered to discuss what to do about this unexpected failure by a star student. As it turned out, they had been searching the list for the wrong last name. Sandra had taken the state bar exam using her soon-to-be-married name, not her maiden name.[8]

In November, Sandra went home to prepare for the wedding. "I love you—and love you—and love you some more," Sandra wrote John. "Only 46 more days—til you're do-o-o-o-omed. What fun." John's mother had given him a pair of nylon pajamas for the wedding night. "I have gotten into the habit of going to bed early while home," Sandra reported, adding drily, "This is preparation, you understand, for our future life together. Fully expect to retire with you each night as the last dish is dried. This is to view your new pajamas."

Sandra had been given a wedding-night gown by her mother. "It is just beautiful," Sandra wrote John, "but suspect, as with your pajamas, it is something on which the money could have been better spent elsewhere. But do hope you like it—for those fun minutes after the bath and before the bed."

Daily letters flew back and forth between Palo Alto and the Lazy B, tender, newsy, playful, and innocently racy. "Your letter about waking me up in the morning with lots of kisses so we could snuggle some more was quite a temperature raiser. More, S.D., more!" wrote John.

The wedding was scheduled to take place at the Lazy B on December 20, five days before Christmas. Sandra and her mother sent out three hundred invitations, knowing that most of their friends would not be able to make the long trek to southeastern Arizona. Somehow, the formal invitations spelled John O'Connor's name wrong—with an *e* instead of an *o*. Sandra was mortified. "I can never tell you how shocked, embarrassed, and horrified I was to receive your letter to-night and find out about the invitations," she wrote three weeks be-fore the wedding. "I couldn't believe my eyes. . . . I could just die. And mother and daddy are terribly embarrassed and ashamed. In fact, Daddy is in a state. . . .

"John," she went on, "just tell me truthfully how your parents have taken this latest shock. I am going to write your mother tonight. It will certainly confirm her worst fears about me as an unsuitable wife for you. I wouldn't have had this happen for anything in the world. Daddy says if he were you he thinks he wouldn't marry me if I couldn't even spell his name right on the invitation."

But John laughed off the mistake, and if his parents had misgivings, he did not share them. He showered her in more love letters. "All I want to convey is my deep, deep love for you, my desire to share what I can offer you and the joy—oh, the lovely joy—in loving you," he wrote one night when he was "a little gassed," as he put it. "I love you so much—don't ever change—just be mine and let me be yours. . . . That's all I want, that's all I care about, that's all I live for."[9]

As the wedding day neared, Sandra went into the mountains to cut pine boughs. She arranged them in the new barn, as yet unused for cattle and horses, filling the corrugated steel and concrete structure with sweet scents. Her mother stretched fabric over hay bales for the guests to sit on. Wedding presents were displayed. Rastus, Sandra's favorite cowboy, gave her a full silver place setting.

The groom arrived a few days before the nuptials. Harry was predictably "terrible" with his new son-in-law, Sandra recalled.[10] According to family legend, Harry made John eat his own "mountain oyster."[11] But John took it all in stride, and kept his own parents on good behavior.

Sandra and John were married in front of the fireplace in the living room of the Lazy B, too small to accommodate the wedding guests, who were mostly local ranchers in their best cowboy boots. In his memoir for his sons, John recalled, "I had been 'Cool Hand Luke' until Sandra came into the living room on her father's arm. She looked petrified. She would try to smile, and the sides of her mouth kept quivering. I had never seen her like that before, and it turned me from casual to semi-shaky."

A local Episcopal priest performed the service. The Days had worried that the O'Connors would insist on a Catholic service, but John, who had very briefly considered the priesthood as a student at St. Ignatius High, had fallen away from the church.

In the barn, a three-piece combo swung into "Put Your Little Foot" and the Virginia Reel and other country tunes. An inebriated immigrant laborer came into the barn and asked Sally O'Connor to dance, John recorded. "Thankfully, she did not create a scene. When M.O. found out about this incident, she about died."[12]

At eight thirty, the newlyweds left the reception and made the long drive to El Paso to catch an early morning flight to Mexico City. On the plane, they were presented with a "huge Mexican breakfast," John recorded. The plane flew south, over the mountains. "SOC began to vomit in an air bag. When she finally got that under control, which was after I was finished eating my breakfast," the insouciant John recalled, "I asked if I could finish her lunch. That almost terminated the marriage." In Acapulco, the young couple stayed in bed, occasionally venturing out to watch young men dive from the cliffs.

SANDRA RETURNED FROM the ten-day honeymoon to take up the search for a legal job. She approached the San Mateo County district attorney and asked for work. He said he could not pay her; she said that would not be a problem. He said he had no desk for her. She noted that there was plenty of space in the outer office where his secretary sat. He offered her a job at no pay, working alongside his secretary. She accepted at once.[13]

"I really like it," Sandra wrote her mother and father in January. She was doing legal research and writing memos, and after a few months, she was paid a small salary. The DA's office "gives opinions to county officials about legal problems that arise," wrote Sandra. "This week I worked a couple of days on an inquiry by the sheriff about just how far he should move a family out when he evicts them from a house after a writ of eviction—whether merely to the sidewalk or street, or into storage. It is a difficult question." She did not say how she answered the question—the first in her long career of reconciling the letter of the law and the emotional and practical demands of real life. Rather, she concluded her letter by writing, "Plenty of time on weekends to clean house."[14]

With the Korean conflict grinding on, John expected to enter the service after graduation that spring, hopefully as a lawyer, and Sandra knew that she would follow him to his posting. He obtained a commission in the Judge Advocate General's Corps as a second lieutenant handling cases for the army. After six months of separation while John endured basic training, John and Sandra spent three months at the JAG school in Charlottesville, Virginia. One cold spring day, they drove three hours north to Washington to visit the Supreme Court. The marble edifice was closed; the massive bronze doors were locked. Sandra and John posed for a picture before the great double row of columns. In his scrapbook, John wrote, "This is first and last time we'll ever see this place."[15]

That summer, John was posted to Frankfurt, Germany (he wrote in his memoir that he obtained a coveted slot in Europe by fibbing to his commander that his lifelong ambition was to swim the English Channel).[16] While John prosecuted AWOL soldiers and petty thieves, Sandra got a legal job with the Quartermaster's Corps, selling off huge amounts of surplus from the American occupation—whole trainloads of equipment and supplies. She churned out contracts and again faced job discrimination. "I received a promotion to a Civil Service Rating of 9," she wrote home. "I am now an 'officer.' I am not too excited because I think that is the rating I should have had all along. But I'm glad of it anyway."[17]

A young American couple could live well on two U.S. government salaries in West Germany in 1955. A couple of blocks from John's office—in the I. G. Farben building, requisitioned by the American army—the O'Connors resided in "an incredible apartment," recalled John. "We had a huge living room, a full-sized dining room, a fantastic bar area, a large bedroom and a big kitchen." They bought a suite of Danish modern furniture and a black Volkswagen with a sunroof.[18] They did not make many local friends. The Germans were still "struggling to eat," recalled Sandra, and they were sullen toward the Americans who were at once occupying their country and defending it from Soviet Communism. "The weather here is unbelievably cold and raining," Sandra wrote home. "Germans blame it on the atomic bomb and there is no reasoning with them to the contrary."[19]

Sandra often talked about feeling a "compulsion to volunteer." Working a day or two a week with German refugees left homeless from the war, she wrote her parents to see if they would welcome one, a girl named Johanna, as a housekeeper at the Lazy B. The reaction from her father was typically dyspeptic. "Your mother has never discussed this business of Johana [sic] with me but knowing her, I am sure she went overboard for it," wrote Harry. "She [Johanna] couldn't be happy here and one of the worst things in life to have to live with is an unhappy female," Harry groused. "All my life I have been surrounded and associated with females whose demands greatly exceeded their contributions towards living (you are the one exception,

Sandra) and I do not relish the thought of assuming responsibility for another one." Ada Mae found a place for Johanna with another family.[20]

In long airmail screeds, Harry sent Sandra a steady stream of complaints: about dying grass, low cow prices, his failing health, and the deficiencies of his wife and two other children. "I came back here yesterday morning from El Paso to this grubby, narrow, and confining life that we lead," he wrote in August 1955. A year later, he wrote, "I can't get along with anybody, my family, my employees, or my neighbors. I don't have any friends. I don't like anyone and no one likes me." When he complained that he was feeling so unwell he wasn't sure he could handle another roundup, Sandra urged him to "please, please" see a doctor. The moaning and groaning was mostly for show. Two months later he chortled, "Ha! Who was it who said I needed medical attention? I have just finished rounding up 240 Sections of range. . . . I have led every drive, branded every calf, selected every old cow to cull from the herd . . . and I am still going strong. I have more pep and energy than any of my men."[21]

Sandra's younger brother and sister were lively company and expert cowhands, but by the mid-1950s, they were both in full teenage rebellion. Alan got into scrapes and Ann picked the wrong boyfriends, causing no end of transatlantic correspondence between Harry and Sandra about the hardship of raising "juvenile delinquents," as Harry sardonically referred to his younger children. Sandra's siblings were in an impossible spot with their father. They "had to live up to a girl who could do no wrong," remarked Diane Porter Cooley. "Sandra was the perfect child, which was too bad for her brother and sister." The comparison was particularly hard on Ann. From Miss Radford's, Ann wrote a poignant note to her older sister about a teacher they shared: "Sandra, she just can't imagine how you and I could be so unalike. You were the quote 'lovely child'—she doesn't have the same tender feelings towards me, I'm afraid."[22]

In response to Harry's fulminations, Sandra wisely did little more than cluck and sympathize. "I spent a sleepless night worrying about you worrying about Ann," she wrote back once, but offered no advice.[23] In truth, she may have been relieved to be seven thousand miles away from the Lazy B, in a place where she and John could forge a marriage far from their judgmental parents.

There was time to travel and to ski. At Kitzbühel, they "rented a little cottage with little hearts and flowers carved on the outside, sitting in the snow in the middle of the Alps," Sandra recalled. Sandra learned a very formal, controlled style of skiing, knees held tight together, erect body gracefully swooping down the mountain in long, smooth arcs.[24]

Après ski, the O'Connors joined other young couples in "shoe dances"—"the ladies all threw shoes into the middle; whoever got your shoe, you danced with him," recalled Lois Driggs Cannon, a friend from Stanford who had run into Sandra at the Frankfurt PX and joined the O'Connors on ski weekends. The best dancers, she recalled, were Sandra and John.

Others stopped to watch when the O'Connors reunited and began to jitterbug. The attraction was obvious. "You know when someone is happily married," recalled Cannon. "You could tell that they were in love with each other."[25]

In September 1956, Sandra wrote her parents that John would be released from the army in January. "John is very anxious to stay over here a little longer," to travel and ski. He wanted to savor their last true free time, unburdened by responsibility. With DA and MO, Sandra played the dutiful daughter: "I am terribly anxious to get home and see you but do not want to make a big issue of it since he wants to stay awhile. Would you be disappointed if we stayed a few months longer than we normally would?"[26]

"We skied until the snow ran out," Sandra later recalled. "We skied all day every day. We skied in the snow and we skied in the rain and we skied in blizzards. We skied on powder and we skied on ice, and we skied on the mud. We skied until there wasn't a bit of snow left and we didn't have any money left, either. So we came home." By then, Sandra was pregnant.[27]

BACK IN THE United States in the spring of 1957, John interviewed at law firms in Los Angeles and San Francisco, staying for a few weeks with his parents, whom he had not seen in three years. But his sights were on Phoenix.

The medium-size (population 350,000) city in the Arizona desert was just becoming a boomtown. John and Sandra had been hearing excited reports from Stanford friends. "Phoenix is going to go!" exclaimed Don Cooley, husband of Sandra's Branner Hall pal, Diane. The Cooleys had moved there so Don could take a job at IBM.[28] A "golden horde" was arriving in the rapidly expanding metro area, sustained by the spread of air conditioning and vast water projects largely paid for by the federal government. World War II veterans stationed at the big air bases outside of town stayed for the sunshine and opportunity. IBM, Motorola, General Electric, and other tech companies were building factories; senior citizens with money were retiring for the balmy winters.[29] From Germany, Sandra had written Bill Rehnquist, who had moved to Phoenix after his Supreme Court clerkship, to ask about the prospects for law jobs. "Ideal," wrote back her former suitor, now friend, who had opened a two-man practice.[30]

"I sensed that Phoenix was where I could make my place and have a greater chance to be a success and be a success sooner," John O'Connor recalled in his private memoir. He took a job as the tenth lawyer at a firm known as Fennemore Craig for the modest salary of $300 a month. For the first month, John and Sandra lived in a motel, then headed to Tucson (site of Arizona's only law school at the time) in the summer of 1957 to study for the Arizona bar exam.

Sandra was having second thoughts about Phoenix. In the month they were holed up in the motel, no one at Fennemore Craig had asked the young couple over to their homes or made any attempt to welcome them. As Sandra and John drove south toward Tucson and the bar review course, Sandra began insisting—in her relentlessly deliberate way—that they should instead live in San Francisco. It was a more civilized, cultivated city, she argued. "I felt it was more romantic," she recalled many years later. "You could listen to Nat King Cole at the Saint Francis. You couldn't do that in Phoenix."[31]

Still quarreling, the couple arrived at a junction with the highway that would lead to Tucson. "We had reached the proverbial fork in the road," John recollected. He pulled over and they argued some more. Finally, he recalled, "we decided to punt" and took the fork to the Lazy

B, "where we could discuss our problems with Sandra's parents." The Days were not much help. "Sandra's mother wanted us to stay in Arizona. Sandra's father was upset by our uncertainty but wouldn't express a view," he wrote. It seems surprising that Sandra was pushing to be so far from the Lazy B, but it may be that it was easier to love her family's ranch from a distance.[32]

Phoenix finally carried the day. Don Kauffman, who hailed from San Francisco and would become very close to the O'Connors in Phoenix, recalled John's thinking at the time. "Status of family was very important in San Francisco. John understood how it worked, how tough it was." John knew Kauffman's own story: He was from the Levi Strauss family in San Francisco that had made a fortune selling blue jeans, but Stanford's social fraternities had blackballed him because he was Jewish. He had moved to Phoenix. "My wife was put in charge of big things at a Phoenix museum at the age of twenty-two. In San Francisco, that never would have happened," Kauffman recalled. "We were an educated group looking for a new frontier, to do things without family history or status."[33] In his memoir, John recorded a more personal and immediate motivation: "My mother was a very critical woman and I did not want to listen to her time and again."[34]

The O'Connors began studying for the bar exam. For the first of many times, they caught the attention of the press. MAGAZINE CUPID FOR LAWYER COUPLE was the headline in *The Arizona Republic* on September 27, 1957. John told the reporter the story of wooing Sandra while proofreading a *Stanford Law Review* article (the "magazine") over beer. The newspaper story mentioned her job in San Mateo and described her as "undoubtedly the prettiest assistant DA to be found anywhere." The reporter asked: Did husband and wife plan to practice law together? The answers were perhaps unintentionally revealing: "'I am happily situated where I am,' emphasized John" to the paper, which named his firm and its office address in the "penthouse of the First National Bank Building." Sandra, then about eight months pregnant, was more circumspect. "I'm pretty well occupied at the moment," she said.[35]

Sandra tried finding a job at a law firm; none was hiring women. "You could fit all the women lawyers in Phoenix around a table," she recalled. Six months after she gave birth to their son Scott, she paired

up with a new lawyer, a graduate of Michigan Law School, whom she
had met at the bar review course, and they opened an office in a shopping center. "It was not the high-rent area," she recalled. Next door
was a TV repair shop. "We took whatever came in the door to pay the
rent." She wrote wills, handled divorces, and took criminal cases assigned by a local judge whose no-nonsense manner she admired. ("He
would admonish lawyers not to touch the bench," she remembered.)
One of her court-appointed clients was charged with forging checks.
He swore that the signature on the checks was someone else's. Out of
her own pocket, Sandra hired an expert—who testified in court that
the signature was indeed her client's. "Live and learn," she remembered.[36]

In the spring of 1959, when Sandra was pregnant again, her baby-
sitter quit and moved away. She left her law practice to become, nominally, a stay-at-home mother, but immediately worried that if she left
the law, she would never be able to return. She began writing questions for the state bar exam, working as a volunteer in the juvenile
court system, and handling bankruptcy work, in between taking care
of a three-year-old (Scott) and a toddler (Brian).[37]

Asked to join the Junior League, the white-gloved ladies' civic organization, Sandra quickly became president. "She learned a lot about
how to run a meeting and stand up on her feet," recalled Beatsie Challis Laws, who continued to visit her Stanford friend. "The Junior
League was an exclusive group. Elitist," recalled Sue Huck, who recommended her. ("We noticed she never mentioned it in later years,"
she added.) Sandra's name came up for membership because her aunt,
Blanche Mason, "was Old Phoenix," recalled Patty Simmons, another
Junior Leaguer. "Because everything was so new in Phoenix, old still
mattered," said Huck. Sandra and John were asked to join the exclusive Valley Field Riding and Polo Club, which had a rustic old clubhouse outside of Phoenix, where 150 members met once a month for
dinner parties.[38]

The O'Connors bought a 1.5-acre parcel of land north of downtown, on Denton Lane in an area called Paradise Valley. They built a
midcentury modern adobe four-bedroom house, full of sharp angles
and plate glass—"custom," recalled O'Connor, "but on the cheap." On
the weekends, the O'Connors sealed the adobe bricks with skim milk,

in the Navajo Indian tradition. Instead of air conditioning, they installed a "swamp cooler," a humidifier with a fan, "which worked until the summer monsoons came," recalled their son Scott.

Nestled in the desert foothills, Paradise Valley still had dirt roads, but it was becoming the favored suburb of both new and old money in Phoenix. A senior partner in his law firm, Phil von Ammon, advised John to join the Paradise Valley Country Club, even though he was making only $6,000 a year (about $54,000 in 2018 dollars). It was a good way to meet clients.[39]

John was a smart commercial litigator, but his greatest strength was keeping his clients, which included mining companies and car dealers, out of court. He had a knack for settling cases and avoiding drawn-out conflict. "He was able to fix things, not in the shady sense, but just by making people calm down and be reasonable," recalled Craig Joyce, a young lawyer at Fennemore Craig who later married the daughter of Sandra's favorite cousin, Flournoy. (Sandra, who liked to play matchmaker so much that she was teasingly dubbed "the Yenta of Paradise Valley," introduced the couple.) John O'Connor was the kind of lawyer who understood that civic engagement was at once good for business and good for the community. He joined the Rotary Club, raised money for the United Way, served on the boards of hospitals, and became involved in politics, at first on the local level.[40] He was instrumental in incorporating Paradise Valley, fending off the City of Phoenix, which wanted to annex the wealthy suburb. His neighbors were eager to keep the strip malls out. "Some people thought that was exclusive, but that's the way it was," recalled Dick Houseworth, a local banker and friend of the O'Connors.[41*]

One of the O'Connors' Paradise Valley neighbors was Barry Goldwater, who lived on a rise overlooking Camelback Mountain. "He lived in the big house on the hill. We lived in the low-rent district," Sandra recalled. "I liked him very much. He had charisma." The O'Connors licked envelopes and passed out leaflets in Goldwater's

---

* "Paradise Valley was a creature of its time," said Arizona historian Tom Zoellner. "No subdivisions or multifamily dwellings. That meant no racial minorities. They never said this; it was expressed through euphemisms like 'low-density.' It wasn't racist. They didn't want poor whites any more than Latinos."[42]

campaign to be reelected a United States senator in 1958. That year, Elva Coor was a nineteen-year-old intern in Goldwater's campaign office. Coor, who became a full-time staffer in Goldwater's Senate office in the early sixties, remembered seeing both John, who was president of the Maricopa County Young Republicans, and Sandra at GOP headquarters at 377 North Third Avenue, meeting with party leaders. "The older group would look to Sandra for advice. Goldwater and [Governor Paul] Fannin were not great intellectuals or highly educated. I would hear them say, 'Get Sandra.' When she walked into a room and spoke, everyone listened." Much of her advice was legal and cautionary—she warned the party elders to steer clear of wild-eyed activists. "We had a nut file," recalled Coor.[43]

John and Sandra were at heart Eisenhower Republicans. They did not want to get rid of the New Deal, but they did want to check the long reach of the federal government. They were pro-business conservatives, but hardly heartless. They did not wish to "stand athwart history, yelling Stop!" like William F. Buckley, Jr., the influential young polemicist and publisher of *National Review*. Rather, they saw themselves as voices of reason and moderation, free speech and fair play. Democrats in their part of the country were not exactly warriors for social justice. In the first half of the twentieth century, Democratic Party control of the "Solid South" extended all the way to the new (1912) state of Arizona. Democrats were funded by rural ranching and mining interests, known as the three C's—cotton, cattle, and copper—which extended their influence by the three B's—broads, beefsteak, and booze.

When Goldwater ran for president in 1964, losing in a landslide to Lyndon Johnson, the outspoken former Air Force pilot, who posed for photos at his Paradise Valley home wearing a cowboy hat and carrying a shotgun, was widely pictured by the Eastern media as a caricature of the Far Right. He was forever tagged by his speech accepting the GOP nomination: "Extremism in the defense of liberty is no vice. Moderation in the defense of justice is no virtue." In Arizona politics, however, he was generally regarded as a reformer.

Booming, sunny Arizona had a shady side. "Land speculators were selling land that was underwater or had no water," recalled Gay Firestone Wray, heiress to the tire fortune, who was part of the O'Connors' wide social circle and helped start a zoo and art museum in Phoenix. "You had to learn who to do business with and who not to do business with." In Phoenix after the war, Barry Goldwater, whose family owned the biggest department store, wanted to clean up the sleazy downtown strip known as the Deuce. The area, with its gamblers and prostitutes, was protected by corrupt politicians who were all Democrats. "In 1958, my boss at the bank told me to make sure to register as a Democrat, because no Republican ever gets elected," recalled Dick Houseworth. "But that was changing."[44] The northerners following the sun to Phoenix were largely Republicans.

The new political establishment was made up of businessmen who might be called progressive, in the sense of wanting government officials who would deliver services and build roads and dams without taking bribes. An informal group of local titans and civic leaders (later more formally known as the Phoenix 40) could meet for drinks at the old Adams Hotel and handpick politicians deemed to be clean (but also loyal to the businessmen). Their herald was Eugene Pulliam, the publisher of *The Arizona Republic* (and grandfather of Dan Quayle, George H. W. Bush's vice president), who was fiercely anti–federal government, anti–Big Labor, but pro–local government—as long as it boosted commercial development. The ideology was not so much conservatism as boosterism.[45]

John and Sandra O'Connor were warmly welcomed by the local powers that be. At charity dances at the Biltmore Hotel, they hobnobbed with the Pulliams and Goldwaters. At dinner parties, they played charades with Bill Rehnquist, who was also becoming involved in Republican politics, and his wife, Nan, a gentle soul who was Sandra's sometime rival in Junior League politics.[46] "It was a privilege to be invited to their house for dinner," recalled Gay Wray, the Firestone heiress, of the O'Connors. "They were invited everywhere." John was becoming a much-sought-after toastmaster, routinely called on after dinner to tell a story. He had a growing collection of jokes and elaborate stories, which he would practice on his children and law partners, making the tales ever more intricate and mimicking Irish brogues and foreign dialects.

His geniality could take the edge off Sandra's more direct manner. "She loved to party, loved to dance—they would be the first out on the floor—loved a naughty joke," recalled Elva Coor. "But she could be bossy as heck." Bossiness was not a virtue for women, who were still supposed to obey their husbands or any male authority. Close friends sensed some residual shyness in Sandra. "To cover up shyness, you become a little gruffer," said Wray. "She'd put up this shield a little."

Sandra could be warm and gracious; also formidable. Her bright hazel eyes were at once inviting and penetrating. It helped that she lit up around the easygoing John. "She acted like John was the most fun guy in the world. You said 'John' and she smiled," said Elva Coor. "Sandra was, in a word, stiff, and John, in one word, was loose," recalled Paul Eckstein, a local lawyer and lobbyist. "Sandra had a strong personality," recalled Patty Simmons, her fellow Junior Leaguer. "We gave a dinner party together. She made all the decisions. I wondered, do I want to do this again?" But Sandra paid no social price for her direct manner, Simmons concluded. "People just admired her so much. They were the golden couple. It just kind of grew."[47]

Gayle Wilson, whose husband, Pete, would later become a U.S. senator and governor of California, arrived in Phoenix in 1965 and met Sandra through the Junior League. "Sandra and John were a team, you could see that, a power couple, though the term didn't exist yet," recalled Wilson. "I was twenty-two, well-educated [Phi Beta Kappa at Stanford], but I telegraphed to her the feeling, 'I'm just a mother.'" Sandra reassured her, "What you're doing"—taking time to raise a family—"is the right thing for you to be doing."[48] Sandra conveyed an unflappable, grounded confidence. If she herself felt a tension between career and family, she was determined not to show it.

Sandra managed to be mother, wife, and civic paragon. (She took on, among other responsibilities, the presidency of the Heard Museum of Native Arts and Culture; "the meetings always ran on time," recalled board member and future Arizona governor Bruce Babbitt.) Her apparent effortlessness was a source of conversation and speculation among her friends. "We would note that John would start a conversation and Sandra would finish it," recalled Don Kauffman. "We wondered: Did they plan it that way?" "We would ask, 'How do you do it all?' She would just shrug," recalled Dick Houseworth.[49]

There was, of course, some resentment. "A little," said her friend

Betsy Taylor. "No one else had done what she had done." There was "some talk that she didn't raise the boys, that she couldn't possibly be doing the right job," said Betsy's daughter, Susan, who was close to the O'Connor children. "The Junior League types thought she had too much power. She was not a girlie-girl at all," said Wray. Even so, while she may have been spending long hours at Republican Party headquarters or on the dance floor at the Biltmore, she was at home in her kitchen. "She loved being a woman, she loved to cook," recalled Julie Folger, a friend from the Paradise Valley Country Club. "We all got hooked on Julia Child. Sandra cooked through the book, recipe by recipe. We said, 'Oh, for God's sake, Sandra, do you always have to overachieve?'"

The other wives "did not feel that she was a threat to their husbands," recalled Gay Wray. She liked men and liked to tease them and flirt with them, "but in a safe, nonsexual way," said Diane Porter Cooley. She had an intuitive, almost uncanny sense of just how far to go—in almost any realm of human endeavor. Her deftness was useful in navigating the politics of the Junior League, but it was obvious to everyone, including the Junior Leaguers, that larger stages beckoned. She did not appear to chafe at the limited opportunities available to a young Phoenix society matron in 1965; rather, she made the most of them. But her ambition was palpable, if not articulated or yet fully formed.[50]

"WE HAD A long leash," recalled her third son, Jay, born in 1963. "We had a few rules: If you go someplace, say where and be back at a certain time. But other than that we could do what we wanted. We didn't call and ask permission. We could ride our bikes everywhere." Scott, the oldest, remembered two rules: "If you can't say something nice about someone, don't say it" and "Don't hit your little brother."

The adventurer in the family was the middle boy, Brian. When he was about twelve years old, he began camping out for the weekend on Camelback Mountain. Earlier, when he was about six, his parents had not been happy to discover he was feeding a hobo living in a nearby arroyo. By the time he was a teenager, he was asking his parents for permission to hang glide (denied) and skydive (accepted; marginally safer). He would go on to scale the highest peaks on all seven continents of the world, culminating with Mount Everest.*

"My mom ran the show," recalled Jay. "She did the schedules, the camps, the schools, and paid the bills. Dad took out the dog but she did the rest. It was totally gender-defined." She was "always active. It was never, 'I just want to sit on the couch and watch TV.'" When Sandra was working full time, she would come home, "walk in the door and immediately start supervising dinner." A series of maids and housekeepers, most of them Mexican immigrants, provided essential help, cooking and cleaning and watching over the boys. Having grown up much of the year in El Paso, just across the then open border from the Mexican city of Juárez, Sandra was the product of a world in which Mexicans and Anglos routinely mixed, in part because every Anglo family in El Paso that could afford one had a Mexican housekeeper. Sandra could be a demanding boss; she expected the household helpers to keep up with her rapid-fire schedule, and a few quit or were let go. At the same time, she never raised her voice, and she invited the help to join the family for dinner. When one of the maids became pregnant, she made sure the mother and child were well cared for.

The boys never heard their mother complain about her hectic life, or anything else. She rarely yelled. "I can only remember one time," Scott recalled, "when we ate all the fried chicken meant for the guests. She blew her stack."

The boys "were a breeze to babysit for," recalled Denise Dravo Eliot, a teenage next-door neighbor who watched over them on some summer mornings and evenings in the late 1960s. "They were polite. They didn't complain. They didn't fuss in the way kids usually do. It was all very orderly," she said. If Denise was to make lunch, "all the ingredients for the meal were measured, in order, laid out in the kitchen by Mrs. O'Connor.

---

* In an age before car seats and seat belts, the O'Connors accepted cuts and scrapes as part of growing up. Once, as Sandra was bouncing along a dirt road, one of the boys tapped her on the shoulder and informed her that his brother Scott had fallen out of the car. She turned the car around, found and dusted off Scott, and they went on their way. She blamed herself for not properly shutting the car door.[51]

"I never saw those boys just watching TV," she added. In the afternoons, teenage boys (the sons of friends) who were athletic—proper
role models—would accompany the O'Connor sons to the country
club for swimming and sports, then later for more cultural uplift at
the Heard Museum. The atmosphere of the house was "not relaxed,"
recalled Eliot. "It was not tense, but not relaxed." She observed that
John O'Connor was fun and playful and could make Mrs. O'Connor
laugh.[52]

"I think I was lucky, in a way, having three boys," Sandra told Jan
Crawford Greenburg of the *Chicago Tribune* in 2003, "because you only
had to buy one set of clothes. Everything else was a hand-me-down.
They don't have the same needs as little girls do in some ways. You
have to keep a close eye on them or they can get into trouble, but they
don't have the same emotional needs that little girls might have."[53]
She may have been thinking about growing up as a little girl separated
from her parents.

In a sense, the boys were raised the Lazy B way, taught to be frugal
and practical. But they were not isolated in Phoenix as they might
have been on a ranch, and the O'Connor household was more cos-
mopolitan than provincial. The boys were exposed to a steady parade
of houseguests and visitors from all over, including foreigners—
diplomats, businessmen, a chef in the Japanese imperial household,
the crown prince of Swaziland—who came to dinner through the
World Affairs Council. The O'Connors arranged for the boys to live
in Mexico for six weeks on an exchange program, and for several
months they cared for a Hispanic couple's son, a star football player
from Duncan, Arizona, who had lost a leg because of medical mal-
practice.

The O'Connor boys learned manners largely by their parents' example. None of the three recalls lectures on the proper way to treat a
lady (or a teenage girl). They had only to watch their mother and father to see a respectful and loving relationship between a man and
woman, husband and wife. If John was not exactly on top of the
housework, the boys themselves learned to iron shirts, do the laundry,
and occasionally cook a simple meal.

From time to time, Sandra and John showed the boys a whimsically
silly side. "When I was in about sixth grade, we were awakened by

mom with a flashlight. 'Boys! Come with me!' she said. We went back to their bedroom and there was Dad dressed up as a clown," said Scott. At Halloween, John would dress up as the Hunchback of Notre Dame and Sandra as a wicked witch. The neighborhood kids would line up to squeal as they plunged their hands into a bowlful of eyeballs (peeled grapes).

To carpool the boys to sports and lessons, said Scott, Sandra would recruit "neighborhood uber-moms" (dubbed "the ladies in waiting" by some of the other mothers, recalled Julie Folger). During a month or two in the summer, the boys were sent out to the Lazy B for a dose of self-reliance. They were put under the tutelage of Sandra's brother, Alan, who was now helping run the ranch and living with his wife in a house connected to the old adobe Headquarters occupied by Harry and Ada Mae. "Alan was the perfect uncle," recalled Jay, "fun, crazy, and exciting." On a roundup, Alan found his twelve-year-old nephew looking a little lost on his horse. "Uncle Alan," said Jay, "is this where I'd be if I was where I was supposed to be?"[54]

The O'Connor family made the four-and-a-half-hour drive to the Lazy B about five times a year. Alan was starting to take over managing the ranch from Harry, and the transition was not smooth. Alan wanted to improve the ranch; his father thought there was nothing to improve. "Sandra was trying to calm the waters, but she couldn't do much," recalled Steve Savage, the family lawyer. "She couldn't really take anyone's side. Sandra," he added, "was not the kind of person to get in the middle of something like that."[55]

IN LATER YEARS, in interviews and oral histories, Sandra would drily joke that she went back to work in 1965, after five years at home, so she could spend more time with her family. She had taken on too much volunteer work. "The only way I can ever unwind these things is if I take a full-time job," she told her family at the time, recalled her son Jay. "She was serious."

A dozen years after graduating from law school, in 1964, she still could not get a job in an established law firm. In the mid-1960s, the Phoenix firms remained closed to women. As late as 1969, John's law firm, Fennemore Craig, rejected Mary Schroeder, a University of

Chicago Law School grad who had been a trial attorney for the U.S. Department of Justice (and would later become a federal judge) because of her sex. The lawyers felt that having a woman lawyer at the firm (as opposed to the female secretaries they already had) would force them to change the way they talked to each other. The older lawyers did not want to have to feel self-conscious about their speech and manners. The Fennemore Craig partner assigned to explain this to Schroeder was John O'Connor. "He was apologetic," Schroeder recalled.[56]

Given later events, it may seem more than a little ironic that John O'Connor was the partner chosen to turn away a highly qualified woman applicant. But in the context of the time, the choice of John as deliverer of bad news made sense. John was, relatively speaking, the *sensitive* one who could explain life as it was because his own wife had faced the same reality. That did not mean John himself could not see the need to change. When the barriers to women lawyers fell a few years later, John would be the lawyer who mentored Fennemore's first woman partner—Ruth McGregor, later the first person hired by Justice O'Connor to serve as her law clerk at the Supreme Court.

But that was in the future. In 1963, Betty Friedan had published *The Feminine Mystique,* her vastly influential book exploring the dissatisfaction of women confined to traditional "female" roles. *The Feminine Mystique* sold a million copies, and so-called Second Wave Feminism was born. In 1966, Friedan, along with a score of other activists, formed the National Organization for Women (NOW). Women could allow themselves to dream of careers in once all-male preserves. Change was stirring—but not so much in Phoenix, not yet. In the mid-1960s, in the socially conservative boomtown, it was considered very ambitious for a woman to practice law at all. When, in 1957, the newspaper reporter had asked the newly arrived "lawyer-couple" if they planned to practice together, John had sounded a bit smug with his answer—that *he* was "happily situated." The irony that his wife, whose grades had been higher in law school, would have to hang a shingle in a strip mall while he took the elevator to the top firm in the First National Bank Building does not seem to have occurred to him.

Her professional ambition at the time, or so it appeared, was to keep her hand in the law while she bore three children. "She just

wanted to be a respectable lawyer," said her oldest son, Scott. Her options as a lawyer were limited, but Sandra's ambitions transcended
mere professionalism. She found meaning in doing. She wanted to
serve, to help others, to make a difference, and she sensed that she had
unusual powers to achieve *something* beyond raising her family and
climbing the Paradise Valley social ladder. Grandmother Wilkey had
stressed: "Be successful." But how? At Stanford, Professor Rathbun
had passionately held forth on the duty to serve. But in what way?

Government jobs were more available to women lawyers in the
Arizona of the mid-1960s, partly because they had a lower pay scale.
Recalling her happy days as an assistant district attorney in San Mateo
County, Sandra found a way to reenter the public sector while maintaining her do-good social profile. In a 1966 photo for *The Arizona Republic* (appearing on the "Lady Fare" women's page), the president of
the Junior League wears a tasteful linen dress and an elegant brooch,
and her hair is carefully coiffed, but Sandra is looking outward with
the gaze of a seeker, not a socialite. The state capitol dome rises in the
background, and she prominently carries a copy of *Arizona Revised Statutes, Annotated*—intended to remind, perhaps, that her service organization was about more than tea dances. At the time—although
unmentioned in the article about the Junior League's volunteer
work—O'Connor already carried the impressive title of State Assistant Attorney General.[57]

The title was grander than her duties, which at first were mundane.
At the end of an era when women weren't even hired as tokens, she
had needed her political connections to get the position. In 1964, the
state attorney general, who was a Democrat, had rejected her; a year
later, he was replaced by a Republican and Sandra got the job.

"They didn't know what to do with me," she recalled. She was sent
out to the state mental hospital, where she occupied a windowless office and worked on legal problems arising in the state mental health
system. She quickly learned not to be a rule-bound bureaucrat but
instead to look for reasonable, humane, and practical compromise—to
ask what is fair and not only what is legal. "Under state law, county
mental hospitals could recover money from the families of those
committed to the institution. The figure was $409 a week," recalled
Jordan Green, a young lawyer who worked with her. "She told me, 'It's

important that the state be reimbursed, but it's more important not to destroy a family by invoking a formula. Your job is to figure out a fair number and get a judge to enter an order."[58]

O'Connor's commonsense efficiency attracted the praise of her superiors. "I wanted to make myself indispensable," she recalled, only half-sarcastically, "so that I could get a deal to work two-thirds of the time for half pay." (She wanted to be home for the kids when they returned from school.) After a year or so, O'Connor was called back to the main office of the state attorney general and put to work on legal problems arising out of the state budget, an eye-opening education in the workings of local administration. Harry Day, on a visit to Phoenix, recalled seeing Sandra engrossed in conversation with a state senator named Isabel Burgess about the need to reform the creaky or broken machinery of Arizona's government. The state was run by a myriad of boards and commissions. The system was intended to decentralize power and keep control in local, often rural communities, but as a practical matter it was an invitation to chaos and petty bribery.[59]

In 1969, Senator Burgess—at the time one of four women in the state senate—moved to Washington to take a political appointment in the Nixon administration. Sandra told her contacts on the Republican-controlled Maricopa County Board of Supervisors that she wanted to fill Burgess's seat in the Arizona senate. On October 30, 1969, she was appointed and became one of thirty senators in the Arizona state legislature, representing District 8-E, a slice of well-to-do suburbia north of downtown, including her home in Paradise Valley. Later, in 1970, she had to run for reelection. Her platform, she recalled, was "Good government. Efficiency." She won easily.[60]

In later years, O'Connor offered a number of worthy or prosaic explanations about why she wanted to become a state senator—"civic duty," "it was where the action was," "to protect the one-acre zoning in Paradise Valley."* She was always circumspect about controversy

---

* She may have thought, incorrectly as it turned out, that getting elected to the state legislature would give her more time at home, since the legislature was in session only about a third of the year. "My salary [$6,000] wouldn't even pay the baby sitter," she noted.[61]

and deft about staying out of fights that were no-win (like family ones between her headstrong father and brother over the running of the Lazy B). But a longtime friend who worked with her at the attorney general's office, where the two officemates often talked about state politics, offered a more blunt assessment: "Why did she join the legislature?" said Jerry Lewkovitz. "Because it was terrible. It was embarrassing. She had a desire to right it. It wasn't to be one of the boys."[62]

CHAPTER FOUR

MAJORITY LEADER

"What a pretty little thing!"

*Sandra poses for the newspapers with a statute book in 1966 as president of the
Phoenix Junior League. Three years later, she joined the state senate. Smarter
and tougher than most of her colleagues, she would walk away
when they jeered or leered.*

IN NOVEMBER 1972, three years after Sandra O'Connor was appointed to the Arizona state senate, she was elected majority leader, the first female leader of any state legislative upper house. Curiously, the national press ignored the story, perhaps because national political reporters paid little heed to state legislatures. Nor did the Arizona press make a fuss about her rapid accession. Female politicians were not new to Arizona, and O'Connor cleverly maintained a low political profile and picked her fights carefully. It also helped that she tended to be smarter, better organized, and tougher than the men around her.

In her speeches, O'Connor would sometimes refer to the tradition of strong frontier women. In the Old West, when their husbands died or ran off, women would often be left to run the ranch. A few made fortunes by starting hotels and bordellos (or, in the case of Arizona's legendary Pearl Hart, by robbing stagecoaches). Women in most states west of the Mississippi, including Arizona, already had the vote by 1920, when the Nineteenth Amendment granting women's suffrage took effect.[1] By taking Isabel Burgess's place in the state senate, "Sandra wasn't all that unusual," recalled Rory Hays, a lawyer who lobbied Senator O'Connor. "My mother had been in the Arizona state legislature from 1958 to 1962. But it wasn't easy. Men would put a hand on her knee and offer to go to Mexico for the weekend if she wanted to get a bill passed."[2]

By the time O'Connor left the Arizona legislature at the end of 1974, one out of five state lawmakers was a woman.[3] But in January 1970, when she walked into the modernist cube that housed the state senate in front of the old Arizona capitol, she might as well have crashed a fraternity house on Saturday night. "There was booze everywhere. Lobbyists delivered bottles to offices," recalled Alfredo Gutierrez, who served in the legislature with Sandra for two years. "People walked around with tea glasses, only it wasn't tea in there." The lawmakers would "tell dirty jokes, use crude names. You had to be one of the guys," recalled Bette DeGraw, Sandra's legislative aide. "What women had to put up with was amazing," recalled Joe Anderson, a lobbyist for the state employees association. "Sexual harassment was the order of the day."[4]

Sandra turned heads. "Arizona's beauteous senator, Sandra O'Connor, is a lively, lissome creature who in January 1970 drew appreciative but sub-sonic wolf whistles from her new colleagues," began a feature piece in *Phoenix* magazine. The magazine quoted one lawmaker: "When you first meet Sandra you think, 'What a pretty little thing.' Next you think, 'My, it's got a personality, too.' "[5] A friend who worked for First National Bank sent her a photo of her swearing-in ceremony. "I have always said there is nothing like a lady legislator," the man wrote, adding, "P.S. You're good looking too. Please don't tell your husband about this letter. What he doesn't know won't hurt him."[6]

On long nights bargaining over legislation, or after liquid lunches with lobbyists, winking could become lewdness. There were stories of how a particularly drunken lawmaker, Tom Goodwin, flipped up the dress of one of his female colleagues. Trudy Camping, an evangelical conservative and one of the four women state senators, was hazed mercilessly when she offered a bill to ban the sale of sex toys, a measure immediately dubbed "the Dildo Bill." ("We asked her to show us exactly how it worked," recalled Gutierrez. "She broke down and cried. Then we tricked her into voting against her own bill.")[7]

But there are no tales of leering lawmakers grabbing for Senator O'Connor. "She just ignored them," recalled Bette DeGraw. While O'Connor laughed at bawdy stories told by her husband and loved dancing on the weekend, at the state senate she was all business. She was dignified, correct, and, when it suited her, stone cold. Years later, her friends would joke about "that look," a sharp-eyed, don't-mess-with-me glare that she occasionally leveled. "You'd have to be a real weirdo to think you could hit on her," said former Arizona governor

Bruce Babbitt, who was at the time a lawyer-lobbyist. (In 1971, he worked on drafting Arizona's adoption of the Uniform Commercial Code with her "line by line.")[8]*

Through the 1930s, '40s, and '50s, legend had it, the state budget of Arizona was written by mining company and railroad lobbyists over drinks in a suite at the old Adams Hotel in downtown Phoenix. In 1970, the lobbyists' suite still existed (and still supplied lawmakers with booze and call girls, according to Gutierrez), but the state legislature, under Republican rule after years of Democratic domination, was reform-minded.† The goal was to modernize state government by getting rid of the dozens of local commissions that had become corrupt and to replace them with a few well-run state agencies. The goal was not less government but better government.[10] Drawing on her experience in the state attorney general's office, Sandra O'Connor took a lead role, rewriting archaic laws (and getting them passed) and updating antiquated procedures, all aimed at boosting efficiency and stamping out cronyism. Using her knowledge of *Robert's Rules of Order* from the Junior League, she quickly mastered the senate's own quirky rules and was soon named senate parliamentarian, charged with keeping regular order on the floor. "She worked all the time, and she read what was in the legislation. The other legislators did not," said Fred Koory, a state senator.[11]

Her partner in getting laws passed was the majority leader of the state house of representatives, Burton Barr. A genial, self-deprecating deal maker, Barr was once described by a newspaper columnist as

---

* Sandra told her family about only one untoward incident. At a lawyers' convention at the Valley Ho Hotel in Scottsdale, Arizona, in the late sixties or early seventies, a senior federal government official asked, "How would you like to sleep with the [he gave his official title]?" She responded, "I wouldn't like that at all."

† The Republicans took over after the one-man, one-vote decision by the U.S. Supreme Court in *Baker v. Carr* (1962) transferred legislative power from the Democratic rural areas to the more densely populated (and Republican) metropolitan areas. The reform movement began with the 1967 "Gung-ho" legislature; its first act, according to *Time* magazine, was to "replace pretty girl pages with less distracting males."[9]

"flexible as overcooked spaghetti."[12] He liked to gently poke fun at O'Connor's self-discipline. "With Sandy, there is no Miller Time," Barr told reporters in 1981 when O'Connor was nominated to the U.S. Supreme Court, referring to a popular TV commercial that showed men and women relaxing while drinking Miller beer.[13] Barr and O'Connor were seen by their colleagues in the legislature as unmatched bookends. One came off as a log-rolling pol, the other as a civics professor. A decorated combat veteran who was much smarter than he pretended to be, Majority Leader Barr was vividly profane about winning votes by favor swapping and handing out campaign contributions from lobbyists. "Once he heard a way to get to somebody, he would say, 'Music to my fucking ears,'" recalled Ned Creighton, a newspaper reporter who covered the senate. O'Connor was meticulous and precise. She once offered an amendment to correct a single comma, which, she argued, changed the intended meaning of a bill. She handed out organizational charts. "The other senators would say, 'Here she is, the know-it-all from Stanford,'" recalled Creighton, who was often on the senate floor taking notes. "She had a Very. Direct. Way. Of. Talking. She was never casual."[14]

Still, Barr and O'Connor admired and liked each other and made a formidable team. "You would never catch O'Connor swapping three votes for a sewer culvert," recalled Gutierrez. But "because Barr did, she didn't have to," noted lobbyist Anderson. And for all her apparent primness, O'Connor knew how to pull on the strings of money and politics. A major beneficiary of her skill at this was her old Stanford beau, Bill Rehnquist.

AFTER PRESIDENT NIXON'S election in 1968, Rehnquist had been recruited by fellow Arizonan Richard Kleindienst, by then Nixon's deputy attorney general, to take a high-ranking job at the Justice Department in Washington. On the famous White House tapes, Nixon can be heard referring to Rehnquist as "Renchberg" and as a "clown" because he wore loud ties and sported long sideburns. Nonetheless, Rehnquist had won the president's attention for his intellectual heft and his willingness to endorse rounding up anti–Vietnam War protesters in the capital. Looking to push his law-and-order agenda, Nixon, in October 1971, appointed Rehnquist to fill a vacancy on the United States Supreme Court.*

In Phoenix, John and Sandra O'Connor were electrified by the news. Sandra took out a notepad and wrote at the top, "Assignments." She began listing everyone she knew—or who knew someone—who could help lobby for Rehnquist's confirmation by the U.S. Senate. One of the names was that of her husband, who was supposed to start working his political connections.[16] They were many, varied, and deep.

John's law firm lobbied the state legislature, and though he steered clear of conflicts, John was by now an important member of the Republican business-political establishment that essentially ran Phoenix. "The talk was that Sandra entered the legislature as John's wife," recalled Scott Bales, a former law clerk to Justice O'Connor who later became chief justice of the Arizona Supreme Court. In his after-dinner speeches, John joked about Sandra's election to the state senate: "I think it is a tribute to American democracy when a cook who moonlights as a janitor can be elected to high public office." The joke may sound insensitive, but Sandra often repeated it. At home in the evenings, he worked closely with her, helping her draft speeches and legislation. Their son Scott recalled seeing his parents poring over yellow legal pads after dinner ("I thought, Is this what it's like to be a grown-up? More homework?"). John was sitting in the senate gallery to hear his wife give a speech when a house member turned to him and said that Sandra's oration "sounded like Winston Churchill." John, who had written the speech, agreed: "She did, didn't she?"[17]

As Rehnquist's confirmation hearings drew near in October 1971, Sandra and John offered to cancel a long-awaited vacation to Puerto Vallarta to come to Washington to testify. Not necessary, came the reply, but Rehnquist stayed in almost daily contact with Sandra. Collecting testimonials and examining old records, she worked behind

---

* Nixon's earlier failed Supreme Court choices had included a judge from the South, G. Harrold Carswell, who was attacked as racially insensitive and mediocre. Nixon had also suggested he was looking for a woman appointee. Surprised by his appointment, Rehnquist drolly told a reporter that he had thought he had no chance "because I'm not from the South, I'm not a woman, and I'm not mediocre."[15]

the scenes to rebut charges (never proved) that as a Republican activist, Rehnquist had harassed black and Hispanic voters at a polling place.[18] She and John also reached out to friends, or friends of friends, who knew bankers in western states. These contacts were important to winning over senators, who typically have bankers as their campaign committee finance chairmen. Particularly useful was the O'Connors' friend Sherman Hazeltine, the president of the First National Bank of Arizona—which had recently made Sandra its first-ever female board member. (It was a trust officer of the same bank who, two years before, had written Sandra, on her appointment as a senator, "You're good looking, too.")

The effect of this shrewd political move by the O'Connors can be seen in Rehnquist's thank-you letter in mid-November, after his confirmation had been assured by the endorsement of the Senate Judiciary Committee:

Dear John and Sandra:

Words are inadequate to convey my appreciation for what you have done for me in connection with the nomination to the Supreme Court. I feel that a very effective organization has somehow suddenly been called into being, largely as a result of your doing. There are numerous personal messages of thanks to others which are richly deserved, and which I hope in due time to get off, but your efforts have been so special I wanted you to know that I deeply appreciate them. Parenthetically, I was virtually bowled over by Sherman Hazeltine's contacts among the western bankers—not only from deep appreciation of his efforts, but from extraordinary admiration of the effectiveness of their congressional contacts. Maybe that is why bankers have more influence than lawyers.[19]

In January, Sandra and John flew to Washington to Rehnquist's swearing-in and, for the first time, went inside the Supreme Court, where the O'Connors walked the marble halls looking at the portraits of justices. As they paused before one bearded or balding gentleman after another, she told her friend Gail Driggs that she imagined the likeness of a woman.[20] When Rehnquist and Lewis Powell were named to the Court on the same day in October (filling seats left by the retirements of Justices Hugo Black and John Marshall Harlan),

she told the local Kiwanis Club that their appointments were "superior . . . but for the fact that neither wears a skirt."[21] Less than a month
before, Sandra had written President Nixon urging him to appoint a
woman to the High Court.[22] She was unaware, but her own name had
been mentioned by Barbara H. Franklin, a White House aide who
had been tasked with finding possible women justices. Since only 300
of more than 8,700 judges in the United States were women (and
only 8 of 520 federal judges), Franklin had widened the search to look
for any promising woman with a legal background and political experience.[23] In her file on Rehnquist's nomination, Sandra kept a newspaper cartoon published the day he was approved by the Senate
Judiciary Committee: A haggard father in a maternity ward looks into
the crib of his newborn and tells the nurse, "Just think, she might
someday become a Supreme Court Justice."[24]

SENATOR O'CONNOR TOOK to heart Abigail Adams's request to
her husband John in 1776, "Remember the Ladies. . . . Do not put
such unlimited power into the hands of Husbands. Remember all
Men would be tyrants if they could."[25] O'Connor began moving on
issues that mattered to women almost at once—but always keenly
sensitive to political realities.

Less than two months after taking her seat in the Arizona senate,
she passed a bill to abolish a 1913 state law limiting women to an
eight-hour workday. The "law has outlived its usefulness," she said on
the floor of the senate. Rather than protecting women, she argued
that the law impeded them.[26] The issue was wisely chosen; she attracted Republican votes by embracing free market principles. The
opposition came from labor unions and Mormons, who were popu-
lous and politically well organized in Arizona.

Encouraged by her initial foray, she sat down and wrote, in her clear
Miss Radford's School script, "Laws Affecting Women in Arizona."
For seven single-spaced pages of legal pad, she detailed the way property laws discriminated against women—who could not buy a car or a
share of stock in the state of Arizona without their husband's permission.[27] As the next legislative session began, she introduced S.B. 1321,
a bill "to eliminate certain provisions of law that discriminate against

or favor, without adequate justification, the female sex." House Majority Leader Burton Barr did not support Senator O'Connor's bill; he was more concerned with winning votes to authorize water projects. S.B. 1321 died in the House Rules Committee. O'Connor realized she needed more political clout to advance women's rights.[28]

IN THE NEWSPAPER story announcing her appointment as the first female director of an Arizona bank, Sandra was referred to as "Mrs. John J. O'Connor."[29] In public, O'Connor always wore skirts, never pants. (She favored linen dresses and sporty knits, topped with a colorful scarf, often bright blue to bring out her hazel eyes.) But the news clippings kept in her legislative file suggest some consciousness raising. She saved a special issue of the March 1970 *Atlantic Monthly* on the status of women, brimming with the stories of aggrieved women who were paid half as much as men for the same work or harassed on the job. One article noted that "if [women] are vital and assertive, they are rejected as 'aggressive bitches.' "[30]

Around the country, "women's liberation" was stirring some of the same passions that had been so evident in the Vietnam War protests and the 1960s civil rights movement. At the 1968 Miss America Pageant, women tossed girdles, hair curlers, and false eyelashes into trash cans to protest sexist beauty standards. Newspaper accounts conflated the incident with draft card burning, and a new epithet was born: "Bra Burner." Mrs. John J. O'Connor was no bra burner. "I come to you," she told the Rotary and Kiwanis Clubs, "with my bra and my wedding ring on."[31] "She was not an angry feminist," recalled newspaper reporter Ned Creighton. Nor did she act like a coquette or a supplicant. "Early on, women had to use their feminine wiles—oh, you're so big and I'm so small. She wasn't like that. She didn't play it that way," recalled lobbyist Rory Hays. "But she wasn't a crazy feminist, either."[32]

Navigating the unpredictable political currents swirling around women's rights, O'Connor could not always avoid the rocks. In the winter of 1972, at the beginning of her third year in the Arizona senate, the Equal Rights Amendment easily passed the U.S. Congress and went to the state legislatures to be ratified. The ERA aimed to do for women what the post–Civil War Fourteenth and Fifteenth Amendments had done (or purported to do) for blacks: guarantee their equality before the law. The idea of a constitutional amendment for women's rights had been around since the early 1920s, following passage of the Nineteenth Amendment, and had reemerged in the liberal era of the late 1960s. The ERA seemed—for a time—to be an almost noncontroversial measure. Both Democrats and Republicans included the ERA in their party platforms in 1968 and 1972 (and the GOP kept it on in 1976). More than half of the necessary thirty-eight state legislatures immediately ratified the amendment.

On March 23, 1972, the day after the ERA passed the U.S. Senate by a vote of 84 to 8, Senator O'Connor rose on the floor of the state legislature to urge her colleagues to vote yes on the ERA.[33] The measure went to the Senate Judiciary Committee, where Senator O'Connor held a seat. The chairman, John Conlan, immediately announced that the committee would not rush to vote on the measure, that days of hearing and debate were necessary. Senator O'Connor said nothing.

Sitting in the audience of the Judiciary Committee hearing room, a pro-ERA activist named Irene Lyons Rasmussen was surprised and bothered by O'Connor's silence. Rasmussen was encountering some backlash against the ERA. On a radio call-in show, the first question to her was: "When was the last time you burned your bra?"[34]

Rasmussen, whose husband was a lawyer in John O'Connor's firm, was not a wild-eyed activist. She was working with Shirley Odegaard, a Paradise Valley Republican who had been motivated by reading Betty Friedan's *The Feminine Mystique*. Odegaard was deputized to call on O'Connor at her small, cramped office in the Arizona senate.

"She was a heroine to us. I knew her," recalled Odegaard. "Sandra wanted to delay. She said she didn't want the ERA to come up on the senate floor because she was afraid we'd lose." Odegaard argued for a floor vote to find out which members were in favor of the bill (and not just saying they were). But O'Connor, who could count the true votes, put her off.

When the bill continued to languish in committee, the ERA proponents became suspicious. "She was playing games with us," said Stanley Lubin, a United Auto Workers lawyer who was secretary to the Arizona Coalition for the ERA. "She was telling us she supported it when she was working behind the scenes to defeat it." In interviews

almost a half century after the failure of the ERA, Lubin and Odegaard revisited their complaints against O'Connor. "She was not the
kind of person to sit around and do nothing, but all of a sudden she
got very quiet," said Lubin. "She never asked a question at hearings.
She sat there like a piece of deadwood. I don't think Sandra was sincere on this issue. I think she was looking for a federal judgeship."
Odegaard likewise claimed, without proof, that Senator O'Connor
sold out the pro-ERA forces for her own advancement.[35]

It is true that O'Connor's ambitions lay beyond the state senate,
but her personal calculus was more subtle and complex. On April 10,
two weeks after the ERA passed the U.S. Senate, she received a letter
from Goldwater, who, along with Arizona's other U.S. senator, Paul
Fannin, had been one of the eight U.S. senators to vote against the
amendment. Hearing of her support for the ERA, Goldwater wrote
O'Connor that he did not like "tampering with the Constitution" and
that any changes in the law could alter "the design of the Lord by
making men and women identical."[36] O'Connor valued Goldwater's
friendship and support. She—and certainly her husband, John—were
not insensitive to the need for political accommodation. What was
she really thinking? O'Connor was usually motivated by a mix of real-
ism and idealism. She disagreed with Goldwater's reflexively retro
views. But at the same time, it wasn't worth it to her to cross him unless she was sure that the Equal Rights Amendment would pass.
O'Connor kept an accurate tally of the ERA's political chances, and
those odds quickly began to decline. The ERA was a provocative in-
strument and, in O'Connor's careful analysis, not the only way to get
from here to there on women's rights.

Indeed, in 1970—two years before she introduced the ERA for
ratification by the state senate—she told a gathering of Arizona State
University law students, "I'm not sure the Equal Rights Amendment
is necessary. I am inclined to believe that a few well-chosen cases
brought before the federal courts would establish the equality of
women under the equal protection clause of the Fourteenth Amendment, and the Civil Rights Act, in a meaningful way."[37] She could not
have known that, a little over a decade later, she would author just
such a decision as a justice of the U.S. Supreme Court.

O'Connor's handling of the ERA reveals her approach to societal problems that are inevitably political problems. The Equal Rights Amendment was (and, decades later, arguably still is) a laudable proposal aimed at guaranteeing the rights of women. But the nation, and certainly the state of Arizona, was not ready for such sweeping change in the early 1970s. The women's movement generated a severe backlash from both men and women who felt threatened by disruptions in traditional gender roles. O'Connor had keen political instincts, and she preferred to live in the world of the possible, to go for better if best was not immediately obtainable. She understood the importance of compromise, of taking more roundabout roads when a direct route was blocked. In the case of the ERA, women's rights, she had believed, could be won case by case in the courts, through existing civil rights laws. On the state and local level, laws could be amended to rid gender bias. This was a task perfectly suited to a careful, patient, persistent legislator like Senator O'Connor. Women's rights would become a quiet cause for Justice O'Connor—never frontally embraced as an activist on the model of Ruth Bader Ginsburg (who came to the Court twelve years after O'Connor), but slowly and surely furthered and fostered in her judicial opinions.

In the Arizona legislature, the backlash confronted O'Connor in the disagreeable personification of John Conlan, the Senate Judiciary Committee chairman who initially held up the ERA for further hearings and debate. A fine-featured, smooth-talking, Harvard Law School–educated evangelical Christian, Conlan was regarded by many of his colleagues as smarmy and insincere. "You knew he was lying when his mouth was open," said Diane McCarthy, a member of the House. "He'd pretend to cry with widows at funerals," recalled Marc Spitzer, a state senator.[38] "To put it nicely, Conlan was a bad guy," wrote John O'Connor in his memoirs. John had been able to "block him from ever becoming state chairman of the Young Republicans," but as a state senator, Conlan was a constant source of exasperation to Sandra O'Connor.[39] Scott O'Connor recalled his mother coming home after long days and describing how Conlan would try to kill a bill in private and then publicly claim credit when it passed. "She would tell us, 'That's what it's like to work with the worst of them,'" recalled Scott.[40]

Conlan disturbed O'Connor not just because he was slippery but also because he represented a new force that threatened to split, if not take over, the Republican Party. The GOP was evolving in a way that O'Connor did not like. Barry Goldwater was a conservative, but he was a libertarian. He supported Planned Parenthood and joked that he liked all the vices that the social conservatives wanted to ban. Both Goldwater and O'Connor, who worshipped occasionally at the same Episcopal church in Paradise Valley, preferred to keep their religious views low-key. In the early seventies, in Arizona—and in many other parts of the country, particularly in the South, Midwest, and West—the fundamentalist and evangelical Christian Right was on the rise. Phyllis Schlafly, the highly effective conservative activist, brought her "Stop ERA" campaign to Phoenix. Before long, there were protesters on the plaza of the state capitol waving placards with messages like WHO'S GOING TO NURSE ME WHEN MOMMY'S DRAFTED? and I LOOK BETTER IN GO-GO BOOTS THAN COMBAT BOOTS.[41]

In the Republican caucus of the state senate, Conlan and the "family values" social conservatives controlled enough votes to undo the Republicans' narrow (18–12) majority. O'Connor was willing to stand up to Conlan, especially when he postured outrageously. Vowing to introduce a bill to outlaw bingo in church basements, Conlan declared, "This is gambling and I intend to stop it!" O'Connor pointedly informed him that if he went ahead with the bingo ban she would be obliged to tell "all those ladies in churches in your district" that the ban was his idea. Conlan came around. But such duels were wearing on O'Connor and distracting.[42] She knew she had to choose her fights carefully to get anything done. The ERA, she decided, was not worth protracted fencing with the likes of Conlan—especially if, at the end of the day, the amendment lacked the votes to pass the legislature.

The legislative leadership appreciated her discretion and political judgment on many matters (not just the ERA). The president of the Arizona senate was a chain-smoking hail-fellow-well-met who sported a silver pompadour and the powder-blue-and-buff saddle shoes favored by University of Arizona alumni. Bill Jacquin was outgoing and, by some accounts, a little lazy, and he was fed up with his obstinate majority leader, David Kret. "Kret would use his 'point of personal privilege' to stand and lecture the senate," recalled Jacquin's chief of staff, George Cunningham. "Finally Jacquin deposed him in a closed-door caucus over one weekend" in November 1972. The Republican caucus lost no time in voting in Sandra O'Connor as the new majority leader. "Jacquin chose Sandra because she was an up-and-comer and a team player," said Cunningham. Bette De-Graw, O'Connor's legislative aide, recalled, "He picked Sandra because she was smart. Smart really narrowed the field." It helped that she had backing from Burt Barr, who ruled the House. "Burt really pushed for Sandra," recalled Barr's wife, Louise. "He adored her."[43]

The reality of a woman in a government leadership role in 1973 was so unexpected that it barely registered. O'Connor was not just first, she was far ahead of the pack. It would be over eight years before O'Connor herself became the first female U.S. Supreme Court justice, then three years after that before Geraldine Ferraro was picked as the first female vice presidential nominee, and then almost another decade before Janet Reno became the first female U.S. attorney general, and four more years after that before Madeleine Albright was named the first female U.S. secretary of state. (Early women governors and senators often succeeded their dead husbands.) The reaction of Bernie Wynn, *The Arizona Republic*'s political editor, was more arch than congratulatory toward O'Connor: "Sandy O'Connor should be quite good at this if she can learn to smile while the minority is trying to shove a political knife in her ribs. She has a lovely smile and she should use it often."[44]

RACE, NOT GENDER, was O'Connor's first testing ground as majority leader. At the opening meeting of the 31st Session of the Arizona state senate in January 1973, another first took place: A native American was sworn in to the Arizona legislature. Art Hubbard, a Navajo Indian, stood to take the oath of office—and was immediately met with an objection. David Kret, the deposed majority leader who was not trying to hide his bitterness, insisted that Hubbard, who had joined the U.S. Marines during World War II (he served with the Navajo "code talkers"), could not be seated because he was not a true Arizona citizen—that as a member of an Indian tribe living on a reservation, he was not subject to state law. Normally, the senior Democrat, Harold Giss, could have been expected to defend his fellow party member. But Giss sat silent.

The Republicans were on the spot; their own former majority leader was leading the attack on Hubbard. But Leo Corbet, the new Republican chairman of the Judiciary Committee, who was taking his orders from the new majority leader, Sandra Day O'Connor, stood to rebut Kret by pointing out that the senate made its own rules and could decide whom to seat. Unsupported by his own party, Kret was forced to back down.

At her desk in the front row, O'Connor could be seen conferring with Corbet. Watching and listening to it all play out from his seat behind O'Connor, a new senator, Alfredo Gutierrez, took note. "I thought to myself, 'there's no racial problem with this woman,'" said Gutierrez. He was a Vietnam veteran who had never finished Arizona State University because he was busy leading demonstrations to support Cesar Chavez and his union of Mexican migrant workers. He had not expected to see progressivism from a woman who looked as if she had just stepped into the dining room at the all-white Paradise Valley Country Club.[45]

Across the capitol plaza in the house of representatives, a similar petty drama of racial harassment was playing out. Art Hamilton had been elected as a state representative—the only black among sixty members in the house. On his first day, Hamilton recalled, house speaker Stan Akers looked straight at him, leaned in to the microphone, and started whistling "Dixie." Not one lawmaker in the chamber objected.[46]

Feeling isolated at first, Hamilton searched out more sympathetic members of the legislature to forge alliances. He naturally turned to the tiny band of Hispanic and female lawmakers, but he wasn't sure about O'Connor. Almost all of Phoenix's small African American population (about 5 percent) lived on the south side, far from Paradise Valley. Still, over the next two years, he learned by working with O'Connor that she was, he said, "by her nature a fair person. She had a basic sense of fairness as the core of her being."

Hamilton observed O'Connor closely when she chaired a committee that was reconciling house and senate versions of a bill regulating auto emissions. "I was being trained by Burt Barr [the house majority leader had recognized Hamilton's potential], so I spent a lot of time watching how it all worked. No one in Arizona liked the idea of a mandatory emissions program. I watched her work the room, member by member, trying to understand where there was give and where they wouldn't budge. She had a far better feel for these people than the fellas. They used big clubs. She knew how to find the spaces in between."[47]

Another O'Connor watcher was a twenty-one-year-old student named Barbara Barrett, who worked as an intern on the senate floor. "For me to see her standing there with a microphone, being the first, carrying the day, this was a whole new image to me. Women can do this." (Like O'Connor a ranch girl, Barrett would later become a qualified NASA astronaut and U.S. ambassador to Finland.) Barrett noticed that O'Connor always dressed professionally—"no fluff or frou-frou, no ruffles or flowers"—and that she was doing things "different[ly] from what the guys were doing. She was sober, strong, deliberate, there to get the job done."

O'Connor was gracious and generous, most of the time, observed Hamilton. But "if there was anybody who was prepared to stand up to the good old boys, it was her." Leo Corbet, who often worked with O'Connor on sticky issues like the disputed swearing-in of Art Hubbard, recalled her fixing one undecided lawmaker in a close vote "with her steely blue eyes." (Her eyes were hazel, but so luminous that they were often remembered as blue.) Usually, O'Connor stuck to prim exclamations like "Oh my goodness!" or "Hot diggity-dog!" This time, she said to the wavering senator, "You know, the only thing you get from sitting on the fence is a sore crotch."[48]

O'CONNOR NEVER WENT to the local bars to drink with her fellow lawmakers. Instead, once or twice a year, she invited all of them, Republicans and Democrats alike, to her home on Denton Lane for chalupas—a Tex-Mex treat made from corn chips, melted cheese, and ground beef—and beer. In February 1972, the O'Connors had installed a swimming pool and a patio large enough to accommodate all thirty state senators and their spouses. (Their friends celebrated the new construction, which included a bridge over a small arroyo, with a mock British colonial ceremony. BRIDGE OVER THE RIVER O'CONNOR was the headline on the society page.)[49]

Alfredo Gutierrez wasn't sure he wanted to go. "I had never been up there [to Paradise Valley] except to work in the gardens," he recalled. "But I went with Lito Peña, who had been with the UFW [United Farm Workers] with Cesar. He said, 'You have to go.'" They were greeted by a broadly smiling John O'Connor, tending bar. "John knew what to give Lito," Gutierrez recalled. ("Canadian Club. He drank the whole bottle," said Gutierrez.) John O'Connor "made everyone feel at home," said Gutierrez. "Sandra was charming, but cold and diffident. She had good manners, but she wouldn't let you in. I realized these barbecues were highly ritualized." O'Connor also invited a few newspaper reporters. Athia Hardt of *The Arizona Republic* recalled about Sandra, "She came up to me and asked, 'Athee, what is your ten-year plan?' I wasn't sure about tomorrow. She seemed like a Junior League type. She wasn't warm but she was friendly. She was not candid but she was professional. I never saw her loosen up. Everything was in the right place."[50]

The floor of the Arizona senate was initially unruly. Most procedural votes, like a simple motion to adjourn, were, by custom, automatically unanimous. Nonetheless, when the brand-new majority leader stood up to make a routine motion, the embittered David Kret and some other misogynistic troublemakers insistently called for votes and raised trivial arguments over the use of the words "shall" versus "may." Sitting back in her seat while her automatic majority crumbled, O'Connor began anxiously smoothing her skirt. Some of the men began mocking her by smoothing their pants. The derision increased. There were ugly mutterings about "the fucking bitch," recalled Gutierrez, and a reference to her menstrual cycle.

O'Connor omitted such crude details from later oral histories, but she did describe how her "heart pounded" and her "legs trembled" at the thought of just standing up before her colleagues. Her legislative aide, Bette DeGraw, recalled, "Sandra could get flustered when confronted, but she'd exit, always gracefully. She would just turn and leave, rather than engage. But on the floor, she couldn't just turn away."

She finally fled to the ladies' room, where a staffer, Donna Carlson West, found her crying. "They need you out on the floor," West gently told her.[51]

Already tough, she hardened some more and regained control of the floor. The job of an Arizona state senator is in theory part time— the legislature usually sits about half the year—but as majority leader, "my phone started ringing first thing in the morning and kept ringing into the night," she recalled.[52] She did not want to waste time and she avoided ego-butting quarrels. "She would stop the meeting and just walk away," said Rick DeGraw, a legislative aide. Rather than say something she would later regret, "she'd go to her office and close the door for a period." She was brusque with her staff. "I'd pick up the phone and she'd start in. There was no 'Hi, Rick,' no 'This is Sandra.' She would just begin speaking. When she was finished she would hang up. No 'Goodbye,' no 'Have a good day.' We were done."[53]

O'Connor rationed her influence as well as her time and energy. "She'd stay out of hot fights, like where to put new prisons," recalled Gutierrez. "She'd say, 'You guys work it out.' As long as they didn't put the prison in Paradise Valley."

Gutierrez enjoyed trying to get a rise out of O'Connor. When she was stressed, she would twitch; her upper body would make a slight involuntary jerk. "Watch," Gutierrez would tell his Democratic colleagues, "I'm going to make her twitch." Years later, he recalled with a laugh, "Sandra was a frustrated English teacher and she spent much of her time correcting grammar, and I spent much of my time making fun of her correcting grammar."[54] "Alfredo was lighthearted about it," recalled state senator Spitzer. "He made fun of her as a rich Paradise Valley doyenne who didn't know how to let it go when it came to grammar."[55]

Gutierrez was mostly playful in his gibes at O'Connor. Other foes were more malignant. Sandra was relieved when John Conlan left the state senate to go to Washington as a U.S. congressman in 1973, but she was often annoyed and sometimes deeply angered by the powerful chairman of the Arizona House Appropriations Committee, Thomas Goodwin.

Goodwin was well known to be a drunk. A senate staffer, Alan Maguire, would pick up Goodwin at a bar at ten in the morning and physically help him to the floor. "But he could remember every number in the budget and conduct a two-hour debate," Maguire recalled. Goodwin controlled the state budget, literally—he once put the document, marked up by the appropriations committee for final passage, in the trunk of his car and disappeared on a bender for a few days. On the payroll at the University of Arizona in Tucson, Goodwin protected his parochial interest. "Goodwin and the Tucson delegation had to get more money for the U of A than ASU [in Phoenix], period. Non-negotiable," said Art Hamilton. Goodwin would hold the budget hostage until he got what he wanted. O'Connor was fed up with Goodwin's wandering off to bars. "I saw them have harsh words," said Hamilton. "Noses incredibly close. She was explaining how it was going to be. He was explaining how she was wrong."[56]

Their mutual animosity finally came to a head over a bilingual education bill that was hung up in the House. At a meeting in the office of Speaker Stan Akers, O'Connor blamed Goodwin for the delay. Goodwin said to her, "I hear you said I was a drunk." O'Connor replied, "I did." They parried on:

GOODWIN: If you were a man, I'd hit you in the nose.
O'CONNOR: If you were a man, you could.

"Sandra was not going to be bullied," recalled Rick DeGraw. Goodwin backed down and let the bill go through.[57]

The senate majority leader had other, more subtle ways of showing who was in charge. One day in the middle of the 1973 session, she had made up a tray of cookies and lemonade for one of her boys to share at school. He dropped it. Called by the school, she left her office, went home, "and reassembled the whole thing and took it to his school," recalled Bette DeGraw. "We stopped all floor action until she got back. The guys were going, 'Where is she?' But she didn't bat an eye."[58]

The end of session, with its final passage of controversial bills, was always a good excuse for carousing and round-the-clock card games. (Art Hubbard, known as "Art the Navajo," turned out to be the big winner at poker.) At midnight on the last day of the 1973 session, Senate President Jacquin announced, "Well, boys, we're going back out on the floor" to conduct some more legislative business. "I'm not," said

Majority Leader O'Connor. "My boys are going to camp tomorrow. I'm going to make sure their clothes are cleaned and their bags are packed." She gave the senators five minutes to resolve some unfinished business, then O'Connor went home and the men went back to their card games.[59]

THE EQUAL RIGHTS Amendment was not going away. The pro-ERA forces continued to push for a vote on the floor of the senate, and the anti-ERA forces staged noisy demonstrations on the capitol plaza. Most lawmakers just wanted to avoid a vote, so as not to antagonize their constituents (or their wives). O'Connor had the idea of submitting the ERA to a statewide referendum, but even that step was too bold for the rest of the Republican leadership. Eventually, the Senate Judiciary Committee declined, by a 5–4 vote, to send the ERA to the floor.[60] O'Connor was one of the four who voted to permit the ERA an up-or-down floor vote.

Still, the ERA backers remained suspicious of her. ERA activist Marcia Weeks claimed that Leo Corbet, the chairman of the Judiciary Committee, told her that he voted no on sending the bill to the floor so that O'Connor could vote yes and preserve her standing with women's groups.[61]

Asked whether he had an arrangement for "pairing" his no vote with O'Connor's yes vote, Corbet recalled, "I don't think that happened. My vote on ERA was always a no. But," he added, "if she'd asked me, I would have." O'Connor, he said, "was caught in the middle between a bunch of ERA ladies and the right-wingers. I felt it was my duty to keep her safe from the right-wingers."

Corbet said he performed this duty when it came to the controversial subject of abortion. "I sat on antiabortion bills to protect her," Corbet said. "I carried her water. She never said to do it, and I never asked, but I knew she did not deserve to take any heat, and as chairman of judiciary, I could do this for her."[62]

SANDRA DAY O'CONNOR'S true views on abortion would become a source of intense speculation when she was nominated to the U.S.

Supreme Court in 1981. She was circumspect with everyone, including her family. "It wasn't a topic around the house," recalled her son Jay.[63] While she often said she was opposed to abortion "as a personal matter," she ducked the question of whether, and under what circumstances, the state could limit a woman's right to an abortion.* It is almost certain that she never favored outlawing abortion altogether, but it is also likely that she struggled in her own mind to settle on the proper legal limits.

In 1970, as a new member of the Senate Judiciary Committee, she cast an unrecorded vote to repeal an old Arizona statute making it a crime to provide an abortion except to save a woman's life. The measure never made it to the senate floor, and O'Connor failed to remember her vote when she was first interviewed eleven years later by the Reagan administration as a potential Supreme Court justice. She was brand-new in the legislature, she explained to her later questioners, and too overwhelmed by the pace of legislation to remember every vote on every committee bill.[65]

If O'Connor had been overwhelmed by work, it was the first and last time. The newspaper coverage from 1970 suggests she was more engaged than she later recalled. When the bill to decriminalize abortion came up in the Judiciary Committee, she had tried to find a compromise, offering an amendment to require that abortions be performed only by licensed doctors.[66] After lengthy debate, the abortion bill was tabled because it was too controversial. Catholic groups opposed legalizing abortion as a "moral evil," while some Protestant ministers and rabbis issued a letter defending the ethical right of a woman to choose. Over the course of a month, the conflict drew several headlines in the Arizona papers.[67]

In 1973, the U.S. Supreme Court ruled, 7 to 2, in the landmark case

---

* In an oral history in 1992, she was asked by a friend, New York Law School professor James Simon, about charges that she had not "taken a strong enough position in favor of pro-life when you were in the state senate." She began her answer, "My memory fades," and later protested, "I don't remember, Jim," and "The specifics don't come clearly to mind." O'Connor, who had a phenomenal memory until she began experiencing cognitive issues late in life, very rarely, if ever, expressed forgetfulness about other subjects in her many interviews and oral histories.[64]

of *Roe v. Wade* that women have a constitutional right to abortion. In an epic miscalculation of the mood of American politics, the majority of justices seemed to believe they were merely putting the Court's imprimatur on a social liberalization whose time had come. Almost immediately, a backlash erupted from the new Christian Right. Various GOP-controlled state legislatures began passing laws seeking to outright overturn *Roe v. Wade* or testing whether they could limit a woman's choice.

It is almost impossible to overstate the impact of *Roe v. Wade* on American politics. By bringing the so-called social issues to the fore, the Supreme Court gave vent to the sense of unease and dislocation felt by many Americans whose lives were shaken by the simultaneous revolutions of the 1960s: the sexual liberation enabled by the Pill, campus unrest and anti–Vietnam War draft card burners, the cracks in the old social order caused by the women's movement and the battle for civil rights. Ten years before, in the case of *Engel v. Vitale,* the Supreme Court had already fed the rise of a religious right by outlawing school-sponsored prayer as a violation of the First Amendment prohibition against "establishing" religion. Years later, angry demonstrators at an Ellijay, Georgia, rally would hold up signs tracing the rise in divorce, crime, and abortion back to the date of the Court's school prayer decision in 1962.

The Court's pro-abortion ruling was even more inflammatory. The Reverend Jerry Falwell claimed that he had an epiphany when he read news of the *Roe v. Wade* decision on January 23, 1973. He instantly knew in his heart, he said, that evangelicals needed to organize into a vast pro-life movement to undo the Supreme Court's decision. By 1980, Falwell's organization, the Moral Majority, would try to make abortion a litmus test for millions of voters all over the country, particularly those voting in Republican primaries. For the cautious, moderate, Main Street GOP, the thunder on the right was an ominous sound.

As Arizona senate majority leader in 1973–74, O'Connor treaded carefully, showing up on both sides of the issue. She backed a couple of measures that indirectly narrowed the opportunity of women to get abortions. One bill that became law gave hospitals and doctors the right not to participate in abortions. Another bill provided that the state would not have to pay for the abortions of needy women. At the same time, she voted against a "memorial"—in effect, an exhortation—urging Congress to amend the Constitution to protect the unborn except where pregnancy would be fatal to the mother.[68]

"She was closeted pro-choice," said George Cunningham, chief of staff to senate president Jacquin. "The Arizona legislature never voted on a measure that would overturn *Roe v. Wade*. As majority leader she controlled what got to the floor. If she wanted to be pro-life, it would have happened." As a legal expert, O'Connor understood that under the supremacy clause of the Constitution, the states do not have the power to overturn federal law. Of course, that did not stop avid pro-life legislators in other states from passing unconstitutional bills in hopes of forcing the Supreme Court to reverse *Roe*. Under O'Connor's rule, the Arizona state senate made no such attempt.[69]

O'Connor could not always keep the pro-lifers at bay. House member Tom Skelly, a gadfly known as the Great Amender, managed to bar abortions at the University of Arizona hospital. He did this by attaching an amendment to a bill authorizing funds to increase the seating capacity at the University of Arizona football stadium. Ever the parliamentarian, O'Connor tried to get the rider knocked off as "nongermane," but the lawmakers wanted a bigger stadium, and she lost.[70]

Denizens of the Arizona state legislature watched O'Connor perform her balancing act—weighing practicality and principle while enduring crudeness and caprice—with a kind of fascinated, if sometimes grudging, admiration. Dealing with shenanigans by looking the other way did not come naturally to her. "She was exacting. She wanted to deal in specifics and facts and truth," said Cunningham. "She did not tolerate fools and she did not like bullshit." Her legislative aide, Bette DeGraw, remembered that "you had to provide her with good information. If you did not, she did not mince words." On the other hand, said DeGraw, "when I saw her with her kids, there was a softer side. She was loving. Not warm and cuddly, but loving."

O'Connor served at a time when the legislature was reforming and modernizing—yet clinging to its tribal ways. She helped push the former and had to put up with the latter. Keven Willey, a young woman political reporter for *The Arizona Republic* who covered the legislature after O'Connor—and who saw Tom Goodwin topple over drunk while rising to make a motion on the House floor—spoke realistically about the world in which O'Connor operated. "She was astute about picking her spots," said Willey. "An ideological purist would say she was a coward but that's ridiculous. She was more effective than if she had stood on principle."[71] Irene Lyons Rasmussen, one of the ERA activists who felt that O'Connor had put her own career ahead of the ERA in 1971, had a more forgiving view when, some years later, she brought her daughter to visit the chambers of the first woman justice of the U.S. Supreme Court. Justice O'Connor gave them the grand tour, she recalled, and invited them to lunch in her chambers.[72]

AS MAJORITY LEADER, O'Connor never lost sight of trying to reform state laws that discriminated against women. The breakthrough came as the legislature was trying to duck an up-down vote on the ERA. At the University of Arizona, a group of law students put together a list of scores of state statutes that favored men over women (not unlike the list that O'Connor was privately keeping herself). In January 1973, the students presented their report to Diane McCarthy, a new member of the house of representatives. She took the list of discriminatory state statutes to Stan Akers, the Speaker of the House, and suggested that by changing discriminatory laws at the state level, they would no longer need to vote on the ERA, since it would effectively be made redundant in Arizona. "Akers said, 'Get out of my office, it's a stupid idea,'" recalled McCarthy. "But two days later, he called me back and said, 'I've been thinking about it. It's a good idea. Call Sandra.'"

McCarthy approached Senate Majority Leader O'Connor, who immediately saw the possibilities. Her earlier efforts to reform the state's gender-biased laws had died in the house. Here was a chance to have the house lead the effort. The measure, which amended more than four hundred statutes that discriminated against women in ways large and small, proved to be surprisingly popular, passing both the house and senate and becoming law later that spring. On the day of the vote in the house, Tom Goodwin, O'Connor's nemesis, put a tape recorder on his desk and, laughing at his own joke, played Helen Reddy's hit song "I Am Woman (Hear Me Roar!)." But he voted for the bill. "McCarthy's bill was the way out on the ERA," recalled Art Hamilton. "But Speaker Akers didn't really care. It wouldn't have happened without Sandra O'Connor." Akers wanted to finesse a messy controversy. O'Connor wanted to change the laws.[73]

THE O'CONNORS LIVED comfortably, though not lavishly. Sandra made only $6,000 a year as a state senator, but John made at least ten times as much as a partner in one of Phoenix's two top law firms. There was money for ski vacations and rafting trips and private school for the O'Connor sons. For a brief period, two of the boys, Brian and Jay, were sent to public school, partly because "funds were tight," recalled the eldest, Scott. A swimming pool and a small guesthouse, where the housekeeper lived, enlarged the Denton Lane establishment, "but the guesthouse was a prefab bolted onto a cement slab. Dad bought it on the cheap from a client," recalled Scott. "A tennis court would have added $12 or $13 a month to the mortgage. Mom said no."[74]

Sandra dressed tastefully, even fashionably, in smart, brightly colored suits and dresses, but she bought her clothes on sale and off the rack. As a Depression-era child, she had watched her father, working at his desk at night, meticulously write down every dime of the Lazy B's expenditures. She shared some of Harry Day's fiscal conservatism, both in her own home and when it came to spending the taxpayer's dollar.

In 1972, Governor Ronald Reagan of California came to speak at the Arizona GOP's annual Trunk 'n Tusk dinner. Governor Reagan was already a rising star in a party that was stirring with taxpayer revolt against Big Government. (He had made a respectable bid for the GOP nomination at the 1968 Convention.) He outlined a proposal to enact a cap on the public spending of his state as a percentage of taxpayers' income; basically, the state government could only grow as fast as the private wealth of its people. Sandra liked Reagan, whose hand she shook at the dinner and whose genial warmth she felt. She liked his proposal so much that she wanted to adopt it for her own state.[75]

In the fall of 1973, O'Connor put together a committee of worthies—economists, lawyers, and tax experts—to study the alarming fact that the state budget was growing about twice as fast as the incomes of Arizona taxpayers. At O'Connor's prodding, the committee recommended a Senate Concurrent Resolution (CR 1012) to cap state spending as a percentage of taxpayers' total income—at roughly 8 percent, with some flexibility built in for hard times. The measure would be put up for the voters' approval in a referendum in the fall of 1974.[76]

The resolution garnered some good publicity—the *Phoenix Gazette* dubbed O'Connor "the Taxpayer's Sweetheart"—and it passed the senate.[77] But then the bill arrived in the House Appropriations Committee, where it languished.[78] The chairman of the committee, Tom Goodwin, once again O'Connor's nemesis, was not about to allow Old Steely Eyes, as he called her, to put artificial constraints on his power to hand out money to his favored projects. O'Connor was disappointed she was not getting more help from her friend Burt Barr. The house majority leader was caught between his alliance with O'Connor and his need to grease the legislative skids with pork. "On the spending bill, Burt left—literally," recalled Representative Diane McCarthy. "He didn't want to take on Sandra. He'd say, 'Sorry, got to go pick up the kids!'"[79]

Barr "has been strangely quiet" on the spending bill, wrote John Kolbe, the *Phoenix Gazette*'s political correspondent, as the legislative session drew to a close in late April. Kolbe, a shrewd observer, credited O'Connor with a "near miracle" in "conceiving the idea, assembling the experts, writing a simple bill, and shepherding it this far through the legislative process. But," he continued, "the plain fact is that her name is a red flag in the 'lower' chamber (partly personality, partly—one suspects—resentment of her keen mind)."[80]

O'Connor leaned on Barr and Goodwin, calling on her old friend Barry Goldwater to use his influence.[81] The push, at last, worked: On the final night of the legislature, CR 1012 narrowly passed, putting a statewide referendum on the November ballot (where it failed—the same fate met by Reagan's spending cap bill in California the year before).[82]

As the lawmakers swapped deals, drank, and played poker into the last night of the 31st Arizona legislature, O'Connor was observed holding on to Burt Barr, who, after long evasion, had swung his clout behind O'Connor's bill. Tears of exhaustion and pent-up anxiety were running down her face. (Years later, when O'Connor was nominated to the Supreme Court, Barr—with a reporter present—called his old friend on the phone and recalled how she had hugged him and wept on that final evening; Barr compared the passage of CR 1012 to "mass murder," meaning that a lot of arms had to be twisted right off.)[83]

Ron Carmichael, a lobbyist for the building industries who had joined the late-night folderol, recalled watching O'Connor cry. "I had never seen her break down. It was the stress of the moment. She wanted to do the right thing. It showed me she was a real person. It wasn't a sign of weakness. It made her more real."

Chris Herstam, another lobbyist who was later elected to the state legislature, observed that the men "were vulnerable. They lost their tempers, they got depressed. But she was always a calm, cool customer." She had to be, said Herstam; the men could afford to act out and misbehave; she had to keep up a brave front and not showboat or dawdle, certainly if she wanted to get home to see her family.*

Also watching O'Connor clasp Barr, Alfredo Gutierrez thought she was more fed up than grateful. "She was sick of it," he said. "She got tired of dealing with Burt, who was irrepressible—he brought the horse trading right into the senate chamber." Come the November elections, O'Connor had already announced, she would not be running for reelection. "Sandra just sort of slipped away," recalled her legislative aide, Bette DeGraw. She wanted to be a judge.[85]

---

* In oral histories and interviews, O'Connor brushed off questions about her colleagues in the state legislature. When PBS interviewer Bill Moyers ventured, "Western politics are pretty tough," Justice O'Connor cut him off. "Well, they weren't so tough in Arizona." James Simon asked her, "Did you experience any sexism while you were in the senate?" O'Connor answered, "Well, I don't know. I was treated well . . ." She said she left the senate because she was tired of being "flattered"—compliments, sincere or not, were legislative currency—though she added, "I was never one of the boys."[84]

. . .

SANDRA O'CONNOR DID not "fit in" to the favor-swapping, back-slapping man's world of the Arizona legislature, but she was not, in the larger political sense, an outsider or an outlier. Although she may not have quite realized it at the time, she was arguably the embodiment of a political movement that would soon emerge as the Reagan Era. She was neither a New Deal liberal activist nor an anti–Big Government libertarian nor a social issues conservative. Rather, she lived with a deep ambivalence about the role of government that characterized so much of the politics of the late twentieth century. She was almost perfectly attuned to the major contradiction of political life.

To be a self-aware Arizonan was to live with an anomaly. The state was dependent on the federal government for its prosperity, even its survival. The vast water projects greening the desert and populating the Phoenix suburbs were paid for largely by the American taxpayer, via the lawmakers and regulators in Washington. Being human, the people who lived in Arizona, as well as other western states, often felt more hostility than gratitude for this largesse, which of course came with strings attached. They denounced Big Government as they drove down interstate highways. They waxed nostalgic about the Wild West even though the federal government owned much of it, including most of the land grazed upon by Harry Day's cattle.

Sandra O'Connor did not want to do away with government, but she wanted it to be more sensible and less intrusive. She was a Republican, to be sure. There were very few Democrats in the environs of the Paradise Valley Country Club. (Living a few miles away at the retirement oasis around the Biltmore Hotel was Dr. Loyal Davis, who helped tutor his new son-in-law, a onetime Democrat and Hollywood actor named Ronald Reagan, on the evils of socialized medicine.)[86] But O'Connor was innately moderate, a balancer, the kind of person who could reconcile competing demands—like how to raise a family while making a successful career.

Her political party kept veering rightward in the 1960s and early '70s. She was able to make do without compromising her principles by a subtle balancing act. She embraced the Barry Goldwater who wanted to clean up Arizona politics; less so the one who voted against the 1964 Civil Rights Act and definitely not the one who talked as if he wanted to lob a missile into the Kremlin men's room. She was named cochair of Richard Nixon's presidential campaign in Arizona in 1972, and took her kids to see one of Nixon's last rallies before he resigned in 1974. "Now here's a lady who understands phone banks," said Thomas C. Reed, the Nixon campaign's southwest regional director. (O'Connor was particularly intent on turning out Mexican Americans to vote Republican.)[87] But she had been wary of the bullyboys at the Committee to Re-elect the President and found Nixon's race-baiting Southern Strategy to be offensive. She wanted a sunnier, gentler, more genial standard-bearer. Before too long, she, and the Republican Party, would find one in Ronald Reagan.

O'Connor always had an almost uncanny instinct for the popular mood and mores. She read the papers and followed the news, but she did not need to look at the polls to know where people stood. Because she had lived so long with competing and sometimes conflicting exigencies, she was almost perfectly suited to be Solomonically wise—to be a judge.

CHAPTER FIVE

ARIZONA JUDGE

"Don't let fate take over. You can influence your destiny."

Judge O'Connor met Chief Justice Warren Burger on a houseboat on Lake Powell in the summer of 1979. A friend remembered that they talked until 2:00 A.M.

W HEN SANDRA DAY O'Connor ran for election as a state court judge, she wanted to break the mold. The system for choosing judges in the state of Arizona, at the time when Sandra O'Connor was hoping to gain a seat on the bench in the fall of 1974, was "very unattractive," O'Connor recalled in a 1995 oral history for the Federal Judicial Center. "Very," she emphasized.[1]

Sandra O'Connor had a rule against speaking ill of others. Her view of human nature was tolerant and nuanced. Nonetheless, she had a way of dividing people—and sometimes, it seemed, the whole world—into two categories: "attractive" and "unattractive." She (and John) used these qualifiers in a way that was at once offhand and pointed. In later years, after Justice O'Connor became a fixture on the Washington cocktail circuit, some of her brilliant but socially insecure Supreme Court clerks wondered where they fell on the O'Connor attractiveness spectrum.

Was she judging people by their physical appearance and social graces? It could seem that way if you were an eager-to-please law clerk working for a boss whose favorite soiree was a four-times-a-year event called the Waltz Group. The more astute ones, however, quickly realized that when she called someone "attractive," she was not talking so much about their looks or manners (she found some homely men, like Solicitor General Rex Lee, to be attractive and some handsome smoothies, like State Senator John Conlan, to be unattractive). Rather, she was using verbal shorthand to describe an ineffable but, to her, appealing mix of integrity, decency, and modesty—or their opposite. She used the term not just to describe people but institutions and ways of doing business, such as the way judges were chosen in Arizona in 1974.

Judges were elected by the voters. Some judges on the superior court—the trial court level—managed to remain neutral and objective, with their personal dignity intact; others barely pretended. "We'd take briefcases of whiskey bottles to the courthouse to give to judges," recalled Bill Jones, who practiced personal injury law and who knew Sandra through the Phoenix Country Day School, which their children attended, and from lobbying her in the state senate on behalf of the American Insurance Association. "Young associates in law firms would be assigned to take envelopes with cash to the judges at Christmas. Sandra could not have avoided knowing about this," he added. Jones told of one particularly notorious judge who played golf with the defense lawyers the day before trial. When the plaintiffs' lawyers objected in court, the wounded judge responded, "Fellas, we didn't talk about the case! And besides, I'm free for dinner tonight." Such loose behavior was endemic, Jones recalled. One judge sat on the floor of his courtroom and drank beer and played poker with the lawyers from both sides. "It was all out in the open," said Jones. "Nobody thought anything about it. Just good old boys."[2]

Having to run for reelection every four years made judges susceptible to the cash- and booze-bearing good old boys. As senate majority leader, O'Connor "worked very hard," she recalled, to change this disreputable system. She introduced a bill to have judges appointed by the governor, choosing from candidates recommended by a nonpartisan merit selection board. In her last year in the state legislature, O'Connor won senate passage, but the bill died in the house of representatives, where lobbyists from the personal injury bar had more clout. Undeterred, O'Connor led a statewide petition effort to make "merit selection" of judges a referendum on the ballot in November. The measure was a compromise—judges in the urban counties, Maricopa (Phoenix) and Pima (Tucson), would be chosen by merit selection; judges in the rural counties would still be elected.[3]

The merit selection referendum passed, narrowly, in November 1974. On the same ballot, among the last group of Phoenix judges who had to run for office, was Sandra Day O'Connor.

She had wanted to avoid an electoral campaign. "I wanted the Governor, Jack Williams, who was a wonderful governor, to appoint me to a vacancy. He didn't want to do that," recalled O'Connor. "He thought I should run." (Eager-to-please politician that he was, Wil-

liams was backing two people for the same job.)[4] O'Connor had never
had to press the flesh to win office. After filling a vacant seat in the
state senate, she had faced only nominal Democratic opposition in
her heavily Republican district. (No door-to-door canvassing required; the property lots were too large to make it worthwhile.) But
now she had to run countywide against a Republican judge named
David Perry, who attacked his opponent as "not a real lawyer" and
claimed that he was Governor Williams's preferred choice. Sandra's
father recalled that the O'Connor boys, then aged eleven, fourteen,
and seventeen, put out signs for their mother. "She was scared to
death. She was really uneasy, afraid she wasn't going to make the
grade," recalled Harry Day. "She hated campaigning," said her senate
legislative aide, Rick DeGraw. "She liked talking to groups, but she
wasn't warm. She was still stiff. But she had a good name and people
knew her." After spending $13,000 to send out a mass mailing to
115,000 Republican households in Maricopa County, she defeated
Perry with 70 percent of the vote.[5]

As always when she took a new job, she suffered a bout of anxiety.*
"I was scared to death," she recalled. "All of a sudden, I was it. When
the motions were made, I had to rule on them. When the objections
to evidence were made, I had to rule on them. It was frightening."[7]
Before taking the bench, she sat in the courtrooms of other judges,
observing and studying. She was learning what to do, but also what
not to do. Watching judges treat the lawyers appearing before them as
their pals, she saw ample evidence of the latter.

EVERY OTHER YEAR, the Arizona Bar Association asked its members to rate the judges before whom they appeared. In 1978, after she
had served three years as a Superior Court judge, O'Connor received
the lowest score of the eight judges ranked.[8] In 1981, when O'Connor

* A young O'Connor friend from Phoenix, Susan J. Taylor, was asked to be the
1995 chair of the Stanford Alumni Association. "I didn't think I could handle it,"
Taylor recalled. "Sandra said to me, 'Susan, I have never done a job I didn't think
was a stretch. There is no manual for Supreme Court justice. I couldn't even find
my way around Washington. You must accept this job." Taylor did.[6]

was nominated to the U.S. Supreme Court, legal journalist Steven Brill decided to look more deeply into her low ratings from the Arizona bar. He was expecting, he wrote, to find "someone who did not belong on our highest court." Instead, he discovered a profile in courage.

O'Connor was well regarded for the quality of her written opinions and as a fair judge. But her overall grade was always pulled down by the bottom marks she received in the category of "courtesy to lawyers."[9] Recalled personal injury lawyer Bill Jones: "She ranked low. She was tough and lawyers didn't like it. We were used to getting away with stuff." It was common practice, for instance, for lawyers to ask for delays in the privacy of the judge's chambers. Judge O'Connor made them do it in open court. If a lawyer arrived inexcusably unprepared, Judge O'Connor would say, "Proceed. Call your first witness." Lawyers soon learned to come to her courtroom ready to make their cases.

"She was tough, terse, curt," recalled Andy Hurwitz, a lawyer who tried cases in her courtroom and later became a federal judge. "You couldn't find some judges in the morning—or in the afternoon after a long lunch," said Hurwitz. "She tried cases during the lunch hour with no jury." The leisurely pace of the Superior Court allowed plenty of time for beer, golf, and running up clients' fees. Judge O'Connor wanted to get her work done, in a thorough but efficient way, and go home. (Lunch was often a chunk of cheese nibbled in her chambers.) "The practice at the time was to let lawyers go on as long as they wanted to," recalled Hurwitz. "She had spent time with the record of the case, so the trial moved much more quickly. She would say, 'Well, you've already asked that question,' or speed it up if she already knew the answer."[10]

O'Connor was brave about standing up to lawyers who had been getting away with sloppy work for years. Renz Jennings had been a former justice of the Arizona Supreme Court before returning to the bar. In 1978, in open court, Judge O'Connor told one of Jennings's clients that Jennings was representing him so badly he should get a new lawyer. O'Connor proceeded to complain to the state bar disciplinary board that Jennings, who was seventy-nine, was senile and should be removed from practice. "For Sandra to do that took a lot of gumption," said Barry Silverman, a Maricopa County prosecutor. "Jennings's problem—missing deadlines, mishandling cases—was something all of us had winked at." O'Connor objected to more than Jennings's incompetence in court. "Renz was a notorious ass-grabber and an old fool," recalled Jack LaSota, chief of staff to Arizona governor Bruce Babbitt. "Renz Jennings was the most aggressively dirty old man I have ever known," said Hattie Babbitt, Governor Babbitt's wife, who also argued cases before Judge O'Connor. "No woman would ever get on an elevator with him."[11]

As a newcomer, one of three women on the Maricopa County Superior Court bench, O'Connor was given the worst courtroom, a dark, noisy, poorly air-conditioned chamber in the basement. The overpopulated drunk tank of the county jail was next door. O'Connor sometimes stepped over or around slumbering bodies in the hallway, and she kept handy a large can of bug spray. She joked to a reporter that she needed "a meat ax" to kill the larger cockroaches.[12]

O'Connor once described her time as a trial judge, hearing both civil and criminal cases, as like "sitting all day in a soap opera. And hearing the stories. Some happy, some sad, some angry, some not."[13] She was neither a hanging judge nor a soft touch, but rather a strict arbiter who was mindful of the limits of the law. She sentenced a drug dealer convicted of murder to the death penalty—but reversed her own sentence and ordered a new trial when she discovered that the prosecutor had withheld evidence. In another murder trial, a man was accused of burning his children to death. The police produced uncontestable evidence of the man's guilt. But because they obtained it without a search warrant, Judge O'Connor excluded the evidence, and the man was acquitted.[14]

At the same time, she was not afraid to assert herself to both humanize the law and make it more just. "I tried to be creative with sentencing," she recalled in a later oral history. "I would try to impress people that I put on probation with the fact that if they didn't do exactly what I said, they were going to come back and see me. Not somebody else, me. I tried to devise creative ways by letting them spend the night in jail but having jobs during the day. I tried to get restitution paid to victims where I could." Dividing up assets in a divorce case, she drew on her experience as a mother who would have one child slice the pizza, the other child choose which slice. When a couple divvying up forty thoroughbred greyhounds threatened to consume days of trial by offering evidence on the value of each dog, Judge O'Connor had one side's lawyer divide the dogs into two lists and the other lawyer choose one of the lists. The case was over in fifteen minutes.[15]

Hard cases could make bad law. A woman confessed to shooting her abusive husband. The jury convicted her of murder. Judge O'Connor, who believed that the woman had acted in self-defense, gave the woman the lightest sentence possible under the law and supported a request for a reduced sentence. Imposing the penalties required by law or sending recidivists back to jail was part of the work of a judge, and O'Connor accepted her role in a system that could seem harsh. Still, the limits of justice and the revolving door of human misery took a toll. O'Connor was sometimes "discouraged" by "the futility of it all," she confessed in the oral history.[16]

In the summer of 1978, O'Connor was confronted with a particularly difficult case. A woman pleaded guilty in her courtroom to forging $3,500 in checks. She had probably kited many more checks—perhaps $100,000 worth. The woman was a college grad from a well-off Scottsdale family. Deserted by her husband, an NFL football player, she sold real estate, but not enough to keep her in the manner to which she wished to be accustomed. Under the law, she deserved jail time.

But O'Connor was faced with a dilemma. The woman had two very young children—one sixteen months and the other only three weeks old. If she sentenced the woman to prison, the children would become wards of the court and might wind up in foster care. The woman threw herself on the mercy of the court, begging for probation instead of jail.

From the bench, O'Connor told the woman, "I can empathize with you as a mother. I've been anguishing over this case for weeks. It is the most difficult case I have had to resolve. You have intelligence, beauty, and two small children. You come from a fine and respected family. Yet, what is depressing is that someone with all of your advantages must certainly have known better."

O'Connor proceeded to sentence the woman to five to ten years in prison. As the defendant was led from the courtroom, she screamed, "What about my babies? What about my babies?" Afterward, a reporter for *The Arizona Republic* found Judge O'Connor sitting in her chambers, still wearing her black robe. She was weeping. (The woman rejoined her children after eighteen months in prison.)[17]

IN THE MID-1970S, the ripples of the Watergate scandal in Washington, D.C., were felt across the country and in Phoenix. Thanks to President Nixon's serious misdeeds, the reform-minded GOP was now cast as the party of corruption. The Republicans lost control of the Arizona statehouse; the Democrats rode a coalition of newly empowered minorities and fed-up white voters to power. Alfredo Gutierrez, O'Connor's friend-and-foe in the state senate, became majority leader, and the voters elected (for the first time) a liberal Hispanic, Raul Castro, as governor.

Then, suddenly, an odd series of events created political opportunity for Sandra O'Connor. She was, by dint of two decades of work in Republican politics, her friendships with the likes of Barry Goldwater and party elders, and her husband's wide web of political connections, a kind of Favorite Daughter of the party establishment. She was an obvious candidate for higher office: at once a reassuring figure of femininity and a New Woman who could attract the votes of women and men alike. The twists and turns of politics opened the way for her—while testing her independence and true desires.

In the fall of 1977, President Jimmy Carter appointed Governor Castro to be ambassador to Argentina. The secretary of state, Wesley Bolin, a business-friendly placeholder regarded as politically weak, automatically succeeded Castro. Some Republican leaders thought Judge O'Connor should run for governor against Bolin in the 1978 election. "We tried to raise money," recalled Dick Houseworth, a Paradise Valley banker active in the GOP. "But there was resistance from Republican donors. The new governor—the old secretary of state—he'd give you everything you wanted. So why bother to change?" Bolin was a Democrat, but he was a creature of a system that had rewarded the business community under the nonpartisan ideology of boosterism.

Then in March 1978, after only five months as governor, Bolin died. There was no secretary of state, so Bolin was in turn succeeded by the state attorney general, Bruce Babbitt. A young, reformist patrician whose ranch family was the largest owner of federal grazing permits in Arizona (Harry Day was the second largest), Babbitt was "less pliable" than Bolin, recalled Housewerth. The GOP establishment could not count on the budding environmentalist Democrat in the governor's office to look favorably on new tax breaks, highways, and water projects. "This led to a move to draft Sandra" to run for governor, said Housewerth. She was deemed by most—but not all—of the party elders to be a trustee of their civic interests.[18]

On most Friday nights, the power brokers of the Republican Party had dinner at a Mexican restaurant to plot strategy. On a Friday night in March 1978 shortly after Bolin died and Babbitt was sworn in as governor, Leo Corbet, O'Connor's ally from the state senate, was deputized to approach Judge O'Connor. "I went to the courthouse to tell her," recalled Corbet. "She was interested, but she said, 'I've got to talk to John.'"[19]

Word of the Draft O'Connor movement quickly spread. Chris Herstam, a lobbyist, ran into Judge O'Connor at lunch and said, "Boy, I hope you run for governor." O'Connor replied, "I'm thinking about it, but I'm not sure I want to get into this." She was reluctant to enter "the political hurly-burly," he said. Peter Kay, a friend who was chairman of the House Judiciary Committee, warned her against running. "I didn't think she'd win," recalled Kay. "Babbitt was popular. Half of Flagstaff [in northern Arizona] was owned by his family." Barbara Bentley, who had lived at Cubberley House at Stanford with Sandra, encountered John O'Connor. "We're trying to decide if Sandra should run for governor," he told her. He seemed calm; "Sandra's success never seemed to bother him," recalled Bentley. But it was also true that his support was critical to her success, and that she would listen closely to his wishes.[20]

At the end of March, an assemblage of Republican worthies gathered at the O'Connor house on Denton Lane. "It was all hands," recalled Scott O'Connor, who had been summoned home from Stanford, where he was in his junior year (and an All-American swimmer). "Crowded. We had to pull in extra chairs." Around the

O'Connor living room, with its polished concrete floor and Danish modern furniture, sat Senators Goldwater and Paul Fannin, Congressman Eldon Rudd, Majority Leader Burt Barr, Arizona GOP Chairman Burt Kruglick, and O'Connor's particular patron, Marshall Humphrey, a former president of the state senate and wealthy farmer. (Known to the O'Connors as "Uncle Marty" from their time together at Iron Springs, a shabby-chic camp in the mountain forests where Old Phoenix went to cool off in the summer, Humphrey was a gentleman reformer who had led the way on modernizing state government.)

Another close friend in the circle of solons was Gary Driggs. His presence was cautionary. The Driggs family owned Western Savings and Loan, a major local bank. His brother, John, a Stanford grad and the former two-term mayor of Phoenix, had run for governor in 1974 and regretted it after he was caught in a nasty five-way primary race that had drained family resources without delivering the governorship. "Driggs had put a lot of money in his race and lost," recalled Scott O'Connor. "Mom worried it was going to be more of the same."

In the crowded O'Connor living room, "each made his pitch," said Scott. "Then Mom said, 'I'm not willing to put in more than so many dollars.' [He could not recall the figure.] She was being totally practical. She used one of her can't-prove-the-negative arguments. How could she be sure she wouldn't be left holding the bag on money?"[21]

Gary Driggs recalled, "Sandra basically said, 'Look, if you want me to run, I've got to be sure there is enough money. So don't talk to me until you've raised enough money to run a campaign.' She had learned there is a lot of loose talk in politics. People are loose with talk, not money. She wanted to see the money before she ran. It was 'show me the money.'"[22]

No one did. The Draft O'Connor movement fizzled out before it caught on. Robert McConnell, a former Arizona State student body president and aide to Congressman John Rhodes, had been persuaded to put aside his law practice and to begin organizing a campaign for O'Connor. "I had been approached by Marty Humphrey, who thought the world of her," recalled McConnell. "I was told she was going to announce on Monday. But on that Monday morning, I was told, 'It's off, she changed her mind.' "[23]

O'Connor's decision was driven by more than a fear of insufficient funds. In private letters to two GOP stalwarts, Congressmen Rhodes and Sam Steiger, O'Connor laid out the obstacles confronting her. The social conservative movement that had bedeviled her in the state senate was again dividing the party, threatening to stage a primary fight for the gubernatorial nomination that would "leave scars," she warned. From the far right, Evan Mecham, a reckless showboat, was gearing up to run.[24] Looking back years later, her son Scott described his mother's thinking, in more colorful terms than she might have used: "Mecham was a goofball car dealer who wore white socks with business suits. He was a clown.* But he was crazy enough to run even if the Establishment greased the skids for mom. Plus, she remembered how hideous the legislature had been."[25]

At least a few movers and shakers were reluctant to commit their money to O'Connor because they did not trust her to do their bidding if she won. "Some of the people she thought were movers weren't really moving," recalled Peter Corpstein, a member of the Arizona house of representatives from Paradise Valley. Like Bruce Babbitt, Sandra O'Connor was not as "pliable" as some donors might wish. "She has a moral integrity that scares some lobbyists," Corpstein told *The Arizona Republic*. "They knew they couldn't just walk into her office and get something done, right or wrong."[26]

Gary Driggs detected "no driving desire" in O'Connor to become governor. "Sandra and John had a good, normal, happy life," he observed. O'Connor, in his view, did not need to feel the rush of ego that motivates most politicians. She was not compelled to win elected office to know that she was serving some greater purpose—or, for that matter, to have meaningful influence in public life. In Phoenix, Sandra and John O'Connor were powers in their own right. "People were just more involved in the community back then," said Driggs, whose

---

* Mecham was elected governor of Arizona in 1986 and was impeached and removed from office in 1988. He was accused of misusing state funds and widely criticized for using the word "pickaninnies" to describe black children.

own large Mormon family was a pillar of the Phoenix business-friendly political establishment. "It was a small enough place. We knew all the powers that be. You could get together with a few people and get it done."

Still, O'Connor's competitive juices had been stirred, then stanched. "I have very mixed feelings," she wrote Congressman Steiger, explaining her decision not to run. She suggested that she had been held back on the home front. "My husband was less than enthusiastic about my candidacy," she wrote. Maybe, as Gary Driggs contended, the O'Connor family did not need to put Sandra into the governor's chair to feel fulfilled in civic life. Even so, O'Connor once told a young family friend who was interviewing her for a school paper that not running for governor was "the hardest decision I ever had to make." O'Connor was not one to second-guess herself, but to her friend Barry Goldwater, she wrote, "I shall always wonder if the decision was correct." Years later, she spoke to Walter Dellinger, a friend and U.S. solicitor general, about her dalliance with elected politics. "She fixed me with those steely eyes," said Dellinger, "and told me, 'Babbitt was a good governor. But I could have taken him.'"[27]

LIKE SANDRA O'CONNOR a decade earlier, Harriet "Hattie" Babbitt had trouble finding a job at a major law firm in Phoenix. After graduating near the top of her class at Arizona State University Law School in 1972, Hattie, by then married to Bruce Babbitt, clerked for a state supreme court justice for a time, then finally found a job at a firm. "My first solo jury trial was in Sandra O'Connor's court," she recalled. "I got to know her pretty well. She wanted to know what the law was. She didn't like hip-pocket arguments [from lawyers winging it]. This gave me an advantage." Babbitt, like O'Connor, relied more on doing her homework than cracking wise with the good old boys.

Judge O'Connor "went out of her way to mentor women," Babbitt recalled, noting that as late as the midseventies, "you could still count on two hands the number of women practicing law in Arizona." Babbitt learned to avoid the groping hands of Renz Jennings in the elevator and managed to keep arguing cases through two pregnancies. Judge O'Connor was particularly solicitous of her during the ever-hot

Phoenix summer of 1975. "I was a baby trial lawyer and she was a baby trial judge. I was 'out to here' with my first child," said Babbitt, and Judge O'Connor wanted her to "take it easy." When Hattie gave birth in early September, Judge O'Connor wrote her, "I hope it doesn't take a court order to tell you to not rush back to work too soon."[28]

In the spring of 1979, President Carter appointed Judge Mary Schroeder of the Arizona Court of Appeals to become a federal court of appeals judge. That left a vacancy on Arizona's second-highest court for Governor Babbitt to fill. Under the merit system adopted with a strong push from Sandra Day O'Connor in 1974, the governor was to choose from one of three nominees proposed by a bipartisan panel of lawyers and civic leaders. But backroom politics had not been entirely eliminated, and before the panel chose a formal list, the governor put together an informal list, which included three names, all male. "Can't you do any better than that?" replied Hattie Babbitt. "There aren't any women on it." She suggested Judge O'Connor.

Governor Babbitt later recalled that his wife was passionate in advocating for O'Connor. ("It was, 'Don't bother coming home unless you put her on the court,'" said Babbitt's chief of staff, Jack LaSota.) Babbitt dutifully approached William Riley, the head of the Arizona Corporation Commission and a member of the Republican establishment who served on the judicial nominating committee, and asked him to find out: Might Judge O'Connor be interested in an appellate judgeship? Inquiries were made; the formal list of recommended nominees now included the name of Judge O'Connor. In December 1979, she was elevated to become a judge on the Arizona Court of Appeals.[29]

For years after, the rumor—accepted in many political circles as fact—was that Governor Babbitt put Sandra O'Connor on the appeals court to remove her as a potential opponent when he came up for reelection as governor in 1982. Babbitt himself joked that "the fact that Sandra O'Connor was twenty points ahead of me in the polls had nothing to do with it."[30] Ruth McGregor, O'Connor's first law clerk on the U.S. Supreme Court, recalled that she asked Justice O'Connor about the rumor. "She smiled and said, 'There may be something to that,'" recalled McGregor. There was also talk around Phoenix political circles that John O'Connor had quietly swung into action when he learned that there might be an opportunity for his wife to move up on the bench. Indeed, years later, Justice O'Connor told her friend Judy Hope that her husband had lobbied the governor's wife to get Sandra on the court of appeals. "'John had a talk with Hattie' was the way she put it," said Hope.[31]

"I don't have any memory of getting a call from John O'Connor, and I think I would remember," Hattie Babbitt told the author. It is doubtful that there was any kind of explicit understanding between the Babbitts and the O'Connors. Nonetheless, friends of both families detected signs of wire pulling in the well-connected machinery of Arizona politics. Judge Hurwitz, who was later Governor Babbitt's chief of staff, said he did not know if John O'Connor called Hattie, but he added, "If there was an opportunity to advance Sandra, John would have grabbed it. I can't imagine John wouldn't take advantage to pitch it. He was a deal maker in his law practice. He was someone that everyone in town liked." As for Bruce Babbitt's role, "I never heard Babbitt make an explicit deal, but he talks up to the edge of implication," said Fred DuVal, who managed Babbitt's 1978 gubernatorial campaign. Said Judge Schroeder, whose court of appeals seat Judge O'Connor filled: "The Babbitts' denial of a fix and 'John called Hattie' are not mutually exclusive. I wouldn't be surprised if John called Hattie. Everyone was speculating. Babbitt needed to fill that seat with a woman."[32] Regardless of the lingering hints of political intrigue, there is no question that Sandra Day O'Connor received a crucial helping hand in her career from Hattie Babbitt, the up-and-coming lawyer whose legal skill she appreciated and whose pregnancy she had sought to protect in the small, hot courtroom in the basement of the old Maricopa County Courthouse in the summer of 1975. When O'Connor was nominated to be a justice on the U.S. Supreme Court in July 1981, she wrote Hattie a note that said: "What can I say? No one was more surprised than me. Of course it is your fault for putting me on the Arizona Court of Appeals."[33]

IN 1976, SANDRA O'Connor was elected to the board of trustees of her beloved alma mater. On her monthly trips to Stanford, she befriended a fellow trustee, Sharon Percy Rockefeller, daughter of Senator Charles Percy of Illinois and wife of Senator John D. "Jay" Rockefeller IV of West Virginia. "We stayed in the Faculty Club," recalled Rockefeller. "We were good conscientious girls. We made our reservations a year in advance. They'd overbook and ask us, 'Would you girls like to share a room?' So we doubled up."

The roommates bonded over hair. "I had blond angel hair from hell," said Rockefeller. "She used bobby pins. I told her to use rollers for full body." O'Connor was "nicely dressed, but she didn't put as much thought and attention into it as some women. She was practical, not overly elegant or expensive." Rockefeller observed that O'Connor was "feminine—she knew how to talk to women. Not soft and mushy, but she cared. You could do it quickly—she didn't overexplain. I was around a lot of feminists. She was different."

But she was no less determined. Rockefeller was commuting to Palo Alto from her home in Charleston, West Virginia. "I said, 'Sandra, this is getting to me. I need to resign.' She said, 'Don't you do it! If you resign, the only thing they'll remember is not that you were on the board but that you resigned.'" Rockefeller stayed on the board. "It was a board of men, dominated by conservatives," said Rockefeller. "It was an old boys' get-together. I had been instructed, 'Don't speak for at least a year.' But Sandra was relentless, never backed down, not one iota." O'Connor stood up to a board member on an arcane real estate issue. "Everyone was thinking, 'Whoa, maybe we should cut it off,'" said Rockefeller. "I thought, 'Whoa, she's not going to give an inch.' She knew she was right."

One day, O'Connor told Rockefeller that she was toying with the idea of running for Congress. Rockefeller asked, "What does John think?" O'Connor answered, "We'll figure it out." Rockefeller interpreted that to mean, "I'm going to do it if I want to do it."[34]

SHE WAS NOT ready to try for a job in Washington, not yet. But she—and, perhaps even more so, John—were inveterate networkers. They liked to meet and get to know interesting, powerful people, for the pleasure of their company, and because they understood that one thing could lead to another. In the summer of 1979, Sandra met and charmed the chief justice of the United States.

That August, Warren Burger was scheduled to come to northern Arizona for a judicial conference. His chief of staff, Mark Cannon, called his sister-in-law, Lois Driggs Cannon, and asked if she had any ideas about how to entertain the chief justice. Lois suggested a short voyage on a houseboat on Lake Powell, the enormous crystal-clear water reservoir made from flooded canyons on the Arizona-Utah border. Her brother John, the former mayor of Phoenix and savings-and-loan mogul, agreed, but asked, "How will we entertain him?"

The Driggses immediately thought of John and Sandra O'Connor. "They knew all the right people," recalled John Driggs's wife, Gail. "We played charades together. Sandra was good at charades. She was good at everything." In January 1972, John and Gail Driggs had traveled to Washington with John and Sandra O'Connor for the swearing-in of their fellow charades player, William Rehnquist. As they looked at the portraits in the vast marble hall of the Supreme Court, Gail had said to John O'Connor, "Sandra's picture is going to be there someday." John responded, "Oh, that'll never happen. They'll never take two from Arizona." ("I teased him about this for years," Gail recalled.)

John Driggs called John O'Connor and asked if he and Sandra would like to join them on the houseboat on Lake Powell with Chief Justice Burger. "Would we ever!" exclaimed John.

Floating on the lake in the August sun beneath the thousand-foot sheer red cliffs, the Driggs and O'Connor families water-skied and ate grilled fish with a marinade made by Sandra. The erect, silver-maned chief justice, who liked the trappings of office, was formal at first. "Call me Chief," he said. But he softened as he sat into the darkening evening, chatting about the law and politics with Sandra. "She and the Chief hit it off right away," recalled Mark Cannon. "It was obvious in his bright eyes. He looked like a guy who had made a discovery." Cannon was accustomed to his boss appearing "skeptical" around lawyers trying to curry his favor. "He fell in love," said Gary Driggs, John's brother, who had come along on the trip. "They talked until two A.M."[35]

On the flight back to Washington, Burger's chief of staff wondered aloud to his boss if Sandra O'Connor might make a Supreme Court justice. She was only a lower court judge at the time, but the pool of Republican women judges was still tiny, and a growing number of voters were getting restless about the historically white-male composition of the judiciary. The Democrats were already moving ahead; President Jimmy Carter was on his way to appointing forty-one female federal judges, five times as many as all his predecessors combined.[36] Recalled Cannon, "President Carter was thinking of Shirley Hufstedler of the Ninth Circuit [federal court of appeals and another Stanford Law graduate] for the Supreme Court. It was clearly coming."

Growing more enthusiastic about O'Connor as they flew east, Burger and his aide talked about "how to make her better known," recalled Cannon. It was obvious that she was ambitious and locally well connected. "We could see that she was calculating," said Cannon. "She was slightly on the liberal side but had [Senators] Goldwater and Fannin in her pocket." To boost her judicial credentials, Chief Justice Burger put her on a council of worthies, the Judicial Fellows Committee, whose members included former Harvard Law School dean and solicitor general Erwin Griswold. He also included her on the Anglo-American Legal Exchange, a high-level annual gathering of jurists from both sides of the Atlantic.

In the summer of 1980, the O'Connors were thrilled to go to London, courtesy of the chief justice, to hobnob with the international legal elite. Both enjoyed costumes and putting on amateur theatricals, so they were duly impressed by the wigs and robes of their British counterparts and noted wryly that even lower magistrates were addressed as Your Worship. Sandra kept a diary: The Royal Garden Party at Buckingham Palace was a "fantastic show" and, sitting in the Visitors Gallery of the House of Commons, she was "impressed" by watching Prime Minister Margaret Thatcher stand up to the "hooting" of Labor MPs with "well chosen responses." Her diary is sprinkled with the word "attractive" (and the occasional "unattractive"). Describing one prominent politician as "very large and unattractive," she asked, "How did he win an election?" By contrast, she wrote, "Judge Winslow Christian [California Courts of Appeal and Stanford grad] is attractive." When Chief Justice Burger arrived, Sandra recorded, "I was glad to see him. He is warm and friendly."[37]

. . .

IN PHOENIX SOCIETY, the O'Connors were by now the local equiv-
alent of royalty. In 1979, John and Sandra and other civic leaders
started a program called Valley Leadership to encourage "younger
bright people in the Phoenix area to learn about the community, to
become active in it, and, in time, to become civic leaders," John
O'Connor wrote in his family memoir.[38] The O'Connors began hosting dinners at which they would put on a little show, passing a pink
Styrofoam football back and forth as they traded turns talking about
what it took to be civic leaders—and how to get along as husband and
wife. The title of their skit was "999 Tips for a Successful Two-Career
Marriage." It was all very lighthearted. They teased and pretended to
upstage each other. John bragged about his "unbroken record of in-
competency" at household chores (the best way to get out of doing
them, he explained). Dick Houseworth recalled going to a speech by
Sandra at the Pointe Hilton Hotel. "She began her remarks and three
minutes in, John walked into the room and said, 'I had on my calendar
that it was me!' "[39]

John liked to poke fun at himself. His successful campaign platform for president of the Phoenix Rotary was: "Beautiful Wife. Rich
Father-in-Law; Pool Hustler; Tennis Bum; Rounder; Currently Employed (as of June 22, 1977); Poor, but Dishonest; A Real Dummy."
When Sandra asserted herself a little too directly at home, he "rolled
his eyes and made a joke out of it. He wouldn't get upset. He might
say, 'Here we go again,' but he never got mad," said son Scott O'Connor.
"John was the cheerleader," recalled Sandra's brother, Alan. "He never
got his nose out of joint. Their deal was she would laugh at his jokes if
he took out the trash."[40]

Sandra did laugh at his jokes, uproariously and genuinely, no matter
how many times she had heard them. But her demeanor on the job
was not light. "She was not hail-fellow," said Jim Kolbe, a state senator
who served with her on a commission to write criminal sentencing
rules. ("Her view was 'let's clean this up.' Sentencing was way out of
whack," recalled Kolbe, who later became a U.S. congressman.) "Sandra held herself ramrod straight and spoke in a sing-song voice. She
was very circumspect and cautious, but her face was expressive. It

would show impatience by the twist of her mouth. You knew when she was not happy. Her eyes would narrow. Her mouth would set."[41] She had small but telling ways of showing off her authority. At the sentencing commission, she came straight from court and seemed, to some of the participants, to make a show of taking off her black robe and draping it on the back of her chair. No one doubted who was the judge in the room.

To her brother, Alan, Sandra always seemed to have a sense that she was destined for a more eminent future than mere wealth or social success. In the late 1970s, as corporate America was awakening to the women's movement, she refused to consider joining the boards of a few national companies. "They really put the bite on her," Alan recalled, mentioning United Airlines and Bethlehem Steel, but she "didn't want to take that course in her life." (In part, because she could not remain a sitting judge while serving on corporate boards.) Alan, who dabbled in mysticism, recalled that he once asked if she felt a "sense of predestiny." He described her reaction as "doing a Sandra," by which he meant graceful evasion. "She didn't acknowledge it, but she didn't deny it, either," he said. From early days, a few of her girl-friends at Stanford thought she held herself aloof, as if she sensed she was meant for more than a "ring by spring" or a big house in the suburbs. "I think she always knew there was something special," said Nina van Rensselaer, her Branner Hall mate.[42]

O'Connor herself once spoke to an interviewer of "an indefinable signal within me which has told me each time when I'm faced with a tough choice, which way to go."[43] She was not waiting on fate. In her files was a note to herself, written in her careful script sometime in the late 1970s. It read: "Don't let fate take over. You can influence your destiny."[44]

WHILE SANDRA AND John O'Connor soared in their happy world of Paradise Valley in the late 1970s, the nation seemed to be in decline. The economy was caught in a vicious cycle of rising inflation and low growth, so-called stagflation that produced a "misery index" of double-digit interest rates and high unemployment. The final, sour loss of Vietnam in 1975 was followed by the shock of the Iranian hostage crisis of 1979. America increasingly looked like a helpless giant. President Jimmy Carter worried about a malaise in the American spirit, but he did not seem to be able to do much about it.

Americans looked to answers from the right—the ascendancy of the anti–Big Government conservatism championed by Ronald Reagan—and from the left—the rise of social movements that sought to cast off the old order holding back minorities and women. Curiously, these two forces came together at a fortuitous moment for Sandra Day O'Connor.

In the swing state of Illinois in mid-October 1980, two weeks before Election Day, Governor Ronald Reagan, the Republican candidate for president, led the Democratic incumbent, President Jimmy Carter, by eleven points among men. But he trailed by nine points among women. Stuart Spencer, Reagan's chief political adviser, warned that the candidate needed to do something to close the gender gap with women. So Reagan made a "campaign plane decision," recalled Kenneth Cribb, an aide to Ed Meese and the deputy counsel of the 1980 Reagan campaign. At a press conference on October 14, Governor Reagan announced that he would name a woman to "one of the first Supreme Court vacancies of my administration. It is time," said Reagan, "for a woman to sit among our highest jurists."[45]

CHAPTER SIX

THE PRESIDENT CALLS

"Who's O'Connor?"

President Reagan and Attorney General William French Smith chat with O'Connor in the Oval Office in July 1981. At her formal interview two weeks earlier, they finessed the issue of abortion. Reagan and O'Connor preferred to talk about ranching.

A T THE JUSTICE Department in the early days of the Reagan
administration, the young aides to Attorney General William
French Smith hoped that President Reagan wasn't serious
about his promise to put a woman on the Supreme Court, at least not
as his first appointment. "We dissected candidate Reagan's speech to
mean 'best efforts,'" recalled Ken Starr, the young counselor to Attorney General Smith. The Young Turks in the office of the attorney
general wanted the president to pick their choice—Robert Bork, former U.S. solicitor general under Presidents Nixon and Ford and now
an outspoken professor at Yale Law School.

To the conservative Republican lawyers at the Justice Department,
the Reagan Revolution against Big Government meant rolling back
the wave of judicial liberalism begun in the Supreme Court under
Chief Justice Earl Warren in the 1950s and '60s. Ronald Reagan had
personally campaigned against abortion, the busing of schoolchildren
to desegregate schools, striking down the death penalty, or using legal
technicalities to let criminals go free. The Supreme Court under
Nixon appointee Warren Burger had begun a course correction, but
the counterrevolution was stalled. Bob Bork would bring a compelling voice for conservatism to the High Court, or so the young Rea-
ganauts hoped and believed.[1]

The president disappointed them. At a staff meeting in late March,
Attorney General Smith confided to his aides that he had momentous
news: Justice Potter Stewart planned to step down, opening a vacancy
on the High Court. Smith called the news a "state secret." The announcement would not be made until June, giving Smith's team ample
time to find his replacement. But any hopes for a Justice Bork were
quickly dashed. The attorney general said he had spoken to President
Reagan shortly after his inauguration. He quoted the president as say-

ing, "I promised to have a woman on the Supreme Court. Now, if there are no qualified women, I understand. But I can't believe there isn't one." To the dismay of his restless young aides, Smith eliminated any wiggle room: "It is going to be a woman," he said.[2]

Already, Smith had begun a list of potential woman justices, writing down their names, in pencil, on the back of a telephone message slip that he kept on a corner of his desk. There were five women candidates on the list. As he left the meeting, Smith handed the slip to Ken Starr. Glancing at the list, Starr asked, "Who's O'Connor? All you've got here is a last name."

Smith replied, "That's Sandra O'Connor. She's an appeals court judge in Arizona."[3]

The candidate with the most impressive judicial credentials on Smith's list was Amalya Kearse, who had been elevated to the U.S. Court of Appeals for the Second Circuit by President Jimmy Carter. Kearse was a brilliant African American woman—but she was also a liberal Democrat. Smith's search committee, led by Assistant Attorney General for Legal Policy Jonathan Rose, moved on. Cornelia Kennedy, another U.S. Court of Appeals judge elevated by Carter, had the right credentials and she was more conservative, but she was also lackluster. "She was an old-school professional woman, she had paid her dues," recalled Hank Habicht, who was on the search committee. "But she was not colorful, nothing to write home about." Sandra O'Connor was "the spoiler," recalled Habicht.*

As Smith's team began its search, the Arizona intermediate court judge "was not as well known. She had no constituency"—with one important exception. Justice William Rehnquist "came on strong for O'Connor," recalled Habicht. He did so "privately, behind the scenes. He volunteered, just popped up. This was a boost for O'Connor. It made a difference." Habicht added that he thought that Rehnquist's intervention was "very out of character for Rehnquist," or, for that

* In addition to Kearse, Kennedy, and O'Connor, there were two other women on a list of eighteen candidates in the files of White House legal counsel Fred Fielding when Stewart announced his retirement in June: Los Angeles Superior Court judge Joan Klein and North Carolina Supreme Court chief justice Susie Marshall Sharp.[4]

matter, for any sitting member of the Supreme Court to actively lobby the Justice Department on behalf of a potential candidate. Exceptional or not, Rehnquist's word carried weight with the search team. On the Court, Rehnquist was the one justice who was actively pushing back against the activism of the federal judiciary. "He was a god among conservative lawyers," said Habicht.

It may have been Rehnquist who first suggested O'Connor's name to William French Smith. "That was my strong impression," recalled Ken Starr. "Smith never said so. He was very discreet," said Starr, but, from remarks and asides made by his boss, Starr concluded that Rehnquist had persuaded the attorney general to put O'Connor's name on his phone slip.[5]

ON JUNE 25, one week after Potter Stewart publicly announced his retirement, Sandra O'Connor was in bed at her home on Denton Lane, recovering from a hysterectomy. The phone rang and it was William French Smith. The attorney general was circumspect. Could she come to Washington to be interviewed for a "federal position"?

O'Connor knew full well the momentousness of the call, but she answered with a sly dig. "I assume you're calling about secretarial work?" she inquired. Before becoming attorney general, Smith had been a partner at Gibson, Dunn & Crutcher—the same Los Angeles firm that had, almost three decades earlier, asked the aspiring lawyer Sandra Day how well she could type.[6]

Smith's call did not catch O'Connor by surprise. The day before, the attorney general's assistant, Hank Habicht, had been sent to Phoenix to check on her record in the legislature and on the bench. The man from Washington did not exactly arrive incognito. He was the only one at the state capitol wearing a suit and tie in the hundred-plus-degree heat (he also burned his hands on the steering wheel of his rental car). Habicht had been advised by Robert McConnell, a former aide to Arizona congressman John Rhodes, now serving as the Justice Department's congressional liaison, to quietly seek out Republican insiders who knew O'Connor. Since one of the insiders picked by McConnell was Marshall Humphrey—"Uncle Marty" to the O'Connor family—Sandra was immediately tipped off.[7]

O'Connor was not overeager with Smith, whom she knew slightly; they had played tennis once in California.* She told Smith that she was recovering from surgery. When did he want her to come to Washington? Within a week, Smith answered. O'Connor said that might work out—she was already scheduled to go to a conference in Washington. She said she would ask her doctor if she could travel. (He approved, as long as she lifted nothing heavier than her pocketbook.) Smith asked if he could send a couple of his aides—Ken Starr and Jonathan Rose—to Phoenix to interview her. She said she would be pleased to welcome them to her house for lunch.[9]

By late June, O'Connor had already become aware of a formidable lobbying campaign on her behalf. She may have entered the Justice Department search process from a position of relative obscurity, but Rehnquist's early advocacy had been joined by other influential voices. Charles Munger, an investor and partner of Warren Buffett, had written his friend William French Smith to say that O'Connor would do for conservatives what Justice William Brennan had done for the liberals on the Warren Court—use hands-on political skills to fashion five-vote majorities.[10] On June 18, the day Stewart announced his retirement, Arizona senator Dennis DeConcini, a moderate Democrat, had issued a press release calling on President Reagan to appoint O'Connor to the Court. Working across the aisle with DeConcini, Senator Barry Goldwater had privately called on President Reagan to push for his old friend Sandra O'Connor. "I told the president, he has to do this!" Goldwater exclaimed to DeConcini on the Senate floor. The White House listened closely to Goldwater; he was chairman of the Senate Armed Services Committee, which would soon be voting on President Reagan's defense buildup. [11]

Meanwhile, the chief justice of the United States approached the president's chief counsel, Fred Fielding. A decade earlier, Warren Burger had told President Nixon that he was "totally against" having a female justice. By floating around Lake Powell on a houseboat with the chief justice, then hobnobbing with him at the Inns of Court in

---

* With his aides, Smith was defensive that his law firm had offered to hire O'Connor as a secretary, not as a lawyer. "Well at least we offered her a job!" he protested.[8]

London, Sandra O'Connor had changed Burger's mind. While Justice Rehnquist was working the attorney general, the chief justice was sidling up to the White House chief counsel, who would also have a voice in the selection of a justice. "By the time Reagan was elected, he was ready to make his move," recalled Burger's chief administrator, Mark Cannon. "Burger had a relationship with Fred Fielding and talked to him about Sandra O'Connor." Recalled Fielding: "Burger invited me to his house for lunch on a Sunday. He talked around it for a while then raised her name. He had spent time in London with her and regaled me. He was planting her."[12]

Sandra O'Connor's husband was soon doing his part. As he had on behalf of Justice Rehnquist a decade earlier, John O'Connor plugged into his network of well-connected clients, including Bill Franke, a Stanford grad and wealthy businessman (at the time, the head of a Fortune 500 company, Southwest Forest Industries). "In 1981, I got a call from John," recalled Franke. "He said, 'Reagan says he is going to appoint a woman to the Supreme Court. You know Baker [White House chief of staff James A. Baker]. Could you call him about Sandra?'"

Franke dutifully telephoned Baker, who, as a partner of a big Houston law firm, had also done some legal work for Franke's business empire. "He said, 'What can I do for you?'" Franke recalled. "I said, 'Reagan's going to appoint a woman to the Supreme Court.' He said, 'Yeah, that's being batted around.' I said, 'I've got someone in mind: Sandra O'Connor.' He said, 'Sandra O'Connor?'" Over the phone, Franke could hear the sound of Baker turning pages. After a short moment, Baker said, "Here she is, she's on the list." The president's chief of staff, known for his cool pragmatism, advised Franke that the process was "political" and that he should rally support for O'Connor from the Arizona congressional delegation (John O'Connor was already on the case).[13]

Jim Baker recollected searching his briefing book for O'Connor's name in his call with Bill Franke. ("I'm surprised I said it was a political process. I don't think I would have said that," Baker told the author, though he added, "I could have.") As Baker tells it, by the time the president's top advisers—the so-called Troika of Chief of Staff Baker, White House counselor Ed Meese, and Assistant to the President Mike Deaver—sat down to consider their recommendation to President Reagan, O'Connor was "the front runner." On June 23, the Troika, along with Attorney General Smith, met with President Reagan to discuss Potter Stewart's replacement. The one-hour talk was almost entirely about O'Connor. Smith told Reagan that Judge O'Connor had "a strong record" of favoring judicial restraint and—importantly—that she was "from the West." As Baker recalled, "There was not much debate. There wasn't any really close competition. We had trouble coming up with conservative résumés." He added, "Nancy Reagan was on board. If she hadn't been, we would not have done it."[14]

O'CONNOR HAD TO pass one last test. At ten o'clock on the morning of Saturday, June 25, the two emissaries from the attorney general—Ken Starr and Jonathan Rose—appeared at the adobe-and-glass house on Denton Lane. Starr, thirty-five, Smith's top assistant, had clerked for Chief Justice Burger; Assistant Attorney General Rose, forty, was Yale (Skull and Bones) and Harvard Law. Both men were of a type that John and Sandra might have described as "attractive."

The O'Connor house was "very informal, nothing fancy, open-air. Very Phoenician," recalled Starr. "We sat on twin facing couches. I sat with Jon Rose; she sat with her husband, John." Starr thought it "a little odd" that John O'Connor "sat in our session," but "he never tried to guide the conversation. It was not offensive."

In his private diary, John O'Connor wrote, "I sat with SOC the entire meeting. The conversation began on an essentially social nature. We all got along quite well." The conversation turned to O'Connor's record as a legislator and judge. Inevitably, the visitors asked her about abortion. As John recorded her response, "she said she considered abortion personally abhorrent. She said the issue was not a major one at the time she was in the legislature. She said she had never been regarded as a crusader on either side of the issue." Starr and Rose asked "whether she felt the Court should reverse past decisions if she felt they were wrong." O'Connor chose to tread carefully; she knew, without anything being said, that the Reagan emissaries were politely fishing for what she would do about *Roe v. Wade,* the High Court's 1973 decision giving women a constitutional right to an abortion. As reported by John, Sandra skillfully finessed the question. "She referred to the fact that she felt courts should construe rather than make laws. She said, however, that in a limited number of cases, it would be appropriate for the Court to reverse old decisions. However, she said this power should be used sparingly."

John O'Connor found Starr, who asked "about 75 percent of the questions," to be "obviously quite bright. He had read all of Sandra's appellate decisions." The conversation was "quite relaxed, and I entered into it on a limited basis," he wrote in his diary. "It was a hot day, and I spent a lot of time ferrying the soft drinks back and forth. Sandra interrupted the conversation to fix a lunch of salmon mousse."[15]

Jon Rose was taken. "Salmon mousse in hundred-degree heat!" he exclaimed many years later. "She did everything at the highest level a woman could possibly do in Phoenix." Ken Starr recalled noting the tight, well-reasoned quality of her state court of appeals opinions (which dealt with local issues like workmen's compensation, not questions of U.S. constitutional law). But he was far more impressed with—and more interested in—her personal manner. "She carried herself very well, with a combination of informality, dignity, and charm. She was impressive," he recalled. "Whoa. Very impressive." He knew his boss, Bill Smith, to be "very relational. It was important that there be a sense of chemistry." As a Los Angeles lawyer, Smith had picked judges for Governor Reagan in California. Smith cared about ideology but more about judicial bearing, as well as finding a personality pleasing to his friend the president.

"She disarmed them," recalled Judge Charles Renfrew of California, a close friend of the O'Connors who later spoke with Starr about his trip with Jon Rose to Denton Lane. "They went out there to quiz her and came back talking about the salmon mousse." Renfrew understood how O'Connor had turned these two dazzling but all-business young men into well-mannered guests. Renfrew had met Sandra O'Connor on one of the Anglo-American Legal Exchanges in London. "She was comfortable with herself. Rejection by law firms could have destroyed others, made them cynical. But she had confidence."[16]

When lunch was over and the conversation done, John O'Connor walked Starr and Rose to the car and said that he "wanted to ask them something they didn't have to answer," as he put it in his diary. "I asked if anyone else was on as fast a track as Sandra was. Without hesitation he [Starr] said 'No.'"

John returned to the house, where Sandra was washing the dishes. "I turned to Sandra and I said I thought for all practical purposes the decision had been made, that barring something totally unforeseen, she would receive the appointment. She agreed."[17]

IN YEARS TO come, O'Connor would say that she had strongly doubted her chances. "It seemed so unlikely that a cowgirl from Arizona would end up on the Supreme Court. It seemed very unlikely that two people [Justice O'Connor and Justice Rehnquist] who had been in the same class in law school and had known each other and lived in Arizona would serve at the same time on the Court," she told James Simon, the dean of New York Law School, during a 1992 oral history interview. "The whole thing seemed unlikely. I just thought it wouldn't happen."[18]

In the moment that Starr and Rose left her house on Denton Lane, O'Connor could let herself share John's conviction that the appointment was hers—as, indeed, it was. John's own faith in Sandra was deep. Ever since he had seen her star rise in law school, he had been dazzled by her drive and intellect. He believed others would be too, once they discovered her. But Sandra's self-effacement was real. Perhaps she could not permit herself to imagine taking a seat on the Supreme Court. The dream had seemed so far-fetched for any woman as to be simply impossible.[19]

Three weeks before the Justice Department lawyers' visit, Sandra had said as much to a friend of Scott's at a Memorial Day pool party at the O'Connors' house. Brett Dunkelman was about to head to Washington as a Supreme Court clerk for Justice Rehnquist. Scott's mother was "serving enchiladas," Dunkelman recalled. "She took me aside. She said that she and Rehnquist had gone to law school together. She told me how much she envied him. He got to clerk for Justice Jackson. She said, 'I always wanted to have that experience. I always envied Bill. But I couldn't have it; it wasn't an opportunity available to me. I hope you appreciate what an opportunity it is for you.'" She conveyed an almost palpable sense of longing—not just to have been a Supreme Court clerk but to have had the career that could follow. Standing by the pool, dressed in a party apron, "she went on and on," recalled Dunkelman. (Less than four months later, Dunkelman attended Justice O'Connor's swearing-in ceremony at the Supreme Court. Standing in the paneled reception room, "her eyes and my eyes met," said Dunkelman. Elated, O'Connor "was sort of laughing.")[20]

On June 29, O'Connor flew to Washington. That night, she had dinner with William French Smith and his wife, Jean, at the Jefferson Hotel. "Jean Smith began the conversation," recorded O'Connor in the journal she began that night. "'I understand you were President of the Junior League of Phoenix,' she said. 'Yes,' I responded. 'Are you a Junior Leaguer?'" (The answer was yes. Jean Smith was also a Junior League president.)[21] In the morning, O'Connor had breakfast with Reagan confidant William P. Clark, the deputy secretary of state (and a cattle rancher), and Deputy Attorney General Ed Schmults. In the afternoon, she was spirited to a hotel suite at the L'Enfant Plaza to meet Fred Fielding and the White House Troika: Baker, Meese, and Deaver. Her plainspoken, woman-of-the-West intelligence won over even Meese, who had preferred a more doctrinaire conservative.[22]

Only Reagan remained. To maintain secrecy, she was told to wait the next morning outside the Peoples drugstore on Dupont Circle. Standing in a pastel suit (bought for the occasion from Saks Fifth Avenue) on a muggy, overcast day, she was picked up by William French Smith's secretary and driven to the White House. No one recognized her.

At 10:15 A.M., she was ushered into the Oval Office. Reagan recalled that the two had met at a Trunk 'n Tusk dinner in Phoenix in 1972. He asked her a little about her judicial philosophy—judges should interpret the law, not make it, was her by-the-book response—and then he raised what he called "the sensitive subject" of abortion. He noted that there was "disagreement" about when life begins. "It seems to me," he said, "that if we are in doubt, we must respect the chance that life is there." But, O'Connor recorded in her notes on the meeting, "No question was asked." She had already said that she thought abortion was "personally abhorrent," but neither the president nor his men pressed her to say whether she favored overturning *Roe v. Wade*. Instead, the president and O'Connor chatted amiably about ranch life. Reagan seemed to be enjoying himself. After forty minutes, the job was obviously hers.[23]

And yet, in later years, she pretended—or actually believed?—that she still had no chance. "I had an airplane flight that afternoon going back to Arizona, and I just remember so clearly my reaction," she told James Simon (and many others, repeating the story almost word for word). "I sat back and thought all about the remarkable meetings that I had held over a two- or three-day period, and how interesting it was to meet people that one reads about day in and day out and to be in the Oval Office and see the president. But I breathed a big sigh of relief, because I felt certain that I would not be asked to take on the job of being the Justice."[24]

The next day, July 2, *The Washington Post* reported that Judge Sandra O'Connor was at the top of the short list of candidates to be appointed to the Supreme Court. With their home phone ringing with the calls of inquiring reporters, the O'Connor family drove to their cabin at Iron Springs, up in the mountains, for the Fourth of July.

Wearing a Western shirt and skirt, O'Connor read the Declaration of Independence from the steps of the Iron Springs clubhouse to a crowd of vacationers. Among those closely watching her was Ruth McGregor, the first female lawyer to be hired by John O'Connor's law firm, Fennemore Craig. ("The firm assigned mentors. I got John, probably because they thought he was used to dealing with women.") Back in 1974, McGregor had been impressed by the way Senator O'Connor had handled Phyllis Schlafly at a hearing on the ERA. "They were talking about unisex bathrooms. It could have gotten out of hand. But Sandra was poised and organized." Now, as stories of her impending appointment to the nation's highest court swirled around, O'Connor was "very dismissive. She gave the impression that nothing was going to happen," said McGregor. "All I can say is that they must have been very good actors."[25]

At about three thirty on Monday, July 6, Sandra O'Connor called her husband at his office at the law firm and told him to come to her chambers at the court of appeals. "Things are popping," she said. When John, trying not to rush, walked into her chambers ten minutes later, she was on the phone. She cupped her hand over the mouthpiece and said, "It's happened." She was talking to the president's chief of staff, Jim Baker. She had already spoken to the president. She had been on the line with Chief Justice Burger when Reagan called, and before that, with Senator Barry Goldwater. Her patrons had queued up to give her the good news.

"I got up off the couch on which I had been sitting and walked back and forth, not surprised on a logical basis, but somewhat in wonderment that that which I had anticipated had now occurred," John wrote in his diary.

Sandra hung up after she finished talking to Baker. John came over and put his arms around his wife. They stood for a moment holding hands, looking out the window. Sandra said, "This will change our lives." John responded, "You have to do it."[26]

IN LATER YEARS, O'Connor would say that her "heart sank" when Ronald Reagan called. "I had a very happy life in Arizona. I was a judge. I liked my lifestyle. I liked my family. I liked where we lived and I didn't want to move to Washington, D.C." She had never served on the federal bench. She wasn't sure she could do the job.

"That's ridiculous," her husband told her. "You'll do fine."[27] Sandra O'Connor would always remember—and cherish—her husband's unwavering support. Their sons noticed, too. "Of course he would never say no," recalled their youngest son, Jay O'Connor, who was a sophomore at Stanford. John O'Connor was in line to be named managing partner at Fennemore Craig. He knew that he was about to go from a position as one of the most powerful lawyers in Phoenix to "second fiddle" in Washington, said Jay. "He walked away from a firm he loved, a city he loved, a practice he loved, and never gave it a second thought."[28]

The O'Connor family was in the kitchen at Denton Lane at six thirty on July 7, the morning after the president called, when Peter Roussel knocked on the door. An assistant in the White House press office, Roussel had taken a late-night flight from Washington to

Phoenix in order to help the first woman ever to be named to the U.S. Supreme Court deal with the waiting reporters. She made him eggs.

Heading downtown, the two were caught in rush hour traffic at 7:45 A.M. when Roussel turned on the radio to hear the words ". . . that was President Reagan from the White House." Reagan had just announced O'Connor's nomination, calling her, resonantly if a little vaguely, "a person for all seasons." Roussel looked at O'Connor and said, "May I be the first . . ." He leaned over and lightly kissed her on the cheek.

At her press conference, O'Connor expressed gratitude, ducked questions about her opinions, and "looked nervous," according to *The New York Times*. She seemed "calm and composed" to Roussel. In her chambers at the court of appeals, she rolled her eyes at the growing stack of pink telephone messages and started calling back well-wishers. She got on the line with her old pal House Majority Leader Burt Barr. He laughingly reminded her, "With Sandy, there ain't no Miller time."[29]

Ruth McGregor, by then John O'Connor's partner at Fennemore Craig, was driving to work that morning when she turned on the radio and heard President Reagan describing the virtues of his choice for the Supreme Court. McGregor had missed the nominee's name. "Who is it? Who is it?" McGregor wondered, then she heard Reagan repeat the words "Judge O'Connor." She pulled to the side of the road and burst into tears. McGregor, thirty-eight, would become Justice O'Connor's first-hired law clerk and, some years later, chief justice of the Arizona Supreme Court.

Molly Powell, the youngest daughter of Justice Lewis Powell, was also driving in her car when she heard the news on the radio. "It was just so exciting! The first woman!" she recalled. "I still get goose bumps. You remember where you were." Just a few years before, she had been so anxious about her father's approval that she took the law school admission test without telling Justice Powell. "I remember the look on Dad's face when Molly told him she had taken the LSATs, scored well, and was headed to law school," recalled her brother, Lewis III. It was one of shock, almost bewilderment—but pride, too.

Eric Motley grew up poor, black, and parentless in Montgomery, Alabama. He was adopted by his grandparents, a carpenter and a maid. The day after O'Connor was nominated to the Supreme Court, his grandfather clipped out the news account from the *Montgomery Advertiser* and taped it to the living room mirror, beneath quotes from Martin Luther King, Jr., and Frederick Douglass. "The message was 'All things are possible,'" recalled Motley, who went on to get his Ph.D. and who, in later life, as an executive of the Aspen Institute, became a friend of Sandra O'Connor.

All over the country, women and young girls (and even a few young boys) were imagining a future once closed to them. In Scotch Plains, New Jersey, nine-year-old Michelle Friedland, a fourth grader, heard her parents talking about the first woman to be appointed to the Supreme Court. "Because of her, I realized this is something I could do," recalled Friedland, who by seventh grade was passing notes in class saying she wanted to be a judge. Friedland graduated high in her class from Stanford Law School in 2000 and clerked for Sandra Day O'Connor at the U.S. Supreme Court in 2002. In 2014, she was nominated by President Obama to sit on the U.S. Court of Appeals for the Ninth Circuit. At Judge Friedland's confirmation hearing before the Senate Judiciary Committee, Justice O'Connor, now a frail eighty-four-year-old, sat directly behind her protégée. "When the senators came up to greet her, she kept saying, 'I am here because Michelle would make a great judge,'" recalled Friedland.[30]

AT THE LAZY B ranch, a reporter for *The Arizona Republic* found Harry Day sitting in his office. Barely looking at the reporter, he was balancing his checkbook and pretending to be cranky. "I used to call her for legal advice every once in a while," said Harry. "But since she became a judge, she couldn't give me any more. . . . She'd just say, 'Well, this is what the law says.' And I'd say, 'Well, hell, I know what the law says; I want to know how to get around the law.'"

In a grudging tone, he allowed that his daughter would be a good justice because she would be better than former chief justice Earl Warren. Standing nearby, Ada Mae said, "Now, Harry, you don't want to be quoted saying that." "Well, hell," said Harry, "why not? It's the truth and I'll say it again."[31]

. . .

ON THE MORNING of Reagan's announcement, while Sandra and
the White House press officer were driving to her judicial chambers,
John O'Connor was on his way to the office of the secretary of the
Arizona state senate. He wanted to do some belated research on his
wife's record on abortion legislation.[32]

Five days earlier, the White House had leaked the likelihood of
Sandra Day O'Connor's nomination to *The Washington Post* for a reason: to test the sources and level of opposition against her. The reaction had been quick. Fed by O'Connor's right-wing foes in the
Arizona state senate, the National Right to Life Committee and
the Moral Majority claimed that Senator O'Connor had voted in the
legislature "six times for unlimited abortion." On Capitol Hill, the
administration's legislative liaison, Max Friedersdorf, passed on a
warning from Senator Don Nickles of Oklahoma and Representative
Henry Hyde of Illinois: O'Connor's appointment would "cause a fire-
storm among Reagan supporters; a betrayal of the platform; resentment would be profound, and she was anti-Reagan." A few hours
later, Friedersdorf followed up: "Add Senator Jesse Helms (R-N.C.)
and Senator Steve Symms (R-Idaho) to the list of senators calling in
today in opposition to Sandra O'Connor for Supreme Court nomination. Both objections were based on the abortion issue."[33]

The opposition of conservative senators—Jesse Helms in particular—was a serious concern in the Reagan White House. As a rising
star of the Republican Party, Ronald Reagan had skillfully exploited
the anger of voters on the New Right, but, to govern, he needed to
contain their disruptive wrath. The Far Right, with its evangelical
Christian base, was pushing a social agenda of "family values"—against
abortion, against pornography, for school prayer. Republicans had
taken over the U.S. Senate for the first time since 1955, but their one-
vote majority included at least a dozen social conservatives, led by the
courtly but adamant Jesse Helms.[34] Reagan was more interested in
cutting taxes and building up the military than engaging in a drawn-
out political battle over the so-called social issues. He could not afford
to agitate his right wing. Indeed, the White House rushed Reagan's

announcement of the O'Connor nomination in the hopes of cutting off the opposition before it could build.[35]

The right-to-lifers' attack on O'Connor's abortion record in Arizona was exaggerated or misleading; she never once "voted for unlimited abortion," much less six times.[36] But O'Connor herself had forgotten to tell her interviewers from the Justice Department about her 1970 committee vote to repeal Arizona's harsh criminal law against abortion.

At the Justice Department, there was consternation. Hank Habicht, who had been sent to research her record, described his initial reaction as: "Oh crap! Did I miss it! Was she secretly pro-choice?" He rushed back to Phoenix, where he met at an out-of-the-way roadhouse with two of O'Connor's fellow legislators. One of them was Leo Corbet, "who talked with great affection about how he had coached her to avoid hot button issues," Habicht recalled.[37] Ken Starr anxiously reinterviewed O'Connor, who said she had simply forgotten about the vote. ("We never had the sense she misled us," said Starr.)[38]

O'Connor's best friend in the U.S. Senate, Barry Goldwater, pushed back against the Religious Right in his inimitable fashion. When Jerry Falwell of the Moral Majority came out against O'Connor's nomination, Goldwater told reporters, "Every good Christian should kick Jerry Falwell in the ass."[39]

O'Connor's best defender was herself. She began calling on individual senators. "A tsunami of cameras came out" as she emerged from her car on Capitol Hill on July 13, recalled Bob McConnell, the Justice Department congressional liaison. Right to Life protesters were chanting "Vote No on O!" With Jesse Helms, her manner was disarmingly friendly and open. "Well," she said, flashing a gap-toothed smile, "what would you like to know?" Standing behind her, McConnell held his breath. He was afraid that Helms would ask O'Connor what she planned to do about *Roe v. Wade,* the Supreme Court's 1973 abortion rights decision. During the vetting process, even the White House had not been so direct, and O'Connor had not volunteered, saying instead that she "personally abhorred" abortion and that she could see permitting some state regulation—but never directly stating that she would overturn the controversial precedent.[40]

But Helms did not ask whether she would vote to reverse *Roe v. Wade*. Perhaps, like the others, he did not want to know, realizing that a direct answer—either "yes" or "no"—could force a political collision that no one wanted in the opening days of the Reagan Revolution. Instead, Senator Helms engaged Judge O'Connor in earnest but bland admonitions against judges who overreached their power. Helms played the Southern gentleman, O'Connor the warm woman of the West. "Fortunately," recalled a relieved McConnell, "he really liked her."

So did senator after senator. Strom Thurmond, the former Dixiecrat turned Republican chairman of the Senate Judiciary Committee, warned her against getting "pinned down" by the questions of senators at her hearings.[41] Then he indicated his wife, Nancy, wanted to give a lunch or tea in her honor and invite the wives of all the senators. O'Connor played a game of tennis with the wife of Senator John East, Jesse Helms's protégé from North Carolina. Meeting Senator Edward Kennedy, the leading Democrat on the Judiciary Committee, O'Connor began the interview by asking, "How is your mother?" When O'Connor emerged from the office of Senator Howard Metzenbaum, she said in a stage whisper—loud enough for the waiting reporters to hear—"Faint praise, Senator, faint praise." In his office, the liberal Democrat Metzenbaum had just lavished praise on O'Connor, but she wanted it to be reported—for the edification of conservative audiences—that the Left was lukewarm on her. Watching her perform this burlesque of indirection, Powell Moore, the White House senate liaison, thought, "Man, this gal can count votes." John O'Connor did a little lighthearted lobbying of his own. With Democratic senator Max Baucus of Montana, he joked that he was excited to be sleeping with someone who was disapproved of by the Moral Majority.[42]

The charm offensive triumphed. On July 18, Max Friedersdorf wrote President Reagan that Judge O'Connor had returned to Arizona that morning after visiting with thirty-nine senators over the course of five days. "At this juncture, there is not a single vote committed or announced against Mrs. O'Connor," he reported.[43]

Her confirmation hearings were scheduled to begin in early September. Her preparations were relentless, bordering on the manic. At the Justice Department, a pair of assistants to the attorney general prepared briefing books on various questions that might be asked by the senators. "We couldn't keep up," recalled one of her briefers, Carolyn Kuhl. "She was always calling up. Where's the next briefing book?" In Phoenix, O'Connor "was not happy with the briefing materials," recalled Ruth McGregor, who agreed to take a leave from her partnership at Fennemore Craig and go to Washington to clerk for the new justice. "So six of us went to the law firm library and began writing memos."[44] (At the Justice Department in Washington, the other assistant working on the briefing materials was John Roberts, who later became chief justice of the United States. Told in 2017 that O'Connor had been less than satisfied with his output back in 1981, the chief justice smiled and said, "What can I say? I was new on the job.")[45]

O'Connor had a near-photographic memory, and she had taken a speed-reading course as a young lawyer to accelerate her productivity. Her predecessor on the Arizona Court of Appeals, Judge Mary Schroeder, recalled witnessing O'Connor's prodigious powers of recall. One day they were standing in a crowded elevator in a Phoenix skyscraper, and just as the elevator was about to lift, the power failed and the lights went out. After a few anxious and claustrophobic minutes, the power went back on. Working from her snapshot memory, O'Connor effortlessly recalled the destinations of the dozen or so people in the elevator car and punched them back on the floor number board.[46]

"She was like a sponge," recalled Bob McConnell, who was helping to coach her for the hearings. "You'd tell her something. . . ." But there was an extraordinary amount to learn and remember. "She had a really steep study curve," recalled Kuhl. "Constitutional jurisprudence? She had none. She had been studying casebook stuff in Arizona." O'Connor was preparing not just for the hearings, but in a larger sense for her career on the Court. The strategy for answering senators was polite evasion—essentially to bore them. "Our plan was to avoid answering questions, to describe at considerable length recent developments in the law, so the senator would forget what the question was," said Kuhl. But that required mastering the ongoing work of the Supreme Court. In civil cases, Judge O'Connor had been dealing with state law—

property rights, personal injury, broken contracts—not overarching questions of equal rights or free speech. In law school, her least favorite course had been constitutional law. In 1981, the U.S. Supreme Court was deciding about 150 cases a year. Many of them involved arcane questions of constitutional law and the interpretation of federal statutes that were unfamiliar to Judge O'Connor.

O'Connor lost so much weight that summer that her clothes hung on her.[47] In August, Richard Hauser, deputy White House counsel, was sent to Phoenix with a team of lawyers to help coach the first female Supreme Court nominee. As usual, O'Connor insisted on cooking a fine meal for her guests. As Hauser and the other coaches sent down from Washington sat on O'Connor's patio discussing the intricacies of federal law with the president's nominee, Hauser could smell acrid smoke. O'Connor had uncharacteristically burned dinner.[48]

BILL KENYON, THE press secretary of the Senate Judiciary Committee, was accustomed to senators with large egos and outsized eccentricities. His boss, Senator Thurmond, had orange-tinted hair implants and liked to stuff his pockets with chicken wings at fundraisers. (His staff had to line the senator's suit pockets with cellophane.) On September 8, the day before the start of the hearings, Kenyon was in his office, wondering about Judge O'Connor, whom he had never before met, when there was a knock on his door.

It was Sandra O'Connor. She was alone. "Hi," she said. "May I see the hearing room?" Kenyon walked her down to the massive, high-ceilinged chamber, where the technicians were setting up dozens of cameras, and showed her the table where she would sit before a raised podium for eighteen senators. "She was very quiet and assured. Pleasant, soft-spoken, and considerate. Not shy, not overwhelmed," recalled Kenyon.

If she was afraid of the media, she did not show it. Two nights earlier, she had accepted the invitation of David Hume Kennerly, the Pulitzer Prize–winning photographer who had shot her for *Time* magazine, to come to a barbecue at his house in Georgetown. Many famous reporters were there, including ABC's Sam Donaldson, known for shouting "Mr. President!" whenever he got anywhere near Reagan.

O'Connor joked easily with the newsmen, and when dinner was over, "she came in and did the dishes!" exclaimed Kennerly. "She was so normal. She was a working mom who was good at young men. She liked guys. No question about it. It was not a flirtatious thing. She was natural. When I took her to the Court to shoot her, she said, 'Wow! I'm really here.'"[49]

On the morning of the hearings, she walked from Senator Thurmond's office to the hearing room arm in arm with Thurmond and Barry Goldwater, conservative icons both. The room was "jam-packed," recalled John O'Connor, who was following behind. Every senator came down from the dais to greet her. Democrats and Republicans alike had fallen for her during her courtesy meetings. Senator Pat Leahy, Democrat of Vermont, had been stuck between floors on a stalled elevator with her. "She said, 'On the count of four, we all jump,'" recalled Leahy. "We counted to four and jumped. Damned if it didn't work! You should have seen the look on the faces of her security guards."[50]

After the usual long-winded senatorial introductions, the microphone was opened for O'Connor. She made it clear—coolly, politely, succinctly—that she would not discuss her possible vote on any particular issue that might come before the Court. She spoke of how her experience as a state legislator and a state judge had given her "a greater appreciation" of the separation of powers between state and federal governments as well as between the different branches of government, and strengthened her view that "the proper role of the judiciary is one of interpreting and applying the law, not making it." In other words, she would not be a Warren Court–type judicial activist.

Lest anyone question her devotion to family values, she read from a lovely, moving marriage ceremony she had written and performed as a judge at weddings:

> Marriage is far more than an exchange of vows. It is the foundation of the family. It is mankind's basic unit of society. It is the hope of the world and the strength of our country. It is the relationship between ourselves and the generations which follow.

Then she introduced her own handsome family, who stood, one by one. "Scott graduated from Stanford two years ago. He was our state swimming champion. . . . My second son, Brian, is a senior at Colorado College. He is our adventurer. He is a skydiver with over four hundred jumps. . . . I look forward to his retirement from the activity [laughter from the audience]. . . . My youngest son, Jay, is a sophomore at Stanford. . . . Finally, I would like to introduce my dear husband, John. . . . John has been totally and unreservedly supportive of this whole nomination and this endeavor, and for that I am very grateful."[51]

Tens of millions of television viewers were watching. Roughly nine out of ten TV sets in America—more than a hundred million viewers—tuned in to the three evening network news broadcasts. All of them led their broadcasts with the O'Connor confirmation hearings and showed extended clips of her testifying. Mary McGrory, the *Washington Post* columnist known for her sharp-eyed performance critiques of politicians, was sitting in the hearing room. She captured exactly O'Connor's appeal. "For a historical figure, Judge Sandra O'Connor is an unpretentious sort. She has bright hazel eyes, brown-gray hair, a metallic western voice," McGrory began her column, entitled "Cautious." While the senators "ransacked their minds" to find adjectives glowing enough to describe the first woman to be nominated to the Supreme Court, O'Connor "sat with her ankles crossed, gravely heeding each speaker with composed attention." McGrory understood O'Connor's perfect balancing act between assertion and deference, self-regard and self-deprecation. "She is an achieving woman without an edge. She is good looking without being alienatingly beautiful and bright without being alarmingly intellectual," wrote McGrory.[52]

Her performance was not an act, but it was hardly effortless. "I sensed destiny weighing her down from the start. She couldn't be perceived as failing in any way," recalled Carolyn Kuhl, the young Justice Department lawyer who was at her side throughout the hearings. "It was grueling, exhausting, but she did beautifully." From the morning hearings to Mrs. Thurmond's lunch for the Senate wives, back to the hearings, O'Connor never took a break. "I could tell it was tiring. She exhibited physical tension"—a tightening around the eyes and mouth, a recurrence of her slight upper-body twitch—"but it was extremely well concealed. It was stressful. I could feel the stress," recalled Kuhl.

In the car on the way back to the Watergate apartment where she was staying, O'Connor asked Bob McConnell, the Justice Department congressional liaison, "How did I do?" Her voice was "tense," recalled McConnell. "I'm thinking, I've got to calm her down." But when McConnell knocked on her door after dinner, she greeted him wearing a Groucho mask—bushy eyebrows, oversize glasses, large red nose. John was also wearing a goofy mask. McConnell burst out laughing and realized he didn't have to worry about her mood.[53]

The hearings went on for three days. O'Connor gracefully parried the occasional probing question. Thoroughly prepared, she was formal and correct, even prim, for the most part, and yet, at critical moments, she was disarmingly intimate with the senators. She said she was opposed to abortion as "birth control or otherwise," but added, "I'm over the hill. I'm not going to be pregnant anymore, so perhaps it's easy for me." On the forced school busing of children, she recalled her seventy-five-mile round-trips into Lordsburg in the winter darkness. "I found that very disturbing to me as a child," she said.[54]

At lunch on the last day, Senator Thurmond seated O'Connor at a table with Senators East, Charles Grassley of Iowa, and Jerry Denton of Alabama. "Very crafty," observed John O'Connor in his diary. "I'm sure it was not an accident that these three senators had to be charmed by Sandra on a personal basis just before they had to examine her on a very sensitive issue [abortion] in front of TV cameras that were carrying the hearings live from coast to coast."[55]

Senator Denton, a former naval aviator, did try to penetrate O'Connor's defenses. As a POW in North Vietnam, Denton had once blinked the word "torture" with his eyelids (using Morse code) during a forced confession aired by Hanoi. Now playing the role of interrogator, he pressed O'Connor about her forgotten 1970 committee vote to decriminalize abortion in Arizona. Smiling, with her hands tightly folded, O'Connor deflected his questions for a half hour, fifteen minutes past Denton's allotted time. She was polite, but steely. She didn't remember voting for the bill, and in any case, "the votes were never there. It was a dead bill." Chairman Thurmond asked the frustrated Denton if he wanted fifteen more minutes. "I don't know whether another month would do," the senator grumbled.[56]

The hearings over, a final receiving line graciously endured, the O'Connor family was "really in a good mood" in the limousine ride back to the Watergate, Bob McConnell recalled. The O'Connors immediately changed into formal wear for the annual Wolf Trap Ball that night. As the dance band swung into a fast fox-trot, John and Sandra swept around the floor. The other dancers, a good swath of Social Washington, stopped and watched. Some began to applaud. Late in the evening, the O'Connors' eldest son, Scott, was watching as Sandra was introduced to the head golf professional at Burning Tree, the men-only golf club patronized by presidents, senators, and lobbyists. O'Connor could not resist teasing him: "I can't wait to play your course," she said.[57]

When it came time to vote on O'Connor's nomination, the only possible holdout was Senator Denton. In the carefully orchestrated Reagan White House, an aide wrote out some arguments and inducements for the president to make in a phone call to the balky lawmaker. On the memo to the president listing the talking points, a line labeled "Action" was left blank. After calling Denton, Reagan filled in the blank with his distinctive script: "He's with us."[58] The final vote was 99 to 0.* On the Capitol steps, photographers snapped a radiantly smiling Sandra O'Connor with her equally giddy backers, Senators Thurmond and Goldwater and Vice President George H. W. Bush.[59]

They all wanted credit. So did President Reagan, who most deserved it. "This is a ten strike," he had privately told Senator Alan Simpson on the day he announced O'Connor's nomination.[60] Reagan's own involvement in the campaign to confirm O'Connor is revealing. It suggests that Reagan was not the genially detached figurehead he sometimes appeared to be, but rather a true advocate from the moment he decided to fulfill his campaign promise of putting a woman on the nation's High Court.

---

* Senator Max Baucus was out of town. He would have been the hundredth vote. At the hearing, he had asked what words O'Connor would like to see on her tombstone. "Here lies a good judge," she replied.

As soon as O'Connor's name was leaked in June, the antiabortion forces had found an insider, a Phoenix doctor named Carolyn Gerster, to make the case in opposition. Alleging (inaccurately) that O'Connor had voted to uphold abortion six times, Gerster, a social acquaintance of O'Connor's (their children swam together at the Paradise Valley Country Club), also claimed that O'Connor had not supported Reagan as the Republican nominee in 1980. But Reagan had his own sources in Arizona. Moving in the O'Connors' social circle in Phoenix, his in-laws, Nancy's mother and stepfather, Edith and Loyal Davis, were able to reassure the First Lady that Sandra O'Connor was, as she might herself say, "attractive." Informed of Gerster's claim, Reagan called Barry Goldwater, the senior senator from Arizona, and asked if it was true. Goldwater "hit the ceiling," the president recalled in a letter to a friend. Goldwater was able to tell Reagan that O'Connor had been for him all the way in the 1980 election and his fan long before that. So, a few days later, when Senator Jesse Helms met with Reagan in a private Oval Office meeting and repeated Gerster's allegations, Reagan airily dismissed the right-to-life doctor as a "fanatic." From then on, Helms understood there was no point in trying to stand in the way.[61]

Reagan was enamored of O'Connor. To be sure, he was moved partly by political considerations. O'Connor's path to becoming the first woman justice had begun with a political consultant's alarm over polls that showed Reagan trailing President Carter among women in the 1980 election. The vision of a woman on the Supreme Court continued to enhance the optics for the media-savvy Reagan administration. During his presidency, whenever the pundits accused Reagan of running his government as a club for rich white men, his aides would trot out the appointment of Sandra Day O'Connor to the Court. By the summer of 1984, Reagan's chief of staff, Jim Baker, made a note to himself that Reagan led his opponent, Walter Mondale, Carter's vice president, among women even in Mondale's home state of Minnesota. The gender gap, wrote Baker, had become "the reverse gender gap."[62]

But Reagan's attachment to O'Connor was personal as well. After the swearing-in ceremony in late September, O'Connor said to Reagan, "As far as I'm concerned, the best place to be in the world is on a good cutting horse working cattle." To Reagan, who dreamed of escaping to his coastal mountain ranch in California and who doodled horses on a notepad at cabinet meetings, such sentiments made for a deep and easy bond. To make sure the world knew about it, White House aides fed O'Connor's quote to a *People* magazine reporter for a cover story that appeared the next week. JUSTICE SANDRA O'CONNOR, read the headline. A RANCHER'S DAUGHTER BECOMES THE MOST POWERFUL WOMAN IN AMERICA.[63]

ON THE THIRD day of his mother's confirmation hearings, Scott O'Connor noticed a diminutive figure walking past the line of anti-abortion protesters who had gathered on the sidewalk outside the Dirksen Senate Office Building to chant "Vote No on O!" The man had a small, impish smile. With a double take, O'Connor realized that the man was Justice Harry Blackmun—the author of *Roe v. Wade,* the Supreme Court's landmark opinion granting women a constitutional right to an abortion. No one else seemed to recognize Justice Blackmun. Maybe, thought Scott, when the hubbub died down, no one would recognize Sandra O'Connor, either.[64]

CHAPTER SEVEN

INSIDE THE
MARBLE PALACE

"It was like I put my hand in a vise."

Justice O'Connor required her female clerks to attend morning aerobics with her in "the highest court in the land," the basketball court above the courtroom. Every woman in the building was invited to join in.

I N THE FALL of 1980, Justice John Paul Stevens traveled to Notre Dame Law School to judge a "moot court" competition, a mock Supreme Court hearing at which students practice their skills at appellate advocacy. U.S. Court of Appeals judge Cornelia Kennedy played the role of another Supreme Court justice. The student advocates addressed Stevens as "Mr. Justice" and Kennedy as "Madam Justice." She interrupted, "Why do you keep referring to me as 'Madam Justice'? Why not just 'Justice'? It's not a sexist term." Stevens turned to Judge Kennedy and asked, "You feel strongly?" "Yes, I do," she answered.

Returning to the Supreme Court, Justice Stevens recounted this episode to his brethren, as the brotherhood of male justices had long been known. Justice Potter Stewart, perhaps contemplating his own retirement and the possibility that his successor would be a woman, said that the justices should agree to get rid of the "Mr." before "Justice" and simply be known as "Justice." After some discussion, a vote was taken. Only Harry Blackmun voted to keep the "Mr." Recalling the incident many years later, Justice Stevens was a little puzzled by Blackmun's resistance. After all, he was the author of *Roe v. Wade*. "I guess he liked 'Mr. Justice' and didn't think it was important. I don't know," Justice Stevens recalled.* "I do know he was the least welcoming of Sandra, maybe because Reagan wanted to overrule *Roe v. Wade*."[2]

Harry Blackmun was a gentle soul, empathetic with his law clerks (notably, he was the first justice to regularly hire women clerks), and

---

* Blackmun wrote the chief justice, "It seems to me of late we tend to panic and get terribly excited about some rather inconsequential things. I regard this as one of them." Burger and Lewis Powell also wondered if the name change was premature.[1]

he was solicitous of O'Connor when she arrived at the Court. When she seemed unsettled after a month, he even offered the services of his staff to help the new justice set up her chambers.[3] But he was also thin-skinned and insecure, especially about his opinion in Roe v. Wade, which had become a target of the Republican Right. He regarded O'Connor as a likely ally of conservatives who wanted to overturn Roe v. Wade.

Blackmun was prideful about his independence. Named to the Supreme Court by Richard Nixon in 1971, Blackmun and Chief Justice Burger were dubbed "the Minnesota Twins." The two men had grown up together in St. Paul, and both had conservative judicial records. But as Blackmun moved to the left and out of Burger's orbit, the chief justice cooled on his old friend. "CJ picks on me at conference," Blackmun wrote in his diary, sounding a bit, wrote one commentator, "like a wounded teen-ager."[4] Blackmun chafed when Chief Justice Burger sometimes used his power to assign opinions in a way that seemed manipulative; he increasingly saw Burger as pompous.*

So did other justices. Richard Nixon had elevated Burger from the federal appeals court largely because he had boosted the president's "law and order" agenda during the riot-torn 1960s. Justice Potter Stewart compared Burger to a "show captain" aboard a cruise ship— the one who went to dinner with the passengers, as opposed to the captain who steered the ship. Stewart's judgment was caustic, but even the gentlemanly Lewis Powell, who tried to defend Burger from his critics in the press, found the chief justice to be so vacuous and long-winded in the justices' weekly conference that he likened him to a Southern senator staging a filibuster.[5]

On Tuesday, September 22, the day after O'Connor appeared triumphantly on the Capitol steps with Senators Goldwater and Thurmond and Vice President Bush, Chief Justice Burger wrote his brethren: "Now that Judge O'Connor has been confirmed by the Sen-

---

* By custom the first to vote at conference, the chief justice in a close case would, Blackmun felt, occasionally pass until he saw which way the other justices were voting, then go with the majority so he could keep his assignment power. If the Chief was in the minority, the senior justice in the majority—usually the liberal Brennan—would assign the opinion.

ate, we can proceed with plans that have been evolving over the last five weeks. The event being unique, the pressures for attendance at the ceremony and the reception and for press coverage are far beyond our capacity. This has given rise to a good many problems, most of which have been worked out." He concluded, "I should like to add that the aggregate amount of time working out the plans for this novel occasion have involved the diligent work of a half dozen of the court's staff to say nothing of a substantial number of hours I have devoted myself." On his copy of the memo, next to the last sentence, Harry Blackmun made an exclamation point. He was stewing about the chief justice grandly referring to O'Connor's swearing-in as an "investiture" (a term now commonly used by the Court). Blackmun had already written two letters to the Court's marshal huffily insisting that his family and law clerks were entitled to their "usual" front row seats.[6]

At a Supreme Court reception before O'Connor's swearing-in, a reporter asked Justice Blackmun if he was ready for the "big day." "Is it?" snapped Blackmun. Justice Thurgood Marshall was more light-hearted with the reporter. He recalled that his swearing-in ceremony was celebrated by a plate of cookies.[7] (Marshall had been sworn in at a closed ceremony—at his request by Justice Hugo Black, who had once been a member of the Ku Klux Klan.)[8]

WHEN THE ARCHITECT Cass Gilbert designed the Supreme Court building in 1932, he was not aiming for subtlety. For more than a century, the High Court had been housed in an elegant but cramped chamber on the ground floor of the Capitol building, beneath the passageway connecting the House and Senate. Gilbert wanted the third branch of government to have its own presence and due. To enter the building, advocates and petitioners would need to climb forty-four steps, between two fifty-ton marble statues (a seated female figure, *Contemplation of Justice,* and male figure, *Authority of Law*) to massive bronze doors beneath a broad frieze that declared EQUAL JUSTICE UNDER THE LAW. With its double row of eight towering marble columns supporting the pediment, the building's architect aimed to echo the Parthenon high above Athens on the Acropolis.[9]

Some of the justices at the time thought their new home was a little too grand, too imperial. Half tongue-in-cheek, they called it the Marble Palace.[10]

At noon on Friday, September 25, Chief Justice Burger took the arm of Sandra Day O'Connor and walked her down the Supreme Court steps as hundreds of photographers, there for the photo session, snapped away. When Burger reached a plaza midway down the steps, he stopped and exclaimed to the reporters, "You've never seen me with a better-looking justice!"[11]

O'Connor kept smiling. She was grateful to Burger and, by now, accustomed to him. He was no more smug or patronizing than some earlier patrons. O'Connor had long since learned to ignore minor diminishments. At the same time, she was perfectly aware of the importance of a dignified image. While most of her friends called her Sandra, she had put up with men who wanted to show they were pals by calling her Sandy (and some genuine old friends, like Bill Rehnquist, who had always called her Sandy). After her arrival in Washington, "Sandy" O'Connor increasingly became Sandra Day O'Connor.[12]

Justices of an earlier era had arrived at the Court with surprisingly little fanfare. When Bill Brennan, named by President Eisenhower, first greeted his brethren in October 1956, they were eating sandwiches and watching a World Series game in the Court's third-floor lounge. After some pleasantries, one of them called out, "Sit down so we can see the game!"[13] When Sandra Day O'Connor entered the justices' private conference room to shake hands with the men who would be her colleagues, she was accompanied by President Reagan.

By custom, there were to be two swearing-in ceremonies, the Judicial Oath in the conference room, the Constitutional Oath in the courtroom. At the first ceremony, John O'Connor noticed that his wife was "a little nervous, which was unusual," he wrote in his diary. "I could feel her hand shaking a bit and she said 'impersonally' rather than 'impartially'" in her judicial vow, which includes the wonderful phrase to "do equal right to the poor and to the rich."

After the private ceremony, O'Connor was escorted to the Court's grand and formal courtroom, with its forty-four-foot ceiling and marble friezes depicting, with serpents writhing, the struggle between Good and Evil. In the foreground of the Court, she was seated in the

chair once used by Chief Justice John Marshall, who had established
the Supreme Court as the final arbiter of federal law two centuries
before. Behind her, the audience of three hundred people included
President Reagan, the First Lady, and as many Arizonans as the
O'Connors could wangle tickets for. They all stood as the Court's
marshal intoned, "The Honorable, the chief justice and the associate
justices of the Supreme Court. Oyez! Oyez! Oyez! All persons having
business before the Honorable, the Supreme Court of the United
States, are admonished to draw near and give their attention, for the
Court is now sitting. God save the United States and this Honorable
Court!" From behind the red velvet curtain, eight justices entered the
courtroom and took their seats in high-backed black-leather chairs
arrayed behind the elevated, wing-shaped "bench." An empty ninth
chair awaited.

After O'Connor had taken the constitutional oath (more confi-
dently this time), the Court's deputy marshal helped her put on her
black robe, the one she had worn on the court of appeals in Arizona,
and escorted her to her chair on the far right end of the long dark
mahogany bench, alongside the other eight justices.

From her seat, she caught sight of her mother and father sitting in
the audience, and she could not hold back tears.[14] DA and MO were
now old and frail; both had emphysema from smoking, and Ada Mae
was suffering from early Alzheimer's disease. President Reagan came
over to greet Ada Mae in her wheelchair. "I think I've seen you some-
where before," she said. That night, there was a family dinner; the
next morning, a White House tour and a cocktail party for the scores
of Arizonans who had come to Washington to celebrate their Favorite
Daughter. John, meanwhile, began looking for a job.[15]

JUSTICE O'CONNOR WAS entering a secretive, cloistered world.
The Marble Palace contained its own security force (who memorized
the faces of the Court's employees), woodworking shop, barbershop,
shoeshine, seamstress, nurse, gymnasium, and library for its four-
hundred-odd employees. In the basement, in room 22-B, there was a
screening room (actually, a movie projector and some chairs) where

Justice Stewart had watched a pornographic movie and famously declared in a 1964 decision on obscenity, "I know it when I see it."[16]

In 1974, seven years before the first female justice arrived, an up-and-coming young reporter named Nina Totenberg wrote an article titled "The Last Plantation." She noted that two decades after the Court outlawed racial segregation in public schools in 1954, black men and women still occupied only menial jobs at the Supreme Court. The great liberal Justices Earl Warren, William Brennan, and William O. Douglas used their Court messengers to cut their grass at home or serve drinks at cocktail parties (for no extra pay). When he arrived, Chief Justice Burger made sure that black employees were better paid and better treated. Even so, there was "still an uncomfortable racial cast," recalled Deborah Merritt, one of Justice O'Connor's law clerks. "The messengers and elevator operators tended to be black. Everyone else was white."[17]

The High Court was grand and imperial outside but fusty and antiquated within. Elevators were still manually operated. On the day Justice O'Connor was sworn in, "the operator . . . tried to go from the 3rd floor to the 2nd floor and missed it and ended up on the 1st floor. It took him 5 minutes to get to the 2nd floor," John O'Connor wrote in his diary. "We went to Sandra's offices. They had just been vacated by Justice Stevens [who was moving into the chambers of retiring justice Stewart]. They were pretty bare and plain."[18]

There was no furniture, not even a filing cabinet. Stacked up along the walls were piles of paper, some five thousand petitions for "writs of certiorari"—requests for Supreme Court review. Litigants disappointed by the results of their cases in appellate courts across the land can ask the Supreme Court to overturn the results where there is a point of constitutional or federal law. (Until 1988, the Court was also required to hear certain cases, such as those involving a federal statute or treaty invalidated by a state court.) The petitions range from elegantly reasoned briefs, written by seasoned practitioners (often former Supreme Court law clerks), to handwritten scribbles from impoverished, semiliterate prisoners. The justices examine them all, usually using their law clerks for the task. A vote of four of the nine justices is required to take a case. In O'Connor's first year or "term" on the Court—scheduled to begin in just a few days, on the traditional first Monday in October—the justices would decide 167 cases.

The workload was staggering. A justice must read hundreds of legal briefs (O'Connor later estimated that she had to read over a thousand pages a day) and write dense, tightly argued memos to the other justices and then judicial opinions by the score. Arriving for her first official day of work on Monday, September 28, O'Connor confronted a chaotic puzzle of paper. The thousands of "cert petitions" for Supreme Court review seemed to be arranged in no particular order. Together with Ruth McGregor, who by then had moved to Washington, Justice O'Connor and John sat down and began sorting the petitions by date, which seemed like a logical thing to do. They also looked for cases that might require Justice O'Connor to recuse herself because of a possible conflict of interest with John's law firm in Phoenix. John took a quick skim through the petitions and pronounced them to be "all fine." "Now, John," Sandra said. A more thorough review found two cases with possible conflicts of interest.[19]

The next morning, Sandra walked down the marble hallway to her first conference with the other justices. Most weeks during the Court year, the nine justices gather around a long polished table in an oak-paneled room dominated by a portrait of John Marshall. For secrecy's sake, no one else is permitted to enter the room. When John F. Kennedy was assassinated in November 1963, Earl Warren's secretary hesitated to knock on the door; she did not want to interrupt.[20] By custom, the junior justice answers the door, takes notes, and fetches the coffee. The brethren briefly worried that O'Connor might find the role demeaning for the first female justice, but decided that custom must go on.[21] The Court had just removed the "Mr. Justice" plaques on chamber doorways, but there was no ladies' room near the conference room. She had to borrow a bathroom in the chambers of a justice down the hall.[22]

By ritual, each justice shakes hands with every other justice before going out into the courtroom or into conference. On her first day, Sandra O'Connor grasped the meat-hook hand of Justice Byron White. While the top student in his class at Yale Law School in 1940, Byron "Whizzer" White had led the National Football League in rushing for the Detroit Lions.[23] He was known for throwing sharp elbows in pickup basketball games with his clerks. "It was like I had put my hand in a vise," recalled O'Connor. "He just kept the pressure on and tears squirted from my eyes. It was very embarrassing, my first day on the court and here I am in tears." It is unlikely that White was trying to intimidate her; he crushed everyone's hand. Nonetheless, after that, O'Connor made sure to shake White's thumb.[24] As junior justice, O'Connor was supposed to keep notes on which cases the justices agreed to review. In her journal entry about her first conference, O'Connor noted that "the Chief goes faster than I can write," and added, "It is my job to answer the door and receive messages." On the other hand, she added, "I do not have to get the coffee." Apparently, no justice had dared to ask.[25]

Traditionally, at the first conference of the year, the justices decide which cases to accept for review. As the discussion commenced, O'Connor quickly realized the notebook she had assembled on the cert petitions was out of order. She, John, and Ruth had wrongly guessed that the petitions would be considered in the chronological sequence in which they were filed at the Court. She had to flip back and forth to find her place. At lunch, "she was upset," recalled McGregor, "but there were no recriminations. It was, 'Let's get it fixed.'"

STANDING AT THE top of Round Mountain at the Lazy B, one could see, with the exception of an occasional truck rumbling down Route 70 in the far distance, no sign of nearby civilization.[26] There was no one to call, and, for that matter, no telephone to call them with. While young people who might become future Supreme Court clerks were reading Ralph Waldo Emerson's essay on self-reliance in college libraries, the Day family was living it.

Sandra was accustomed to looking after herself. Still, she was a little lonely and a little lost—figuratively but also literally in the Court's confusing matrix of marble hallways. As the light died on ever shorter fall days, she would step out into one of the open-air interior courtyards and turn her face toward the pale sun.[27] She missed the Arizona brilliance. In a way, she even missed the Arizona legislature, with all of its glad-handing and arm-twisting. She was surprised to find that within the Marble Palace the justices rarely spoke to each other outside of conference. Their chambers were "nine separate one-man law firms," as one justice put it. With few exceptions, they did not visit each other or pick up the phone.[28]

In part, this was because, out of all Washington institutions, the Supreme Court comes closest to the Platonic ideal of disinterested government.[29] Much of the discussion among the justices is legalistic and technical. Conversation is an imprecise form of communication, subject to misunderstanding. Better to write it down, to argue by memo, with words of commonly understood meaning in the law, rather than debate face-to-face through ambiguous gesture and intonation. Human feeling can be distracting and can muddy the shaping of jurisprudence. In the law, sticking to process helped guard against arbitrariness.

The justices are not Plato's "Guardians," his all-wise philosopher kings. Nor are they always immune to outside suasion or political pressure. Justice Abe Fortas, appointed by President Lyndon Johnson, kept a red phone on his desk connecting him straight to the White House.[30] But Fortas was the outlier, and he did not last long; he was soon exposed for minor financial impropriety and forced to resign. (Fortas was something of a tragic figure, caught up in the politics of the day; his more serious crime was being too close to an unpopular president.) Most justices are courteous but formal and correct with one another, and some choose to stay insulated from the outside world.

Thrown together by the presidents who appoint them, they do not necessarily like each other. They could be "nine scorpions in a bottle," in the words of one of the greatest justices, Oliver Wendell Holmes, Jr. In the 1940s, Felix Frankfurter, who had been a Harvard Law professor, regarded Chief Justice Fred Vinson, a former Kentucky congressman and Harry Truman crony who never went to law school, as an intellectual mediocrity, and he let others know it. Finally, Vinson threatened—in the middle of the Court's weekly conference—to punch Frankfurter in the nose. On the train home from Vinson's funeral in 1953, Frankfurter remarked, "This is the first indication I have ever had that there is a God."[31]

Spiteful personal feuds, like those between Vinson and Frankfurter, or, during the same era, between Justices Hugo Black and William O. Douglas, flared up from time to time.[32] When O'Connor arrived in 1981, Blackmun and Burger had already cooled, and she found a subdued, wary atmosphere at the Court's conferences and the sparsely attended weekly lunches. (On days they heard oral arguments, the justices dined in an elegant but austere dark-paneled room on the second floor; the food was not known for its quality, and O'Connor may not have improved it by bringing spicy beef jerky to share with her brethren.) The justices were still smarting over Bob Woodward and Scott Armstrong's book *The Brethren,* which had come out a couple of years earlier to great fanfare and high sales. The two *Washington Post* reporters played up (and perhaps overplayed) the occasional backbiting and petty jealousies of the justices.[33] The stories were harshest about Chief Justice Burger, who was portrayed as at once overbearing and lightweight. The main sources for the book were the justices' law clerks. Unsurprisingly, a few of the law clerks (average age about twenty-seven) presumed themselves to be the hidden powers. But several justices (particularly Potter Stewart) also spoke to the authors. Now the justices were treading lightly around each other.[34]*

With O'Connor, Burger usually meant well, but he could have a tin ear about his own advice. In November, after she had been on the Court for less than two months, the chief justice sent the newest justice an academic paper entitled "The Solo Woman in a Professional Peer Group" with a note that it "may be of interest" to her. Examining the ways men behave toward a lone female in their group, the paper's abstract concluded that the woman's presence "is likely to undermine the productivity, satisfaction, and sense of accomplishment of her male peers." Unless the group openly discusses her status as a woman, the paper counseled, the woman should be willing to accept a more passive role as a pragmatic accommodation to the men in the group.

This was not the sort of message that the first woman on the Supreme Court, and certainly not Sandra O'Connor, was likely to

* Shortly after the book was published in the late fall of 1979, John O'Connor wrote his friend Justice Bill Rehnquist, "Sandra and I read *The Brethren* over the holidays. It may contain a lot of gossip and garbage, but it certainly is interesting reading."[35]

welcome. Justice O'Connor routinely answered any and all communications, sometimes perfunctorily, usually warmly. There is no record in her Court papers that she answered this one. Under Burger's covering note, she simply wrote, "file the article."[36]

Justice O'Connor felt isolated.[37] She had hoped—and expected—that she would get a helping hand from her friend Bill Rehnquist. In her journal, she regarded her old friend coolly. While noting that "Brennan, Powell, and Stevens seem genuinely glad to have me there," with "Bill R., it is hard to tell. He has changed somewhat. Looks aged. His stammer is pronounced. Not as many humorous remarks as I remembered from years ago."[38] Another friend visiting from Phoenix, Betsy Taylor, recalled that "there was something about Rehnquist that was irritating her at this time." Cynthia Helms, wife of former CIA director Richard Helms and later perhaps O'Connor's closest Washington friend, recalled that at first "she had been very disappointed because Rehnquist didn't help her at all. 'You get there,' she said, 'and you're in this big office and you have all these briefs, and Bill was no help at all.' She couldn't understand, she couldn't figure out, why he wouldn't help her."[39]

Brett Dunkelman, the Rehnquist clerk who knew O'Connor from Phoenix, could see "the perception that he didn't help Justice O'Connor. He wasn't around a lot." Rehnquist's health was poor; he was arriving late to the Court and leaving early. He had been laid low by pneumonia in the summer, and in the autumn his chronically bad back worsened. At oral arguments, it was obvious to casual members of the audience that his speaking was impaired. "He had to take increasingly large doses of painkillers," said Dunkelman. "He had an adverse reaction [to the sleep drug Placidyl, later taken off the market] in December and was hospitalized for two weeks. He had to be totally taken off the painkillers, which were making him slur his words, slightly, though the syntax was all there. When he came back to the Court he would lie on the floor to read. He winced a lot and couldn't sit for long periods. We'd get up and walk around the block with him, discussing cases, a few times a day." At some point O'Connor registered Rehnquist's poor health, recalled their mutual law school friend Beatsie Challis Laws, but Rehnquist did not reach out to her. Nor did she reach out to him.[40]

Rehnquist had another reason to keep his distance from O'Connor, said Dunkelman, speaking to the author in 2017. "They had been such lifelong friends. He didn't want . . ." Dunkelman paused, searching for the right words. "Not to show favoritism, exactly, but he didn't want his personal relationship to color his professional relationship."[41] Rehnquist knew that his brethren were aware that he had dated O'Connor in law school. Justice Blackmun did not let him forget it. When O'Connor joined the justices on the bench in October, Blackmun leaned over to Rehnquist and whispered, "No fooling around."[42]

If Justice O'Connor was even aware of the boys' club jokes, she ignored them. She tried to cheer up her severe surroundings. She decorated her cold, empty chambers with Western flair—gorgeous black-and-white photographs of the desert landscape, a cactus topped with a cowboy hat, Navajo blankets on the walls, large tribal drums as a coffee table. From the National Gallery of Art she borrowed five prints by George Catlin, the great portrait painter of Native Americans.[43] But her outer office resembled a post office sorting center before Christmas. Sacks of mail piled up. She received some sixty thousand letters in her first year—more than any other justice in history. Some of the letters were pointedly addressed to "Mrs. John O'Connor." One said, "Back to your kitchen and home, female! This is a job for a man and only he can make tough decisions." O'Connor began by trying to answer every letter, but in time there was so much mail that O'Connor and her staff could not open it all. She had brought in a secretary from the Arizona Court of Appeals. Overwhelmed, the secretary fled back to Phoenix after six weeks.[44]

Justice Lewis Powell came to the rescue. "Dad told me Justice O'Connor's secretary was a train wreck, and Justice O'Connor needed help," recalled Powell's daughter, Molly Powell Sumner. "He gave her a secretary from his own chambers." The secretary, Linda Blandford, "whipped us into shape," Justice O'Connor recalled. "We hadn't any idea how the court did its work, how the paper flowed." O'Connor was eternally grateful; it was the beginning of a deep friendship with the courtly Powell.[45]

Powell was an old-school Virginia gentleman. In the conference room, he pulled out O'Connor's chair for her and stood when she entered the room. O'Connor appreciated Powell's manners. Years later, Powell's biographer and former clerk John Jeffries asked Justice O'Connor if it made her uncomfortable to be treated by Powell with such elaborate old-world courtesy, to be singled out, in an old-fashioned way, as a lady among men. "She almost shouted, 'No!'" recalled Jeffries. O'Connor did not see a conflict between such courtesies and contemplating consciousness-raising. That November 1981, when Betty Friedan sent Justice O'Connor a copy of *The Second Stage,* her follow-up to *The Feminine Mystique,* O'Connor wrote back, "I look forward to reading it one of these days. I am a bit overwhelmed at the moment."[46]

O'Connor enjoyed the same tony recreations as Powell. "I hear she's an excellent horsewoman, a good shot, a good golfer. . . . She is an excellent ballroom dancer," Powell told a reporter that fall. He had indeed waltzed with her at a ball, a soiree at Washington's posh Sulgrave Club, competing with Justice White to be the first Supreme Court justice to dance with another justice.[47]

Powell's clerks loved to poke fun at their justice's curiosity about the modern day. "Are those blue jeans?" Powell asked one denim-clad clerk. "My, I've tasted doughnuts before, but what do you call these?" he asked, holding up a bagel. One of his clerks from that year, John Wiley, recalled that his boss was "Southern in his graces and tastes. He told us clerks, 'One of my favorite things is to put on my white gloves and Jo [his wife] and I will go out fox-trottin'.'"[48]

Powell was a "genuinely kind, generous man," said Wiley. He was also a "hardline moderate," according to his biographer, John Jeffries. As head of the Richmond School Board in the 1950s, Powell tried to steer a middle course between court-ordered racial desegregation of the schools and "massive resistance" by Virginia state authorities.[49] He moved slowly and deliberately from his conservative views, but he did move. He had also made his peace with his daughter's decision to go to law school and was, with Harry Blackmun, among the first of the justices to hire female clerks.[50]

He was impressed, and possibly surprised, by O'Connor's acute intelligence as well as her charm and manners. When he wrote his family on October 24, only three weeks into the Court term, that "it is quite evident that she is intellectually up to the work of the Court," it was obvious he had been measuring her. He added, "Perhaps I have said that she is the number one celebrity in this town!" Six weeks later, he wrote, "You know by now that we find the O'Connors socially attractive, and she is little short of brilliant. She will make a large place for herself on the Washington scene."[51]

O'Connor's social graces had been the source of considerable media attention (some of it illicit; a reporter was caught rooting through her garbage). On November 30, underneath a photo of Justice O'Connor and husband John in black tie, hobnobbing with Elizabeth "Liddy" Dole at a society ball, the *Washington Post* headline read O'CONNOR PROVES JUSTICES CAN BE POPULAR.

Harry Blackmun saved a copy of the article for his files. The fifth paragraph of the story began, "Nobody cares much about the comings and goings of, say, Justice Harry A. Blackmun." With a black pen, Blackmun underlined the words "Nobody cares."[52]

JUSTICES HIRE LAW clerks to help them research and write their judicial opinions. Since the early 1970s, most justices have hired three or four clerks; Justice John Paul Stevens, who wrote his own opinions, hired two for many years. Eventually, even he hired four. Clerks generally provide justices with at least a first draft, which may explain the declining literary quality of Supreme Court opinions since the days of Holmes, Cardozo, and Brandeis.[53] The clerks stay a year, working day and night six and often seven days a week; some work until they can work no more. Coming to the Supreme Court with the highest grades at the best law schools and the most prized appellate clerkships under their belts, the clerks can be cocky, but also a touch insecure.

"The Supreme Court is like an Upton Sinclair novel. The assembly line keeps accelerating. Even if you're arrogant, it's intimidating. You get performance anxiety," recalled Brian Cartwright, who clerked for Justice O'Connor in her first year on the Court. Cartwright was typical of the super meritocrats clerking for the justices. After getting his Ph.D. in astrophysics at Yale, he had been president of the *Harvard Law Review,* winning the prize for highest grades in his class. In the cafeteria one day, Cartwright, who had clerked for a federal court of appeals judge but never actually practiced law, tried to engage Thurgood Marshall about an opinion the justice was working on. "I asked if he would emphasize this or that aspect, and he looked at me, with a twinkle in his eye, and said, 'Oh, I don't know about that. I've got a smart white boy to write that up for me.'"[54] Marshall, the first black Supreme Court justice, probably did have a smart white boy writing his opinion; the pool of black top law students was tiny. But he was having fun with Cartwright. Marshall, who had memorized the U.S. Constitution in high school as punishment for clowning around in class—and had argued for the winning side in one of the most important Supreme Court cases in history, the landmark school desegregation case *Brown v. Board of Education* in 1954—was amused by the self-importance of the people around him. He liked to greet Chief Justice Burger in the hallway by exclaiming, "What's shakin', Chiefy Baby?" (Burger was not amused.)[55]

Cartwright and two others, John Dwyer and Deborah Merritt, had originally been hired as law clerks by Potter Stewart. When Stewart stepped down before their term began, O'Connor agreed to take them on to work alongside Ruth McGregor. In early September, donning their dress-for-success best, the three Stewart clerks had presented themselves at the Watergate apartment rented by the O'Connors. "We looked like pointy-headed little nerds," recalled Debby Merritt. "She opened the door and said, 'Well! You don't have to dress like that for me! You can wear jeans in chambers.'"

Merritt's first assignment from O'Connor was to form an early morning exercise class. "I nearly fell over," she recalled. "I was not someone who did exercise."[56] Dutifully, Merritt found an aerobics instructor from the local YWCA to run the class from 8:00 to 8:45 every morning. The class met on the basketball court directly above the justices' courtroom. The "highest court in the land" was grim and spare, painted ice-blue, with an unyielding hard floor. "The boys would play basketball at three. They all got hurt. They were not coordinated but they were so competitive!" recalled Mary Mikva, who clerked for Justice Brennan that year.[57] "There was only one locker room and no mirrors," recalled Diane DiMarco, the aerobics instructor. "Justice O'Connor bought a full-length mirror." The class quickly became popular. Any woman in the courthouse could join in. Female clerks and phone operators and the occasional senator's wife began showing up every morning at eight. One male clerk, who had a background in ballet, was turned away. Before long, the participants were thinking up jokey lines for T-shirts—EXERCISE YOUR CONSTITUTION, MOTION SUSTAINED. O'Connor vetoed LIGHTENING THE SCALE OF JUSTICE, said DiMarco. "It implied we were too fat."

O'Connor appeared five days a week, usually attired in gym shorts and a brown shirt with butterflies. "She didn't shower. She didn't sweat," recalled DiMarco. "She hides everything well. Many times she was tired in class, but you never saw it." While excluded from aerobics, O'Connor's male clerks knew they were supposed to stay in shape, too. One of them was eating an ice cream cone at his desk. Seeing her coming, he put the cone in a drawer.[58]

Justices treat their clerks with varying degrees of respect and warmth. Justice William O. Douglas notoriously terrorized his, describing them, inexplicably, as the "lowest form of animal life." On Saturday afternoons, Chief Justice Earl Warren invited his clerks to the University Club to watch a football game and have a couple of Scotches.[59] On Saturday mornings, Justice O'Connor cooked a pot of chili or some other Tex-Mex concoction and served it to her clerks in chambers. Before and after lunch, the clerks would present, in summary form, their "bench memos" on each case that the Court would be hearing the next week. These were twenty to forty dense pages of background and analysis of fact, precedent, and doctrine. Then the clerks would debate the proper outcome.

"It was an intense experience," recalled Cartwright. "We'd square off in intellectual battle. She did not participate much. She wanted to hear." Partly, O'Connor was refraining from tipping her hand in order to let the debate go on. She was also letting the clerks educate her.[60] "We had come from constitutional law classes taught by great professors at the top of their game. She was coming from the Arizona Court of Appeals," said Cartwright. He was being patronizing, perhaps, but truthful. O'Connor's fine law school record and years of practical experience in all three branches of government did not prepare her for the arcana of Supreme Court practice. That first term, he said, "we scripted her questions for oral argument. She read them aloud. I would have been more sensitive to appearance." At the time, the Court heard oral arguments three days a week, two weeks a month. At oral argument, the justices engage the lawyers for each side—and, in-

directly, each other—in a fast-moving, demanding, sometimes tentative, other times highly argumentative back-and-forth.

The clerks worried about how their justice would come across during her first weeks and months. "The East Coast Washington establishment, the Ivy League law school grads, viewed her as affirmative
action," said Merritt. "They never said that to your face, but it was
clearly in the background. She came from the West, and in the East
people are full of themselves," said Merritt, a middle-class New Jersey
girl who went to elite schools (Harvard and Columbia, where she was
on the *Law Review*). But, Merritt added, "She was always quite confident and in command."[61]

None of her clerks doubted who was in charge. She had no record,
no experience with constitutional law, no clearly articulated views or
established doctrine to follow. Yet she did not have any trouble deciding. She was rarely relaxed, but she was almost always calm. "She occasionally lost her temper, but in a very reserved way. She never yelled
or screamed, but we knew who was the disfavored clerk that week.
There was a sharpness in tone, a cutting off of discussion," recalled
Merritt.

In the Court's weekly conference, the junior justice votes last.
O'Connor recalled that she felt "electric" about her first vote, on October 9, 1981. On the very first case, the justices were split four to four
and then it came to her. She felt "overwhelmed" to be at the table at
all—and yet thrilled to be "immediately" in the position to cast the
decisive vote. This was a power she had never felt when she was herding fractious lawmakers in the Arizona senate. The stakes were far
higher than any judicial docket she had ever faced in the state courts.[62]

Behind O'Connor's mask of self-control was an exuberance, a joy-
ous exultation, a fulfillment of her father's bursting pride. Deborah
Merritt was in the front room of O'Connor's chambers when the justice returned from that first October 9 conference. "She came back
almost girlishly excited," recalled Merritt. "I know that sounds sexist.
But she wasn't in her stoic mode. She had found it so amazing. How
they went around the table. She was surprised there was not as much
discussion as she expected, but also at how weighty the issues were.
And she seemed to be saying, 'I did it! I survived! I held my own!'"

. . .

AT THEIR SENATE confirmation hearings, judges nominated to the federal courts (including Sandra Day O'Connor) typically tell the senators what they want to hear, that they will not "make" law but rather "apply" it, or at most, "interpret" it. This myth—classical theory might be the more polite way to put it—was unraveled more than a century before by no less a legal authority than Oliver Wendell Holmes, Jr., in his late-nineteenth-century treatise on the common law. Judges—who at the federal level are appointed for life, and can be held accountable only by extremely rare impeachment proceedings—do not want to appear to be usurping or arrogating power. Judges are mindful of precedent, and they know that the public values predictability and stability in the law.[63] But, as Holmes pointed out, of course judges make law.[64] They usually make law incrementally—adjusting the law to the facts case by case, in the tradition of centuries-old English common law—and occasionally sweepingly, when, for instance, they reverse their own precedents or find new meaning in the U.S. Constitution. Ever since *Marbury v. Madison* in the early days of the Republic, when Chief Justice John Marshall exerted the Court's power to strike down a political attempt to stack the judiciary, the courts have had the last word on whether laws passed by Congress violate the Constitution.[65] With such power, argued Holmes, comes the responsibility to be modest—to show "judicial restraint." At the same time, judges need to shape the law to meet what Holmes memorably called "the felt necessities of the time."[66]*

The tension between these obligations has played out most dramatically—and, for society, most meaningfully—in the history of one amendment to the U.S. Constitution. For Justice O'Connor, the story of the Fourteenth Amendment—which guarantees "due pro-

---

* At Yale Law School in the 1930s, the "legal realists" decided that judges should be more open about their politics and policy preferences and "not hide behind legal mumbo jumbo," as one commentator put it. Partly in reaction, at Harvard Law School in the 1960s, the "legal process" school argued back that judges should guard against personal arbitrariness by closely following legal procedures and precedents.[67]

cess" and "equal protection" under the law—is the backdrop of her most difficult and most important decisions.

The Fourteenth Amendment, adopted in 1868 during the Reconstruction Era, was added to the Bill of Rights after the Civil War to guarantee the rights of freed slaves. It was soon interpreted by the laissez-faire justices on the Supreme Court to protect economic interests, from those of small shopkeepers to wealthy tycoons. The justices of the Gilded Age found in the due process clause of the Fourteenth Amendment a "liberty of contract," meaning that agreements between people—generally speaking, between employers and employees—should be free of government interference. The justices used the Fourteenth Amendment to strike down state and federal laws passed to regulate businesses and labor conditions, including minimum wage and worker safety laws.[68] By the 1930s, President Franklin Roosevelt was so infuriated by the Supreme Court invalidating New Deal programs that he threatened to expand the Court by appointing justices until the Court voted his way. Congress rejected FDR's "court packing" legislation, but the justices were not politically deaf. In the much discussed "switch in time that saved nine," the Court began upholding laws passed by Congress and state governments that protected workers and consumers from the extremes of free enterprise.[69]

Then, the pendulum swung again. In the 1950s and '60s, the Supreme Court under Chief Justice Earl Warren began using the Fourteenth Amendment as a tool of individual liberty and social justice. The justices applied the amendment's guarantee of "due process" to state and local law, in order to protect free speech and freedom of the press; religious freedom; the right against unreasonable searches and seizures; the rights of the criminally accused, including the right to counsel and the right against self-incrimination; and the right to privacy, including sexual freedom. They applied the "equal protection" guarantee to outlaw segregated schools and voter discrimination and protect the rights of those traditionally discriminated against.[70]

The "Rights Revolution" of the Warren Court was epochal, but in some ways just a start, initially aimed at upholding the rights of black people (the original intended beneficiaries of the post–Civil War amendments). Over time other "historically marginalized" minorities, including women and gays, would feel the protective embrace of the nine men—and, in time, women—of the nation's highest court.

Revolution always breeds counterrevolution. In the 1970s, with federal judges redesigning local school systems and taking over the management of state prisons and mental institutions, conservatives began decrying the "imperial judiciary."[71] Richard Nixon vowed to roll back the excesses of the Warren Court, but his four appointees at the Supreme Court—Warren Burger, Harry Blackmun, Lewis Powell, and William Rehnquist—proved to be less than dependable "strict constructionists." Chief Justice Burger was insufficiently clever to marshal a consistent majority, and he pushed his "Minnesota Twin" Harry Blackmun into the arms of the liberals. While conservative, Powell was no hard-liner. Only Rehnquist was adamant about reining in the federal judiciary, but he was in sole dissent so often that he picked up the nickname "the Lone Ranger."

Rehnquist seemed to relish the sobriquet (a toy model of the Lone Ranger, given by his clerks, stood on the mantel of his chambers). Sandra O'Connor's onetime study buddy on the *Stanford Law Review* could be willfully provocative. As a young law clerk to Justice Robert Jackson, he had written a memo recommending that Jackson vote to affirm *Plessy v. Ferguson,* the discredited late-nineteenth-century precedent upholding segregated schools as separate but equal. He later disavowed the memo, but during his clerk days, he enjoyed getting a rise out of the liberal clerks from Harvard and Yale as they argued around the lunch table in the Supreme Court cafeteria.[72]

As a justice, Rehnquist's outspokenness—and his ability to set off his more liberal colleagues—sometimes showed in open court. In 1972, in a splintered decision, the Supreme Court outlawed the death penalty, but essentially invited the states to bring it back as long as they followed certain procedural safeguards.[73] When O'Connor came on the Court in the fall of 1981, the justices were still hotly debating the issue. At an early oral argument, Justice Rehnquist asked a lawyer from the state of Oklahoma if it wouldn't be cheaper "from the taxpayer's point of view" to execute a defendant rather than confine him for years of psychiatric treatment. From the other side of the bench, Justice Marshall growled, "Well, it would be cheaper just to shoot him when you arrested him, wouldn't it?"[74]

Behind the scenes, the friction between Rehnquist and Marshall flared in early December when the justices met to vote on whether the children of undocumented aliens had a right to public education. The case, *Plyler v. Doe,*[75] was fought on the familiar ground of the Fourteenth Amendment. Were these children entitled to "equal protection" under the law? By a 5-to-4 vote, the answer was yes. At the Court's Friday conference, when Rehnquist used the term "wetbacks" to describe undocumented workers, Marshall bristled. Rehnquist explained that the term "wetback" was still in common usage in Arizona. "Under that theory, I used to be referred to as a 'nigger,'" Marshall spat back.

In the *Plyler* case, Justice O'Connor voted with Rehnquist and two other justices in the minority. But at conference, she told the other justices that she was "troubled" by the plight of the children affected by the decision. "This was still relatively early in the term," wrote William Brennan (or one of his clerks) in his annual private history of the Court's term, "and SOC had not yet adopted the conservative reflex that seemed to control her votes later in the term."

Brennan was watching O'Connor closely. He saw her as a "swing vote"—and as a potential recruit in his rearguard action to preserve the liberal legacy of the Warren Court.[76] Brennan, at age seventy-five, was in the twilight of a remarkable career. The Warren Court might as well have been called the Brennan Court. Every morning or afternoon before the Court's weekly conference, Chief Justice Warren would appear in Brennan's chambers, gruffly acknowledge Brennan's secretary by the wrong name (calling her "Miss Fuller," not "Miss Fowler"), and go into Brennan's office and close the door. There, for an hour or so, the two men would plan strategy. No one was better at forging Court majorities than the warm, tactile, impish Bill Brennan. He was the exception to the rule that justices do not lobby one another. He liked to arrive at conference arm in arm with his most famous recruit to the liberal cause, Harry Blackmun. Every year, Brennan would quiz his new clerks: What is the most important word in constitutional law? After they had stumbled through some wrong answers, he would hold up his hand, fingers spread. "Five," he would say. With five votes, he told them, "you can do anything."[77]

But at the beginning of the 1981 term—Brennan's twenty-sixth year on the Court—he was "not his usual self," recalled Mary Mikva, one of his clerks. His wife had been diagnosed with breast cancer over the summer. "He was very distracted," said Mikva. He left the Court in midafternoon to attend to his sick wife, and he was seriously thinking about retiring.[78] When O'Connor arrived, "at first he thought, great, new blood! But he didn't have the energy, the bandwidth. His skill was personal—his personality. To be pragmatic. But I remember how sad he was. He was not able to turn it on fully for her," said Mikva.

O'Connor was wary of Brennan. She had seen his kind, or the Arizona variant, in the state legislature. She may have slightly misjudged him. "Brennan had a reputation as a Svengali, a master of getting people," said Cliff Elgarten, another Brennan clerk from that year. "He wasn't like that at all. He wasn't devious. But she thought he was more Machiavellian than he really was."

Brennan's pixie-ish "Hiya, pal" greeting hid a shy side. He was matey, but only with men. A creature of an early generation of lawyers, he was uncomfortable with women in the office. Mary Mikva was only Brennan's second female clerk, and he was reluctant to say so much as "damn" around her. In a 2017 interview, Mikva imagined, with a mixture of affection and bemusement, her old boss's free associations: "He loves women. But you can't talk dirty. Women are a mystery. You have to be careful."[79]

Brennan tried, in his way. He invited O'Connor to join him and his "pals" for lunch at Milt Kronheim's, an unlikely lunch spot for the Supreme Court justices, federal judges, and Washington power lawyers who ate there—a converted liquor distributor's warehouse in a nondescript part of town. Dirty jokes were told there, though not, presumably, on the day O'Connor visited.[80]

In his private history of the Court, Brennan lamented his failure to make an ally out of the newest justice. That spring, she switched votes on a case—abandoning Brennan and voting instead with Rehnquist, costing Brennan "his" Court and swinging the 5–4 vote to the conservatives. The case, *Clements v. Fashing,* ruling that a Texas state official could not run for two offices at once, was insignificant.[81]* But

* O'Connor wrote Brennan that she switched her vote after "considerable soul searching." A few clerks in other chambers believed that she was motivated to

O'Connor's switched vote gnawed at Brennan. "My opinion in this case and my rather angry dissent in *Engle v. Isaac* reached her chambers at the same time, and I heard via the clerks' grapevine that the combination did not please her at all," Brennan wrote.[83]

Engle v. Isaac was an important case for O'Connor. It involved the writ of habeas corpus, once referred to as the Great Writ by legal scholars. The doctrine of habeas corpus, as old as the Magna Carta, is a foundation stone of due process. In a dictatorship, the man in charge (or woman in charge) can lock up anyone he or she wants on a whim, indefinitely. In a free liberal democracy, the state cannot deprive individuals of property or liberty without legal justification. The Great Writ is a formidable safeguard of individual rights. Indeed, only because the Civil War broke out could President Lincoln justify suspending habeas corpus, and his exigent act remains controversial.

In essence, habeas corpus gives someone arrested for a crime the right to appear before a judge. In the era of the Warren Court, habeas corpus became the tool that indigent prisoners, particularly those on Death Row, could use to get from state court—where individual rights were sometimes ignored or spottily protected—to federal court, where prisoners stood a better chance of having their rights vindicated. The Court's opinion in the landmark habeas case *Fay v. Noia* was written by Justice Brennan, using the due process clause of the Fourteenth Amendment—the guarantee of personal liberty that had made its way down through the English common law into the U.S. Constitution.[84] In *Fay v. Noia*, a man convicted of murder failed to file his state appeal on time. The Supreme Court ruled that he could still seek relief in federal court.

By the time O'Connor arrived at the Supreme Court, conservative judges and politicians were beginning to complain about convicted prisoners gaming the system, using habeas corpus petitions to stall or subvert justice by winning endless new hearings on trivial or bogus

---

vote with Rehnquist that term (more than 80 percent of the time) in gratitude for his help in getting her onto the Court and by fealty to "the Reagan Revolution." O'Connor's own clerks strongly resisted the implication that she voted against her conscience. "It's unsurprising that she followed Rehnquist in areas where he had knowledge, and she genuinely held Reaganite views," said Merritt.[82]

issues. Ever efficient, determined to clean up "messiness," O'Connor was impatient with protracted or circular litigation. She liked what the law refers to as "finality." Unlike Justices Brennan and Thurgood Marshall, she was not against the death penalty as a matter of absolute principle. Having been a state court judge, she was hardly blind to local hackery, but she also believed state courts were improving and that a virtually parallel system of state and federal courts could be unnecessarily redundant.

So, writing for a 5-to-4 Court in *Engle v. Isaac,* O'Connor cut back the ability of federal prisoners to use habeas corpus to get to federal court without first exhausting their claims in state court. In dissent, Brennan was scathing. He called her opinion "incomprehensible" and mocked its "tortuous reasoning." When his clerks warned him to tone it down, he replied (with words he later regretted), "She has to learn to play in the big leagues."[85]

In her occasional journal, O'Connor wrote, "Bill Brennan circulated his dissent in Engle yesterday. It is too harsh and misses the point."[86] Lewis Powell, who voted with O'Connor, was taken aback by Brennan's tone. "No one is kinder or more generous than WJB until he takes up his pen in dissent," wrote Powell. But Harry Blackmun, who voted against O'Connor, seemed gleeful about the slashing attack. "WOW!" he wrote on the top of his copy of Brennan's opinion and made exclamation points next to the juicier passages.[87]

Blackmun was nurturing his resentment of the newest justice. Still learning the unwritten rules of the Court, she had unwittingly invaded his private space, a small library in the Supreme Court set aside for the justices where Blackmun liked to hole up to do his own research. Blackmun was unique in his attention to minute detail, and he did not want any company as he flyspecked the opinions of other justices, looking for tiny errors. When she entered his sanctuary, he was "most surprised," she recorded.[88]

Blackmun's gentle side deserted him when O'Connor dissented from his majority opinion in *Federal Energy Regulatory Commission v. Mississippi* that spring. The case seemed technical—it dealt with the power of the federal government to dictate energy policy to the states—but the underlying issue was dear to both O'Connor and Bill Rehnquist. In earlier cases, Rehnquist had taken the lead in cutting back the broad reach of Congress and the federal government to interfere with state government. In a vigorous twenty-three-page dissent to Blackmun's majority opinion in *FERC v. Mississippi,* O'Connor wrote, with unusual expressiveness, that "state legislative and administrative bodies are not field offices of the national bureaucracy." In other words, state officials do not exist to merely carry out the orders of far-off bureaucrats out of touch with local realities.* In his own opinion, Blackmun wrote that O'Connor's "apocalyptic observations . . . are overstated and patently inaccurate." In his "chronology of significant events" for 1981, Blackmun wrote for April 16, "FERC case blast at O'C."[90]

O'Connor could not help but notice Blackmun's small-bore sniping at her in this and other cases. But she had long ago learned—from the provocations of her father and less benign males in the Arizona courts and legislature—not to take the bait. In June, Blackmun circulated some seemingly personal criticisms of her reasoning in another case, *Ford Motor Company v. Equal Employment Opportunity Commission,* accusing her of being "far removed from the real world." She underlined his harsh words on her copy of his opinion draft and then added a formal footnote to her own opinion "declining the opportunity" to address Blackmun's "ad hominem" attacks.[91]

Around her clerks, O'Connor, unlike some justices, tried to contain her frustrations. She did not always succeed. Debby Merritt recalled that "after Blackmun dissed her by not accepting a couple of her footnotes"—refusing to incorporate a few of her minor additions to his majority opinion—O'Connor exclaimed, "I even went to his damned prayer breakfast!"[92] In her private journal, she wondered if Blackmun was "affected by some subtle desire to frustrate what he may see as a possible new force on the Court. He referred in conversation to the 'competitiveness' which appears at the end of the term. If such a feeling exists, it is a pity. It does not belong here."[93]

On the last day of the term, she dutifully penned Blackmun a gra-

---

* O'Connor's one piece of legal scholarship before she got on the Court echoed Rehnquist's crusade to restore power to the states. She had help researching the piece from a Supreme Court judicial fellow working in the chambers of Chief Justice Warren Burger, as part of his campaign to boost her legal credentials.[89]

cious note, calculated to calm his ire. "Your knowledge and the care you exhibit with all you do sets a wonderful example," she wrote.[94] In her clear girls'-school hand, she also wrote Bill Brennan,

> Dear Bill,
>   Since I will not see you again until September, I wanted to express my appreciation for your kindness on my first Term on the Court. It has been one of the special treats to get to know you and to learn first hand of your remarkable intellect. It has been a joy to hear you express your views in Conference. I trust your summer will be restful and happy. Until September,
>
>   Sandra[95]*

She also had to mend fences with her friend Lewis Powell. "I made a strategic blunder," she wrote in her journal on June 25. She had suggested that a complex tax case that had already been argued be put over and not decided until the next term. "Lewis could hardly speak to me," she wrote. Powell told her he would "stay here all summer" to get the tax case finished, if necessary. "He was visibly upset. I was amazed," wrote O'Connor. "Of all the Justices, he is the most thoughtful, kind, and gentlemanly. I would never intentionally cause him a minute's grief or anguish." Powell did not answer a conciliatory note from O'Connor, but finally agreed to an "awkward" conversation as they walked to their chambers. O'Connor teared up as they talked; she had not realized the extent of his ire. "It will be years before I learn all the habits and customs of this unusual place," she wrote in exasperation and concern in her journal.

The spat with Powell did not last. On the final evening of the term, he came to O'Connor's chambers "to apologize for upsetting me," she wrote. "He extended both his hands—which I took in mine. He kissed my cheek and I repeated my feeling of respect and admiration and affection for him. All is well . . ."[97]

---

* Brennan responded with equal grace: "I am deeply touched by your gracious and generous note. As I've said before, it's been a delight to watch how easily and effectively you have become one of us. I cannot remember any other new colleague who had mastered the job so quickly."[96]

CHAPTER EIGHT

SCRUTINY

"Did you write this?"

*When Sandra and John danced, people would stop and watch.
Sociable and wishing to give her husband a chance to shine,
O'Connor went out most evenings, although never on
nights before oral argument.*

B Y 1982, DURING O'Connor's first full year on the Court, women had just started entering the law in significant numbers. Law schools had enrolled few women before the 1970s. Dressed in boxy suits with padded shoulders, wearing silk shirts with bow ties, female junior lawyers were trying not to attract too much attention in the formerly all-male precincts of law firms. The few women judges were not sure whether to venture pantsuits under their robes.

Justice O'Connor wanted to help these women and others to follow. She would make hundreds of speeches aimed at inspiring women in the law in every state and all over the world. In April 1982, toward the end of her first term on the Court, she spoke at a national conference of about forty women state judges held in Racine, Wisconsin. The women were thrilled to see her, recalled Barbara Babcock, who was attending the conference as the first female professor at Stanford Law School. In the ladies' room before the speech, the first female justice was greeted with something like reverence. "There was a line of women, but everyone made way for her. She said, 'No, no, I don't mind waiting,' but we bowed her in," recalled Babcock. "She was humble. But she enjoyed it."

Most of the women in the audience were freshly appointed municipal court judges, coping with overcrowded crime and domestic-dispute dockets. From the audience, a judge from Detroit asked O'Connor, "How do you take care of your family and have a career?" The justice answered, "Always put your family first." In the audience, Babcock felt "a wave of disappointment fill the room." Babcock herself did not believe Justice O'Connor's simple answer, for her or for any other woman trying to get ahead in the law. At the time, and reflecting back many years later, Babcock reckoned that the true answer was "By constant struggle."[1]

The judges in the room felt let down, according to Babcock. They were looking for a story. O'Connor might have talked about her own sometimes amusing battles with the male-dominated legal establishment, or how she had raced home to feed the kids after school before working late into the nights. Or at least clarified what she meant, given that she herself had raised a happy family on the way to the top.

Years later, she would be more candid. Balancing work and family was "desperately hard," she told an oral history project in 2001.[2] But O'Connor always resisted whining, and personal confession, or even public introspection, was not O'Connor's style at a time when she and other women were still provisional members of the legal fraternity. On the role of women and on women's rights, she was a cautious crusader. In Arizona, she had irked the feminists by backing off her support of the Equal Rights Amendment. The pro-ERA supporters had not wanted to hear her incremental approach: to change laws locally and to let women's rights advance through the courts, by individual lawsuits challenging gender discrimination.

As it turned out, O'Connor had been prescient as well as patient. In 1982, the ERA finally died a decade after passing Congress, unable to meet the deadline required for ratifying a constitutional amendment by the votes of two-thirds of state legislatures. But, by then, a score of legal cases had gradually chipped away at laws that discriminated against women. Many had been argued by Ruth Bader Ginsburg, an American Civil Liberties Union lawyer before she became a federal judge.[3] The Supreme Court, which had finally, slowly, embraced civil rights for blacks, was even slower with women. Still, the victories were coming. In the 1976 case of *Craig v. Boren,* the Court ruled that the state of Oklahoma had violated the equal protection clause of the Fourteenth Amendment by allowing girls to drink beer at the age of eighteen while requiring boys to wait until age twenty-one. The "beer case" sounds trivial, but it was actually shrewdly chosen by the women's rights advocates. It showed that men, too, could be affected by outdated gender stereotypes. (The lead plaintiff in the case was a thirsty fraternity brother.)[4]

At the Supreme Court in late March 1982, Justice O'Connor heard her first sex discrimination case, *Mississippi University for Women v. Hogan.* Joe Hogan was a twenty-six-year-old man who wanted to be a nurse.

The Mississippi University for Women had a nursing school, but it did not accept men. He won a lawsuit to gain admission, but the state of Mississippi, wishing to preserve its all-women's college (known as the W), appealed. The case made its way to the Supreme Court, where it was scheduled for oral argument before the justices.[5]

Oral arguments at the Supreme Court are intended to awe as well as inform. At the marshal's cry of "Oyez! Oyez! Oyez!" the nine justices emerge in groups of three from behind the red velvet curtain and take their high-backed black-leather seats behind the mahogany bench. At the lectern below the justices, just a few feet distant, stands the lawyer arguing the case. Some advocates, especially the newer ones, understandably quake. In ways that can seem downright rude to the uninitiated, the justices can be abrupt during oral argument, especially when a lawyer fumbles or refuses to give a straight answer. They scowl, cross-talk, and interrupt; sometimes they chat and tell jokes to each other; occasionally they close their eyes and appear to nap.

The votes of the justices are rarely swayed by oral argument. They use the interrogations to parley with each other, to sharpen points of reasoning or tease out loose ends. Often, an advocate has barely begun before a justice begins firing off questions, sometimes involving head-spinning hypotheticals.

In later years, O'Connor would usually be the first justice to ask a question, boring in as soon as the advocate had uttered a sentence or two. In the *Hogan* case, she waited eight minutes. Enunciating slowly in a soft but metallic Western voice, she asked the lawyer for the Mississippi University for Women, Hunter Gohlson, "What level of scrutiny do we have to apply?"[6]

The question seems esoteric and legalistic, but it goes to the heart of how the Supreme Court rules on equality in America. Generally speaking, when the justices consider whether a government policy or law infringes on a right, they ask if the purpose of the law is reasonable. Can the state require nearsighted people to wear corrective lenses when they drive? Obviously, yes, public safety demands it. This is known as the "rational basis" test. But if the law discriminates against a minority group for whom there is a history of exclusion and oppression—in particular, African Americans—then the bar gets higher. The state must now come up with a rock-solid reason for the discrimination. That test is called "strict scrutiny," meaning that the justices will look very closely at the history and circumstances behind the discrimination. There must be a "compelling government interest" for the policy—for example, national security—and the law or policy must be "narrowly tailored" to achieve that goal. Strict scrutiny can be a difficult test to pass. Most famously, public schools that exclude racial minorities flunk it.[7]

Racial discrimination requires "strict scrutiny" by the courts. But discrimination against women? Against gay people? They, too, had been historical victims of discrimination, but when Sandra Day O'Connor joined the Court in 1981, the justices were still working out whether gays and women enjoyed the same Fourteenth Amendment protection as African Americans did. In legal terms, the question was whether laws that classified people by gender or sexuality were "suspect" and thus subject to "strict scrutiny," thereby requiring the government to show a "compelling interest" in order for the law or policy to be upheld. Hence Justice O'Connor's question: "What level of scrutiny do we have to apply?"

Lawyer Gohlson, representing the nursing school, wanted to duck it. He wanted a level of scrutiny that was as watered down as possible—more "rational basis" than "compelling interest"—and he sensed O'Connor was antagonistic to his cause of keeping the school all-female. He hoped that he would be able to convince O'Connor and Justice Marshall—the only woman and only African American on the Court—that the all-women's college was a form of affirmative action for women. He quickly tried to change the subject, raising the specter of lawsuits to force coed dorms. He was right to be worried about O'Connor's vote.[8]

Oral arguments usually took place on Monday and Tuesday mornings and afternoons, as well as Wednesday mornings. On Wednesday afternoons and Friday mornings, the justices met in conference to discuss cases and vote on them. On the afternoon of Wednesday, March 26, O'Connor, careful to grab Justice White's thumb and not his hand, joined her colleagues in the paneled conference room next to the chambers of the chief justice. Chief Justice Burger and Justices Rehnquist, Powell, and Blackmun voted to allow the state to keep "the W" all women. Justices Brennan, White, Marshall, and Stevens voted to let in the men. With the Court divided four to four, it was up to O'Connor, the junior justice and the only person in the room who had ever experienced sex discrimination, to cast the decisive vote.

This time, she took her lead from Bill Brennan. He argued that it was not necessary to decide for all single-sex schools, rather just the nursing program at "the W," which was the only nursing program in the state. O'Connor agreed.[9] Brennan was being canny; he knew the best way to win a majority was to narrow the grounds for the decision. Normally, the chief justice decides which justice will write the Court's opinion in the case. But if, as in the *Hogan* case, the Chief is in the minority, the senior justice in the majority has the power to assign the opinion. That was Brennan, and he chose O'Connor, knowing that if she wrote the Court's opinion, she would not switch over to the other side.

In the O'Connor chambers, shaping the opinion was a long and arduous process. Ruth McGregor wrote the draft, but O'Connor ran the show. Carts filled with law books crowded her office. "It seemed like a pretty clear-cut case," recalled McGregor. "She didn't expect special treatment for women. She just didn't want them to be prevented from doing certain things." But there were still tricky questions about how far to go on the all-important issue she raised at the oral argument: What level of scrutiny should the Court apply? She was thinking about future sex discrimination cases. In *Craig v. Boren*, the beer case, Justice Brennan, writing for the majority, had chosen a middle road, more demanding than "rational basis," but just short of the "compelling interest" required to uphold the law. O'Connor followed his example. She wrote that the state of Mississippi lacked the "exceedingly persuasive justification" for the ban on men. Excluding males from nursing training, she wrote, tends to "perpetuate the stereotyped view of nursing as an exclusively women's job."

O'Connor's ruling on the facts was narrow; she was opening the door of a Mississippi nursing school program to male applicants. But in a broader sense, she wanted to leave the door open to lawsuits by women who had faced discrimination in similar or even different circumstances. She told her clerks that she wanted to add a footnote stating, "We need not decide whether classifications based on gender are inherently suspect." Even this modest, limiting statement was a red flag, warned several of her clerks. Because the word "suspect" has a specific meaning in Fourteenth Amendment cases, triggering "strict scrutiny," O'Connor could be seen to be throwing down a gauntlet. Was the justice—writing for the Court's majority—signaling that women might, in the future, qualify as a "discrete and insular minority," like African Americans or religious groups, who had been afforded special constitutional protection beginning in the 1930s? Why arouse speculation that she was open to making women a "suspect class," entitled to the same legal protection as blacks? She was earning a reputation for judicial restraint; why even hint that she might become an activist? But O'Connor insisted. "Her attitude was 'Let's not shilly-shally around. Why hold back and pretend?" recalled Debby Merritt. Importantly (and as time went on, increasingly), O'Connor saw the Court as a party to an ongoing debate on the great and hard questions of fairness, furthering a centuries-long conversation with the other branches of government. Her footnote was added.

O'Connor believed in moving incrementally, but she did not like to waver or retreat. She had seized some ground in the long fight for women's rights. She wanted to secure it and leave open the possibility of gaining more ground, as this opinion did by challenging future lawmakers and jurists to engage in the question: Do women deserve the same protection as blacks?[10]

O'Connor's best friend on the Court was bothered by the implications for the old, genteel world he held dear. Justice Lewis Powell worried about distractions in the classroom at an age when hormones rage; he was concerned that, thrust into the same classroom as young men, young women might be anxious that they were coming across as too smart or too dumb to be attractive to the opposite sex. Notions that would later seem antiquated and "patriarchal" in their protectiveness were essential safeguards in Powell's vanishing world. His wife and daughters had attended proud all-female schools for Virginia gentlewomen; these sanctuaries now seemed threatened. Powell doubted that the movement to do away with single-sex schools would stop at a single nursing program. He feared, not unreasonably, that single-sex schools would be eventually swept away altogether.

"To him, the idea that a single-sex institution was per se illegal was startling and wrong," recalled one of his law clerks, John Wiley, who worked on the case. "Normally, Powell assigned opinions to the clerks, but he kept this one for himself. I remember getting his opinion. The first sentence was jarring: 'The Court's opinion bows deeply to conformity.' It was a clever rhetorical move. He was saying to O'Connor, 'You think you're striking out on a bold new path. You're really just doing what's trendy.' I imagine she inhaled deeply when she read this," said Wiley.[11]

Powell's dissent "did not upset her," recalled Ruth McGregor. "Because he was her friend. She understood it. There was no animosity, no feeling of tension." Nonetheless, O'Connor got a chuckle out of the reaction of Justice Thurgood Marshall, who regarded the gentlemanly Powell as a throwback to the days of Old South plantations. In her journal, O'Connor wrote, "When Lewis's dissent came around in the Miss. U. for Women, I was struck by the lack of any legal authority for it. . . . Word came back via the clerks that when Thurgood read Lewis's dissent, he said to his female clerk, 'Tell Justice O'Connor not to worry. The dissent has only gone back to 'Gone with the Wind.'"[12]

Two days before the opinion was announced at the Supreme Court, on the last day of the Court's October-to-July term, O'Connor had lunch with Ruth Bader Ginsburg, who was now a judge on the U.S. Court of Appeals for the District of Columbia Circuit, a sometime farm club for the Supreme Court. The lunch was arranged by Debby Merritt, who had clerked for Ginsburg the year before Merritt clerked for O'Connor. In January 1981, Merritt and her fellow clerks had watched Ronald Reagan's inaugural parade from the window of Judge Ginsburg's chambers "with an air of mourning," she recalled. "We knew our judge would not be the first woman justice."

When Merritt suggested that O'Connor invite Ginsburg to lunch, O'Connor responded, "Oh absolutely!" The lunch was served in O'Connor's chambers. "Judge Ginsburg was quiet. She is an incredibly slow eater. Justice O'Connor was talkative, though not a chatterbox. With RBG, there were long silences," recalled Merritt. "You'd start to wonder, is she going to respond? But the body language was positive." There was no discussion of the *Hogan* case, no recognition—overt, that is—that the two most important women in the law were breaking bread together.[13]

Two nights later, Ginsburg brought home a copy of Justice

O'Connor's majority opinion in *Hogan,* announced that day. Her husband, Marty, read the opinion, looked up at his wife, and asked, "Did
you write this?"[14]

SUPREME COURT JUSTICES have the summer off. As it happened,
the O'Connors had won a round-trip ticket to Morocco as the door
prize at a charity ball. When they arrived in early August, King Hassan II insisted that Justice O'Connor come to a party in the Moroccan desert for his son, Crown Prince Mohammed. "It was a scene out
of the Arabian Nights," recalled Brian O'Connor, the twenty-two-
year-old middle son, who was along for the trip. "Enormous tents,
rugs in the sand. Mom was seated next to the prince. He did not speak
English, so they both spoke French. It was fascinating to watch my
mom engage him. She had him laughing. I thought to myself, I have
to learn some of that French." Back at the palace, Justice O'Connor
was granted an audience with "the Mother of the Children," who bore
the king his firstborn son. It was explained to O'Connor that the
crown prince is sent the best-looking girl from every tribe and that he
sleeps with them all. She kept a diplomatic straight face.[15]

Before the O'Connors' trip to Morocco, John had spent seventeen
days in an all-male environment that was far tamer than the king's
harem but, in a twentieth-century context, almost as exotic. As a
member of the Bohemian Club, a private men's club in San Francisco,
he attended the club's annual "encampment" at the Bohemian Grove
in the California redwoods, where captains of industry and statesmen
go for a week or two each summer to "escape care," to unwind and
refresh. "The Grove" is a mix of high and low, foreign policy speeches
and off-color jokes, violin concerts and ribald revelry. Bohemia's
members and guests, numbering over a thousand a year, have included
Republican presidents (Herbert Hoover, Richard Nixon, Ronald
Reagan, and George H. W. Bush were members; Dwight Eisenhower
and George W. Bush were guests); politicians and generals; and mul-
titudes of tycoons—but never women.

"Dad had heard about the Grove forever," recalled his son Jay. A
Stanford fraternity brother invited John as a guest in 1977. "When he
came home from his first trip in the Grove, he had gained fifteen

pounds in seventeen days. We looked at him and said, 'Oh my God, what happened? You look terrible.' He said, 'It was absolutely fantastic!' He had died and gone to heaven," recalled Jay. In his family memoir, John wrote, "When I first entered the Grove, I was overwhelmed. It was so large. It was so beautiful. It was a magical playground."[16]

Because he was funny, charming, and sociable—and game to stay up most of the night—John O'Connor skipped the twenty-year waiting list to become a member. "He had been admitted six months before Sandra was nominated to the Court," recalled Frank Saul, a wealthy Washington banker and fellow Bohemian. "It meant a lot to him—he had got there on his own."[17]

Sandra O'Connor was initially "irritated" by the Bohemian Club and the Grove, said her friend Betsy Taylor. (When O'Connor had asked Taylor to host a reception for Arizona visitors to O'Connor's swearing-in, she had stipulated that the party not be held at a men's club.) O'Connor had heard the usual stories of men peeing on the trees at the Grove and otherwise reliving delayed adolescence. But she held her tongue. "We saw her after John got home from the Grove, and she said, 'I'm going to be good now. I'm not going to say anything,'" said Taylor. Sandra saw John's joy in the Grove, and she knew how important it was for her husband to have his moment to shine without her. "For John O'Connor, the Bohemian Club was his salvation, for being an important person, for getting recognition," said Charles Renfrew, a federal judge prominent in San Francisco social circles and a close friend of the O'Connors. It was a formula for marital harmony, Renfrew added, "to which Sandra subscribed one hundred percent."

When Sandra O'Connor was appointed to the Supreme Court, a Paradise Valley friend of the O'Connors, Joan Myers, wrote Harry Day, "Everyone says, 'What about John?'"[18] The friends had reason to wonder. The big law firms in Washington were wary of hiring the husband of a Supreme Court justice; there were worries about potential conflicts of interest, and concern that a general business lawyer from Phoenix might not fit into the highly specialized practice of a Washington lawyer. John found a spot with a medium-sized firm, Miller & Chevalier. In October, Homer Moyer, a Miller & Chevalier partner, went to dinner at the O'Connors' new apartment in the posh

Kalorama neighborhood. (They had decided to move into a condominium apartment rather than a house, partly because the justice had
received some death threats.)[19] The last to arrive, Moyer walked into
a living room decorated in the warm colors of the Arizona desert. He
was charmed by the insouciance of his hosts. He gratefully accepted a
cocktail from John, sat down heavily in a fragile chair, and toppled
over backward as the chair splintered. "John offered me a gin and
tonic, I sat down and did a backward summersault in my chair. John
said, 'Not a problem, just sign here.' After dinner, Sandra said, 'Shall
we go into the living room and break up some more furniture?'"[20]

The O'Connors were invited everywhere. They hired Nancy
Kauffman, the attractive daughter of Arizona friends, to serve as an
all-purpose assistant and social secretary. "It was crazy," she recalled.
"Some people just don't sleep. They were out more nights than they
were in. I was twenty-two years old and I couldn't keep up with her."
The O'Connors became instant social stars in Washington, among
both the old-time society "cave dwellers" and the prominent journalists and top government officials who went to the Georgetown parties
of Katharine Graham, the owner and publisher of *The Washington Post*.
"If Sandra was invited, that was the thing to do. If she was invited, that
was the place to be," recalled Ann Hoopes. She and her husband,
Townsend ("Tim"), a former Yale football star and secretary of the
Air Force in the Johnson administration, were a sporty, popular couple, and the O'Connors were soon part of their crowd at the Chevy
Chase Club, the capital city's establishment country club.[21]*

John jumped into the social whirl. His diary recounted the many
evenings out: the menus, the guest lists, the chatter, the exhilaration,
the occasional awkward moments. He rated the "attractive" against
the "tacky." After a dinner at the White House, he narrated: "Then
Nancy Reagan motioned Mrs. Astor to sit down with us on the sofa.
So that I was between SOC, the highest ranking woman in American
history, and Mrs. Astor [Brooke Astor, the philanthropist and social-

---

* John O'Connor's sponsor for membership at Chevy Chase was Justice Potter
Stewart, who had met John at the Bohemian Grove and was able to favorably
report to his former brethren on the husband of the justice who had taken his
place.

ite] and across the aisle from the President and the First Lady and Princess Alexandra [a cousin of Queen Elizabeth] and her husband. Later in the evening [Cy] Coleman played: 'If My Friends Could See Me Now,' and I thought that was just how I felt."[22]

He made light of his subordinate status in the Washington hierarchy. "John and Sandra were everywhere," recalled Gayle Wilson, wife of Senator Pete Wilson. "If the president was there, Sandra was seated at his right. John would be put at the back of the room. He'd joked about it: 'Back of the room, near the kitchen, with women on either side I don't know and don't like.'" But the grousing was mild and infrequent, and in his diary, John took note of his appeal on the dance floor. After a tea dance at the Chevy Chase Club, he wrote, "The ladies began to flow in my direction. I guess that 30 women asked me to dance. . . . Two or three said they had waited all night to dance with me. They would cut in on me all night. I never even got to the food table. That band was just average, but I had a lot of fun." After a night with the Waltz Group, he wrote, "It killed me to leave at 1 A.M. because the music was still playing."[23]

Justice O'Connor's clerks wondered about how often she went out at night and whether she could keep up the pace. So did the other justices.[24] She made it a rule to stay home the nights before oral argument in order to prepare, but other nights the O'Connors were often out. Their close friends understood the subtle marital dynamic at play. "John was never a shrinking violet. He was always the life of the party. Sandra would back off and let him show his skills," said their friend Bill Draper, a wealthy venture capitalist appointed by President Reagan to run the Export-Import Bank. "She took a back seat in social situations. She waited for him to tell his jokes." When John stood up after dinner to tell "The Diesel Fitter," a mildly risqué, pun-filled story involving a factory assembly line worker and a pair of pantyhose (the punch line to "The Diesel Fitter" was "Dese'll fit 'er"), Sandra would laugh until she cried, time and again. Years later, in a conversation with the author and her son Scott, Justice O'Connor allowed that she had perhaps skimped on sleep in order to give John the chance to play the social lion. "I might have stayed home a little more reading briefs," she said.[25]

At his first State of the Union address on January 26, 1982, President Reagan declared how happy he was to have appointed the first woman to the Supreme Court. Below him on the floor of the House of Representatives, Justice O'Connor, robed in black, was sitting with the other justices alongside cabinet members and the bemedaled Joint Chiefs of Staff. "Sandra had not known he [the president] was going to say this," John wrote in his diary. "The remark brought the biggest applause of the night; it was unanimous and very extended. Also, it was very happy."

The next night, it was off to the Washington Press Club's "Salute to Congress." On the night after that, John wrote simply, "How nice. We stayed home." Two nights later they were guests (for the second time in three months) at the home of Katharine Graham, with whom Sandra had played tennis that afternoon. Old Washington, top government officials, and journalists were seated at three tables of eight. John recounted his cocktail conversation with presidential aide Mike Deaver: "He spoke of how happy everyone was with Sandra; that she was the absolutely perfect person for Ronald Reagan to have put on the Court. He said her manner and charm had captivated everyone." In her formal toast to Justice O'Connor, Katharine Graham pronounced, half tongue-in-cheek, "And now, I happily relinquish to you the title of 'The Most Powerful Woman in America.'"* John noted that the guest list included Bob Woodward, the coauthor of *The Brethren* and *Washington Post* reporter of Watergate fame, "who was thrilled to meet Sandra and kept pressing her for her reactions to the Court."[27] In November, the World Almanac Survey reported that O'Connor had edged out Kay Graham as the most influential woman in the world. Tennis star Billie Jean King finished third.[28]

The O'Connors began to worry that Sandra's social profile was too

---

* John delighted in the acclaim for his wife. In his diary, after the Naval Academy's Brigade of Midshipmen gave her a dress parade and nineteen-gun salute, he noted that "the only other woman so honored was Queen Elizabeth." At a reception at the National Portrait Gallery, "when SOC arrived, every flashbulb within 20 miles went off." When she read Bible passages at the Bethlehem Chapel of the National Cathedral, "people nudged each other when they realized who she was." At a Marine Corps birthday dinner, when the commandant announced her presence, "people all over the room, spontaneously and excitedly, gasped approvingly out loud. It was symbolic of the country's view toward SOC."[26]

high. After the annual Corcoran Gallery Ball, John wrote that he had spotted the *Washington Post* Style section reporter Lois Romano following him. He tried to explain to the reporter, off the record, that the O'Connors did not want publicity. John appreciated the "upbeat tone" of the *Post* article, "Justice on the Party Circuit," that appeared a week later. "What is really funny," he noted, "is that the writer talks about our busy schedule and recreational calendar without having any idea that she has just seen the tip of the iceberg." Sandra was less sanguine. "She talked about the publicity being bad for the Court when it is claiming there is an overload of work," noted John. She was particularly bothered by one sentence in the article: "Just a week ago, O'Connor, in flowing purple silk, charmed guests at the Corcoran Gallery Ball, dancing with a string of partners while most of her court colleagues were at an intimate dinner celebrating Justice William Brennan's recent marriage." After Brennan's wife died of cancer, he had married his longtime secretary, Mary Fowler. John wrote, truthfully but a little defensively, "The statement could give rise to an inference that SOC and Brennan and Marshall don't get along that well or that SOC puts the 'social life' before her life with other Justices; either inference would be wrong."[29]

Both Sandra and John worked hard at getting along with the brethren. They were a little taken aback that December in 1982 when Harry Blackmun gave an hour-long interview and divulged some inside-the-room stories. He described how O'Connor had exclaimed over a "buzzing sound" in the conference room and how she had wondered aloud if the room was bugged. Mischievously, Blackmun had not told her that the sound was coming from his hearing aid. Sandra was irked by Blackmun's little story but, as was her custom, pretended not to be. At a Christmas brunch at the house of Vice President George H. W. Bush, she and John talked to Blackmun about his TV interview: "We both laid it on in praising his calmness, the precision with which he spoke, etc. He was obviously very, very interested and deeply appreciative for the nice things we said about his remarks," John wrote. "No one talked about whether he should have given the interview."

Two days later, the O'Connors were standing in a receiving line with Justice Blackmun and his wife when retired justice Arthur Goldberg came over and said, "Harry, I don't want you to be mean to her [Justice O'Connor]. I read your opinions and sometimes you're pretty mean. I want you to be nice." In his diary, John noted that "Blackmun just smiled and said nothing. I think Mrs. Blackmun was startled. SOC said, 'Oh he's just fine. Everybody has to hang in there.' Later, SOC and I really chuckled over Goldberg's statement."[30]

Over the holidays, John wrote in his diary his wife's assessment of her first year and three months on the Supreme Court. Sandra never discussed pending cases with John, and she was discreet about Court doings in general, but "in two separate conversations" that December, she described "her feelings about her own performance on the Court to date and about the abilities of the other members of the Court." John wrote:

> She entered her job knowing it would be challenging, but without any real feeling as to what it would be really like. When she arrived, no one came in to give her any suggestions as to how to manage the paper flow, organize her office or do anything else. The clerks and SOC had to figure out what was logical, and the clerks tried to find out what some of the other chambers did. As she begins her second term, she feels light years ahead in terms of organization and control.
>
> She has never once suggested or implied that the job was, even for a moment, beyond her. She feels she is not on a par with some of the great intellectual justices of history of the Court, like Holmes, but she feels she understands very well everything that is going on about her and has the ability to express herself clearly, to persuade and to do a great job.

"The great mind on the Court," Justice O'Connor told her husband, "is Bill Rehnquist." John continued: "SOC feels he is incredibly bright, but they really see little of each other even though their chambers adjoin and he sits next to her on the bench. He never just wanders in. They have a good relationship, but they are not close in terms of spending any real time together."

O'Connor effused over Powell. "SOC feels closer to Lewis on a personal basis than to any member of the Court. He is as kind a man as there is. . . . Any time she has gotten brickbats, he has made a point of walking down the hall and telling her everything is all right."

As for her sometime nemesis Harry Blackmun, John wrote, "she feels [he] has a very good mind." She praised his research and preparation, but she told John that he "has the shortest fuse on the Court. He gets mad when a conference is called for a different time than normal. He communicates always in writing. He is somewhat accusatory. Toward the end of the session, he really feels under pressure and is brittle. SOC," wrote John, "is determined to get along with him and is going to make special efforts to do things with him socially to carry this off. Lewis Powell said to me once regarding Blackmun, 'I never know what he's going to do.' This from Powell is harsh criticism."

O'Connor was generous in her opinion of Justice Brennan: "She thinks Bill Brennan is very bright. He is also shrewd in how to play the game in order to achieve the results he seeks," wrote John. O'Connor told her husband that "[Byron] White has a good mind" and that Thurgood Marshall "hardly ever talks on the bench." In conference, she added, his most common refrain is, "I'll go along with Bill (Brennan)." John Stevens she described as "very pleasant" and a "maverick" who "seems to take delight in going his own way and is proud of it." O'Connor had kind words for Burger. "The Chief has been incredibly friendly and supportive of SOC at all times," wrote John (Sandra had apparently not begrudged the Chief for passing along the patronizing article of advice on how to be a woman in a man's world). "Periodically, he has her into tea and talks turkey with her in terms of lobbying her on just a few cases or talking about Court problems. The latter includes more anticipated difficulties with Blackmun in the '82–'83 term." O'Connor did not spell out those problems, but just about the time she was confiding in her husband, the court was agreeing to revisit Justice Blackmun's beloved, and now threatened, ruling on abortion in *Roe v. Wade*.[31]

WHEN HIRING LAW clerks, O'Connor made it her practice to choose men and women, conservatives and liberals, in roughly equal measure. She told one candidate, Gary Francione, that she wanted her clerks to argue with her. "I'm your boy," responded Francione, who was hired to work for the justice for the 1982–83 Court year. Graduating from the University of Virginia with a law degree and a master's in philosophy, Francione was a passionate animal rights activist. When another clerk told him he had just seen a dog hit by a car on the street outside, "I brought the dog into the Court," Francione recalled. "There was blood spilled on the oriental rug. Justice Rehnquist got really mad at me, really upset with me for making a mess. Justice O'Connor heard the fuss and came out of her chambers. She talked to Rehnquist: 'You know, Bill, he feels strongly about the animal issue.' There were justices who routinely yelled at clerks, in harsh, humiliating ways. That was never the case with Justice O'Connor and us. Ever."

Like many clerks, Francione felt overwhelmed by the Supreme Court's role as court of last resort on cases involving the death penalty. Prisoners on death row routinely made last-minute habeas corpus pleas to the Supreme Court for a stay of execution, and the justices had to say yes or no, sometimes in the middle of the night. On one of these cases, "I went into her office eight times. I was trying to come up with some argument to keep the guy from being executed," recalled Francione. "After the eighth time, she got up and closed the door. She sat me down on the couch and took my hand. Very solemnly, she told me, 'Gary, you have to accept something. God made me the justice.' I said, 'No God didn't! Ronald Reagan did!' 'Very good!' she said, with a laugh. 'But the bottom line is the same. I have to make this decision.'" She voted to allow the execution to proceed.[32]

The clerks sensed that beneath her warmth, the justice was steeling herself. "Justice O'Connor was fairly confident, but cautious," recalled Stewart Schwab in an interview with the author in 2016. "The pressure she was under was phenomenal. We forget that now. She felt, accurately, that if she messed up in a public, obvious way, there wouldn't be another woman justice for another fifty years." In the early years, O'Connor scrupulously checked every case cited by her clerks. They were instructed to put the casebooks on carts, in order, left to right, with the pages marked. Wheeled into her office, the carts would rest by her desk, sometimes three deep.

Most justices delegate to their clerks the job of reviewing the thousands of "cert" petitions for review. A pool of law clerks write memos about the cert petitions to share with the other chambers, which they

sign with their last names or initials. When the case of *Hishon v. King &*
Spalding came up for review in the fall of 1982, Stewart Schwab was the
pool clerk. A woman turned down for partnership by a prominent
Atlanta law firm had filed suit, claiming a violation of her civil rights.
Schwab recommended that the Court "deny cert"—refuse to hear the
case. Often, the Court will refuse to hear cases until there is a conflict
between federal courts of appeals, and there was, as yet, no conflict on
the narrow legal issues of whether an associate up for partnership in a
law firm was an employee covered by Title VII of the Civil Rights Act
of 1964.

"The justice popped into my office," recalled Schwab. "Stewart, I
saw your initials. Did you write this?" she asked, holding up Schwab's
"denial of cert" memo. "When I saw this was one of my clerks, I
wanted to wring your neck." O'Connor was smiling, but not warmly.
"What were you doing?" she asked. "We are going to take cert in this
case! This is an important issue. It affects thousands of women lawyers trying to make partner." While O'Connor was generally, or at
least nominally, a believer in the notion of "judicial restraint," she was
also intensely practical. At their Saturday Tex-Mex sessions to discuss
cases, Schwab and the other clerks had observed that she was impatient with legal abstractions and philosophical debate. "She was always thinking of the real-world consequences," said Schwab. (In
Hishon, the woman, Elizabeth Hishon, won her Supreme Court appeal
unanimously. The law firm, which had once held a bathing suit beauty
contest featuring its female summer interns, began making women
partners.)[33]

THE "REAL WORLD" showed up at the Supreme Court on January
22, 1983, on the tenth anniversary of the Court's right-to-abortion
decision, *Roe v. Wade.* Thousands of protesters thronged outside, in
part because the justices had agreed to take another abortion case,
City of Akron v. Akron Center for Reproductive Health, Inc. Around the country, states and cities had begun enacting restrictions aimed at stopping
or discouraging women from having abortions. In Ohio, the City of
Akron put in rules requiring women to sign "consent forms" that included a lecture from the doctor that a fetus is "human life from the

moment of conception" and a twenty-four-hour waiting period before the abortion could be performed.

The Reagan administration backed the local rules. At oral argument, Justice Blackmun held up the government's brief and glared at the solicitor general, Rex E. Lee. "Did you write this brief personally?" he demanded. Clearly taken aback, the government's lawyer answered, "Very substantial parts of it."[34]

To Harry Blackmun, the law on abortion was highly personal. When the abortion cases first came to the Supreme Court, Blackmun had spent the summer of 1972 back home in Minnesota in the library at the Mayo Clinic, where he had served as counsel before donning judicial robes. He had researched the medical history of abortion and deeply pondered the constitutional law of privacy, which was murky at best. In his fifty-five-page opinion for the Court in *Roe v. Wade,* Blackmun tried to balance a woman's privacy, her right to control her own body, against the state's interest in protecting the health of the woman and the life of the unborn. He worked out a formula. For the first three months, or trimester, of a woman's pregnancy, her right to abortion was absolute. During the second three months, the state could intervene, but only to protect the health of the woman. During the last three months (when the fetus could potentially survive outside the womb of the mother), the state could assert its interests to protect both the mother and her child. Blackmun's opinion was heavy on medical analysis; his concern seemed to be as much to protect doctors from being punished as to protect the privacy rights of women.[35]

In Justice O'Connor's chambers, the clerks had divided up the cases so that each of the four clerks wrote a roughly equal number of "bench memos" for each of the 162 cases the Court decided that term. In the *Akron* case, Gary Francione wrote the bench memo. "I was pro-choice on privacy grounds," said Francione. "I argued that the state should never tell a woman not to have an abortion. This was not about the doctors. It was about the women." At their usual Saturday lunch, cooked by the justice, the clerks debated the facts and law in the case. O'Connor asked a few questions but, as usual in big cases, gave little indication of her own views. One of her clerks, Jane Fahey, sensed from her questions and a stray remark or two that the justice was uncomfortable with the notion that the right to privacy, which is not explicitly guaranteed in the Constitution, could be found in the due process clause of the Fourteenth Amendment—the fundamental underpinning of Blackmun's opinion in *Roe v. Wade*. Preparing for the *Akron* case, O'Connor had read a famous law review article by the newly appointed Stanford Law School dean John Hart Ely, who argued that inferring moral rights from the Constitution was undemocratic. Justice O'Connor may have been swayed by Ely's attack on *Roe v. Wade*. But the clerk could only guess; O'Connor never came out and explicitly said so.[36]

After the justices had voted at their conference the next Friday, Justice O'Connor called Francione to her chambers so that he could get his marching orders to draft an opinion. "It was just us," he recalled. "It was clear she didn't agree with me."

Justice O'Connor had succinctly laid out her views in her personal notes of the Court's conference, which considered the *Akron* case in early December. In her steady-handed script, she wrote: "There is simply no justification in Constitutional theory for having a different standard or test for the different trimesters. Seems it puts us in the business of being a science review board. The interest of the state in protecting the unborn is essentially the same at all stages of pregnancy. I would permit state regulations at every stage which do not unduly burden the right of the woman to terminate her pregnancy."[37]

In other words, she rejected Blackmun's formula set out in *Roe v. Wade*. She was moved less by constitutional theory than by the purely practical problems of judges trying to decide when a fetus was "viable," able to live outside the womb. Medical progress meant that "viability" would become earlier and earlier, which meant, as she later put it, that Blackmun's trimester framework in *Roe* was "on a collision course with itself." As always protective of states' rights, O'Connor was willing to let the states restrict abortions, as long as they did not put an "undue burden" on the woman's right to choose. The phrase "undue burden" had appeared in the Reagan administration's brief— the same document that Justice Blackmun excitedly waved at its author, Solicitor General Lee. It was a purposefully vague term; "undue burden" left plenty of room for the states and the courts to maneuver— and litigate—in the years to come. But, significantly, the Reagan administration had not tried to overturn *Roe v. Wade* completely. In June

1983, six justices voted to knock down *Akron*'s restrictions, while three—O'Connor, Rehnquist, and White—voted to uphold them. *Roe* survived intact. Women still had a constitutional right to terminate their pregnancies.

Blackmun might have been satisfied, but he stewed that eventually the justices would overturn *Roe*. He saw O'Connor as the first in a series of future justices appointed by Ronald Reagan seeking to reward the "pro-life" vote.[38] He had some reason to be worried about O'Connor, who had agreed with Justice White that the state had a "compelling interest" in protecting potential life "throughout pregnancy." He was especially riled when he read a draft of O'Connor's dissent, which called Blackmun's trimester framework "completely unprincipled and unworkable." The words had actually been written by Francione, who had perhaps too sharply expressed his boss's opinion.

A Blackmun clerk complained to Francione, who went to Justice O'Connor. "It was a misunderstanding—we weren't trying to say Blackmun lacked moral principles," recalled Francione. "I told Justice O'Connor. She said, 'Well, take it out!'" The word "unprincipled" was deleted, leaving the adjective "unworkable."[39]

The contact between the O'Connor and Blackmun clerks, in those early years, was rare. "If we were talking to other chambers, she would ask, 'What are you doing there? What were you saying?'" recalled Schwab. "She didn't want us negotiating with other chambers," recalled Francione. Some justices allowed their clerks to act as emissaries, even as spies, but O'Connor was wary of using her clerks that way. "She didn't like the brethreny stuff of clerks running the show," said Francione.[40]

IN JULY, AT the end of the term, the O'Connors flew to Wisconsin for some golf and relaxation with friends. On the plane, Sandra told John that during her second year on the Court, "she had become more fully aware of how to get things done." She did not have a lot of influence on Brennan, Marshall, or Blackmun, she confided, but "she does have a lot of impact on the Chief and Lewis Powell and periodically on Bill Rehnquist," wrote John. She had been "in the cat bird seat; she

was the fifth vote." A month earlier, O'Connor had told her husband
that she enjoyed the "jockeying" as the justices maneuvered to put
together majorities at the end of the term. "She just lights up physically and in her manner of speaking when she talks about it," John
wrote. It was obvious to her husband that Justice O'Connor may have
been humble about her jurisprudence, but she was not exactly averse
to exercising power on the Court.[41]

Later that summer, O'Connor went on a hiking trip to Vermont
with Peggy Lord, a frequent golf partner. The two ladies attended a
golf school at Stratton Mountain, where the instructor told them to,
as Lord put it, "stick our butts out." Somewhat brashly, Lord broached
the question of what O'Connor thought about *Roe v. Wade*. O'Connor
may have indicated that she thought Justice Blackmun's reasoning in
Roe v. Wade was wrong, but that she felt states should not be able to ban
abortions altogether. In Lord's recollection, she answered, "Oh, Peggy,
it's bad law, but I have to think about all the women in the United
States." (Hearing this story, some of O'Connor's former law clerks
were surprised. They guessed that O'Connor would have responded:
"Hmmm.")[42]

CHAPTER NINE

FWOTSC

"I can't have you profoundly disturbed on my account."

Justice O'Connor leads a conga line at a judicial conference. She made sure she spoke in every
state in the Union and was soon trying to spread the rule of law through Eastern Europe,
Africa, Asia, and South America.

AT A BLACK tie dinner at the Watergate in January 1983, Jack Valenti, the head of the Motion Picture Association and Washington's highest-paid lobbyist, came up to Justice O'Connor during cocktails. The garrulous Valenti, a former aide to LBJ, said he had been at the Supreme Court that morning for a copyright case involving Sony Pictures and that he wanted to talk to the justice. O'Connor "abruptly walked away," John wrote in his diary.[1]

Members of the Supreme Court are supposed to be above influence and removed from politics. O'Connor had to be careful on the cocktail circuit. Both at the Court and out in the world, she never hid that she was a Republican. She liked to make side bets with Justice Rehnquist, who ran low-stakes betting pools among the justices on election results, sporting events, anticipated snowfall, or whatever came to his curious and competitive mind.[2] But she steered away from political conversations, even with close friends. "She was not pompous about it," recalled Bill Draper. "It was not, 'Oh no! I can't get into that!'" When John O'Connor voiced his political opinions, she would sometimes "raise her eyebrow and distance herself," said Ruth McGregor. If people pressed her about her own views, she would ask about their children, just to distract them. "I watched her as people started talking about Little Suzy," said her friend Cynthia Helms, who would catch her eye. "She couldn't have cared less," said Helms, "and she knew that I knew it." O'Connor did not appreciate the chatter speculating about her own political ambitions. "I mentioned her as a potential vice president and she gave me hell. I said, 'It was just cocktail conversation!'" recalled Frank Saul.[3]

O'Connor was circumspect with high-level journalists making the social rounds. After a party for Ambassador Sol Linowitz, John wrote in his diary that they had run into Sally Quinn, "the society columnist who ate everyone alive. . . . Miss Quinn is to be dealt with," he wrote, "with great care."[4] In 1984, *Washingtonian* magazine gushed over O'Connor with a story entitled "She's a Lady—and She's Tough, Smart, Funny and the First Woman on the Supreme Court." But the piece included some personal details, like the price of her condominium in Kalorama ($355,000) and her approximate net worth ($1.5 million). O'Connor had warily cooperated, including permitting her aerobics instructor, Diane DiMarco, to speak to the reporter. "We're never going to do that again," O'Connor told DiMarco.[5]

An exception to the "no reporters" rule was Jim Lehrer, the cohost of the nightly PBS news program that the O'Connors regularly watched. O'Connor and Lehrer had become friends as cotrustees of the Colonial Williamsburg Foundation. Lehrer recalled observing Justice O'Connor at a function at which a "senior official in the Reagan administration [Lehrer would not identify which one] said something inappropriate during an after-dinner speech." Lehrer looked over from his seat at Justice O'Connor, "who looked stricken." O'Connor got up—to go to the ladies' room, assumed Lehrer—but as she passed by Lehrer's seat, she handed the newsman her place card. Inside, she had written her one-word opinion of the after-dinner speaker: "Fool."

O'Connor's fires, while carefully banked, needed an outlet. She did not hold back on the tennis court or golf course or at the bridge table. In 1984, she and John befriended a particularly attractive and athletic couple named Jim and Diana Holman, with whom they regularly played doubles. "She played with me because I never lost and she didn't like losing," recalled Jim. Diana remembered, "She rejected John as a partner. 'I want *Jim*,' she said. She kept score: 'Thirty–fifteen!' she said. I said, 'Wasn't it fifteen–thirty?' 'Thirty–fifteen!' she repeated and said, 'Diana, if you don't keep score, someone else will keep it for you. I learned that on the Court.'"

Jim Holman fared less well as O'Connor's bridge partner. "I tried to finesse and lost the finesse and four tricks. She looked at me with an expression no one has ever used on me, including my father and mother. 'Jim,' she said, 'I just don't know what you were thinking,'" recalled Holman. "I never played bridge again."

Her nonstop energy could wear out her friends. On skiing trips with the Holmans and their friends Skip and Kim Nalen in Sun Valley, O'Connor would make breakfast for everyone (huevos rancheros, her favorite Mexican egg dish) and announce, "Let's play a rubber [of bridge] before we go skiing!" "Everyone would hide," said Jim. She did not hesitate to instruct others, including champions, at their own sport. "She would say, 'Don't hit the golf ball there, hit it straight,'" recalled Ann Hoopes, who had the lowest woman's handicap at the Chevy Chase Club. Nor could O'Connor, who was tone deaf, resist offering helpful hints to professional musicians. Jukka Valtasaari, the Finnish ambassador, recalled that after a famous jazz trio had performed at his embassy, Justice O'Connor said to the piano player, "Young man, if you play so intensely, you should lose some weight." She could turn a classical concert into a campfire sing-along. When the Holmans gave a party for Thomas Stewart, one of the world's greatest Wagnerian baritones, O'Connor joined him in singing the cowboy song "Don't Fence Me In" with full-throated gusto. "She was wailing," said Holman.

Her favorite shot in tennis was a vicious crosscourt forehand. Former congressman James Symington recalled her body language as she stood, taut, at the serving line. "It was like, this is the most important moment of the day. She was ready to play. Nothing else mattered." When she became too intense, John pulled her leg. Playing doubles one day, she shouted, "John! John!" to make him move on the court. For the rest of the game, he would randomly pipe up, "Sandra! Sandra!"[6]

Some friends bridled at her bossiness. Richard Helms, the former director of the CIA, enjoyed talking to O'Connor more than playing tennis with her. "In the car on the way to Chevy Chase, Dick would imitate her giving orders: 'You stand here, you stand there, and you serve.' I'd have to hold him down," recalled his wife, Cynthia. But mostly, the O'Connors' friends were, like John, amused and even glad to be told what to do. To be sure, some were slightly intimidated when they engaged her in conversation. "There'd be a certain expression of silence, ominous silence," recalled Symington. "If you knew her, you could see it coming. You could tell when a subject was exhausted and it was time to move on. There was no point in trying to outflank her. She'd give you a look and that would be the end of it."

But they saw O'Connor's sweeter side as well. "There was not an ounce of meanness in her. No anger or spite," said Symington. "I've seen people fawn," said Diana Holman. "She would not embarrass them. In the ski lodge, a young woman came up to her, going on and on about her achievements. 'Aren't you nice,' Sandra said. 'Tell me where you are going to law school.'" She was rarely snide or catty, even in her private remarks to John, though she scorned braggarts. "SOC's worst comment on people is 'He has a pretty high opinion of himself,'" he wrote in his diary.[7] People who played the victim got the cold shoulder. "I was crying about getting paid five thousand dollars less than the men in the same job [Director of Industrial Relations for the U.S. Synfuels Project]," Diana Holman recalled. "She just looked at me. 'That's the way it is. Why did you think it would be different?'" She was bored if parents boasted about the achievements of "Little Suzy." But she would envelop them in warmth and solicitude if the child was sick or in trouble.

She knew her own power and how to use it. "She was miffed that women had to wait until 11:00 A.M. on Saturdays to play golf at the Chevy Chase Club," recalled Peggy Lord. "So we'd sit there on a bench by the first tee around 10:30 and greet all the men, 'Oh, hello Pete, hey George, hi John.' Within a month they had changed the rule."[8]

"When she wasn't a schoolmarm, she could be goofy," said Gary Francione. She howled at the clerks' end-of-the-term skits making fun of her. She was grave and reverent about the place where she worked, but not always. When Arizona state senator Carl Kunasek dropped by, she showed him the justices' robing room and suggested he put on one of their black robes "to feel what it was like." Draped in black, Kunasek on a goof strode out into the courtroom—and scurried back when he saw a group of gaping tourists.[9]

In his diary for October 31, 1984, John recounted Sandra's efforts to loosen up the Court's conference:

> On the way home, she told me about a Halloween trick she played at the Court today. She had wanted to do something funny on Halloween since her first days on the Court, but she was afraid that if she did, they'd think she was a nut.

When they got to conference, SOC put on Groucho Marx type glasses that have a big nose, a moustache and bushy eyebrows. She sat there and did nothing. Lewis Powell and Byron White spotted her disguise first, but kept quiet and watched the others. Then, John Stevens saw her and roared. Then Thurgood came in, sat down, looked around for a minute or two as he could see something had happened. Finally, he realized it was SOC's get up and he, too, had a big laugh. It was a great success. Everyone enjoyed it.

Naturally, O'Connor's friends would wonder what drove her. "There was always a bit of 'what made Sammy run,'" said Jeannette Brophy, a friend from Arizona who had moved to Washington with her husband, Ray. Few friends asked her about her lonely upbringing on the Lazy B and at Grandmother Wilkey's. Aside from spinning a few well-worn ranch stories, she did not tell them. Unsure what motivated her, they were quite sure that she felt a sense of purpose, and that, while she disliked show-offs, she was determined to be a role model. In the fall of 1983, in an article poking fun at government acronyms, The New York Times wrote, "The chief magistrate responsible for executing the laws is sometimes known as the POTUS (president of the United States). The nine men who interpret them are often the SCOTUS." O'Connor wrote the Times reminding them that for two years "SCOTUS has not consisted of nine men." She signed the letter FWOTSC—for "first woman on the Supreme Court." Her tone was lighthearted, but the letter was prominently published on the paper's editorial page—as she surely assumed it would be. "It would have been wholly understandable for her to find us guilty of a mindless mistake and throw the book at us," publicly apologized the editors of the Times. "Instead, she offers clemency in the form of a sly reproach about our information."[10]

"She knew her role. She wanted to be out there," said her Washington pal Cynthia Helms. "She was an icon, always on. She had a great public following, particularly among women. She did have a sense of destiny. I never knew it to fail her, not once in the thirty-five years I knew her," said Helms in 2016. "It wasn't a burden. It was a pleasure."

. . .

ON THE MORNING of April 10, 1984, Justice O'Connor called her
husband, John. She was crying. "DA died," she said. Her father, eighty-
five years old and emphysema-ridden, had passed away from a stroke
as he slept in his bed with MO the night before. "I went to the Court
to try and console her, but there was nothing I could do," John wrote
in his diary. "She sat there in her chambers with mountains of correspondence in front of her, red-eyed, crying and thinking of DA."

Two days later at the Lazy B, Sandra stood in front of about 150
people, ranchers in their best suits, cowboys in their boots, her husband and sons, and started to speak. "How do you say farewell to
someone you've loved as long as you have lived?" she asked. "She
choked up on those first words, as did I," John recorded in his diary.
"She had to struggle to keep her composure, but she did." Sandra
spoke of her father's work ethic, his frugality, his resourcefulness, his
endless curiosity, and his basic decency. John recorded how she spoke
of MO and DA: "They had a truly happy marriage, although I'm sure
it was not always easy. He used to say, 'MO tells me what to do and by
God, I do it!' Then he would laugh and do what he wanted to do. But
MO was tolerant and they shared a magnificent life together in this
barren part of the West that we call the Lazy B."

At sunset, the Day and O'Connor families climbed Round Mountain. The evening was mild and clear, and they could see for fifty to a
hundred miles all around. Alan scattered some of DA's ashes on the
ground and then put the rest into a rock cairn, to await MO's. At Sandra's instruction, the family stood in a circle and said the Lord's
Prayer.[11]

Two days later, Sandra achingly wrote to her son Jay from Washington:

The trip to the ranch to bid farewell to DA was a sad one indeed. I always knew it would be unbearable to lose him; it is
even worse than I feared. I feel a tremendous sense of loss and
"rootlessness." I feel cut off from the strong support he always
provided. MO is pathetic. She feels she has nothing left to live

for and that her world is shattered. She knows she cannot take care of herself. She forgets what has happened and looks for DA, and then must relive the horror of knowing he is gone.

Alan and Ann are as sad about it as I am.[12]

BY THE TIME O'Connor came on the Court in 1981, the justices were occasionally hiring female law clerks. O'Connor always did. Although O'Connor rarely defined herself—or even her jurisprudence—in terms of gender, she was acutely conscious that she could give young women lawyers opportunities that had been closed to her. She was creating a pipeline for future female prosecutors, Supreme Court lawyers, law professors, and judges.

Top women law students vying for clerkships in her chambers created an early (and largely apocryphal) mythology around her interview process. It was important to wear a red dress, or the right makeup, they said. One clerk was told "that she liked to seat you so you'd be facing into the sun, so she could see your facial expressions and body language—what you can least control," recalled Iman Anabtawi of Stanford Law. Like several other O'Connor clerks, Anabtawi, who clerked in 1990, was an athlete. After a tennis game with Justice O'Connor against a pair of Rehnquist clerks, Anabtawi recalled, "I said, 'That was fun, wasn't it?' She looked at me. 'We didn't win,' she said."

All of O'Connor's clerks had tip-top grades and the usual honors, but she also hired clerks who could play concert piano—or juggle, or sing in an opera, or, in one case, swim the English Channel. She hired the children of poor immigrants, the first-ever clerk who was disabled (born with malformed limbs), and one who was blind. She asked Viet Dinh, whose family had fled Vietnam in an open boat, "Can you work hard?" Dinh, who had picked strawberries as a ten-year-old farmworker and did not consider researching cases in a library to be real work, brushed off the question. O'Connor repeated it. "Can you work hard?" "Yes, ma'am," answered Dinh, and got the job.[13]

Shirley Woodward attended night law school, unusual for a Supreme Court clerkship applicant; even more unusual, she had come from a small town in West Texas and served in the CIA as an under-cover operative. She was hired by O'Connor (and, some years later, was chosen to be inspector general of the CIA). Judge J. Harvie Wilkinson III of the U.S. Court of Appeals for the Fourth Circuit recommended one of his clerks, Sri Srinivasan, for a Supreme Court clerkship with O'Connor. "Unknown to me, Sri asked to reschedule his interview with Justice O'Connor from a Friday to a Monday so he could have a romantic weekend out West," recalled Judge Wilkinson. "Sandra immediately called me, not pleased. She asked if Sri was more interested in his professional obligations or his social obligations? I promised that he wakes up thinking about the law every day!" Sriniva-san recalled: "It was a miscommunication. When I saw her, she asked, 'Are you really interested?' with those piercing blue eyes." Srinivasan assured her he was, and, as he left, mentioned to her that he was a golfer. O'Connor had set up a putting green out in the clerks' area. She said to Srinivasan, "Let me see you putt." Srinivasan replied, "What?" His hands shaking, he lined up a ten-footer and sank it. "Okay," she said. "I'll call you." Some years after his clerkship with O'Connor, Srinivasan became a judge on the U.S. Court of Appeals for the District of Columbia Circuit, and his name showed up on President Barack Obama's short list for a nomination to the Supreme Court.[14]

O'Connor looked for expertise as well as experience outside the law. "She wanted someone who had economics and math, because as a junior justice she got tax and antitrust cases. I had just finished a graduate degree in economics," recalled Kent Syverud, a clerk apply-ing to work for O'Connor for the 1984–85 Court year. Syverud, who went on to be the dean of Vanderbilt Law School and then president of Syracuse University, would become a lifelong friend of O'Connor's. His initial reaction to her—awed, but at the same time slightly patronizing—was typical of the highly credentialed clerks, as was his surprise at finding a deeper, more complex—and ultimately mysterious—woman beneath her brisk façade. "I approached her as the most famous woman in the country, but one the elite regarded as a state court judge who was a friend of Ronald Reagan's and a light-weight," recalled Syverud. "She had laserlike blue eyes and an extreme fixed stare. She completely focused on you and nothing else. She quickly established that she had a deep range of experiences as a human being and mother. She was not what I expected."

One night during Syverud's first month, O'Connor worked late on a habeas petition, voting (in a 5–4 case) to deny the prisoner's appeal; the convict was executed after midnight. Syverud, who was both liberal and deeply religious, was in the chambers when the justice arrived early the next morning and said she had "fabulous" plans for an event later that day. ("Fabulous" is a favorite O'Connor adjective.) "I called her on it," said Syverud. "She said, 'Look, you've got to move on.'" The time to worry about a decision, she said, is before it is made.[15]

"She is the most private person I ever worked for," said Syverud. "Very, very few people know her well. She kept a hard shell around her innermost thoughts. She showed an outer persona—a Chamber of Commerce, Junior League positive presence who liked to dance. But there was an inner core of how she was brought up, in solitude, on her own."

Over the years, Justice O'Connor's hundred-plus law clerks generally regarded her with a mixture of admiration, affection, loyalty, and not a little trepidation. Maggie Dupree, who served as O'Connor's number two secretary for over two decades, watched as a generation of clerks learned to live with her abrupt manner. Whether she was displeased or just wanted to move on, O'Connor did not waste time with stroking her subordinates. "She'd just turn away. It was hard for some of them to deal with it," said Dupree. "They'd cry."

Julie O'Sullivan, who clerked for O'Connor in 1985–86, recalled, "I spent a lot of time crying by the soda machine in the basement. I'd take a pounding at the Saturday lunches. She once said to me, 'What are you, my bleeding heart?'" But O'Sullivan, who in later years became close to O'Connor, also observed, "Sandra is the only woman I know who doesn't say sorry. Women would say, 'Sorry, I can't do that.' She would just say, 'No.' I really admired that."

Many clerks felt protective of "the Justice," as they all called her. In the early days of her celebrity, when she wore large dark glasses and a hat to avoid being recognized, some of the clerks addressed her by the pseudonym Mrs. Brown in public. The clerks need not have worried about whether she could withstand the glare of media fame. In January 1985, at a Salute to Congress dinner, the O'Connors went as guests of *People* magazine. Another guest, the Washington Redskins star running back John Riggins, had too much to drink and exclaimed, "C'mon, loosen up, Sandy baby!" before passing out beside the table. (In his diary, John recorded, "At about 10:50 p.m., I stepped over John Riggins, and SOC and I left the room.") The morning papers gleefully recorded the incident. "We were aghast," said Scott Bales, one of her clerks. "She just laughed about it." She was privately a little less blithe: After a dinner party in mid-March, O'Connor recorded in her occasional journal, "Kay Graham told me I would never escape John Riggins' tag of 'Sandy Baby'—it had been the topic of conversation for weeks. I am sure she is right. It will stick— not to my face, but certainly out of my presence."[16] A few years later, when Riggins, his football career over, appeared as an actor in a local play, the O'Connors showed up at the stage door with a bouquet of roses and a note saying that while his performance was fine, he needed to loosen up a bit.[17]

The clerks vied to show their fealty. Aware that other chambers—particularly Justice Blackmun's—were poised to pounce on the tiniest error emerging from Justice O'Connor's chambers, they checked and carefully annotated each other's opinion drafts and memos. They competed to carve the best possible Halloween pumpkin and joined in their own O'Connor-staged birthday celebrations with manic, if slightly forced, hilarity. "There was a crazy tradition of trying to pop off the champagne cork [actually, Martinelli's Sparkling Cider] so it ricochets off the ceiling into the basket under the ceiling lamp. We tried like a bunch of monkeys. Nobody ever did it," recalled John Setear, who clerked in 1985–86.

In later years, clerks liked to pass around the story of the day O'Connor took her clerks on a white-water rafting trip in the Pennsylvania mountains during spring thaw. The rafting guide instructed them that if one person in the raft fell out, the others were not to jump in to rescue the person—because, the guide explained, "then I'll have to rescue both of you." At the first rapid, Justice O'Connor bounced out of the raft. All four clerks jumped in after her. Or so the story was improved over time. Actually, one clerk jumped in; one or two others may have jumped in or fallen in.[18]

To broaden their cultural horizons, O'Connor would take her

clerks on "outings" to Washington's various museums and galleries. As O'Connor exhaustively interrogated the tour guides, the clerks would troop past the Rembrandts and Renoirs, grumbling amongst themselves about all the work they had to do. O'Connor did not want to hear excuses. She told Norma Schwab, the pregnant wife of her clerk Stewart Schwab, that she wanted to see her every morning at exercise class until the day of birth. Recalling her own hesitation, Norma imitated the justice's pep talk: "Pregnancy is not a disability! You can work through that! We're not hothouse flowers here!" That March, O'Connor told the clerks they were going to walk to the Cherry Blossom Festival at the Tidal Basin, more than two miles away. A clerk had the temerity to point out the cold and rainy weather outside. "We're going out! And we're going to have a good time!" the justice exclaimed. The elements be damned. The justice loved nature; the clerks needed to learn to love it, too.[19]

The clerks liked to complain about the "field trips," but they usually, if grudgingly, enjoyed them, and they were flattered and touched by the attention O'Connor gave their personal lives. The justice liked to plan their futures, advising on careers and where to live and suggesting when and whom to marry. Any clerk progeny were deemed to be "grand clerks." "When I went to Phoenix, she introduced me to a nice young man and told me what neighborhoods to go house hunting in," remembered Kathy Smalley, a clerk in 1982–83, who became a lifelong friend.

A few of the older clerks had children, and she was attentive to them. During her clerk year 1984–85, Barbara Woodhouse lived apart from her twelve-year-old son back home in New York and her fifteen-year-old daughter at boarding school in Massachusetts. "It's my son Kenny's birthday," Barbara told the justice. "Oh, we have to call him!" replied O'Connor and picked up the phone. "I want to thank you for lending me your mother," she told the boy. "I know you must miss her. I know how that feels. When I was a little girl, I lived with my grandmother, and I missed my mother." She went on to tell the rapt little boy how important his mother's work was. Listening, Woodhouse was wiping away her tears. Later, she told the justice that her daughter was singing in a Gilbert and Sullivan operetta at her boarding school. "Aren't you going?" asked O'Connor. "Too much work," said Woodhouse. O'Connor called her travel agent and booked her clerk on a plane to Boston. "The message was family comes first," recalled Woodhouse. "But also, you shouldn't be choosing. You should be able to do both."[20]

EVERY JUSTICE'S CHAMBERS had its own rituals. Justice Brennan liked to meet his clerks for coffee and talk about cases in the morning. On conference days, at ten minutes before ten in the morning, he would wrap up with the clerks and stand at the threshold to the broad marble hallway, waiting for Harry Blackmun to walk by. Brennan would step out and announce, "Harry, old pal!" and put his arm around his shoulder or link arms as they headed down to confer with their brethren and sister.

"It was relentless. It wasn't just strategic. They really liked each other. But it was also strategic," recalled Don Verrilli, a Brennan clerk in 1984–85 (and later U.S. solicitor general in the Obama administration). "He didn't have that with O'Connor. Did he charm her? I'm not sure he even tried. He just wasn't comfortable dealing with women in positions of authority." There was also an age gap. Brennan was twenty-four years older than O'Connor. When she arrived at the Court at the age of fifty-two, she was a generation younger than most of her brethren. Even Rehnquist was six years older. O'Connor, for her part, continued to be circumspect around Brennan and the older brethren, holding her bossy side in check.[21]

When Brennan's wife died of cancer in 1982, he had seemed so low that his clerks expected him to retire. But after his marriage to his feisty secretary, Mary Fowler, in March 1983, the clerks began to notice a renewed zest for the fight.[22] With the rise of the Reagan Revolution, the liberal legacy of the Warren Court—and, in no small part, Bill Brennan's legacy—still hung in the balance. "We were living in an ideological time," recalled Verrilli. "We felt we were fighting a very important battle." Newly revived as he neared his eightieth year, Brennan roused himself to "get five" in the cases that most closely divided the Court and the country.

O'Connor had limited interest in the sort of academic theorizing that preoccupied legal scholars. She did not invoke, or even mention, the names of the eighteenth-century statesman Edmund Burke, or Justice John Marshall Harlan II, or Yale law professor Alexander Bickel, all of whom were her intellectual and spiritual forebears in the cause of judicial humility and measured, gradual change. "But she did talk about 'constitutional avoidance,'" recalled Gail Agrawal, a clerk in 1984–85. By that, O'Connor meant respecting the rights of state courts and legislatures from activist liberal judges who used the constitution, in particular the Fourteenth Amendment guarantees of due process and equal protection, as a crusader's sword.

Agrawal had clerked for John Minor Wisdom, a federal court of appeals judge who played an instrumental role in desegregating the South. The child of a working-class family in New Orleans, Agrawal had been overcome when O'Connor offered her a clerkship. Head spinning as she left her interview, she had sat down on the steps of the Marble Palace and wept. Agrawal was deeply respectful of O'Connor, but she felt she came from a different place, literally and figuratively. "In the Deep South, we viewed the federal government as the place we went for protection from the states," she said. "Louisiana was a racist, sexist place where you didn't trust state officials, who were white, male Christians, usually not Catholic." O'Connor's judicial philosophy, insofar as she was willing to admit to one, came from a different perspective. Agrawal recalled her laying it out one afternoon as the justice and her clerk sat in one of the Court's private courtyards on a spring day. As O'Connor saw it, said Agrawal, "Arizona was a free country. A person raised in the West is so different. We can take care of things, or get out of the way."[23]

In the case of *Garcia v. San Antonio Metropolitan Transit Authority,* argued in March 1984 and reargued in October 1984, O'Connor wanted the Court to take a strong stand against federal interference with state government.[24] The case involved a suit by the U.S. Department of Labor to impose its minimum wage and overtime rules on the San Antonio Transit Authority. O'Connor believed that the Court was presented with a clear-cut case, that local authorities should be left alone to run their own basic government functions, like mass transit, without federal interference. She thought she had all four Nixon appointees on her side—Rehnquist, Powell, Burger, and Blackmun—to rule in favor of the city transit authority. But at the last minute, Harry

Blackmun changed his vote and sided with the U.S. Department of Labor.

"Wow!" wrote Lewis Powell when he heard that Blackmun had switched his vote. O'Connor was about as angry as she allowed herself to be. Blackmun "is clearly not a 'Team Player,'" she wrote in her journal. "He seemingly relishes any discomforts suffered by others. Curious!" Bill Brennan was delighted. "Wonderful Harry! Splendid, just splendid!" he declared. As the senior member of the new liberal majority, Brennan promptly assigned Blackmun to write the Court's opinion.[25] By a 5-to-4 vote, the Court in *Garcia* reversed a 1976 decision, *National League of Cities v. Usery,* that had sharply limited Congress's power to impose its will on state and local governments. With *Garcia,* the liberalism of the Warren Court—which favored the federal hand to protect workers against the miserliness or injustice of local authorities—lived on, at least one more day, against the conservative retrenchment led by Justice Rehnquist and usually (but not always) joined by Justice O'Connor. On the day the *Garcia* decision was announced, February 18, 1985, Justice O'Connor gave John a lift home from his office, and they discussed Blackmun's switched vote. In his diary, John wondered, "Could his feelings of jealousy regarding SOC be motivating his substantive decisions, especially on an issue strongly identified with her?"[26]

It was a significant victory for Brennan, who had not lobbied Blackmun—at least not in any obvious way. On Friday nights, after the Court's computer system shut down at midnight, clerks from all chambers would convene at the nearby Irish Times bar for refreshments. "Who has the best political skills on the Court?" asked one clerk. "O'Connor, of course," answered another clerk. "Have you ever seen her work a room?" Another clerk interjected, "Yes, I have, that's true. But the best politician on the Court is Brennan, because when he works the room, you don't know he's doing it."[27]

O'Connor made a concerted effort to get along with Brennan. Her husband sent him Irish jokes and was in return invited to lunch in Brennan's chambers; they became friendly (at one get-together, the two men discussed the unfairness of forcing men's clubs to take women).[28] O'Connor gave a party in her chambers to celebrate Brennan's thirty years on the Court, complete with T-shirts listing all his landmark cases in a single footnote. The footnote was an inside joke. Brennan was notorious for trying to slip little surprises into the footnotes that supported his opinions. "Brennan planted little Easter eggs in them," said Julie O'Sullivan, who clerked for O'Connor in 1985–86 and helped plan the party for Brennan. Always looking for ways to broaden the mandate of the federal courts to enforce "equal justice," Brennan craftily salted broad constitutional language into the footnotes of cases, in the hopes that down the line, judges would use the language and build on it.*

O'Connor was wary of Brennan's less-than-straightforward approach to making law, and offended by the Court's increasingly free use of footnotes in the 1970s and '80s. Both sides could play the game, of course. O'Connor also warned her clerks to watch out for Justice Rehnquist's conservative agenda-driven footnotes. "You know Bill!" she would say.[30]

But Brennan was the more practiced gamesman. "He had a system, a very well executed system to write as much constitutional law as possible," said Steve Gilles, a clerk during the 1985–86 Court year. "She would say to him, 'I can't join your opinion unless you take that out.'" In the back-and-forth, there was none of the personal animosity that characterized Blackmun's pot shots. "She loved Brennan but didn't trust him as far as she could throw him," said Julie O'Sullivan.[31]

OF ALL THE liberal decisions of the Warren Court, the most unpopular may have been *Engel v. Vitale* in 1962, striking down state-sponsored prayer in public schools. The First Amendment both guarantees freedom of religion and bans the establishment of a state religion—a tension that can be hard to reconcile when free speech,

---

* In later years, O'Connor would wage a campaign against footnotes in judicial opinions, in part to make the opinions clearer and more accessible. While the language in the footnotes might seem like mere marginalia, and not central to the Court's ruling, from little acorns mighty oaks may grow. It had happened before—in 1938, in the famous Footnote Four of *United States v. Carolene Products Co.*, Justice Harlan Stone slipped into the majority opinion some language about protecting minorities that became the foundational text for using the Fourteenth Amendment as a tool of social justice.[29]

like the saying of prayers in public school, collides with the ban on the state propagating or "establishing" religion. Requiring schoolchildren to say prayers violated the First Amendment's establishment clause, the Court had ruled. The justices of the Warren Court received more hate mail after *Engel* than any other case. They were excoriated for taking God and moral teaching out of education. In the 1970s, the issue helped propel the rise of the Religious Right, which campaigned to put prayer back in the schools. State legislatures tried to work around *Engel* by passing laws allowing for a "moment of silence" during which schoolchildren could choose to pray, thereby exercising their freedom of religion.[32]

Alabama passed such a law. In Mobile, Alabama, some parents sued, saying their children were being ostracized by their playmates for not saying their prayers. At the Supreme Court, Chief Justice Burger and Justice Rehnquist wanted to uphold the "moment of silence" laws to allow prayer in schools and open a crack in the door closed more than twenty years before by *Engel v. Vitale*. But O'Connor did not go along with them. In *Wallace v. Jaffree*, she joined the liberals, forming a majority to knock down the state law allowing a "moment of silence" as a violation of the establishment clause.[33]

Her vote surprised some—especially Chief Justice Burger, who wrote a strongly worded dissent. It reveals an important side of her approach as a justice. Her experience as a state legislator and judge made her sympathetic to "states' rights" when federal bureaucrats came calling. At the same time, she was realistic about what went on in state government. Her clerk, Kent Syverud, who worked on *Wallace v. Jaffree* with her, remembered one exchange: "I suggested, as a point of argument, that we should assume good faith and proper motives of the legislature. She set me straight. 'You may want to presume that,' she said. 'But some state legislators can be the most venal, self-important people you can imagine.'"

The real world, and her experience in it, was always important to O'Connor, and it informed her independent-minded judgment. In her concurring opinion in *Wallace v. Jaffree*, she took apart the Alabama "moment of silence" law to show its true purpose: to push prayer in schools. Her opinion caught the attention of Justice John Stevens, the Court's cerebral iconoclast. "It was the only time I saw a justice walk down the hall," recalled Syverud. "He walked in holding her opinion. He was pleased. To Stevens, it was evidence that she was a serious judge. It was the first moment when he saw he had a colleague."

O'Connor was deeply gratified—and a little surprised—by Justice Stevens's reaction. She had "struggled," she wrote in her journal, "with trying to put together a sensible framework of analysis for Establishment Clause and Free Exercise Clause claims—one that adheres generally to precedent but which is faithful to history and the underlying purposes of these clauses. It is not easy." Indeed, for months, she staged an ongoing mini moot court in her chambers, pitting Syverud arguing from the extreme establishment clause perspective and another clerk, Barbara Woodhouse, from the extreme free exercise side, while she probed for a middle ground. When Justice Stevens arrived in her chambers holding her opinion in *Wallace v. Jaffree,* it was the first time Stevens, whom she regarded as a somewhat solitary maverick, had come to see her since the day she arrived at the Court. She wrote in her journal:

> John had a copy of my opinion in his hand, and I assumed he would urge me to join his opinion and offer to make necessary changes. I was wrong. He said, "Sandra, I just came by to tell you I read your opinion and it is really terrific. You should be very proud of it in years ahead. It has a very good analysis which will be helpful—probably better than my own."
>
> I was astonished and rather misty-eyed. . . . We seldom hear compliments from other Justices about our work.[34]

To the chief justice, on the other hand, her 1985 opinion in *Wallace v. Jaffree* was further proof of O'Connor's perfidy. She had not been the go-along, get-along justice (and passive female) he had hoped for (and not so subtly suggested that she be). Years later, after O'Connor retired, she described to a class of University of Virginia students the chief justice's practice of inviting her to tea to persuade her to join his opinion. "You could tell how she felt about these sessions by the way she spat out the word *tea*," said Jim Todd, the UVA professor who arranged her talk. O'Connor's clerks felt the tension. "You had the sense Burger was unhappy with her," said Scott Bales, who also clerked for

O'Connor in 1985. "Just because Burger and Rehnquist thought something didn't mean that she did."[35]

O'Connor had her own view of when a state violated the establishment clause, and it did not completely jibe with Burger's. O'Connor believed that the test should be whether the state's use of religious symbols or words made a person feel like an "outsider." Again, she was drawing on her own experience, as a woman in a man's world, and more specifically as a lonely girl taken by Grandmother Wilkey to a Baptist church service in El Paso. With the demonstrative Baptists, she had felt pressure to declare belief in Jesus publicly. To her—to the daughter of Harry Day—born to the church of nature under the stars high above the Lazy B, religious faith was private and personal.[36]

In the case of *Lynch v. Donnelly*, the Court was asked to decide whether including a crèche, the tableau of Christ's birth, in an elaborate Christmas holiday display owned by the city of Pawtucket, Rhode Island, violated the establishment clause.[37] O'Connor agreed with the chief justice that it did not—but she refused to go along with his reasoning and wrote a separate, concurring opinion laying out her own test of whether the state's actions "endorsed" a particular religion.* Burger was beside himself. The justices were increasingly criticized for an overabundance of concurring opinions that narrowed and sometimes muddied majority opinions, confusing lawyers and lower court judges. "I am profoundly distressed," he wrote O'Connor in a personal, longhand note. She wrote back, with the tiniest hint of mockery, "I can't have you profoundly disturbed on my account." But she refused to back off.[39]

Burger rewarded her independence by assigning her "second tier" opinions—dealing with economic issues, like taxes and water rights, not the major constitutional disputes. O'Connor resignedly told her clerks not to expect to work on high-profile cases. She ruefully revealed to her clerk Barbara Woodhouse that during her first term on

---

* As one clerk explained it, "If you see a crèche in front of City Hall, you think, 'My government loves Jesus and I don't.' But if it has 'Season's Greetings' and reindeer and Santa Claus and candy canes as it did in *Lynch v. Donnelly*, it's just part of the wider holiday celebration. It's all in the context." O'Connor's test became known as "the reindeer rule."[38]

the Court, when the chief justice assigned the first major opinion to her by saying, "Sandra, would you like to take a crack at it?" she had answered (somewhat uncharacteristically), "Well, I'm not sure." There had been a silence, and O'Connor realized that she had given the wrong answer. Over time, tensions had grown between the Burger and O'Connor chambers. But she avoided gratuitous shots at the Chief. When Barbara Woodhouse put a small dig into the draft of an opinion, O'Connor drew a line through it. "Barbara," she said, "we don't need to say that." (Steven Gilles recalled that when he wrote in a draft dissent that the majority opinion was a "constitutional temper tantrum," O'Connor "got a big laugh. Then she crossed it out.")⁴⁰*

Burger was feeling unloved and beleaguered as Chief, and he showed his frustration in petty ways, complaining bitterly about Harry Blackmun's use of a Court car to be driven to work and telling O'Connor she could not have dancing or more than eighteen guests at parties in the Court's formal rooms.⁴² Without telling his brethren, Burger sought out a new job as head of a commission planning celebrations for the bicentennial of the Constitution. On April 30, 1986, as they walked to their chambers after oral argument, Lewis Powell told O'Connor that he had picked up "certain indications" that Chief Justice Burger was planning to retire at the end of the year.

Then came an intriguing confidence: Powell told O'Connor that "he [Powell] intends to support SOC's nomination as Chief Justice," John wrote in his diary that night. "He told her that she has the vision that the others don't have to look beyond the cases they have and see the impact the decisions will have in the long run."

Surprised, O'Connor told Powell that it might be better to bring "someone in from the outside." When she reported this to John, he responded that "what Lewis told her was the greatest compliment

---

* At the annual clerks' skit, "the Chief was the butt of remarks," John noted in his diary. Using the Scarecrow in *The Wizard of Oz* as inspiration, a clerk portraying the chief justice sang "If I Only Had a Brain," while another clerk portraying Rehnquist sang "If I Only Had a Heart" and a clerk portraying Brennan sang "If I Only Had a Court." Thurgood Marshall was portrayed as waking up and saying, "I vote with Bill." John wrote: "I think SOC was as shocked as I was about the number about the Chief, but there was nothing that could be done."⁴¹

anyone could ever have." Always confident in his wife, he predicted that President Reagan would make her chief justice.

Six weeks later, when Burger announced his resignation, the president appointed William Rehnquist as chief justice. Justice O'Connor was neither surprised nor disappointed, John wrote in his diary. While she would have been William French Smith's choice to replace Burger, the more conservative Edwin Meese was now attorney general. Her "goose was cooked" after she voted with the liberals against allowing the "moment of silence" in the Alabama case, she told John. She said she was relieved not to endure the additional loss of privacy and extra duties that came with the job of chief justice.

It is hard to imagine that O'Connor did not entertain some desire for the highest job in the nation's highest court. She certainly knew she had the political skills to bring the Court together in ways others might not. But she had long learned to bank her fires while keeping her steam up.[43]

Mindful of the circumstances behind her own appointment, O'Connor could temper her ambition with philosophical detachment. At a Miller & Chevalier firm dinner in March 1986, she remarked to John's partner, Robert Huffman, that Henry Friendly, a highly esteemed U.S. Court of Appeals judge often mentioned as a possible U.S. Supreme Court justice, had taken his own life. (Friendly, eighty-two, had been in poor health and was recently widowed.) Huffman asked her, "Do you know why Friendly was never nominated to the Supreme Court?" O'Connor replied, "Being nominated to the Supreme Court is like being struck by lightning."[44]

THE ELEVATION OF William Rehnquist to chief justice of the United States marked a turning point for the Supreme Court—but not, somewhat surprisingly, a turn to the right. As O'Connor had long known, Bill Rehnquist was an intriguing man, whose bluntness concealed sensitivity and whose restless mind was not always predictable.

To be sure, Rehnquist, unlike O'Connor, had a deeply felt conservative philosophy. (O'Connor had no agenda per se, though she often voted with conservatives.) At his annual lunch with O'Connor's clerks in 1983 at a restaurant on Capitol Hill, he had downed a martini and held forth on what he called the "sinuosity" of the law. The law might take twists and turns, he said, but it was possible to nudge it and shape it, and he meant to do so.[45] Rehnquist could come across as brash, even bumptious, particularly when trying to tweak the liberal graduates of elite East Coast law schools. Every year, he boisterously led the Court employees in Christmas carols. "He skipped past all the songs that didn't have Jesus in them," recalled Brian Hoffstadt, an O'Connor clerk. "The Jewish clerks would be looking around as he sang 'Hark, the Herald Angels Sing,'" said another, Dan Bussel.[46]

Yet, increasingly, Rehnquist had a live-and-let-live attitude toward the other justices. While Burger could be stiff and formal, Rehnquist was offhand and easygoing. The gangly chief justice became close to his liberal opposite, the impish Bill Brennan. They were often seen walking arm in arm, one man tall, one man short, but both seemingly in on a private joke.[47] Rehnquist took the view that the justices had largely made up their minds before coming to conference, so there was no point in having elaborate or long-winded debate. Burger had exasperated the justices by his habit of passing rather than casting the first vote, apparently to see how the sides lined up. Rehnquist, with O'Connor's enthusiastic approval, kept the conference moving smoothly and efficiently.[48] By securing congressional relief from mandatory judicial review of some cases, he also found ways to cut the Court's crippling workload—eventually slicing the caseload in half—to the relief of the justices (and their beast-of-burden clerks).

When she first arrived at the Court, O'Connor had been puzzled and a little hurt by Rehnquist's aloofness. He still rarely visited her chambers. Once when he complimented an O'Connor opinion in a memo, O'Connor exclaimed to her clerks, "We don't often hear praise from that corner."[49] Rehnquist's romantic pursuit of O'Connor in law school was a distant memory, but perhaps not entirely forgotten. At a later annual lunch with the O'Connor clerks, one had asked Rehnquist, lightly as an ice breaker, if he could "give us any dirt" about their time together in law school. Rehnquist's expression turned cold. "If I had any stories, I wouldn't tell you," he said. "There was no spark of humor," recalled one of the clerks, Bill Nardini. "He shut us down."[50] With her clerks, O'Connor was largely silent on the subject of

Rehnquist, allowing that they had "gone to the movies" once or twice at Stanford. Even so, later clerks thought they noticed a close, if largely unspoken, connection between Rehnquist and O'Connor.

In June 1993, O'Connor sent Rehnquist a *Peanuts* comic strip "for your humor files," she wrote. The strip showed Charlie Brown, reclining against a tree, saying to his dog, Snoopy, "I can see you now sitting on the bench of the Supreme Court. They'd probably put you right next to Judge Sandra Day O'Connor." The thought bubble over Snoopy's head says, "Is she cute?"[51]

In the private journal she kept from time to time, O'Connor wrote that when she heard the "surprising" news of Rehnquist's elevation to chief justice, she was

> delighted with the selection. . . . I have only admiration for Bill Rehnquist. He is an able and adept legal analyst and his manner is friendly and low key. He will run a fine operation. In a sense it is a relief to know I was not asked to serve as C.J. The job requires even more time and effort and skill than my present job, which is already all-consuming. I have no doubt that WHR's jurisprudence is more to Ed Meese's liking than mine, which has not always followed the Administration's views. . . . It will be hard to call Bill "Chief" though we will all adjust to it. He has laughingly told us to call him "Bill" if we prefer, at least socially. I still do.

Of the transition from Burger to Rehnquist, she wrote, "The atmosphere at the Court is as though everyone, from Justice to janitor, breathed a big sigh of relief now that our Chief has changed."[52]

SANDRA O'CONNOR AND Byron White were in some ways mirror opposites. John called his wife the "world's best enunciator," and a British journalist once wrote that when Justice O'Connor spoke with her emphatic, perfect diction, every subordinate clause securely in place, "you can almost hear the punctuation."[53] Justice White spoke from the bench in an incomprehensible growl. O'Connor was invariably polite, if sometimes coolly so. When Justice White did not like a lawyer's argument, "he would do a 180-degree turn in his chair so he didn't even have to look at the guy," recalled Scott Bales.[54]

O'Connor's aerobics classes in the morning were so unstrenuous that the justice did not bother to shower afterward. Byron White's basketball games with the clerks in the afternoon were Darwinian in their savagery. "He would throw elbows," recalled Dan Bussel, an O'Connor clerk in 1986–87. "A clerk kept making a set shot from the corner. White said, 'Don't make that shot.' The clerk thought he was kidding and made another shot. White decked him with his forearm," Bussel continued. "How do you elbow back a seventy-five-year-old Supreme Court justice?"[55]

O'Connor stressed to her clerks that she wanted consistency—her opinions should cohere and not contradict one another.[56] White claimed that he didn't even reread his old opinions, that he didn't have to, that after more than two decades on the Court he knew what he wanted to say. "Justice White would race his clerks to finish a draft," recalled Susan Creighton, an O'Connor clerk in 1986–87. "If the clerks lost, they could throw [their draft] in the circular file." Two of them, a pair of White opinions in relatively inconsequential cases, arrived in O'Connor's chambers in the end-of-the-term rush. Creighton recalled that she had protested to the justice, "You can't join these without changes!" O'Connor responded, "I can't propose changes to Byron on both. You pick which one."[57]

O'Connor indulged White because she was practical and needed his goodwill, but also because she liked him. She found him to be straightforward and manly. He flirted with her, in an innocent, Big Man on Campus way. "Good night, beautiful," he was overheard saying as he gave her a warm kiss going out the O'Connors' front door after a dinner party.[58] White had been a John Kennedy appointee and had, in his early years, often voted with the liberals; O'Connor was regarded as right of center. But the two justices in fact shared the middle ground on the Court, voting together about 80 percent of the time.[59] White liked to practice his golf putting in his office and he would challenge his clerks to beat him. Few did. O'Connor accepted his challenge and would wander down to his chambers to sink a few, especially if she needed his vote.[60]

It was White who wanted O'Connor's vote in *Thornburgh v. American College of Obstetricians & Gynecologists,* which the Court heard on November 5, 1985.[61] Abortion was back at the High Court; in the O'Connor chambers, the mail included photos of dead fetuses. The issue the Court addressed was the same as it had been in the 1983 *Akron* case: To what extent can the state—this time, Pennsylvania—restrict abortions through regulations? Justice White had been one of two justices to vote against *Roe v. Wade* (the other was William Rehnquist). He did not find a woman's right to terminate her pregnancy in the words or meaning of the Constitution, and he wanted to overturn *Roe.* He hoped O'Connor would join him. She did, although not in a way that would prove fatal to the right to choose.

By a 5-to-4 vote, *Roe* survived. Justice Blackmun, writing for the Court, knocked down Pennsylvania's attempt to restrict abortion. O'Connor wrote a dissent, in which she stated, "Suffice it to say that I dispute not only the wisdom, but also the legitimacy, of the Court's attempt to discredit and preempt state abortion regulation regardless of the interests it serves and the impact it has." In other words, she attacked Blackmun's cherished opinion in *Roe* as an illegitimate usurpation of state power.

On his copy of O'Connor's draft opinion, Justice Blackmun put an exclamation point next to that sentence and wrote in pencil, "She just is against abortion."[62]

But Blackmun was wrong.* O'Connor was not against abortion. She was willing to let states restrict abortion *unless* the restrictions imposed an "undue burden" on a woman's right to an abortion. Significantly, she had not joined White's dissent seeking the reversal of *Roe v. Wade.* Steve Gilles, O'Connor's clerk who worked on the case, was a right-to-life conservative, and he wished that the justice would be persuaded by White's dissent. He had a glimmer of hope: In the *Akron*

---

* Blackmun's gloomy state of mind was understandable; about eighteen months earlier, someone had fired a bullet through the window of the justice's apartment in Rosyln, Virginia. (Police decided the shooting was random.) Since then, Blackmun, instead of driving his own car like most justices, had been driven to work in a Court car, eliciting some grumbling from Chief Justice Burger (the only justice entitled to a Court car).[63]

case, O'Connor had declared that the state *had* a "compelling interest" in protecting the fetus "throughout pregnancy." But O'Connor was not willing to go all the way to overrule *Roe v. Wade*.[64]

The reasons why are rooted in her jurisprudence, her incremental, pragmatic approach to the law. While O'Connor's jurisprudence is not easily pigeonholed, her method of deciding cases falls into the philosophic tradition of pragmatism. Legal pragmatists believe, as it were, that the proof is in the pudding, that the truth of a belief rests in the success of its practical application. "The life of the law has not been logic; it has been experience," wrote Oliver Wendell Holmes, Jr. Like Holmes, O'Connor was more mindful of outcomes than theories.[65]

Her friend, former federal judge and FBI and CIA director William Webster, called her a "consequentialist." Being a consequentialist made her wary of the consequences. In her own opinion in the *Thornburgh* case, Justice O'Connor stated simply that "because Pennsylvania has not asked the Court to reconsider or overrule *Roe v. Wade,* I do not address the question." She may have been wrestling in her own mind with what to do about *Roe v. Wade*. In any case, she saw no need to resolve a question that was not, strictly speaking, before the Court. More subtly, and significantly, she may have been weighing the practical consequences of Justice White's sweeping language. Gilles, her clerk, recalled that O'Connor "was well aware" that White's opinion insisted that the state's compelling interest in protecting the unborn began "at conception." That could mean that the states could ban certain contraceptives as well. In Justice O'Connor's *Akron* opinion, she had spoken of the state's compelling interest in protecting the unborn "throughout pregnancy," a more ambiguous phrase than "at conception." It appears that O'Connor was wary of calling for *Roe v. Wade* to be overruled in a way that could interfere with contraception and new birth control technologies. In major cases, she always wanted to weigh carefully the long-term import, the practical impact on the people affected, to be certain of her decision.[66]

At the same time, she may have been hoping that the whole issue would go away. A year or two before the *Thornburgh* case reached the Supreme Court, John's law firm, Miller & Chevalier, was considering whether the firm should take on an abortion rights case representing a pro-abortion-rights group "pro bono" (free of charge, for the public good). John came to one of his partners, Robert Huffman, and cautioned that taking the abortion case would be a "terrible mistake" because, if the Supreme Court then agreed to review it, Sandra would have to recuse herself—to avoid the appearance of a conflict of interest with her husband's law firm. "You'll lose Sandra's vote, and she could be a key vote," said John. Shortly after—in May 1984—Huffman recalled, he was at a dinner party at the O'Connors' apartment in Kalorama, and he came into the kitchen to find Justice O'Connor, in an apron, doing dishes. Huffman told her that the firm had decided not to take on an abortion case. According to Huffman, she responded, "These abortion cases are going to be going away. The issue is going to be mooted by a new drug. It will eliminate the need for abortions."[67]

Justice O'Connor was being wishful, as well as atypically open about her inner thoughts. She may have been referring to the "morning after" pills that came on the market some years later and saved millions of women from unwanted pregnancies—but did not end abortions or remove the contentious issue from the Court's docket.

O'Connor's efforts to bring the real world into her jurisprudence raise an uncomfortable issue about judges wrestling with great social policy questions. Supreme Court justices may be experts at the law, but they are typically not experts at science, social or natural, and their attempts to render as "legal" the challenging moral and scientific issues that confront society can lead to unanticipated consequences.

Abortion poses a particular quandary. The Constitution is a moral document. It recognizes that people are rational beings, rational enough to govern themselves, but also that they are irrational, susceptible to baser urges like the lust for power and tribal hatred. The Framers meant to enable and encourage the former and rein in the latter. When justices interpret the Constitution, inevitably they make moral judgments. Sometimes they reflect society's moral norms, sometimes they follow, and very occasionally, they push ahead. Does a woman's right to privacy give her the right to terminate her pregnancy? Justice O'Connor ultimately answered yes, subject to state control so long as the state did not impose an "undue burden."

But Harry Blackmun's opinion in Roe v. Wade had gone further, into the realm of science and medicine. With his complex trimester system and page after page of medical evidence, his opinion in *Roe* set up the justices as all-knowing experts, pushing into areas normally left to policy makers and elected lawmakers. State legislatures were beginning to liberalize abortion law in the late sixties and early seventies. If the Court had stayed out of the political thicket, would abortion have been widely legalized? Would Congress have stepped in to ensure abortion rights? It is impossible to know, since by inserting themselves in the abortion fight, the justices may have helped guarantee a backlash.

Abortion was one societal conflict that engaged—and threatened to overwhelm—the nonlegal expertise of the justices. Affirmative action was another. In the years to come, using racial preferences to boost minority hiring and school admissions would present Justice O'Connor with a trying task. By allowing university admissions committees, government contractors, and corporate HR departments to explicitly use race, the Court sanctioned practices that have caused prolonged resentment and litigation on all sides. The battle may have been necessary. Overcoming centuries of discrimination is a problem with no easy answers, and involvement by the Court was unavoidable. Still, mixing constitutional theory with real-world practices can, and did, lead the justices into labyrinths. As time went on, Justice O'Connor would have to grapple with the conundrum of how to cure the effects of racial discrimination without at the same time discriminating by race. Like many judges before her, she saw no choice but to "fix" the problem through the law, albeit by trying to find the least intrusive means. She was cautious and tried to be clear-eyed as she made her way across uncertain ground, but the inherent degree of difficulty bears noting.

BEFORE ARRIVING IN Washington, O'Connor had limited real-world experience with African Americans. She had rarely had contact with black people growing up in Arizona or at Stanford, and while she had won the respect of Art Hamilton, the only African American in the Arizona state legislature, her only frequent contact with minorities was with Hispanics.

Her job, as one of the nation's chief interpreters of the Fourteenth

Amendment guarantee of equal protection under the law, required her to learn more about the experience of a racial minority that had been enslaved and then systematically discriminated against for most of the nation's history. Her tutor, in a manner of speaking, was Thurgood Marshall, an "Afro-American," as he preferred to be called, who had done as much as any to set his people free.[68] O'Connor had first heard Marshall's voice on the radio in 1954 when she was a civilian lawyer for the army in Germany. Marshall was speaking about *Brown v. Board of Education,* the landmark case he had just won before the Court as the lawyer for the NAACP. Marshall continued O'Connor's education in the conference room of the Supreme Court, where he regaled the justices with stories of his days as a civil rights lawyer, somehow never telling the same story twice. Marshall liked to shine a light on unconscious bias. "People don't know they are prejudiced," Marshall once declared at the Court's conference. He was specifically referring to white jurors in a death penalty case, but it was obvious from his remarks that he meant to include his white brethren and sister around the table.[69]

Marshall disagreed with O'Connor on many cases, but he grew fond of her. "*Saaandra,*" he would call out. "Did I ever tell you about the welcome I received in Mississippi?" And he would be off, eyebrows shooting up as he re-created what it was like to be run out of town by a sheriff with a gun or threatened with jail for defending an innocent man.[70] Marshall's stories were deadly serious, but he could also be wickedly droll. While drafting the Kenya constitution, he met Prince Philip, who asked, "Do you care to hear my opinion of lawyers?" To which Marshall responded, "Only if you care to hear my opinion of princes."

Marshall defiantly wore white athletic socks with his baggy business suits. He spent a lot of time watching soap operas and quiz shows on the small black-and-white TV in his office, or hanging around, teasing his clerks, whom he called "girl," "boy," "shorty," and "knuckle-head." He could be sarcastic with other justices, addressing them as "massa," and he could grow morose.[71]

One day, Marshall came to O'Connor in a funk about his time on the Court. "I haven't really accomplished anything," he said. She looked at him. "Thurgood, what are you talking about?" she said. "You are the only member of this Court who, if he had never been on the Court, never heard a single case, would have been a genuine American hero."[72]*

By the time O'Connor got to the Court, the great civil rights cases on school desegregation had long been decided. The Court had moved on to the vexing issue of affirmative action, or as the lawyers phrased the question, When is it constitutionally and legally permissible to use racial preference? To remedy proven past discrimination, in a narrow, time-limited way, was one thing, But what if the goal was a little gauzier, like the need to promote "diversity" in the workforce or in higher education? More fundamentally, is it right to discriminate now to cure discrimination then? The answer of the liberals (Marshall and Brennan) was usually yes and the answer of the conservatives (Rehnquist and later Nino Scalia and Clarence Thomas) was almost always no. O'Connor was in the middle—feeling her way case by case, almost instinctively in sync with public attitudes, looking for ways to balance competing interests. Can you discriminate against an *individual*, whose rights are clearly protected by the Constitution, to do justice to *groups* long discriminated against? Her attempts to reconcile dueling imperatives would, over time, define her role on the Court.

* When Marshall died in 1993, O'Connor wrote in her distinctive script on the cover of his funeral program, "Remembered: At a Court Conference when someone said we 'had to' do something, Thurgood said, 'Had to? There are only 2 things I got to do—stay black and die.'"[73]

CHAPTER TEN

CANCER

"I don't know if I want to go on."

Wearing a wig after breast cancer treatment,
O'Connor cradles her first grandchild.

I N THE SUPREME Court cafeteria, in a lunchroom walled off so tourists and nosy reporters would not overhear their conversations, the justices' overworked clerks would sometimes gossip about their bosses' quirks and habits. The inside jokes included wordplay, some of it cleverly revealing. The name Powell became a verb, as in "to powell." A justice who "powelled" a case wrote an opinion that, in its desire to accommodate and find a middle way, was so narrow that it muddled the Court's decision.[1]

Possibly the most powelled-up case in history was the famous "reverse discrimination" case, *Regents of the University of California v. Bakke,* handed down in June 1978.

Allan Bakke wanted to be a doctor. But when Bakke, who was white, applied to the University of California, Davis, Medical School, he was rejected, even though students with lower grades on their entry exams were accepted under a program that set aside sixteen places for minorities. Bakke sued, claiming "reverse discrimination." When the case got to the U.S. Supreme Court, four justices voted to knock down the UC Davis program because, as the elder justice John Marshall Harlan had put it in his famous dissent from *Plessy v. Ferguson* in 1896, the "Constitution is color blind."[2]

By this reading, racial preferences are on their face unconstitutional. Another four justices voted to uphold the Davis program because, as Harry Blackmun noted, "to get beyond racism, we must first take account of race." Justice Powell was in the middle. He wrote an opinion that no other justice joined in full and legal scholars criticized, but that found a compromise. Powell said no to explicit racial "quotas" but yes to fuzzier racial "goals." Since there was no proven past discrimination at UC Davis, he embraced a whole new rationale for racial preference: to increase "diversity" in the student body. A

Harvard Law grad, Powell invoked Harvard College's "holistic" approach to admissions, which gave an advantage to minority applicants (as well as an edge to legacies and athletes) without setting explicit quotas. EVERYONE WON! editorialized *The Washington Post,* and Powell's split-the-baby decision took some of the heat off an issue that was polarizing and confusing to many. Still, the Court would spend the next several decades trying to figure out exactly what Justice Powell meant.[3]

In *Wygant v. Jackson Board of Education,* Justice Powell found himself in the awkward position of trying to resolve some of the many unanswered questions about affirmative action left by *Bakke.*[4] In the early 1980s, during an economic downturn, the City of Jackson, Mississippi, had laid off some white teachers while protecting the jobs of black teachers with less seniority. Due to a previous collective bargaining agreement with the teachers' union, the city school system had been banned from lowering the overall percentage of minority teachers. The white teachers sued, claiming reverse discrimination.

At the Court's conference on November 8, 1985, the conservatives, Chief Justice Burger and Justice Rehnquist, voted to strike down the affirmative action program, as did Justice White, who had been moving to the right on race cases. Justice Powell, who had been the head of the school board in Richmond and was no fan of teachers' unions, voted against the percentage plan as a "quota." The liberals wanted to uphold the lower court's decision in favor of affirmative action; the capital of Mississippi had a long history of racial discrimination.

The vote was 4 to 4 when it came to Justice O'Connor. She wanted to temporize—to send the case back down to the lower court to be reargued rather than to vote up or down on affirmative action. She told the other justices her vote in the case to overrule the courts below was "tentative."

"Very tent[ative]!!!" Harry Blackmun wrote next to O'Connor's name on his scorecard of the conference votes. Back in his chambers, regaling his clerks, he mimicked O'Connor in a schoolmarm's voice, "I vote tentatively, very tentatively . . ."[5]

Justice Powell had coined the expression "nine one-man law firms" to describe the surprising isolation of Supreme Court justices, but from time to time he would walk down the hall to learn O'Connor's

thinking—and seek her vote. The O'Connor clerks were accustomed
to Powell's gaunt figure (always thin, he was lately suffering from
prostate cancer) and his gentlemanly inquiry, "Does Sandra have
some time for me?"[6]

As the holidays approached in December 1985, Justice Powell
wanted to see O'Connor about the *Wygant* case because, as a practical
matter, O'Connor was "powelling" him. She wanted to decide the
case before the Court and nothing more, to avoid carving in stone an
answer that might be wrong for other cases—but leaving future outcomes uncertain. Powell had been assigned the majority opinion by
the chief justice in the hope that he could bring his friend Justice
O'Connor on board as the fifth vote to knock down the Jackson affirmative action program.

Ever the moderate, Justice Powell, in drafting his majority opinion,
did not argue that the Jackson School Board could never discriminate
against whites. But he wrote that the state would need a compelling
interest—i.e., to remedy proven discrimination against blacks and
other minorities—and only then if the remedy was "narrowly tailored" to redress wrongs without perpetrating new ones.

Even this compromise formulation was too definitive for Justice
O'Connor. She wanted to find a more open-ended approach to affirmative action. Her "tentativeness" may have annoyed Justice Blackmun, but it shows the merits of O'Connor's approach to her job as a
Supreme Court justice. She understood, better than many of her
brethren, that the commonplace impression of the Supreme Court as
the last word, the final authority, is fundamentally misleading. The
Supreme Court is a political institution—not in a partisan sense, but
rather in terms of the balance of power set forth in the Constitution.
In momentous and hard cases, judicial review can be less a resounding
judgment from On High than a kind of ongoing conversation between courts and legislatures—"no" to this, "yes" to that, and, on particularly sensitive cases like the death penalty or affirmative action,
"try again."

O'Connor had been on both sides of this dialogue. She had served
in a state legislature; she had, unlike every other justice on the Court,
run for office and asked for votes. While confident like Oliver Wendell Holmes, she knew, like Judge Learned Hand ("the spirit of Lib-

erty is the spirit which is not too sure that it is right"), the importance of doubt. "The least dangerous branch," as Alexander Hamilton called the judiciary (because it lacked the power of the executive and the political passions of the legislature), is engaged in a long and elaborate minuet with the other branches of government, both state and federal. The Supreme Court gets the toughest cases, the ones in which the "correct" outcome is not obvious or clear. Abortion and affirmative action are prime examples. Some societal questions do not lend themselves to black-and-white answers, partly because the American people are divided and feeling their way, or because social attitudes are evolving, sometimes slowly, occasionally all in a rush. Americans may believe something about gun control or the death penalty—and then change their mind.[7]*

The Court is an essential part of a long process of melding attitudes and mores with the law of the land. Rarely is there a last word. Sometimes the Court gets ahead of public opinion, or at least some well-entrenched sectors of opinion—notably in the 1954 school desegregation case, *Brown v. Board of Education,* and the 1973 abortion case, *Roe v. Wade.* (The country eventually caught up on desegregation; it remains divided on abortion.) O'Connor was very aware of the Court's obligation to step in and resolve some festering disputes, but she was also sensitive to the need to allow some vexing issues—such as, when is it right to use race to overcome the effects of race?—to evolve over time, albeit with some gentle nudging by the Supreme Court. Though she could be steely and decisive, hers was a fundamentally humble approach. It was born of wisdom and personal experience. She herself was a product of both discrimination and, later, affirmative action; in time, she would become the savior of (limited, time-sensitive) affirmative action.

So, in *Wygant v. Jackson,* O'Connor was reluctant to shut the door. When Powell wrote a requirement that the layoffs of the white teachers could be justified only on a showing that the school board had "engaged in purposeful discrimination," O'Connor penciled in the

---

* On the ERA, thirty-five of the thirty-eight required states ratified the amendment by 1977, but before the 1979 deadline, five of the states voted to rescind their ratifications.

margin of his draft opinion, "No—too strict?" When he declared that the layoff plan was not "sufficiently narrowly tailored," she wrote, "Never?"

Justice O'Connor wanted to leave the door open a little wider to future affirmative action programs. She wanted to signal that cities could use racial preferences in hiring their employees even if they could not definitively prove past discrimination against minorities, and she wanted them to have some flexibility in finding ways to make a more diverse workplace.

In rare moments of indecision, when the right course was not clearly apparent to her, she would use a phrase familiar to her brethren, "I am not at rest," meaning she had not finally decided on her vote. Affirmative action was a subject that kept her awake. She wrote Justice Powell, "I am not at rest on this, but I am inclined to think there is a legitimate state interest in promoting racial diversity in public school faculties." In later years, the term "diversity" would become a byword on college campuses, but in 1985, it still sounded a little vague, and Powell noted that the City of Jackson had not offered diversity as a rationale for maintaining a certain percentage of minorities during teacher layoffs. But he agreed with O'Connor on one very practical dilemma. It was in society's interest to encourage employers to voluntarily set goals (but not quotas!) in hiring minority employees. Yet if the law required employers first to prove prior discrimination, they were in a bind: Did they have to admit they had violated antidiscrimination laws before taking affirmative action to hire minorities? In other words, did they have to invite lawsuits for past discrimination just because they wanted to create a more diverse workforce, one that better mirrored their community? This was a no-win, catch-22 situation the Supreme Court had tried to avoid in an earlier landmark case involving affirmative action in industry, *Fullilove v. Klutznick,* decided in 1980.[8]

Back and forth Powell and O'Connor went in the winter of 1986. "I need your vote rather badly," pleaded Powell on March 19. Without O'Connor, he would lose his majority and the opinion would be reassigned to a liberal justice.

"These affirmative action cases are very difficult, at least for me," responded O'Connor on March 28. She was torn. As a woman, she knew that employers sometimes had to be compelled to hire people who did not look like them. On the other hand, she understood that a better-qualified person might be denied a job, and she was sensitive to the resentment that built up when well-meaning but distant Higher Authorities uttered decrees. Back on the Lazy B, when the functionaries of the Bureau of Land Management had laid down some new rules, she had seen the scowl on her father's face.

Finally, in April, O'Connor and Powell found a way for her to join most of his opinion as the fifth vote, knocking down the Jackson layoff plan while allowing her to signal that affirmative action was still viable. O'Connor's own concurring opinion tried to help lower courts pick their way through the confusing labyrinth of affirmative action while also preserving judicial flexibility. As ever, Powell was gracious. "It has been exceedingly helpful to me to be able to discuss the affirmative action cases with you during the Term," he wrote O'Connor on April 8. "We should perhaps do this more often within the Court in trying to resolve some of the more difficult cases."[9]

When Powell wrote that letter, he was recovering, though slowly, from complications from an operation for his prostate cancer during which he had almost bled to death. He was nearly eighty years old and exhausted. What's more the 1988 election was coming up, and if a Democrat won, it was possible that Powell's replacement would be to the left, possibly far left, of center, and of Powell.

On June 26, 1987, the last day of the Court's term, Justice Powell announced that he was retiring.[10] John O'Connor was in the courtroom that day, as dismayed as his wife. "I went to SOC's chambers," John wrote in his diary that night. "She was still teary about it all. She said she couldn't help but cry when Lewis told them. She didn't even want to go on the bench because she hadn't recovered emotionally when it was time to go out. She said that Lewis had been her best friend on the Court and that, for her, Lewis's announcement was like learning her best friend had just died."

The O'Connors walked together down to Powell's chambers. "He was standing there in shirt sleeves with cookies and milk on his desk," John wrote.

SOC walked over to Lewis at his desk, and they stood in each other's arms. SOC said, without tears, but close to them, that she simply couldn't talk yet about Lewis's decision because if she tried to, she would break down. Lewis turned to her and said: "John, you know what a jewel you have. If Sandra weren't married to you, I would have chased her myself." He then said to SOC: "Maybe we should do that and have Jo and John go off together." SOC then said: "Well, I guess it's a little late for that." I couldn't help feeling that the superficially light statement Lewis had made expressed a deeper feeling about SOC. I think he truly loves her in a wonderful way.

Four days later, the O'Connors were packing for summer vacation when they got word that President Reagan had nominated Robert Bork, a conservative judge, to replace Justice Powell. Bork had been the favorite of some of the ardent conservatives in the Reagan administration from the very beginning; in their zeal, the president's men could not see that his nomination would become a lightning rod for liberals pushing back against the Reagan Revolution.

Like many revolutionary movements, the one led by Ronald Reagan was stronger on rhetoric than reality. Reagan did succeed in lifting the public mood after the economy improved in the early eighties, and his fattened defense budgets and defiant talk about the "Evil Empire" of the Soviet Union pushed the Cold War toward an uncertain and possibly precipitous end. But part of Reagan's genius was to compromise. After shaking his fist at the Kremlin, he began to look for arms control agreements. At the same time, he shied away from insisting on the social agenda of Movement Republicans. He did not push for a constitutional amendment to ban abortion or a "Family Protection Act" in Congress that might have threatened the progress of women's rights. Rather, he preferred to work through Supreme Court appointments. The true-believer conservatives at the White House and Justice Department began looking for judicial nominees who would push back against the liberal activism of the Warren Court—and, as it happened, be more reliably conservative than Sandra Day O'Connor.

One of the great powers of the presidency is the opportunity to fill openings on the Supreme Court. In theory, a president can reshape the Court in his or her own ideological image. The reality is rarely so neat or predictable, but with the retirements of Chief Justice Burger in 1986 and Justice Lewis Powell in 1987, President Reagan had a chance to push the Court rightward by finding more dependable and forceful conservatives than the clumsy Burger and the courtly Powell.

The year before Powell resigned, President Reagan had chosen Antonin Scalia to take Bill Rehnquist's seat when Rehnquist moved up to chief justice, replacing Warren Burger. Bork and Scalia, judges on the D.C. Circuit Court of Appeals, were both darlings of the conservative movement, outspoken in their opposition to the liberalism of the Warren Court. President Reagan had picked Scalia before Bork "for actuarial reasons," recalled Ken Cribb, the top assistant to Attorney General Ed Meese. "Scalia was ten years younger and smoked cigars, not cigarettes."

Bork's appointment "will mean that SOC will have three conservatives to her right," John wrote in his diary that night, meaning Rehnquist, Scalia, and now Bork. "She had predicted several years ago that appointments to her right would end up putting her in the middle of the Court. The big impact of the Bork appointment will be on abortion. Presumably, his will be the fifth vote that will overturn Roe v. Wade.* It will be interesting to see how the pro-choice groups fight the Bork nomination," John wrote, with understated prescience.[11]

WHEN NINO SCALIA had first taken his seat on the Court in October 1986, Sandra O'Connor had welcomed his high intelligence and verve. Brennan, Blackmun, and Marshall were visibly slowing and allowing their clerks to do much of their work; Scalia, she believed, would be a tonic. "Nino Scalia will have a dramatic impact here," she wrote in her journal—her last entry before she discontinued her rela-

---

* John O'Connor's presumption is intriguing, for it appears to count his wife as a vote to overturn Roe v. Wade: Rehnquist, White, Scalia, Bork—and O'Connor. Yet at other times, he appeared to guess that she would vote to uphold abortion rights. It appears likely that he was indeed guessing—that she did not even confide to John her true (and perhaps unsettled) leanings on this most difficult subject.

tively discreet, on-again, mostly off-again record of her time on the Court. "He is brilliant, confident, skillful and charming."[12] It did not take long, however, for her to realize that a full dose of Scalia could be a little too bracing.

The O'Connors and Scalias were social acquaintances. The two couples had taken a trip to Amish country in 1984 with their mutual friends, Ivan and Nina Selin. "The trip was Sandra's idea," recalled Nina Selin. "She wanted to invite Nino—she knew he was going to get to the Supreme Court." When the White House announced Scalia's nomination, the O'Connors feted him with a small dinner party of close friends.[13]

After Scalia's first Court conference, on October 8, 1986, Scalia arrived at O'Connor's office, shut the door, and asked, "Is that the way conferences always are? They're even worse than the D.C. Circuit conferences. I can't tell you how shocked and disappointed I am. There doesn't seem to be room for any give-and-take." O'Connor's response, according to John's diary, was "generally speaking, that was the way it was. The justices were well prepared, knew how they were going to vote, and did so without much discussion."

John continued: "She likes Nino very much, but wonders how others may react as he had come on so strong so soon."[14]

Scalia was the Court's first Italian American, a Catholic with a large family (nine children), undeniably brilliant, charmingly ebullient, but also domineering at times. Rejected by Princeton, still a WASP bastion in the 1950s, because he was, as he put it, "not quite the Princeton type," Scalia was notably undeferential. He and Lewis Powell, then serving his last year on the Court, were a poor mix. Powell valued courteous manners; Scalia was immediately in the face of his more senior brethren, sending them sharply worded memos, "Ninograms," correcting everything from their grammar to their understanding of the Constitution. During the Court's first oral argument, Scalia asked so many questions that Powell turned to Thurgood Marshall, who sat beside him on the bench, and whispered, "Do you think he knows the rest of us are here?"[15]

As the junior justice, O'Connor had been delegated such tasks as improving the Court's cafeteria and testifying before congressional committees to argue for the Court's annual budget appropriation. The latter duty had been passed on to the Court's newest justice, Scalia, but on his maiden trip to Congress, Scalia's brashness had offended the lawmakers. In January, Chief Justice Rehnquist appeared in Justice O'Connor's chambers asking if she could go across the Capitol plaza and make peace with the Court's appropriators.[16]

Congressmen may have been put off by Scalia's manner, but Supreme Court clerks—liberal as well as conservative—were enthralled by him. "There was a lot of Scalia envy in the building," recalled the clerk of a liberal justice. Scalia was anything but a remote figure, and his chambers were virtually a salon of stimulating constitutional analysis. This was precisely the fresh breeze that O'Connor had welcomed.

That is, until she began to feel the blowback. Scalia continued to reach out to O'Connor, to call on her with bluff good cheer. But within his own chambers, he was too frank with his clerks, and he began scoffing that O'Connor was a politician not a judge; and that he thought she was not a rigorous legal thinker but rather felt her way to crowd-pleasing outcomes.[17]

O'Connor was far more discreet, but her clerks sensed a change in her mood. At first, "she was excited about him, felt warmly," recalled Steve Catlett, one of her clerks that year. "Early on, he was courting her. She was impressed. But by the end of the year, it wasn't happening. When you're creating a middle road [as O'Connor tended to do], you have to fudge to make things work. Scalia would call her out. He was an intellectual purist. She cared about decorum, and she did not like to be called out."[18]

Sandra did not confide to her husband the extent to which she was offended by Scalia during his first year, October Term 1986 (OT '86 in Court jargon), at least not in a way that surfaced in John's diary. In time, Scalia became an irritant to Justice O'Connor, but during Scalia's first year on the court, 1986–87, she tried to ignore his barbs. There were, in any case, two Scalias, the bombastic pedagogue at conference and the puckish charmer at cocktails.

John, for his part, was delighted by the bon vivant Scalia. They shared a love of jokes and wit, music and culture, and a taste for the grape. John invited Scalia to be his guest at the Bohemian Grove and have lunch at his favorite new club, the Alibi.[19]*

In April 1988, as John and Sandra were driving home after a dinner at the Supreme Court with "the family," as the justices and their wives called themselves, they talked about "how dull the evening was in some respects," John recorded in his diary. Cooped up in their Court, avoiding discussion of their one shared interest—the cases before them—the justices could be less than scintillating company when they all gathered socially. Judges, O'Connor noted, could be dulled by their monastic lives.

John tried to look on the bright side. "Nino Scalia, Byron White, and Lewis Powell aren't dull," he wrote, "and I think Anthony Kennedy may be fun, though careful. To my surprise, Tony asked me tonight if I would like to play at Augusta with him this fall." ("Augusta" was the Augusta National Golf Club in Georgia, home of the Masters Tournament and, to John and many others, the number one golf club in the country.)[21]

That February in 1988, Anthony Kennedy, a federal court of appeals judge from Sacramento, had been confirmed as the Court's newest justice, filling Powell's empty seat. John O'Connor's weather eye had been right; four months earlier, in October, Robert Bork's nomination had perished before a liberal onslaught under the television lights of the Senate Judiciary Committee Hearing Room. Another nominee, Judge Douglas Ginsburg, had withdrawn in November 1987 when it was reported that he had smoked marijuana as a profes-

---

* John was a clubman. In 1988, the O'Connors, either individually or together, belonged to ten clubs (at several the fees were waived or discounted for Supreme Court justices): in California, the Bohemian Club; in Phoenix, the Arizona Club, the Paradise Valley Country Club, and the Valley Field Riding and Polo Club; and in Washington, the Metropolitan Club, the University Club, the Sulgrave Club, the Chevy Chase Club, the Alfalfa Club (an annual movers-and-shakers dinner), and what John described as "maybe the most exclusive club in the United States," the Alibi Club, which had a small house a few blocks from the White House. John was put up for the Alibi by Lewis Powell. Its fifty members, John proudly noted, included Vice President George Bush, two Supreme Court justices (Burger and Powell), the Republican Senate minority leader, the FBI director, the former heads of the CIA and the Federal Reserve, and various retired top military commanders.[20]

sor in law school. (Ginsburg, like Bork, had a beard. O'Connor's only comment to her clerks when Ginsburg appeared on TV during his nomination was "Another beard?")²² Kennedy, a Californian close to Ronald Reagan, arrived at the Court with a studied gentility; he was conservative, but not deterministically so. He was upbeat and gracious with the O'Connors, who gave him a welcoming dinner at the Court. John O'Connor was prepared to like him, whether they went to Augusta or not.

JOHN O'CONNOR LIKED to look on the bright side. At a party at the Canadian embassy at the end of December 1987, Solicitor General Charles Fried heard Justice O'Connor say that the United States had not suffered a total economic disaster—"yet." In his diary for the evening, John recorded, "Fried picked up on her 'yet' and said: 'Are you basically a pessimist, a chicken little?' She confessed that she was and that her mother had purchased two funny wooden dolls years ago that showed an upturned mouth on one of them—the optimist—and a downturned mouth on the other. Sandra's mother said—accurately— that the former represented me [John] and the latter her."²³

Most people regarded Sandra O'Connor as an optimist, or if a pessimist, only in comparison to her ebullient husband. Determined to show effortless grace, Sandra had been raised by her father to anticipate the worst and, with as much cheer and resolve as one could muster, to carry on without looking back. John was far more blithe; he wanted to savor the moment. His Washington diary, notwithstanding a few acerbic asides, is an upbeat chronicle of "superb" meals, fine wines, charming company, funny stories, and fascinating conversation. He was no longer the wide-eyed arriviste in Washington society; he was an accepted member of the inner circle. In September 1987, he described going to the Metropolitan Club during a break in the Bork nomination hearings. Entering the Members Grill, he sat at the Long Table. "Paul Nitze [Reagan's arms control adviser] was just getting up, so I took his place. Others at the table were William Howard Taft III, the grandson of the president and chief justice; Eddie Hidalgo, formerly secretary of the navy; Les Douglas [son of a famous diplomat]; and [CIA official] Cord Meyer, whose wife had an affair with J.F.K.

both during and after their marriage. There are interesting people here in D.C."[24]

Later that fall, he noted that he "spent most of the night talking to Kay"—Graham, *The Washington Post*'s grande dame and O'Connor's predecessor as "Most Powerful Woman in America." Mrs. Graham told John "that she thought it was great the way I accepted SOC's fame with grace," he wrote in his diary. "She said she had gone around a fair amount with Warren Buffet[t], and he couldn't handle playing second fiddle to Kay on these occasions, despite the fact that he is one of the richest and most respected men in Washington."[25]

John kept his pride in check. Wearing a jaunty lapel badge proclaiming himself to be the Supreme Court Male Auxiliary, he had attended the regular lunches with the wives of the justices in the wood-paneled chamber formerly known as the Ladies' Dining Room—renamed, after the O'Connors' arrival, the Spouses' Dining Room. He made a show of dubbing himself Honorary Chairman of the Association of Male Auxiliaries of the United States, appointing Denis Thatcher, the dutiful husband of British prime minister Margaret Thatcher, as chairman of the international counterpart. Their motto was "To the stars by virtue of our wives."[26]

But over time, inevitably, the jokes wore thin. In November 1987, he attended his first spouses' lunch at the Court in a year and a half. He knew he did not really belong there.[27] "John did not like the lunches," recalled Maureen Scalia. "He wanted to bring a male guest and Cissy Marshall vetoed it. She said, 'This is the only place I can talk about Thurgood.'" The ladies' lunch had been a kind of sanctuary for the wives. "Having husbands who like audiences, it was their turn to talk," explained Maureen.[28]

John's steady—and genuine—good cheer masked the less happy reality of his professional life. At his law firm, Miller & Chevalier, "John was a not a natural fit," said his partner, Homer Moyer. (The firm was known for expertise in tax law; John was assigned to government procurement contracts, "a subject he knew nothing about," said one of his partners.) "He was a generalist, not a specialist. The thought was maybe he could develop his contacts in Phoenix, but it never really worked," said Moyer.[29] In the spring of 1988, John began looking for a new firm, but he did not want to play the role of hard-charging hired

gun. When he heard that Brendan Sullivan, made famous by his defense of White House aide Colonel Oliver North at the Iran-Contra
scandal hearings in 1987, billed three thousand hours a year, John
wrote in his diary, "How sad." John might have made some easy money
by serving on corporate boards—but he worried about the appearance
of conflicts with his wife's judicial role. In his diary for March 9, 1986,
John recorded a conversation with Senator Paul Laxalt: "I told him
the practice of law was different in D.C. than elsewhere and wasn't
that much fun."[30]

The O'Connors' closest friends saw the effort that John put into
his role as husband of the Most Powerful Woman in America. "He
was rather on his best behavior around her," recalled Rawdon Dalrymple, the Australian ambassador to Washington and John's regular
golf partner and joke teller. "There was a line in the sand and John
knew exactly where it was and was at pains not to cross it."[31]

Sandra herself felt free to be outrageous—but only in safe company.
En route home from a fishing trip with the O'Connors and her old
Stanford friend Beatsie Challis Laws in the Sierra Nevada, Judge
Charles Renfrew drove through the agriculture checkpoint on the
California-Nevada border in the wrong lane. "A guy came out scream-
ing that I had committed about six moving violations and should be
arrested," Renfrew recalled. "Sandra leaned over from the back seat
and said, sotte voce, 'also for taking women across state lines for im-
moral purposes.' I said, 'Sandra, that's not funny!'"

The rest of the time, she was on public display and carried herself
accordingly. John sometimes wearied of tagging along. At the Anglo-
American Exchange in London in July 1984, Sandra O'Connor, Judge
Renfrew, and the other jurists had a full schedule of legal confabs at
the Inns of Court. The spouses were supposed to go to a fashion show.
Barbara Renfrew said she was going to the theater instead. "John said,
'Can I come with you?'" Barbara recalled. "We went every afternoon.
I could see that he was unhappy. He said that he was 'at sea.' But he
wouldn't change it."[32]

JOHN ALWAYS MARVELED at his wife's robustness. "SOC actually
said she was tired just before she went to bed," he wrote in his diary

on May 4, 1985. When she got a bad cold a year later, he recorded that she "was dragging, which is unlike her."[33] On March 7, 1988, she went into the hospital for an emergency appendectomy. The next day she was on the phone to a law clerk, Nelson Lund, to talk about a case. "She sounded like she was calling me on an ordinary day. Her voice was strong and her mind was clear and entirely focused on the case." But her aerobics teacher, Diane DiMarco, recalled that she was kept waiting outside O'Connor's hospital room for several minutes while the justice readied herself. "She did not want me to see her lying down in bed," said DiMarco.[34]

On the Fourth of July 1988, the O'Connors went to Lake Owen, Wisconsin, as they did most years, to play golf at the private course of some friends who were heirs to the Johnson Wax fortune. "SOC said she lost energy," John wrote that night, "words seldom spoken by her."[35]

At fifty-eight years old, O'Connor appeared to be fit and healthy. But in late August, a routine mammogram detected a mass in her right breast. She was told to have a biopsy, just in case, but she put it off for a month, until September 29, less than a week before the traditional opening of the Court's term.

On that first Monday, October 3, she got a call from the doctors "saying they wanted to talk to her," John wrote in his diary. "It was clear that the news is not going to be good."[36]

The diagnosis was cancer. The biopsy had found cancer in situ, a small tumor that was not—yet—invasive. Justice O'Connor put on her stiff upper lip. "What an annoyance," she told her secretary, Carolyn Sand.

For the next two weeks, Justice O'Connor consulted a series of doctors. Like many cancer patients, she came to learn that the experts do not always agree. Each of her doctors gave her different advice. The doctor at Bethesda Naval Hospital—her first stop, where presidents and other high government officials often go—recommended a mastectomy, surgery to remove her breast. The doctor at Washington Hospital Center, where she went for a second opinion, recommended a mastectomy and the removal of some lymph nodes, in case the cancer had migrated beyond her breast. A doctor at Georgetown Hospital—her third opinion—recommended another biopsy, but no mastectomy. Rather, he recommended a "lumpectomy," removing only the cancerous portion of the breast, followed by radiation. On October 11, she talked to all three doctors, who continued to disagree with one another's advice. Understandably, she was upset. She allowed to John that she was now "distracted" at work.

On Wednesday, October 19, the news was more ominous: The pathology from the second biopsy showed that her cancerous cells were "invasive." A mastectomy was now in order, along with the removal of some lymph nodes under her arm—to be performed two days hence. "SOC was really down," John wrote that night. She confided that she dreaded "mutilation" and feared losing full use of her right arm—the arm that had edited opinions longhand and that had so forcefully hit crosscourt shots on tennis courts and driven golf balls down fairways.

O'Connor had agreed to speak at Lewis Powell's alma mater, Washington and Lee University, the next day. And speak she did, even though it meant riding eight hours in a car with John to Lexington, Virginia, and back—on the eve of major surgery. During a question-and-answer session, she turned a question in legal ethics into a passionate talk about "the pure pleasure of helping people who need help," John recorded. He wrote: "I got misty because I knew that she was not only speaking so well, but . . . it could not have been far from her mind that tomorrow she would have a mastectomy." They did not get home until after midnight, and John recorded that she awoke at four thirty in the morning with what seemed to her to be a painful urinary infection. Still, she was determined to go ahead with the operation. She needed to be back at work for oral arguments on Monday, October 31—in ten days.

It was "raining cats and dogs" on Friday, October 21, when she arrived at Georgetown Hospital. Joining her outside the operating room, John found his wife in a hospital gown, "not happy about what was to happen."

The operation appeared to go well, although the surgery to reconstruct her breast was unexpectedly long and difficult (and left some troublesome scar tissue). On Friday afternoon and evening she rested and slept. At eight thirty Saturday morning, "SOC called and began giving orders again," wrote John. "I laughingly told her that I was going to ask the doctors to give her more morphine so we [John and their son Jay] could have some peace and quiet." (Jay was living with them while he took the business school boards.)

That Monday, John went to his office to explain to his partners at Miller & Chevalier that he was moving to a new firm, Bryan Cave, a St. Louis–based firm with offices in Washington and Phoenix, where John's old contacts could presumably be useful. (In his diary, John pronounced his new partners to be "gentlemen.")[37] From there, he was supposed to have lunch at the University Club with a friend, but shortly before that, Sandra called from her hospital bed. John's diary captured the conversation in heartrending detail:

> She said: "You'd better come over. We've got the report." I said, "You sound sad." She replied, "I'm afraid it's bad news" and broke down crying. . . . I drove to Georgetown as quickly as I could.
>
> I went to SOC's room. She was sitting in her bathrobe. I knew the news would be bad. I leaned over and kissed her. She started to cry and said: "They discovered cancer in the lymph nodes." SOC then began to sob and said: "They want me to go into chemotherapy. I don't know how much of this I can stand."

The cascade of bad news—the progressively worse diagnoses, the maddeningly mixed medical advice, the multiple trips to operating tables for surgeries, the sheer uncertainty—had finally taken a toll. Worse, for her, was the prospect of chemotherapy, which she now needed with Stage II cancer. She told John that she was terrified of ending up like their friend Ash Taylor, a prominent Phoenix doctor who had just died, his body ravaged by the effects of cancer and the awful side effects—the nausea, vomiting, and exhaustion—of "chemo," the medical toxins administered to fight cancer cells.

For Sandra O'Connor, it was not enough just to weather debilitating treatments that would go on for months. She had built a persona of extraordinary achievement. It was necessary for her to be "on" at all times. That was how she had sustained the burden and challenge of being "the first." Being "on" was how she had accepted with good grace the sobriquet of Most Powerful Woman in America, even though she was humble enough to know there was no such thing. She had been blessed with endless energy; now it would be sapped, if not drained, with a poison that might not buy much time. With John, she began to grieve, as if she were trying out—with her beloved husband—her own elegy. "I've tried to be a role model, but I can't be on this," she told John. "I'm sorry but I can't help it." She let herself go:

> I have had a good life. We've been very lucky. I've tried to do the best I could and to succeed and I've been able to do that. I don't know that I want to go on taking treatments.

Sandra had been a role model in the unremitting glare of the public spotlight for so many years, and now she was spent. "She was dissolved," John wrote. "She was saying that she didn't even want to struggle because the future seemed so bleak."

It was finally too much for John, too. "I couldn't help but cry," he wrote in his diary that night. "I thought I held back pretty well, but I couldn't hold it all. It was too awful. It was the worst moment of my life. I could think of reasons why she was wrong in her pessimism and be convinced that she would change her views, but it didn't help at that moment because she honestly thought she was going to die in the near term one way or the other."

Sandra's doctor, Marc Lippman, the chair of the department of oncology at Georgetown University, was out of town. Another oncologist, a woman whom John described as "the coldest professional person I have ever seen," told the O'Connors that Sandra had a fifty-fifty chance of living for five to ten more years. John thought he heard her say "with or without chemotherapy," but he probably misunderstood her—she may have meant without aggressive chemotherapy. "The fact of the matter is that fifty-fifty wasn't far off without chemotherapy," Dr. Lippman told the author in 2018.

Sandra was, in a way she had never been before, desperate. She called her friend Nancy Ignatius, who came right over. A Wellesley graduate and wife of Paul Ignatius, former president of *The Washington Post* and secretary of the navy, Nancy had played tennis with Sandra and had recruited her to do Bible readings at the National Cathedral's Bethlehem Chapel on many Sunday mornings, before Sandra went off to make sandwiches at a soup kitchen.

"Nan was wonderful," John wrote in his diary. "She described how she had had the same reaction when she found out she had cancer in her lymph nodes. She had been told she only had a 50/50 chance of survival. Faced with that, she didn't know whether she wanted to take chemotherapy, but she did, and it worked."

The two women "shed some tears," Nancy Ignatius recalled. Nancy told her that treatment was "essential" and "livable." Sandra seemed doubtful. "She worried that she would not be at her best," recalled Ignatius. She worried that the chemo "would somehow affect her thinking" and her "behavior." She worried about "feeling so weak," recalled Ignatius. "She worried about social events, where she had been in the spotlight."

Breast cancer, Ignatius saw, "was an unusual attack on Sandra's belief that she could be good at everything. She needed someone who had been through it all who could say that it would be okay."[38]

Over the summer, the O'Connors had moved from their apartment on California Street close to downtown to a roomy, comfortable house just over the Maryland line, conveniently across from the Chevy Chase Club and its golf course and tennis courts. On Wednesday, October 26, O'Connor was discharged from the hospital and returned home. For three days, she repeated what she had told John at the hospital, an incantation of sorrow and letting go, or trying to let go.

"SOC collapsed emotionally several times," John wrote. "She said she just didn't know if she could go through chemotherapy, that we had had wonderful times and she had had a good life and perhaps we should just let whatever happens happen. My eyes kept watering during these moments, but I was able to keep from breaking down." Jay, who was home to greet his mother, recalled, "I was stunned. It was the first time I saw her lose it emotionally."[39]

But she rallied. Dr. Lippman returned and told her about an aggressive cancer treatment called Adriamycin, a powerful strawberry-colored toxin known as "the red devil." She would, for a time, lose her hair and her eyebrows, but her survival odds would improve to 75 percent. A day later, he upped the odds to 85 percent. Dr. Lippman may have seen that after so much bad news, his patient needed to hear something more hopeful. "I remember her as intensely shy and private in the doctor-patient relationship," Lippman recalled. He was not surprised that the fiercely upbeat O'Connor felt overwhelmed in the moment. The patient's normal personality, he said, "has little to do with how she feels when she suddenly feels the rustle of wings around her."

There were other risks to Adriamycin. The drug could cause heart damage and it would make her very nauseous, as well as bald. For Sandra, who had worried about her thin hair as a girl, losing her hair was no small issue. Still, she characteristically decided to start taking chemo right away—her first dose of Adriamycin/Cytoxan was on Friday, November 5. That was two weeks before John expected it. She was back in the saddle.

She had already returned to the Court to work; she scheduled her chemo doses (every three weeks) on Fridays so that she would be sickest over the weekend. John reported that the first weekend was "not bad"—just some "dry heaves" at 4:30 A.M.

She felt "lethargic," she told John. Incredibly (or in O'Connor's case, predictably), she was determined to go to the Saturday dinner dance at the Sulgrave Club the next night. She napped until seven, when cocktails started. The partygoers had all seen or read the news of O'Connor's surgery and were not expecting to see her. "We got to the Sulgrave Club at 7:30," John wrote. "When we walked in, you could see the endless heads turn because here was SOC at a dinner dance just fifteen days after surgery."[40]

Nancy Ignatius was at her table. "She looked ashen," Ignatius recalled. "But she was there." The next day, her friend Judy Hope called her to tell her she was bringing dinner. "She resisted," recalled Hope. "I took over a chicken dish and a cold lemon soufflé. When she saw the soufflé she started to cry. 'Nobody takes care of me,' she said. I said, 'The reason why is you don't let them.'"

O'Connor's moment of self-pity was so out of character that it shocked Hope, but O'Connor was in the highly unusual position of dependency. Helplessness, like lasting fatigue, was an entirely foreign feeling for her.[41]

It was not true, by a long shot, that there was "nobody" to take care of her. Her sister, Ann, had come right away. The two siblings were not close—active in Arizona politics, Ann would sometimes introduce herself by saying, "I'm Ann Day, not Sandra's sister."[42] But John's diary records that Ann stayed a week and "really helped a great deal during a difficult time." Meanwhile, John wrote, many friends were bringing her food ("enough to feed two armies") and trying to comfort her.

John saw himself as a traditional male, whose role was to be stoical. But he had the good sense to let his wife mourn and grieve without arguing with her. He listened. He was also anything but a cold, unsentimental person. Len Bickwit, John's friend at Miller & Chevalier, recalled a conversation with John during this period. "He came into my office to talk about something else and broke down, involuntarily. He was surprised by it. In the middle of a sentence. He couldn't finish."

Sandra felt the love of her family, just as she had felt her mother and father's love from the very beginning. But her identity was partly built on helping others. "I am a compulsive volunteer," she liked to say. It was very hard to think of herself as needy, as dependent. She had seen her dear friend Lewis Powell struggle with the complications from surgery for his prostate cancer and how it inconvenienced the Court because he kept missing oral arguments and conferences, and thus could not vote on cases. She told John that if she felt disabled after two months, she would have to step down from the Court—an enormous concession. She knew she was being watched closely. On her first day back on the bench, she was horrified to see Tim O'Brien, the Supreme Court reporter for ABC News, watching her from the press gallery, perhaps fifty feet away—through binoculars.

Her family meant everything to her. She spoke often to Scott and Brian by phone and was grateful to have her youngest, Jay, living at home. In Arizona, the outspoken Ann had tried to escape the shadow of her successful, highly self-disciplined sister since childhood, and the younger sibling's rebelliousness and resentment had caused some painful moments in the family. But Sandra was touched and grateful for her sister's help. Sandra's free-spirited brother, Alan, arrived a few days after Ann. A larger-than-life cowboy whose fun-loving manner belied a sensitive, spiritual streak, Alan offered to arrange a lesson in self-hypnosis from a parapsychology organization called Silva Mind Control, which Sandra gamely agreed to do.[43]

Sandra's faith had always been quiet and personal, but she more openly turned to religion.[44] Her friends Gail and John Driggs, the for-

mer mayor of Phoenix, came to Washington and brought Bill Marriott, the head of the Marriott Corporation and an elder in the Mormon
Church, to perform a faith-healing ceremony on Sandra in the
O'Connors' living room. "Bill took a small bottle of oil out of his
pocket and poured a few drops on SOC's head," John O'Connor recorded. "He crossed his hands on top of her head and, with closed
eyes, asked the Lord to bless and heal SOC. He spoke for perhaps a
minute. John, whose eyes were now filled with tears, but who never
lost control, then crossed his hands and put them on top of Bill's
hands. John spoke for about three or four minutes, imploring the
Lord's assistance and referring to the good work SOC was doing.
That ended the blessing."

O'Connor almost always wrote thank-you letters immediately, but
she waited a week to write John Driggs about his hands-on prayers.
Her note was sincere, if a little stiff: "I have faith that our action will
have material results. Your intercession with God on my behalf is
something I believe will help."[45] Two days later, the justice cooked
Thanksgiving dinner for her law clerks. "After we went into dinner,
SOC said grace," John wrote. "I was quite content that she do so . . .
but she usually asked me to say 'something' rather than Grace as such.
Her 'grace' was much longer and more religious than usual; I was surprised."

The next day, she picked up a wig from her hairdresser, Eivand
Bjerke, in Georgetown. "The man did a good job," wrote John, "but it,
of course, looks quite different from SOC's own hair. . . . The wig
gives her a much fuller head of hair than she has ever had. Her hair is
really coming out a lot now. She thinks she may switch to the wig in
three days."[46]

Justice O'Connor was devastated when she lost her hair, according
to Bjerke. "During her cancer treatment, I'd sneak her through the
back parking lot at the end of the day. About every two weeks I'd clean
her wig. One of the first things she said to me was, 'I don't have time
for this.'"[47]

There was hardly a pause in the O'Connors' social calendar. The
night after she was fitted with her wig, she had dinner with Laura and
George W. Bush, who had worked on his father's successful presidential campaign and said he was "keeping his options open." George told

O'Connor that he had suggested that his father consider O'Connor as his running mate, and asked if she would have taken it. "She said, unhesitatingly, that she would not have," John wrote. "I think he was pretty surprised. He is a pleasant fellow, but certainly nothing unusual."[48]

BEFORE SURGERY ON Friday, October 21, O'Connor had sent a message to her brethren, with more optimism than she may have felt: "This is to let you know before you read about it in the newspaper that I am undergoing surgery today for breast cancer. Please do not be unduly concerned about it. The prognosis for my full recovery is in the range of 100 percent, and I do not anticipate having to miss any of the court's oral arguments as a consequence of it. I will be back very soon among you. No flowers—just good thoughts. Sincerely, Sandra."[49]

A week after the surgery, Nino Scalia had called his friend John to ask about the patient. Scalia had already spoken to the distraught Sandra. "He is the only Justice to whom SOC really unloaded her emotions when she was most devastated," John wrote. Scalia told O'Connor to "put her health first." If she missed some cases, "that would not be earth shattering," he said. John warned Scalia against coming to the house because "she'd break into tears again, and that wouldn't be desirable. I told him that when SOC called him and unloaded on him that was a real compliment. He said he took it that way."[50]

She returned to the Supreme Court on Monday, October 31, ten days after surgery. Incredibly, but not surprisingly, she went to her 8:00 A.M. aerobics class in the "Highest Court of the Land." "She stood in the back—for one day," recalled Diane DiMarco, her instructor. "Soon after, she was back in the front row."[51]

O'CONNOR HAD NOT wanted breast cancer to define her, and she did not speak publicly about her cancer for six years. But when she did, in an informal talk to the National Coalition for Cancer Survivorship, she was remarkably candid. "I remember her being pretty nervous about the talk," recalled Dr. Lippman, who had encouraged her to speak. As she often did, she mastered her nerves and forged ahead. The C-SPAN video of her speech is worth watching by anyone facing cancer, and by anyone wanting to see O'Connor, the private person, as her friends and family saw her.

She stood erect at the podium, still handsome at age sixty-four, her hair a blondish-gray, her eyes bright and, at moments, blazing. Speaking animatedly in her flat cowgirl accent, she was warm and funny. At times a lovely smile would spread across her face. She was earnest, intent, and at the same time beguiling. She said she was speaking for everyone in the room, and she did:

"We begin with the anxiety of going through the testing. Something is seen in a mammogram, or there's a little spot on your back, whatever it is, and then you start the tests. . . . The initial impact in me was one of utter disbelief. I felt fine, just fine! I was told that I had a potentially fatal disease. Now that gets your attention," she told the audience, emphasizing the word "that" with a twang that made the audience laugh. "The Big C! The word 'cancer.' It overwhelms the psyche. Just the word. I couldn't believe it. I was unprepared for the enormous emotional jolt. . . . I can remember all of a sudden my face and my hands, my whole body tingled. I couldn't believe I was hearing this. It couldn't be true. I'm too busy. I feel fine! You can't be serious!"

She described the toll of her treatment: "I was tired . . . and I'm not used to being tired. I had a lot of energy in my life and I couldn't believe I needed all that sleep. I'm a person that didn't sleep much. Well, I could hardly get up, and in the afternoon, I felt like I needed a nap. And this was frightening. . . . In my exercise class, there was a lot I couldn't do. But I did a little, I did what I could. . . . I still had a fat stomach, so I could work on that. . . ."

Having said, on learning she needed chemotherapy, that she could not be a role model, six years later she was just that. The way she chose to be one was to be honest, practical, and ultimately optimistic. She ticked off steps to improve the scarily mystifying process: Do some research. Call on friends. Try to get the doctors together in one room. She spoke of the strain on her family, and of doctors who talked past each other. Then she described "the upside to all of this," as she put it.

"Having this disease made me more aware than ever before of the transitory nature of life here on earth, of my own life. And it made me value each and every day of life more than ever."

SHE DID NOT tell the whole story. She left out some of her own unmatchable moments, like the time, late in her chemotherapy, when she was giving a speech and felt a wave of nausea. She excused herself, went offstage to throw up, returned, and finished the speech as if nothing had happened.[52] Sandra O'Connor was not Everywoman. But on the day of the National Coalition for Cancer Survivorship speech, she opened her heart to a gathering of women and men in a meeting room in Washington. When she finished, the audience stood and clapped and clapped. Then Sandra went back to work.[53]

CHAPTER ELEVEN

A WOMAN'S ROLE

"Beams of fire!"

Sandra did not lavish praise on her superstar law clerks, and some feared her, but she cared deeply about them. Almost all came to appreciate that she was giving them "an apprenticeship in life."

O'CONNOR'S LAW CLERKS had been stunned in October when the justice told them, in a matter-of-fact voice, that she was going to the hospital the next day to undergo surgery for breast cancer. They were ordered to share the news with no one. The clerks drew straws for the duty of bringing her briefing materials while she was bedridden. "I lost," recalled Adalberto Jordan, one of her clerks, who did not look forward to seeing his revered boss so diminished.

Justice O'Connor was "gaunt and pale" during the winter of 1989, recalled Jordan. "She put on her game face," said Daniel Mandil, another clerk. The Saturday lunches were now held at O'Connor's house in Chevy Chase, not in her chambers at the Court. But she still cooked the lunch. The clerks installed a "nerf pong" table (Ping-Pong with a soft foam ball) in their office at the Court. O'Connor, her right shoulder drooping from surgery, would join in. "She challenged Chief Justice Rehnquist, who came more than once. She loved to beat him," recalled Jane Stromseth, her sole female clerk that year.[1]

"She gutted it out," recalled Andrew McBride, the fourth clerk. "She'd come into chambers in the morning, and you could see her eyes were red." This made her stare seem more intimidating to clerks from other chambers, noted McBride. "A Kennedy clerk told me, 'Andrew, I just don't want to face those beams of fire.' Beams of fire!" exclaimed McBride. "I loved that. If she stared at you and she was upset or disappointed, you knew it."

McBride, twenty-eight years old, a burly ex–football player who graduated near the top of his class at Stanford Law and went on to be a major crimes prosecutor, was well matched with O'Connor. The Court's 1988–89 term, filled with major cases, was highly contentious, particularly among the clerks. McBride was a battering ram in the new conservative assault on liberal judging. O'Connor enjoyed McBride, opened up to him to a degree, and handled him with a sure and light touch, all the while sick and exhausted.

As soon as he met her, McBride had been impressed by the justice's grit and toughness (and by John's, too: "A lot of men are threatened by strong women. He never showed any reduction in his masculine mojo," McBride said). The son of a librarian, educated at Holy Cross, a small, rigorous Catholic college outside Boston, McBride revered the school of hard knocks. As a football player at Bergen Catholic High School in blue collar New Jersey, he had once been ordered by his coach, as a punishment for "dogging it" during wind sprints, to get on his stomach and push a ball the entire length of the field—with his nose—as his teammates cheered and jeered.

The brash McBride was a central figure in a group of ten conservative Supreme Court law clerks that year known by other clerks and by themselves as "the Cabal." Members of the Federalist Society, an increasingly assertive minority that had grown up to resist the perceived liberal slant in elite law schools, the Cabal strove to persuade their justices to embrace the doctrine of "original intent." The Constitution, they argued, should be read as the Founders originally intended, not as it had been interpreted by later (liberal) judges.* Their heroes were Robert Bork—a political martyr, according to McBride, who had clerked for Bork on the court of appeals—and Nino Scalia, who believed in bright line rules and "textualism." (According to the "textualists," the Constitution and statutes should be interpreted by their literal meaning, not by judges trying to fathom legislative purpose.) The Cabal met once a week in a local Chinese restaurant to plan strategy, and they communicated by their own email network.

A Justice Blackmun clerk named Edward Lazarus later wrote a controversial book, *Closed Chambers,* about the pitched battle between the Cabal and the more numerous but less well organized liberal clerks in October Term 1988—OT '88—a struggle that climaxed, or flamed out, with McBride and another clerk wrestling in one of the Court's fountains on the last day of the term.[3]

---

* "Originalism" has evolved to mean not so much the "intention" of the Founders as the original public meaning and purpose of their words.[2]

Justice O'Connor "stayed above it all," said her clerk Adalberto Jordan (who later became a federal court of appeals judge). "She was not consumed or concerned. She knew the justices decided, and we were the kids who thought we knew everything. And some of us thought it more than others." The clerks quickly learned who was in charge in the case of a man prosecuted for burning an American flag. All four clerks agreed the flag burning was political speech protected by the First Amendment. O'Connor did not argue with them or even explain her views; she simply went the other way.[4]

McBride relished the give and take between the conservative and the liberal clerks. Nonetheless, he had few illusions that he, or any cabal of clerks, could "control" O'Connor. From time to time, O'Connor would gently put McBride in his place. "The Cabal would compete—who could write the shortest cert pool memo? I won," he recalled. Some drug traffickers, arrested and in prison, had tried to get their arrests thrown out by claiming that there was no marijuana aboard their ship, even though they had been seen pitching it overboard. McBride's memo read, "Facts: plaintiffs seen pitching marijuana overboard. Plaintiff's argument: no marijuana on boat. Analysis: Res ipsa loquitur" [Latin for "the thing speaks for itself"]. Justice Blackmun called Justice O'Connor to complain about McBride's flippancy about what Blackmun saw as the larger issue, the habeas corpus rights of indigent convicts. "She thought it was funny," said McBride. "She was laughing as she said, 'Rewrite this to not displease Justice Blackmun.'"

O'Connor wanted to accommodate Blackmun and his fellow liberals on the Court—up to a point. On the day she came back to the Supreme Court from surgery, she was on the bench to hear oral arguments in a case with real resonance for professional women trying to break the glass ceiling. Ann Hopkins's candidacy for partnership at the accounting firm of Price Waterhouse had failed in part because she was described by some of the partners as "too macho"—apparently, she used profanity, just like the men. The partner who delivered the bad news told her that her professional prospects would improve if she would "walk more femininely, talk more femininely, wear makeup and have her hair styled and wear jewelry." She sued and won under Title VII of the 1964 Civil Rights Act, which bars discrimination on the basis of sex as well as race. The Supreme Court took the case to decide the proper standard in sex discrimination cases, and which side bears the burden of persuasion when sex stereotyping plays a role in the employment decision.

O'Connor was the only justice to have actually faced sex discrimination in the workplace. She was the sixth vote with the liberals and Justice White to put the burden on the defendant, Price Waterhouse—making it easier for a plaintiff to recover in these cases. She was the logical candidate to write the majority opinion. But Justice Brennan assigned the opinion to himself. Justice O'Connor insisted on writing a concurrence rather than sign on to his opinion, despite Brennan's repeated cajoling. "Poor employers, she feels," harrumphed Justice Blackmun, suggesting that O'Connor was oversensitive to defendants in these civil rights cases. But the reasoning in her concurrence is so close to Brennan's—with differences involving semantic shadings over the words "substantial" and "motivating"—that one senses personal pique at play on both sides.[5]

In several other cases that year, she voted with the conservatives to limit the reach of the civil rights laws. In a dissent to one of the cases, Justice Blackmun complained, "One wonders if the majority still believes that discrimination . . . is a problem in our society, or even remembers that it ever was."[6]

The Court's aging liberal lions, Brennan, Blackmun, and Marshall, often walked to conference arm in arm, but their step was slowing. During the winter of 1989, Brennan went into the hospital with a gallbladder infection and returned visibly weakened; in conference, he began to read his arguments from three-by-five cards. O'Connor felt that the clerks of all three liberals were starting to wield too much influence over their justices. Indeed, she told her clerk from the 1985 term, Kent Syverud, "that she did not want to stay on so long that it happened to her," recalled Syverud. She asked Syverud to keep an eye on her level of engagement and energy and to tell her if she was failing. For the next two decades, until Justice O'Connor retired, Syverud faithfully checked in with her every year. (He never told the justice that she was flagging.)[7]

In the winter of 1989, O'Connor knew that at least one, if not all three, of the liberals would have to step down before too long, and she did not want them to be replaced by other liberals. O'Connor, who played tennis with Barbara Bush every Tuesday morning, had rooted hard for George H. W. Bush to win in November. A week before the election, she had written to her friend Barry Goldwater, "I will be thankful if George wins. It is vital for the Court and the Nation if he does."[8]*

O'Connor did not like to be a political prop and was annoyed when, without prior notice, she was swept up in President George H. W. Bush's inaugural parade on January 20. As they sat in their black limousine on Constitution Avenue waiting to be driven to the reviewing stand (as guests of the newly sworn-in president), "we realized we were going to be in the parade," wrote John. "No one had told us that." The surprise turned out to be pleasant. "As we began going down the street and people realized from the sign on the side of the car that SOC was in it, they began to wave and holler: 'Hey, it's Sandra Day O'Connor,' 'Sandra' etc. It is impossible to describe the upbeat, absolute enthusiasm of the crowd when they realized it was SOC. This went on for miles. Literally, thousands of people took pictures of her in the car, tens of thousands waved. It was very, very, very moving," especially to a husband who had feared for his wife's life a few weeks earlier.[10]

THE ADMINISTRATION OF President George H. W. Bush was, in historical hindsight, an Edwardian summer of moderation and comity in the nation's capital. For establishment figures like Sandra Day O'Connor, Washington was a comfortable environ in the late 1980s. Media barons of the pre-Internet age dined at Katharine Graham's with the grandees of the Bush administration, men of the center like Secretary of State James A. Baker—and, often, John and Sandra

---

* O'Connor and Goldwater remained close. "I've always said you're the best woman I've ever known," Barry Goldwater once wrote her. Retired from the U.S. Senate (his seat was taken by John McCain), Goldwater gave O'Connor photographs he had taken of the Southwest to hang in her chambers, including one of an old Native American woman worn by care and time. "The Navajo woman looks like I feel at some of the Court's Conferences," O'Connor wrote Goldwater.[9]

O'Connor. No one paid much attention to a conservative rabble-rouser in the House of Representatives, Newt Gingrich of Georgia, who was fomenting a political revolution from the Right. Populism was but a distant rumble. Still, though Reagan had returned to his ranch, the Reagan conservatives had not abandoned their think tanks and political action committees, and they had their heroes. One of them was Antonin Scalia.

From his first days on the Court, Scalia waged a fierce campaign to end affirmative action. In a case involving a woman bus dispatcher who was promoted over a man who scored slightly higher in the job interview, Justice Brennan, writing for the majority, tried to get O'Connor to go along with a sweeping endorsement of affirmative action for women. As usual, she wanted to avoid overreaching, so she wrote a narrow concurring opinion sticking closely to the facts of the case. In the conference, Justice Scalia, who never hesitated to instruct his fellow justices on points of law, launched a jeremiad against any hiring preferences based on race or sex. "Why, Nino," O'Connor interjected, deadpan, "how do you think I got my job?"[11]

In the spring of 1989, Andrew McBride saw an opening to bring O'Connor over to Scalia's conservative point of view on racial preferences. As a rancher's daughter, O'Connor had long experience with affirmative action in a different context. She was admiring of Native American culture, and, as head of the Heard Museum in Phoenix, she had done much to preserve it. But like many ranch families, she chafed at the preferences the tribes received on state and federal water rights. She grumbled to McBride that she felt uncomfortable when a delegation of Native Americans, in tribal dress, stared at her from the audience throughout an oral argument in a water rights case.[12]

To O'Connor, affirmative action was too often not so much about social justice as about divvying up the spoils of political power. Or so it looked to her in the case of *City of Richmond v. J. A. Croson Company*. After the voting rights revolution of the 1960s and '70s had swept through the South, African Americans, who made up roughly half the population of Richmond, gained control of the city council by a 5-to-4 vote. The city council promptly enacted a law requiring the city's prime contractors to award 30 percent of their subcontracts to minority businesses (defined, as in the federal law, to include "Eskimos and Aleuts," of whom there were few in Richmond). Directing government contracts to minority businesses—known as set-asides—was becoming commonplace in cities with large minority populations, but the practice was contentious. Denied a contract to supply toilets, a white-owned company in Richmond sued the city for "reverse discrimination."

When six justices voted to knock down Richmond's minority set-aside, Chief Justice Rehnquist assigned the majority opinion to O'Connor. "To her, the Richmond set-aside looked more like Boss Tweed than affirmative action," said McBride, meaning more like old-style political machine patronage than justified preferences. In her opinion, Justice O'Connor zeroed in on the crassness of the city council, whose motivation smacked of "now it's our turn" racial politics. It troubled her that in coming up with the 30 percent figure, the city had not tried to determine how many qualified minority construction firms there were or even what percentage of city construction dollars went to minority contractors.

In dissent, Thurgood Marshall cited Richmond's long and "disgraceful" history of discrimination against blacks. "This is the capital of the Confederacy!" Blackmun spluttered as he marked up his copy of O'Connor's draft majority opinion with question marks, exclamation points, and expressions of "Wow!" and "Really?" But O'Connor did not want to look back; she wanted to move society toward a day when racial preferences would be a relic of the past.[13]

In drafting a proposed opinion for O'Connor, McBride hoped that she would follow Scalia's lead, and take a hard line against racial preference by asserting that the Constitution is "color blind." As usual in an affirmative action case, the key was the standard of review. O'Connor opted for "strict scrutiny," which, as a practical matter, could make it hard for any affirmative action plan to pass constitutional muster. Among legal scholars, the expression is "strict in theory, fatal in fact," because the test is so challenging: a history of proven past discrimination and a narrowly tailored remedy when no other alternative would do.

But O'Connor, as she so often did, left the door open. "Strict in theory" did not mean "fatal in fact" if the facts were right. In her edit of McBride's draft, she indicated that if the local government could do a better job than Richmond did of identifying specific instances—or even a clear statistical inference—of past discrimination, it could tailor a narrow remedy, including setting aside contracts for minority-owned firms. This was not the precedent that Scalia (or Andrew McBride) wanted to set. "Andrew wanted to push her into a broad legal proposition, to make her jurisprudence more pure. But that's not who she was," said McBride's fellow clerk Adalberto Jordan. "She was an incrementalist and minimalist at heart. One or two steps at a time. Strict scrutiny in affirmative action was a big step. But she was not willing to go all the way."

McBride, ruefully, accepted the reality. "She didn't like affirmative action," he recalled years later, after O'Connor had provided the decisive vote in upholding affirmative action in higher education, "though she was the one to save it."[14]

THE CROWDS KEPT getting larger. On January 22, 1989, the sixteenth anniversary of *Roe v. Wade*, more than sixty thousand demonstrators assembled on the Mall to protest the Court's famous abortion decision. Over loudspeakers, they heard the newly inaugurated President George H. W. Bush tell them—and send a not-so-subtle signal to the Supreme Court—that the time had come to overrule *Roe*. The political pressure of the antiabortion movement had continued to mount: President Bush, once a Planned Parenthood–supporting moderate, had felt compelled to champion the right-to-life cause. Moderation may have had its reigning moment in the Bush administration, but the president himself knew to cover his right flank.[15]

Two weeks earlier, the Court had agreed to rule on a Missouri law sharply limiting abortion. Missouri legislators called it the "kitchen sink" law because they had put in every restriction to abortion they could think of, from a preamble declaring that "life begins at conception" to prohibiting public hospitals from performing abortions that were not necessary to save the life of the mother. The case was called *Webster v. Reproductive Health Services*.[16] In O'Connor's chambers, the mail stacked up again—letters with photos of dead fetuses in one pile, letters with photos of coat hangers (symbol of back-alley abortions in the pre-*Roe* era) in another.

Harry Blackmun was morose. He referred to O'Connor, Scalia, and Kennedy as "the Reagan crowd cabal" and predicted they would vote with Rehnquist and White to affirm the Missouri law and reverse *Roe v. Wade*.[17] He was right about Scalia, who was busily working on Kennedy, the newest justice and a fellow Catholic. Kennedy regarded *Roe v. Wade* as a modern-day *Dred Scott,* the Supreme Court's discredited pre–Civil War decision upholding slavery.

O'Connor was again the swing vote. ALL EYES ON JUSTICE O'CONNOR read the cover line of *Newsweek* the week the *Webster* case was argued before the Supreme Court.[18] In the cover photo, she looked thin and obviously bewigged, but she was on the mend. The week before, O'Connor had finished her last chemo treatment and celebrated by dancing with John at the Chevy Chase Club, where, impromptu, they began swing-dancing, doing the jitterbug and the Charleston.[19]

Andrew McBride put his heart into trying to persuade his justice to join Scalia in voting to reverse *Roe*. He wrote a long memorandum arguing (as Scalia had in another case) that the privacy right found in the due process clause of the Fourteenth Amendment should be restricted to historical, traditional rights, like marriage—not abortion.[20]

McBride's rival for O'Connor's attention on the abortion case was his fellow law clerk Jane Stromseth, a Rhodes Scholar from Yale. She wrote a long memo arguing that a woman's right to decide whether to terminate a pregnancy was fundamental to her "liberty" (guaranteed by the Fourteenth Amendment's due process clause), even if Blackmun's trimester system in *Roe* was not the best way to go about protecting it. All four of O'Connor's clerks remembered a tense, emotion-laden confrontation between the two brainy and strong-willed clerks at the weekly Saturday lunch. "Everyone knew it was Jane v. Andrew for O'Connor's soul," McBride recalled, taking on a jocular tone he may not have shown at the time.

O'Connor listened, asked questions, and did not tip her hand. Years later, she recalled her feelings as she watched McBride and Stromseth square off. "It was a confrontation, and I never liked that. I tried not to be obviously upset, but it was upsetting."[21] Still, she did not show her disquiet. She liked to tease McBride, the Holy Cross grad, about the Catholic bond between Scalia and Kennedy. "I find it unseemly when Catholic justices get together," she said, kidding (but not entirely).[22]

Stromseth was reasonably confident her view would prevail. "I knew the justice understood what was at stake for women," said the clerk. "She had experienced childbirth. She understood the challenge of carrying a child to term, what it meant." After the intense Saturday meeting with her clerks, Stromseth recalled, "Justice O'Connor put her arm around my shoulders as we walked out of her chambers." Stromseth felt as if O'Connor was conveying something beyond mere comfort or companionship—that, as Stromseth put it, the justice "fully appreciated what women can face in these deeply personal decisions."[23]

O'Connor's understanding had deepened over the past few years as her eldest son, Scott, and his wife, Joanie, had struggled to conceive. Finally, through a fertilization procedure, Joanie had become pregnant. On Mother's Day 1989, just over two weeks after oral arguments in *Webster v. Reproductive Health Services* and her appearance on *Newsweek*'s cover, O'Connor sat down with her husband, son, and daughter-in-law to view an ultrasound video of her first grandchild. "We watched a terrific video of 'Baby O'Connor' at 4½ months since conception and about six inches long," John wrote in his diary that night. "I couldn't help reflect that SOC was watching pictures of a fetus of her grandchild at a time when she was concurrently being viewed as the swing vote on the abortion issue."[24]

At the Court, O'Connor liked to be first: first to hire her law clerks (to get the pick of the crop); first to write an assigned opinion (to get assigned more opinions); first to ask a question at oral argument (to establish the issue before the Court). But in *Webster,* she was slow to produce her concurrence to the Court's majority opinion. In Blackmun's chambers, the justice and his clerks waited anxiously and warily. On May 1, Blackmun clerk Eddie Lazarus wrote his boss, "My sources inform me that Justice O'Connor does indeed have a pregnant daughter-in-law. Apparently, this relative has been trying to have a child for years." Seven weeks later, as the term drew to an end, Lazarus cattily wrote Blackmun, "The expected circulation from SOC has been delayed until sometime later this afternoon. Apparently, her tennis game with Barbara Bush this morning, and her luncheon appointment, have precluded her final pre-circulation review."[25]

In the end, O'Connor went with an approach recommended by a third clerk, Daniel Mandil, and entirely consistent with her jurisprudence: to say as little as possible and to let the argument evolve through the delicate balance between legislatures elected by the people and judges sworn to protect the Constitution. She concluded that, properly read, the Missouri regulations did not impose "an undue burden" on a pregnant woman (her test from the *Akron* and *Thornburgh* cases) and that there was no need to revisit the constitutional validity of *Roe v. Wade*.[26] In other words, the battle would return to the states, which could keep trying to restrict abortion—and keep trying to persuade the Court to throw out its embattled precedent in *Roe v. Wade*.

"A chill wind blows," Blackmun wrote in his dissent from Rehnquist's majority opinion upholding the Missouri law. But, thanks to O'Connor's just-the-facts concurrence, the core holding of *Roe*— that a woman's right to an abortion is protected by the Constitution— survived. In his opinion, Scalia fumed and frothed that O'Connor's refusal to overturn *Roe v. Wade* had exposed the Court and the country to more turmoil by ducking her essential duty. "We can now look forward to at least another Term with carts full of mail from the public, and streets full of demonstrators, urging us—their unelected and life-tenured judges who have been awarded those extraordinary, undemocratic characteristics precisely in order that we might follow the law despite the popular will—to follow the popular will. Indeed, I expect we can look forward to even more of that than before, given our indecisive decision today." With scorn verging on contempt, he wrote that Justice O'Connor's concurring opinion "cannot be taken seriously."

On July 3, after Chief Justice Rehnquist announced the decision in *Webster v. Reproductive Health Services* and gaveled the fraught term to an end, some clerks had a few drinks and ended up going outside to one of the Court's interior courtyards. Taunts were traded between the liberals and the Cabal. Pretty soon, Andrew McBride and a Brennan clerk, Tim Bishop, were shoving and swinging at each other until they wound up in the courtyard fountain.[27]

O'Connor did not wait for the formalities of the final day. She had gone to the private golf resort in Wisconsin, owned by Arizona friends, where she often went to celebrate Independence Day. On the night of July 3, John wrote in his diary, "SOC won closest to the hole for ladies in both 9 hole contests and was second in the ladies contest."[28]

Her friend Lewis Powell was worried about her. "I cannot recall a previous term in which there were as many concurring and dissenting opinions," Powell wrote O'Connor on July 10 from his home in Richmond. "Some of the intemperate language in dissents reached the level of personal criticism. This, if the trend continues, could lessen respect for the Court as an institution." Though he had retired, Powell may have felt she needed reinforcement. "You must know that I am fond of you personally and have a high opinion of you as a thoughtful and conscientious Justice. I have said publicly that the President could not have found a more conscientious woman to be the first to serve on this Court. I also admire John. He has made a place for himself in this critical city, and is widely liked. My affectionate best to both of you."[29]

John was more bemused than angry with Scalia, who had agreed to be his guest and make a speech at the Bohemian Grove the following summer. After a lunch for a Franco-American legal exchange on September 5, John wrote, "Nino Scalia was at my table, and we exchanged jokes. After SOC made remarks, I whispered across the table to him: 'Any rebuttal remarks?' In the context of SOC's position in the Webster abortion case, that was particularly funny. He howled."[30]

"Scalia could be tough on me," Justice O'Connor acknowledged many years later. But Supreme Court justices have to work together "whether they like it or not," she said.[31] That fall of 1989, determined not to let history repeat itself, she read *The Antagonists,* an account of the divisive rivalry between Felix Frankfurter and Hugo Black during the years of the Warren Court.[32] Before Christmas, she told Justice Scalia that "ever since he had come on the Court, it was a much better Court," John recorded in his diary. "Nino told her that was the best Christmas present he ever could have received. SOC thinks Nino has been very hurt and is sensitive to the statements in the press that he had 'lectured' SOC in his concurring opinion in the Webster case. During the visit today, Nino made reference to that and said to SOC, in effect, 'Don't believe all that junk.'"[33]

THE WIG CAME off in October. Her hair had grown back slightly thicker. "It was terrific," wrote John. "She looked like a grey-haired Ingrid Bergman in 'For Whom the Bell Tolls.'" That month, O'Connor "quietly wept" as she held her first grandchild, a baby girl named Courtney. In December, she proudly wrote a friend that her golf handicap was unchanged from her precancer game.[34]

JUSTICE SCALIA WAS not wrong to predict that the Court's irresolution over Roe v. Wade would invite more political and legal struggle. Right-to-life state legislatures continued to test the limits of how far they could go. Minnesota began requiring teenage girls to get permission from both parents before obtaining an abortion, and the case reached the Supreme Court in late November 1989, less than six months after the Webster decision. This time, O'Connor drew the line. For the first time, she voted to strike down a state restriction on abortion as an "undue burden" on a woman's right to terminate her pregnancy.[35]

O'Connor was worried about the teenage daughters of abusive parents, said her clerk, Marci Hamilton, who wrote the bench memo in the case. "She was unhappy about putting children at risk. She was influenced by her own kids." O'Connor did not shed motherhood when she put on the robes; her clerks were well aware of her care for her children. O'Connor's sons were impressive young men, but they had the usual challenges of starting careers in an uncertain economy. Scott and Joanie O'Connor were finally able to have a baby—but the little girl had heart problems that required surgery. "Half the time when I went into her chambers she was on the phone with one of her sons," said Hamilton. "She told us, 'Be a parent first.' Once I came in while she was hanging up the phone. 'It just never ends,' she said."

The Minnesota abortion case reopened O'Connor's rift with Scalia, who filed a scathing dissent. "I didn't like what Scalia had said about her, so I wrote a fiery response," said Hamilton. "I got called into her chambers. 'Now, we don't talk like that,' Justice O'Connor said. 'But I like it!' I said. 'We don't talk like that. Take it out,' she said."[36]

O'Connor's sensitivity to children showed up in another case that year. Under the Sixth Amendment, a person accused of a crime has the right to confront the witnesses against him. For a child in a sex abuse case, that can mean taking the stand, looking at the defendant seated a few feet away in the courtroom, and seeing a monster. The state of Maryland tried to protect molested children by letting them testify by video camera. To the literal-minded Justice Scalia, the amendment meant what it said—the accuser had the right to confront witnesses face-to-face. But Justice O'Connor wrote the majority opinion allowing children to testify by one-way closed-circuit TV. She was persuaded by social science showing that children forced to confront their abusers became traumatized—and proved to be unreliable witnesses, said Ivan Fong, the clerk who worked on the case.[37]

Scholars and court watchers were noticing that O'Connor was notably sensitive to women and children in her rulings and opinions, and they began writing about it. Some elevated her to the role of a "new feminist" who brought a "unique perspective" to the differences between men and women. Others saw her playing the traditional woman's role of trying to bring warring sides together through compromise. After the *Webster* case, Ellen Goodman, a widely read columnist for *The Boston Globe,* wrote a piece entitled "O'Connor Tries to Be the Supreme Court's 'Mom.'"[38]

O'Connor did not want to be seen as either a "new feminist" or the Supreme Court's mother. "She was a gender equality person all the way. No 'women are different' for her," recalled Linda Meyer, a clerk in the 1991–92 term. In the fall of 1991, Meyer edited a major speech on gender and the law for O'Connor entitled "Portia's Progress." While a band of feminist pro-choice demonstrators outside chanted "Sandra Day, you can't hide! Undue burden is a lie!" the justice told an NYU Law School audience that asking whether women attorneys speak with a "different voice" was not only "unanswerable" but "dangerous." It risked conjuring up the Victorian myth of the "true woman" whose femininity needed to be protected by "stronger" males—the same rationale used for keeping women out of the professions for generations. Though she had been subject to discrimination during her career, she bridled at notions of "victimhood" and refused, ever, to play the martyr. "Do women judges decide cases differently by virtue of being women?" O'Connor asked her audience at NYU. She answered by quoting another judge who said, "A wise old man and a wise old woman reach the same conclusion."[39]

It was a strong speech, and she reprised the themes in many writings in the years ahead.[40] But her clerks, with the hubris of twenty-seven-year-olds, sometimes shook their heads at her lack of self-awareness, if not willful denial. Without question, her experience as a woman, daughter, wife, mother—and now grandmother—influenced her jurisprudence. It was true that she had no overarching agenda on women's issues, no "gender-based" approach to the law. At the same time, by judging in her one-case-at-a-time fashion—by looking closely at the facts and broader social context—she did bring a uniquely female perspective: her own. She was determined to anchor her jurisprudence in reality. In a 1994 case ruling that a state criminal court could not exclude female jurors, O'Connor wrote, "one need not be a sexist to share the intuition that in certain cases a person's gender and resulting experience will be relevant to his or her view of the case." Gender, she declared, should make no difference as a "matter of law"—but that didn't mean that gender made no difference as a "matter of fact."[41]

It should be no surprise that O'Connor remained guarded and protective of hard-won ground for women. She was constantly reminded, in ways large and small, that the battle for equality was not yet won. Ten years before, when Democratic presidential nominee Walter Mondale chose Congresswoman Geraldine Ferraro as his running mate in July 1984, O'Connor had written in her journal, "It makes even my Republican heart beat faster. National politics will be irrevocably changed. It *is* historic. Never again, whether the Democrats win or lose this one, can either party fail to seriously consider diversity on the National ticket. It is high time. It is a very happy day."[42]

But progress was painfully slow. A month before she gave her "Portia's Progress" lecture in 1991, O'Connor was listening to a Supreme Court argument from an unreconstructed Southern lawyer named

Harry McCall, Jr., who was defending the state of Louisiana in a prisoners' rights case. "I'd like to remind you gentlemen," he said at one point, prompting O'Connor to lean over the bench and say, with a slightly mischievous smile, "Would you like to remind me, too?" McCall, who was seventy-five years old, tried again. "Justice O'Connor and gentlemen," he began. Byron White interjected, impatiently, "Just 'Justices' would be fine."[43]

O'Connor's approach to most things was not to intellectualize, and certainly not to wring her hands, but rather to do. In a speech titled "Women in Power" in the fall of 1990, she directly and memorably stated:

> For both men and women the first step to getting power is to become visible to others, and then to put on an impressive show.
>
> As women achieve power, the barriers will fall. As society sees what women can do, as women see what women can do, there will be more women out there doing things, and we'll all be better off for it.[44]

While putting on "an impressive show," O'Connor liked to have some sport. In May 1990, when Gibson, Dunn & Crutcher asked her to speak at a hundredth-anniversary celebration of the firm, she accepted. But first she pointedly asked Gibson Dunn partner Ted Olson: How many woman lawyers work at the firm? How many women are partners? What is the gender breakdown of recent hires? Before an audience of eight hundred in the Beverly Wilshire Hotel ballroom, including the mayor of Los Angeles, the governor and chief justice of California, and all of the firm's top clients, O'Connor began by drily noting that thirty-eight years earlier, Gibson Dunn had allowed her to apply for a secretarial job. Had they hired her as a lawyer, she calculated, she might be number ten in a firm of 650 lawyers. As it was, she had settled for a smaller firm, where she had only been able to rise from number nine to number seven. In the audience, the nervous chuckles grew into a roar of laughter. She went on to say, with a big grin, that it was a Gibson Dunn partner, William French Smith, who had recommended her for the Supreme Court, so "all is forgiven." She reported to her husband, who had helped write the humorous part of her remarks, that the audience "howled and loved it." Some years later, the late-night TV host David Letterman asked her about her speech to Gibson Dunn. "It was the most fun I ever had," she said.[45]

AFTER HER CANCER, her clerks speculated that the justice might ease up. She did seem to slow a little, leaving her chambers earlier, traveling less, going out at night not quite so often. Then after a year or so, her tempo resumed its hectic pace. When her chambers secretary, Maggie Dupree, retired in 2004 after twenty years of service, she was worn out from calling airline presidents to hold flights and juggling competing speaking invitations that her boss had accepted. "I was semi-insane!" she recalled. "I couldn't work for another year. You had to be on top of everything."[46] "My strongest memories from clerking all involve trying to keep up with her," recalled Stuart Banner, who clerked in OT '91. An outing to the National Arboretum was anything but relaxing. "This wasn't quite stopping to smell the roses," Banner remembered. "It was more like speeding up to smell the roses. And learning why they smelled the way they did. And how one could become a better rose smeller. And what steps one should take to improve the quality of roses and the breadth of their distribution. And then moving on to the next set of roses down the road."[47]

O'Connor was relentless about making sure her clerks and family never passed up an educational opportunity. A few years later, during one of Washington's every-seventeen-years eruptions of dormant cicadas, O'Connor collected a batch of the large, dead insects and sent them in a shoebox to her grandchildren in Arizona (by this time, her son Scott and his wife, Joanie, had three children). Recounting the cicada story to a friend, Mary Adams, she explained that "one of the most important things to me is that my children and grandchildren are curious. Because, if you're not curious, you're not smart."[48]

Relaxation was, for O'Connor, a relative term. Outings for the clerks were more about kicking in than kicking back. In the spring of 1990, her clerk Ivan Fong carried his two-year-old daughter on what he thought was to be a three-mile hike in the Shenandoah Valley. It turned out to be a nine-mile trek. "Justice O'Connor would go off ahead, we'd straggle along. As soon as I got there, off she'd go again. We finally got to the lodge and collapsed into chairs. She came in and announced, 'Time to make dinner!'" On an earlier occasion back at the chambers, she had challenged Fong to a game of nerf pong. Fong had spent time in Hong Kong and played a lot of Ping-Pong there. Finding himself with a bigger than expected lead, he had "a dilemma," he recalled. "Do I toy with her? Or finish her off? Either way, it was a bad result! After I won, she just walked out without a word. We never played again."[49]

BILL BRENNAN WAS the first of the old liberals to go. Traveling to Europe after the end of term in the summer of 1990, he fell at the airport and hit his head. He had suffered a small stroke. The great cocreator and preserver of the Warren Court resigned a few days later.[50]

John Sununu, the chief of staff in the Bush White House, at first touted Brennan's replacement, David Souter, as a "home run" for conservatives. But after watching Souter ruminate unpredictably through a practice session for his Senate confirmation hearings, White House Counsel Boyden Gray said to his confreres, "My God, did we ever pick the wrong person."[51]

Souter, fifty-two, sailed through his hearings with a modest, well-spoken charm, but he was unusual. Unmarried, he lived alone in an old New Hampshire farmhouse. He owned a television set but never turned it on. When O'Connor came to see Souter at his new chambers in the Supreme Court, the lights were off, and Souter was straining to read by natural light. He explained that he liked to save electricity. She urged him to come to lunch and he asked to be served his usual meal—an apple and a cup of yogurt—dutifully served on the Court's fine china.[52]

O'Connor was close to Bill Webster, the former head of the FBI, now director of the CIA, and his vivacious young wife, Lynda. In October, the justice invited herself for Sunday lunch at the Websters' house in suburban Bethesda. The O'Connors showed up with Justice Souter in tow. In the kitchen, Sandra told Lynda, "I'll bet you wondered why I was so bold. Here's the deal. Barbara Bush and I were talking. We're thinking that Justice Souter should be married. Barbara and I thought that if he were constantly surrounded by happily married people, he'd want to be one, too."

Lynda was amused. "I'll do my best to act happy today," she replied. She whispered to her husband, the CIA director, "Act happy!"[53]

Justice Souter did go on a date or two arranged by Justice O'Connor. After one, he thanked the woman and said, "That was fun. Let's do it again next year." O'Connor asked him to join the O'Connors for Thanksgiving. Souter said no. She insisted. He said no again. She asked, "What else are you going to do?" He answered, "I'm a social minimalist."[54] In his diary, John recorded that "SOC had asked him for dinner, but he declined. He was going to be alone. However, he told his mother he was going to be with us, apparently so she wouldn't feel he was not with someone this Thanksgiving. She is in a New Hampshire rest home."[55]

Souter was a deep-dive thinker who reworked and rewrote his clerks' drafts, making them denser and more complex. By mid-April, he had circulated only two opinions (O'Connor had already circulated fourteen). On the drive home from work, Justice O'Connor told her husband that Souter's slow pace "was a real problem. No one knows what's going to happen because this problem has never happened before."

Six weeks later, Souter agreed to go with the O'Connors on a hike along the C&O Canal that runs by the Potomac River. His mood was much improved: He had circulated a raft of opinions. He admitted, "most frankly," wrote John, that he had really "fought the Court" until March or April, but that "he had finally relaxed a lot more. He is a very open, easy conversationalist," noted John, with some surprise.[56]

Long after Souter had retired from the Court, in the winter of 2016, he came to Phoenix to toast O'Connor at a prize dinner at the Sandra Day O'Connor College of Law (Arizona State's law school had recently been renamed in her honor). Souter found O'Connor, who was in a wheelchair. "Hiya, toots," he greeted her and held her hand as they entered the ballroom. He described her as his "first friend on the Court." Through his first twenty-four decisions on the

When Sandra was born, the Lazy B ranch had no electricity, telephone, or hot water. "It was no country for sissies," she recalled. "We thought of it as our own country."

When the windmills broke, they had to be fixed in forty-eight hours, before the cows started to die. With Sandra's father, there were no excuses.

As a young girl, Sandra tried to make wild creatures into pets, including a bobcat named Bob and a baby coyote. Her favorite horse, Chico, waited for her to climb back on if she fell off.

At a swimming hole near Yosemite, on vacation from college. Sandra was an A student in Western Civilization, liked to dance "crazy" at fraternities, and described Stanford as "Utopia."

SWIMMING HOLE ON BIG OAK FLAT
ROAD — NEAR GROUGLAND

Only the best students made *Stanford Law Review*. Graduating near the top of her class, Sandra applied to about forty California law firms. None would hire her. Only one even interviewed her, asking how well she could type.

Sandra dated her classmate William Rehnquist, later chief justice of the United States. In the spring of 1952, he asked Sandra to marry him. But she had fallen in love with John O'Connor.

Sandra's mother, Ada Mae, and father, Harry, at her wedding to John. Harry could be charming, blunt, and difficult. Ada Mae was loving and patient. Sandra saw a strong physical attachment between them.

Sandra gave up her job as an assistant district attorney to follow John to Germany, where he was an army lawyer and she worked for the Quartermaster's Corps. They stayed for three years and skied until the snow melted.

In evening dress. When John and Sandra went out dancing, other couples would stand and watch.

While John took a job with a top law firm in Phoenix, Sandra had to hang her shingle with another lawyer in a strip mall and take any case that walked in the door.

The O'Connors moved to Paradise Valley, a high-end Phoenix suburb, and custom-built a midcentury modern house. But they could not afford air conditioning and sealed the adobe bricks with skim milk themselves.

Elected the first female majority leader of a state senate, Sandra was known for a certain no-nonsense look. She managed to ignore or rise above most of the tomfoolery and change dozens of laws that discriminated against women.

Sandra, John, and their three sons, Scott, Jay, and Brian. The boys were given free rein, as long as they didn't sit around watching TV. One year, Sandra cooked nearly every recipe in the Julia Child cookbook for dinner.

Testifying at her confirmation hearings in the summer of 1981. Among the young Justice Department lawyers helping O'Connor prepare was future chief justice John Roberts. He struggled to keep up with her demands.

Chief Justice Warren Burger parades O'Connor down the Supreme Court steps after her swearing-in as the first woman justice. Burger was warm with O'Connor but could also be patronizing.

O'Connor said she learned a great deal from Justice Thurgood Marshall, who used the weekly private conferences of the justices to recount his experiences as a black defense lawyer in the Deep South.

"The Most Powerful Woman in America" shakes hands with the most powerful woman in Great Britain, Prime Minister Margaret Thatcher. John jokingly made her husband, Denis, a member of his husbands-of-powerful-women club.

Chief Justice Rehnquist and Justices Byron White, Antonin Scalia, Anthony Kennedy, Sandra Day O'Connor, William Brennan, Harry Blackmun, and John Paul Stevens. O'Connor did not like to be called "the swing vote" because that implied fickleness. But her vote was often decisive.

With Jim Symington and President George H. W. Bush at the Alfalfa Club dinner in 1994. O'Connor was later elected president of Alfalfa, which conducts a bibulous annual banquet of mostly male movers and shakers.

O'Connor golfing in Scotland. She had a long drive and a low handicap. She would go out on the course "even if it was thirty-four degrees and sleeting," according to her golf pro.

O'Connor loved fly-fishing. She had to use a can of bear spray to ward off this grizzly in Alaska. Her guide said he had never been so anxious; she shrugged it off.

John seated between friends Diana Holman and Kay Evans at a dinner in 2000. That morning, he had been diagnosed with Alzheimer's. He and Sandra still performed a skit, which did not go well.

With Ruth Bader Ginsburg in Statuary Hall at the Capitol. Ginsburg was grateful for O'Connor's counsel when she wrote her first opinion and later had to cope with cancer. The two were friendly but not close.

O'Connor teased Chief Justice Rehnquist about putting gold stripes on his robes. Rehnquist, who could be puckish, said he was inspired by a Gilbert and Sullivan operetta.

Justice O'Connor retires from the Court. She wanted to take care of John, whose dementia was worsening. But six months after she stepped down, she had to put him in a memory care facility.

Supreme Court of the United States
Washington, D. C. 20543

CHAMBERS OF
JUSTICE SANDRA DAY O'CONNOR

July 1, 2005

Dear President Bush:

This is to inform you of my decision to retire from my position as an Associate Justice of the Supreme Court of the United States effective upon the nomination and confirmation of my successor. It has been a great privilege, indeed, to have served as a member of the Court for 24 Terms. I will leave it with enormous respect for the integrity of the Court and its role under our Constitutional structure.

Sincerely,

Sandra Day O'Connor

The President
The White House
Washington, D. C.

Weeping as Bill Rehnquist's coffin passes by. The two had talked for months:
Who should leave first? The Chief decided to stay—but soon died. O'Connor
later regretted stepping down prematurely.

President Obama about to award O'Connor the Presidential Medal of
Freedom on August 12, 2009. The president praised the justice for building
"a bridge behind her for all young women to follow."

At the New York Public Library with former secretary of state Madeleine Albright in March 2013. O'Connor was testy and impatient; her staff began to notice she was forgetful. A year later, she was diagnosed with early dementia.

Applauded by Justices Ruth Bader Ginsburg, Sonia Sotomayor, and Elena Kagan. O'Connor's appointment "changed everything," said Sotomayor. "No one could have done it better," said Kagan.

Court, October Term 1990, he voted with O'Connor one hundred percent of the time.[57]

JUSTICE THURGOOD MARSHALL soon followed his "pal Billy Brennan," retiring from the Court a year later, in October 1991. O'Connor wept when she heard the news that summer; she would miss the civil rights hero's storytelling, even if she had rarely voted with him on major constitutional cases.

President Bush nominated Clarence Thomas to be the Court's second African American justice. At his confirmation hearings, Anita Hill, a lawyer who had worked for Thomas at the Equal Employment Opportunity Commission, accused him of making unwelcome sexual comments to her. During the televised spectacle, Justice O'Connor remained grimly mute around her clerks. She may have tolerated her husband's coarser private jokes with the guys, but she was perfectly aware that many people were appalled by Anita Hill's testimony, and she was surely disheartened by it, even if she did not let on. John's private reaction was more lighthearted. At breakfast at home during the hearings, John O'Connor opened his newspaper to see a cartoon of Thomas sitting next to Justice O'Connor for the Court's annual photo portrait with his hand on her knee. "It really is a funny cartoon," John wrote in his diary.[58]

Thomas, who had denied Hill's claim, appeared to be bitter and lonely when he arrived at the Court. Raised dirt poor in Georgia, educated at Yale Law School, he seemed to feel betrayed by the liberal Eastern elite. On the mantel of his chambers, Thomas put a YALE SUCKS bumper sticker. Asked to lecture at Harvard and Yale, he responded, "I don't do Ivies."[59] Gingerly, he agreed to follow the custom of meeting over lunch with the clerks of other justices. One O'Connor clerk, Vaughn Dunnigan, who graduated high in her class at Columbia Law School and, like Thomas, came from a working-class background, later recalled her impressions:

> When we met Justice Thomas, maybe he was still reeling [from Anita Hill's testimony], but I was sort of shocked. He wasn't

nice. He had a chip on his shoulder. It was almost unpleasant. We were so uncomfortable. And we were not wealthy and entitled kids.[60]

Thomas had his own clerks watch the 1949 movie *The Fountainhead,* a dramatization of Ayn Rand's novel extolling individualism. (The hero is an architect who refuses to bend to conformity.) On the Court, Thomas was content to be a judicial loner, to the right of Scalia. He wanted to restore "the Constitution in Exile" by discerning the intent of the Founders and stripping away the layerings of post–New Deal activist judges.[61]

Thomas was the mirror opposite of O'Connor's balancing act moderation. She rarely joined his opinions even when she voted on the same side in a case. At the end of Thomas's first year, she wrote a concurrence criticizing him for his slipshod analysis in a habeas case. Years later, in an interview with the author, Thomas shook his head and chuckled ruefully as he recalled, "I had the unmitigated gall in *Wright v. West* to write an opinion she didn't agree with. It was 'Welcome to the Court! Welcome to the NFL!' My clerks were upset, but I said, 'No, no, no, I'm the new guy!' She was that sort of Maggie Thatcher firm about what she wanted. She could not be pushed around."

Looking back on his first days at the Court, Thomas recalled his sense of feeling overwhelmed. "I was young, I was forty-three years old, I had been hammered really badly. I had a ton of work, every area of the law I had to get up to speed with, so I was always lugging two big L.L.Bean bags around. I wasn't going to lunch," he said, referring to the justices' tradition of having lunch together in the Court's formal dining room on days when they held oral argument.

O'Connor began walking with Thomas back to his chambers after oral argument. On their very first walk, she brought up Thomas's rough confirmation hearings. "They did a lot of damage," she said. Thomas wasn't sure whether she meant damage to the Court or damage to him. A bit of both, he guessed, but, not knowing quite what to say, he said nothing.

She continued to walk with him after their conferences. "She kept saying, 'You should come to lunch, you should come to lunch.' One day, she looks at me, 'Now, Clarence, you need to come to lunch.' She wagged her finger!" Thomas roared with laughter as he recalled the scene. "So then I said, 'Yes, ma'am!' So then I started going to lunch."[62]

O'Connor had always believed that breaking bread was a way to make peace and foster understanding and unity. The traditional role of homemaker was, in O'Connor's hands, a gesture of hospitality and generosity. Anxious, high-achieving law students applying for a Supreme Court clerkship were sometimes startled—then soothed—when the justice not only offered them a cup of coffee, but poured it and served it to them, asking, "Sugar or cream?"[63]

Some years later, Thomas noted in a talk at the Bohemian Grove, duly recorded by fellow Bohemian John O'Connor, that it was harder to be mean when you've had a nice lunch together.[64]

Thomas, at first, may have been sullen around Ivy-educated law clerks, but he was warm and funny with the Court's support personnel, the security guards and elevator operators who appreciated his kindness. In time, his good nature showed through to his colleagues and their clerks (he even reconciled with Yale Law School). He also became a friend of John O'Connor's. "I had a long talk with Clarence Thomas," John wrote in June 1994. "Among other things, he said he will never forget how thoughtful and kind SOC had been to him but added, laughingly, 'Does she drive a hard bargain!' I chuckled and said, 'Oh, really? That isn't the way it is at home.' We both laughed then."[65]

SUPREME COURT JUSTICES, liberal or conservative, hired very few African American clerks in O'Connor's time. Only one of the first forty clerks hired by Justice Thomas was black. Sandra O'Connor selected her first African American clerk in the fall of 1991, two months after Thurgood Marshall retired.* James Forman, Jr., came from a remarkable family—his father, James Forman, Sr., had been head of the Student Nonviolent Coordinating Committee, or SNCC, at the peak

---

* When Thurgood Marshall retired, following Court custom, he had shared one of his clerks, Crystal Nix-Hines, with Justice O'Connor's chambers. An African American woman and graduate of Princeton and Harvard Law, Nix-Hines put Forman's résumé in Justice O'Connor's in-box.[66]

of the civil rights movement, and his mother, Constancia Romilly, was the daughter of the British journalist Jessica Mitford, one of the famous socialite Mitford sisters of the Bloomsbury set in interwar London.

But as he took the train from New Haven, where he was attending Yale Law School, to Washington for his clerkship interview in the fall of 1991, Forman was just another overaccomplished law review editor trying to figure out how to impress the justice. Would he remember a blur of cases? Would he flatter too much? Not enough? Would he be required or tempted to somehow sacrifice his dignity? His almost comically stream-of-consciousness account of the interview is revealing about a meritocrat's rite of passage to the tippy-top of the ziggurat. More subtly, it suggests what O'Connor was really looking for:

> I was warned that she might ask who my favorite Justice was. Thurgood Marshall was without question my favorite Justice. He embodied the civil rights movement. Should I say "Marshall" or was that too obvious? Should I be more interesting? I thought about Marshall on the way to the Court. I was scared. I was surprised to see the elevator operators [the only other African Americans he saw]. My head was full of cases—I had been warned to study her opinions—so I was thrown off when she started, because she just wanted to talk about her family. She wanted to talk about her three boys. Did birth order correspond to personality? I was surprised—relieved—but worried still. Where were the legal questions? She talked about the job of clerking, how hard it was, how she expected her clerks to work hard. She asked, "Are you a hard worker?" "Yes!" I said.

Pausing to take a breath, Forman plunged ahead:

> But maybe she wanted more! Of course I'd say yes. . . .
> She never asked who my favorite Justice was. She did say, "Now James, I see from your résumé that you've been involved in a lot of civil rights causes and social justice issues in college and law school." She looked at me. "I imagine there are some of my opinions that you disagree with." This was a hard question.

Clearly, the answer was yes. She had written the *Croson* case
[striking down racial set-asides in Richmond]. To me, both her
outcome and reasoning were troubling. I didn't know what to
say. But I thought of my dad. . . .

Forman's father, veteran of so many trials, literal and figurative,
during his movement days, had advised his son, "Just tell the truth."
Forman sensed he was near his own moment of truth:

I said, "Yes, there are decisions I disagreed with." I modified it
a bit—"Of course, I'm a law student and haven't studied the
record in the case"—but, "Yes." She nodded. That was the end
of the interview! She said, "I'd like to offer you a position in the
'93 Term."
I was not prepared for this. I'd never been offered a job that
way. It was unimaginable to me. I smiled. I smiled. "Yes! This is
the best news I've ever received. Yes!" We shook hands. I was
jumping for joy.

Recounting this story years later, Forman could barely contain his
joy and sense of wonder. Getting the O'Connor clerkship was like
"winning the legal lottery of life!" he exclaimed. "All of a sudden, you
have an incredibly interesting job. It was life-changing. I understood
that." After the clerkship, O'Connor seemed slightly disappointed
when Forman took a job as a public defender representing indigents
instead of a more high-impact post with the Justice Department. She
need not have worried. Forman went on to found a successful charter
school in the District of Columbia, teach law at Yale, and, in 2017,
author a highly influential, Pulitzer Prize–winning book, *Locking Up
Our Own: Crime and Punishment in Black America*.[67]

HER MIND NEARLY gone from Alzheimer's, Ada Mae Day died in
1989. Alan Day had taken over the Lazy B, but the ranch was in a financial squeeze. The family blamed government overregulation; increased grazing fees threatened to put the ranch out of business.
Painfully, regretfully, the family decided to sell the ranch, piece by

piece.[68] By Thanksgiving 1992, only the parcel around Headquarters remained. At lunch that day at the ranch, Sandra was in a blue mood, Alan Day noticed, though not just over the loss of the Lazy B. The abortion issue, she told her brother, "is making me grit my teeth. It is wearing me down."[69]

O'Connor was deft at changing the subject when abortion came up in social conversation, as it sometimes did among unthinking guests sitting at O'Connor's table as she made the Washington social circuit. "Sandra, so when does life begin?" asked one overly curious dinner partner. "When the kids are out of college and the dog dies," answered Justice O'Connor, with a forced smile. But with Ross Dalrymple, the wife of Australian ambassador Rawdon Dalrymple—friends of the O'Connors trusted for their discretion—she was unusually open. "She took me aside and said, 'What do you think about this [Roe v. Wade]?'" recalled Mrs. Dalrymple. "I said a woman has every right to choose and it's no one else's business. She was very intent, listening and waiting."[70]

The issue would not go away. In the winter of 1992, at the annual right-to-life protest march on the anniversary of Roe v. Wade, a hundred thousand people showed up. With the replacement of the liberal Thurgood Marshall by the conservative Clarence Thomas, it appeared likely that the Court would find five votes to overturn Roe. The state of Pennsylvania had enacted the most restrictive law yet: Women wanting an abortion had to wait twenty-four hours after contacting a clinic to get one; they had to undergo a mandatory lecture on fetal development; and if a woman was married, she had to notify her husband.

Planned Parenthood of Southeastern Pennsylvania v. Casey was argued on April 22, 1992.[71] Justice O'Connor awoke at 4:15 A.M. in "real pain," recorded John. "She began shaking like a leaf and continued to shake for 5 to 10 minutes." She was up by six and on her way to the Supreme Court.[72] The immediate cause of her pain was a back injury sustained during her aerobics class, but she may have also been feeling the accumulated stress of too many years in the eye of the abortion storm. At the time of the Webster case, two leading feminist lawyers, Susan Estrich and Kathleen Sullivan, had authored a widely read, passionate defense of Roe v. Wade entitled "Abortion Politics: Writing for an Audience of One." The one, as the legal and political world well understood, was Justice O'Connor.[73]

The lawyer arguing to strike down the Pennsylvania abortion restrictions, Kathryn Kolbert, representing Planned Parenthood, adopted a radical strategy. She wanted to force the court to either affirm *Roe* outright—or reverse it. With polls showing most people supporting a woman's right to choose, Kolbert was playing politics. Assuming that the Court reversed *Roe*, the pro-choice movement planned to make abortion a central issue of the 1992 presidential election to boost the chances of electing a Democrat who would appoint liberal justices.

Justice O'Connor was irked by Kolbert's all-or-nothing argument. Asking the first question, her flat voice radiating thinly disguised annoyance, O'Connor stated, "Ms. Kolbert, you're arguing the case as though all we have before us is whether to apply stare decisis and preserve Roe against Wade in all its aspects. Nevertheless, we granted certiorari on some specific questions in this case. Do you plan to address any of those in your argument?"[74]

At the conference, Chief Justice Rehnquist counted five votes to reverse *Roe* and assigned himself the Court's opinion. When he circulated a draft in late May, Harry Blackmun wrote in the margin, "Wow! Pretty extreme!" The author of *Roe v. Wade* despaired that he had lost his beloved landmark decision. Then, just a few days later, on May 29, he received a letter from Justice Kennedy. "Dear Harry," it began, "I need to see you as soon as you have a few free moments. I want to tell you about some developments in *Planned Parenthood v. Casey*, and at least part of what I say should come as welcome news."[75]

The "welcome news" was that three justices—Kennedy, Souter, and O'Connor—had been meeting secretly to save a woman's right to abortion. The Troika, as they became known, was cobbling together a joint opinion that, when added to the pro-abortion votes of Blackmun and John Stevens, would effectively negate Rehnquist's effort to gut *Roe v. Wade*.

It was not so surprising that Souter had joined forces with O'Connor. As a disciple of Justice John Marshall Harlan II, Souter revered precedent and took an expansive view of the right to privacy in the Constitution. He and O'Connor voted almost as one in the conference. Anthony Kennedy was the more remarkable member of the Troika.

In his first three years on the Court, Kennedy had voted so often with Scalia (about 85 percent of the time) that some of his own law clerks referred to him as "Nini," signifying "Little Nino."[76] Kennedy was a Roman Catholic and receptive to sweeping arguments and fixed rules. Scalia, his neighbor in suburban McLean, had courted him on walks around the leafy streets.[77] But Scalia's irrepressible need to lecture and needle—and write ad hominem dissents—had chafed at Kennedy. By 1992, he was on Scalia's side far less often—voting with him about 60 percent of the time.

Brad Berenson and Michael Dorf, two Kennedy clerks, observed their boss with O'Connor. She was not personally close or even particularly warm with Kennedy, they said. But, crucially, she did not patronize the Californian justice, who was gracious and gentlemanly but could seem a little insecure.[78]

Unlike O'Connor, whose legal writing style was almost willfully dull (a blandness she enforced on the clerks who drafted her opinions), Kennedy liked lofty flourishes. In *Casey,* he began the Troika's joint opinion, "Liberty finds no refuge in the jurisprudence of doubt." O'Connor did not quibble with Kennedy's flight of rhetoric. She understood that it took some courage for the Catholic Kennedy to countenance any compromise or middle way on abortion rights. Furthermore, to lay down ground rules actually *facilitating* the termination of pregnancies was sure to invite criticism of Kennedy, and not just from his neighbor Scalia. Souter and O'Connor had been able to persuade Kennedy to change his initial vote in conference, from overturning *Roe* to sustaining it. O'Connor and Souter were able to persuade Kennedy to take a personal risk by appealing to his basic sense of decency and fairness.

With Souter handling so-called stare decisis—the importance of following by now well-established precedent—O'Connor undertook the nuts-and-bolts part of the opinion. She did away with Blackmun's creaky trimester system and firmly implanted her "undue burden" test in abortion law, signaling the states that any restrictions on abortion would still have to pass judicial review protecting a woman's right to choose. She voted to uphold most of the Pennsylvania law but, significantly, struck down the requirement that wives formally notify their husbands before obtaining an abortion. Taken as a whole, the Court's opinion is a clear defense of a woman's liberty.[79]

O'Connor had seen many abusive husbands as a state judge and assistant attorney general. More broadly, her concern was with the health and safety—and autonomy—of women, while Blackmun's opinion in *Roe v. Wade* had focused on medical science and doctors. With *Casey*, the law on abortion was imprinted with O'Connor's pragmatism—written craftily, with as few fingerprints as possible, but coming from a woman's heart and experience.

CHAPTER TWELVE

CIVIC RELIGION

"There is a little bad girl in there."

A second female justice, Ruth Bader Ginsburg, finally joined the Court in October 1993. They were not close friends, but Ruth was always grateful that Sandra showed her, in ways large and small, how to navigate a world that had been all-male for almost two centuries.

S ANDRA DAY O'CONNOR was an athletic Arizona ranch girl. Ruth Bader Ginsburg was a tiny, almost birdlike creature raised in Brooklyn. At a judicial conference in Mumbai, India, in the early nineties, O'Connor was down in the lobby meeting and greeting early every morning, while Ginsburg ran about a half hour late and had trouble looking anyone in the eye. "We had a rather exhausting schedule," Ginsburg recalled. "Sandra moved very fast and would make the most gracious remarks to our hosts."[1]

When President Bill Clinton appointed Ginsburg to replace the retiring Byron White in 1993, making her the second female Supreme Court justice, O'Connor was grateful and relieved, and not just because the Court finally installed a women's bathroom in the robing room behind the bench. "I was so glad to have company," O'Connor said to ABC correspondent Jan Crawford Greenburg, who had become friendly with the justice. "Immediately, the media started treating us as fungible justices, not so much focused on a single woman. It made an immediate big difference."[2]

Ginsburg would become a pop-culture feminist icon, but when she first came to the Court, she was known as an incrementalist, more of an activist than O'Connor to be sure, but, like O'Connor, cautious and deliberate in her jurisprudence. The two women were not natural pals; their relationship was not cozy. Over their next twelve years together on the Supreme Court, O'Connor never visited Ginsburg's chambers to talk over a case, Justice Ginsburg recalled. Ginsburg did not attend O'Connor's morning aerobics class.

Then there was the matter of Ginsburg's driving. Sandra began driving tractors at the age of ten; Ginsburg did not learn to drive a car until she moved to Washington in middle age. They were assigned adjacent parking spaces in the Supreme Court garage. "Sandra was furious because Ruth would come in late and hit her car," recalled Patricia White, an O'Connor friend who was dean of Arizona State University College of Law. "Multiple times. Sandra bribed the parking attendants to take Ruth's car and park it." Romeo Cruz, O'Connor's chambers "messenger" and occasional driver, recalled, "In the Court parking lot, she was rear-ended twice by Justice Ginsburg." Asked by the author if she had hit Justice O'Connor's car, Justice Ginsburg threw up her hands and responded, "Oh, dear!" She explained, "My parking space was between Sandra's and Scalia's. I was so anxious not to scrape Scalia's car that I scraped hers. I came upstairs and told her I had done something bad. She said, 'Oh, Ruth, you never do anything bad.' But when I told her, she said, 'I just got the car out of the body shop yesterday.'" (Romeo Cruz had been in a minor accident while driving Justice O'Connor.)[3]

Fender benders aside, when it really mattered, the two women helped each other. When Ginsburg was diagnosed with cancer in 1999, O'Connor was able to guide her through a maze of conflicting medical opinions and oversolicitous well-wishers. Ginsburg followed O'Connor's advice to have chemo on Fridays, so she could be done with her nausea in time for oral argument on Monday.[4]

The two women were bonded by their trials as women pioneers. In the 1950s, Ginsburg had been one of nine women in a class of five hundred at Harvard Law School. Her nickname bestowed by the guys was "Bitch." ("Better 'Bitch' than 'Mouse,'" said Ginsburg.) Both women had been rejected by male law firms and battled for women's rights, though in different ways.[5] At the Court, they got more death threats than the other justices. (For security reasons, O'Connor did not vote and never used her home address. She refused to see the movie *The Pelican Brief* because it involved the assassination of two Supreme Court justices.)[6]

After one of her first conferences, Ginsburg turned to O'Connor when Chief Justice Rehnquist assigned her a difficult first opinion. "The legend is that the new Justice gets an easy first opinion," Ginsburg recalled. "And instead our old Chief [as she referred to Rehnquist] assigned me an ERISA opinion [involving highly technical and knotty questions about insurance law]. I went to Sandra and said, 'Sandra, he wasn't supposed to do this.'"

Justice O'Connor said, "Ruth, now you just do it! Just do it! And get your opinion in circulation before he makes the next set of assignments, so you can get another." Ginsburg recalled, "That's the way she was about everything. Like it or not, just do it." By the next year, O'Connor and Ginsburg were competing to be the first justice to circulate an opinion.

Ginsburg suspected that Rehnquist had punished her, she later recalled, "because he thought I talked too much. He thought a new Justice should be tamer."[7] While the older justices had grown quieter on the bench during oral argument, both Ginsburg and Scalia peppered advocates with questions. O'Connor was hardly shy about asking questions, but she, too, felt that the junior justices were monopolizing the time at oral argument. In November 1993, the O'Connors gave a formal dinner at the Court to welcome the Ginsburgs (and John jokingly invited Ruth's husband, Marty, to become a fellow member of "the Denis Thatcher Society"). In her toast, Sandra said the Court was considering a gag rule: Each justice would have only three minutes to speak at each half-hour oral argument in order to assure that the lawyers would have at least three minutes left over to make their cases. "While this concept was superficially a joke," John O'Connor wrote in his diary, "SOC made it serve a purpose: to get the Justices, especially Nino and Ruth, to restrain themselves when asking questions. SOC said it's really become a serious problem. When SOC finished this point, Ruth said (in a laughing way) that a reporter had told her Nino asked one more question than she had."[8]

In Court, O'Connor and Ginsburg put on a sister act. Nervous lawyers occasionally confused their names, even though they looked nothing alike. The National Association of Women Judges presented them with T-shirts reading I'M SANDRA, NOT RUTH and I'M RUTH, NOT SANDRA.[9] On the path of women's rights, O'Connor did not always have Ginsburg's activist agenda, but she knew when to get out of the way.[10] In 1996, the Court agreed to hear a sex discrimination challenge to the all-male Virginia Military Institute. At the conference, six justices voted for the admission of women. The chief justice initially voted no, leaving it to the senior justice, John Paul Stevens, to assign the majority opinion. He chose Sandra Day O'Connor. Generously, shrewdly, O'Connor demurred, saying, "This should be Ruth's

opinion." She knew Ginsburg would be honored to cap her long career in the field of women's rights by opening up a last male bastion
while advancing the law on sex discrimination. "Of course, I loved her
for that," recalled Justice Ginsburg. When Justice Ginsburg announced the result in *United States v. Virginia* on June 26, 1996, ruling
that government agencies must have an "exceedingly persuasive justification" for discrimination based on gender—and citing O'Connor's
precedent in *Mississippi University for Women v. Hogan*—the two women
justices exchanged a knowing smile.[11]

JUSTICE O'CONNOR TRAVELED so much and spoke at so many
events that the secretaries in Justice Ginsburg's chambers joked that
there must be two Justice O'Connors, the real one and a stand-in
double to give speeches. In October 1997, O'Connor achieved her
goal of speaking in every state in the Union (the last was West Virginia). Her clerks struggled to write speeches that were supposed to
be inspiring and entertaining—but not quotable or revealing. "We became experts at writing boring speeches," said Stuart Banner, a clerk
in OT '91 (who also drafted O'Connor's just-the-facts portion of the
Casey opinion).

By the 1990s, O'Connor was traveling all over the world when she
was not hearing cases—to Asia and India, to Argentina, Africa, and
the Middle East, Australia and New Zealand, and particularly, beginning in the early 1990s, to Eastern Europe. Her capacity to race across
time zones was jaw dropping. She did like to retreat to old haunts,
spending a week or two every year at Iron Springs, her somewhat
ramshackle mountain resort north of Phoenix, where she could sit on
the porch and smell the pines or look at the stars (in between reading
briefs). But she could also interrupt a trip to a legal conference in
London to fly to Tokyo and back—eighteen hours in the air, each way,
over one weekend—to address a women's conference. "It is <u>not</u> a
pleasing prospect," she wrote in her journal, "but I cannot disappoint
the Japanese women who are counting on me and who are trying to
attain better opportunities in the work force."[12]

The woman who had pored over stacks of *National Geographics* as a
girl was drawn to exotic and far-off places by her love of nature. She

had always found time to leave her desk for the wilderness, taking her city-slicker young husband on horse-packing trips into the Sierra, introducing her sons to spelunking in Indian caves, fishing and bird watching wherever she went. She was intensely curious, relentlessly quizzing her guides, but she was not notably patient about either catching fish or watching birds. She liked to snag a mountain stream trout or spot a rainbow lorikeet, but she did not like to wait too long to do either. No destination was too distant. She had hiked across New Zealand and gone to see gorillas in Rwanda in 1992, stopping en route to speak to Rwandan judges about the rule of law.[13]

When, in 1994, those same Rwandan judges were massacred in a horrific genocide, she was reminded about the fragility of legal institutions in a world given to mayhem and power exercised at the end of a gun. She was particularly concerned about building a sturdy judicial system in countries emerging from years of misrule and authoritarian governments. During the 1990s, she beat a regular path to Poland and Hungary, Romania and Bulgaria, the Czech Republic and Slovakia, with excursions to the warring republics of the former Yugoslavia.

With the fall of the Berlin Wall in 1989 and the collapse of Communist rule in the old Iron Curtain countries, a great need had arisen for lawyers and judges to help spread the rule of law. While the former Eastern Bloc countries were drafting Western-style constitutions, they were a long way from building independent legal systems that would guarantee equality and individual rights. "There was no experience, no history, and the judges were not independent. They reported to the party and the government," said Mark Ellis, the director of the Central and Eastern European Law Institute, better known as CEELI. Judges practiced "telephone justice"—they would pick up the telephone and ask their political bosses how to decide.

As it happened, one of John O'Connor's former law partners at Miller & Chevalier, Homer Moyer, was the head of the American Bar Association's International Division. The ABA recruited an astonishing five thousand American lawyers to go abroad and spend months of their time working pro bono publico, free for the common good, drafting laws and training judges. ("Lawyers are bored. We were dying to go," said one of them, Mary Noel Pepys, a land use lawyer from Kansas who went to Bulgaria and slept in her coat in the winter.)

Moyer, who had become friendly with Justice O'Connor, recruited her to serve on the board of CEELI.

O'Connor instantly became America's ambassador for the Rule of Law. "She knew how to use her celebrity," said Moyer. "She'd say, 'This is really important,' and look them in the eye." CEELI director Ellis traveled all over Eastern Europe with O'Connor for week-long stretches during the summer months for more than a decade. "When she walked in the room, wow! She got attention," said Ellis. "It was as if you were bringing the U.S. Constitution alive. If she wanted to point a finger, she had enormous power. She might even be a little rude. If she decided it was time to go, it was time to go. She was aware, she knew what her position meant. It became natural to her; this was how people responded. No one ever tested her, no one ever second-guessed. Ever." Pepys, the Kansas land use lawyer in Bulgaria, recalled eating lunch with Justice O'Connor and some judges in Sofia. "Halfway through lunch, she said, 'Isn't it time to go now?' We all jumped up. It was like an E. F. Hutton ad. We took it as a command."[14*]

O'Connor was impressive partly because she was heartfelt. "It wasn't intellectual. It wasn't reading a book. She loved that lawyers were giving back," said Pepys. At a reception in Sofia in 1994, an older gentleman, a professor at the university, walked up to her and pulled out a badly frayed copy of the U.S. Constitution and said he had been reading it for forty years. O'Connor, who always carried a copy of the Constitution in her pocketbook, choked up. "It will serve you well," she told the man, "and guide you as it has us."[17]

O'Connor was not an American exceptionalist, not a Western triumphalist, her fond memories of Western Civ at Stanford notwith-

---

* It is hard to gauge Justice O'Connor's and the other recruits' long-term effectiveness; they were battling deeply entrenched forces resisting and undermining the rule of law. John's diary from a dinner with an Argentine supreme court justice in November 1993 gives a hint of what she was up against in just one country: "Unfortunately, since we were in Argentina, there has been public bickering and accusations between the Peronistas, which constitute a majority of the Court, and the radicals. The 'radical' justices had never met with SOC and Tony Kennedy, which, I believe, is a terrible breach of courtesy."[15] As for CEELI, she wrote a friend in 2002, "The result of our efforts there have been mixed, I would say."[16]

standing. She admired Ronald Reagan but had watched his "Morning in America" campaign ads in 1984 with a "raised eyebrow," she told one clerk. She was too unsentimental for that. What moved her was a powerful sense of civic duty. If O'Connor had an overarching faith, a kind of secular religion beyond her belief in God, it was the duty to serve one's community. She was a relentless apostle for service. She would try to steer her brainy clerks away from comfortable academic careers into hands-on jobs like working in the U.S. Attorney's office prosecuting cases. "Do something! Help someone!" was her command to go forth. In the 1990s, she became a global civic activist. Asked to speak about the "New Millennium" as the 1990s ended, she said that just as the work of the twentieth century had been about removing barriers facing women and minorities in the United States, the work of the twenty-first century would be to break down some of the barriers that divided the United States from the rest of the world. When it came to community, the pragmatist was an idealist.[18]

Traveling with her girlfriends, the justice could be exuberantly unsubtle. Carol Biagiotti was one of a dozen or so women friends who joined O'Connor every summer in late July when John was off with the fellows at the Bohemian Grove. The women called themselves the MPU—Mobile Party Unit—a name adopted after dancing with some enthusiastic cowboys at a honky-tonk in Idaho in 1991. Biagiotti recalled taking O'Connor to a small working-class bar in Florence, Italy. "This is a communist bar," Biagiotti said as they walked in. *"This is a communist bar!"* exclaimed O'Connor, and the patrons all turned to look at her. On a trip to Washington, Biagiotti arrived at the O'Connors' house on Oxford Street in Chevy Chase as Justice O'Connor was conferring with a group of Argentinian judges. O'Connor interrupted the conversation to ask Biagiotti what was wrong with her living room furniture arrangement. Pretty soon, the Argentinian judges were pushing around couches and chairs as O'Connor gave commands, changed her mind, and gave some more commands.[19]

At home as well as abroad, O'Connor's willfulness could become amusingly over-the-top. In the midnineties, during the annual mass protests on the anniversary of *Roe v. Wade*, the justice decided she wanted to go shopping. "There was a huge crowd as we came back," recalled her driver, Romeo Cruz. "We couldn't get through. She got out of the car. She stopped traffic so I could get through. I couldn't believe it. The justice is doing traffic?"[20] It was not the only time the justice played traffic cop. During the holiday season in Bethesda, when cars and pedestrians started mixing dangerously at the intersection by the Barnes & Noble bookstore and the Landmark Movie Theater, Justice O'Connor walked into the middle of the street and began giving orders to the astonished motorists.

IT IS EASY and fun to depict O'Connor as Miss Bossy Bull-in-the-China-Shop through such anecdotes. She once even told a clerk how many children to have. But as Sandra O'Connor, who turned sixty in 1990, entered midstream in her long career as a Supreme Court justice, she was a far more subtle being, capable of clever indirection as well as frontal assaults. She was no martinet; indeed, she loosened up over time. "She was very straitlaced when she came to Washington, very careful," said her friend Ann Hoopes. "But she became more open, more at ease. She would argue at dinner parties."[21] Still, she was always determined to be in control. She knew when to let down her guard but also when to defend her ground, fiercely when necessary, usually with a sort of stoical grace.

Though O'Connor had told a friend that getting appointed to the Supreme Court was "like getting struck by lightning," her rise was hardly accidental: She rose by a combination of shrewd political skills, well-defended probity, and subtle human intuition. She could be mindful and quietly deft dealing with people. "She had real fingertips," said John Macomber, who came to Washington in 1989 to run the Ex-Im Bank for President George H. W. Bush and often socialized with the O'Connors. "She could instinctively get a feel for what made people tick and what they were sensitive about." Macomber recalled watching O'Connor hosting an amateur "entertainment" at which it was apparent that one of the entertainers was starting to lose her voice. "She let the person sing long enough but not too long," recalled Macomber.

In a world still dominated by males, Sandra "preferred men, she treated men differently," said Macomber. But, in Washington as in Phoenix, she managed to do so without offending their wives. "She was sort of a flirt. She used her feminine wiles. Like body language. She'd look at you with her head cocked. Blink, blink, blink, and say, 'Now John, do you really think that?' I'd say, 'Yes, I do,' and she'd say, 'Let's think at this . . .' and put her hand on your arm and tease you a little."[22]

At the same time, O'Connor could be an attentive and loyal girl-friend, When Judy Hope was divorced from Tony Hope (son of co-median Bob) in 1991, O'Connor "didn't say she was sorry for me, but every week for the next six months she called me and said, 'Let's go to the movies.' Never, 'Your heart must be broken.' It was, 'We're not going to cry. We're going to do something.'" O'Connor also said to Hope, "Thank God John is not afraid of smart women."[23]

O'Connor was sometimes depicted as a country club matron, and her politics as old-fashioned country club Republicanism. She did, in fact, live across the street from the Chevy Chase Club, and she used it constantly, playing golf and tennis during the day, dining and dancing by night. Many of her friends were members of the club, as well as other posh clubs. But she was hardly a WASP social snob like some Washington "cave dwellers"; she was comfortable with all kinds of people and sought a variety of experience. She liked party games. At one all-girls dinner in Phoenix, the hostess asked: "If you could have a tattoo anywhere, what would it say and where would you put it?" "That's easy," she answered, "the Lazy B on my left hip."

A few of her Chevy Chase Club friends were sniffy when she went to an all-night sleepover at a fancy downtown hotel with some women they regarded as social climbers (while the women had a champagne brunch in the morning, O'Connor left to work in a soup kitchen, as she often did on Sunday mornings).[24] Her host at the sleepover was Adrienne Arsht, the widow of Myer Feldman, who had been White House counsel in the Kennedy administration. Arsht inherited a bank in Miami, which she ran herself, and moved in wider circles than O'Connor's Chevy Chase crowd. "I was different from her women friends," said Arsht. "She wanted new experiences and I could give them to her."

Arsht took O'Connor on trips to New York, backstage at the American Ballet Theatre and to lunch with Jacqueline Kennedy Onassis. "She was very curious, she wanted to look, to see. I think I

introduced her to her first openly gay woman." Raquel Matas, assistant dean at the University of Miami Law School, recalled that
O'Connor was "polite" but not very curious. (In all likelihood,
O'Connor had interacted with a number of openly gay women by
then.) O'Connor's curiosity was not limitless. "She heard about the
Broadway play *The Book of Mormon* and told me she wanted to see it,"
said Arsht. "She said, 'I'm probably the only one who's read the Book
of Mormon.' I told her one of the songs in the show was '[Expletive]
God.' She said, 'Oh, I don't want to see that.' "[25]

Arsht took O'Connor to buy a new judicial robe at Josie Natori, a
clothing designer in New York. (O'Connor had been wearing a small
man's robe bought for under $50.) When O'Connor fretted that her
black robe made her look too austere, Arsht gave the justice her own
mother's white lace jabot, or neck scarf, of the type worn by *avocats* in
France. (Arsht's mother, Roxana Cannon Arsht, had been the first
woman judge in Delaware; over time, O'Connor collected several
more white ascots.) "I tried to dress her up," said Arsht, but O'Connor
liked to shop at Chico's, which sold moderately priced dresses and out-
fits that didn't wrinkle and were easy to pack. O'Connor wasn't as
fashion-conscious as her mother, who would wear dress shoes on the
ranch even when she was hunting for arrowheads. Still, with her many
public appearances and regular partygoing, O'Connor wanted to wear
nice clothes, as long as she didn't have to spend too much for them. She
had a good eye as a shopper, recalled her friend Carole Biagiotti, but
she was "totally uninterested or unaware of important brand names."
She liked turquoise Indian jewelry and her color choice often recalled
Arizona sunsets.[26] According to John's diary, she bought a few heavily
discounted designer dresses in New York, once paying $700 for a dress
that cost more than $2,000 at full retail.[27] In her office closet, she kept
a hair dryer, she told Barbara Renfrew, "so I can look like a girl."[28] John
noted in his diary that she would from time to time skip church on
Sunday mornings to get her blond highlights touched up.

She wanted to set an example for her clerks, who closely studied
her. "She was classy but not overly formal," recalled Silvija Strikis (OT
'97). "She wore earrings—button style, black with a gold trim—and
flats, not heels, and fashionable business suits and dresses. Her jackets
were soft and tailored, and she often wore a colorful blouse and a

flowered bow. She didn't wear too much black and she was not afraid of pink." O'Connor's waistline had grown by the midnineties, but she lifted weights to strengthen and tone her muscles (and compensate for a skiing injury to her shoulder). "I'm in the best shape of my life," she told Strikis.[29]

O'Connor cared about preserving her good looks. She had cosmetic surgery to "nip and tuck" the skin around her eyes, and she told her friend Lynda Webster, "You should use Botox. I do." When O'Connor was eighty-five years old, Sarah Suggs, the head of the O'Connor Institute in Phoenix, complimented her on her eyeliner. "When I look people in the eye, I want my eyes to have definition," said O'Connor.[30]

IN HER CHAMBERS, the clerks made light of O'Connor's stern and demanding demeanor. Accustomed to glowing encomiums from their parents and teachers, the clerks had to adjust to a boss who grew up on a ranch where the extent of the patriarch's praise was a desultory "That'll be all right, then." In the late eighties, the clerks taped on the wall a photocopy of Justice O'Connor's hand with a message printed below: "If you want a pat on the back, lean here."

But O'Connor was in on the joke. She played along and let the clerks photocopy her hand. After Kevin Kelly, a clerk in the 1990 October Term, wrote a good draft of an opinion, O'Connor appeared in the clerks' room and said, "Kevin, get up." She marched him over and backed him up against the picture of her hand.[31]

The clerk rumor mill declared that O'Connor had been "mellowed" and "softened" by her bout with cancer. It was true that she was, marginally at least, more solicitous of the clerks' workload. When Silvija Strikis (OT '97) had to pull an all-nighter to monitor a death penalty case, O'Connor showed her the pillow and blanket she kept in her office and offered her couch as a bed. But the work still had to be done. Assigned O'Connor's first opinion of the year, Viet Dinh (OT '94) tried to explain that he was scheduled to have his wisdom teeth taken out. "Is this elective surgery?" the justice asked. She continued to play mother hen. Woe to the clerk who forgot to get his or her flu shot and came down with the flu. One clerk was more or less ordered to stop chewing gum. (The clerk offered her a stick, and she responded, "No. What a disgusting habit.") When Brian Hoffstadt (OT '96) picked a single grape from the bunch, she corrected him to snap off a whole stem. Matt Stowe (OT '97) was so worried about his manners that he bought a book on etiquette by Letitia Baldrige, social secretary in the Kennedy White House. Spotting the book on his desk, O'Connor said, "Oh, Tish, she's great."

She remained the champion of marriage and family and an indefatigable, if only occasionally successful, matchmaker. Still, O'Connor was willing to bend with the times. When one of her former clerks, Julie O'Sullivan, had a child, O'Connor came into the clerks' office and said, "She's not married, but it's an option these days." Silvija Strikis noticed that O'Connor was looking at her with "her eagle eye. I was in my thirties and I had been divorced," said Strikis. "She was saying you can be divorced and still have a family."[32]

The clerks understood that they were undergoing more than legal training in her chambers. "She was actually modeling a balanced life," said Lisa Kern Griffin (OT '97). "Make time for your family. Take care of yourself. Experience the outdoors and get some exercise. Have a sense of the wider culture. Enjoy lively dinner parties and a varied circle of friends. Never be above taking care of people. It was really unusual. We were getting not just an apprenticeship in law but an apprenticeship in life." O'Connor's message of "you can do it all" was the subject of some uneasy conversations among the justice's female clerks. "She was so energetic and extraordinary," said Griffin, "that we would think, well, that works for *you*."

When clerks were in the company of O'Connor, they had her absolute attention. Several noted that when O'Connor was concentrating on one thing, which was often, her body would grow unnaturally still. She would not gesture or stir or fidget. Her eyes would fix and lock on. O'Connor, Griffin observed, was "mindful before there was a word for it. She was completely in the moment with you. We all think we were her favorite clerk. It seems impossible that she was invested in every single one of us."[33]

The clerks may have missed O'Connor's well-hidden vulnerability. As a clerk in 1985, Julie O'Sullivan felt she had not won O'Connor's confidence, but the two women had become close as O'Sullivan went into the world to work at a high-powered law firm, then teach at Georgetown Law—and, along the way, become a single mother. In the midnineties, O'Sullivan could tell that O'Connor was hurt by the sparse attendance at a clerks' reunion, and so she invited a group of former clerks to her own house for a more informal gathering with the justice. "You're the only clerk who ever invited me to her house for a party," O'Connor told her. O'Sullivan was fascinated by the earthy woman behind the carefully crafted persona. "There is a little bad girl in there," O'Sullivan said. "I've seen her salsa and have an extra glass of wine or two. She can be funny and a little naughty. There's something under there."[34]

IN HER EARLY years on the Court, O'Connor had been wary of the clerks' network, the web of relationships among the justices' law clerks, many of whom had served together on the law reviews at Yale or Harvard or Stanford. The chatter and shared notes between clerks of different chambers sometimes worked in crafting majority opinions and sometimes stirred mischief, depending on the skills, ideologies, and egos of the clerks involved. O'Connor warned her clerks against exaggerating their roles and communicating with other chambers without her approval.

But as she grew in confidence, and as she secured a pivotal role in the middle of the Court's lineup, O'Connor became more comfortable plugging into the clerks' network. As she forthrightly explained to the author in 2017, "I wanted to know what was going on."[35] "Clerks are very self-important," said Vaughn Dunnigan (OT '92). "We like to think our lobbying and kvetching are important. In fact, it's the information we supply our bosses that matters. Justice O'Connor wanted to know, what if we do this? What if we do that? She was subtle about it. We were never directed to be spies."

Kate Adams (OT '93) agreed. "She would never say go find what people are doing. But where it was close and contentious, we clerks would go to other chambers thinking it would be good to see where they were. We sensed our job was to get from A to Z, and that might mean saying some things to get there. Brennan would tell his clerks, 'Go find out!' Justice O'Connor handled it subtly."

Like Brennan—and unlike a loner like Stevens or an absolutist like Scalia—O'Connor wanted to cobble together majorities however she could. She was less expedient than Brennan, more likely to go her own way and write separately to narrow or limit the Court's holding, but if she could patch together five votes on an issue she cared about, she was willing to compromise. "She was one sharp cookie when it came to thinking about the dynamics of the players on the Court," said Adams. She knew which justices could be coaxed (Justice Kennedy) and which ones were not worth trying (Justice Thomas).

When O'Connor and her clerks were done with cobbling together an opinion designed to "hold a Court"—win the necessary five votes to make a majority—the final result could look like patchwork, not elegant but serviceable. She excised clever turns of phrase from clerks, especially if they were aimed at the work of another justice. "A little snippy, aren't we?" she said to Viet Dinh, as she deployed her red pencil. O'Connor was "not worried about being quoted in *The New York Times*," said Griffin. "She would say she could tell how the *Times* felt about her opinions by the picture they ran—frowning and dour versus smiling and attractive."

To some clerks, she was inscrutable. Mark Perry (OT '93) recalled watching her at oral argument. After jumping in with the first or second question, "she would sit back and listen. She would adopt a calm, relaxed smile and just absorb," he observed. "She would be still. She would get to a position of rest and stay there. No jiggling around. She would not move for a long time."[36]

O'CONNOR DISLIKED LAWYER advertising. She believed that bar associations should devote themselves to preserving civility in the profession. "Ambulance chasing"—the practice of lawyers seeking out victims in order to represent them in lawsuits, usually for hefty contingency fees (typically a third of the award or settlement)—"disgusted her," said Elizabeth Earle Beske (OT '94). In Florida, the bar association enacted a rule that lawyers had to wait thirty days after an accident before sending direct mail solicitations to potential clients. Some plaintiffs' lawyers sued, claiming a violation of their right to free speech.

When the case was argued at the Court on January 11, 1995, Justice O'Connor peppered the attorney representing the plaintiffs' lawyers with pointed questions. The attorney struggled to answer, addressing her inadvertently as "Justice Connor." "O'Connor," she corrected him, in the voice she reserved for people who were "unattractive." At conference, O'Connor was in the minority, on the side of the bar association. Justice Kennedy was assigned the majority opinion. O'Connor circulated a dissent that persuaded the Court's newest justice, Stephen Breyer, to switch his vote. "She got his vote by focusing on the practical," recalled one of her clerks. "She basically argued, 'You know these guys [the plaintiffs' lawyers' firm, Went For It, Inc.] are scumballs [the clerk's word; O'Connor would have used a more refined term] and it [the rule barring client solicitation] is only for thirty days.'" O'Connor's dissent became the majority opinion. When she returned to her chambers after winning Breyer's vote, she came into the clerks' room and embraced Elizabeth Earle Beske, who had drafted her opinion. "She literally picked me up and swung me around," recalled Beske.[37]

STEPHEN BREYER HAD replaced the retiring Harry Blackmun, O'Connor's aged nemesis, earlier that year. "SOC thinks Steve is brilliant and the perfect choice," John wrote in his diary.[38] Breyer soon became O'Connor's best friend on the Court since Lewis Powell. Educated at Stanford and Oxford, married to the daughter of a British viscount, Breyer was said to resemble an absentminded professor or, physically, the nefarious Mr. Burns from the animated satire *The Simpsons,* but he was approachable, happy to debate another justice's clerk over a slice of pizza.[39] "Steve is intelligent, pleasant, and witty but one would never characterize him as a 'regular guy' like Nino and Tony," wrote John. "Joanna [Breyer's wife] is smart, somewhat elfin, very different and far from a 'good old girl.'"[40*]

---

* The justices' spouses generally deferred on the relatively rare social occasions when the justices spoke up about substantive issues, though not always. During a bridge game with Sandra O'Connor and Cynthia Helms, when her husband

O'Connor and Breyer shared a deep civic-mindedness. Breyer's center of gravity was more to the left. A product of San Francisco's best public school, Lowell High, and a former staff director of the Senate Judiciary Committee for Senator Edward Kennedy, he had more faith than O'Connor in the efficacy of government.[42] "He liked the Conseil d'État, the highly professional French bureaucracy," said Kate Adams, an O'Connor clerk who had clerked for Breyer when he was on the U.S. Court of Appeals. "He believed you should let the machinery work correctly." But Breyer was far from dogmatic in his beliefs, and he was always eager to debate them in a spirited but friendly way.[43]

He began showing up in O'Connor's chambers. "I like to talk, and she liked to talk," Breyer recalled of their unusual (for Supreme Court justices) togetherness.[44] O'Connor poked the gentlest fun at Breyer's propensity for long-winded, convoluted questions on the bench, but she welcomed his counsel. The fact that Breyer was self-consciously an intellectual did not faze her; indeed, although she sometimes scoffed at theorizers, she was curious about ideas of all kinds and fully capable of deep intellectual exploration and exegesis on complex subjects ranging from spirituality and religion to tax law.[45]

O'Connor made it her business to get along with every justice, but Scalia was beginning to test her forbearance. When O'Connor took the side of the federal government to protect habitats for endangered species, Scalia was withering. Should the Court worry about hurting the feelings of slugs by draining the ponds in which they "frolic"? Scalia sneered.[46] "Oh, Nino," O'Connor sighed when she read his dissent.[47] In conference, Scalia suffered from smartest-kid-in-the-class syndrome, and in private he could be rude. "He just hung up on me," a startled O'Connor told one of her clerks, who was sitting across from her at her desk.

Justice Ginsburg observed Scalia's baiting manner with some alarm. Ginsburg was personally close to Scalia—they shared a love of opera and often dined together with their spouses. "I told him he was losing

was waxing expansive on the subject of race, Joanna interjected, "You know absolutely nothing about race."[41]

friends and not influencing people by turning off his colleagues," Ginsburg recalled. "It didn't make any difference." O'Connor "did not say anything to me" about Scalia, Ginsburg recalled. "On the surface, she ignored him. She certainly did not try to answer him in kind."[48]

O'Connor's feelings emerged on a court away from the Court. Every Sunday, Bill Leahy, a neurologist, played tennis with Scalia. John O'Connor invited them to play doubles—Scalia and Leahy against the two O'Connors. "It was one of the most uncomfortable hours I've ever spent," recalled Dr. Leahy. "The justices were two people who did not like each other. He'd get the ball and ram it down her throat and she did the same to him. It was tense from the get-go. She was the better player. When it was over, he said, 'We're not playing doubles anymore.'"

The relationship between Scalia and O'Connor "got less warm, but it was always courteous," insisted Maureen Scalia, the justice's widow. "If playing doubles was John's idea," she added, "he didn't read Nino too well."

Although Maureen Scalia was not a lawyer (she met Nino when she was an undergrad at Radcliffe College and he was a student at Harvard Law), she understood with lawyerlike acuity the profound philosophical divide between her husband and Sandra O'Connor. Aside from shared competitiveness, O'Connor and Scalia stood apart in ways that transcended mere temperament. Their differences went to the very nature of the role of a Supreme Court justice. Her husband believed that O'Connor, unlike Breyer and Ginsburg, was "not passionate about the law itself," said Maureen. Scalia viewed O'Connor as more concerned with practical, specific outcomes than shaping broad legal doctrines. A judge willing to fit or mold the law to arrive at an outcome is known as "results oriented," a pejorative term among legal purists. Maureen Scalia noted, "The worst thing you could say in the Scalia house was 'results oriented.'"[49]

Scalia and O'Connor took fundamentally different approaches to judging. Scalia believed in bright-line rules and fixed principles. O'Connor preferred to set more flexible standards to accommodate the facts and changed circumstances. Scalia's world was governed by absolute "thou shalt nots." O'Connor leaned more toward three-part tests: If this condition were met, or that circumstance arose, or this event happened, how would a "reasonable" person feel or act? Context and circumstances were important, sometimes decisive.

O'CONNOR WAS DETERMINED to maintain civility on the Court. She was able to help keep peace among the justices in part by insisting that they eat lunch together. "She would make you go to lunch," recalled Justice Thomas. "She was right! She was the glue! The reason this place was civil was Sandra Day O'Connor." When O'Connor had joined the Court in 1981, so few justices came to lunch that they used a smaller, more intimate room off their main dining room. But by the midnineties, after years of prodding by O'Connor, eight or all nine justices were coming to every lunch, and they moved back into their larger formal dining room to eat their sandwiches. "No Court business was discussed. We would talk about whether Shakespeare wrote all his plays, talk about movies—Scalia loved movies—or we'd tell stories. It was a ton of fun," said Thomas.

At the head of the table, with O'Connor usually by his side, sat Bill Rehnquist. Thomas, a warm, feeling man with a huge laugh, observed the interplay between O'Connor and the chief justice. "The Chief would have his apple at the end of lunch, and a glass of milk, and we'd tell jokes. He could make her laugh. She could lecture him. It was, 'I know you're Chief, but . . . When it came to her, he was the more equal among equals. They were friends first.

"He loved her, he respected her," said Thomas. "You have love, you have respect, you have affection up here. That part never gets written about," Thomas told the author in 2018.

Thomas felt a little guilty when O'Connor complained one day after lunch that intemperate language in some of the justices' dissenting opinions was hurting the Court's public standing. "I remember begging off and saying, 'I dissent a lot, too, and I'm sorry.' She looked at me, and she got that look of hers, and she said, 'But *you* are never mean.'" (She was apparently thinking of Thomas's acerbic partner on the right, Justice Scalia.)

In 1999, when Thomas and his wife, Ginni, went to Phoenix to buy a custom motor home (for summertime excursions around the country), they stayed with the O'Connors. "We all went over to the motor

home lot to look. She knew nothing about coaches, but it was an ad-
venture. She gave me a Lucille Ball movie, *The Long, Long Trailer* [a 1953
comedy about the trials of Lucy and Desi in their new motor home],"
said Thomas, still chortling.[50]

The human relations on the Court—warm bonds formed over
time—were essential. "The Court becomes a small family. It may be
dysfunctional in some ways, but it is a family nonetheless," said
Thomas. But the different approaches to the law were fundamental,
too, and there were some gaps in the murky realm where law met society that could not be bridged. So-called reverse discrimination was
one.

THE MID-1990S WERE by and large a prosperous, progressive era for
America. The advent of computers and the dawn of the Internet age
unleashed a rip-roaring tech sector that rippled into the rest of the
economy, improving productivity and raising many—but not all—
boats.

Beneath the boom times, old gaps remained. Deep wounds of racial division persisted. Affirmative action had given middle-class black
America a boost, opening avenues to advancement in the military, in
universities, in corporations and in many jobs, from policeman to
building contractor, throughout the ranks of state, local, and national
government. But an achievement gap persisted in the school test
scores of the races, and life in the inner city improved little, if at all.
The crack cocaine scourge of the 1980s abated, but prisons were filling with young black men, many of them serving long sentences for
minor drug offenses. Occasionally, racial tensions would erupt, and
they did so with deadly force in the Rodney King riots in Los Angeles
in 1992.

At the Supreme Court, the justices continued to struggle to find
tools that could be used to promote the advancement of African
Americans as well as other historically marginalized groups—without
running afoul of the guarantees of equality written into the U.S. Constitution. If the arguments appeared technical and narrow, it was because the Court was trying to find ways of finessing societal problems
that defied sweeping solutions and yes-or-no answers, as well as buy-

ing time to nudge other democratic institutions to wrestle with the issues.

On the question of race, the Supreme Court had struggled and stumbled after its ringing decision in *Brown v. Board of Education* in 1954. Yes, the schools had to be desegregated, but how, and how quickly? By busing schoolchildren long distances? By merging black urban school districts with white suburban ones? The Burger Court gave uncertain, tangled answers.[51] Affirmative action led the court into an even denser thicket. The justices came at the problem in different ways, none entirely satisfactory.

The long-standing battle between Scalia and O'Connor and their basic approaches to deciding cases arose when the Court faced, yet again, the nearly intractable problem of fairness in racial preferences. Just before he retired in 1990, in literally his last strike in favor of Warren Court liberalism, Justice Brennan had forged a one-vote majority to uphold federal set-asides—those government contracts "set aside" outside the normal competitive bidding process—for minority-owned companies seeking federal broadcast licenses. White-owned Metro Broadcasting Company had sued, claiming reverse discrimination after the FCC gave a license to Rainbow Broadcasting, whose ownership was 90 percent Hispanic. Congress's rationale for the minority set-asides—to encourage diversity on the airwaves—met the Supreme Court's approval, winning the votes of Brennan, Marshall, Stevens, Blackmun, and White and deciding in favor of affirmative action.

Five years later, with Brennan, Marshall, Blackmun, and White gone, Justice O'Connor led a 5-to-4 majority to reverse *Metro Broadcasting, Inc. v. Federal Communications Commission* and to put brakes on the use of racial preference in federal contracting. In *Adarand Constructors, Inc. v. Peña,* a guardrail construction company had challenged a Transportation Department program favoring firms that awarded subcontracts to minority-owned businesses. Once again in an affirmative action case, the issue was the standard of scrutiny used by the justices. O'Connor wrote that the federal courts should apply "strict scrutiny" to federal programs that discriminated on the basis of race, the same level of scrutiny she had set out in *Richmond v. Croson* for state and local affirmative action programs favoring minority contractors.

But—as in her earlier affirmative action and abortion cases—
O'Connor avoided a clear-cut answer. Strict scrutiny was not, as the
saying went, "fatal in fact." O'Connor's majority opinion preserved
the possibility that the federal government could design minority set-
asides that passed constitutional muster because they were (arguably)
"narrowly tailored" to redress past discrimination or encourage diversity in a time-limited way.

As a practical matter, O'Connor left the door not just ajar but
nearly wide open. Justice Scalia, naturally, was livid. The bright line
Scalia wanted was to say no, period, to racial preferences. To do otherwise, he wrote, was to "preserve for future mischief the way of
thinking that produced race slavery, race privilege, and race hatred."

The Clinton White House set up a committee to refashion set-
aside programs in light of the Court's ruling against racial preferences
in *Adarand*. Yet little changed in practice: The federal government routinely continued to award contracts that favored minority-owned
companies. Walter Dellinger, the White House counsel who ran the
post-*Adarand* committee, said that Justice O'Connor was no doubt
aware that after *Adarand,* affirmative action went on almost, if not just,
as before. O'Connor clearly had doubts about the fairness and efficacy
of affirmative action, but she apparently believed that the social experiment should go on so long as the political system and the business
community, by and large, wanted it to. "She was a pragmatist," said
Dellinger, approvingly.[52]

Race can provoke arguments with deep emotions but endless shadings. What did O'Connor really believe? The question arose once
again when she approached the age-old question of "gerrymandering," whether it is constitutionally permissible to manipulate the
boundaries of electoral districts to favor a class, party—or race. As a
state legislator, O'Connor had been "shocked" to see how far her colleagues would go to draw the lines to protect their own seats, recalled
her son Scott. Race added another complex dimension.[53] "On racial
gerrymandering, I never understood where she drew the line," said
Simon Steel, a clerk in the 1995 term. Steel worked with O'Connor
on a voting rights case, trying, and failing, to fashion an overriding
theory to decide when state legislators could use race to create congressional districts.

By using census data, it was possible to draw the lines of a congressional district to make virtually certain there were enough black voters to elect a black member, given that voting often followed racial patterns. Two years before, in *Shaw v. Reno,* O'Connor, writing for a 5–4 majority, ruled that North Carolina had gone too far by trying to guarantee that the 12th Congressional District would elect a black representative. The district was oddly shaped, snaking down Interstate 85, and it seemed to have offended O'Connor partly on aesthetic grounds. "It was unseemly. That was the word she used for it," said another clerk, Sean Gallagher. "Unseemly" was a cousin to "unattractive." It was less a rationale than a gut reaction, like Justice Potter Stewart's famous line about obscenity, "I know it when I see it."

On the great questions facing the Court—on abortion, race, gay rights—the clerks rarely (if ever) knew what O'Connor really thought. She didn't tell them. "She was poker-faced," said Steel. For all her decisiveness in these difficult cases, O'Connor sometimes was unsure. Uncertain, she thought it wise to essentially get out of the way and let the societal debate unfold.[54]

JUSTICE O'CONNOR WEPT when Nan Rehnquist died in 1991, after a long bout with ovarian cancer. She worried about the chief justice, who began going to movies alone. Looking for a more social way to keep her old friend entertained, she thought about the upstairs of the Alibi Club, the small band-of-brothers club John had joined with a great sense of pride a few years before. "Bill doesn't know anyone," Sandra told Sylvia Blake, whose husband, Ambassador Robert Blake, was a long-standing Alibi member. She proposed a monthly bridge game at the Alibi for five or six couples, including Chief Justice Rehnquist and the occasional appropriate (and eligible) widow or divorcée.[55]

The Alibi Club, a Dickensian two-story brick building tucked anonymously in among the glass-and-concrete office buildings downtown, serves a high-calorie lunch on Fridays but otherwise sits empty. Occasionally, the O'Connors had played poker or bridge in the upstairs card rooms with other couples. One wife had been shocked to see a giant mural of two very curvaceous ladies sitting stark naked at a table playing cards. "If you looked like that, you'd pose, too," said O'Connor, who disliked gratuitous sex scenes in movies but laughed at raunchy jokes in private (John had a vast collection, including a volume entitled *Best Dirty Jokes Ever, Vol. III*).[56]

Once a month during the Supreme Court's October-to-June term, the Alibi Bridge Group met, usually on a Friday night. Attendees included several Supreme Court justices (the gregarious Scalia loved the Alibi), the former CIA director Richard Helms, and the former White House counsel Boyden Gray.[57]

"When is dinner coming?" Cynthia Helms asked Chief Justice Rehnquist as they sat on a couch in the club's quirky, artifact-cluttered living room. "Don't worry, Sandra will tell us," Rehnquist said, drily. Mrs. Helms brought in a bridge expert, the women's world champion, Sharon Osberg, who had taught Bill Gates and Warren Buffett how to play. "Sandra spent the whole evening telling Sharon how to play!" exclaimed Helms. "Sharon never got over it."[58]

The evenings were deemed a great success and went on even after the chief justice died in 2005. The only person who appeared not to have fun was John O'Connor. In his diary, he referred to being trapped in "bridge hell."[59] Bridge requires the ability to remember what cards have been played. Sandra's grandmother Wilkey was a famously good bridge player; like her granddaughter, she had a near-photographic memory.[60]

John, while nearly as bright, noticed that he was having trouble remembering cards. And not just cards. At his law firm, Linda Neary, his secretary, began wondering why he was asking her to copy the same documents twice.[61]

CHAPTER THIRTEEN

BUSH V. GORE

"Half the country is going to hate me."

O'Connor's new best friend on the Court was Justice Breyer. "When she reached a decision," said Breyer, "that was it. She told me, 'This is what we should do.'"

THE PLAN HAD been that Sandra would step down from the High Court in 1996, when she was sixty-six. After fifteen years, a Supreme Court justice can retire at full salary and still "ride the circuit," sitting as an occasional judge on federal courts of appeal around the country. Freed from the daily grind, the O'Connors imagined a more relaxed life of travel and sports with family and friends, while they were still young enough to enjoy it.[1]

But when 1996 arrived, Bill Clinton was president and likely to be reelected, and Justice O'Connor did not want her successor to be chosen by a Democrat. She was comfortable in her role. O'Connor was in the majority so often that the pundits were beginning to write about the "O'Connor Court." She bridled at being called "the swing vote," a term suggestive of fickleness and expediency. "It makes it seem like you are not consistent," she told the author. "Very unattractive. Very unattractive."[2] She was not as overtly political and opportunistic as Bill Brennan (motto: "It takes five"), but she did have a strong desire to be in control.

So there was no more talk of retirement. In between judging seventy-five cases a year and delivering speeches by the score, O'Connor still managed to find ample time for tennis, golf, skiing, and her newest passion, fly-fishing. "Hot diggity dog!" she would yell after hooking an elusive trout on some remote mountain stream, recalled her frequent fishing partner, Lynda Webster. Apt to get his line tangled up, John was a less enthusiastic angler. Asked at one fishing camp whether he wanted a monthly, weekly, or daily license, he inquired, "Is there an hourly one?"[3]

At Sun Valley, Idaho, the O'Connors could fish in the summer and ski in the winter. They went to the mountain resort as guests of their

Washington friends Skip and Kim Nalen, who had built a luxurious
"log cabin" with sweeping views down the valley. Skiing at the end of
January 1996, O'Connor caught an edge and crashed badly. She insisted that she could ski down the mountain, but the ski patrol required her to be strapped onto a sled. She had broken her shoulder.[4]
(Hopeful that her accident would cause the aerobics class to be can-
celed, her female clerks were disappointed when she participated
wearing a sling.)[5]

At a bibulous dinner party two nights after O'Connor's fall, Skip
Nalen invited John to tell one of his funny stories. "He said, 'I don't
want to.'" Nalen recalled. "I figured he'd just had too much to drink.
Sandra said, 'Don't push him,' but the crowd said, 'Oh come on, come
on.'"

John stood up and launched into a complicated tale involving pen-
guins and people in formal attire. After a game start, his voice became
softer and softer, then quieted altogether. "He just stopped," recalled
Jim Holman, who was also at the dinner. Gently, Sandra grabbed
John's sleeve and sat him down. The revelers grew quiet. "It was very
uncomfortable. We all changed the subject," recalled Nalen.[6]

On the same trip, John lost his wallet. Back in Washington, he
stopped a friend, Ray Brophy, after lunch at the Metropolitan Club.
"Ray," he said, "I have a problem. I find that when I'm writing, I can't
think of the word, and it frustrates me so." To Ivan Selin, he said, "I
have moments of clarity, then I can't remember what I did fifteen
minutes ago." Other friends began to notice he was not himself. On a
boat trip on Lake Pleasant, Arizona, that summer, "he seemed really
strange, he said odd things. And he was drinking too much," recalled
Gail Driggs (who, as a Mormon, disapproved of drinking altogether).[7]

His son Brian later recalled that he tried to hide his memory lapses
from his wife, but of course, she saw and worried, too. Quietly, she
reached out to a few friends. Adrienne Arsht's husband, Mike Feldman, had developed dementia. Justice O'Connor called Arsht out of
a board meeting at her bank in Miami and anxiously said, "Adrienne,
I think it's happening to John. What do you know? What did it feel
like?" "She was perplexed," recalled Arsht. At the beginning of 1998,
O'Connor responded to her husband's spotty memory in characteris-

tic seize-the-bull-by-the-horns fashion: She encouraged him to write his memoirs, which he did. (Intended for family reading, they are crisp and clear; they convey a sense of gratitude for his life.)[8]

At his law firm, Bryan Cave, John was having trouble filling his days. His legal work was drying up; there was little demand for a generalist lawyer in his late sixties. He mentored young lawyers, but he lamented that they no longer had time or inclination for "civic engagement." In their drive to rack up billable hours, fewer big-firm lawyers were serving on hospital boards or getting involved in local politics, as he had in his day.[9] No longer a rainmaker for his firm, John gave up his partnership and went "of counsel." He was still spending ten days a month in Phoenix, but he was bored by the dinner-party talk of real estate prices.

He yearned for his favorite refuge, the seventeen-day "summer encampment" at the Bohemian Grove, where he was always the first to arrive and the last to leave. His wife understood. "He loved the Grove. He had fun. That was good for John," she told the author in January 2017. "Because being the husband of me was not an easy job."[10]

"Sandra was the queen of Washington, but he was king of the Grove," Alan Kirk recalled. The road running down the middle of the Grove leads to the Russian River, with campsites rising into the Redwoods on either side. "He was the social genius of the Grove," recalled former senator Alan Simpson of Wyoming, whom John drafted to join his camp, Pelican. "He knew everything happening in the camps off River Road. He'd stand there—'Kissinger at three at Mandalay!' Or 'Bush at Cave Man at four!'" said Simpson. Former congressman Jim Symington recalled, "In the evening, when people were going to bed, he'd start down the road, looking to find a piano being played, a song being sung, a joke being told. He would walk into any camp [there are more than a hundred] and be welcome. He would not go to bed until the last dog died."[11]

Beneath the determined cheer, the perhaps not so effortless bonhomie, there were signs of stress and strain. After breakfast one day, he told his friend Phil Schneider that he had to go back to his cabin to study his jokes. Telling a story at lunch that day, "he stumbled," said Schneider. "It was tough to watch," recalled Simpson. "He had been so sure about telling you what to do—'Now Al, you will sire [host] Herman Wouk at lunch.' Suddenly, there was this angst, as if he was trying to remember."[12]

John's diary records very little of this struggle. "I thought perhaps my memory was failing me," he wrote in February 1996 when he misplaced his golf clubs. But then the journal returns to its catalog of dinners and parties. The only telltale sign of his slowly encroaching dementia is the length of his sentences: Beginning with his entries in 1996, they are progressively shorter and simpler, dimming like a bulb. He may not have wanted to see what was happening. In one entry he described Alzheimer's—in someone else—as "horrible."[13]*

In the spring of 1997, John became ill with a high fever and went to see his internist, Dr. Tab Moore. Observing his fogginess, Dr. Moore sent him to Dr. Stanley Cohan, a neurologist at Georgetown Hospital. Dr. Cohan ran some tests and decided, tentatively, that John's problem was not dementia but alcohol: He was drinking too much. He told John to cut back, and he did (or tried to). But his cognitive abilities continued to slowly, inexorably decline.[15]

IT WAS KNOWN as the "courtesy vote." In the 1980s, the Court had been racked by a macabre anomaly in last-minute death penalty cases. It took four votes to grant "certiorari"—to agree to review a case. But it took five votes to grant a stay of execution. Thus a prisoner on death row could find himself in the ultimate good news–bad news situation: Yes, the Supreme Court has decided to review your case, but, no, they won't be able to, because you'll be dead.

When a Georgia death row prisoner, caught in this gothic limbo, was executed in 1985, the New York Times editorial headline was KILL HIM, 4–4. To prevent such inhumane outcomes, Justice Powell, most courteous of gentlemen, determined that he would be the "courtesy" fifth vote, always voting to stay an execution if there were only four votes for "cert."[16]

* According to Dr. Robert Stern of the Boston University School of Health, "Part of Alzheimer's is a progressive lack of awareness and insight into the disease. The condition is called anosognosia. It's not psychological denial but neurologically based. You feel as if nothing is wrong."[14]

Since the liberal justices generally voted to stay executions and the conservative justices to permit the executions to go on, it fell to the justices in the middle to provide the fifth or "courtesy vote." After Powell retired, that usually meant O'Connor and Kennedy, who volunteered when their clerks called in the middle of the night with the pleas of convicts facing imminent execution.

With Marshall, Brennan, and Blackmun gone, a new group of liberals—usually Ginsburg, Stevens, Breyer, and Souter—continued to need O'Connor's or Kennedy's help on staying executions. But by the late nineties, Justice Kennedy stopped automatically sharing "courtesy vote" duty. "It often, if not always, fell to Justice O'Connor to provide the courtesy vote. She was frustrated," said one of her clerks, Brad Joondeph (OT '99). "I never spoke to her about it directly, but she may have read it as an unstated assumption that the women would look out for the collective good and allow men to vote their individual preferences."[17] Recalled his fellow clerk Shirley Woodward: "There were times when it appeared that Justice Kennedy's chambers were avoiding our phone calls. So there may have been some frustration there."[18]

The relationship between O'Connor and Kennedy, never personally warm, had grown cooler. They had agreed on *Casey,* the landmark abortion case, and still often voted together, but they had different styles and approaches. Kennedy was more earnest, dramatic, and emotional. He made no effort to hide his agonizing over hard cases and employed sweeping rhetoric when he decided.

Kennedy criticized O'Connor as a nitpicker. He scoffed that the fact-specific "reindeer test"—weighing holiday banality in judging religious intent—introduced by Justice O'Connor in crèche cases would lead to "a jurisprudence of minutiae" relying on "little more than intuition and a tape measure."[19] But others, including some of her own peers, regarded O'Connor as more personally secure. "Sandra was more comfortable being the one who had to cast the deciding vote," Justice Ginsburg told the author in 2017. "For Tony it was more difficult. Maybe she had more confidence in her judgment. Sandra could accept the role of being in the middle without excessive worrying."[20]

O'Connor gravitated instead toward Justice Breyer. "We liked each other a lot," recalled Justice O'Connor. "Some Justices were easier to talk to than others," she added. Justice Breyer reciprocated. "We enjoyed each other. It was fun. When she reached a decision," said Breyer, "that was it. She told me, 'This is what we should do.' Then move on to the next. 'Tomorrow's another day.' She said that a lot."[21]

But before she reached a decision, Breyer might try to subtly work on her. He saw that while she could not be pushed, she might be ever so gently pulled, at least on cases where they shared common ground. They both had a practical bent. When the doctrinal purists on both the Left and the Right combined to effectively undo the Federal Sentencing Guidelines by requiring that juries, not judges, play a greater role in criminal sentencing, both O'Connor and Breyer dissented. As a member of the United States Sentencing Commission, Breyer had helped write the sentencing guidelines. O'Connor, the former trial judge, understood that requiring more jury trials would create "a mess," said her clerk Noah Levine, using a favorite O'Connor euphemism to describe the inevitable backlogs and justice delayed.[22]

Justice O'Connor did not like "messes." She liked real-world solutions, and she was fairly flexible about how to get there. Looked at case by case, she was not entirely predictable and certainly not constrained either by rigid doctrine or by another justice. Still, she was a person of opinions, emotions, and beliefs, and they affected her, consciously or not. She had a shape, and over time it changed.

Many justices evolve on the Court. More often than not, as they age they move to the left, sometimes surprising the presidents who appointed them (Brennan and Blackmun, appointed by Eisenhower and Nixon respectively, are the two obvious examples). Though routinely used, the labels "liberal" and "conservative" are not always useful and can even be misleading to describe justices; after all, Justice Scalia has been called an unlikely hero of liberal criminal defense lawyers because of his defense of the Fourth Amendment prohibition of "unreasonable searches and seizures."[23] Still, the Court is, broadly speaking, a political institution, and though she resisted categorization, Justice O'Connor could not entirely escape it. From one decade to the next, her votes on the Court began to show a pattern. The movement is subtle, but identifiable.

Throughout her first decade on the Supreme Court, Justice O'Connor could be fairly described as a center-right jurist. But judged by her votes on important constitutional cases, she moved—not dramatically, but measurably—in a leftward direction toward the center and sometimes a little beyond.

A PROMINENT MEASURE OF JUDICIAL IDEOLOGY CHARTS O'CONNOR'S LEFTWARD SHIFT:
MARTIN-QUINN SCORES FOR SANDRA O'CONNOR
(the higher the number, the more conservative)
(Data generated by Andrew D. Martin and Kevin Quinn)[24]

TERM	IDEOLOGY
1981	1.563
1982	1.715
1983	1.687
1984	1.5
1985	1.28
1986	1.38
1987	1.563
1988	1.501
1989	1.52
1990	1.12
1991	0.693
1992	0.855
1993	1.017
1994	0.829
1995	0.838
1996	0.976
1997	1.077
1998	0.964
1999	0.869
2000	0.584
2001	0.356
2002	0.243
2003	0.196
2004	0.12
2005	0.071

Various explanations have been offered, some more persuasive than others. Some friends, particularly Westerners, have argued that her hearty Western individualism was altered by spending time hobnobbing with the Washington establishment, which was largely liberal. Judge Laurence Silberman, an outspoken conservative on the U.S. Court of Appeals for the D.C. Circuit, suggested that O'Connor was co-opted by what he called the Greenhouse Effect, referring to the influential, liberal-minded *New York Times* Supreme Court correspondent Linda Greenhouse, whom both Kennedy and O'Connor respected.[25] Others argued that O'Connor began to hire more liberal clerks (true, but it is unclear how much she was influenced by them);* that she didn't so much move to the left as the Court moved to the right; that she was softened up and "liberalized" by her cancer scare; and that she was driven to the left by Justice Scalia's intemperate dissents. That last view was offered by Justice Stevens in an interview with the author in 2016. "He [Scalia] was critical of her opinions in a way that was unfair and unkindly from time to time," said Stevens.[27]

The simplest explanation is the most obvious one: that O'Connor became increasingly willing to go where the facts and her sensitive judgment led her. Generally speaking, O'Connor subscribed to the notion of "judicial restraint," the obligation of judges to follow precedent and procedure and not impose their personal views on the law. But, increasingly over time, she did not shy away from activism if her conscience was moved, or if she believed that the law was drifting out of sync with the tenor of the times. "She believed that law exists to shape society," said her clerk Brad Joondeph, OT '99. "It doesn't exist as a Platonic ideal."

While O'Connor professed to have minimal regard for legal philosophizing, there was one doctrine she did champion, certainly in her early years: federalism. Though "states' rights" took on a sour connotation before the civil rights movement did away with the Jim Crow laws in the 1950s and '60s, O'Connor always saw the states as an im-

---

* Though not necessarily by design, O'Connor generally hired a balance of liberal and conservative clerks, but by the 2000s, the balance had tipped leftward, at least as crudely measured by the donations of her clerks to liberal political candidates.[26]

portant part of the American polity, endowed with powers reserved to them by the Constitution. When she first came on the Court, she joined William Rehnquist in his effort to push back the encroachment of federal power on state and local government, sticking up for governors, mayors, and local public servants in their delicate balance of power with Washington officialdom. She had even allowed herself a rare burst of rhetoric, declaring in her first term that state and local governments are "not field offices of the national bureaucracy."

But she was never a hard-liner against federal intrusion, and she became less so in her later career. She paid close attention to the facts of the case, especially if the facts involved women and children. She would delve down into the record made in the courts below, looking for the real-world consequences for the individuals involved and the potential impact on society at large.[28]

In one case, LaShonda Davis was a fifth grader tormented by a classmate. The boy said, "I want to feel your boobs" and "I want to get into bed with you." He purportedly put a doorstop inside his pants and thrust his pelvis at LaShonda in gym class. This behavior went on for five months. Her father complained, but the teachers and administrators essentially ignored him, while the girl's grades fell and she grew despondent and suicidal. Finally, LaShonda's father sued the school for creating a "hostile environment" under Title IX of the Civil Rights Act.

For the first time, the Supreme Court, by a 5-to-4 vote, ruled that a school could be sued for student-on-student sexual harassment. Justice O'Connor wrote the Court's decision in *Davis v. Monroe County Board of Education,* and she led with the alleged facts, recounting them in graphic detail. O'Connor was joined by the Court's liberals: Ginsburg, Breyer, Souter, and Stevens. The Court's conservatives— Rehnquist, Scalia, Thomas, and Kennedy—dissented. The dissenting opinion, by Justice Kennedy, accused O'Connor of betraying federalism by allowing the federal government to interfere in local schools. At the end of the 1998–99 term, Kennedy took the unusual step of reading his dissent from the bench.

Justice O'Connor took the even more unusual step, for her, of taking a public, sarcastic shot at a fellow justice. Reading her own opinion from the bench, she retorted that Kennedy's dissent accused the majority of giving "little Johnny a perverse lesson in federalism." On the contrary, she declared, the Court's decision ensured that "little Mary" might learn her school lessons without being sexually harassed by "little Johnny."[29]

Kennedy and O'Connor fell out again in the next term of 1999–2000 over the ever vexing question of abortion. Their joint opinion in the *Casey* case in 1992 had quieted the abortion question for a time, but it came roaring back to the Court seven years later. Once again, the facts, or rather the personal lens through which each justice viewed the facts, made all the difference.

A physician in Ohio had developed a procedure for abortions late in pregnancy (after sixteen weeks) and for late-term miscarriages that involved dilating the cervix and pulling out the fetus feetfirst, then crushing the head to fit through. This procedure was thought to reduce the risk of damaging the woman's cervix, but to antiabortion activists, the procedure smacked of infanticide, since the fetuses looked fully formed. More than half the states passed laws banning these "partial birth abortions" (a somewhat loaded description—the medical term is "dilation and extraction").

When the case, *Stenberg v. Carhart,* arrived at the Supreme Court, Kennedy and O'Connor split. Kennedy, a devout Catholic, could not abide so-called partial birth abortions, and he rejoined Scalia in the antiabortion camp. With all four liberals lined up on the other side, O'Connor was in her now familiar position of casting the decisive vote. As described by Jeffrey Toobin in *The Nine,* Justice Breyer carefully and cleverly lobbied Justice O'Connor to provide the fifth vote for his opinion striking down Nebraska's law, which made these abortions a felony. While Breyer waited to see if O'Connor would join him, he persuaded both Ginsburg and Stevens not to circulate their own opinions, lest O'Connor be put off by their liberal theorizing and pushed into the conservative camp.[30]

At oral argument, O'Connor had asked the one question that mattered to her: Did the Nebraska law banning partial birth abortions make an exception to protect the health of the mother? Because the answer was no, O'Connor voted with Breyer and the liberals to strike down the law. But she left open the possibility that the states or Congress could rewrite the law to pass constitutional muster (which, in fact, happened after O'Connor left the Court in 2006).³¹

"Justice O'Connor was genuinely humble about leaving things undecided," said one of her clerks from that year, Brad Joondeph. "She didn't want to prejudge cases." While she rejected all labels, she was aptly described by Cass Sunstein, at the time a professor at the University of Chicago Law School, as a "minimalist."

Nothing illustrates O'Connor's ability to narrow the meaning of a decision to just the facts better than her role in the highly controversial right-to-die cases. In 1997, she joined a 9–0 decision to uphold New York State's ban on physician-assisted suicide. The ruling seemed, "at first glance, like very big news," wrote Sunstein. The Court seemed to be saying there was no constitutional right to privacy, which would have enormous implications for abortion and gay rights. "But wait," wrote Sunstein. "O'Connor wrote a (characteristic) separate opinion, suggesting that any new development was small and incremental. In her view, all the Court held was that there was no general right to commit suicide. She cautioned that the Court had not decided whether a competent person experiencing great suffering had a constitutional right to control the circumstances of an imminent death. That issue remained to be decided on another day." She was content to let the issue simmer a little longer in the lower courts and legislatures.³²

By June 2000, *USA Today* was calling O'Connor the "go-to" justice. "On a divided bench, no one else has shaped the law as much or played such a key role in helping reach compromise," wrote Joan Biskupic, the newspaper's veteran Supreme Court correspondent (and later O'Connor biographer). "It's all about O'Connor," wrote Edward Lazarus in the *Los Angeles Times*. "As Justice O'Connor votes, so goes the Court."

Lazarus, a former Supreme Court clerk and author of a telling book on the inner workings of the Court, pointed out that in the 1999–2000 term the Court split 5 to 4 in twenty-one of seventy-four cases, the highest percentage of one-vote margins in a decade. O'Connor voted in dissent only four times, tying the modern record. "The O'Connor Court" indeed: Nobody played a more important role in determining what the Supreme Court decided—and, especially, what it did not decide—than Justice O'Connor. "Nineteen years after her appointment as the High Court's first female Justice," wrote Biskupic, "O'Connor has become, in today's vernacular, 'The Man.'"[33]

THE JUNE RUSH is a frantic time around the Supreme Court, as the justices and their overburdened clerks labor to finish the hardest opinions in the biggest cases on the eve of the traditional end-of-term finale, usually just before the Fourth of July holiday. O'Connor told her husband that she found late June to be a relaxing time—she prided herself on finishing her opinions first, and was mostly waiting around for the other justices to catch up.

O'Connor loved amateur theatricals, both watching them and putting on her own skits with John. In mid-June 2000, she and John were practicing a complicated duet to be performed at a surprise eightieth birthday party for her friend Jean Douglas. "My own view is that it was too complicated," John wrote in his diary for June 16. "The concept is that I stand in front with my arms in back of me, but SOC moves her arms. We did something like that years and years ago, but this is more complex. We will see."

For John, who liked performing even more than Sandra did, such cranky self-doubt was uncharacteristic. But he was, at the moment, deeply worried about his cognitive state. That same morning, without telling Sandra, he had taken a cab to Georgetown Hospital and asked to see a neurologist—any neurologist. He was given an appointment for the following Tuesday.

At noon on June 20, John met with Dr. Paul Aisen, who had replaced Dr. Stan Cohan, the Georgetown neurologist he had consulted in 1997. Dr. Cohan had told John that his memory lapses probably came from drinking too much alcohol. Now, with Dr. Aisen, John recorded, "I was given a short test, and then I had a long, long very good visit. Dr. Aisen asked me about a lot of things. He asked me about my alcoholic intake. I said I didn't take any hard liquor, but I do have 2–3 Merlots. In short, and in a nice way, he said I shouldn't take any wine at all. . . .

"In substance, he said that I have a certain level of Alzheimer. As I told him, I forget things I would not have forgotten in years past."[34]

In 2017, Dr. Aisen told the author, "The first time I saw him, I gave him a diagnosis. 'You probably have mild Alzheimer's,' I said. He was, if anything, relieved to hear it. He had suspected as much."[35]

That night was the surprise birthday party for Jean Douglas, co-hosted by the O'Connors but held at the home of Tim and Ann Hoopes, whose "Hoopes' Troops" delighted the O'Connors' social set with sprightly renditions of Broadway show tunes.[36] Sandra, who had spent the afternoon playing golf with her clerk Brad Joondeph, arrived at the Hoopeses' carrying her favorite corn pudding. John lugged in the other groceries. "John was mad," recalled Ann Hoopes. "He said, 'I've been doing all the scut work and no one gives me credit.' He was really mad." The O'Connors' hostess was caught by surprise; John was "no longer his usual jovial self." After dinner, John recorded, "Eventually, SOC and I had to do our thing. I did not look forward to that. I thought the act that SOC had selected was much too difficult. I was right. It was not a good idea, but SOC would not accept anything else. I tried to look funny at appropriate times, and I got some laughs, but I was not a happy camper."[37]

John continued to try to hide his condition from Sandra. Frank Saul, the owner of a Maryland bank, was close to John and grateful for his having arranged Saul's membership in Pelican, John's "camp" at the Bohemian Grove. Saul, who had known the O'Connors only since their arrival in Washington, was candid about his perception of the O'Connor marriage. "Every marriage has a weakness," he said. "Sandra dominated him. John didn't tell her about his illness because she would dominate him even more." Other friends saw in John's evasions a brave attempt to spare his wife undue anxiety. John had strongly supported the Bohemian Club membership of LaSalle Leffall, a distinguished surgeon and the first African American member in Pelican. At the camp that July, John told Dr. Leffall, "I think I'm not all there, but I don't want Sandra to know about it. I think I can get around it. I think I can control my dementia. I don't want to worry her."[38]

But of course she did know, or strongly suspect, that something was seriously wrong with her beloved husband. Knowing that Leffall would be John's guest and roommate at Pelican, she had quietly asked the doctor to make sure John took his medication, Aricept, an enzyme blocker used by patients experiencing cognitive fuzziness. ("The pills didn't really work," recalled Leffall.) She was more oblique with some friends. She asked their old Phoenix pal Dick Houseworth to keep an eye on John's ball on the golf course, she explained, "because he forgets where it is." "It was my first inkling that something was wrong," Houseworth recalled. She was more direct with Phil Schneider, another longtime Phoenix friend. On their way to a ski trip in the winter of 2000, she confided, "I am dealing with a husband who is losing his mind." Recalled Schneider, "It was the first time I heard her express it so clearly."[39]

Ruth McGregor, Sandra's original law clerk and the only one close enough to call her Sandra, was visiting the O'Connors in Chevy Chase when she witnessed an odd moment. On the way to the car, Sandra's jacket belt slipped off, and, momentarily at a loss, she exclaimed, "Where is my belt?" John became agitated. "Really, Sandra," he said, "that is so embarrassing! You are just so embarrassing!" The normally smooth, debonair John was "just like a little kid," observed McGregor. John was becoming unpredictable, even a little uncouth. "She didn't know what he'd do in social situations," recalled McGregor.

O'Connor's approach, said her friend and former law clerk (who had just been appointed to the Arizona Supreme Court), was "Just deal with it. Like rain at the ranch. Sandra started assigning people to keep an eye on John." Another longtime Phoenix friend, Don Kauffman, recalled, "She took it in stride and said, 'That's the way it is. That's the way it's going to be.'"[40]

The O'Connor way—to do the impossible without complaint, or even without acknowledging the difficulty—was a source of rueful mirth to her clerks. Late on a winter's night in 2000, the justice returned to her chambers after a social engagement to pick up some papers. Encountering her clerks still grinding away, she said, "Go home, you're working too hard!" Noah Levine responded, "Okay, does that mean you don't need this memo first thing in the morning?" O'Connor responded, "No, I want the memo in the A.M." Shirley Woodward recalled, "So we packed up and went with her to the elevator. She went down to her car in the garage. We went out, walked around the block, made sure the coast was clear, and went right back to her chambers, laughing."[41]

Understandably, her sons were less blithe about their parents' just-deal-with-it stoicism in the face of John's creeping dementia. "Mom would say, 'Oh, your dad is losing his memory,'" Jay said. "Mom would start to confide in us. . . . But you don't know what to think. We didn't know what it was. We thought she was exaggerating. Then you'd see things yourself—see him lose track or forget a punch line." Said Brian: "It was not talked about. We just lived it. There were never any big group sessions or anything." Added Scott: "He wouldn't talk about it with us. He called it 'this thing,' or 'my thing.' He couldn't use the word [Alzheimer's] because it was too terrifying."[42]

JOHN O'CONNOR DID not like Al Gore. During the second term of the Clinton-Gore administration, he criticized the vice president more than half a dozen times in his diary, referring to him as "pompous" and "fake." On the final night of the Democratic National Convention, August 17, 2000, the O'Connors started to watch Gore's acceptance speech as the party's nominee for president. "SOC couldn't stand it and went to bed," wrote John.

The O'Connors watched the first presidential debate between Gore and Governor George W. Bush of Texas on October 3. "I find Al Gore to be a very unattractive person," wrote John. "He is a 'know it all.' He never stops talking. He interrupts when he shouldn't. I simply can't stand the guy."[43] In these years, John was increasingly aware of his dementia, and perhaps his outbursts to his diary reflected his own anxiety.

Sandra's own feelings about Gore—or about his opponent, George W. Bush—are hard to ascertain. (Halfway through both the second and third debates, Sandra had fallen asleep, recorded John.) She was a loyal Republican and a friend of the Bush family. "Keep your fingers crossed for a Bush victory," she had written to Arizona governor Jane Dee Hull in March. Still, she was careful, even within her own family, not to fulminate about politicians who might appoint her successor. The revelation of President Clinton's affair with a White House intern, Monica Lewinsky, in January 1998 was a subject best not discussed. With her clerks, she generally concealed her tartness, certainly on the subject of presidential infidelity. ("Her way of expressing shock was to say, 'Good night nurse!'" recalled Leslie Hakala, a clerk in the '99 term.) Noah Levine had just finished interviewing for his clerkship in the winter of 1998 when one of O'Connor's secretaries came into the office and said, "Justice, the president is about to make a statement." O'Connor and Levine went into the outer office to look at the small black-and-white TV on the secretary's desk. The president was responding to press reports of a sexual relationship between Clinton and Lewinsky. "I did not have sexual relations with that woman," President Clinton said. "Well, isn't that interesting," said Justice O'Connor. She abruptly turned and went back into her chambers, recalled Levine.[44]

ON ELECTION DAY, Tuesday, November 7, Justice O'Connor called—for the first time—John's neurologist, Dr. Paul Aisen. John had finally confided in his wife by putting a name—Alzheimer's—to his dementia. Dr. Aisen's notes recorded, "I spoke to Justice O'Connor and discussed diagnosis and treatment. She indicated she was eager for him to participate in experimental studies."

That night, John and Sandra attended an election-viewing party at the home of Mary Ann Stoessel, the widow of a prominent ambassador. Televisions were set up all over the house, and the O'Connors watched a tiny black-and-white one in the basement den as they ate off plates from the buffet with a few other guests. Shortly before eight, all the networks called Florida for Gore, who had already won two critical swing states, Illinois and Michigan. O'Connor looked "unhappy, troubled," recalled her friend Paul Ignatius. She was "upset, agitated. It was obvious," recalled Cynthia Helms. "This is terrible," O'Connor said. "That means it's over." The justice got up and walked out of the room. John stayed behind. He said to the others that his wife was upset because they wanted to retire and move back to Arizona, but she wouldn't leave the Court as long as there was a Democrat in the White House to appoint her successor.[45]

O'Connor later explained, unconvincingly, that she was upset about the networks' calling the election before the polls closed in California, not about Gore's apparent victory. John's indiscretion may have flowed from his incipient Alzheimer's. But their son Scott believed that his parents were at least considering retirement if a Republican won the White House in 2000. "They both had their infirmities," he noted. After she broke her shoulder skiing in 1996, doctors told Justice O'Connor that she suffered from osteoporosis, which made her bones more brittle, possibly because of her chemo treatments for cancer. Forced to curtail her skiing, she lamented to Cynthia Helms, "I'm going to be a bent-over old lady." Possibly, she wanted to move with John back to Arizona before one or both was enfeebled. On the other hand, said Scott, "you could have pushed her to stick around with a feather. She loved her job." He also noted that "her office had become a bit of an escape from Dad."[46] It may be significant that O'Connor had delayed hiring the next batch of law clerks, a sign to Supreme Court watchers that a justice is pondering retirement.[47]

The 2000 election was, incredibly, a virtual tie. Neither candidate had won enough electoral votes. Florida, as it turned out, had not gone for Gore but rather for Bush—but by so few votes that an automatic recount was called for. O'Connor did not know it, but the closeness of the election was about to draw her into the most dramatic and controversial episode of her time on the Supreme Court.

On the day after the election, the O'Connors drove to Colonial Williamsburg, where O'Connor was a trustee. She had been brought on the board by Lewis Powell in 1985 and was trying to recruit Justice Kennedy or Justice Breyer as her replacement. "Most famous board members kiss off their boards," recalled Jim Lehrer, the *PBS NewsHour* host and fellow board member at Colonial Williamsburg, the Rockefeller-funded restoration of Virginia's capital during the pre-revolutionary era. "She was engaged in the smallest details." Colin Campbell, the director of Colonial Williamsburg at the time, recalled how, during a restoration of the Inn, she objected to clear glass doors on the showers. "So they have fogged doors," said Campbell. O'Connor was most engaged in how to make history interesting to kids. The popular historian David McCullough had told her that American schools were failing at teaching civics, which disturbed her.[48]

O'Connor was unmoved by political theory, but she was passionate about history. She would often take houseguests to Mount Vernon,

George Washington's home on the Virginia bank of the Potomac. "She never referred to the slaves," recalled her friend Craig Joyce, who each year came to visit Justice O'Connor on the first Monday in October. "She was relentlessly positive: 'Isn't this fabulous? Isn't this fabulous?'" What inspired her was the way the Founders and the Framers created "a society of laws and not men," how they fashioned a system that peaceably transferred power and maintained civil government through checks and balances. James Madison, the father of the Constitution, was her favorite Founder.[49] Like her other hero, George Washington, she was particularly concerned with the rules of civility. In the mid-1990s, when Senate Republicans and Democrats began to shed the traditional courtesies and attack each other personally, she summoned the Senate leaders of both parties, Democrat Tom Daschle of South Dakota and Republican Trent Lott of Mississippi, to her chambers and lectured them on the need for civil discourse in politics. "She was very determined to express herself," Daschle recalled. "No one had reached out to us that way."[50]

On November 8, 2000, a modern civics lesson intruded as she stood with some other Colonial Williamsburg trustees outside a meeting room. Already, the Bush and Gore campaign lawyers were gathering to do battle over the recount in Florida. O'Connor was asked, "Do you think it will go to the Supreme Court?" "Oh, heavens no," she answered. Later, when her son Brian remarked, "Mom, this is going to end up in the Supreme Court," she responded, "Don't be ridiculous."[51]

Events quickly proved her wrong. Old voting machines, old voters, and politics had collided to produce chaos in Florida. The ballots had confused voters, especially in the retirement condos in southern Florida, so that conservative independent candidate Pat Buchanan had picked up hundreds, possibly thousands, of votes almost certainly cast in error by lifelong Democrats. Voting machines were unable to count punch ballots with "dimpled" or "hanging chads." Partisanship threatened to paralyze or skew the recount. Republicans wanted to freeze the process to preserve Bush's razor-thin margin; Democrats wanted to keep the recount going, believing Gore would win. Florida's Republican secretary of state, Katherine Harris, was ready to certify

Bush's victory; a Democratic-controlled state supreme court was poised to overrule her. In retrospect, it was inevitable that the justices of the U.S. Supreme Court would be called in to break the logjam.[52]

Normally, the Supreme Court tries to steer clear of "the political thicket" of elections.[53] The first time the case that became known as *Bush v. Gore* came to the nation's highest court, over Thanksgiving, the justices batted it down in a 9–0 ruling requesting that the Florida courts clarify their reasoning. But the case came right back. On December 8, by a party-line 4–3 vote, the Florida Supreme Court (while brushing off the justices' questions) ordered a statewide recount of every "undervote"—the votes, including those by now famous "hanging chads," not counted by the faulty machines. Such a sweeping recount seemed almost sure to favor Al Gore. The Bush camp immediately went to the U.S. Supreme Court to stop it.

The Supreme Court, by careful design, does not appear to be a partisan political institution, even on close inspection. To read the court files of a Supreme Court justice is to plunge into a world of arcane legal technicality. Log-rolling, vote-swapping, deal making—the legislator's lubricants—rarely, if ever, show up in the paper trail of memos and opinion drafts between justices. Their arguments are high-minded, cloaked in legalisms and channeled by precedent. The words "Republican" and "Democrat," "party" or "partisan," are never uttered as a rationale or justification for voting to decide cases. After a decade on the Court, Justice Thomas said, "I have yet to hear any discussion of partisan politics." He was telling the truth, as was Justice Breyer when he told the author in 2017, after he had served twenty-three years on the Court, "We never had a voice raised in anger in the conference."[54]*

---

* Of course, over the years the Court has had its share of politicians, most notably Chief Justice Earl Warren (governor of California), Justice Hugo Black (U.S. senator from Alabama), and Chief Justice William Howard Taft (former U.S. president). Some legal scholars like Judge Richard Posner have argued that the Court is, at bottom, political, and would do well to have more justices in touch with public opinion. In 2018, every current justice on the Supreme Court with one exception (Elena Kagan, a former solicitor general) is a former U.S. Court of Appeals judge. Politicians running for president often campaign on picking

Yet the final votes do not lie: At the end of the day, on the big cases, the ideological liberals and the ideological conservatives usually end up on opposite sides, with the moderate pragmatists shuttling between them (and holding the balance of power). So it was in *Bush v. Gore,* only more obviously than usual.[55]

On that Friday evening, December 8, Justice John Paul Stevens and Justice Stephen Breyer, both highly civilized, cultured men, bumped into each other at the National Gallery of Art's annual Christmas holiday party. They had just heard about the Florida Supreme Court's ruling and knew that Chief Justice Rehnquist had called the justices to meet in conference on Saturday morning to decide what to do. The Bush campaign had immediately filed papers with the U.S. Supreme Court to demand a "stay," stopping the recount (and thereby securing Bush's victory, since he was still narrowly ahead).

Stevens later recalled, "I remember both of us saying to one another, well, I guess we're going to have to meet tomorrow on this but that'll take us about ten minutes because it had . . . obviously no merit to it. Because in order to get a stay . . . the applicant has to prove irreparable injury." Stevens continued: "There just, obviously, wasn't any irreparable injury to allowing a recount to go through because the worst that happens is that you get a more accurate count of the votes."[56]

Stevens was in for a rude surprise. The next morning at ten, the justices shook hands, filed into the conference room, took their seats, and split in a way that seemed, to him at least, to be shockingly political. The five Republicans—Rehnquist, Thomas, Scalia, Kennedy, and O'Connor—voted to grant a stay to stop the recount. The two Democrats, Breyer and Ginsburg—joined by the two Republicans turned liberals, Stevens and Souter—voted against the stay. There was no real debate or discussion. With this decision, for all intents and purposes, it appeared, the election was over. Bush had won.

The Court had just engaged in power politics of the rawest kind, or

---

conservative or liberal appointments to the Court, and if elected find it easier to tell if potential nominees have prior records of judicial service. Perversely, the politicization of Court nominations seems to have ruled out former politicians.

so it appeared to Breyer and Stevens. All that remained was for the justices to find a reason, other than naked partisanship, to justify their decision.

The three most conservative justices—Rehnquist, Thomas, and Scalia—didn't even see the need for oral arguments. They based their decision on a narrow, literal reading of Article II, Section 1 of the Constitution: "Each State shall appoint, in such manner as the Legislature thereof may direct, a Number of Electors. . . ." The Constitution spoke of state legislatures, not courts. The Florida Supreme Court had no business second-guessing the voting rules set by the state legislature (never mind, as U.S. Supreme Court author Jeffrey Toobin has pointed out, that courts routinely interpret state election laws). The votes had been certified by the secretary of state under the rules set by the Florida state legislature. Game over.

Such summary justice on a technical point was not good enough for Justice O'Connor or Justice Kennedy—it was a little unseemly, given the enormous national attention and the high stakes. They appeared to want to hear oral arguments to see if there wasn't a more persuasive rationale, a grander reason to justify intervention by the highest court in the voting procedures of a state. The stay could still be lifted if the Gore team could come up with a persuasive argument to let the recount go on.

Oral argument was set for two days later, Monday morning, December 11, with a decision due the next day. That is breakneck speed for the Supreme Court, and, inevitably, the justices bounced off a few guardrails. Some would say they crashed.

Scalia was in a white heat when he appeared at the indoor tennis court of the Chevy Chase Club on Sunday afternoon for his weekly game with Dr. Bill Leahy. "He walked on the court very red-faced," Leahy recalled. "Maureen had warned me, 'He's very wound up.' He said something to me like, 'Why did the Florida Supreme Court throw this in our lap? Okay, let's play. No more talk.' For two hours, I was his battering ram. I was exhausted. I bought him a bottle of wine and said, 'This is how the Irish handle constitutional crises.' "[57]

Justice Kennedy, meanwhile, was having second thoughts. The justice felt the weight of decision in big cases. Before he went to the Court to announce the *Casey* decision in 1992, he told a reporter,

"Sometimes you don't know if you're Caesar about to cross the Rubicon or Captain Queeg cutting your own tow line." He asked the reporter to leave so he could "brood" some more.[58] Now, walking the Supreme Court's marble corridors, he was still wrestling with whether to make the stay permanent—or to let the recount resume.

The Court was like a castle, surrounded by a moat, but under siege. Justice O'Connor's middle son, Brian, had asked if he could come to the oral arguments on Monday and bring a couple of friends. "When we got to the Court, it was like a scene from *Apocalypse Now*," Brian recalled. "There were mounted riot police. Demonstrators were burning justices in effigy. We got to her chambers, overlooking the plaza and the Capitol. It was eerily quiet, even serene." His mother got up from her desk and warmly greeted his friends by name, engaging them in conversation. Watching her, Brian thought, "When you talk to her, you are the most important person in the room." Justice O'Connor nodded to the window and the muted chaos outside. "Isn't this crazy?" she said, with a smile and a shrug.[59]

For O'Connor, as for any good ranch hand, it was important to shrug off hardship and danger. One of her clerks that year, Stan Panikowski, recalled her impish side. For years, the clerks had made light of her parsimonious praise by that photocopy (now a bit frayed) of the palm of her hand. Panikowski had the idea of taking a similar image of her foot and putting it on the wall with the sign, "If you want a kick in the butt, lean here." Hesitatingly, he asked O'Connor if she would let him photocopy her foot. "That's fantastic!" she replied. Said Panikowski, "We took her to the copying machine and had her put her foot on the glass." She gamely climbed on a chair and stuck out a foot while the clerks hooted with laughter. "She understood that at heart, we were all ambitious and insecure," said Panikowski. Recalled another clerk, Tamarra Matthews-Johnson, who was sitting in an upstairs office, "We got a call from her secretary, 'Please get here to save us from catastrophe!' The justice was balancing on a chair—scary!—and we were going to get blamed."[60]

Panikowski decided to have some fun with the media mob assembled for *Bush v. Gore*. In the dark of a mid-December night, the Court was ringed by cameras and TV trucks, as well as protesters shouting through bullhorns. Panikowski put on a spare judicial robe and lady's wig (used for the annual clerks' skit making fun of the justices), went into the justice's empty office, flipped on the light, and stood by the window pretending to read a federal case reporter, a heavy brown leather volume. "The cameras and lights immediately swung," Panikowski recalled. "The networks reported that O'Connor was in her chambers, working late into the night." The next morning Panikowski recounted the scene to Justice O'Connor, who had been at home asleep. "She thought it was hilarious," said the clerk.

Other clerks, however, noted that O'Connor had seemed troubled by the media circus. Left unresolved, the election standoff risked stressing the rule of law. Two weeks earlier, there had been a distasteful "Brooks Brothers riot" of scuffling lawyers at a meeting of election canvassers in Miami-Dade County. The press was playing up the possibility of civil unrest if the country stumbled on too long without a winner in the presidential race. At a dinner party at their friend Julie Folger's, John O'Connor let slip that he and Sandra were disturbed by reports that the Gore campaign had brought in machine hacks from Boston and Chicago to try to "steal" the election.[61]

Brian O'Connor was surprised by the celebrity star power packed into the courtroom when he took his reserved seat in the justices' family box for the oral arguments in *Bush v. Gore* on Monday, December 11. "Jesse Jackson was there, and Geraldo [Rivera], too," he recalled. His mother, others observed, was in full schoolmarm mode. When David Boies, the lawyer for the Gore camp, pointed out that some voters had become confused and had trouble properly filling out their ballots, O'Connor interjected, "Well, why isn't the standard the one that voters are instructed to follow, for goodness' sake? I mean, it couldn't be clearer. I mean, why don't we go to that standard?"[62] O'Connor did not disguise her annoyance at the Florida Supreme Court. Normally, O'Connor wanted to let the dialogue go on between the Supreme Court and other institutions of government, to let the law evolve as public views evolve. But in this case, the judges on the Florida high court had essentially ignored the gentle nudge from the justices in Washington to come up with a fair method of counting votes and a rationale for doing so. Now time was running out.

One of her clerks, Richard Bierschbach, felt her familiar—and powerful—urge to fix the problem and move on. "Justice O'Connor likes to make decisions," he recalled. "She doesn't like things messy and drawn out. My impression is that she was trying to put an end to it. It wasn't political. It was . . ." Bierschbach paused as he spoke. "She wanted certainty."[63]

Watching her colleague, Justice Ginsburg saw some of the same motivation at work. "I think Sandra thought that if the Court stayed out of it, it would have been weeks" before a resolution, Ginsburg recalled. Florida could have remained deadlocked, riven by partisanship. The state might have chosen two opposing sets of electors—the one already certified by the Republican secretary of state, the determined Katherine Harris, the other the product of the recount ordered by the Democratic-controlled state supreme court. With both candidates claiming Florida's electoral votes, the election would have wound up in the Congress, where Bush probably would have ultimately won anyway, but only after a chaotic struggle among politicians, whose civility O'Connor had come to doubt.[*] "Sandra believed that it was better to get the country out of the agony," said Ginsburg (who disagreed; she wanted the recount to go on, particularly because she felt that historically disenfranchised black voters had been disproportionately undercounted).[65]

The Monday afternoon after the oral argument was a free-for-all in the normally sedate, slow-moving Court. "That day! That was some day, when a lot of people tried to influence other people," recalled Ginsburg. "Sandra knew where she wanted to be. And that was it. There was no possibility of persuading her."

Justice Breyer—"more than anyone else," according to Ginsburg—tried to bring his friend around. But she was dug in, determined to end the recount and declare a winner. Justice Kennedy, on the other hand, was still waffling. Breyer had an inspiration. Kennedy liked ar-

---

[*] According to 3 U.S. Code Sec. 15, if there are two sets of electors, the matter goes to Congress and both the House and the Senate vote to accept one. The Republican-controlled House would have voted for the Bush electors, the newly elected Democratic-controlled Senate for the Gore electors. Section 15 provided that where the two houses disagree, the slate certified over the governor's signature would prevail. The governor of Florida was Jeb Bush, George W.'s brother. With charges of conflict of interest and nepotism flying, the furor would have gone on and on.[64]

guments that resonated with the broad sweep of history. He could see at oral argument that Kennedy was drawn to the argument that Florida, by using different standards to count votes in different counties—and even in different polling places—had violated the equal protection clause of the Fourteenth Amendment. That was, superficially at least, a meaty rationale, more powerful than the legal technicality trotted out by the conservatives to prop up their vote. Breyer suggested to Kennedy that he join himself as well as Justices Stevens, Ginsburg, and Souter (the four liberals) to rule that Florida needed to establish a uniform standard for counting votes—and then let the recount go on.

For a moment, Kennedy seemed to waver and tip into the liberal camp. But then he pulled back. Now it was Justice O'Connor's turn to use her political wiles. She worked with Kennedy to fashion an opinion that used the equal protection clause of the Fourteenth Amendment to reverse the Florida Supreme Court—but to end the recount. O'Connor was a utilitarian. Finding the right constitutional theory to support an outcome was a little like finding the right spare part, from the piles around the ranch, to fix a broken windmill. If one old part didn't work, find another. Somewhat amazingly, O'Connor persuaded the three conservatives—Scalia, Rehnquist, and Thomas—to sign on to the equal protection rationale (even though Scalia privately scoffed that it was, "as we say in Brooklyn, a piece of shit"). Using the Fourteenth Amendment had the advantage of allowing the Court to say that seven of the nine justices agreed on the reasoning—even if only five agreed on the result. The opinions of the justices in the minority offered lofty criticisms of the majority—for "lend[ing] credence to the most cynical appraisal of the work of judges throughout the land," wrote a scornful Justice Stevens. But the liberals' solution was problematic, too. Had Gore ultimately won, the Court would have become a punching bag for outraged Republicans.

There could be no happy ending. Kennedy wrote the florid language of the Court's opinion, and O'Connor inserted the most banal—and telling—phrase: The holding of the Court's opinion was "limited to the present circumstances, for the problem of equal protection in election processes generally presents many complexities."

In other words, the Court's opinion was extremely narrow—a one-time ticket to get out of a jam.[66]

At home on the Monday night before the decision was announced, she "made us a Scotch," Brian recalled, and watched the *NewsHour* on PBS. The analysis of the legal arguments by the legal experts brought on the show was so off the mark that she visibly "flinched," said Brian. John was in Arizona (where he still kept an office at Bryan, Cave), so O'Connor took her son and his two friends across the street to the Chevy Chase Club for a hamburger. No cellphones were allowed in the clubhouse, but she ignored the rule and took four calls. When Brian went to bed, his mother was still dressed, standing in her study, and "there was a lot of faxing going on."

His mother was up when Brian arose at five fifteen to catch a flight back to Phoenix. She toasted her son an English muffin. "Well, we made our decision," she said. Brian knew enough not to ask what the decision was. "Half this country is going to hate me," she said. The justice's tone was "matter-of-fact," Brian recalled. But, he said, "I could see that she was really bothered that people would despise her."[67]

WHAT MOTIVATED JUSTICE O'Connor during the days and nights she decided the most difficult and momentous case of her life? That she wanted George W. Bush to win the election over Albert Gore, Jr., is no doubt true. But it would be wrong to say that she was driven by partisan politics. More likely, she was moved by values she had learned growing up on the Lazy B—of self-reliance and responsibility, of the duty to step up to face dirty and hard tasks, without hesitation and without complaint. She knew she would be splattered with mud when the job was done. But her motivations were not so much selfish—in fact, by voting for an outcome that secured Bush's election, she was, she knew, robbing herself of the chance to retire, at least right away. To take advantage of a Republican that she had helped put in the White House would be unseemly—unattractive, as she used the word in its deepest meaning. Had the Court allowed the recount and had Bush ultimately won, either in Florida or in Congress, she would have felt free to step down. It is an irony of her vote in *Bush v. Gore* that it guaranteed she could not retire anytime soon.

O'Connor was in a difficult position; indeed, they all were. She was willing to expose herself (along with the institution she cherished) to harsh criticism—temporary, she hoped—for the greater good, to spare the nation political chaos. She believed that the country faced a deep existential crisis that tested the rule of law and civil society. She did not trust a fractious Congress—and certainly not the Florida courts and political system—to solve it. So she did what her father had taught her to do. Making no excuses, she fixed the tire (or, more like it, grabbed the bull by the horns). Then she moved on, or tried to.

CHAPTER FOURTEEN

AFFIRMATIVE ACTION

"What's fair?"

With John and Justices Thomas and Scalia in the old Supreme Court chamber at the U.S. Capitol before George W. Bush's inauguration. "Oh, Nino," Sandra would sigh when Scalia aimed a sharp dissent at her. "She was the glue" that kept the Court together, Thomas says.

A T TEN O'CLOCK on the night of December 12, 2000, the Supreme Court press office handed out the Court's decision in *Bush v. Gore*. The per curiam, unsigned opinion of the Court, accompanied by a welter of concurrences and dissents, was so convoluted that the journalists lined up outside on the cold marble steps visibly struggled to make sense of it for the cameras. Within a minute or two, it was apparent that the next president would be George W. Bush. Most of the justices had already left the building, driving in their cars from the Court's underground garage.

The criticism of the Court came right away, and it was merciless. "A travesty," wrote Mary McGrory of *The Washington Post*. Maureen Dowd, the sharpest pen on the *New York Times* op-ed page, crafted a wickedly funny send-up of the justices asking questions from the bench. Justice O'Connor was depicted as quoting from her friends at the Chevy Chase Club and asking David Boies, the lawyer for the Gore campaign, "Are you aware that if I side with you I could put in jeopardy the membership of my husband, John, in the Bohemian Grove?" In his diary, John wrote about Dowd, "She zapped SOC and me."[1]

The more serious questions revolved around the Court's use of the Fourteenth Amendment to justify stopping the recount. Many commentators noted that the equal protection clause had been a tool for liberal judicial activists to expand federal power. So why were all five of the Court's conservatives, who usually took up the cause of states' rights, borrowing it to justify the outcome in *Bush v. Gore*? Pure politics was the answer given by skeptical Court watchers across the ideological spectrum.[2]*

---

* According to Gallup, public approval of the Supreme Court dipped sharply

The cynics had a point. Justice Scalia told his ally on the D.C. Court of Appeals, Judge Laurence Silberman, that he signed on to Tony Kennedy's Fourteenth Amendment rationale in order to keep Kennedy from swinging over to the liberals and costing the conservatives their majority vote to stop the recount. "Tony was like a depth charge loose on deck," he told Silberman. There were some principled defenses of *Bush v. Gore,* most notably by Richard Posner, a brilliant free-market-oriented federal court of appeals judge in Chicago, who praised the Court's (and O'Connor's) pragmatism. But the criticism from the legal and journalistic establishment was bitter and unrelenting.[4]

Justice O'Connor left town for Arizona right after the decision. At a Christmas dinner at the Valley Field Riding and Polo Club, she told her friend Betsy Taylor, "Oh, we'll never get over this." Taylor recalled, "She was really upset."[5] Nevertheless, during the vacation, she scored her first-ever hole-in-one at the Paradise Valley Country Club.

Back in Washington, at a New Year's party thrown by Najeeb Halaby, the former head of Pan American World Airways, Justice O'Connor came up behind Ann Hoopes and grabbed her arm. "Ann, everybody hates me," she said. "I felt like saying, 'Well, you deserved it,'" said Hoopes. Her husband, Tim, wrote Sandra a blistering letter: "I was shocked, along with millions of others, by the naked partisan power play executed by a narrow majority of the court. . . . And I was profoundly disappointed that you chose to be a part of this." O'Connor defended the Court, and, for a time, Tim Hoopes and Sandra O'Connor, old friends, avoided each other.[6]

Bush v. Gore was a "burr under her saddle," recalled former senator Alan Simpson. "She'd say, 'I really don't want to talk about this.'" Normally, her friends knew not to ask her about Court business, but after *Bush v. Gore,* some could not resist. Her standard answer, if pressed on why the Court did what it did, was short, cool, and mildly enigmatic: "We just had to move on." She never pointed out that there were four other justices in the majority or made a cogent defense of their actions.[7] At public speaking events, she would begin the Q&A

after *Bush v. Gore,* quickly recovered, then gradually slumped again as President Bush's approval ratings fell.[3]

session by announcing, "Don't ask me about *Bush v. Gore.*" Former president Jimmy Carter told friends that he was so incensed with Justice O'Connor that he determined not to speak to her when they were both fly-fishing in the summer of 2002 at Silver Tip in Montana, a lodge part-owned by Ralph Davidson, the former Time-Life president. President Carter's vow of silence melted as soon as he and the justice started tying flies together.[8]

O'Connor had a way of disarming people with her vivacious good cheer and joy at games and entertainment. In the wake of *Bush v. Gore,* Hattie Babbitt, whose intervention two decades before had helped lift O'Connor to the Arizona Court of Appeals, was grievously disappointed. "My emotions ran from appalled to depressed to disgusted," she recalled. "People who liked Sandra were walking out of the room when she walked in. Not to be rude, they just didn't want to face her." In April 2001, four months after the decision, the Babbitts ran into the O'Connors at a showing of the movie *O Brother, Where Art Thou?* at Mazza Gallery near their Washington homes. "We couldn't avoid them," remembered Hattie. "Sandra said, 'Why don't you come over to our house for dinner?' Bruce said, 'Sure!' She made dinner, spinach and peas salad. She knew what she was doing. Coming together over food, a gesture to old times." Hattie's husband, the former governor, Bruce Babbitt, added, "We didn't talk at all about the case. We talked about ranching."[9]

No one was more determined to move on from setbacks, large and small, than Sandra O'Connor. At the annual New Year's Eve party at Frank Saul's country house on the Eastern Shore of Maryland, O'Connor led the partygoers in writing lists of everything that had gone wrong in their lives that year, crumpling them up, and throwing them in the fire.[10] (Possibly encouraged by John, she also tried to make light of the *Bush v. Gore* imbroglio: The O'Connor Christmas card for 2000 read, "May Your New Year Be Free of Hanging Chads.") Still, the questions about the case nagged at her for years. Speaking to the London School of Economics after she retired, she was asked if she regretted *Bush v. Gore.* "I did what I had to do. It's over. Get on with it," she responded. She seemed uncharacteristically defensive, recalled Mark Ellis, her colleague and friend who ran CEELI. "Everyone was taken aback," he said.

O'Connor liked to point to Florida recounts sponsored by large media organizations showing that Bush would have won anyway if the recount demanded by Gore and ordered by the Florida courts had gone on. "Now, there were three separate recounts of the four critical counties in Florida . . . because the ballots were all saved, so they could go through and count them. And in none of the recounts would the results have changed, so, you know, I don't worry about it anymore," she told one audience in 2009. "I think, okay, if there were something wrong we would have heard about it. The press would have told us, right? So I'm going to let sleeping dogs lie."[11]

Over a decade after the decision, the editorial board of the *Chicago Tribune,* one of the media organizations sponsoring the recount, asked O'Connor again about *Bush v. Gore.* The Supreme Court "took the case and decided it at a time when it was still a big election issue. Maybe the Court should have said, 'We're not going to take it, goodbye.' . . . Probably, the Supreme Court added to the problem at the end of the day," said O'Connor, in a rare moment of second-guessing. Asking not to be named, one of O'Connor's law clerks recounted to the author in 2016 that O'Connor had told the clerk that she regretted *Bush v. Gore.* Apprised of this unusual confession, Justice Stevens said, "She didn't care enough about it [referring to the blow to the Court's credibility]. She voted incorrectly. She made a terrible mistake."[12]

In January 2017, asked if she had any regrets about *Bush v. Gore* as she sat in a wheelchair at her assisted living facility, she answered, "I'm sure I did, but second thoughts don't do you a lot of good. It looked like a party-line vote, I know." Her craggy face softened and grew sad.[13]

When President Bush was inaugurated in January 2001, Justice O'Connor and her family had not joined in the celebrations. "After Bush was elected, she blackballed going to any social events for Bush '43," recalled Brian O'Connor. "She never wanted people to feel there was a tit-for-tat."* There was no more talk of retiring.[15]

---

* Less than forty-eight hours after the Court's decision, Justice O'Connor encouraged a mutual friend to recommend to Bush's recount adviser Jim Baker that the president-elect "immediately communicate his intention to play down lavish inaugural celebrations, the high-profile parties with costly catering, the

. . .

ON A CHAIR in Justice O'Connor's office was a pillow, the cheeky gift of some friends, embroidered with the motto MAYBE IN ERROR BUT NEVER IN DOUBT. In the spring of 2001, a few months after *Bush v. Gore,* the justice agreed to see Jeffrey Rosen, a George Washington Law School professor who was writing a cover profile of the justice for *The New York Times Magazine.* She was wary of Rosen, who had written critically about her. "There is nothing moderate or restrained about Justice O'Connor's jurisprudence," Rosen had penned in an earlier op-ed for the *Times.* "Rather than being guided by consistent legal rules, lawyers and judges must try to read her mind." On the top of a photocopy of the piece, the justice had scrawled, "Save a copy of this nasty article."[16]

Turning down Rosen's request for an interview, she gave him a cursory tour of her chambers. She was herding him out the door when he noticed the pillow with the inscription. In his June 3, 2001, cover story for the *Times* ("A Majority of One"), he wrote, "Contrast O'Connor's embroidered motto—'Maybe in error but never in doubt'—with the judicial tradition . . . of judicial humility." Against O'Connor's pillow, Rosen contrasted Learned Hand's quote, "The spirit of liberty is the spirit which is not too sure that it is right." Rosen concluded, "O'Connor's jurisprudence has not been judicial restraint but a kind of judicial imperiousness: she views the court in general, and herself in particular, as the proper forum to decide every political and constitutional question in the land."[17]

O'Connor was not pleased with the cover drawing, which made her look like George Washington, and not pleased with Rosen's biting critique. Her secretary, Linda Neary, was instructed that in the future, whenever a journalist called, she was to remove the pillow.[18] Five years after O'Connor left the Court, Rosen wrote an article entitled "Why I Miss Sandra Day O'Connor." He warmly praised her moderation

---

expensive parades with exotic floats, etc., and perhaps somehow redirect those celebration funds toward underwriting the costs of an extensive study of the election flaws and inconsistencies in this country." The suggestion went nowhere.[14]

(relative to the newer justices) and pragmatism. When he became president of the National Constitution Center in 2013, she was on the board of trustees.[19]

But in 2001, Rosen cut with a sharp edge. His misgivings about her jurisprudence were widely shared by other constitutional scholars, including a few of her otherwise protective former law clerks. Still, having barely met O'Connor, Rosen could not know her. Certainly in later life she could come across as too sure of herself, but she was not, in any real sense, an arrogant person; she did not have an exaggerated sense of her own importance. She knew that she was performing a large public role as FWOTSC, and she did not shy from the responsibility.

O'Connor is easy to caricature and harder to understand. She could present a confusing or contradictory image. She could be charming or brusque. She could be disarmingly straightforward; she could also be roundabout and sly. It is difficult to reconcile the "bossy" O'Connor, who would tell passengers exactly where to sit in a car, with the modest O'Connor, who practiced judicial "minimalism," preferring to stick to the facts and let the law slowly evolve rather than making broad pronouncements. ("I guess you could say she was bossy about minimalism," quipped Cass Sunstein, the author of the book on judicial minimalism.)[20]

O'Connor liked to be in control, and she could warm to the challenge of putting together a majority of justices in a big, close case. But "she didn't like those 'Most Powerful Woman in the World' articles," said RonNell Andersen Jones, who clerked for O'Connor in the 2003 term. A Mormon who graduated from Ohio State Law School, Jones got to know O'Connor as well as any clerk other than Ruth McGregor, seeing subtleties and complexities that even the most astute journalists missed.

Jones rejected the "trope" of the "Maybe in error but never in doubt" pillow. "It misconstrues a layer of vulnerability . . . not vulnerability, but humility. Humbleness," said Jones. Although O'Connor could take pleasure in shaping majorities—enjoying her spot in "the cat bird's seat," as John O'Connor once wrote in his diary—on hard, close cases with heavy societal ramifications, "she did not relish her role as the fifth vote," said Jones. "I heard her agonize over it. She never came back from the conference saying, 'We are for sure driving this train!'" On the big cases, Jones—and many other clerks—would hear her say simply, "Oh, help!"

As Jones understood her, the justice wasn't beseeching her clerks, or anyone in particular, for help. It was more of an existential plea. "To God? To the universe?" said Jones. "She was not full of trepidation, but she did find the work weighty. The justice's attitude was, 'We have a job to do, and somehow we'll get through it.' There was no victory dance."

Jones, like O'Connor, had grown up on a cattle ranch where the reward of the Almighty was the hope, and self-reliance was the rule. Over time, the older woman and the younger woman became close as they talked about their fathers, both charismatic, strong-willed men who were benign autocrats in their domains. They talked about the "ranch mentality," the obligation to "dig in," the faith that "work was the solution to a whole lot of things."[21]

O'Connor did not like show-offs, but she did want to be a role model, which required—as she forthrightly acknowledged—a certain amount of showing off. The trick was to do so modestly and humbly. O'Connor wanted to tell her story, but on her own, carefully modulated terms.

As it happened, just as Jeffrey Rosen came for his quick noninterview tour of Justice O'Connor's chambers in the spring of 2001, O'Connor had just finished putting the last touches on her own memoir of growing up on the Lazy B. The book had been several years in the making. Since the midnineties, O'Connor had been pursued by Sam Vaughan, the Random House editor whose authors included Wallace Stegner, Sandra Day's old Stanford writing teacher who had gone on to be a Pulitzer Prize–winning novelist of the West.[22] In 1998, just as John O'Connor was starting to write his own unpublished memoirs, Sandra began talking to her brother, Alan, about telling the saga of the Lazy B. "Write what you want and send it to me," she instructed Alan. He struggled with a narrative, and then hit on the idea of writing six cameo chapters, one each about MO and DA and the other four about different cowboys on the ranch. He and Sandra got together for a few days in Iron Springs and roughed out the rest.

"We laughed about our genes," Alan recalled. "Some great ones and some you would not want." Sandra "ratcheted back the chapter on DA about five notches," he added.[23]

The structure of *Lazy B* is random, perhaps intentionally so; one chapter is entitled simply "More About Jim" (Brister, one of the colorful cowboys). But the prose is at once simple and highly charged—not unlike Wallace Stegner's—and the impressionistic quality allowed O'Connor to reveal much about her upbringing without actually revealing too much about her own inner life. "*Lazy B* provides a palimpsest of the adult author," wrote Linda Greenhouse in *The New York Times Book Review*. (A palimpsest is a manuscript from which the original writing has been effaced to make room for later writing but of which traces remain.) The book makes no "explicit attempt" to reconcile the "Sandra Day O'Connor the public knows: the prim and button-down onetime president of the Phoenix Junior League . . . who grew up to become the first woman on the United States Supreme Court" with the little ranch girl raised to be "no sissy." But it was nonetheless an "engaging memoir," wrote Greenhouse, which it was, selling well enough to make the *New York Times* bestseller list. Greenhouse's review was respectful of the Day children's reverence for the austere and demanding country they called their own. O'Connor inked a warm thank-you to "Dear Linda," whose writing about the Court she admired. "No column by you will ever capture my heart more than this," she wrote.[24]

JUSTICE O'CONNOR WAS in India, spreading the gospel of the rule of law, when the terrorists struck New York and Washington on September 11, 2001. A month after she arrived home, she and the other justices had to evacuate their chambers when a letter dusted with anthrax spores showed up in the Supreme Court's mailroom. Crammed into the chambers of a court of appeals judge in the federal courthouse downtown, "she was not happy about the whole thing," recalled Michelle Friedland, a clerk (and later a judge on the Ninth Circuit Court of Appeals). "She was at a judge's desk and we were sitting on the floor. It was makeshift and she liked order. She said, 'We can't let this distract us. We have to keep going.'" Recalled Anup Malani, another 2001 clerk: "She had a way of saying 'calm down' without saying calm down."[25]

The clerks responded by trying too hard, carving "Osama bin Pumpkin" at Halloween. One of the clerks, Jeremy Gaston, recalled that he was "very worried" about the prospect of another terrorist attack. "I was truly scared," he recalled. "It was all I could do to continue focusing on work." Gaston had the skills of a professional juggler and pianist (he had auditioned as both for the justice, who had inquired, "Can you juggle three cantaloupes?"), but he was more of a computer scientist than a constitutional scholar. "I was always worried I wasn't doing well enough," he remembered. "But she had confidence in me. I'll never forget the big hug she gave me at the end. It meant so much to me. I had done my best and it was good enough."[26]

For the clerks, there were the ritual tests to be passed. On the morning of the annual end-of-March trek down Capitol Hill to view the cherry blossoms, a gale-force wind whipped freezing rain. "Surely we are not going," a clerk, Carolyn Frantz (later deputy general counsel at Microsoft), said to O'Connor's secretary, Linda Neary. "Justice O'Connor does not change because of the weather," replied Neary. "The weather changes because of Justice O'Connor." On the walk down the Hill, "it was slippery," recalled Frantz. "I put my arm out [to steady her]. She just hit it."[27] She did not want to be reminded of her age.

She had become a grandmotherly figure, but she still dyed her hair blond, and when she was inducted into the Cowgirl Hall of Fame that June in 2002, she spoke of the code of self-reliance she had learned at the Lazy B.[28] Fishing at Silver Tip the summer before, she had slipped on a wet rock and badly hurt her arm, John recorded in his diary. "She didn't want anyone to know about it, so she had a woman in the kitchen help her put on a bandage."[29]

She was determined not to show weakness or fragility, especially as John drifted further into dementia. John's Georgetown neurologist, Dr. Paul Aisen, met regularly with the justice and John during 2001 and 2002 as his struggle deepened. Her keep-calm-and-carry-on approach—making the usual round of parties, letting John get himself around town—was no longer sustainable. "I began to suggest in 2001 that she get more involved," Dr. Aisen recalled. "I was urging him to quit drinking and begging him to stop driving, and she needed to watch him take his meds."

On April 22, 2002—less than a month after O'Connor swatted away her clerk's helping hand on the frozen march to the cherry blossoms—the O'Connors met with Dr. Aisen to hear his report that John was "declining." "He's having trouble writing down his thoughts. He can't remember his words," Dr. Aisen wrote in his notes. Justice O'Connor began crying "discussing his condition," then "John teared up." Two weeks later, on May 5, John "reported insomnia—several sleepless nights each week," a common condition with Alzheimer's. On June 26, Justice O'Connor told the neurologist that her husband "is not able to fulfill simple instructions." In September, she reported that John was depressed. In a phone conversation on October 1, she said that he was having trouble making simple statements and was putting the trash in the wrong place. She was "upset by loss of intimacy," Dr. Aisen wrote in his notes. By then, John had given up his diary. On May 21, he had noted, in one of his last entries, that sleeping in the same bed—which they had loved—was more of a challenge. He wrote: "SOC fixed a low-key dinner. It was fantastic. We went to bed. Once again, it was difficult for us. I couldn't sleep and my movements were waking SOC up. It is a very, very bad problem." But here he was, too, still appreciating her cooking.[30]

JUSTICE O'CONNOR CONTINUED to devote herself to mentoring her clerks. Carolyn Frantz's self-image when she arrived in Justice O'Connor's chambers in the summer of 2001 was not unusual for a newly minted Supreme Court clerk. "I was a bit of a snot," she said. "I thought it was all about being an intellectual powerhouse." From her boss, she learned "the importance of being socially gifted and human."

Frantz got a lesson in simple humanity while laboring over a habeas corpus case, an appeal from a convicted prisoner. "It was very complex, hard intellectually. I parsed subsection B and so forth and decided the prisoner should get no relief," Frantz recalled. She presented her conclusion to Justice O'Connor. "She just asked, 'Do you think this is fair?'" Frantz thought for a moment and answered, "Well, no."[31]

But is it fair? That had been Earl Warren's famous question. The chief justice of the Warren Court was known to cut through legal niceties and obfuscations to get to the heart of the case, especially when it came to expanding the Fourteenth Amendment's guarantees of due process and equal protection. O'Connor may have entered the Court as an ally of William Rehnquist to roll back the incursions of federal power on states' rights, but by the beginning of her third decade on the High Court, she sounded more like Earl Warren when the facts compelled her, as they did in the case of *Atwater v. Lago Vista,* decided in the spring of 2001.

Gail Atwater was driving her two small children back from soccer practice in the town of Lago Vista, Texas, when a local policeman pulled her over because she and her children were not wearing seat belts. Mrs. Atwater was handcuffed and carted off to jail for an hour or so and ultimately paid a $50 fine. She sued the police for violating her constitutional rights. The "Soccer Mom" case went to the Supreme Court, where a majority of the justices—the four conservatives plus Justice Souter—ruled that she had no case. "It's not a constitutional violation for a police officer to be a jerk," said Justice Kennedy at oral argument. O'Connor, voting with the liberals, filed an impassioned dissent. "She really dug into the record to get the human dynamics," recalled Jennifer Mason McAward, one of her clerks. Justice O'Connor noted that Atwater's three-year-old had been "traumatized" by knowing that his mother was being taken to jail. Although race had not been involved in the case (Atwater was a white woman), O'Connor accused the majority of unintentionally encouraging racial profiling by police. What message was the Court sending the cops, she asked, who pulled over and harassed young black men for petty traffic violations? Molly Ivins, a liberal commentator, hailed O'Connor for her real-world vision, applauding her "best ever" dissent.[32]

The plight of women and children reached a deep place in O'Connor. So, too, discrimination against minorities. But she continued to see no easy answer for the legacy of racism in society. Race, or rather racial preference, continued to be a bedeviling question for Justice O'Connor, partly because she occupied an ever lonelier no-man's-land between the conservatives, who wanted to end affirmative action, and the liberals, who wanted to preserve it.

O'Connor wished to believe that the day was coming when racial preferences would no longer be necessary. In 1995, the Court, with O'Connor voting with the conservative majority, struck down an effort by the Georgia legislature to design congressional districts that guaranteed black representation. The editorial page of The New York Times accused the Court of "gutting" the 1965 Voting Rights Act, but O'Connor was heartened by the reaction of a black Republican congressman who said he was "thrilled" with the decision. John O'Connor described his wife watching the coverage of the case on her favorite news show, PBS's MacNeil/Lehrer NewsHour. The congressman, "whose district is 90 percent white," was "very articulate, friendly, and sharp," wrote John. "SOC was overwhelmed by his presentation and his thesis that whites will vote for blacks whose views are similar to theirs." O'Connor clung to her faith that the power of ideas could be more persuasive than skin pigmentation.[33]

At the same time, O'Connor, the realist, was mindful of more pessimistic views. She knew that her old friend and mentor on race matters, Thurgood Marshall, had believed it would take at least another century before racial preferences were no longer required to cure the historic effects of segregation and racial oppression. (Her other, closer friend, Justice Powell, had been rendered speechless when Marshall made his hundred-year prediction at the justices' conference on the Bakke case in December 1977.)[34]

At the University of Michigan Law School, affirmative action was entering its third decade when O'Connor toured the school in December 1996 after receiving an honorary degree. Her tour guide was her former clerk, now the law school's associate dean, Kent Syverud. As they walked through the basement of the main legal research building, O'Connor noticed that the corridor's billboards were plastered with notices from various race- and gender-based student groups: blacks, Hispanics, Asians, women. "She was appalled," Syverud recalled. O'Connor asked, "Is this what diversity is going to be all about?" She disliked victimhood and identity politics. "She was very annoyed about the idea of a 'woman's point of view,'" said Syverud. "She had a lot of experience of her own to know that the playing field was not always level, but she disliked explicit recognitions of race." O'Connor was an old-fashioned integrationist who believed in the mixing bowl; to her, separatism and tribalism undermined the civic understanding she held as her greatest ideal.

Standing in the basement, O'Connor and Syverud discussed affirmative action. O'Connor wanted to know "When is long enough? How do we get to that point?" She wanted a temporary way to force racial inclusion. She was willing to take practical measures to reach her goal, but she wanted them to be just steps along the way toward a more unified whole. Syverud characterized her views as "Reparations? Terrible! Victim-based solutions? Ugh." O'Connor was "nervous and worried about affirmative action," he recalled—in part because she knew she would, before too long, be ruling on it once again.[35]

Six years later, in December 2002, the University of Michigan's affirmative action program was before the Supreme Court. There were actually two cases. One challenged undergraduate admissions; the other challenged law school admissions.[36]

The undergraduate admissions system, dealing with vastly greater numbers of applicants than the law school admissions, awarded points for grades, class rank, SAT scores, extracurricular leadership, and legacy status. Any applicant who got to 100 points was automatically accepted. Minority candidates started off with a hefty 20 points. As a practical matter a minority B student with 1200 SATs got in; a white student with the same record did not. At the much smaller law school, the system was more "holistic" and individualized; the admissions committee considered each applicant on the merits. Race was a "factor," but not determinative. In theory, that is; one year, one of fifty-one whites with a B average and middling-to-high LSATs was admitted, while ten of ten blacks were. Racial preference was probably no less a leg up at the law school than it was at the college. It was, however, less overt.[37]

The University of Michigan had hired the high-powered Washington law firm Wilmer, Cutler & Pickering to defend its affirmative action programs in the Supreme Court. Working on the case was O'Connor's former clerk Stuart Delery. Lawyers often specifically target particular justices when they make their arguments. After the publication of Lazy B in early 2002, O'Connor soon tired of briefs making allusions to ranch life.[38]

It was obvious that O'Connor's vote would be critical in the affirmative action cases, so Delery and the other Wilmer lawyers (he was on a team led by John Payton, a noted civil rights lawyer) crafted their arguments with her in mind. Delery had worked in Justice O'Connor's chambers during 1995, the year she had written the Court's majority opinion in *Adarand*, the case subjecting federal "set-asides" for minority contractors to strict scrutiny. He knew that she would apply "strict scrutiny" to racial preferences, but that, as she saw it, strict scrutiny was not "fatal in fact"—that context always mattered.[39] The model was the opinion written by O'Connor's old friend (and role model) Lewis Powell in *Bakke*. Explicit racial quotas were out. But "holistic" admissions policies that used race as one factor among others—like the Harvard College approach recommended by Powell, whereby race could tip the scales, but not obviously—were more likely to pass O'Connor's constitutional muster.

Delery had started his clerkship shortly after Justice O'Connor had written the Court's opinion in one of the first cases testing how far state legislatures could go using race to draw congressional districts. "In *Shaw v. Reno*, all the evidence suggested she just recoiled at drawing racial lines. It was unattractive. It was unseemly. She disliked race as a predominant factor," recalled Delery.

"We knew she had deep respect for Powell. We set out to prove that Powell was right in *Bakke*—that diversity is good for whites as well as blacks, and to show that race was not a predominant factor in admissions," Delery recalled. "So we got social scientists talking about the effects of diversity, and we got statisticians to show that race was one of many factors. We knew if race was predominant, we were dead."

One wise step taken by the Wilmer team was to enlist Kent Syverud, the former associate dean at Michigan Law and former O'Connor clerk, as an expert witness at the trial court. Because the grades and test scores of racial minorities continued to lag behind those of white students, doing away with affirmative action at top schools like the University of Michigan would mean classrooms with very few minority faces. Indeed, virtual resegregation had happened at the University of California Law School in Berkeley when a state referendum had abolished racial preferences in the midnineties. Giving minorities a boost was the only way to reach "a critical mass," Syverud had testified. His words were aimed straight at the justice who had been made uncomfortable by the identity-group pleadings of the posters in the basement of Michigan Law School. In her opinion in *Grutter v. Bollinger*, the law school case, O'Connor would cite Syverud's expert testimony and sum up his argument with a slightly labored syllogism of legal argumentation: "When a critical mass of underrepresented minority students is present, racial stereotypes lose their force because non-minority students learn there is no 'minority viewpoint' but rather a variety of viewpoints among minority students." Syverud had in effect said to his old boss that if you want to get a place where ideas matter more than skin color, you need to double down on affirmative action to create a "critical mass."[40]

Perhaps the smartest play by Delery and the University of Michigan legal team was to make sure O'Connor could, as he put it, "split the baby." O'Connor's clerks knew she preferred to compromise by rejecting extremes in the search for solutions in the middle. The clerks called it "baby-bearing," from the fable "Goldilocks and the Three Bears," in which Papa Bear's porridge is too hot, Mama Bear's too cold, and Baby Bear's "just right."[41]

In the case involving undergraduate admissions (*Gratz v. Bollinger*), affirmative action was "too hot"—it was based on numbers, with a whopping 20 points (out of 100 needed to gain admission) assigned purely for race, which sounded like a quota. But no affirmative action at all was too cold. It would slash minority enrollment. The tippy-top law schools—Harvard, Yale, Stanford—would use full scholarships to scoop up the relatively small number of African Americans with high LSAT scores, leaving merely excellent schools like Michigan with unacceptably low numbers of blacks. In the law school admissions system challenged in the *Grutter* case, however, there was a formula for "just right"—race as a factor, but not a determining factor, and the whole process artfully fuzzed up as "holistic."

In a strategic move, the University of Michigan encouraged the Supreme Court to review both cases at once, even though the undergraduate case was not through the appeals process in the courts below. It is likely that O'Connor instinctively saw a middle way even before she began to seriously delve into the case.

She did not welcome her role as the decisive vote. She knew she was alone in the middle, that the other swing vote, Anthony Kennedy, would go with the conservatives to reject affirmative action in state universities. Justin Nelson, one of her clerks, recalled, "She pulled me over and said, 'This is going to come down to me.' "[42]

"The cases loomed over our chambers," recalled Emily Henn, another of her clerks in 2002–2003. "She was reading the newspapers, to see how the country was grappling with affirmative action. Not just the law books and briefs." During the oral arguments that winter, large crowds of demonstrators collected outside the Court. O'Connor suggested to Justin Nelson that he go outside and talk to the people. "She wanted to know what the world was saying," recalled Cristina Rodriguez, another OT '02 clerk.

The diversity in O'Connor's own chambers was "very deliberate," noted Henn. Though she didn't pay close attention to ideology per se in hiring clerks, O'Connor wanted to hear from different points of view. Rodriguez was a Hispanic woman from Yale Law School, a Rhodes Scholar, and deeply committed to civil rights. "I thought because I was involved in a human rights clinic and a labor law clinic I would be too liberal. Later, I realized she wanted balance." One clerk, Allyson Newton Ho, was a conservative activist—the head of the Federalist Society at the University of Chicago Law School—while the other two that term fell along the spectrum toward the left. Rodriguez believed that O'Connor herself was farther to the left than she let on. "'What's fair?' definitely motivated her thinking," said Rodriguez. Asked about O'Connor's claim that a "wise man and a wise woman" would reach the same result as a judge, Rodriguez answered, "Judges have to say that. There is no question that because she was a woman it informed her decision making. A man could not have written *Hogan* [her first gender rights case]. She wanted to believe that she was an independent thinker, that she had no gender inclination, but I don't know how a woman could say that seriously."

As usual in fraught, high-profile cases, O'Connor was careful not to tip her hand around the clerks. "We got a few hints," said Rodriguez. "She said, 'We said this ["narrowly tailored" affirmative action] was okay in *Bakke*.' But she never told us what she was reading. I recall an extended debate in her chambers. She didn't say a word."

Dozens of legal briefs in the *Gratz* and *Grutter* cases were stacked high in her office. "There was a chart showing the impact on California schools after the referendum abolishing affirmative action. That's what got to her," said Rodriguez. "It showed a steep drop-off in minorities. She couldn't accept the effect on elite institutions." One amicus curiae ("friend of the court") brief supporting affirmative action was signed by a raft of top military officers, including Colin Powell and a number of former chairmen of the Joint Chiefs of Staff. It argued that affirmative action was necessary at the military academies and in the officer corps to make sure there was no yawning racial gap through the ranks. The military—indeed, all major institutions—needed to look like society at large. "She sometimes wouldn't read friend-of-court briefs but I know she was interested in that one," recalled Emily Henn. "She wanted to know how affirmative action affected society and institutions." The polling data on affirmative action tends to be murky, since the answers depend on the questions. (Do you approve of quotas? No. Do you approve of affirmative action? Yes. Do you approve of racial preferences? Maybe not; it depends.) But opinion among the establishment elite was clear: Affirmative action was necessary to make their institutions "look like America." O'Connor, who often mixed with corporate executives, may also have been affected by pro-affirmative-action briefs from major businesses.[43]

Because of the demands of John's illness, Justice O'Connor no longer cooked crock pots of chili for the clerks on Saturday. But the clerks still wrote "bench memos" and argued them out with each other while the justice listened and occasionally interjected. Rodriguez wrote the bench memo for *Gratz,* the undergraduate admissions case. She staunchly defended affirmative action. Allyson Newton Ho attacked affirmative action in the bench memo for *Grutter,* the law school case.

"Allyson and Cristina really battled," recalled Henn. "It was a long, heartfelt debate. It wasn't that they were arguing with each other, it was not a fight between them. They were making points to her. It was always her decision."

Rodriguez recalled, "We were fighting over language. She told us to cut it out. She said, 'This is what is going to happen. Put an end to it.' "[44]

O'Connor turned to a third clerk, Justin Nelson, to look for a middle-of-the-road approach. At conference, Justice O'Connor had voted with Chief Justice Rehnquist and four other justices to knock down the rigid numbers-based system of admissions in the undergraduate case. She joined Rehnquist's majority opinion in that case. But in the law school case, she voted with the four liberals to uphold the more flexible affirmative action plan. The senior justice in the majority, John Paul Stevens, assigned the opinion to O'Connor. (Stevens chose O'Connor because, he explained, "I always gave it to the person with the most risk involved. There's a greater chance she'll adhere to her original vote if she writes the opinion herself.")

Writing for the Court, O'Connor relied heavily on Justice Powell's split-the-difference reasoning in *Bakke* and cited the briefs of the military and business leaders. She emphasized that law schools had a history of providing leaders to the nation (a quarter of the current U.S. Senate), and that it was important to include minorities in the "civic life of the nation," her holy grail. She bought the argument of the University of Michigan—and her old clerk, friend, and former Michigan Law associate dean Kent Syverud—that a "critical mass" was necessary to ensure that minorities did not feel isolated or tokenized, and that nonminority students heard their diverse voices.

On this last point, she was perhaps not totally persuaded. Affirmative action had succeeded in increasing the numbers of minorities at top schools. But it had hardly put an end to identity politics. Minorities increasingly clamored for their own identity-group housing and ethnic studies. The spirit of togetherness was difficult to implant on campuses where students sometimes self-segregated at tables in the dining hall. O'Connor was all for the inclusion of different groups, but she wanted them to meld into one civic society. O'Connor was unhappy that at her beloved Stanford, the mandatory course on Western Civilization had been eliminated as "patriarchal" and "hegemonic," although she was careful not to be vocal about her complaints.[45]

In the law school case, O'Connor registered her ambivalence about racial preferences by suggesting a time limit. It had been twenty-five years since Justice Powell upheld "narrowly tailored" affirmative action in *Bakke*. Since then, the numbers and percentages of minority students in higher education had greatly increased, to the point where student bodies at even the most selective schools closely mirrored society at large. In a sentence that she—and not her clerks—wrote, Justice O'Connor declared, "We expect that 25 years from now, the use of racial preferences will no longer be necessary."[46]

Not quite fourteen years later, she told the author, "That may have been a misjudgment."[47] Shortly after she retired from the Court, her African American friend Eric Motley, a senior official at the Aspen Institute, asked her to predict how long affirmative action would be necessary. She answered candidly: "There's no timetable. You just don't know."[48]

IN THE MARBLE Palace, the justices are sometimes a beat or two behind the times. In 1986, when the Court upheld a state antisodomy law that criminalized homosexuality in Bowers v. Hardwick, the fifth and deciding vote was cast by Lewis Powell. In his separate concurring opinion, Powell suggested that he was troubled by the law but rationalized that it was rarely enforced against gays. "I don't think I've ever met a homosexual," Justice Powell told one of his law clerks who was working on the case. The law clerk, who was homosexual, assured the justice that he had, he just didn't know it. Powell, in retirement, later said his vote had been a mistake.[49]

Justice O'Connor also voted to uphold the antisodomy law in Bowers. But her fondness for family helped awaken her to gay rights. When her clerk Stuart Delery, who was gay, adopted a child in 2001, she sent the child a tiny T-shirt claiming him as one of her "grandclerks." "This is okay, right?" she asked her clerks, seeking (somewhat unusually) their reassurance.[50] In 2003, the Court once again ruled on a state antisodomy law in Lawrence v. Texas. This time, O'Connor voted to strike down the law. She based her vote on the equal protection clause—that it was unfair to treat straights and gays differently—rather than on a right of privacy analysis grounded on the Fourteenth Amendment's due process clause, the rationale of the rest of the Court's majority. (This allowed her to be consistent, since she had joined the conservatives back in the Bowers case to find that gays were *not* protected by the due process clause.)

She was not happy with some of the language of Justice Kennedy's majority opinion, which waxed on about the importance of sexuality in human behavior. As she read the draft of his opinion, she exclaimed to her clerks, "This 'joy of sex' paragraph is coming out!"[51]

A decade late, Justice O'Connor presided over one of the first marriages of a gay couple at the Supreme Court (the ceremony was held in the Lawyers' Lounge). One of the couple, Jeff Trammel, thanked her for her vote in *Lawrence,* as he put it, "for making sure my partner and I are no longer felons in our country." Eyes twinkling, she smiled.

JUSTICE O'CONNOR WAS determined to show her clerks, by word and deed, that it was possible to have it all—career and family, health and well-being. But as she struggled to balance the demands of work and family in her own life, she began to seem frenetic, in ways that made the clerks laugh but also caused them to worry about her.

She could seem like a hyper version of herself, teaching self-reliance while meddling protectively in the lives of her clerks. Emily Henn became pregnant before she was scheduled to begin her clerkship for the 2001 term. "Nervously, I went to Justice O'Connor and asked what to do. She told me to talk to my co-clerks and work it out." Henn swapped with another clerk and reported for duty in the 2002 term. Justice O'Connor arranged for Henn to use an empty office while she pumped breast milk, and she excused her from the morning aerobics class—for a while. "At Christmas, she said to me, 'I think it's time to join aerobics. Don't you?'"

Henn got a job at Covington & Burling, Washington's top old-line law firm, after her clerkship, but her husband, a journalist, was offered a job at *Marketplace,* the public radio show based in Los Angeles. Henn asked O'Connor what she should do. "You have to go," said Justice O'Connor. Henn told her she wasn't so sure. That night, at a party, O'Connor ran into a Covington partner. "You've heard that Emily is moving to Los Angeles," bustled O'Connor. The next morning, Henn received "a long, hysterical email" from the partner who had not heard this news, because Henn had not yet decided. At the same time, Henn began to receive job inquiries from former O'Connor clerks at law firms in Los Angeles. When Henn protested to O'Connor that she hadn't yet made up her mind, the justice insisted, "It's time you let him [her husband] be the priority. You'll be fine." Recalled Henn, who stayed in Washington: "It took all I had to resist the pressure to move to L.A." Another clerk, RonNell Andersen Jones, observed that O'Connor's meddling could seem "controlling, except when you're in the middle of it. You realize she is anguishing over you."

Justice O'Connor was increasingly preoccupied with her own husband, though she tried not to show it. During early 2003, John O'Connor began spending his days sitting on a couch in the justice's office, reading, or pretending to read, a newspaper or a book. He had gotten lost once trying to go to his office and lost another time trying to find his way around the Chevy Chase Club. "He'd often join us for lunch," recalled Justin Nelson. "If you didn't know, you'd think he was mostly with it. She made only the briefest, passing comment, 'I'm taking care of him.'" On some days, she would take John home in the midafternoon. "It was increasingly obvious that his brain was not functioning right," recalled Cristina Rodriguez. "He had a great sense of humor, but he'd say off-color things. He lost his filter. I never saw her flinch, or say anything. She just let it go."

Giving a tour of the Court to some friends that year, Justice O'Connor pointed to a portrait of Chief Justice John Marshall and said "he was my favorite justice"—not because of his great opinions, she said, but "because he went home every night to serve dinner to his sickly wife."

Emily Henn recalled, "Sometimes John was quiet, sometimes he was lucid, sometimes he said things that made no sense. The justice would say, 'Oh, John, you don't mean that.' She wouldn't ignore him, but she wouldn't get bothered. He'd say weird things and she managed as best she could. She was patient and loving." A few times, John wandered off down the Court's marble hallways. After that, Justice O'Connor asked a young assistant to take John on walks around the Court. He would cheerfully introduce himself to the guards, again and again.

John could still dance. One evening in the winter of 2003, Allyson Newton Ho took a break from her duties and peeked in on a formal dance in the Great Hall of the Court. "I was awed by the grandeur and majesty of it," recalled Ho. "All the beautifully dressed people. She had silver hair and a brightly colored shirtwaist. She was dancing with John. I saw a glimmer of what it must have been like."[52]

The chambers still teemed with visitors from all over, including, over one three-day stretch, a princess from Thailand, a nun from a silent nunnery, and several Sherpas who had led her son Brian up Mount Everest. The world's tallest mountain, which Brian ascended in May 2003, was the latest conquest of her adventuresome son; he had already climbed the tallest peaks on each of the world's other six continents (and would also dive to the wreck of the *Titanic*). Justice O'Connor was in conference when Brian called on a satellite phone to say that he had reached Everest's summit and was now back at a base camp. O'Connor's secretary, Linda Neary, decided to break the conference's "do not disturb" rule. "The one time I saw real emotion was when her son called her that he had just made it down Mount Everest," recalled Ruth Bader Ginsburg. "You could just see the relief."[53]

IN SEPTEMBER 2004, the new clerks in Justice O'Connor's chambers were feeling overwhelmed. The McCain-Feingold law regulating campaign contributions had been challenged as a violation of the First Amendment's free speech guarantee. Spending money to influence a political campaign, it was argued, was an expression of free speech. With the elections coming in November, the Court had to rule quickly.[54]

The O'Connor clerks were in the weeds, working eighteen hours a day, discussing doctrine, quibbling over technical details. O'Connor, meanwhile, was focused. She knew the case was really about the fungibility of money and the threat of corrupt influence. On one of the clerks' drafts, which was full of complex legalisms entangled in the intricacies of campaign finance legislation, she wrote the phrase, "Money, like water, will always find an outlet." That phrase became the heart of the Supreme Court's decision upholding most of the congressional statute, which had been passed in 2002 to regulate so-called "soft money" contributions, money raised by the national political parties and used to get around earlier campaign finance laws limiting donations to individual candidates.

"She wanted us to bring her what mattered," recalled Sean Grimsley, one of the clerks most directly involved in the case. "But she could identify before we could what *really* mattered. She would have been an extremely good executive, a great governor or president. She could cut to the chase, put aside what was not important, not get sucked in by irrelevant detail. And do it with grace. It never seemed to take much effort."[55]

CHAPTER FIFTEEN

END GAME

"Where's Sandra? Where's Sandra?"

Saying farewell to her friend Bill Rehnquist. Later, Sandra would wonder whether the chief justice had been forthcoming about the state of his health when the two justices were discussing who should step down first.

BEFORE HE CLERKED for Justice O'Connor in the 2003–2004 term, Sam Sankar had been a boat captain and a welder. He had an engineering degree from Cornell, a master's from Stanford, and a law degree from Berkeley. In his interview Justice O'Connor said nothing about the small gold hoops in his ears, but she asked the lower court judge for whom Sankar had clerked, "Does he always wear those earrings?" Word got back to Sankar. He never wore them again.

O'Connor was broadminded in many ways, inclusive, tolerant, and generous. Sankar was a typically eclectic hire. But the justice liked things a certain way. "She had an easy manner, but she was Old School and proper," said RonNell Andersen Jones, an OT '03 clerk who put on lipstick for the first time for her interview. She would later advise female applicants for an O'Connor clerkship to avoid pantsuits. There was an O'Connor code of conduct, a right way of carrying yourself and dealing with others, said Jones. Thank-you notes were to be written on time. Civility, not snark, was the currency of discourse. Extremism of any kind was to be avoided. Absolutism was for demagogues.

In the fall of 2003, the Court heard a challenge to the phrase "under God" in the Pledge of Allegiance, which children recited routinely in school. The phrase, tacked on to the original (1892) pledge by Congress in 1954, was a relic of the Cold War struggle against godless Communism, but a parent had protested that "under God" violated the First Amendment prohibition against the state's "establishing" a religion. At lunch, Justice O'Connor and her clerks discussed the case and the meaning of "under God." The justice regarded the phrase as essentially ceremonial, a nicety, a way to solemnize official business. Sam Sankar, who came from a Hindu family in India, mustered the courage to argue with his boss. He told the justice that the words "under God" did mean something to him: They referred to the singular god of Western monotheistic religions. Hindus, after all, worshipped "gods," plural. Using the justice's own phraseology, Sankar explained that from his point of view, the pledge "conveyed a belief that a particular set of beliefs are favored or preferred," and that he therefore shared the perspective of the atheist plaintiff, who felt that the language of the pledge branded him a "political outsider." O'Connor listened carefully, politely, and ultimately made it clear that Sankar was to draft the concurring opinion her way, upholding the pledge.

"Her basic approach was 'Can't we just get along?' I knew what she was going to say. 'Are we really going to fight over this? Congress put "under God" in there so we could tell each other that we aren't like these godless Commies. They weren't trying to be mean to Hindus and atheists!'" recalled Sankar. "I wrote the opinion. I slipped a reference to Hinduism into a footnote and she let it slide."[1]

O'Connor knew her role on the Court and her place in American public life, and, as she began her twenty-second year as a justice, she enjoyed it. "Once, we had to cross the Great Hall," recalled Sankar. "You could walk around it, but we marched through. She just gently turned her head to the tourists, gave a half smile and a little wave. She knew exactly who she was."

She continued to quarrel with Justice Scalia, in a polite, almost ritualized kind of way. "At the end of each term, I'd ask, 'What happened?'" recalled Scalia's weekly tennis partner, Dr. Bill Leahy. In June 2003, when Justice O'Connor announced the Court's decision upholding affirmative action at Michigan Law School, Scalia was "furious" at O'Connor, said Leahy. "He pointedly said to me, 'You know, one of my colleagues is a politician with legal training. This [her opinion in *Grutter*] is very Clintonian. It's what do the polls show? That's not the way this court is supposed to be run.'"[2]

During that same Court term, the two justices had crossed swords over a case dealing with the right to counsel guaranteed by the Sixth Amendment of the Constitution, a subject O'Connor cared deeply about from her days as a trial court judge. Writing for the Court's 7–2 majority, O'Connor had ordered a new sentencing trial for a convicted murderer because his court-appointed lawyer had incompetently failed to offer mitigating evidence. (The defendant had been badly beaten and burned by his alcoholic mother and sexually abused by one of his foster parents.) Scalia was withering in dissent, describing O'Connor's reasons for ordering a new trial as "incredible" and "feeble."[3]

O'Connor disliked Scalia's incivility, but she was determined not to show it. When the Sierra Club tried to get Scalia disqualified from a case involving federal energy policy, based on his having gone duck hunting with Vice President Dick Cheney, O'Connor backed Scalia when he refused to recuse himself. She did guffaw, however, when, at the annual clerks' skit, Scalia was portrayed as Elmer Fudd chasing "wabbits with wascally Dick Cheney."[4]

O'Connor used her public speeches as a way of preaching her civic religion. Like Thurgood Marshall, she liked to convey moral messages by telling stories, sometimes her own story. When she spoke of the rights of women, "she did not see herself as victimized," said RonNell Andersen Jones, who helped draft many of her speeches in 2003–2004. In recounting how she had been rejected by seemingly every major law firm in California, she emphasized how "lucky" she was to have been forced into the public sector.

For speeches on the legacies of Barry Goldwater and Ronald Reagan, O'Connor wanted to "play up their selflessness, their devotion to hard work, their concern for finding solutions," said Jones. Reagan and Goldwater were different from each other and, in any case, not notably hardworking. But this was another chance for the justice to reinforce a narrative about her role as a pioneer. In her Reagan speech, O'Connor underscored the significance of a conservative president naming a woman to the Supreme Court—that it was a monumental decision, breaking down barriers and building a bridgehead to the future.

Jones could see that for O'Connor, there was a time to be decorous and restrained, and a time to cut loose and go for it. One of the justice's favorite movies was *Legally Blonde,* the 2001 film about a sorority queen who turns stuffy Harvard Law School on its head. In the bustling, bossy Reese Witherspoon character there was a touch of Sandra Day O'Connor. Sharing her boss's ranch upbringing, Jones appreciated the justice's cowgirl sense of humor. In one speech, Jones included an earthy joke about a conversation between Calvin Coolidge and Herbert Hoover. (Coolidge: "You can't expect calves as soon as you put together cows and a bull." Hoover: "But you'd expect some happy cows.") The other clerks protested, "The justice can't make a joke about cow sex in the speech!" Jones recalled. "But she laughed long and hard." The joke stayed in the speech.[5]

THE O'CONNOR FAMILY was at ease with the Bush family. In the 1980s, Sandra had played tennis with Barbara as often as once a week. At Washington dinner parties and official functions, George H. W. Bush charmed the justice with his gracious warmth, and she approved of his pragmatic, conciliatory brand of politics.

The forty-third president was, perhaps inevitably, a less comfortable fit in O'Connor's social and political milieu. George W. had seen his father punished politically as a one-term president for lacking "the vision thing." The son was determined to be rhetorically bolder. After 9/11, as he inveighed against the "Axis of Evil" (North Korea, Iran, and Iraq) and took a hard line in the "War on Terror," the junior Bush became a more polarizing figure. Some of his macho pronouncements, like saying that he wanted Al-Qaeda's Osama bin Laden "dead or alive," seemed more suitable for Rush Limbaugh's talk radio show than the staid, evenhanded PBS *NewsHour with Jim Lehrer* watched by Sandra O'Connor.

Within her own family, O'Connor did not hide her disappointment with the direction taken by the Republican Party since the rise of Newt Gingrich and Fox News. Politics was getting harsher and more partisan, she believed. She regarded the Bush administration's hard-line attorney general, John Ashcroft, as "unattractive." At the same time, after 9/11, she reached out to First Lady Laura Bush, inviting her to her chambers for lunch with some wives of cabinet members and lawmakers. She wanted to put on a show of normalcy and togetherness.

O'Connor felt that too many people in authority had panicked over the terrorist threat. In October 2002, a sniper in a vehicle was randomly shooting people on the streets of greater Washington. Asked by her clerk Justin Nelson if she planned to take any protective steps, O'Connor answered, "No, why would I do that? Of course not! You've got to keep on going."[6]

The administration's way of dealing with suspected terrorists captured outside the United States was to lock the door and throw away the key. So-called "unlawful combatants" in the "War on Terror" had no legal rights. They were neither criminal defendants, who had constitutional protections ranging from the right to counsel to the right to confront their accusers, nor were they prisoners of war, protected from harsh interrogation by international law. Hundreds of "unlawful combatants" had been indefinitely locked away in far-off prisons like Guantanamo, the U.S. naval base in Cuba, or at CIA "black sites," where some were tortured.

O'Connor was uncomfortable with the Bush administration's absolutist position. In the spring of 2004, she was assigned to write the Court's opinion in the case of Yaser Hamdi, an American citizen living in Saudi Arabia who had been arrested by local warlords in Taliban territory in Afghanistan and turned over to American forces. The administration argued that Hamdi was essentially a nonperson, not entitled to any due process. In time of war, the executive had to be given great license to protect national security.[7]

There was little precedent. Lincoln had suspended habeas corpus during the Civil War, and, in the infamous case of *Korematsu v. United States,* the Supreme Court had upheld the internment of Japanese Americans during World War II.[8] It was hard even to know what questions the justice should be asking. On the day of oral arguments, one of her clerks told Justice O'Connor that she assumed they would not be going to aerobics class. "Of course we will," responded the justice. "The most important thing is to stick with routine and take care of yourself."

But little seemed routine in the months and even years after 9/11. The OT 2003 clerks had heard about the anthrax scare from O'Connor's secretary, Linda Neary, who became choked up just remembering it. On a morning in early June at the end of term, while O'Connor was working on the case of *Hamdi v. Rumsfeld,* suddenly there was a horrific alarm. On the walls, emergency lights started flashing red. One of the marshals came running into the chambers, physically grabbed Justice O'Connor, and hustled her out the door.

Down the stairs in the Court's garage, black sedans were whizzing up and screeching to a halt, doors flung open. Court marshals were shoving the justices in (a clerk ran up and tried to jump in, too). Back in the chambers, the clerks all thought Washington was under attack.

It was a false alarm. A plane carrying the governor of Kentucky to Ronald Reagan's memorial service at the National Cathedral had wandered into restricted airspace and not responded to queries from the control tower. The plane seemed to be on a course for the Capitol or the Supreme Court, and National Guard jets were preparing to shoot it down.[9] For some tense minutes at the Court, it was 9/11 all over again.

"That was the tenor of the building," RonNell Andersen Jones recalled. "National security was not some abstract, distant principle. It was Justice O'Connor being shoved into a speeding sedan." When the justice returned to the Court sometime later that day, she recounted that her car had roared off and driven at full speed until it reached the Maryland border.

Unflappable as ever, O'Connor went back to searching for a middle way in the *Hamdi* case. The Court was split in different directions. Justice Thomas, whose hard-line former clerks had gone to work in the Bush Justice Department, backed the government all the way. Justice Stevens wanted to give Hamdi the due process accorded any American citizen charged with a crime. So did Justice Scalia, whose "originalism"—his focus on the literal original meaning of the Constitution—led him to say that only Congress, not the executive branch, could suspend habeas corpus. O'Connor was looking for a compromise that would hold the votes of the rest of the justices. She understood that it was impractical to give "enemy combatants" a full evidentiary hearing on the battlefield. But they were entitled, she believed, to some kind of due process before rudimentary military tribunals. O'Connor was put off by the all-or-nothing brief from the executive branch. From the outset, she built the opinion around a declaration that was, for her, unusually memorable: "A state of war is not a blank check for the President when it comes to the rights of the nation's citizens."[10]

The decision reasserted the essential role of the judiciary in the constitutional balance of power, even in time of war. Handed down with two other prisoners' rights cases on the last day of the term at the end of June 2004, the *Hamdi* decision cemented O'Connor's standing as the true rudder of the Court.[11]

Court watchers noted that Chief Justice Rehnquist, who had been a strong advocate of executive power as a high-ranking Justice Department official in the Nixon administration, had merely signed on to O'Connor's opinion scolding the Bush administration.[12] There was more talk that O'Connor should be chief justice, since she seemed to be functioning like one. At oral argument, Donald Verrilli, a frequent Supreme Court advocate (and later solicitor general of the United States), took his cues from Justice O'Connor. "Other justices tried to knock you off course," he remembered. "But she was giving you the chance to engage. She was intensely pragmatic. She was saying, 'Let's talk turkey here. Is this what you want. Or isn't this what you want?'"[13]

THE CLERKS WATCHED John O'Connor's decline, day by day. "Every day, he would sit with us at lunch," recalled RonNell Andersen Jones. At the beginning of the year, he knew us. At the end of the year, he thought he should know us. 'Well,' he'd say. 'There's a familiar face.'"

Justice O'Connor was now bringing her husband to the Court every day and leaving with him around three o'clock. The care of John was "a huge part of her life," said Jones. "It was incredibly fortunate in a way. How many others could bring a spouse with Alzheimer's to work? In other respects, it was the exact opposite. She was the critical fifth vote on the Supreme Court. The weight of the world was on her." Jones and the other clerks could see how loving she was. "Madly, deeply, the real deal," said Jones.[14]

"He is at severe stage," Dr. Paul Aisen, John's neurologist, wrote in his notes after seeing John in May. "But good natured, friendly, cooperative. These qualities must be deeply entrenched. Quite unusual at this stage. He is not unable to dress himself. She lays out his clothes. He is content to spend time reading or looking at an open book. He is not able to read."

Dr. Aisen was now more worried about John's wife. "She refused an anti-depressant," he wrote.[15]

Sandra did her best to hide the pain from her friends. "John would wander around, and she could be sharp with him," recalled Ginny Chew, a regular tennis partner. "'John! It's time to go home!' she would say. To us, it was kind of a joke. We didn't know the trauma. She did it all so well."[16]

As time went on, friends could not help but notice John's odd behavior. At a dinner party, Sandra had to stop him from eating a stick of butter, which he had mistaken for cheese. On the tennis court, Sandra would have to very deliberately instruct, "John! The balls! Are in! Your pocket!"[17]

Trying to improvise, she recruited friends to keep an eye on her husband while she worked. But John was not a burden easily shared. In January 2004, Claire Cox, a close friend, took John to an oral argument at the Court. During the argument, a messenger arrived with a note for John, saying that he was supposed to go to lunch with another friend at the Metropolitan Club. "John got quite confused," recalled Cox. "He said, 'I'm here, I can't get there.' John looked beseechingly at his wife, who was in her high-backed black leather chair about fifty feet away. "I could see her, on the bench, watching him watching her," recalled Cox. Another note arrived, explaining that John should meet a driver to take him to the club. Claire asked to see the note and explained that all would be fine. John just said, over and over again, "I don't want to go."[18]

John became increasingly agitated when he was separated from Sandra, even for a few minutes. As she took a walk on the Shenandoah Valley farm of Joe and Lucia Henderson one bright May day, John, sitting on the porch, kept crying out, "Where's Sandra? Where's Sandra?"[19]

The annual pilgrimage to the Bohemian Grove, once such a ritual delight, had become an ordeal, although one that he was determined to endure. In his cabin at night, John was waking up every twenty minutes, asking where he was. His son Brian had to sleep beside him under a blanket on the floor.[20]

John's social governor was slipping. He could suddenly blurt, during the cocktail hour before dinner, "Goddamn it, where's the food!" Seated next to Lynn Garland, the wife of federal court of appeals judge Merrick Garland, he could only repeat, like a refrain, "I am married to the most powerful woman in the world." Still, there was a sweetness about him. On a walk with his friend Michael Boskin, former chair of the Council of Economic Advisers in the George H. W. Bush administration, at the Sun Valley Writers' Conference in 2003, John said to Boskin, "Didn't we used to tell jokes to each other?" Boskin choked up. On a family trip to Ireland in 2002, as John was saying goodbye to his daughter-in-law Joanie, Scott's wife, he said "Joanie, I love you so much" and wrapped her in his arms. Sandra, watching, dissolved.[21]

The physical and emotional toll mounted. On their travels or at the theater, the justice would sometimes have to stand with John by the men's room door until a stranger came along who would take him in.[22] John began to awaken and roam at night, on one occasion shouting that there were burglars in the house. The O'Connor sons began to actively worry about their parents. Searching the Internet, their oldest son, Scott, found a Harvard Medical School study showing that caregivers of seriously ill patients had higher mortality rates themselves. The highest rates were for family members taking care of Alzheimer's patients. "Mom, this is killing you," he told her. He urged his mother to begin the process of finding institutional care for John. She wouldn't hear of it.[23]

One day in 2004, Sandra brought John along to the hairdresser in Georgetown. Sharon Rockefeller, the president of the Washington public television station WETA and her old friend from the Stanford board of trustees, was also in the salon getting her hair done. "I said, 'You can find someone to care for John,'" Rockefeller recalled. "'I can help you.'" Rockefeller had experience lining up minders for her father, former Illinois senator Charles "Chuck" Percy (and John's Pelican campmate at the Bohemian Grove), who also suffered from Alzheimer's. "She said she didn't want to spend the money. I thought maybe she was feeling too guilty," Rockefeller recalled.

The O'Connors' longtime friend from Phoenix, Betsy Taylor, and her daughter Susan (whom O'Connor had persuaded to take the job as chair of the Stanford Alumni Association) also tried to help. Susan's godmother was Lorraine Percy, Chuck Percy's wife. "By this time, Sandra was bathing him, clothing him, and attending to his personal

needs," Susan recalled. "We got together with Lorraine, who was dealing with Chuck's problems. She suggested getting help. But Sandra
said to me, 'It will not work. He will not tolerate anyone but me.' "[24]

Justice O'Connor was determined to continue to care for John
herself. She told another friend that she worried that she had not
spent enough time with her boys growing up. She was not going to
sacrifice or slight John.

Although O'Connor was a realist, she fought the reality. More than
anyone, she knew how hard it was to take care of John and do the
work of a justice of the Supreme Court. Bringing John to the Court
had become untenable; the situation was, as she had once said about
the deadlocked vote in Florida, "a mess." In between reading the
newspaper, which he sometimes held upside down, the justice's husband had begun lying on the bench in the outer office by Linda Neary's
desk and falling asleep.[25] Visitors could not help but notice. He had
left home a few times and gone looking for Sandra while she was busy
at the Court, once dangerously crossing Connecticut Avenue up by
the Chevy Chase Club in rush hour. In the mornings, three days a
week, John began attending a group for Alzheimer's patients called
the Friends' Club. But for the rest of the day, and all through the long
and fitful nights, Sandra remained his caregiver.

On August 9, 2004, less than six weeks after she announced the
Court's decision in *Hamdi*, O'Connor was in a Mexican restaurant at
the El Paso Airport with her friend Craig Joyce, the son-in-law of her
cousin Flournoy. They were watching John O'Connor stare into the
middle distance. In a quiet voice, O'Connor told Joyce, "I'm going to
have to step down." She nodded toward John.[26]

STILL, SHE CARRIED on. For years, while they traveled in the summers, the O'Connors had installed an incoming clerk to house-sit
their Maryland home. That summer of 2004, the clerk was Theane
Evangelis, the daughter of immigrants (her father owned a gas station) and number one in her class at New York University Law School.
Although "Mr. O'Connor" (as the justice always referred to him
around her clerks) was "in pretty bad shape," Evangelis recalled, the
justice showed no outward stress. "She told me, 'We all sleep with our

doors open.' It was clear she prescribed how everything was done. I practically slept in my clothes. I didn't want her to see me in my PJs."

Justice O'Connor knocked on her (open) door at six the next morning and announced, "Breakfast in thirty minutes," Evangelis recalled. "By the time I got downstairs, fresh muffins were baking in the oven and she had cut up a fruit salad. By 7:00 A.M., she was reading cert petitions. I thought, talk about Super Woman. Here she was putting Martha Stewart to shame and deciding our nation's most important issues. I was just in awe."

When the O'Connors were away, Evangelis knocked around the O'Connors' roomy house, decorated in the soft sand tones of the desert. A portrait of Harry Day hung over the fireplace. "I was terrified I would break something. The vacuum cleaner, which looked like it was bought when Reagan nominated her, didn't work. I told her the vacuum cleaner was broken. She said, 'Well, fix it.' So I found probably the last place that would repair an Electrolux relic."

When the term began in October, "she and Justice Ginsburg were in a race to get out the first opinion," recalled Tali Farhadian, another clerk. Farhadian was working on an early case when Justice O'Connor told her, "Get your coat. We are going to the Dan Flavin exhibit at the National Gallery [a fluorescent light installation]." Farhadian said, "I know you want the first opinion, but you want me to go to the exhibit. Which do you prefer?" O'Connor answered, "I want both." Farhadian got her coat, and O'Connor delivered the first opinion of the term. "She wanted us to have everything in life," Farhadian recalled.[27]

IT WAS BECOMING increasingly clear that Chief Justice Rehnquist was fading. Though he still jauntily wore his robe with four golden stripes on each sleeve (an idea, he said, he borrowed from Gilbert and Sullivan) and enjoyed leading sing-alongs, he seemed fatalistic. After years of trying to lead a counterrevolution against the activism of the Warren Court, he had written a decision reaffirming the famous "Miranda warning" ("You have the right to remain silent . . .") required when police arrest suspects. Justice Scalia, joined by Justice Thomas, wrote an outraged dissent at this perfidy to the conservative cause.

Rehnquist's opinion (joined by O'Connor) was terse, conceding that the warning had become so routine that eliminating it would be disruptive. In the view of many Court watchers, Rehnquist was not even trying to be an intellectual force on the Court. It was widely noted that his opinions were getting shorter and sparer, as if he felt it was not worth bothering to explain the reasoning on the way to the result.[28]

As the October 2004 term began, Rehnquist was not feeling well; he had a bad sore throat that would not seem to go away. In church, he discovered that he could no longer sing the hymns he loved so well.[29] Later in October, Rehnquist announced that he was going into the hospital for thyroid cancer surgery. He underwent a tracheotomy, which involved placing a tube through a hole in his throat to help him breathe.[30]

His return to the Court was delayed, and then delayed again. In January, when he swore in President George W. Bush for a second term, he had only a few thin strands of hair left from chemotherapy, and his voice was weak and raspy. He remained at home most of the time, hearing the Court's oral arguments on tape and casting his votes and assigning opinions by memo. Only two members of the Court, John Paul Stevens, the senior justice, and Sandra O'Connor were permitted to see him.[31]

A widower, Rehnquist had begun keeping company with Pat Hass, a book editor who was also a friend of Justice O'Connor. Hass was at Rehnquist's house in suburban Virginia several times that winter when O'Connor came by to talk about their futures on the Court. The conversations of the justices occasionally known as the Arizona Twins were at once intimate and wary. "Each thought the other was in decline and should go," recalled Hass. But they agreed that they couldn't both retire: It would be bad for the Court to have two vacancies at once. The two old friends gingerly circled the question: Who should go first?[32]

On Tuesday, February 1, on a visit to San Francisco, Justice O'Connor had dinner with her fly-fishing buddies Charles and Barbara Renfrew. The ties of friendship were deep. A former federal judge and deputy attorney general in the Carter administration,

Charles Renfrew was one of the legal establishment lawyers who had noticed O'Connor when she began going to legal conferences in the late 1970s.

At dinner in the Renfrews' elegant Federalist-style house in Pacific Heights, O'Connor told Renfrew that she had been talking to Chief Justice Rehnquist about retiring from the Court, for John's sake. But she went on to say that the justice who should retire—for the sake of the Court—was her old friend Bill Rehnquist.

O'Connor was warm and protective toward Rehnquist. "She and the Chief had a nice relationship," observed Ruth Bader Ginsburg. But speaking privately with Judge Renfrew over dinner, O'Connor was frank. As Renfrew recalled the conversation, O'Connor told him that the chief justice was "in decline." For Rehnquist to remain on the Court was "not fair to the other justices or the whole legal system."

But she wasn't sure what to do. If Rehnquist was determined to stay, then maybe she should retire.

"I said, 'You're too important to retire,'" Renfrew recalled. He emphasized that she was the true leader of the Court, the essential balance wheel between the liberals and conservatives. "She sort of agreed," said Renfrew. O'Connor could be inscrutable when she needed to be, and Renfrew wasn't sure he could read her. "Actually, I got the feeling that she didn't agree with my analysis," he told the author during an interview in 2017. "But I also got the feeling she wouldn't retire without talking to me further."[33]

ON MARCH 1, when Justice Anthony Kennedy announced the Supreme Court's decision in *Roper v. Simmons*, striking down the death penalty for juveniles, the Republican Right in Congress erupted. Kennedy, who traveled abroad as much as O'Connor, noted in his opinion that only a few countries, including Saudi Arabia and Pakistan, had executed juveniles, and even they had disavowed the practice. Democracies, including the nations of the European Union, had largely stopped executing anyone.

In the House of Representatives, eighty-two Republicans sponsored a resolution criticizing the Supreme Court for relying on foreign law—which the opinion did not do—and one of the members,

Representative Steve King, launched an investigation of the justices' foreign trips (ninety-three between 1998 and 2003).[34]

Justice O'Connor did not go along with Kennedy, dissenting in *Roper*. Mindful of the importance of popular opinion on sensitive social issues, she did not discern a national consensus to do away with the death penalty for seventeen-year-olds. Notwithstanding her personal view that eighteen might be the appropriate minimum age for capital punishment, she wrote in her dissent, it was up to the legislature, not the courts, to decide. But she was upset by the congressional attack on the judiciary. Her concern turned to alarm a month later, when the branches of government became entangled over a highly emotional "right to die" case.

By 2005, Terry Schiavo had been in a "persistent vegetative state" for fifteen years. When her husband decided to have her feeding tube removed eight years after her coma began, her parents had objected. Because Schiavo did not have a living will, the case wound up in a whirlpool of litigation with multiple suits in the state and federal courts. After a state judge again sided with the husband in 2005, Congress rushed back from recess to pass a one-time law giving federal courts jurisdiction over the case, while President Bush flew to Washington from his Texas ranch to sign the bill.

The federal and state judges refused to reinsert the feeding tube, and the Supreme Court again declined to hear the case. Terry Schiavo passed away on March 31. Congressman Tom DeLay, the fiercely partisan House majority leader known as "the Hammer," promptly threatened to punish all the judges involved. At about the same time, in unconnected cases, there were murderous, vengeful attacks on judges and their families in Chicago and Atlanta. Recklessly, Senator John Cornyn of Texas took to the Senate floor to wonder, as he put it, about "the perception in some quarters, on some occasions where judges are making political decisions yet are unaccountable to the public." The resentment "builds up and builds up and builds up to the point where some people engage in violence," he said. He wasn't condoning the violence, but he seemed to be suggesting that it could be expected.[35]

Justice O'Connor watched this spectacle with mounting consternation. She had been the target of numerous threats. On the Internet,

a "hit man" was vowing to shoot her, and in April, her chambers received a box of cookies laced with rat poison. She was deeply put off
by Senator Cornyn's remarks. "It doesn't help," she later told some
appellate judges, "when a high-profile senator suggests there may be a
connection between violence against judges and decisions that the
Senator disagrees with."[36] But her worries transcended personal safety.

Democracies, O'Connor believed, do not exist just because of
some rules on a page. For the rules to work, leaders have to show forbearance and tolerance. A country can have a perfectly crafted constitution, but it won't mean anything if the rulers do not limit their own
power. Judges have no armies; they count on respect and obedience.
From her personal experience visiting countries abroad, she knew a
great deal about "telephone justice," practiced by party bosses in
Communist countries who picked up the telephone to tell judges how
to decide cases. (In the fall, she had hosted the Supreme People's
Court of China, which was wholly subservient to the party.) Closer to
home, in Arizona she had served as a judge in a state court system that
was just beginning to reform from a favor bank for political cronyism
to a merit-based system. Essential to the rule of law was civility, and
that required self-control.

She had watched her mother cope with her irascible father by refusing to be provoked. There were times to push back, of course. She
had handled the drunken Tom Goodwin in the Arizona legislature,
when he threatened to punch her in the nose, by slyly mocking his
manhood. But the political parties needed to know when to back off
and when to compromise. They should never, ever try to intimidate
the judiciary that guarantees individual rights and equality before the
law. "Statutes and constitutions do not protect judicial independence," she liked to say. "People do." On April 14, ten days after Senator Cornyn's provocative speech, O'Connor wrote federal court of
appeals judge Cynthia Holcomb Hall, "I have never seen worse relations between the Third Branch and Congress in my lifetime."[37]

SHE WAS THINKING about her legacy while trying not to be heavy
about it. The Phoenix federal courthouse already bore her name, and
she was sitting for an official Supreme Court portrait, to be hung

when she retired. In the glass atrium of the Phoenix courthouse, a nine-foot bronze statue shows her, in robes, standing atop shattered glass to symbolize the broken ceiling. She claimed to be annoyed that the statue made her head look too small and her feet and her hands too big, but she may simply have been joshing with her portrait painter, Danni Dawson. The two women enjoyed teasing each other. "It was like being her girlfriend," recalled Dawson. "She complained, 'You didn't try to put in my French fingernails.' I told her they'd be out of style in twenty years. In truth, I really wanted to distract from her hands. She has truck driver hands."[38]

John's situation continued to deteriorate. While watching Sandra play golf at Augusta National in March, he took off across the fairways in a golf cart. Alan Day had to run down the cart and take away the key. In the middle of the night, Alan woke up to see John standing over him. "It was spooky, unsettling," Alan recalled. In January, Sandra wrote a friend, Owen Paepke, "It is sad to see John lose the capacity to converse and tell jokes. There is no happy ending." In March she wrote Peggy Lord, "Because of John's situation, I am not going to make an MPU plan [Mobile Party Unit, her ladies' traveling group] for this summer. I have no good way to care for him."[39]

Sometime late that spring, Justice O'Connor saw Danni Dawson at a cocktail party and said, "You're going to get to see your portrait of me because I'm going to step down." Dawson, her feisty and blunt friend, responded, "That is a mistake." The justice put on a long face and said, "I'm going over here to talk to some people who like me." Dawson urged O'Connor to get John professional help. But Justice O'Connor "didn't want to hear me," said Dawson. "She just looked at me and said nothing." Dawson, like others who had given similar advice, was frustrated; she thought that her friend was being stubborn, driven more by a guilty sense of obligation than by common sense.

Cynthia Helms, who knew O'Connor as well as anyone outside her family, also believed that her friend was torn by guilt over uprooting her husband from his high-flying Phoenix career and making him a second fiddle, albeit a highly polished one, in Washington. "She never forgave herself. She never said that, but I felt it," said Helms.[40]

On June 23, Justice Rehnquist, his breathing labored, his voice distorted by a tube sticking out of his throat, announced that Justice Stevens would deliver the Court's opinion in *Kelo v. City of New London.* The Court held that the City of New London could, using eminent domain, compel private homeowners to sell their property to a private company to further the city's economic redevelopment plan. The case, which seemed incremental, might have gone largely unnoticed outside the real estate business—except for Justice O'Connor's dissent, which began slowly and built into a powerful attack on the unbridled power of government.

She began by noting that the house of one evicted owner, Wilhelmina Dery, had been in the family for more than a century (about the same length of time the Day family had owned the Lazy B). She wrote, "Under the banner of economic development, all private property is now vulnerable to being taken and transferred to another private owner, so long as it might be upgraded. . . . Nothing is to prevent the State from replacing any Motel 6 with a Ritz-Carlton, any home with a shopping mall, or any farm with a factory." (For similar reasons, the O'Connors had worked to stop Phoenix from annexing Paradise Valley during the 1960s.)

Once again, O'Connor was more in sync with the public mood than her fellow justices. The backlash, on both the political Right and Left, was immediate: Within a few years, nearly every state in the country passed laws outlawing such "public takings" for private purposes.[41]

On the afternoon that *Kelo* was decided, Justice O'Connor called Cynthia Helms and asked her to a bridge game the next morning with the chief justice in his chambers. The fourth player would be Admiral Tazewell Shepard, the former naval aide to President John F. Kennedy.

Assembling at ten o'clock, the foursome played for an hour. Chief Justice Rehnquist, looking thin and pale, announced, "I've had enough." He meant bridge. He made it clear that he was determined to hold on to his job for another year. "He told us, 'I've decided to stay on for another term,'" Helms recalled.

The bridge party broke up. With Rehnquist's words echoing in O'Connor's head, the two women headed back toward her chambers. Mrs. Helms could see that her friend was wound up. "She turned to me and said, 'If he's going to stay, well, then I can go.'"[42]

O'Connor had been telling a few friends, like Danni Dawson and Judge Renfrew, that she was planning to step down. Always prepared, she had quietly taken other steps in the direction of retirement, asking her friend Ginny Chew, who sold real estate, to find a buyer for her house in Chevy Chase and hiring three, but not four, law clerks for the next year. A legal blog, "Underneath Their Robes," noticed that she was one shy on hiring clerks but guessed that she planned to pick up a Rehnquist clerk, probably a woman, as her fourth.[43] But she had never been so definitive. Rehnquist's declaration sealed her decision.

In her chambers, O'Connor wrote President Bush a letter saying she would be retiring. The letter was to be delivered a week later, on the day she was scheduled to leave town. She also wrote letters to her three sons, timed to arrive on the same day, Friday, July 1. On Monday, she took her clerks on a final outing, a hike in the hills around the historic site of Harpers Ferry, West Virginia. The justice packed lunch. "It was a disgusting D.C. day," recalled Tali Farhadian. "The air was thick and smelled awful. For me in my twenties, the hike was a challenge. Mr. O'Connor made the hike with us and did not struggle. He was not physically diminished."

"It was hot," recalled Josh Klein. "She out-hiked us." During the drive back to Washington, she asked the clerks to come to her house for a glass of wine. "Back at the house, she poured us a glass and sat us down," recalled Theane Evangelis. "She had something to tell us. She had not told the president yet."

In an even voice, the justice said, "The time has come for me to retire. John needs me."

"I wanted to cry," Evangelis recalled. "I tried not to cry in front of her. She was the swing vote, the first woman. I thought of the importance of her, what she had meant to the Court and our country. She was very matter-of-fact. I got the feeling she wasn't quite ready, but that it was the right thing for John."

As the stunned clerks got up to leave, John said, "She should have been president."[44]

On Friday, the other justices all received letters from Justice O'Connor, including a poem, an old chestnut titled "The Indispensable Man," arguing that there is no such person. The justices started calling. After she hung up with Justice Kennedy, who phoned to wish her farewell, she said about his conservative clerks, who saw her as an impediment to Federalist Society purity, "You could hear the corks popping in his office." She also spoke with Justice Stevens, who said, "The way I feel now is how you must have felt when Justice Powell retired." In front of her clerks, she choked up.

At the White House, President Bush opened the letter and called Justice O'Connor, asking her to come see him. She politely declined, saying, truthfully, that she had a plane to catch. (She wanted to be out of Washington when the news broke; reporters had been staking out Rehnquist's house for days, expecting him to quit.)

"For an old ranching girl, you turned out pretty good," said the president. "You're one of the great Americans." O'Connor later told her friend the *Chicago Tribune* reporter Jan Crawford Greenburg that she was overcome with emotion, and that her voice began to break. "I wish I was there to hug you," said Bush.

In her chambers at the Supreme Court, Ruth Bader Ginsburg picked up a pen and wrote her friend Sandra, "I have been trying to hold back the tears." Nino Scalia warmly scrawled: "I have (despite my sometimes sharp dissents) always regarded you as a good friend— and indeed as the forger of the social bond that has kept the Court together." He wondered, "Who will take that role when you are gone?" From his sickbed, Chief Justice Rehnquist dictated a note that was cryptic but allusive: "We met more than half a century ago—can you believe it—in law school, and I admired you then for more than one reason. . . . I shall miss you greatly."[45]

JUDGE RENFREW HEARD the news of Justice O'Connor's retire- ment on the radio. "I called her and said, 'We talked about this!'" Renfrew recalled. "She said, 'I don't know if this is right or wrong, but I have to do it. John gave up his career for me. We want to have these last few months.'" She wanted to take John back to Arizona before he could no longer recognize home.[46]

Justice O'Connor had dutifully told the president that she would not step down until her successor was confirmed. Expecting Rehnquist to retire, the White House had been vetting candidates for two months. On July 19, Bush nominated U.S. Court of Appeals judge

John Roberts to fill O'Connor's seat. His confirmation hearings were scheduled for September 6.

O'Connor was satisfied by the choice of Roberts. "That's fabulous!" O'Connor told reporters, employing her trademark enthusiasm when she returned from a fly-fishing trip and heard the news. "He's good in every way except he's not a woman."[47] With her clerks, O'Connor had used her other favorite adjective—"attractive"—to describe Roberts, who, as a deputy solicitor general under George H. W. Bush and as a private lawyer, had argued nearly forty cases before the Supreme Court. When he came before the Court, he was always well prepared, always quick on his feet, and always attuned to her. He did not exactly direct his arguments at the Court's first woman justice and perennial decisive vote, Roberts told the author in 2017, because "if you focus on the swing vote, right away there are eight people who don't like you." But he knew that O'Connor would usually ask the first question, the one that went right to the heart of the case. He always came prepared. "I would have one sentence ready I thought was important," said Roberts.[48] O'Connor thought so highly of Roberts, a clean-cut midwesterner via Harvard, that she told her friends Jeannette and Ray Brophy, "He was born to be chief justice."[49]

The comment was offhand, but it turned out to be prescient. Chief Justice Rehnquist's determination to serve one more term was no match for the aggressive form of thyroid cancer ravaging his body. At the end of August, the ailing Chief was rushed to the hospital. Rehnquist kept his puckish sense of humor to the end; asked, in the emergency room, to name his primary care physician, he answered, "My dentist." On September 3, he passed away.

Justice O'Connor was asked by Rehnquist's family to give a eulogy at St. Matthew's Cathedral on September 8. Using a cowboy metaphor, she spoke admiringly of the Chief's leadership. "He never twisted arms to get a vote on a case," she said. Instead, "he guided us with loose reins and used the spurs only rarely."[50]

To the reporters outside the church, Justice O'Connor said but one word: "Sad." Watching her old beau's casket carried down the marble steps of the Supreme Court, she appeared uncharacteristically careworn and bent over. "It's like an earthquake hit," she told her friends and former clerks.[51]

According to two friends who knew her well, she was bothered by a troubling thought: In their tortured conversations about who should go first, had the chief justice been fully honest with her?[52] He had not told her the severity of his disease; she did not know that his doctors had given him no more than a year to live when he was diagnosed in October 2004. In her eulogy, O'Connor made affectionate, poignant fun of Rehnquist's fondness for laying bets: "I think the Chief bet he could live out another term despite his illness. He lost that bet, as did all of us, but he won all the prizes for a life well lived." Still, she may have wondered: Had she been subtly outmaneuvered? Speaking carefully but deliberately to the author in 2016, Justice Stevens recounted that O'Connor had talked to him about her misgivings. "She expressed regret to me. She wished she had it to do all over again," said Stevens. Reflecting his own view but perhaps hers as well, he continued: "She was too deferential to Bill. She should have stayed on. That was an unfortunate decision." The longtime senior liberal on the Court added, somewhat mournfully, "The Court has never been this far to the right."[53]

On Capitol Hill in the summer of 2005, a group of women senators, all of them pro-choice on abortion, had worried that O'Connor's departure and Rehnquist's demise would lead to the appointment of Nino Scalia as chief justice. In June, as reports spread of Rehnquist's decline, speculation grew that Scalia was angling for the chief's job, with strong conservative support. "An informal Scalia boomlet is under way—and Scalia may be leading it," wrote Charles Lane, The Washington Post's Supreme Court reporter.[54] Scalia had support among the strong Federalist Society activists embedded in the White House and Justice Department, who saw an unexpected opportunity to install the movement's hero on top of the judicial branch. (Scalia's wife, Maureen, would later tell the author that her late husband "never expected to be Chief. It was not his thing.") On July 14, Senators Barbara Boxer, Democrat of California, and Susan Collins, Republican of Maine, had written Justice O'Connor asking her to reconsider her decision to retire so that she could come back to the Court as chief justice if Rehnquist stepped down. O'Connor did not respond to the letter.[55]

The senators need not have worried about a Scalia Court. Before he died, Rehnquist himself had suggested to President Bush that he make John Roberts, a former Rehnquist clerk, the chief justice and find someone else to fill O'Connor's chair. In early September, the president announced that Roberts would be the nation's seventeenth chief justice. A month later, he picked his personal lawyer, White House counsel Harriet Miers, to fill O'Connor's seat.

Having extolled Roberts, O'Connor said nothing about Miers. The chief virtue of the president's counsel was loyalty to George W. Bush. Miers was diligent but narrowly focused, and she was not conservative enough for congressional hard-liners. She lacked the charm of John Roberts—or Sandra O'Connor. Senate Democrats had privately implored Bush to send up a noncontroversial middle-of-the-roader—no more Robert Borks—but as she made the rounds visiting senators on Capitol Hill, Miers struggled to impress. After twenty-three days of unfriendly leaks and uncomfortable interrogation, Miers called the president to ask him to withdraw the nomination. The White House began looking again.[56]

O'CONNOR'S FRIENDS CONTINUED to wonder and worry if she had done the right thing. Eric Motley asked her, "Wasn't there a way John could be cared for that would allow you to remain on the Court?" She answered, "At some point, you have to do what you're supposed to do." Then she asked Eric who took care of his grandfather. "My grandmother," he replied. "That is what duty is," she said.

Ruth McGregor, her first clerk and longtime friend, remembered that a few years before John's dementia set in, the justice had told a friend in the same predicament, "You can't keep him in your own home." Yet that was precisely what she intended to do for John. "I think she thought she could go on taking care of him," said McGregor. The plan was to live part time in a small Phoenix home, bought after the sale of the Lazy B in the midnineties as an Arizona pied-à-terre, and part time in a Washington apartment complex known as the Colonnade. (Selwa "Lucky" Roosevelt, President Reagan's chief of protocol, had found the spot in Washington.) O'Connor had bought the Colonnade apartment sight unseen. "Does it have closets?" was all she asked.

She plowed straight ahead. "After she moved into the Colonnade, we'd have lunch nearby at Chef Geoff's," recalled Lou Davidson, wife of former Time Inc. CEO (and fellow Stanford alum) Ralph Davidson. "She acted as if it was all the same. For me it was devastating. John was just 'there.' He couldn't cut his own food. She did it like it was the most natural thing in the world."[57]

BACK AT THE Court, still a sitting justice, she continued to hear cases as she waited—and waited—for her replacement. "It was a strange period," recalled Ben Horwich, one of her law clerks. "It seemed like the justice was always six weeks from retirement." Because she was a lame duck, O'Connor's mood was "ever so slightly exasperated," said Horwich, "but accepting. It couldn't be helped."

Horwich had been editor of the *Stanford Law Review*. Like so many clerks before him, he came to O'Connor's chambers with a head full of abstract legalisms and doctrinal complexity. He ended up getting a lesson from the realm of human experience, the real world so vigorously and decisively inhabited by Sandra Day O'Connor.

For most of her time on the Court, O'Connor had joined the conservatives in resisting, under the banner of "federalism," congressional intrusion into matters more properly left to state control. States generally had "sovereign immunity," an ancient doctrine, long part of British common law to protect the crown, which held that the sovereign, or state, cannot commit a legal wrong and is thus immune from civil lawsuits or criminal prosecution. In a case testing whether, under the bankruptcy clause of the Constitution, Congress could override the doctrine of state sovereign immunity to allow bankruptcy trustees to sue a state government, Horwich figured O'Connor would follow precedent and conservative doctrine to say no. Instead she said yes, voting with the liberals in a 5-to-4 ruling involving a community college and a bankrupt bookstore.[58] Her reasoning was simple and, as ever, pragmatic: Bankruptcy laws cannot work unless states are treated like other creditors. "There was a long line of precedents a 'C' student could have figured out [supporting sovereign immunity]," recalled Horwich. "But she said, 'How does this make sense?' She could size it up, much faster than the clerks." O'Connor was letting the clerks know the real business of judging, as she had understood her role and practiced it for a quarter of a century. "It was, wait a minute, we're not doing this as an intellectual exercise. We're doing this to run society. It's just us people running things," said Horwich.

O'Connor was brisk, cheerful, and matter-of-fact as she played, for the 330th time in twenty-four years, the role of swing vote. "There was no grand sit-down with us. She was very comfortable doing it quickly," said the clerk. "She just said, in a nice way, 'We're not going to do that' [follow sovereign immunity precedent]. She didn't need a long philosophical discussion."

Justice O'Connor's last majority opinion was, fittingly, on the subject of abortion. In the case of *Ayotte v. Planned Parenthood of Northern New England,* O'Connor put together a unanimous Court to do as little as possible.[59] A federal court of appeals had knocked down a state law requiring minors to notify their parents before having an abortion, because the law lacked an adequate exception for the health of the mother. O'Connor "effectively kicked the can down the road," said Horwich, by instructing the lower court to shape a remedy that did not involve throwing out the whole statute. She did not want to put the Court to the test of ruling once more on the constitutionality of restrictions on abortion, and the other justices were willing to duck the issue. Practicing her own jurisprudence of "consequentialism," she was saying, once again, that the answer to hard constitutional questions can depend on the context.[60]

Horwich, like many clerks excited to be working behind the curtains at the High Court, was initially let down that the Court did not directly take on a big abortion case, its first in five years. But he was learning more valuable lessons from his boss. "A decision that avoids making a big decision, sure, some people will see that as vacuous," he recalled. "But if you can get nine people to decide not to decide, that is something." The doctrine-driven jurists, he noted, like to make pronouncements that will be carved on their tombstones, or at least quoted in law reviews. "People who do rules are looking for immortality," said Horwich. "She recognizes we are just muddling along. I felt it had something to do with her close acquaintance with mortality and death." (He had read *Lazy B.*) "She was saying we can't always resolve the big questions. I felt I was learning something. A moral lesson. It wasn't taught, rather observed. Decide what you have to decide and move on."

O'Connor announced the Court's decision in *Ayotte* on the morning of January 18, 2006. Less than two weeks later, at 11:30 A.M. on January 31, the U.S. Senate confirmed U.S. Court of Appeals judge Samuel Alito to be a justice on the Supreme Court, filling O'Connor's seat. In the high-columned building across the plaza from the Capitol, a whirlwind moved down the marble corridors. "A whole team of carts descended on our chambers," recalled Horwich. "They took off the labels of O'CONNOR and put on the labels of ALITO. It was sudden, but it didn't seem to bother her."[61]

That night, President George W. Bush was scheduled to give his annual State of the Union address to a joint session of Congress. The White House called Justice O'Connor and asked if she would like to sit in the gallery with the First Lady. She declined, saying, as she had six months earlier, that she had a plane to catch. The White House offered a presidential plane to fly her to Arizona after the speech. Politely, O'Connor again declined. She had her own speech to give in Phoenix the next morning, for the Barry Goldwater Lecture Series at Arizona State University. She wanted to get on with life.*

---

* When Rehnquist died and Roberts was elevated, President Bush personally asked Justice O'Connor to stay on the Court while he searched for her replacement. She had no constitutional obligation to fill the seat, but the president appealed to her sense of duty. After she retired, Bush thanked her with a lavish private dinner at the White House, attended by most of the cabinet. (The centerpieces were hollowed-out law books filled with flowers, the menu was all-ranch, and the dessert was a Scales of Justice cake.) First Lady Laura Bush, whose father had suffered from Alzheimer's, took John by the hand and stayed with him throughout the evening.[62]

CHAPTER SIXTEEN

LABOR OF LOVE

"What am I going to do with myself?"

The bridge builder: Sandra with Justices Sotomayor, Ginsburg, and Kagan. As the first woman on the Court, O'Connor "changed everything," says Sotomayor.

A T HER SPEECH in Phoenix on February 1, the day after she stepped down from the Supreme Court, Justice O'Connor ran into her old friend Sue Huck. "John gave up his position in Phoenix to come with me," she explained, "so now I am giving up my job to take care of him." But it was already too late.

At the end of April, the O'Connors and five friends went on a cruise off the Turkish coast on a 50-foot motorsailer yacht. "John was never sure where he was," recalled Don Kauffman, a close friend from the early years in Phoenix. "He'd get up in the middle of the night. He was arguing with Sandra. He couldn't understand what he was doing." Frank Wallis, John's former law partner who was also the O'Connors' estate planner, recalled that John would "get up at two or three A.M. to socialize." Bleary-eyed, their friends would help Sandra coax John back to their cabin.

Late-stage Alzheimer's patients can become angry or even violent, but John, so far, had not. Mostly he sat silently, staring blankly at a book. Occasionally he would complain that he was cold. None of this was terribly new to his wife. But for the first time, he could not be consoled by her.[1]

The trip to Turkey was a "disaster," recalled Scott O'Connor. "They were afraid he would jump overboard." The moment Sandra had long resisted had finally arrived. She could no longer take care of John. "When she got back, she cried," recalled Scott. "'I'm ready,' she said. 'Show me what you've researched.'" Scott and his wife, Joanie, had identified a care facility for Alzheimer's patients in Phoenix, the Huger Mercy Living Center. In July, the O'Connor family took John to his new home. Sandra could not bear to go along. "I told a white, therapeutic lie," recalled Joanie O'Connor, Scott's wife. "I said to John, 'We're taking you to a hotel while Sandra goes fishing.' He hated

fishing so he wouldn't want to be there." To allow the patients to adjust to their new surroundings, the families of patients at Huger were
not allowed to visit for the first two weeks. "I sent one of my friends
to read to John and check up on him," Joanie recalled. "John would say
to her, 'You are normal. The rest of these people are kooks.'" When
Sandra was finally permitted to visit, John wrenchingly pleaded,
"Don't leave me."[2]

Undone, Sandra called one of her oldest friends in Phoenix, Betsy
Taylor, and said, "I need to get away. Let's just go to your place [at a
mountain refuge, Pinetop] and hide out." Taylor put together a group
of her pals—the ladies' group, the MPU—in "about ten minutes," recalled Taylor. Peggy Lord, who flew in from the East Coast, recalled,
"Sandra was teary and upset. She slept for two days."[3]

"WHAT AM I going to do with myself?" Sandra asked her friend Judy
Hope after she had returned to Washington in September. As a retired justice, she was given chambers at the Court and retained a
staff—two secretaries and a part-time law clerk. But, at first, she was
purposeless. She felt idle and—uncharacteristically—regretful. Stepping down from the Court was "the dumbest thing I ever did," she
confessed to Hope. "I'm not doing anything important," she fretted.

"After she retired, she did face a down time," recalled her son Jay.
"Before, there had always been new challenges. Once she stepped
down, she realized it was downhill. It was never going to be the same
level of professional involvement. It was hard for her to make the ad-
justment. She was very sad about that."[4]

She could be cranky. In March, she had joined the Iraq Study
Group, a panel of bipartisan leaders commissioned by Congress to
assess the long-stalled war in Iraq. The chairmen were former secretary of state James A. Baker and House Foreign Affairs Committee
chairman Lee Hamilton. Other members included Reagan's attorney
general, Edwin Meese; Clinton's White House chief of staff, Leon Panetta; Carter's secretary of defense, William Perry; and Senator Alan
Simpson of Wyoming. Highly critical of President Bush's Iraq policy,
Justice O'Connor "was nothing if not outspoken," recalled Jim Baker.
She was as ever practical and incisive, but less diplomatic than usual.

When the report was being edited in November, she criticized the written-by-committee prose, complaining to one of the authors, Senator Simpson—an old and dear friend—that "this is the worst writing I've ever read." When Annie Leibovitz, the celebrated magazine cover photographer, arrived to shoot a group portrait, O'Connor balked, saying, "I'm not going to pose for a picture by that woman." She had been impatient during a photo shoot for *Vogue* with Leibovitz a few years earlier; besides, she did not want to glamorize the work of the Study Group with *Vanity Fair* treatment.[5]

She was cross about her successor, Justice Samuel Alito. On the night of April 28, 2007, when she was receiving a lifetime achievement award from the American Academy of Arts and Sciences, she complained about Alito to the award presenter, former Clinton administration solicitor general Walter Dellinger. The conversation was private, but for O'Connor, who had assiduously avoided speaking ill of other justices, unguarded. In O'Connor's view, Alito was an inflexible believer in conservative jurisprudential doctrine, in the mold of Antonin Scalia. O'Connor believed, not wrongly, that Alito's vote would undermine her pragmatic compromises on abortion, affirmative action, freedom of religion, and other important issues. "She was furious about Alito," said her friend Dellinger. "She viewed him as a betrayal of all her accomplishments. She told me, 'The last thing you needed was a fifth Catholic man.'" (The other four were Roberts, Scalia, Kennedy, and Thomas.)[6]

O'Connor's remark was politically incorrect, but it touched on an old strain: O'Connor regarded the Catholic justices as rule-bound in the way of their faith with its fixed catechism. For their part, Scalia, Alito, and Thomas, and to a lesser degree Roberts and Kennedy, regarded O'Connor as insufficiently attentive to rules that gave the law its consistency and predictability. ("The rule of law," said Justice Scalia, "is the law of rules.") O'Connor, like her role model Lewis Powell, often applied neutral-seeming "balancing tests" to close questions. After the death of his hero Nino Scalia in 2016, Justice Alito joked to their Federalist Society followers, "As Nino told us more than once, if a judge uses a balancing test, then the balance almost always comes out exactly the way the judge wants it to come out." What Scalia and

Alito did not say was that by depriving lower court judges of the flexibility to decide, the conservative justices were trying to freeze the law
a certain way—their way.[7]

What some others saw in Alito as shyness, O'Connor saw as aloofness, and it grated on her. "He has no sense of humor," she told her
friend Jim Todd.[8] Her dislike of Alito, who his friends say can be drily
humorous, has to be seen in the light of her regret about stepping
down prematurely, as well as her sorrow over losing six months with
John as she waited for her successor to be confirmed. Dellinger was
not the only friend (or even acquaintance) to hear her decry the
Court's lurch to the right after her departure.

On a warm spring day in 2007, O'Connor sat in one of the Court's
private patios with her clerk Justin Driver and talked, a little wistfully,
about her time as a justice. She pointed, approvingly, to a decorative
ring of turtles around the base of one of the Court's outdoor lamps.
The turtles, as Driver knew, were meant to be symbolic of the slow,
deliberative pace of the law. (There are also turtles engraved in the
Court's stone décor.) "She worried about her legacy," said Driver. "She
used that word." On the last day of the 2006–2007 term, Stephen
Breyer declared, unusually, in open Court, "It is not often in the law
that so few have so quickly changed so much." He was referring to the
swap of O'Connor for Alito, as well as the direction of the new chief
justice, who, to the dismay of both Breyer and O'Connor, seemed
more intent on pushing a conservative agenda than his predecessor
had been. In a single year, the Court had upheld a ban on what pro-
lifers referred to as partial birth abortion, loosened the rules of campaign spending, and, in a school integration case, chipped away at her
balancing act on affirmative action.

That summer, driving to the airport in Missoula, Montana, after a
fly-fishing trip, O'Connor told her old Stanford dormmate Martica
Ruhm Sawin, "Everything I stood for is being undone." She was over-
reacting, or so it seemed at the time. On the most controversial
issues—abortion and affirmative action—the essence of her decisions
still stood. Turtles notwithstanding, the Court has in its long history
swung right, swung left—and then swung back again. For more than
two decades, during tumultuous times, she had kept the Court cen-

tered. Still, with her keen political instincts, she seemed to have sensed that in an increasingly polarized age, newly appointed justices were not likely to be centrists.[9]

Friends tried to help O'Connor find a cause that would focus her still fierce energy. When O'Connor expressed some sadness that the O'Connors' old adobe house on Denton Lane was about to be torn down and replaced by a "McMansion," some wealthy friends chipped in to move the entire house, brick by adobe brick, to a park next to the Arizona Historical Society in Tempe. The hope was that the stylish midcentury modern adobe house would become a relaxed place where Democrats and Republicans could meet and bond over beer and Mexican food, as they had in the day of Majority Leader O'Connor. But after a few gatherings, "Chats and Chalupas" at "O'Connor House" petered out. The partisans of the twenty-first-century state legislature were more interested in attacking one another.[10]

O'Connor understood that her celebrity was a diminishing asset. She could have chosen to cash in on her fame by sitting on boards and giving paid speeches, but she wanted to focus on civic-minded work. "I've got five years where I'll still be relevant," she said, repeatedly, to friends and family. But how best to make a difference? As far back as her days as a legislator, she had been giving speeches warning about inroads on the independence of the judiciary. The issue, resonant for emerging democracies in the post–Cold War world, was taking on a new urgency at home as well. For O'Connor, bolstering the integrity of the Third Branch—and educating young people about why the Constitution matters—became a last hurrah, as well as a testament of faith in her own civic religion.

The gradual movement away from the popularly elected state judges of the Jacksonian era to the merit-based judicial selection systems of the early and mid-twentieth century had stalled and even reversed by the 1980s and '90s. More states were electing their judges again, and the issue was becoming partisan, with Republicans (to O'Connor's dismay) favoring popular elections and Democrats backing an appointive process. Money was starting to pour in to state judicial races, sometimes with outrageous results. In West Virginia, a coal company was accused of using campaign contributions to buy a favorable result in the state supreme court. When the case came before the U.S. Supreme Court, Justice O'Connor, retired, emerged from her chambers to make a show of sitting in the public gallery, lest the other justices have any doubt about her views on the issue. "She would say, 'Cash doesn't belong in the courtrooms. The last thing you want to see is the parties worrying about how much money the other side was contributing to a judge,'" said Becky Kourlis, a friend of O'Connor's and a close ally as the head of the Institute for the Advancement of the American Legal System.[11]

O'Connor was very disappointed when the Roberts Court's conservative majority, in an opinion written by Anthony Kennedy, opened the floodgates to corporate spending on elections in *Citizens United v. Federal Election Commission*.[12] Corporations and other organizations, wrote Kennedy, have free speech rights, too, and spending to influence elections is protected by the First Amendment. O'Connor thought Kennedy was being naïve and allowing the Court to be used as a political weapon. Unlike other Supreme Court justices, O'Connor had practical experience at the crossroads of money and politics, both as a state legislator and as an elected state judge. Bruised feelings about *Bush v. Gore* heightened her sensitivity to the divide between the bench and the ballot box. Judges, she believed, should never be confused with politicians; the one was impartial, the other partisan. "She doesn't think of the Court as a partisan political institution," said Kristen Eichensehr, her clerk in OT '10, the term after *Citizens United* came down. "That really drove her. She had an allergy to courts being seen that way."

As early as 2006, O'Connor had worked with Georgetown Law Center to sponsor three annual conferences to highlight the issue of judicial independence. O'Connor was a forceful presence. At dinner at the home of Judy Areen, the dean emerita of Georgetown Law School, a Chinese legal scholar tried to suggest that judges had the last word in the Communist system. Ignoring protocol, Justice O'Connor cut in: "No, they don't. The party does." Meryl Chertoff, who ran the program, recalled, "It was awkward, but that didn't bother her."

O'Connor was honored that the "state of the judiciary" conferences at Georgetown were in her name, and she was particularly moved by a speech by Justice Souter, who, in a paean to the engaged citizenry of small-town New England, warned that "the Republic can be lost if it is not understood." At the same time, "there was a lot of 'Oh, what can we do?'" recalled Abby Taylor, a Harvard Law grad who was serving as an assistant to O'Connor. "She's not good at hand-wringing. She likes to get stuff done, not hear herself talk. It was, 'All right, what are we going to do?'"

Stopping the flow of campaign cash to the judges was "not politically possible," said Taylor. "But the justice believed that we could at least educate the next generation." O'Connor threw herself into the role of teacher—on a mass scale. She wanted young Americans to learn that there were three branches of government, checks and balances, a rule of law—and why their freedom depends on the system's working.

She was faced with generations of indifference. "It was clear schools were giving civics education short shrift," said Patricia White, the dean of the Arizona State University Law School, renamed, in 2006, the Sandra Day O'Connor College of Law. "More kids knew the Three Stooges than the three branches of government." (O'Connor liked to say that more kids could name the three judges on *American Idol* than any three Supreme Court justices.) The traditional high school civics book *We the People* felt old and faded, its cover an homage to bewigged white men of long ago. "People said it was dated," recalled Abby Taylor. "Justice O'Connor said, 'Well, that's what we have to fight.'"

It was obvious that better textbooks were not the answer. O'Connor was anything but a "techie"; like most Supreme Court justices of her era, she largely avoided the Internet and could not do her own email. But Arizona State University professor James Gee, who had received funding from the MacArthur Foundation and written a book titled *What Video Games Have to Teach Us About Learning and Literacy,* offered a suggestion: Why not teach civics as a video game?

O'Connor was highly skeptical at first. "She dismissed video games as trivial and violent," recalled Gee. She didn't like the word "game." "How about interactive learning?" suggested Gee. He began to develop interactive online games that the average nonbookish middle schooler might like to play. O'Connor was intrigued and pressed for more. "She acted as if, 'I'm just an old cowgirl,'" recalled Gee. "But the message was pretty clear: Failure is not an option." At Chautauqua,

the high-minded upper New York State retreat where O'Connor
liked to spend a week or two in the summer soaking up culture, the
justice borrowed the son of a neighbor, an eleven-year-old boy named
Charlie Dolan. "She plied me with miniature golf and ice cream to get
me to check out her website," recalled Dolan. The two became fast
friends, and Dolan gave O'Connor a short course on the learning
habits of an early adolescent boy.

In 2009, O'Connor formed a nonprofit organization to develop
free video games to teach civics to middle schoolers. Abby Taylor suggested a name: iCivics. "Well," said O'Connor. "I guess so. Everything
these days has an 'i' in it." After some fits and starts, iCivics got trac-
tion and became a fixture in the curricula of many middle schools
around the country. Florida passed a "Sandra Day O'Connor Education Act" requiring civics to be taught in public schools. By 2017, half
of all middle schoolers in the United States—about five million
students—were playing games like "Win the White House," "Executive Command," and "Do I Have a Right?"

O'Connor was thrilled. Nancy Ignatius recalled her friend sweeping into her favorite Italian restaurant in northwest Washington, De-
Carlo's, spouting the latest statistics about the spread of iCivics to the
nation's schools. "She repeated to me, over and over, that iCivics was
the best thing she had ever done," said Cynthia Helms. "Far more important than what she had done on the Court." Helms thought her
old friend was "laying it on a bit thick," as she put it. She figured what
the retired justice was really saying was that she had found a way to
move on. But iCivics was far more to O'Connor than a consolation.
As she watched the coarsening of civic discourse, the rise in polariza-
tion, and the alienation of large swaths of the nation from public institutions, O'Connor had become convinced of the urgency of
educating the young in civics, in order to make them better citizens.
"She wanted to show them, at an early age, how the system worked so
they could participate in it," said Kathy Smalley, her former clerk who
had joined the board of iCivics. "It's counterintuitive to think that she
thought iCivics was more important than being the first female justice, but in a way it's true. She thought it was more important for five
million kids a year to learn how to participate in public life than it was
to have one woman justice for twenty-five years. Civic education, she

believed, goes on forever." A justice's jurisprudence can be eclipsed. With iCivics, she believed she was building a bridge that would last.[13]

O'CONNOR HAD INTENDED to spend a good portion of her time in Phoenix, where she could visit John, but a sadder reality awaited her. Patients with advanced Alzheimer's sometimes form "mistaken attachments." In their dementia, they "fall in love" with other patients.* In the fall of 2007, a local TV reporter was tipped off to a story of two patients at the Huger Mercy Living Center who had formed a romantic attachment. One was John O'Connor.

In 1994, with her compelling talk to the National Coalition for Cancer Survivorship, Justice O'Connor had turned her own experience with a dreaded disease into an opportunity for public understanding. Now she bravely did the same with Alzheimer's. Her eldest son, Scott, took the Phoenix TV reporter and camera crew to film John, who was holding hands with another woman, identified as "Kay." Scott told the reporter that his father had been depressed, and now he was happier. He said that his mother was "thrilled" to see John's spirits revived.[14]

"I'm happy it makes John happy," Sandra told her friend Lou Davidson, among others. With her old Branner Hall mate from Stanford, Diane Cooley, she described John sitting on a porch swing with his new attachment. "Sandra chuckled and said, 'Can you believe it?'" recalled Cooley. Arriving at the Huger facility to find John happily holding hands with the woman, Sandra adapted. She sat down and held his other hand.[15]

After another visit, Sandra called her friend and estate lawyer, Frank Wallis, and said, "I went to see John. He was sitting there holding a woman's hand, and he said to me, 'Come meet my wife.'" Wallis responded thoughtfully, "That's a great compliment. It means he feels that he was happily married." Sandra "could laugh about it," said Wallis. "But it was tough."

A few months before the story about John's mistaken attachment

* The mistaken attachment condition was dramatized in a 2006 movie, *Away from Her,* with Julie Christie.

appeared in the news (the story made headlines around the world), Sandra had attended a reunion of the MPU at Peggy Lord's house in Hobe Sound, Florida. Sandra shared a room with her friend Carol Biagiotti. "She told me she was brokenhearted," said Biagiotti. "It hurt. It was tragic he had to end his life this way."[16]

AFTER SANDRA WOULD visit John at the Huger Care Center, she would sometimes stop in at the office of Patricia White, the dean of the newly renamed Sandra Day O'Connor College of Law. "It was a depressing time for her," recalled White. "Her voice was flat, matter-of-fact. She said John's new life was a good thing for him. But it was sad and discouraging for her. She didn't want to go home and be alone. She would sit in the anteroom and read our *New York Times*."

In White's opinion, seconded by many of O'Connor's friends, O'Connor was traveling too much, willing to appear before almost any organization that asked. "She would be ridiculous. She said yes to too many things," said White.

During this period, she was like a latter-day Theodore Roosevelt, another speed-reader who was curious about everything; who was at once blunt and diplomatic; who lived a life of work and service; and who loved the West. After his mother and his wife tragically died on the same night in the same house, he had fled west to start a cattle ranch. "Black care," TR once wrote, "rarely sits behind a rider whose pace is fast enough."[17]

O'Connor set a fast pace—and a hard one. Never a spendthrift, she usually flew economy. She did not check her bags, and she overscheduled herself in a way that exhausted her staff, if not her. She liked attention but was impatient when an introduction went on too long. "Oh, couldn't they just get on with it?" she would mutter. She was a notorious backseat driver, telling her drivers, usually U.S. marshals, how fast to go and where to turn (sometimes in the wrong direction).

As a justice with "senior status," she was entitled to "ride the circuit," sitting on panels of federal courts of appeals judges hearing cases all over the country. She was dutiful as ever in her late seventies, yet having turned her attention to iCivics, she appeared to her clerks to be slightly more interested in showing the flag than actually deciding complex cases. "She didn't want the tough cases," said Josh Deahl, her clerk in 2009–10. "She wanted to meet and greet the judges, but she didn't want to get stuck." Justin Driver, her clerk in 2006–2007, recalled, "The courts of appeals would save intriguing cases for her. She would see all the briefs and exclaim, 'My heavens!'" Driver added, "When the spotlight was on, she would shine. I would see her, before she stepped out of the car, straighten her back. She had a way of crinkling her nose and twinkling her eyes. Like a good politician, she would adjust her accent depending on where we were. 'Isn't it?' could become 'Id'n it?'"[18]

JOHN O'CONNOR PASSED away in Phoenix on November 11, 2009. Justice O'Connor was in Washington weeping when Deahl arrived at her chambers that morning. She had been told the day before that John was dying, and there had been some discussion about flying her out to be by his deathbed. She had sadly declined. "She may have been thinking, 'What's the point?'" said Deahl. Her beloved husband had long since stopped recognizing her.

John's memorial service was filled with affectionate remembrances and spiced with humor from his sons and former senator Alan Simpson, his Pelican Camp brother. Sandra did not speak, but earlier at a bibulous festival he had always relished, the annual Alfalfa Club dinner in Washington, she had given him a loving toast. The Alfalfa is a collection of 250-odd titans of industry and politics, often including the president and his cabinet and many members of the Joint Chiefs and Supreme Court, who gather once a year to make fun of each other. In January 2007, Justice O'Connor had been nominated as Alfalfa's first woman president (she had been one of Alfalfa's first women members in 1994). She had giggled her way through corny jokes roasting her fellow Alfalfans and then grown serious talking about her "dear John," about how much he would have enjoyed the camaraderie and good fellowship, and about how he would have loved to see Sandra in the role of Alfalfa president. Toasting John again the year after he died, she brought down the house of movers and shakers by ending her talk with one of his favorite quips: "As my dear husband John used to say, you don't have to drink to have fun. But why take a chance?" Coming to the podium after her, a still laughing President Obama asked, "Who does not love this woman?" The crowd stood and roared.[19]

The honors flowed her way: honorary degrees and lifetime achievement awards, and, on August 12, 2009, the Presidential Medal of Freedom. As O'Connor looked on, at first expressionless, President Obama made her smile by telling the audience the story of how, at her one and only law firm interview after graduating near the top of her class at Stanford, she was asked how well she could type. "I cannot know how she would have fared as a legal secretary," Obama said. "But she made a mighty fine justice of the Supreme Court. A judge, an Arizona legislator, cancer survivor, child of the [El Paso] Texas plains, Sandra Day O'Connor is like the pilgrim in the poem she sometimes quotes, who has forged a new trail and built a bridge behind her for all young women to follow." O'Connor enjoyed chatting up the other Medal of Freedom honorees, who included Billie Jean King, Desmond Tutu, and Senator Edward Kennedy, and introducing them to her sons. "She took it all in stride," recalled Scott.[20]

AND SO, DETERMINED to remain "relevant" for five years after leaving the Court—and then for five more years—she continued to soldier on across the country and around the world, a salesperson for civic virtue and, as she entered her ninth decade, a living memorial to women's progress. She was, if possible, more vibrant than ever. She could be crotchety; also, warm, empathetic, and saucy. "She was so difficult," said Tom Wilner, a top Washington human rights lawyer and iCivics board member who traveled with her and interviewed her on stage. "She would say, 'I don't want to answer that' or just give one-word answers. At dinner, I would say, 'You make it so difficult!' She would say, 'I'm trying to improve your examinations.' She was tough and abrasive. But also funny and sweet. She was a big flirt."

On her foreign swings to preach the rule of law to judges in emerging democracies, "she was not shy about scolding those guys. She would let them have it about 'telephone justice,'" recalled John Jasik, a State Department official who traveled with her and became a close friend. (Among the leaders she chided, in a diplomatic way, was the president of China, Jiang Zemin, who personally asked to meet with her.)[21] "She was the world's biggest sweetheart until you pissed her off," said Jasik. She liked to talk to schoolkids, explaining how she went to work for free at the DA's office out of law school and was forever grateful to have been exposed to a life of public service. On their travels through the Middle East or Asia, O'Connor would enthusiastically wear out her hosts. "She really liked to sample local customs. She was adventurous. She also liked a good drink. It was, 'Ambassador, do you have any Scotch?'" recalled Jasik. "She was not a stiff. She could be a good-time Charlie. She treated everyone the same, whether president or janitor. They loved her. People came up to us with tears in their eyes."[22]

In the summer of 2011, she went on a safari to Botswana with her daughter-in-law Heather (Jay's wife) and a few other friends. Their guide, Anthony Bennett, "was a take-charge guy, and she responded to that," recalled Heather. O'Connor bantered with him like a school-girl. "In the jeep, she'd say, 'Ant, no! Stop!' as we drove over a tree to look at lions. 'Oh Ant, you are so terrible!' She loved it," laughed Heather. "She was strong willed," recalled Bennett. "I had to rein her in. She was up for everything." When the trip was over, she issued certificates to the Fellows of the Blue Ball Society, in honor of her favorite monkey, a dominant male with electric-blue testicles.[23]

She could be a little short with the help when service was slow, but at the same time she called out a bigot who was abusing the waitstaff. At the bar of a private club, a bitter old fool told the waiter bringing him a drink, "I asked for a Manhattan, not an Old Fashioned, you camel jockey." The room grew silent. O'Connor arose from her seat and said, "Sir, you do not belong to the human race. You should be ashamed of yourself."

She was, as ever, in a hurry and willful and a touch outrageous. With her friend and portrait painter Danni Dawson, she went in the fall of 2011 to look at the new Martin Luther King, Jr., Memorial, across the Tidal Basin from the Jefferson Memorial. Their friend Joe Henderson went to get the car to drive them home. There are few parking spaces down on the Mall, and Henderson was gone for some time. "Is he ever coming?" O'Connor demanded. "Let's hitchhike," she said to Dawson. She saw a red car approaching that looked like

Henderson's. O'Connor stepped into the street, hiked up her skirt, and put out her thumb. The car was not Henderson's. The driver stopped, paused, and drove on, possibly wondering if he had just seen the nation's first woman Supreme Court justice hitchhiking.[24]

She was as sporting as ever. Visiting a NASCAR track on one of her speaking tours, O'Connor hopped in one of the racecars. "Step on it!" she commanded the U.S. marshal assigned to protect her and drive her. Fishing in Alaska, she was obliged to repel a lumbering grizzly with a can of bear spray. "The guide said, 'I've never been so scared in my life,'" recalled Lynda Webster. "She said, 'Oh, I wasn't afraid.'"[25]

But she was beginning to have trouble walking—she began fishing while sitting in an inner tube—and her displays of impatience were getting more noticeable, at times embarrassingly so.

ON MARCH 28, 2013, O'Connor was interviewed, along with former Secretary of State Madeleine Albright, before a large crowd at the New York Public Library. The moderator was Anne-Marie Slaughter, a Princeton professor and former State Department head of policy and planning. Slaughter asked about the role of family in their careers. "My husband had Alzheimer's. Don't get it, okay?" said Justice O'Connor. "Just stay away from it. It's an awful thing to go through. Just stay away from it."

During the discussion, Slaughter noticed that O'Connor's answers were getting shorter and shorter. Slaughter asked whether women brought to their jobs different perspectives than men. O'Connor deflected the answer. Slaughter pressed: "No difference?" O'Connor answered, "Very seldom."

At one point, O'Connor announced, "Anne-Marie, you've run out of time." Startled, Slaughter said, "Have I?" O'Connor: "I think you better think about that before launching another topic." There was still a half hour to go in the program. Slaughter struggled on, as gracefully as she could, to stretch out the conversation for another ten minutes.

At about the same time, O'Connor attended an Episcopal funeral service in Phoenix. When the organist seemed to go on and on, O'Connor called out from the congregation, "That's enough already!" There were laughs, but some people exchanged glances.[26]

O'Connor's staff began to notice that she was becoming forgetful and more irascible. Meryl Chertoff wondered if she was "punch drunk" from the relentless travel. Jim Gee observed that she was repeating herself at iCivics board meetings, but he rationalized, "Well, we all repeat things."

That spring of 2013, boarding the Semester-at-Sea ship in Fort Lauderdale for a voyage to Peru, where she would climb to the ancient ruins at Machu Picchu, she told the tour director, "I've always wanted to go on this ship." She had been on the same vessel two years before. The director turned to her friend, University of Virginia political scientist Jim Todd, and asked, "Do we have a problem here?" "She couldn't remember that she had talked to you the day before," recalled Lynda Webster. Even so, she made the long hike up the Peruvian mountain.[27]

Her long-unwavering confidence began to flag. "I first noticed that she was being circumspect," recalled Cynthia Helms. "She would stick to mundane conversation. I could tell she was realizing that something was wrong. She was briefer, more hesitant."[28]

On September 17, 2013, she was scheduled to give the John Paul Stevens Lecture before a thousand people at the University of Colorado Law School. Earlier that day, touring an inner-city school, she had had trouble answering questions. Backstage at the Justice Byron White Auditorium, she turned to her friend Becky Kourlis and said, "What am I speaking about?" She asked Kourlis and Ruth McGregor to go onstage with her; occupying two hastily added chairs, the two prompted her through a labored conversation. "She knew what was happening," recalled McGregor, but she was not ready to confront reality. "Sometimes, she was dismissive: 'I can't remember anything.' Other times she was more serious: 'I just can't remember *anything*.'"

Sandra was well aware that her own mother and her mother's sister, Evelyn, had suffered from Alzheimer's. "Her greatest fear," said her brother, Alan, "was that she would get it."

She rebelled against the formal diagnosis—dementia, most likely Alzheimer's—when it finally came. "She was mad at the doctor and said she wanted a different one who knew what he was doing," recalled her son Scott. "The doctor began calling me because she was refusing to hear him." The denial spluttered along for a time, followed by a restless acceptance. "I'm going to just fade away now," she told Becky Kourlis, her partner in championing an independent judiciary. "You keep on." Back problems consigned her to a wheelchair; she moved to an assisted living facility. But O'Connor continued to show the flag at public events. In March 2017, at the age of eighty-seven, she appeared in her wheelchair on the floor of the Arizona state senate, where she sat at her old spot as majority leader and said a few spontaneous, well-chosen words in support of a resolution endorsing iCivics. Former Democratic majority leader Alfredo Gutierrez sat in his familiar seat across the aisle. The two old foes reached out and held hands.[29]

Later that summer, O'Connor, accompanied by two of her former clerks, Kathy Smalley and Jane Fahey, peeked into the auditorium at the Sandra Day O'Connor College of Law at ASU, where an administrator was holding an orientation for students entering in the fall. After greeting the justice, the administrator asked if she would like to say a few words. "Sure," she said. Her two former clerks "exchanged an anxious glance," recalled Fahey. But they wheeled her forward and handed her the microphone. Speaking in a still firm voice, O'Connor congratulated the students on their decision to pursue a legal education and said they would have the privilege of practicing a profession in which one person really could change the whole system and make it, and his or her community, better. "It was vintage O'Connor," Fahey recalled. "The importance of the rule of law, the chance to make a real difference, the inspiring example of the modest start to her own career that included hanging out her own shingle. It was all there. She saw in these young folks potential bridge builders like herself, and she encouraged them to make the most of it."[30]

Before she left Washington for the last time in 2016, O'Connor had gone out to dinner with Cynthia Helms. In the car, after the usual backseat driving, she turned to Helms and said that she wanted her to know how happy she had been to be her friend all these years. "She was tearful," recalled Helms. "I felt she knew the down slopes were coming. I felt she had come to this moment with herself, that things were changing, things were coming to an end."

In Phoenix in the fall of 2017, Ruth McGregor said of her old mentor and friend, "She has become more angry. Also, more affectionate. She tells people she loves them."[31]

As a law student at Yale in the late 1970s, Sonia Sotomayor would sit in the cafeteria and see that all the portraits on the wall were of white men. "We would speculate: Would there ever be a woman Supreme Court justice?" O'Connor's appointment in 1981 "changed everything," said Justice Sotomayor, speaking to the author in December 2017. "She was so big—such a big figure. For someone like me, she was such an extraordinary woman. The possibility that I could have a full career, to do anything I wanted in the profession, became a reality. Yes, there were other barriers—race, religion, et cetera—but first and foremost was being a woman." On Sotomayor's first day as a U.S. Supreme Court justice in October 2009, Justice O'Connor came to her chambers and told her, "The worst thing you can do is be indecisive. Make a decision, right or wrong. If you're known as indecisive you'll never belong fully." Sotomayor soon realized she was not the first new justice to experience O'Connor's tough love.

After Chief Justice Roberts arrived at the Court in 2005, O'Connor told him it was his responsibility to be present at every Court lunch—and make sure other justices attended. "I heard that if other justices didn't go, she'd sit in their office, inquiring why they were delinquent," said Sotomayor.

In October Term 1987, Elena Kagan had clerked for Justice Thurgood Marshall. Known for her jump shot, Kagan preferred playing basketball to attending Justice O'Connor's morning aerobics. After she tore a knee ligament and wound up on crutches, a sheepish Kagan encountered Justice O'Connor in the corridor. "She looked at me with a (mock) very sad expression," recalled Justice Kagan in 2017. "She said, 'It wouldn't have happened if you had come to my exercise class.'"

Justice Kagan told this story with a laugh as she sat in her chambers—the same chambers once occupied by Sandra Day O'Connor, a grand suite overlooking the Supreme Court plaza across from the U.S. Capitol. Justice O'Connor "had an unerring instinct for what the citizenry could accept," said Kagan. "An instinct for the middle, as a centrist, with respect to every issue. She would find the sweet spot where the settlement of incredibly difficult issues could be accepted. That was her brilliance—at the time, it was the best thing a judge could have done. No one could have done it better. The country is stronger as a result."[32]

WHEN SANDRA DAY O'Connor read the Declaration of Independence to a small crowd of friends at Iron Springs, Arizona, on July 4, 1981, three days before she was nominated to the Supreme Court, she spoke from the heart. She had faith in the work of the Founders. As a justice, she kept a copy of the U.S. Constitution in her purse. "She still does," said Scott O'Connor as his mother turned eighty-eight in 2018.

She was a patriot who did not gush about her patriotism. She was mystical about the Lazy B, less so about Washington. A pragmatist, she was aware from personal experience how long it took to give full meaning to the promises of the Founders' documents.

O'Connor was not one for philosophizing or intellectualizing. She was a doer. The way to happiness, she believed, was through "work worth doing," a favorite phrase of hers. For O'Connor, teaching millions of children the virtues of the American system of government through iCivics was a labor of love.[33]

Toughened by her father's stern love, she learned to make no excuses. When men ranging from drunken boors in the Arizona legislature to Antonin Scalia tried to patronize her, she deftly sidestepped their provocation. Martyrdom was a self-indulgence. She understood that she needed to succeed for the sake of all the women who wished to follow. She could be feisty and, as she aged and became ill, even ornery, but for the most part, she was the embodiment of grace under pressure.

The U.S. Constitution is not a self-executing document. Self-governance requires restraint, forbearance, and the willingness to compromise. The Founders wanted to create, as John Adams put it, a "government of laws and not of men" because they were cognizant of human weakness. More than most, Sandra Day O'Connor was sensitive to those weaknesses but not fazed by them. The way to meet unreasonable expectations was to plunge in, do your best, and not look back.

While her sense of self was strong, she was an avatar of selflessness. Though she was not a devotee of a particular legal doctrine, she was a guardian of the system itself. Her greatest faith was in the collective endeavor of liberal democracy, an ongoing conversation between the branches of government that, over time (sometimes a very long time), can protect the worth of each individual. You could say that her life embodied that process.

She more than once said that she wanted as her epitaph "Here lies a good judge," but she knew better. Her role went far beyond judging. Although her jurisprudence, like her character, was essentially modest, she was well aware of her place in history. She knew that Ronald Reagan chose her (with two others) to speak at his funeral not because she was his friend, or knew him particularly well, but because he wanted to claim her as an epochal achievement.* Like Jackie Robinson, who broke the color barrier in baseball, she understood that as the first woman justice, all eyes were upon her—always. Like Robinson, she carried herself with a self-conscious yet natural dignity.

She was humble, but her humility was born of confidence. Judge J. Harvie Wilkinson III of the Fourth Circuit Court of Appeals (whose own name often appeared on Supreme Court short lists) wisely noted "the irony that a more traditional woman probably contributed more to the advancement of women's rights than, say, a more ardent feminist would have." She would never put it so cheekily, but by not threatening men, she more easily replaced them. The analogy she preferred was from the poem she liked to quote about the pilgrim who built the bridge. "Justice O'Connor *was* the perfect bridge," said Judge Wilkinson. "Someone to her right or her left, or without her flinty pragmatism and indefatigable public energy, could not have carried off the transition nearly so well."[35]

As you walk up the wide steps of the Supreme Court, you pass between two grand marble statues, on the right a man (*Authority of Law*) and on the left a woman (*Contemplation of Justice*). Until Sandra

---

* The other two were British prime minister Margaret Thatcher and President George H. W. Bush.[34]

O'Connor arrived, every justice had been a man. She knew the burden she carried: that she would have to be a paragon of far more than legal acuity, that the nation would want a woman who was, as she might put it, "attractive." More than an activist for women's rights, she had to play the role of Lady Justice, holding the scales. She brought to her job the wisdom that can come from personal suffering, from having a great love and losing it, from being a daughter and a mother as well as a role model for millions of women.

IN JULY 1987, when she was fifty-seven, Justice O'Connor wrote down some instructions for a public funeral, in case she died while still on the Court. At the end of the document, she addressed her three sons:

> I have been greatly blessed by my life's experiences. I have loved dearly my husband, my children, Joanie [her new daughter-in-law], my friends and family. I hope I have helped pave the pathway for other women who have chosen to follow a career. Our purpose in life is to help others along the way. May you each try to do the same.

Two years later, when she buried her mother's ashes alongside her father on the top of Round Mountain at the Lazy B, she told her family that when the end came for her, "This is where I want to be."[36]

As time went on, long after the Lazy B had been sold off, through the painful years of John's illness and the saddening trial of her own decline, she never tired of speaking lovingly of her childhood at the ranch. "That was the best life," she would say. In the spring of 2016, sitting in a restaurant in a strip mall in Phoenix with the author, she kept pointing to the desiccated but strangely beautiful hills, lit by a setting sun, across the highway. In her old age, dimmed yet undaunted, she wished to go home. She dreamed of the land that had made her.

At the Sandra Day O'Connor United States Courthouse in Phoenix.

ACKNOWLEDGMENTS

My wife, Oscie, was essential to this book. We conducted almost every interview together, and she spent many hours with me reading documents in Justice O'Connor's chambers at the Supreme Court and in the Madison Building reading room of the Library of Congress. We talked about the book constantly, and she worked over every word of the manuscript. We traveled together to visit the justice in Phoenix and to speak with Justice O'Connor's clerks and friends in many places around the country. Oscie has been deeply involved in most of my books as an editor and coresearcher, but this one is different. She understood Justice O'Connor in ways that I could not. The portrait here is the work of two people who have grown ever closer over the years. It is a joint project and a labor of love.

The idea to do the book came to us from Kate Medina of Random House, the legendary editor who had been Justice O'Connor's editor for her bestselling memoir of growing up on a ranch, *Lazy B,* as well as two other books by the justice about the Supreme Court and the law. In February 2016, I flew to Phoenix to see Justice O'Connor and her son Scott and Scott's wife, Joanie. In late 2014, Justice O'Connor had been diagnosed with dementia, probably Alzheimer's. She was still alert and vital when we talked, and she had retained some long-term memory, but it was obvious that she could not be a significant source for the book. We spoke a half dozen times over the next year, mostly about family and growing up. With few exceptions, she discussed her time at the Court only in general terms. She did not engage much on the subject of her own jurisprudence. With a gleam in her eye not much diminished by age and illness, she dismissed academic theories of her jurisprudence as "those kooky ideas."

Justice O'Connor wrote a letter to her colleagues, friends, and law clerks asking them to speak with me and cooperate on the book. Seven justices spoke with us at their chambers: John Paul Stevens, Ruth Bader Ginsburg, Stephen Breyer, Clarence Thomas, John Roberts, Sonia Sotomayor, and Elena Kagan. We interviewed 94 of Justice O'Connor's 108 law clerks, almost all on the record. We are indebted to all of them. We want to thank, in particular, Ruth McGregor, Deborah Merritt, Jane Fahey, Kathy Smalley, Julie O'Sullivan, Kent Syverud, Dan Bussel, Steve Gilles, Lisa Kern Griffin, and RonNell Andersen Jones. All of them read and commented on the manuscript. Thanks, too, to Judge J. Harvie Wilkinson III of the Fourth Circuit Court of Appeals; Judge John Walker of the Second Circuit Court of Appeals; and Dean John Jeffries and Professor Paul Stephan of the University of Virginia Law School, for reading and giving us their thoughts on all or parts of the manuscript. Judge Wilkinson taught constitutional law to Oscie and me at UVA in 1975 and Paul Stephan was in my first-year study group, so it was a happy reunion and mini refresher course.

Justice O'Connor gave me access to her papers, most of which are at the Library of Congress but closed to the public, and those private papers which remained at her chambers at the Supreme Court. Her papers include personal correspondence, records, and oral histories; her occasional journal of her early years on the Court; the personal unpublished memoir of her husband, John; and John's daily diary from the time she joined the Court in 1981 until he was overcome by Alzheimer's in 2002. To use the material in John's diary and her journal, I needed permission from her son Jay O'Connor, her literary executor, and for that I thank him. For permission to quote from Justice Rehnquist's letters, I am grateful to Janet Rehnquist.

Justice O'Connor's papers at the Library of Congress include all of her papers from her work as a justice—her draft opinions, notes from conference, and memos back and forth with other justices. I was given full access to those papers from her first term on the Court, 1981–82, through the 1990–91 term, when Justice Clarence Thomas came on the Court. (Justice O'Connor wanted her Court papers to remain closed for any terms that involved a sitting justice.)

I spent many hours talking to Justice O'Connor's three sons, Scott, Brian, and Jay; to Scott's wife, Joanie, and Jay's wife, Heather; and to Sandra's brother, Alan Day. They shared observations and warm memories and more than a few laughs. For this book, Oscie and I conducted more than 350 interviews. I thank Phil Schneider and Phil Edlund in Phoenix for offering to track down old friends and acquaintances of the O'Connors, and also thank Sarah Suggs, the head of the O'Connor Institute in Phoenix, who was supportive throughout. Alfredo Guterriez helped us understand the colorful world of the Arizona legislature, and we learned still more from a number of her aides and colleagues from the time. We are grateful to them all. Sandra O'Connor had wide-ranging and overlapping circles of friends, from her Stanford days to Phoenix to Washington, and in time, all over the world. At CEELI, thanks to Mark Ellis; at the State Department, thanks to John Jasik. Thanks, too, to Sandra's many close girlfriends, including "the Girls of Branner Hall" and the "Mobile Party Unit" (as well as the next generation, Susan J. Taylor) for sharing their recollections. We could see why Beatrice Challis Laws was Sandra's best friend in law school, and we are very thankful for access to her memorable photo albums. In Washington, Sandra's friends Cynthia Helms, Judy Hope, Bill and Lynda Webster, and Adrienne Arsht were especially helpful. I want to thank Alan Kirk for inviting me to lunch several times at the Alibi Club, a special world that John O'Connor loved (and Sandra O'Connor appreciated). We talked to some pillars of the Washington legal establishment, and we thank especially Don Verrilli, Ted Olson, and Ken Starr. Among veteran Court watchers, we thank Nina Totenberg, Jim Newton, and Joan Biskupic, author of an earlier O'Connor biography. With the family's permission, Dr. Marc Lippman of Georgetown answered our questions about Justice O'Connor's breast cancer, and Dr. Paul Aisen patiently discussed John O'Connor's Alzheimer's with us. We are grateful to both.

In Justice O'Connor's chambers, Linda Neary and Marilyn Umali were gracious and tireless in helping us work through the trove of pictures and documents. At the Library of Congress, Jeff Flannery, head of Reference and Reader Services in the Manuscript Division, is an amazing resource (and a lot of fun to hang out with). His excellent staff—Fred Augustyn, Joseph Jackson, Patrick Kerwin, Bruce Kirby, Edith Sandler, and Lara Szyszak—kept us busy. Thanks as well to Janice Ruth at the LOC and Ethan Torrey at the Supreme Court for helping us sort through the permission issues. Kathy Arberg and Tyler Lopez at the Supreme Court Office of Public Information were unfailingly good to us. In the Curator's Office, Catherine Fitts, Franz Jantzen, and Fred Schilling patiently fielded our queries and were a great help with the photos.

Our friend Mike Hill, who researched several of my earlier books, did some valuable digging online and in the Lewis Powell Papers at Washington and Lee University, and he joined Oscie and me on a fascinating tour with Alan Day of the magical realm of the Lazy B. Thanks to the new proprietor of the ranch, Kristen Sorensen, for hosting us. In Phoenix, Paul Bergelin patiently and resourcefully researched Sandra O'Connor's legislative record. Thanks, too, to Nisha Norian, who made available her background paper on O'Connor's Phoenix years. And at the National Cathedral in Washington, our thanks go to master researcher Margaret Shannon.

At Random House, we were expertly guided by Kate Medina and her excellent associates, senior editor Anna Pitoniak and associate editor Erica Gonzalez. Kate is every author's dream as an editor: at once warm and candid, wise and supportive. Anna, a brilliant young author in her own right, helped us see Sandra O'Connor more clearly, and Erica is a generous, sure-handed guide on all matters publishing. For the cover art, I am grateful to Paolo Pepe and Anna Bauer; for interior design, to Simon Sullivan. Picture researcher Carol Poticny tracked down dozens of photos, and copy editor Emily DeHuff worked with production editor Steve Messina to bring clarity and needed corrections to the manuscript. In marketing, Andrea DeWerd and Katie Tull are working hard to sell the book, all under the wise aegis of deputy publisher Avideh Bashirrad. In Random's PR shop, we were in the good hands of London King, Maria Braeckel, and Greg Kubie, and Matthew Martin, Random's fine lawyer, gave us wise counsel.

I feel lucky to count as friends three of the great modern popular historians, Jon Meacham, Michael Beschloss, and Walter Isaacson. It was Jon who brought me to Random House and Gina Centrello. Oscie and I have spent many happy hours with Jon and his wife, Keith, talking over this book, all books, and so much more. Ann McDaniel, our friend from my days as a journalist, has long been a wise and sensitive consigliere. Steve Smith taught me how to write in ways that matter most. Sven Holmes and I have been talking about "the events of the day" for almost fifty years, and he is still teaching me about the Fourteenth Amendment. Our daughters, Louisa and Mary, have lovingly tried to steer me straight, or at least out of oncoming traffic.

My agent of decades is Amanda Urban. The best.

EVAN THOMAS
Washington, D.C.

NOTES

ABBREVIATIONS

AHS Arizona Historical Society	PP Lewis F. Powell papers
ASLA Arizona State Legislature Archive	PUL Princeton University Library
BP Harry Blackmun papers	RL Reagan Library
JOCD John O'Connor Diary	SC Supreme Court
LB *Lazy B*	SOC Sandra O'Connor
LOC Library of Congress	SOCP Sandra O'Connor papers
OT October Term	WLU Washington and Lee University

NOTE ON SOURCES

Most of Justice O'Connor's papers are at the Library of Congress and currently closed to the public. These are designated as SOCP, LOC. Her private collection, including her occasional journal of her early years on the Court and a trove of personal and family letters, including those from the young William Rehnquist and some correspondence with the other justices, has been, until recently, stored at the Supreme Court. These papers are designated SOCP, SC.

PROLOGUE

1. *Time,* July 20, 1981; Bill Kenyon interview.
2. "Sandra Day O'Connor, random notes fall 1981," SOCP, SC; "First Day of Work for Supreme Court Justice Sandra Day O'Connor," Carl Stern, Correspondent, *NBC Nightly News,* October 5, 1981, NBC Learn Web, January 18, 2015; *Watt v. Energy Action,* Oral Argument Transcript, October 5, 1981, SC Public Information Office (tape of the argument can be heard at National Archives II, College Park, MD); Lewis F. Powell to his children, October 24, 1981, PP, WLU.
3. SOC interview; Silvija Strikis, Justice Sonia Sotomayor, Justice Clarence Thomas, Lisa Kern Griffin, Daniel Bussel, RonNell Andersen Jones, Jim Todd interviews. O'Connor included the poem *The Bridge Builder,* by Will Allen Dromgoole, in her 2004 commencement address, *Stanford Report,* June 13, 2004.

CHAPTER ONE: LAZY B

1. SOC interview.
2. LB, vii, 7, 9, 18, 234; author trip to Lazy B Ranch with Alan Day, March 2017.

3. *LB*, viii; SOC interview.

4. Judge J. Harvie Wilkinson III interview.

5. *LB*, 203–208, 213–25.

6. Ibid., 231.

7. Ibid., 29, 44.

8. Ibid., 53–59. Rastus is sometimes spelled Rastas.

9. Ibid., 229–30.

10. Ibid., 33.

11. Ibid., 23, 27–28, 140; Alan Day interview.

12. Ibid., 190, 193.

13. Ibid., 69–71, 275.

14. Alan Day interview.

15. SOC interview.

16. *LB*, 5, 131–34.

17. Ibid., 7–8, 24.

18. Ibid., 25.

19. Alan Day interview.

20. *LB*, 23–24; Harry Day to Eleanor Day, November 19, 1919, SOCP, AHS.

21. *LB*, 30.

22. Harry Day to Ada Mae Wilkey, August 13, 1927, July 7, 1927; AMW to HD, July 15, 1927, SOCP, SC; *LB*, 37.

23. *LB*, 43, 94.

24. Ibid., 43–44.

25. Ibid., 26, 43, 98, 234; Alan Day interview.

26. Ibid., 49; Alan Day interview.

27. Ibid., 29.

28. SOC interview.

29. SOC to Verla Sorenson, June 6, 2005, SOCP, LOC.

30. Harry Day to Ada Mae Wilkey, September 17, 1928, SOCP, SC.

31. *LB*, 115; SOC interview.

32. Alan Day, Molly Joyce interviews.

33. Scott O'Connor, Molly Joyce interviews.

34. SOC oral history by Eugene Griessman, December 12, 1986, SOCP, LOC (hereinafter Griessman OH); SOC interview; SOC oral history by Sarah Wilson, September 18, 1995, SOCP, LOC (hereinafter Wilson OH).

35. Alan Day, Molly Joyce interviews.

36. SOC oral history by James Simon, November 16, 1992, SOCP, LOC (hereinafter Simon OH).

37. *LB*, 40, 45; Wilson OH.

38. Beverly Timberlake interview.

39. *LB*, 116.

40. SOC interview, *Utah Bar Journal*, vol. 22, issue 5, September/October 2009, SOCP, LOC.

41. SOC oral history, *Phoenix Oral History Project*, January 31, 1980, SOCP, LOC (hereinafter Phoenix OH).

42. *LB*, 41.

43. Griessman OH.

44. Beverly Timberlake interview.

45. Molly Joyce interview.

46. *LB, 46.*

47. Ibid., 177–78.

48. "Justice Sandra Day O'Connor," *People,* October 21, 1981; in a letter to an author of children's books, SOC also said her father lassoed her to send her back to school. SOC to Norman Macht, March 19, 1991, SOCP, LOC.

49. *LB,* 117–19; SOC interview.

50. *LB,* 165–70.

51. Alan Day interview.

52. *LB,* 96; Simon OH; "Justice Sandra Day O'Connor," *People,* October 12, 1981.

53. *LB,* 239–44; Allison Beard, "Life's Work: An Interview with Sandra Day O'Connor," *Harvard Business Review,* December 2013.

54. *LB,* 244.

55. See, for example, Beard, "Life's Work."

56. Ruth McGregor interview.

57. RonNell Andersen Jones interview.

58. Newspaper clipping, undated, probably 1945, SOCP, SC.

59. SOC interview; Simon OH; graduation exercises, Austin High School, El Paso, Texas, May 22, 1946, SOCP, LOC.

60. Simon OH; SOC interviewed by Kevin Cool, *Stanford Magazine,* January/February 2006. In SOC's papers is a ticket for the College Board exams administered in El Paso on June 1, 1946; she may have been referring to other placement tests administered by Stanford, SOCP, SC.

CHAPTER TWO: STANFORD

1. Sandra O'Connor, "Harry's Last Lecture," Stanford University, April 28, 2008, youtube.com; Jocas, Neuman, and Turner, *Stanford University: An Architectural Guide;* SOC's answers to 1986 questionnaire from *The Stanford Daily,* SOCP, LOC.

2. Roth, *American Pastoral,* 40; David Kennedy interview.

3. "Regulations for Women Students, Stanford University, 1946–47," SOCP, SC.

4. Sandra Day to Harry and Ada Mae Day, undated, probably 1949, SOCP, SC.

5. Diane Porter Cooley, Nina van Rensselaer, Martica Ruhm Sawin interviews.

6. Andy Campbell interview.

7. SOC interview; Colin Campbell interview; "History 12: History of Western Civilization: A Syllabus" (1943), Stanford University Archives.

8. SOC interview; SOC delivers "Harry's Last Lecture," April 22, 2008, stanford .edu.

9. Martica Ruhm Sawin, Beth Harrelson Growden interviews; Wilson OH.

10. *Lazy B,* 142.

11. SOC interviewed by Kevin Cool, *Stanford Magazine,* January/February 2006; "Harry Rathbun," *Stanford Business School Magazine,* February 1988.

12. Hirshman, *Sisters in Law,* 7–9.

13. Diane Cooley interview; Charles Lane, "Courting O'Connor," *Washington Post Magazine,* July 4, 2004.

14. Sandra Day to Harry and Ada Mae Day, undated, probably spring 1947, SOCP, SC.

15. Graduation Exercises, Austin High School, May 22, 1946, SOCP, LOC; Stanford Yearbooks 1947–1952, Stanford University Archives.

16. SOC interview; SOC to Thomas Lemann, May 8, 2003, SOCP, LOC.

17. Sandra Day to Harry and Ada Mae Day, undated, probably spring 1947, SOCP, LOC; SOC interview; Beth Harrelson Growden interview.

18. Chad Graham, "O'Connor Adds a Light Touch to Economic Event," *Arizona Republic,* January 16, 1991; Alan Day interview.

19. Sandra Day to Harry and Ada Mae Day, undated, probably fall 1948 and winter 1949, SOCP, SC.

20. Sandra Day to Harry and Ada Mae Day, undated, probably spring 1949, SOCP, SC.

21. Simon OH; Beverly Timberlake, Alan Day interviews.

22. Diane Cooley, Martica Ruhm Sawin interviews.

23. SOC was proposed to by Andy Campbell, John Hamilton, William Rehnquist, and John O'Connor; formally engaged to Hamilton and O'Connor; and "loosely engaged" to Richard Knight, according to Beatrice Challis Laws.

24. Sandra Day to Harry and Ada Mae Day, January 28, 1950; Sandra Day to Edith Wilkey, undated, probably winter 1950, SOCP, SC.

25. Craig Joyce oral history of Harry and Ada Mae Day, May 1983, SOCP, LOC (hereinafter Joyce OH).

26. Beatrice Challis Laws interview.

27. "Chronology of Legal Education at Stanford University, 1885–2006," legal research paper, Stanford Law School; David Lempert, "After Five Decades: Stanford Law School's Class of 1952," Legal Studies Forum 2003, law.stanford.edu.

28. *Stanford Daily,* May 17, 1950.

29. Miles Rubin interview.

30. SOC interview; Beatrice Challis Laws interview; Wilson OH; SOC "Fiftieth Anniversary Remarks," 50 *Stanford Law Review* 1 (1997).

31. Charles Lane, "Head of the Class," *Stanford Magazine,* July/August 2005; Jenkins, *The Partisan,* 14–24.

32. William Rehnquist to Sandra Day, March 29, 1952, SOCP, SC.

33. Alan Day, Molly Joyce, Pat Hass interviews.

34. "One-on-One with the Chief," *Stanford Lawyer,* Spring 2005; Beatrice Challis Laws, Diane Porter Cooley interviews.

35. Sandra Day to Harry and Ada Mae Day, undated, probably winter 1952, SOCP, SC.

36. Donald Querio, "Alan Fink," *Stanford Lawyer,* fall 2013.

37. Sandra Day to Harry and Ada Mae Day, undated, probably January 1952, SOCP, SC.

38. Jim Watkinson interview.

39. John O'Connor Memoir, 20–21, 41–42, SOCP, Family Archives.

40. Beth Harrelson Growden interview.

41. Beatrice Challis Laws, Diane Cooley interviews.

42. Ann Day to Sandra Day, undated, probably April 1952, SOCP, SC.

43. Rehnquist Notebooks, 1951, William Rehnquist Papers, Hoover Institute.

44. William Rehnquist to Sandra Day, January 28, February 21, March 11, 29, April 11, 22, 29, May 19, 1952, SOCP, SC.

45. Simon OH.

46. David Gergen, "Still Supreme," *Parade,* September 30, 2012; SOC oral history by Victoria Lawford, July 17, 1987 (hereinafter Lawford OH); Wilson OH 9, SOCP, LOC.

47. NPR interview by Terry Gross, March 5, 2013.

48. SOC interview.
49. Beatrice Challis Laws interview.
50. Simon OH.
51. John O'Connor Memoir, 43, SOCP, Family Archives.
52. Sandra Day to John O'Connor, June 21, 1952, SOCP, SC.
53. William Rehnquist to Sandra Day, June 25, July 11, 19, 23, August 26, 1952, SOCP, SC.
54. Pat Hass interview.
55. John O'Connor Memoir, 77, SOCP, Family Archives.

CHAPTER THREE: THE GOLDEN COUPLE

1. Ada Mae Day to John O'Connor, September 8, 1952, SOCP, SC.
2. Joyce OH.
3. John O'Connor Memoir, 46, SOCP, Family Archives.
4. Ibid., 8–9.
5. Diane Porter Cooley, Beatrice Challis Laws, SOC interviews.
6. Sandra Day to Harry and Ada Mae Day, undated, probably September 1952, SOCP, SC.
7. Sandra Day to John O'Connor, undated, probably September 1952, SOCP, SC.
8. SOC to Harry and Ada Mae Day, undated, probably January 1953, SOCP, SC.
9. Correspondence between Sandra Day and John O'Connor, undated, probably October–December 1952, SOCP, SC.
10. Gergen, "Still Supreme."
11. *LB*, 285.
12. John O'Connor Memoir, 47–49, SOCP, Family Archives.
13. Lawford OH, SOCP, LOC.
14. SOC to Harry and Ada Mae Day, undated, probably January 1953, SOCP, SC.
15. SOC interview; SOC oral history by Mauree Jane Perry, Women's Forum West Legacy Foundation Project, "Pioneering Women of the 20th Century," April 4, 2001, SOCP, SC (hereinafter Perry OH).
16. John O'Connor Memoir, 56, SOCP, Family Archives.
17. SOC to Harry and Ada Mae Day, undated, probably 1955, Phoenix OH, SOCP, SC.
18. John O'Connor Memoir, 70–72, SOCP, Family Archives.
19. Wilson OH; SOC to Harry and Ada Mae Day, undated, probably 1956, SOCP, SC.
20. Harry Day to SOC, January 5, May 2, 1956, SOCP, SC.
21. Harry Day to SOC, August 29, November 24, 1955; SOC to Harry and Ada Mae Day, September 9, 1955, and undated, probably 1955, SOCP, SC.
22. Diane Porter Cooley interview; Harry Day to SOC, undated, probably 1955, SOCP, SOC.
23. SOC to Harry Day, September 9, 1955, SOCP, SC.
24. Konrad Staudinger interview.
25. Lois Driggs Cannon Aldrin interview.
26. SOC to Harry and Ada Mae Day, September 18, 1956, SOCP, SC.
27. Simon OH; John O'Connor Memoir, 75, SOCP, Family Archives.
28. Diane Porter Cooley interview.
29. Jason La Bau, "Phoenix Rising: Arizona and the Origins of Modern Conserva-

tive Politics," Ph.D. dissertation, University of Southern California, August 2010, 72, AHS.

30. William Rehnquist to SOC, December 15, 1955, SOCP, SC.
31. SOC interview.
32. John O'Connor Memoir, 76–77, 98–99, SOCP, Family Archives.
33. Don Kauffman interview.
34. John O'Connor Memoir, 77, SOCP, Family Archives.
35. Pat Smith, "Magazine Cupid for Lawyer Couple," *Arizona Republic,* September 27, 1957.
36. SOC interview; Simon OH; Craig Joyce, "A Good Judge," *Journal of Supreme Court History,* vol. 31, issue 2, 105, 2006. The forged check story may be slightly exaggerated; it seems hard to believe that even the inexperienced O'Connor would use an expert witness to give testimony adverse to her client.
37. Lawford OH; SOC to Elizabeth Marshall White, December 2, 1998, SOCP, LOC.
38. Sue Huck, Patty Simmons, Beatrice Challis Laws interviews.
39. Scott O'Connor, SOC interviews.
40. Craig Joyce, Tim Berg, Tim Burke, Jerry Lewkowitz interviews.
41. Dick Houseworth interview.
42. Tom Zoellner interview.
43. Elva Coor interview.
44. Gay Firestone Wray, Dick Houseworth interviews.
45. Diane McCarthy, Marshall Trimble interviews; David Berman, *Arizona Politics and Government,* passim; Rick Pearlstein, *Before the Storm,* 23–24; La Bau, "Phoenix Rising," passim.
46. Patty Simmons, Sue Huck, Gail Driggs interviews.
47. Elva Coor, Gay Wray, Paul Eckstein, Patty Simmons interviews.
48. Gayle Wilson interview.
49. Don Kauffman, Richard Houseworth interviews.
50. Julie Folger, Gay Wray, Diane Porter Cooley, Susan and Betsy Taylor interviews.
51. Diana Holman interview.
52. Denise Dravo Eliot interview.
53. Jan Crawford Greenburg, "One Woman's Path to the U.S. Supreme Court," *Chicago Tribune,* July 2, 2004.
54. Brian, Scott, Jay O'Connor interviews; Alan Day interview.
55. Steve Savage interview.
56. Mary Schroeder interview.
57. Friedan, *Feminine Mystique;* Lady Fare, *Arizona Republic,* July 3, 1966.
58. Jordan Green interview.
59. Joyce OH.
60. Simon OH; Wilson OH.
61. Perry OH.
62. SOC interview; Jerry Lewkowitz interview.

CHAPTER FOUR: MAJORITY LEADER

1. SOC, speech to Arizona Women's Hall of Fame, June 12, 1982, SOCP, LOC.
2. Rory Hays interview.

3. Carol Palmer, "Challenging Tradition: Arizona Women Fight for the ERA," Ph.D. dissertation, Arizona State University, September 2007, 45–47.
4. Alfredo Gutierrez, Bette DeGraw, Joe Anderson interviews.
5. Dickson Hartwell, "Sandra," *Phoenix,* February 1971.
6. John Casey to SOC, November 4, 1969, SOCP, LOC.
7. Alfredo Gutierrez, Leo Corbet interviews.
8. Bette DeGraw, Bruce Babbitt interviews.
9. *Time,* March 10, 1967.
10. Simon OH; Wilson OH.
11. Alfredo Gutierrez, George Cunningham, Fred Koory interviews.
12. VanderMeer, *Burton Barr,* 6.
13. Leo Corbet interview.
14. Ned Creighton interview.
15. *Time,* November 1, 1971; Jenkins, 108–109.
16. SOC to William Rehnquist, October 27, 1971; handwritten "assignment" undated, SOCP, ASLA.
17. Scott O'Connor interview; John O'Connor Memoir, 124, SOCP, Family Archives.
18. SOC to William Rehnquist, October 26, 1971; William Rehnquist to SOC, November 16, 1971, SOCP, ASLA.
19. William Rehnquist to John and Sandra O'Connor, November 10, 1971, SOCP, ASLA.
20. Gail Driggs interview.
21. SOC speech to Camelback Kiwanis Club, October 28, 1971, SOCP, ASLA.
22. SOC to Richard Nixon, October 1, 1971, SOCP, ASLA.
23. Barbara Hope Franklin interview.
24. "Dunagin," *Orlando Sentinel,* November 10, 1971, SOCP, ASLA.
25. Abigail Adams to John Adams, March 31, 1776, Adams Papers, Massachusetts Historical Society.
26. "State Senate Votes to Repeal 8-Hour Work Day Law for Women," *Phoenix Gazette,* February 28, 1970.
27. "Laws Affecting Women," handwritten notes, undated, probably 1972, SOCP, ASLA.
28. "Sen. O'Connor Authors Bill to Equalize Status," *Phoenix Gazette,* February 8, 1972; Nisha Norian, SOC Research Document, 10, SOCP, SC.
29. "Woman Director: Mrs. O'Connor Is Bank's First," *Arizona Republic,* January 24, 1971.
30. Hirshman, 46.
31. Palmer, 68.
32. Ned Creighton, Rory Hays interviews.
33. "Senate Maneuvers into Equal Rights Debate," *Phoenix Gazette,* March 24, 1972.
34. Palmer, 71; Irene Rasmussen Oral History, ASLA.
35. Stanley Lubin, Shirley Odegaard interviews.
36. Barry Goldwater to SOC, April 10, 1972, SOCP, ASLA.
37. SOC remarks, Arizona State University, May 7, 1970, SOCP, ASLA.
38. Diane McCarthy, Mark Spitzer, Rick DeGraw, Bette DeGraw, Rory Hays, Athia Hardt, Peter Kay, Alan Maguire interviews.
39. John O'Connor Memoir, 152, SOCP, Family Archives.

40. Scott O'Connor interview.

41. Palmer, 55, 66–67; La Bau, 141.

42. Barbara Barrett interview.

43. George Cunningham, Bette DeGraw, Louise Barr interviews; "Akers Named House Speaker; O'Connor Gets New Role," *Arizona Republic,* November 9, 1972.

44. Bernie Wynn, "One Man's Opinion," *Arizona Republic,* November 12, 1972.

45. "Democrat, 24, to Wait for Seat in House," *Arizona Republic,* January 9, 1973; Alfredo Gutierrez, Leo Corbet interviews.

46. Mark Kiefer, "The Work of Art Hamilton," *Phoenix New Times,* October 1, 1998. Art Hamilton said that in later years, he and Akers were friendly and would laugh about it.

47. Art Hamilton interview.

48. Alfredo Gutierrez, Barbara Barrett, Leo Corbet interviews.

49. SOC interview; Margaret Thomas, "Bridge Over the River O'Connor," *Arizona Republic,* February 2, 1972.

50. Alfredo Gutierrez, Athia Hardt interviews.

51. "Floor Debate Tests Sen. Majority Chief," *Arizona Republic,* February 5, 1973; Mark Spitzer, George Cunningham, Bette DeGraw interviews; Lawford OH, SOCP, LOC; Donna Carlson West oral history, ASLA.

52. SOC to Rob Schmults, March 1, 1987, SOCP, LOC.

53. Rick DeGraw interview.

54. Ron Carmichael, oral history, ASLA; Alfredo Gutierrez interview.

55. Mark Spitzer interview.

56. Alan Maguire, Art Hamilton, George Cunningham interviews.

57. Leo Corbet, Rick DeGraw interviews.

58. Bette DeGraw interview.

59. Diane McCarthy interview; Craig Joyce, "A Good Judge," *Journal of Supreme Court History,* vol. 31, issue 2, 2006.

60. "Seesawing Senators Spell Death of Equal Rights Bill," *Arizona Republic,* March 6, 1973.

61. Palmer, 77; notes of interview with Marcia Weeks, courtesy Carol Palmer.

62. Leo Corbet interview.

63. Jay O'Connor interview.

64. Simon OH.

65. Ken Starr to Attorney General William French Smith, July 6, 1981, RL.

66. "Abortion Bill Clears Sen. Judiciary Panel," *Arizona Republic,* April 30, 1970; "Senate Rules Next: Committee Moves on Abortion Bill," *Phoenix Gazette,* April 29, 1970.

67. "Three Catholic Bishops Issue Statement Calling Abortion Bill 'Moral Evil,'" *Arizona Republic,* February 23, 1970; "Clergymen Seek Open Hearings on Abortion Bill," *Arizona Republic,* March 25, 1970.

68. *Engel v. Vitale,* 370 U.S. 421 (1962); Randall Balmer, "The Real Origins of the Religious Right," politico.com, May 27, 2014; Nomination of Sandra Day O'Connor, *Hearing Record,* September 9, 1981, 94–101, SOCP, LOC. As a reporter for the *Chattanooga Times,* Jon Meacham witnessed the rally in North Georgia in 1992.

69. George Cunningham interview; Kathy Smalley interview.

70. Tom Skelly, oral history, ASLA.

71. George Cunningham, Bette DeGraw, Keven Willey interviews.

72. Hirshman, *Sisters in Law,* 50; Irene Rasmussen oral history, ASLA.
73. Diane McCarthy, Art Hamilton interviews; Palmer, "Challenging Tradition," 74–76.
74. Scott O'Connor interview.
75. Simon OH.
76. "Limit on State Income Tax Under Consideration," *Phoenix Gazette,* August 28, 1973.
77. "Taxpayer's Sweetheart," *Phoenix Gazette,* September 4, 1973.
78. "Spending Limit Pressure Reported," *Arizona Republic,* April 16, 1974.
79. Diane McCarthy interview.
80. John Kolbe, "Sandbagging by 'Friends' Dazed Bill to Limit State Spending," *Phoenix Gazette,* April 29, 1974.
81. SOC to Barry Goldwater, March 25, 1974, ASLA.
82. Norian, 14.
83. "A Friend Recalls Legislative Past of a Woman Judge," *Arizona Republic,* July 8, 1981.
84. William Moyers oral history of SOC, SOCP, LOC; Simon OH.
85. "Re-election Ruled Out by Senator," *Arizona Republic,* April 24, 1974; Ron Carmichael, Chris Herstam, Alfredo Gutierrez interviews.
86. Cory Franklin, "The Other Man in Nancy Reagan's Life," *Chicago Tribune,* March 8, 2016.
87. Biskupic, *Sandra Day O'Connor,* 53–54.

CHAPTER FIVE: ARIZONA JUDGE

1. Wilson OH.
2. Bill Jones interview.
3. Scott Bales interview; "Merit Selection Offers Chance to Lift Judges Out of Politics," *Arizona Republic,* November 1, 1974.
4. Simon OH.
5. Rick DeGraw interview; Joyce OH; Norian, 18–19; Scott O'Connor interview.
6. Susan Taylor interview.
7. Simon OH.
8. John Crewdson, "Nominee for High Court: A Record Defying Labels," *New York Times,* July 12, 1981.
9. Steven Brill, "The High Court's New Justice Is Actually One Tough Cookie," *Washington Post,* November 1, 1981.
10. Andy Hurwitz, Bill Jones interviews.
11. Brill, "High Court's New Justice"; Jack Lasota, Hattie Babbitt interviews.
12. Bill Jones interview; Linda Kauss, "A Day in the Court with Judge Sandra Day O'Connor," *Phoenix Gazette,* September 18, 1975.
13. Simon OH.
14. Huber, *Sandra Day O'Connor,* 48.
15. Simon OH; Huber, *Sandra Day O'Connor,* 49; Barbara Woodhouse interview.
16. Simon OH.
17. "Sobbing Mom Is Ordered to Prison for Bad Checks," *Arizona Republic,* August 2, 1978; Huber, *Sandra Day O'Connor,* 46.
18. Dick Houseworth interview.
19. Robert McConnell, Leo Corbet interviews.

20. Chris Herstam, Peter Kay, Barbara Bentley interviews.

21. Scott O'Connor interview.

22. Gary Driggs interview; "Sandra O'Connor to Run for Governor—with 3 Ifs," *Arizona Republic,* March 31, 1978.

23. Robert McConnell interview.

24. SOC to John Rhodes, April 7, 1978; SOC to Sam Steiger, April 13, 1978, SOCP, LOC.

25. Scott O'Connor interview; "Evan Mecham, 83, Was Removed as Arizona Governor," *Washington Post,* February 23, 2008.

26. "Judge Says No to Race for Governor," *Arizona Republic,* October 18, 1977.

27. SOC to Barry Goldwater, April 6, 1978; SOC to Rob Schmults, March 1, 1987, SOCP, LOC; Walter Dellinger interview.

28. SOC to Hattie Babbitt, September 11, 1975, SOCP, LOC.

29. Hattie Babbitt, Bruce Babbitt, Jack LaSota interviews.

30. Simon OH.

31. Ruth McGregor, Judy Hope interviews.

32. Hattie Babbitt, Andy Hurwitz, Fred DuVal, Mary Schroeder interviews.

33. SOC to Hattie Babbitt, July 21, 1981, courtesy Hattie Babbitt.

34. Sharon Percy Rockefeller interview.

35. Mark Cannon, Lois Aldrich, Gail Driggs, Gary Driggs interviews.

36. Gwyneth Kelly, "Jimmy Carter's Most Important Legacy: Female Judges," *New Republic,* August 13, 2015.

37. Mark Cannon interview; SOC speech to Rotary Club of Phoenix, April 3, 1981; SOC, Diary of Anglo-American Exchange, July 6–7, 1980, SOCP, LOC.

38. John O'Connor Memoir, 164, SOCP, Family Archive.

39. "999 Tips," undated, speech file, SOCP, LOC; Betsy and Susan Taylor, Dick Houseworth interviews.

40. Rotary WANTED poster, ca. 1977, SOCP, AHS; Alan Day interview.

41. Jim Kolbe interview.

42. Alan Day, Nina van Rensselaer interviews.

43. Lawford OH.

44. Undated memo [ca. 1978], SOCP, LOC.

45. Kenneth Cribb interview; "Reagan Pledges He Would Name a Woman to the Supreme Court," *Washington Post,* October 15, 1980.

CHAPTER SIX: THE PRESIDENT CALLS

1. Kenneth Starr, Jonathan Rose, Hank Habicht, Kenneth Cribb interviews.

2. Hank Habicht, Kenneth Starr interviews.

3. Smith, *Law and Justice in the Reagan Administration,* 64; "History of the Nomination of Sandra Day O'Connor," William French Smith to SOC, April 4, 1984, SOCP, SC; "A Conversation with Ken Starr," JOCD, February 24, 1982, SOCP, LOC. Asked about the appointment process by John O'Connor in February 1982, Starr told John that Smith "does not believe that any real direction was given by the president as to any kind of person to be selected or whether it was to be a sitting judge, a female etc." At the time, Starr may not have wanted to talk frankly to the candidate's husband about inside-the-administration deliberations.

4. "FFF" [White House legal counsel Fred F. Fielding], June 18, 1981, Margaret Tutweiler files, RL.

5. Hank Habicht, Kenneth Starr interviews; "Conversation with Ken Starr," JOCD, February 24, 1982, SOCP, LOC. According to Justice Department aide Robert McConnell, Smith told him that Reagan himself put O'Connor on the list. Robert McConnell interview.

6. "Sandra O'Connor: A Life in the Law," *Wake Forest Jurist,* winter 2007.

7. Hank Habicht, Robert McConnell interviews.

8. Carolyn Kuhl interview.

9. Smith, *Law and Justice,* 66; "History of the Nomination," SOCP, SC; Simon OH.

10. Charles Munger interview.

11. Dennis DeConcini interview. It was long and incorrectly rumored in Phoenix legal circles that Goldwater single-handedly secured O'Connor's nomination. RonNell Andersen Jones interview.

12. Mark Cannon, Fred Fielding interviews.

13. Bill Franke interview.

14. James Baker interview; "A Conversation with Ken Starr," JOCD, February 24, 1982, SOCP, LOC.

15. Kenneth Starr, Jonathan Rose interviews; JOC, "Contacts leading up to appointment," undated, probably July 1981, JOCD, SOCP, LOC.

16. Charles Renfrew interview.

17. JOC, "Contacts," JOCD, SOCP, LOC.

18. Simon OH.

19. See, for instance, "Conversation with Sandra Day O'Connor," *Bulletin of American College of Trial Lawyers,* summer 2012.

20. Brett Dunkelman interview.

21. SOC Journal, June 29, 1981, SOCP, SC.

22. Kenneth Cribb interview.

23. JOC, "Contacts," JOCD; SOC Journal, June 30, 1981, SOCP, SC; Simon OH.

24. Simon OH.

25. Ruth McGregor interview.

26. JOC, "Contacts," JOCD, SOCP, SC; Jim and Diana Holman interview.

27. "O'Connor Adds a Light Touch to Economic Event," *Arizona Republic,* January 16, 2008; SOC interviewed by Rebecca Blumenstein, *Wall Street Journal,* April 11, 2011.

28. Jay O'Connor interview.

29. Peter Roussel interview; "Honored by Post, Nominee Declares," *New York Times,* July 8, 1981; "A Friend Recalls Legislative Past of a Woman Judge," *Arizona Republic,* July 8, 1981.

30. Ruth McGregor, Molly Powell Sumner, Eric Motley, Michelle Friedland interviews.

31. "Rancher Reflects on Early Years of Girl Who Became a Judge," *Arizona Republic,* July, 16, 1981.

32. JOC, "Contacts," JOCD, SOCP, SC.

33. Max Friedersdorf to Jim Baker, Ed Meese, Mike Deaver, Fred Fielding, Pen James, July 6, 1981, Fred Fielding Files, RL; Fred Fielding interview.

34. Peter Ross Range, "Thunder from the Right," *New York Times Magazine,* February 8, 1981.

35. Fred Fielding to Jim Baker, "Supreme Court Nominee: Game Plan," July 6, 1981, Fred Fielding files, RL.

36. See John Wilke to President Reagan, July 3, 1981, Margaret Tutweiler files, RL.

37. Hank Habicht, Leo Corbet interviews.

38. Kenneth Starr interview; Ken Starr to William French Smith, July 6, 1981, Margaret Tutweiler file, RL.

39. "The Judge Gets Rave Reviews on the Hill," *Washington Post*, July 15, 1981.

40. Robert McConnell interview.

41. Max Friedersdorf to Jim Baker, Ed Meese, Mike Deaver, Fred Fielding, July 14, 1981, Fred Fielding files, RL.

42. Powell Moore interview.

43. Max Friedersdorf to President Reagan, July 18, 1981, Fred Fielding files, RL. Reagan sent her nomination to the Senate August 19, 1981. archives.gov.

44. Carolyn Kuhl, Ruth McGregor interviews.

45. Chief Justice John Roberts interview.

46. Mary Schroeder interview.

47. Greenburg, *Supreme Conflict*, 14.

48. Richard Hauser interview.

49. Bill Kenyon, David Hume Kennerly interview.

50. Patrick Leahy interview.

51. *Hearing Record*, 86–89, SOCP, LOC.

52. Mary McGrory, "Cautious," *Washington Post*, September 10, 1981.

53. Carolyn Kuhl, Robert McConnell interviews.

54. "Here Comes La Judge," *Time*, September 21, 1981; *Hearing Record*, 11–12, SOCP, LOC.

55. JOC, "Contacts," JOCD, SOCP, LOC.

56. "O'Connor's Senate Trial," *Newsweek*, September 21, 1981.

57. JOC, "Contacts," JOCD, SOCP, LOC; she never played the course. Scott O'Connor interview.

58. "Recommended phone call to Sen. Jeremiah Denton," September 16, 1981, Edwin Meese Papers, RL.

59. "O'Connor Confirmed for High Court Seat," *Washington Post*, September 22, 1981; *Hearing Record*, 112.

60. Alan Simpson interview.

61. Ronald Reagan to Harold Brown, August 3, 1981, Reagan, *A Life in Letters*; Rich Williamson to James Baker, July 31, 1981, office/desk files, Baker Papers, PUL; Scott O'Connor interview. Nancy Reagan's parents lived near the Biltmore Hotel in Phoenix. SOC to Nancy Reagan, November 12, 1987, SOCP, LOC.

62. James Baker notes, office/desk files, undated [probably 1984], Baker Papers, PUL.

63. "Justice Sandra Day O'Connor," *People*, October 12, 1981; see Edmund Morris, *Dutch*, 450–51.

64. Scott O'Connor interview.

CHAPTER SEVEN: INSIDE THE MARBLE PALACE

1. Harry Blackmun to Warren Burger, November 17, 1980, BP, LOC. Lewis Powell to Warren Burger, November 17, 1980; Warren Burger, "Memo to the Conference," November 20, 1980, PP, WLU.

2. Justice John Paul Stevens interview.

3. Linda Blandford to Harry Blackmun, November 2, 1981, BP, LOC.

4. Rosen, *Supreme Court,* 14.

5. Woodward and Armstrong, *The Brethren,* 315; Lewis Powell to William Rehnquist, January 18, 1985, PP, WLU.

6. Warren Burger, "Memorandum to the Conference," September 22, 1981; Harry Blackmun to Marshal Wong, September 10, 11, 1981, BP, LOC.

7. Steve Wermiel, "The Burger Years," *Wall Street Journal,* June 14, 1984.

8. DeNeen Brown, "Thurgood Marshall Asked Ex-Klan Member to Help Him Make Supreme Court History," *Washington Post,* November 1, 2017.

9. Supreme Court Information Sheet, Office of the Curator, U.S. Supreme Court.

10. Dan Bussel interview.

11. "O'Connor Takes Oath as Justice," *Washington Post,* September 26, 1981.

12. Scott O'Connor interview.

13. Newton, *Justice for All,* 344.

14. JOCD, September 25, 1981; SOC Journal, September 25, 1981, SOCP, SC; Alan Day interview.

15. *LB,* 299; Alan Day interview.

16. Debra Merritt interview; Stern and Wermiel, *Justice Brennan,* 274; *Jacobellis v. Ohio,* 378 U.S. 184 (1964).

17. Nina Totenberg, "The Supreme Court: The Last Plantation," *New York Times,* July 26, 1974; Robert Fabrikant, "From Warren to Burger: Race Relations Inside the Court," *Mitchell Hamline Law Review* 43:6, 2017.

18. JOCD, September 24–25, 1981, SOCP, LOC.

19. Deborah Merritt, Ruth McGregor interviews; JOCD, September 24, 1981.

20. Stern and Wermiel, *Justice Brennan,* 410.

21. Justice John Paul Stevens interview.

22. Deborah Merritt interview; SOC interviewed by Terry Gross, *Fresh Air,* NPR, March 5, 2013.

23. Hutchinson, *The Man Who Was Once Whizzer White,* 157–62.

24. "A Life in the Law: Sandra Day O'Connor," *Wake Forest Jurist,* winter 2007.

25. SOC Journal, "Fall 1981 Random Notes," SOCP, SC.

26. Scott O'Connor interview.

27. Ruth McGregor interview.

28. Simon OH; Greenburg, *Supreme Conflict,* 67.

29. Bradford Berenson interview.

30. Stern and Wermiel, *Justice Brennan,* 267.

31. Rosen, *Supreme Court,* 6, 9.

32. Ibid., 145; for a history of the period, see Simon, *The Antagonists.*

33. Stern and Wermiel, *Justice Brennan,* 463. Justice Clarence Thomas told the author that when he arrived at the Court in 1981, a decade later, the justices were still recovering from *The Brethren.*

34. Stephen McAllister, "Justice Byron White and *The Brethren,*" *Green Bag,* winter 2012.

35. JOC to William Rehnquist, January 3, 1980, Rehnquist Papers, Hoover Institution.

36. Warren Burger to SOC, November 25, 1981, SOCP, LOC; Carol Wolman and Hal Frank, "The Solo Woman in a Professional Peer Group," Working Paper No. 13 (1972), Wharton School of Management, University of Pennsylvania. Burger received the paper from Dr. Walter Menninger of the Menninger Foundation

during O'Connor's nomination hearings. The paper, which was published with a revised abstract by the *American Journal of Orthopsychiatry* in January 1975, focused on helping a woman avoid depression while working in an entirely male workplace.

37. Greenburg, *Supreme Conflict,* 67.

38. SOC Journal, "Fall 1981 Random Notes," SOCP, SC.

39. Betsy Taylor, Cynthia Helms interviews.

40. SOC was aware that Rehnquist was suffering from side effects of medication. Beatsie Laws to SOC, January 28, 1982, SOCP, SC.

41. Brett Dunkelman interview.

42. Vera Glaser, "She's a Lady—and She's Tough, Smart, Funny and the First Woman on the Supreme Court," *Washingtonian,* May 1984.

43. Gail Galloway to SOC, December 11, 1981, SOCP, SC.

44. Deborah Merritt, Ruth McGregor interviews; "30 Years Ago: the Nomination of Sandra Day O'Connor to the Supreme Court," *Huffington Post,* July 6, 2001.

45. Molly Powell Sumner interview; Simon OH; SOC, "A Tribute to Justice Lewis F. Powell, Jr.," *Harvard Law Review,* 101:2, December 1987, 395; in later years, SOC tried to help new justices as Powell had helped her. See SOC to Tony Kennedy, January 28, 1988, SOCP, SC ("There is no 'how to do it' manual for the new Justices").

46. John Jeffries interview; SOC to Betty Friedan, November 5, 1981, SOCP, LOC.

47. Evan Thomas and Stuart Taylor, "The Swing Vote," *Newsweek,* July 4, 2005.

48. John Wiley interview.

49. Jeffries, *Justice Lewis F. Powell, Jr.,* 131–82.

50. Judge J. Harvie Wilkinson interview.

51. Lewis Powell to family, October 24, December 6, 1981, PP, WLU.

52. Fred Barbash, "O'Connor Proves Justices Can Be Popular," *Washington Post,* November 30, 1981, in files of BP, LOC.

53. Lazarus, *Closed Chambers,* 272.

54. Brian Cartwright interview.

55. Thurgood Marshall, Jr., interview.

56. Deborah Merritt interview.

57. Mary Mikva interview.

58. Diane DiMarco interview; Toobin, *The Nine,* 46.

59. Peppers and Ward, *In Chambers,* 180, 192; Stern and Wermiel, *Justice Brennan,* 84.

60. SOC interview.

61. Brian Cartwright, Deborah Merritt interviews.

62. SOC interviewed by Kevin Cool, *Stanford Magazine,* January/February 2006.

63. See *Dickerson v. U.S.,* 530 U.S. 428 (2000), and *Patterson v. McLean Credit Union,* 491 U.S. 164 (1989) at 172–75, declining to overrule *Runyon v. McRary.*

64. White, *Justice Oliver Wendell Holmes: Law and the Inner Self,* 487.

65. *Marbury v. Madison,* 5 U.S. 137 (1803).

66. See White, *Justice Oliver Wendell Holmes,* 148–224; Holmes, *The Common Law.*

67. Rosen, *Supreme Court,* 190–91; Jack Balkin, "*Bush v. Gore* and the Boundary Between Law and Politics," *Yale Law Journal* 110: 1447 (2001).

68. See *Lochner v. New York,* 198 U.S. 45 (1905). The reach of the Fourteenth Amendment was sharply limited by the famous Slaughterhouse cases, 83 U.S. 36 (1873), which held that the amendment only protected the rights of federal citizenship—at the time, very few—not the rights of state citizenship.

69. *West Coast Hotel Co. v. Parrish,* 300 U.S. 379 (1937). Historians now dispute the causal link. John Jeffries interview.

70. See, most notably, *New York Times v. Sullivan,* 376 U.S. 254 (1964) (free press); *Engel v. Vitale,* 370 U.S. 421 (1962) (school prayer); *Mapp v. Ohio,* 367 U.S. 643 (1961) (unlawful search); *Gideon v. Wainwright,* 372 U.S. 335 (1963) (right to counsel); *Griswold v. Connecticut,* 381 U.S. 479 (1965) (sexual privacy); *Brown v. Board of Education,* 347 U.S. 483 (1954) (school segregation); *Baker v. Carr,* 369 U.S. 186 (1962) (voter redistricting).

71. Evan Thomas, "Have the Judges Done Too Much?" *Time,* January 22, 1979.

72. Adam Liptak, "New Look at an Old Memo Casts More Doubt on Rehnquist," *New York Times,* March 19, 2012.

73. *Furman v. Georgia,* 408 U.S. 238 (1972); *Gregg v Georgia,* 428 U.S. 153 (1976).

74. Fred Barbash, "Court's Rulings Hinged on the Middle Faction," *Washington Post,* July 4, 1982.

75. 457 U.S. 202 (1982).

76. Justice Brennan kept private histories of each Court term, which were made available to the author through an anonymous source. OT 1981, x–xi.

77. Stern and Wermiel, *Justice Brennan,* 183; Tushnet, *A Court Divided,* 35.

78. Mary Mikva interview; Peppers and Ward, *In Chambers,* 406.

79. Mary Mikva, Clifton Elgarten interviews.

80. "Washington Briefing," *New York Times,* May 18, 1982; "Where the Justices Adjourn for Lunch," *New York Times,* July 15, 1979.

81. 457 U.S. 957 (1982).

82. SOC to William Brennan, May 4, 1982, SOCP, LOC; Clifton Elgarten, Howard Gutman, Ruth McGregor, Deborah Merritt interviews.

83. Brennan history, OT 1981, vi.

84. *Engle v. Isaac,* 456 U.S. 107 (1982); *Fay v. Noia,* 372 U.S. 391 (1963).

85. Stern and Wermiel, *Justice Brennan,* 479.

86. SOC Journal, March 26, 1982, SOCP, SC.

87. *Engle v. Isaac* file, PP, WLU and BP, LOC.

88. SOC Journal, January 27, 1982.

89. SOC, "Trends in the Relationship Between the Federal and State Courts from the Perspective of a State Court Judge," *William & Mary Law Review* 22:801 (1981); David O'Brien, Mark Cannon interviews.

90. *National League of Cities v. Usery,* 426 U.S. 833 (1976); *FERC v. Mississippi,* 456 U.S. 742 (1982); Blackmun, "Chronology of Significant Events," April 16, 1982, BP, LOC.

91. *Ford Motor Co. v. EEOC,* 458 U.S. 219 (1982), Blackmun draft opinion in *Ford v. EEOC* case file in SOCP, LOC.

92. Deborah Merritt interview. When Blackmun switched his vote to upend her majority opinion in a death penalty case the same month, O'Connor wrote her friend Lewis Powell, "In this business one must learn to grin and bear it." SOC to Lewis Powell, June 23, 1982, SOCP, LOC; *Enmund v. Florida,* 458 U.S. 782 (1982).

93. SOC Journal, June 21, 1982, SOCP, SC.

94. SOC to Harry Blackmun, July 1, 1982, SOCP, LOC.

95. SOC to William Brennan, June 28, 1982, SOCP, LOC.

96. William Brennan to SOC, undated, probably June 1982, SOCP, SC.

97. SOC Journal, June 25, 1982, SOCP, SC.

CHAPTER EIGHT: SCRUTINY

1. Barbara Babcock interview.
2. Perry OH.
3. Hirshman, 45–125.
4. *Craig v. Boren,* 429 U.S. 190 (1976).
5. *Mississippi University for Women v. Hogan,* 458 U.S. 718 (1982).
6. *MUW v. Hogan* oral argument, March 22, 1982, at oyez.org.
7. The famous Footnote Four in *United States v. Carolene Products Co.,* 304 U.S. 144 (1938), introduced the idea of heightened scrutiny; *Brown v. Board of Education,* 347 U.S. 483 (1954) outlawed school segregation (though the Court did not use the term "strict scrutiny"). See Adam Winkler, "Fatal in Theory and Strict in Fact: An Empirical Analysis of Strict Scrutiny in the Federal Courts," *Vanderbilt Law Review* 59:793 (2006).
8. Biskupic, *Sandra Day O'Connor,* 135.
9. SOC Conference notes in *MUW v. Hogan* file (OT 1981), SOCP, LOC.
10. See footnote 9, page 724, *Mississippi University for Women v. Hogan,* 458 U.S. 718 (1982); Deborah Merritt interview.
11. John Wiley interview; Wiley to Lewis Powell, March 21, 1982; LP memo to file, June 7, 1982 ("The court, in this case, may have departed farther from the intent and purpose of the equal protection clause than in any other case"), PP, WLU.
12. SOC Journal, June 21, 1982, SOCP, SC.
13. Deborah Merritt, Ruth McGregor interviews.
14. Justice Ruth Bader Ginsburg interview.
15. Brian O'Connor interview.
16. Jay O'Connor interview; John O'Connor Memoir, 180–82, SOCP, Family Archives.
17. Frank Saul interview.
18. Betsy Taylor, Charles Renfrew interviews; Joan Myers to Harry Day, July 10, 1981, Harry Day papers, AHS.
19. Ginny Chew interview.
20. Homer Moyer interview.
21. Nancy Kauffman, Ann Hoopes interviews.
22. JOCD, April 19, 1983, SOCP, LOC.
23. Ibid., May 6, 1982, February 26, 1983, SOCP, LOC.
24. Brian Cartwright interview; JOCD, "Conversation with Lewis Powell," February 6, 1982, SOCP, LOC.
25. William Draper, SOC interviews.
26. JOCD, April 15, October 18, 1982; May 1, 1983; November 10, 1982, SOCP, LOC.
27. JOCD, January 26–30, 1982, SOCP, LOC.
28. *Arizona Republic,* November 11, 1982.
29. Ibid., April 22, May 4, 1983, SOCP, LOC; Lois Romano, "Justice on the Party Circuit," *Washington Post,* May 4, 1983.
30. JOCD, December 11, 13, 1982, SOCP, LOC.
31. "Vignette," December 1982, JOCD, SOCP, LOC.
32. Gary Francione interview.
33. Stewart Schwab interview; *Hishon v. King & Spalding,* 467 U.S. 69 (1984); Hirshman, 157.
34. *City of Akron v. Akron Center for Reproductive Health, Inc.,* 462 U.S. 416 (1983). Oral argument November 30, 1982, at oyez.org.

35. Greenhouse, *Becoming Justice Blackmun*, 91–92; *Roe v. Wade*, 410 U.S. 113 (1973).

36. SOC, Gary Francione, Jane Fahey interviews; John Hart Ely, "The Wages of Crying Wolf: A Comment on *Roe v. Wade*," *Yale Law Journal* 82:935 (1973).

37. SOC Conference notes, *Roe v. Wade* file (OT 1982), SOCP, LOC.

38. Greenhouse, *Becoming Justice Blackmun*, 145.

39. SOC first draft of dissent on May 5, 1983, *Akron v. Akron Center for Reproductive Health* file, SOCP, LOC; law clerk to Harry Blackmun, May 12, 1983, BP, LOC; Gary Francione interview.

40. Stewart Schwab, Gary Francione interviews.

41. JOCD, July 1, June 9, 1983, SOCP, LOC.

42. Peggy Lord interview.

CHAPTER NINE: FWOTSC

1. JOCD, January 18, 1983, SOCP, LOC.

2. See, for example, SOC to William Rehnquist, Lewis Powell, John Stevens, undated, probably November 1986 (betting pool), PP, WLU.

3. William Draper, Ruth McGregor, Cynthia Helms, Frank Saul interviews.

4. JOCD, April 26, May 12, 1983, SOCP, LOC.

5. Clark, *Washingtonian*, May 1984; Diane DiMarco interview.

6. Jim Lehrer, Jim and Diana Holman, Ann Hoopes, James Symington, Leonard Bickwit interviews.

7. JOCD, November 26, 1985, November 19, 1986, SOCP, LOC.

8. Peggy Lord interview.

9. Carl Kunasek interview.

10. JOCD, October 31, 1984, SOCP, LOC; "High Court's 'Nine Men' Were a Surprise to One," *New York Times*, October 12, 1983.

11. JOCD, April 10–12, 1984, SOCP, LOC.

12. SOC to Jay O'Connor, April 16, 1984, SOCP, SC.

13. Iman Anabtawi, Viet Dinh interviews. The clerk who was disabled was Leslie Hakala; the clerk who was blind was Isaac Lidsky.

14. Shirley Woodward, Judge J. Harvie Wilkinson III, Judge Sri Srinivasan interviews.

15. Kent Syverud interview; Syverud, "Lessons from Working for Sandra Day O'Connor," *Stanford Law Review* 58:6, April 2010.

16. Maggie Dupree, Julie O'Sullivan interviews; SOC Journal, March 12, 1985, SOCP, Family Archives.

17. Scott Bales interview; JOCD, January 30, 1985, SOCP, LOC; Elizabeth Kastor, "John Riggins' Big Sleep: He Came, He Jawed, He Conked Out," *Washington Post*, February 1, 1985; Scott O'Connor interview.

18. Chris Cerf, John Setear, Julie O'Sullivan, Stephen Gilles interviews.

19. Stewart and Norma Schwab interview.

20. Kathy Smalley, Barbara Woodhouse interviews.

21. Don Verrilli interview.

22. Stern and Wermiel, 486–89.

23. Gail Agrawal interview.

24. *Garcia v. San Antonio Metropolitan Transit Authority*, 469 U.S. 528 (1985).

25. Blackmun to all Justices, June 11, 1984, PP, WLU; Brennan history, OT '83, 38; SOC Journal, July, 1984, SOCP, Family Archives.

26. *National League of Cities v. Usery,* 426 U.S. 833 (1976); JOCD, February 28, 1985, SOCP, LOC.
27. Gail Agrawal interview.
28. JOC to William Brennan and Lewis Powell, March 26, 1984; JOC to William Brennan, May 7, 1985, William Brennan to JOC, May 9, 1985, JOC to William Brennan, May 14, 1985, SOCP, LOC; JOCD, March 8, 1987, SOCP, LOC.
29. *United States v. Carolene Products Co.,* 304 U.S. 144 (1938).
30. Gary Francione interview.
31. Julie O'Sullivan interview. For an example of Brennan wooing a wary O'Connor, see William Brennan to SOC, March 16, 1982, SOC to WB, March 18, 1982, WB to SOC, March 19, 1982, SOC to WB, April 12, 1982 in *Karcher v. Daggett* case file, OT 1982, SOCP, LOC.
32. Rosen, *Supreme Court,* 164; Tushnet, 182; *Engel v. Vitale,* 370 U.S. 430 (1962).
33. *Wallace v. Jaffree,* 472 U.S. 38 (1985).
34. SOC Journal, April 12, 1985, SOCP, SC; Kent Syverud, Barbara Woodhouse interviews.
35. Jim Todd, Scott Bales interviews.
36. Theane Evangelis interview.
37. *Lynch v. Donnelly,* 465 U.S. 668 (1984).
38. RonNell Andersen Jones interview.
39. Warren Burger to SOC, November 29, 1983, SOC to WB, November 28, 1983, *Lynch v. Donnelly* file, OT 1983, SOCP, LOC.
40. Barbara Woodhouse, Steve Gilles interviews.
41. JOCD, June 18, 1985, SOCP, LOC.
42. JOCD, February 19, 1985, June 17, 1985, May 28, 1986, June 12, 1986, SOCP, LOC.
43. JOCD, April 30, June 11, June 17, 1986; October 19, 1987, SOCP, LOC; Ken Cribb [Meese aide] interview.
44. Robert Huffman interview.
45. Glenn Nager interview.
46. Brian Hoffstadt, Daniel Bussel interview; Thurgood Marshall to William Rehnquist, December 14, 1988; petition to the chief justice signed by sixteen clerks, November 21, 1988, LOC.
47. Susan Creighton interview.
48. JOCD, September 29, 1986, SOCP, LOC.
49. Steve Gilles interview.
50. Bill Nardini interview.
51. SOC to William Rehnquist, June 1993, William Rehnquist papers, Hoover Institute.
52. SOC Journal, January 2, 1987, SOCP, Family Archives.
53. Simon Hoggart, "First Lady of the Law," *Times* (London), June 25, 1983.
54. Scott Bales interview.
55. Dan Bussel interview.
56. Viet Dinh interview.
57. Susan Creighton interview.
58. JOCD, December 17, 1984, SOCP, LOC; Buzz Lewis interview.
59. Voting statistics courtesy Lee Epstein, Washington University Law School.
60. Andrew McBride interview.

61. 476 U.S. 747 (1986).

62. SOC to Harry Blackmun, March 14, 1985, Thornburgh opinion draft file, OT 1985, BP, LOC.

63. Greenhouse, *Becoming Justice Blackmun,* 182; JOCD, May 7, 1986, SOCP, LOC.

64. Steve Gilles interview; *City of Akron v. Akron Center for Reproductive Health, Inc.,* 462 U.S. 416 (1983).

65. Thomas Grey, "Holmes and Legal Pragmatism," *Stanford Law Review* 41:4, April 1989.

66. William Webster interview.

67. Robert Huffman interview. The abortion rate dropped by half between 1981 and 2018. Belluck, Pam, and Jan Hoffman, "Medical Gains Are Reshaping Abortion Fight," *New York Times,* July 2, 2018.

68. Williams, *Thurgood Marshall,* 387.

69. SOC notes on Conference, *McCleskey v. Kemp,* 481 U.S. 279 (1987), SOCP, LOC.

70. SOC, "Thurgood Marshall: The Influence of a Raconteur," *Stanford Law Review* 44:1217, summer 1992; Williams, 375.

71. Peppers and Ward, *In Chambers,* 315.

72. Justice Stephen Breyer interview.

73. Handwritten note on "A Funeral Service for the Honorable Thurgood Marshall, 1908–93," SOCP, SC.

CHAPTER TEN: CANCER

1. See Susan Behuniak Long, "Justice Sandra Day O'Connor and the Power of Maternal Legal Thinking," *Review of Politics* 54:3, 429, summer 1992; Judge J. Harvie Wilkinson III interview.

2. *Plessy v. Ferguson,* 163 U.S. 537 (1896).

3. *Regents of the University of California v. Bakke,* 438 U.S. 265 (1978); Jeffries, *Justice Lewis F. Powell,* 455–501.

4. *Wygant v. Jackson Board of Education,* 476 U.S. 267 (1986).

5. Harry Blackmun Conference notes, November 5, 1985, BP, LOC; Stuart Taylor, "Swing Vote on the Constitution," *American Lawyer,* June 1989.

6. Julie O'Sullivan interview.

7. Judge Learned Hand gave his famous "Spirit of Liberty" speech at a patriotic rally in New York in 1944. The author is indebted to UCLA professor and O'Connor clerk Dan Bussel for this analysis of O'Connor's jurisprudence.

8. SOC to LP, December 19, 1985, SOCP, LOC: *Fullilove v. Klutznick,* 448 U.S. 448 (1980).

9. *Wygant v. Jackson Board of Education* file, OT 1985; Lewis Powell to SOC, November 19, 1985; SOC to LP, December 19, 1985; LP to SOC, March 19, 1986; SOC to LP, March 28, 1986; LP to SOC, April 8, 1986, SOCP, LOC.

10. Jeffries, 535–45.

11. JOCD, June 26, July 1, 1987, SOCP, LOC; Ken Cribbs interview.

12. SOC Journal, January 2, 1987, SOCP, Family Archives.

13. Nina Selin, Maureen Scalia interviews.

14. JOCD, October 8, 1986, SOCP, LOC.

15. Biskupic, *American Original,* 23; Jeffries, 534.

16. Dan Bussel interview.

17. Clerk for another justice who asked to remain anonymous.
18. Steven Catlett interview.
19. Maureen Scalia interview.
20. JOCD, December 24, 1986, SOCP, LOC.
21. Ibid., April 22, 1988.
22. Nelson Lund interview.
23. JOCD, December 29, 1987, SOCP, SOC.
24. Ibid., September 19, 1987.
25. Ibid., November 5, 1987.
26. Ibid., May 7, 1987.
27. Ibid., November 6, 1987.
28. Maureen Scalia interview.
29. Homer Moyer interview.
30. JOCD, June 3, 1988, March 11, 1983, March 9, 1986, SOCP, LOC.
31. Rawdon Dalrymple interview.
32. Charles and Barbara Renfrew interview.
33. JOCD, May 4, 1985, March 29, 1986, SOCP, LOC.
34. Nelson Lund, Diane DiMarco interviews.
35. JOCD, March 7, July 4, 1988, SOCP, LOC.
36. Ibid., month of October 1988; for the cancer narrative, SOCP, LOC.
37. Ibid., August 4, 1988.
38. Dr. Marc Lippman, Nancy Ignatius interviews.
39. Jay O'Connor interview.
40. JOCD, November 5, 6, 1988, SOCP, LOC.
41. See SOC Speech to National Coalition for Cancer Survivorship, November 3, 1994, SOCP, LOC.
42. John Kolbe interview.
43. Leonard Bickwit interview; Leonard Bodine, "Sandra Day O'Connor," *ABA Journal* 69:1394 (1983); Alan Day interview.
44. "Without my religious faith, my recovery would have taken a different turn," she wrote a friend. "It has been my daily source of strength." SOC to Mrs. John Eden, February 14, 1989, SOCP, LOC.
45. SOC to John Driggs, November 23, 1988, courtesy Gail Driggs.
46. JOCD, November 15, 25, 26, 1988, SOCP, LOC.
47. Eivand Bjerke interview.
48. JOCD, November 26, 1988, SOCP, LOC. According to George H. W. Bush's biographer, Jon Meacham, Bush mentioned SOC in his diary as a possible running mate.
49. SOC to justices, October 21, 1988, BP, LOC.
50. JOCD, October 28, 1988, SOCP, LOC.
51. Diana DiMarco interview; see SOC, "Surviving Cancer: A Private Person's Public Tale," *Washington Post,* November 8, 1994.
52. Brian O'Connor interview.
53. To view the video, search "Sandra O'Connor, National Coalition for Cancer Survivorship, November 3, 1994" or go to https://www.c-span.org/video/?61342-1/surviving-cancer/.

CHAPTER ELEVEN: A WOMAN'S ROLE

1. Judge Adalberto Jordan, Daniel Mandil, Jane Stromseth interviews.
2. Randy E. Barnett and Evan Bernick, "The Letter and the Spirit: A Unified Theory of Originalism," *Georgetown Law and Faculty Publications and Other Works*, 2018.
3. Andrew McBride, Judge Adalberto Jordan interviews; Lazarus, *Closed Chambers*, 261–66, 419.
4. *Texas v. Johnson*, 491 U.S. 397 (1989). SOC tentatively voted to strike down the statute at conference but later changed her vote to join Rehnquist and White to uphold the statute. SOC conference notes, *Texas v. Johnson* file, OT 1988, SOCP, LOC.
5. SOC to William Brennan, December 13, 1988; WB to SOC, January 6, 1988, BP, LOC; *Price Waterhouse v. Hopkins*, 490 U.S. 228 (1989). Ann Hopkins won her partnership and worked for the firm until she retired in 2002. Her daughter said, "You either loved her fiercely or you couldn't stand being in the same room with her." "Ann Hopkins, Who Struck an Early Blow to the Glass Ceiling, Dies at 74," *New York Times*, July 18, 2018.
6. *Wards Cove Packing Co. v. Antonio*, 490 U.S. 642 (1989); *Patterson v. McLean Credit Union*, 485 U.S. 617 (1989); Biskupic, *Sandra Day O'Connor*, 198.
7. Kent Syverud interview.
8. SOC to Barry Goldwater, November 1, 1988, Barry Goldwater papers, AHS.
9. Barry Goldwater to SOC, January 25, 1995; SOC to BG, undated; Goldwater papers, AHS.
10. JOCD, January 20, 1988, SOCP, LOC.
11. *Johnson v. Santa Clara Transportation Agency*, 480 U.S. 616 (1987); Linda Greenhouse, "Name Calling at the Supreme Court," *New York Times*, July 28, 1989.
12. Andrew McBride interview; see Richard Barnes, "A Woman of the West, but Not of the Tribes: Justice Sandra Day O'Connor and the State-Tribe Relationship," *Loyola Law Review* 58:1, 39 (2012).
13. *City of Richmond v. J. A. Croson Company*, 488 U.S. 469 (1989); *Croson* file, OT 1988, BP, LOC.
14. Judge Adalberto Jordan, Andrew McBride interviews; *Grutter v. Bollinger*, 539 U.S. 306 (2003).
15. "Bush Cites Abortion 'Tragedy,'" *Washington Post*, January 24, 1989.
16. 492 U.S. 490 (1989).
17. Harry Blackmun, "Chronology of Significant Events," 1989, BP, LOC. Blackmun was remarkably emotional about the case in conference. SOC handwritten notes capture his almost stream-of-consciousness resentment: "Overruling Roe directly—media out of control. W[ou]ld not do so. Is a personal attack on me. Roe was correct. I resent fact that media says is a Blackmun op[eration]. 16 years have passed. I don't understand CJ's pos[ition]. Stick with it." SOC conference notes, *Webster v. Reproductive Health Services*, OT 1988, SOCP, LOC.
18. *Newsweek*, May 1, 1989.
19. JOCD, April 20, 1989, SOCP, LOC.
20. See *Michael H. v. Gerald D.*, 491 U.S. 110 (1989).
21. SOC interview.
22. Andrew McBride interview.
23. Jane Stromseth interview.
24. JOCD, May 14, 1989, SOCP, LOC.

25. Ed Lazarus to Justice Blackmun, May 1, 1989, June 22, 1989, BP, LOC.
26. Daniel Mandil interview.
27. Lazarus, 419; Judge Adalberto Jordan interview.
28. JOCD, July 3, 1989, SOCP, LOC.
29. Lewis Powell to SOC, July 10, 1989, PP, WLU.
30. JOCD, September 5, 1989, SOCP, LOC.
31. SOC interview.
32. SOC to Katharine Graham, November 9, 1989, SOCP, LOC.
33. JOCD, December 8, 1989, SOCP, LOC.
34. JOCD, October 7, 13, 1989; SOC to Robert MacNally, December 14, 1989, SOCP, LOC.
35. *Hodgson v. Minnesota,* 497 U.S. 417 (1990).
36. Marci Hamilton interview. See Marci Hamilton to SOC, March 21, 1990, *Hodgson v. Minnesota* file, OT 1989, SOCP, LOC
37. *Maryland v. Craig,* 497 U.S. 836 (1990); Ivan Fong interview.
38. Suzanna Sherry, "Civic Virtue and the Feminine Voice in Constitutional Adjudication," *Virginia Law Review* 72:543 (1986); Ellen Goodman, "O'Connor Tries to Be the Supreme Court's 'Mom,'" *Boston Globe,* July 11, 1989.
39. SOC, "Portia's Progress," *N.Y.U. Law Review* 66: 1546 (1992); Nat Hentoff, "Justice O'Connor and the Myth of the 'True Woman,'" *Washington Post,* November 23, 1991; Linda Meyer interview.
40. See SOC, *Majesty of the Law,* 166–67, 192–93.
41. Tushnet, 124; *J.E.B. v. Alabama* ex rel. T.B., 511 U.S. 127 (1994).
42. SOC Journal, July 1984, SOCP, Family Archives.
43. "She's No Gentleman," *Legal Times,* November 25, 1991.
44. Ruth Bader Ginsburg, "A Tribute to Justice Sandra Day O'Connor," *Harvard Law Review* 119:1240 (2006).
45. JOCD, May 5, 1990, SOCP, LOC; *ABA Journal,* July 26, 2009; Ted Olson interview.
46. Magee Dupree interview.
47. Stuart Banner, "Speeding Up to Smell the Roses," *Stanford Law Review* 58:1713 (2006).
48. Mary Adams interview.
49. Ivan Fong interview.
50. Stern and Wermiel, 537.
51. Greenburg, 102–103.
52. Toobin, *The Nine,* 51–52; Lynda Webster interview.
53. Lynda and William Webster interview.
54. Molly Sumner interview.
55. JOCD, November 22, 1990, SOCP, LOC.
56. Ibid., April 23, June 2, 1992, SOCP, LOC.
57. Author was at the dinner. Linda Greenhouse, "Another Frantic Finish Looms for the Supreme Court," *New York Times,* May 15, 1991.
58. JOCD, October 9, 1991, SOCP, LOC.
59. Toobin, *The Nine,* 123–24.
60. Vaughn Dunnigan interview.
61. Toobin, *The Nine,* 117–20.
62. Justice Clarence Thomas interview; *Wright v. West,* 505 U.S. 277 (1992).

63. Kathy Smalley interview. SOC's favorite holiday was Thanksgiving. SOC, "The Blessedness of Thanksgiving," *Cathedral Age,* spring 1998, 12–13, courtesy Margaret Shannon.

64. JOCD, July 18, 1997, SOCP, LOC.

65. Ibid., June 23, 1994, SOCP, LOC.

66. Crystal Nix-Hines interview.

67. James Forman, Jr., interview.

68. *LB,* 307–11.

69. Alan Day interview.

70. "Sandra O'Connor," *Army Magazine,* April 1990.

71. 505 U.S. 833 (1992).

72. JOCD, April 21–22, 1992, SOCP, LOC.

73. *University of Pennsylvania Law Review* 138:119 (1989).

74. *Planned Parenthood v. Casey* oral argument, April 22, 1992, oyez.org.

75. Chief Justice Rehnquist's draft opinion in *Planned Parenthood v. Casey,* Anthony Kennedy to Harry Blackmun, May 29, 1992, BP, LOC.

76. Murphy, *Scalia,* 192.

77. Maureen Scalia interview.

78. Brad Berenson, Michael Dorf interviews.

79. For an argument that the "undue burden" standard was so squishy that it left the door open to further undermining a woman's constitutional right to an abortion, see Linda Hirshman, "Sandra Day O'Connor and the Fate of Abortion Rights," *Los Angeles Times,* February 28, 2016, and Meaghan Winter, "Roe v. Wade Was Lost in 1992," *Slate,* March 27, 2016.

CHAPTER TWELVE: CIVIC RELIGION

1. Charles and Barbara Renfrew, Justice Ruth Bader Ginsburg interviews.

2. Greenburg, 220.

3. Patricia White, Romeo Cruz, Justice Ruth Bader Ginsburg interviews. See "Sandra Day O'Connor," Ruth Bader Ginsburg, *My Own Words,* 89–93. For Ginsburg's cautious jurisprudence, see Jill Lepore, "Ruth Bader Ginsburg's Unlikely Path to the Supreme Court," *New Yorker,* October 8, 2018, reviewing a new biography of Ginsburg by Jane Sherron De Hart.

4. SOC to Ruth Ginsburg, September 20, 1999, SOCP, SC.

5. Hirshman, xxiii.

6. JOCD, November 6, 1990, April 4, 1994, SOCP, LOC.

7. Justice Ruth Bader Ginsburg interview.

8. JOCD, November 8, 1993, SOCP, LOC.

9. Biskupic, *Sandra Day O'Connor,* 261.

10. Hirshman, 215–19; *Harris v. Forklift Systems,* 510 U.S. 17 (1993).

11. Justice Ruth Bader Ginsburg interview; *United States v. Virginia,* 518 U.S. 515 (1996).

12. SOC Journal, July 1984, SOCP, Family Archives.

13. Jim Todd, Scott O'Connor interviews.

14. Homer Moyer, Mary Noel Pepys, Mark Ellis interviews.

15. JOCD, November 1, 1993, SOCP, LOC.

16. SOC to A. E. Dick Howard, October, 17, 2002, SOCP, LOC.

17. Mary Noel Pepys, Mark Ellis interviews.
18. SOC, *Majesty of the Law,* 269.
19. Carol Biagiotti interview.
20. Romeo Cruz interview.
21. Ann Hoopes interview.
22. John Macomber interview.
23. Judy Hope interview.
24. JOCD, February 26, 1994, SOCP, LOC.
25. Adrienne Arsht, Raquel Matas interviews.
26. Adrienne Arsht, Carol Biagiotti interviews.
27. JOCD, October 22, 1997, SOCP, LOC.
28. Charles and Barbara Renfrew interview.
29. Silvija Strikis interview.
30. Lynda Webster, Sarah Suggs interviews.
31. Kevin Kelly interview.
32. Silvija Strikis, Viet Dinh, Jane Fahey, Brian Hoffstadt, Matt Stowe interviews.
33. Lisa Kern Griffin interview.
34. Julie O'Sullivan interview.
35. SOC interview.
36. Kate Adams, Lisa Kern Griffin, Viet Dinh, Kathy Smalley, Mark Perry interviews.
37. Elizabeth Earle Beske interview; *Florida Bar v. Went for It Inc.,* 515 U.S. 618 (1995), oral argument, January 11, 1995, oyez.org.
38. JOCD, May 13, 1994, SOCP, LOC.
39. Tushnet, 197.
40. JOCD, January 24, 1995, SOCP, LOC.
41. Cynthia Helms interview.
42. Toobin, *The Nine,* 94.
43. Kate Adams interview.
44. Justice Stephen Breyer interview.
45. See her concurring opinion in a complex tax case, *Commissioner v. Tufts,* 461 U.S. 300 (1983).
46. *Babbitt v. Sweet Home Chapter, Communities for a Great Oregon,* 515 U.S. 687 (1995).
47. Elizabeth Earle Beske interview.
48. Justice Ruth Bader Ginsburg interview.
49. Dr. William Leahy, Maureen Scalia interviews.
50. Justice Clarence Thomas interview.
51. *Green v. County School Board of New Kent County,* 391 U.S. 430 (1968), *Swann v. Charlotte-Mecklenburg Board of Education,* 402 U.S. 1 (1971). For an excellent analysis, see Jeffries, 282–332.
52. *Metro Broadcasting v. FCC,* 497 U.S. 547 (1990); *Adarand Constructors, Inc. v. Peña,* 515 U.S. 200 (1995); Walter Dellinger interview.
53. Stuart Delery, David Ellen, David Kravitz, Walter Dellinger interviews.
54. *Shaw v. Reno,* 509 U.S. 630 (1993); Simon Steel, Sean Gallagher interviews. See *Miller v. Johnson,* 515 U.S. 900 (1995).
55. Sylvia Blake interview; SOC to William Rehnquist, October 16, 1995, William Rehnquist papers, Hoover Institute.
56. JOC binders, SOCP, SC.
57. Alan Kirk interview.
58. Cynthia Helms interview.

59. JOCD, July 15, 1995, July 4, 1996, SOCP, LOC.
60. Anderson OH.
61. Linda Neary interview.

CHAPTER THIRTEEN: *BUSH V. GORE*

1. Scott O'Connor interview.
2. SOC interview. See also SOC interviewed by Charlie Rose, March 5, 2013, youtube.com.
3. Lynda Webster, Joe and Lucia Henderson interviews.
4. JOCD, January 28–February 2, 1996, SOCP, LOC; Skip Nalen interview.
5. Silvija Strikis, Julia Ambrose interviews.
6. Skip Nalen, Jim Holman interviews.
7. Ray Brophy, Ivan Selin, Gail Driggs interviews.
8. Adrienne Arsht interview; JOCD, January 18, 1998, SOCP, LOC.
9. JOCD, December 4, 1994, SOCP, LOC; Tim Burke, Frank Wallis interviews.
10. SOC interview.
11. Alan Kirk, James Symington, Alan Simpson interviews.
12. Phil Schneider, Alan Simpson interviews.
13. JOCD, August 19, 1997, SOCP, LOC.
14. Dr. Robert Stern interview.
15. Dr. Tab Moore, Dr. Stanley Cohan, Dr. Paul Aisen interviews; JOCD, May 20, June 12, 1997, January 28, 1999, SOCP, LOC.
16. Lazarus, *Closed Chambers,* 147–65.
17. Brad Joondeph interview.
18. Shirley Woodward interview.
19. *Allegheny County v. ACLU,* 492 U.S. 573 (1989); Dahlia Lithwick, "Crèche Test Dummies," *Slate,* December 21, 2001. As Kennedy chose more clerks with doctrinaire Federalist Society backgrounds, his chambers became philosophically oppositional with O'Connor's chambers, where the clerks arrived as liberals or conservatives but usually ended up appreciating her pragmatic approach.
20. Justice Ruth Bader Ginsburg interview.
21. SOC, Justice Steven Breyer interviews.
22. *Apprendi v. New Jersey,* 530 U.S. 466 (2000); Noah Levine interview.
23. Robert Smith, "Antonin Scalia's Other Legacy: He Was Often a Friend of Criminal Defendants," *Slate,* February 15, 2016.
24. Martin Quinn scores courtesy Lee Epstein, Washington University Law School. See Lee Epstein, Andrew Martin, Kevin Quinn, and Jeffrey Segal, "Ideological Drift Among Supreme Court Justices: Who, When, and How Important?" *Northwestern University Law Review* 101:1481 (2007). SOC moved with the times. On the death penalty, notes her friend Professor Craig Joyce of the University of Houston Law School, she paid heed to evolving public attitudes, which gradually liberalized on the question of what is "cruel and unusual" punishment banned by the Eighth Amendment.
25. Judge Laurence Silberman interview; "Press Is Condemned by Federal Judge for Court Coverage," *New York Times,* June 14, 1992.
26. Adam Bonica, Adam Chilton, Jacob Goldin, Kyle Rozema, and Maya Sen, "Do Law Clerks Influence Voting on the Supreme Court?" unpublished paper, January 5, 2017, courtesy of Adam Chilton, University of Chicago Law School.

27. Justice John Paul Stevens interview.

28. For a case in which O'Connor's personal experience (as a child living for many years with her grandmother) may have informed her judgment, see her opinion giving parents a constitutional right to stop grandparents from visiting a grandchild, *Troxel v. Granville*, 530 U.S. 57 (2000); for a last blow in favor of federalism, see her dissent in *Gonzalez v. Raich*, 545 U.S. 1 (2005), in which she argued that Congress should not be permitted to enforce the federal marijuana laws against those who, under state law, legally possess it for medical use—even though she, personally, would vote against the state law.

29. *Davis v. Monroe County Board of Education*, 526 U.S. 629 (1999), announced May 24, 1999, oyez.org.

30. Toobin, *The Nine*, 156–61; *Stenberg v. Carhart*, 530 U.S. 914 (2000).

31. *Gonzalez v. Carhart*, 550 U.S. 124 (2007); oral argument in *Stenberg v. Carhart*, April 25, 2000, oyez.org.

32. Brad Joondeph interview; Cass Sunstein, "In the Court of Cautious Opinions," *Washington Post*, July 14, 1997; *Vacco v. Quill*, 521 U.S. 793 (1997).

33. Joan Biskupic, "O'Connor the 'Go-To Justice,'" *USA Today*, July 12, 2000; Edward Lazarus, "It's All About O'Connor," *Los Angeles Times*, July 9, 2000.

34. JOCD, June 16–20, 2000, SOCP, LOC.

35. Dr. Paul Aisen interview.

36. SOC office calendar June 20, 2000, SOCP, SC.

37. Ann Hoopes interview; JOCD, June 20, 2000, SOCP, LOC.

38. Frank Saul, Dr. LaSalle Leffall interviews.

39. Dick Houseworth, Phil Schneider interviews.

40. Ruth McGregor, Don Kauffman interviews.

41. Shirley Woodward interview.

42. Scott, Brian, and Jay O'Connor interviews.

43. JOCD, August 17, 2000, October 3, 1996, SOCP, LOC.

44. SOC to Jane Dee Hull, March 2000, SOCP, LOC; Leslie Hakala, Noah Levine interviews.

45. Dr. Paul Aisen interview; Cynthia Helms, Paul and Nancy Ignatius interviews; Michael Isikoff, "The Truth Behind the Pillars," *Newsweek*, December 24, 2000.

46. Scott O'Connor, Cynthia Helms interviews.

47. Justin Nelson interview.

48. Jim Lehrer, Colin Campbell interviews.

49. Craig Joyce, Colin Campbell, Gordon Wood interviews.

50. Tom Daschle interview.

51. Alan Day, Brian O'Connor interviews.

52. Richard Posner, *Breaking the Deadlock*.

53. The famous exception is the one-man, one-vote case, *Baker v. Carr*, 369 U.S. 186 (1962).

54. Charles Zelden, *Bush v. Gore*, 197; Justice Steven Breyer interview.

55. *Bush v. Gore*, 531 U.S. 98 (2000).

56. Justice John Paul Stevens interview; Justice Stevens interviewed by Scott Pelley, *60 Minutes*, November 28, 2010; Stevens, *Five Chiefs*, 198–99.

57. Dr. Bill Leahy interview.

58. Terry Carter, "Crossing the Rubicon," *California Lawyer*, October 1992.

59. Brian O'Connor interview.

60. Stan Panikowski, Tamarra Matthews Johnson interviews.

61. Julie Folger interview; Toobin, *Too Close to Call,* 248; for other narratives, see David Margolick, "The Path to Florida," *Vanity Fair,* March 19, 2014, and Linda Greenhouse, "Bush v. Gore: Election Case a Test and a Trauma for Justices," *New York Times,* February 20, 2001.
62. *Bush v. Gore,* oral argument, December 11, 2000, oyez.org.
63. Richard Bierschbach interview.
64. Zelden, 194.
65. Justice Ruth Bader Ginsburg interview.
66. This reconstruction is based on on-the-record interviews with Justices Stevens and Ginsburg, Judge Laurence Silberman (who spoke to Scalia about the case), and Theodore Olson (the Bush campaign's lawyer), and background interviews with knowledgeable sources involved in the case. The best analysis of motivation and reasoning is found in Charles Zelden's *Bush v. Gore,* 189–229.
67. Brian O'Connor interview.

CHAPTER FOURTEEN: AFFIRMATIVE ACTION

1. Mary McGrory, "Supreme Travesty of Justice," *Washington Post,* December 14, 2000; Maureen Dowd, "The Bloom Is Off the Robe," *New York Times,* December 14, 2000; JOCD, December 14, 2000, SOCP, LOC.
2. See Jack Balkin, "*Bush v. Gore* and the Boundary Between Law and Politics," *Yale Law Journal* 110:1407 (2001).
3. "Do you approve or disapprove of the way the Supreme Court is handling its job?" news.gallup.com.
4. Judge Laurence Silberman interview; Posner, *Breaking the Deadlock.*
5. Betsy Taylor interview.
6. Ann Hoopes interview; Townsend Hoopes to SOC, January 22, 2001; SOC to Townsend Hoopes, February 13, 2001 (O'Connor wrote Hoopes, "I was surprised, and unhappily so, to receive your highly critical letter. . . ." She defended the Court, saying there was no choice but to intervene, that political chaos had beckoned if the battle was allowed to go on). Townsend Hoopes papers, Gottlieb Archival Research Center, Boston University.
7. Alan Simpson, Jim Holman interviews.
8. Lou Davidson, Carol Butler interviews.
9. Hattie and Bruce Babbitt interview.
10. Jack and Donna Pfleiger interview.
11. Mark Ellis, Scott O'Connor interviews; Ford Fessenden and Jonathan Broder, "Examining the Vote: The Overview; Study of Disputed Florida Ballots Finds Justices Did Not Cast the Deciding Vote," *New York Times,* November 12, 2001; Sandra Day O'Connor, "Judicial Independence and Civics Education," *Utah Bar Journal,* September/October, 2009. Gore might have eked out a win if every single vote in the state had been recounted, but that process would have taken months.
12. "O'Connor Questions Court's Decision to Take Bush v. Gore," *Chicago Tribune,* April 27, 2013; Justice John Paul Stevens interview; see Linda Greenhouse, "Who's Sorry Now?" *New York Times,* May 1, 2013.
13. SOC interview.
14. Craig Nalen to James Baker, December 13, 2000, courtesy Craig Nalen.
15. Brian O'Connor interview.

16. Jeffrey Rosen, "Make Up Your Mind, Justice O'Connor," *New York Times,* December 26, 1995, SOCP, LOC.

17. Jeffrey Rosen, "A Majority of One," *New York Times Magazine,* June 3, 2001.

18. Peggy Lord, Linda Neary interviews.

19. Jeffrey Rosen, "Why I Miss Sandra Day O'Connor," *New Republic,* July 1, 2011; Jeffrey Rosen interview.

20. Cass Sunstein, Mark Perry interviews.

21. RonNell Andersen Jones interview.

22. Sam Vaughan to SOC, March 5, 1996; SOC to Sam Vaughan, January 15, 1999, SOCP, LOC.

23. Alan Day interview.

24. Linda Greenhouse, "Happy Trails," *New York Times Book Review,* February 3, 2002; SOC to Linda Greenhouse, February 14, 2002, SOCP, LOC.

25. Judge Michelle Friedland, Anup Malani interviews.

26. Jeremy Gaston interview.

27. Carolyn Frantz interview.

28. "Cowgirl Hall of Fame," NPR, June 2, 2002.

29. JOCD, August 9, 2001, SOCP, LOC.

30. Dr. Paul Aisen, interview; JOCD, May 21, 2002, SOCP, LOC.

31. Carolyn Frantz interview.

32. Jennifer Mason McAward interview; *Atwater v. Lago Vista,* 532 U.S. 318 (2001); oral argument, December 4, 2000, oyez.org; Molly Ivins, "Hey, All of You Petty Criminals, You're Going Straight to Jail," *Chicago Tribune,* May 30, 2001.

33. JOCD, June 29, 1995, SOCP, LOC; *Miller v. Johnson,* 515 U.S. 900 (1995).

34. Jeffries, 487–88.

35. Kent Syverud interview. Michigan Law School had informally practiced affirmative action since the early 1970s; its formal program went into effect in 1992.

36. *Gratz v. Bollinger,* 539 U.S. 244; *Grutter v. Bollinger,* 539 U.S. 306 (2003).

37. Nicholas Lemann, "The Empathy Defense," *New Yorker,* December 18, 2000.

38. Allyson Newton Ho interview.

39. Adam Winkler, "Fatal in Theory and Strict in Fact: An Empirical Analysis of Strict Scrutiny in the Federal Courts," *Vanderbilt Law Review* 59:793 (2006). In about 30 percent of cases, strict scrutiny is not fatal.

40. Stuart Delery interview; expert report of Kent Syverud in *Grutter v. Bollinger, Peabody Journal of Education* 79:136–40 (2004).

41. RonNell Andersen Jones interview.

42. Justin Nelson interview.

43. Emily Henn, Cristina Rodriguez, Stuart Delery, Kent Syverud interviews.

44. Emily Henn, Cristina Rodriguez interviews.

45. Colin Campbell, Gordon Wood interviews.

46. *Grutter v. Bollinger,* 539 U.S. 306 (2003).

47. SOC interview. Cass Sunstein makes the interesting argument that by being so uncertain and conflicted—and confusing—about affirmative action, the Court stimulated democratic public debate, which should properly determine the future of affirmative action. Sunstein, *One Case at a Time,* 117–36.

48. Eric Motley interview.

49. Jeffries, 521; *Bowers v. Hardwick,* 478 U.S. 186 (1986); Ruth Marcus, "Justice Powell Regrets Backing Sodomy Law," *Washington Post,* October 26, 1990.

50. Stuart Delery interview.
51. *Lawrence v. Texas,* 539 U.S. 558 (2003).
52. Emily Henn, Judd Nelson, Cristina Rodriguez, Allyson Newton Ho, Beverly Gunther interviews.
53. Justice Ruth Bader Ginsburg interview.
54. *McConnell v. Federal Election Commission,* 540 U.S. 93 (2003).
55. Sean Grimsley interview.

CHAPTER FIFTEEN: END GAME

1. RonNell Andersen Jones, Sam Sankar interviews; *Elk Grove Unified School District v. Newdow,* 542 U.S. 1 (2004).
2. Dr. William Leahy interview.
3. Cristina Rodriguez interview; *Wiggins v. Smith,* 539 U.S. 510 (2003). O'Connor's opinion was based on her earlier opinion in *Strickland v. Washington,* 466 U.S. 669 (1984), which the justice often said was her decision "with the greatest effect." *The BLT: The Blog of Legal Times,* November 7, 2007.
4. "Scalia Angrily Defends His Duck Hunt with Cheney," *New York Times,* March 18, 2004; Biskupic, *American Original,* 259.
5. RonNell Andersen Jones interview.
6. Jay and Scott O'Connor, Justin Nelson interviews.
7. *Hamdi v. Rumsfeld,* 542 U.S. 507 (2004).
8. 323 U.S. 214 (1944); overturned in *Trump v. Hawaii,* 17–965, 585 U.S. ___ (2018).
9. Spencer Hsu, "Plane That Caused Capitol Evacuation Nearly Shot Down," *Washington Post,* July 8, 2004.
10. RonNell Andersen Jones interview.
11. *Rasul v. Bush,* 542 U.S. 466 (2004); *Rumsfeld v. Padilla,* 542 U.S. 426 (2004).
12. Linda Greenhouse, "The Year Rehnquist May Have Lost His Court," *New York Times,* July 4, 2004; Toobin, *The Nine,* 276.
13. Don Verrilli interview.
14. RonNell Andersen Jones interview.
15. Dr. Paul Aisen interview.
16. Virginia Chew interview.
17. Joe and Lucia Henderson interviews; Jack and Donna Pfleiger interviews.
18. Claire Cox interview.
19. Joe and Lucia Henderson interview.
20. Brian O'Connor interview.
21. Danni Dawson, Lynn Garland, Michael Boskin, Scott and Joanie O'Connor interviews.
22. Judy Hope interview.
23. Scott and Jay O'Connor interviews.
24. Sharon Rockefeller, Betsy and Susan Taylor interviews.
25. Danni Dawson interview.
26. Craig Joyce interview.
27. Theane Evangelis, Tali Farhadian Weinstein interviews.
28. Craig Timberg, "Rehnquist's Inclusion of 'Dixie' Strikes a Sour Note," *Washington Post,* July 21, 1999; *Dickerson v. United States,* 530 U.S. 428 (2000); Toobin, *The Nine,* 144–46.

29. Charles Lane, "Rehnquist Eulogies Look Beyond the Bench," *Washington Post,* September 9, 2005.

30. Lawrence Altman, "Prognosis for Rehnquist Depends on Which Type of Thyroid Cancer He Has," *New York Times,* October 26, 2004.

31. Toobin, *The Nine,* 282.

32. Pat Hass interview.

33. Charles and Barbara Renfrew interview. SOC also told Judy Hope that Rehnquist should resign.

34. Jeffrey Toobin, "Swing Shift," *New Yorker,* September 12, 2005; *Roper v. Simmons,* 543 U.S. 551 (2005). Two Democrats also sponsored the resolution, H. Res. 97.

35. Toobin, *The Nine,* 287–91; Charles Babington, "Senator Links Violence to 'Political Decisions,'" *Washington Post,* April 5, 2005.

36. Nina Totenberg, "O'Connor Decries Republican Attacks on Courts," NPR, March 10, 2006.

37. Julian Borger, "Former Top Judge Says U.S. Risks Edging Near to Dictatorship," *The Guardian,* March 13, 2006; SOC to Cynthia Holcomb Hall, April 14, 2005, SOCP, LOC.

38. Danni Dawson interview.

39. Alan Day interview; SOC to Owen Paepke, January 18, 2005; SOC to Peggy Lord, March 12, 2005, SOCP, LOC.

40. Danni Dawson, Cynthia Helms interviews.

41. *Kelo v. New London,* 545 U.S. 469 (2005); Ilya Somin, "The Political and Judicial Reaction to Kelo," *Washington Post,* June 4, 2005.

42. Cynthia Helms interview.

43. Ginny Chew, Sasha Volokh interviews.

44. Tali Farhadian Weinstein, Josh Klein, Theane Evangelis interviews.

45. Greenburg, *Supreme Conflict,* 22–23; Ruth Bader Ginsburg to SOC; Antonin Scalia to SOC; William Rehnquist to SOC, July 1, 2005, SOCP, SC.

46. Charles Renfrew interview.

47. Rich Landers, "O'Connor," *Spokesman Review* (Spokane, WA), July 20, 2005.

48. Chief Justice John Roberts interview.

49. Jeanette and Ray Brophy interview.

50. Charles Lane, "Rehnquist Eulogies Look Beyond the Bench," *Washington Post,* September 9, 2005.

51. Lisa Kern Griffin interview.

52. Anonymous sources.

53. Justice John Paul Stevens interview.

54. Charles Lane, "Former Clerks Pay Tribute to the Chief," *Washington Post,* June 18, 2005.

55. Charles Lane, "Rehnquist Says He Has No Plans to Leave the Supreme Court," *Washington Post,* July 15, 2005; Maureen Scalia, Sen. Barbara Boxer interviews.

56. Toobin, *The Nine,* 330–45.

57. Eric Motley, Ruth McGregor, Ben Horwich, Lou Davidson interviews.

58. *Central Virginia Community College v. Katz,* 546 U.S. 356 (2006).

59. 546 U.S. 320 (2006).

60. Ben Horwich, Justice Ruth Bader Ginsburg, Steve Gilles interviews.

61. Ben Horwich interview.

62. Scott and Brian O'Connor interviews.

CHAPTER SIXTEEN: LABOR OF LOVE

1. Sue Huck, Frank Wallis, Don Kauffman interviews.
2. Joanie and Scott O'Connor interviews.
3. Betsy Taylor, Peggy Lord interviews.
4. Judy Hope, Jay O'Connor interviews.
5. James Baker, Rich Williamson interviews.
6. Walter Dellinger interview.
7. Adam Liptak, "A Potential Agenda for the Supreme Court in the Era of Trump," *New York Times*, November 29, 2016.
8. Jim Todd interview.
9. Justin Driver interview; Linda Greenhouse, "In Steps Big and Small, Supreme Court Moved Right," *New York Times*, July 1, 2007; Martica Ruhm Sawin interview.
10. Gay Wray, Lattie Coor, Lela Alston interviews.
11. Patricia White, Becky Kourlis, Meryl Chertoff interviews; *Caperton v. A.T. Massey Coal Co.*, 556 U.S. 868 (2009); Josh Deahl interview; Toobin, *The Oath*, 212.
12. *Citizens United v. Federal Election Commission*, 558 U.S. 310 (2010).
13. Meryl Chertoff, Patricia White, Kristen Eichenschr, Abby Taylor, Julie O'Sullivan, James Gee, Charlie Dolan, Louise Dube, Nancy Ignatius, Cynthia Helms, Kathy Smalley interviews; Leslie Brody, "Civics Game Advanced by Former Justice Is Classroom Hit," *Wall Street Journal*, November 13, 2016; Natasha Singer, "A Supreme Court Pioneer, Now Making Her Mark on Video Games," *New York Times*, March 27, 2016.
14. Al Tompkins, "Behind the O'Connor Love Story," *Poynter Institute*, November 16, 2007; Kate Zernike, "Love in the Time of Dementia," *New York Times*, November 17, 2007. Six months later, Justice O'Connor spoke movingly about the ordeal of Alzheimer's disease in a hearing before the U.S. Senate's Special Committee on Aging. She incorrectly testified that her husband had been diagnosed with Alzheimer's in 1990, ten years before he actually was. After the publicity and attention to John's mistaken attachment, it may have seemed to her that his illness had gone on even longer than it had. "Sandra Day O'Connor Makes Alzheimer's Plea," NPR, May 14, 2008; Scott O'Connor, Veronica Sanchez interviews.
15. Lou Davidson, Diane Cooley, Jack Connolly interviews.
16. Frank Wallis, Carol Biagiotti interviews.
17. Patricia White, Abby Taylor interviews; Dalton, *Theodore Roosevelt*, 90.
18. Justin Driver interview.
19. Scott and Brian O'Connor interviews; Lynn Duke, "Court to Jester," *Washington Post*, January 28, 2007; Bill and Lynda Webster interview; SOC Alfalfa acceptance speech courtesy Greg Platts.
20. Medal of Freedom ceremony, August 12, 2009, C-SPAN; Scott O'Connor interview.
21. Robert Henry, John Walker interviews.
22. Tom Wilner, John Jasik interviews.
23. Heather O'Connor, Ant Bennett interviews.
24. Danni Dawson, Christian Thorin interviews.
25. Becky Kourlis, Lynda Webster interviews.
26. Anne Marie Slaughter interview; "Live from the New York Public Library," March 28, 2013, youtube.com; Jerry Lewkowitz interview.

27. Jim Todd, Lynda and Bill Webster interviews.
28. Cynthia Helms interview.
29. Alan Day, Ruth McGregor, Becky Kourlis interviews; the author was at the Arizona legislature.
30. Jane Fahey interview.
31. Cynthia Helms, Ruth McGregor interviews.
32. Justice Sonia Sotomayor, Justice Elena Kagan interviews.
33. Scott O'Connor interview.
34. "A Nation Bids Reagan Farewell," CBS News, June 5, 2004.
35. Judge J. Harvie Wilkinson III interview.
36. Scott and Jay O'Connor interviews.

BIBLIOGRAPHY

Berlin, Isaiah. *The Proper Study of Mankind: An Anthology of Essays.* New York: Farrar, Straus and Giroux, 1998.

Berman, David. *Arizona Politics and Government.* Lincoln: University of Nebraska Press, 1998.

Biskupic, Joan. *American Original: The Life and Constitution of Supreme Court Justice Antonin Scalia.* New York: Farrar, Straus and Giroux, 2009.

————. *Sandra Day O'Connor: How the First Woman on the Court Became Its Most Influential Justice.* New York: Harper Perennial, 2006.

Carmon, Irin, and Shana Knizhnick. *Notorious RBG: The Life and Times of Ruth Bader Ginsburg.* New York: HarperCollins, 2015.

Dalton, Kathleen. *Theodore Roosevelt: A Strenuous Life.* New York: Knopf, 2002.

Day, H. Alan. *Cowboy Up! Life Lessons from the Lazy B.* New York: Morgan James, 2018.

De Geest, Gerritt, and Boudewijn Bouckaert, eds. *Encyclopedia of Law and Economics.* London: Edward Elgar, 2000.

Friedan, Betty. *The Feminine Mystique.* New York: W. W. Norton, 1963.

Garrow, David. *Liberty and Sexuality: The Right to Privacy and the Making of* Roe v. Wade. Berkeley: University of California Press, 1994.

Ginsburg, Ruth Bader. *My Own Words.* New York: Simon and Schuster, 2016.

Graetz, Michael J., and Linda Greenhouse. *The Burger Court and the Rise of the Judicial Right.* New York: Simon and Schuster, 2016.

Greenburg, Jan Crawford. *Supreme Conflict: The Inside Story of the Struggle for Control of the United States Supreme Court.* New York: Penguin, 2007.

Greenhouse, Linda. *Becoming Justice Blackmun: Harry Blackmun's Supreme Court Journey.* New York: Times Books, 2005.

Hirshman, Linda. *Sisters in Law: How Sandra Day O'Connor and Ruth Bader Ginsburg Went to the Supreme Court and Changed the World.* New York: HarperCollins, 2015.

Holmes, Oliver Wendell, Jr. *The Common Law.* Boston: Little, Brown, 1881.

Huber, Peter. *Sandra Day O'Connor: Supreme Court Justice.* New York: Chelsea House, 1990.

Hutchinson, Dennis. *The Man Who Was Once Whizzer White.* New York: Free Press, 1990.

Jeffries, John. *Justice Lewis F. Powell, Jr.: A Biography.* New York: Fordham University Press, 2001.

Jenkins, John. *The Partisan: The Life of William Rehnquist.* New York: PublicAffairs, 2012.

Jocas, Richard, David Neuman, and Paul Turner. *Stanford University: An Architectural Guide.* New York: Princeton Architectural Press, 2006.

Lazarus, Edward. *Closed Chambers: The Rise, Fall, and Future of the Modern Supreme Court*. New York: Penguin, 1998.

Maveety, Nancy. *Justice Sandra Day O'Connor: Strategist on the Supreme Court*. Lanham, MD: Rowman and Littlefield, 1996.

Morris, Edmund. *Dutch: A Memoir of Ronald Reagan*. New York: Random House, 1999.

Murphy, Bruce Allen. *Scalia: A Court of One*. New York: Simon and Schuster, 2014.

Newton, Jim. *Justice for All: Earl Warren and the Nation He Made*. New York: Riverhead Books, 2008.

O'Brien, David. *Storm Center: The Supreme Court in American Politics*. New York: W. W. Norton, 2011.

O'Connor, Sandra Day. *Majesty of the Law: Reflections of a Supreme Court Justice*. New York: Random House, 2004.

—————. *Out of Order: Stories from the History of the Supreme Court*. New York: Random House, 2013.

O'Connor, Sandra Day, and H. Alan Day. *Lazy B: Growing Up on a Cattle Ranch in the American Southwest*. New York: Random House, 2002.

Pearlstein, Rick. *Before the Storm: Barry Goldwater and the Unmaking of the American Consensus*. New York: Hill and Wang, 2002.

Peppers, Todd, and Artemus Ward, eds. *In Chambers: Stories of Supreme Court Law Clerks and Their Justices*. Charlottesville: University of Virginia Press, 2012.

Peppers, Todd, and Clare Cushman, eds. *Of Courtiers and Kings: More Stories of Supreme Court Law Clerks and Their Justices*. Charlottesville: University of Virginia Press, 2015.

Posner, Richard. *Breaking the Deadlock: The 2000 Election, the Constitution, and the Courts*. Princeton, NJ: Princeton University Press, 2001.

Rosen, Jeffrey. *The Supreme Court: The Personalities and Rivalries that Defined America*. New York: Times Books, 2007.

Roth, Philip. *American Pastoral*. New York: Houghton Mifflin, 1997.

Simon, James. *The Antagonists: Hugo Black, Felix Frankfurter, and Civil Liberties in Modern America*. New York: Simon and Schuster, 1989.

—————. *The Center Holds: The Power Struggles Inside the Rehnquist Court*. New York: Simon and Schuster, 1995.

Skinner, Kiron, Annelise Anderson, and Martin Anderson. *Reagan: A Life in Letters*. New York: Simon and Schuster, 2003.

Smith, William French. *Law and Justice in the Reagan Administration: Memoirs of an Attorney General*. Stanford, CA: Hoover Institution Press, 1991.

Starr, Kenneth. *First Among Equals: The Supreme Court in American Life*. New York: Warner Books, 2002.

Stegner, Wallace. *Crossing to Safety*. New York: Modern Library, 2002.

Stern, Seth, and Stephen Wermiel. *Justice Brennan: Liberal Champion*. New York: Houghton Mifflin, 2010.

Stevens, John Paul. *Five Chiefs: A Supreme Court Memoir*. New York: Little, Brown, 2011.

Stout, Lee. *A Matter of Simple Justice: The Untold Story of Barbara Hope Franklin and a Few Good Women*. University Park: Pennsylvania State University Libraries, 2012.

Sunstein, Cass. *One Case at a Time: Judicial Minimalism on the Supreme Court*. Cambridge, MA: Harvard University Press, 1999.

Toobin, Jeffrey. *The Nine: Inside the Secret World of the Supreme Court*. New York: Anchor Books, 2007.

—————. *The Oath: The Obama White House and the Supreme Court*. New York: Anchor Books, 2013.

———. *Too Close to Call: The Thirty-Six-Day Battle to Decide the 2000 Election.* New York: Random House, 2001.

Tribe, Laurence, and Joshua Matz. *Uncertain Justice: The Roberts Court and the Constitution.* New York: Henry Holt, 2014.

Tucker, Lisa McElroy (with Courtney O'Connor). *Meet My Grandmother, She's a Supreme Court Justice.* New York: Millbrook Press, 2000.

Tushnet, Mark. *A Court Divided: The Rehnquist Court and the Future of Constitutional Law.* New York: W. W. Norton, 2006.

VanderMeer, Philip. *Burton Barr: Political Leadership and the Transformation of Arizona.* Tucson: University of Arizona Press, 2014.

White, G. Edward. *Justice Oliver Wendell Holmes: Law and the Inner Self.* New York: Oxford University Press, 1993.

Williams, Juan. *Thurgood Marshall: American Revolutionary.* New York: Three Rivers Press, 1998.

Winkler, Adam. *Gun Fight: The Battle over the Right to Bear Arms.* New York: W. W. Norton, 2013.

Woodward, Bob, and Scott Armstrong. *The Brethren: Inside the Supreme Court.* New York: Simon and Schuster, 1979.

Yarborough, Tinsley. *Harry A. Blackmun: The Outsider Justice.* New York: Oxford University Press, 2008.

Zelden, Charles. *Bush v. Gore: Exposing the Hidden Crisis in Democracy.* Lawrence: University Press of Kansas, 2010.

ILLUSTRATION LIST AND CREDITS

ILLUSTRATIONS IN THE TEXT

TITLE-PAGE SPREAD (PAGE IV): Justice O'Connor on the steps of the U.S. Capitol after her Senate confirmation, September 21, 1981. With her are (left to right) Attorney General William French Smith, Senator Barry Goldwater, Vice President George H. W. Bush, and Senator Strom Thurmond. BETTMANN/GETTY IMAGES

PROLOGUE (PAGE XI): Sandra on horseback at the ranch. COURTESY OF THE O'CONNOR FAMILY

CHAPTER ONE (PAGE 3): Sandra, about age eleven, with her mother, Ada Mae, and siblings, Alan and Ann. COURTESY OF THE O'CONNOR FAMILY

CHAPTER TWO (PAGE 25): Sandra at sixteen, outside the Lazy B ranch house, with the caption in her writing "Ready to go to Stanford." COURTESY OF THE O'CONNOR FAMILY

CHAPTER THREE (PAGE 47): Sandra and John O'Connor at their wedding reception at the Lazy B, December 1952. COURTESY OF THE O'CONNOR FAMILY

CHAPTER FOUR (PAGE 71): Sandra O'Connor carries the Arizona Statutes book, as president of the Junior League, for a newspaper photo published July 3, 1966. FROM THE ARIZONA REPUBLIC, JULY 3, 1966/EARL McCARTNEY/© 1966 GANNETT-COMMUNITY PUBLISHING. ALL RIGHTS RESERVED. USED BY PERMISSION AND PROTECTED BY THE COPYRIGHT LAWS OF THE UNITED STATES. THE PRINTING, COPYING, REDISTRIBUTION OR RETRANSMISSION OF THIS CONTENT WITHOUT EXPRESS WRITTEN PERMISSION IS PROHIBITED.

CHAPTER FIVE (PAGE 101): Judge O'Connor and Chief Justice Warren Burger at Lake Powell, Arizona, in July 1979. COURTESY OF THE O'CONNOR FAMILY

CHAPTER SIX (PAGE 121): President Reagan and Attorney General William French Smith talk with nominee O'Connor in the Oval Office, July 15, 1981. COURTESY RONALD REAGAN LIBRARY

CHAPTER SEVEN (PAGE 147): Justice O'Connor at morning aerobics at the Supreme Court. COURTESY OF THE O'CONNOR FAMILY

CHAPTER EIGHT (PAGE 175): Sandra and John O'Connor dancing at the Smithsonian Ball, March 1982. GUY DELORT/WWD/SHUTTERSTOCK

CHAPTER NINE (PAGE 197): Justice O'Connor leads a conga line at a judicial conference, July 1983. COURTESY OF THE O'CONNOR FAMILY

CHAPTER TEN (PAGE 227): Sandra O'Connor holds her first grandchild, October 1989. COURTESY OF THE O'CONNOR FAMILY

CHAPTER ELEVEN (PAGE 253): Justice O'Connor with her clerks in her chambers at the U.S. Supreme Court, June 2002. DAVID HUME KENNERLY/GETTY IMAGES

CHAPTER TWELVE (PAGE 283): Justice O'Connor and Ruth Bader Ginsburg at Justice Ginsburg's investiture, October 1, 1993. PHOTOGRAPH BY KEN HEINEN, COLLECTION OF THE SUPREME COURT OF THE UNITED STATES

CHAPTER THIRTEEN (PAGE 307): Justice O'Connor and Justice Stephen Breyer at the Sandra Day O'Connor Project, Georgetown University Law Center, May 20, 2009. CHIP SOMODEVILLA/GETTY IMAGES

CHAPTER FOURTEEN (PAGE 335): Justice O'Connor with John O'Connor and Justices Clarence Thomas and Antonin Scalia at the U.S. Capitol before President George W. Bush's inauguration, January 20, 2005. PHOTOGRAPH BY STEVEN PETTEWAY, COLLECTION OF THE SUPREME COURT OF THE UNITED STATES

CHAPTER FIFTEEN (PAGE 359): Chief Justice Rehnquist's coffin arriving at the Supreme Court for the lying in repose ceremony, September 6, 2005. PHOTOGRAPH BY STEVEN PETTEWAY, COLLECTION OF THE SUPREME COURT OF THE UNITED STATES

CHAPTER SIXTEEN (PAGE 385): Justice O'Connor with Justices Sonia Sotomayor, Ruth Bader Ginsburg, and Elena Kagan at Justice Kagan's investiture ceremony, October 1, 2010. PHOTOGRAPH BY STEVEN PETTEWAY, COLLECTION OF THE SUPREME COURT OF THE UNITED STATES

END OF TEXT (PAGE 406): Justice O'Connor at the Sandra Day O'Connor United States Courthouse in Phoenix in 2000. PHOTOGRAPH BY FRED SCHILLING

INSERT (ILLUSTRATIONS IN THE ORDER IN WHICH THEY APPEAR)

1. Headquarters at the Lazy B ranch. COURTESY OF THE O'CONNOR FAMILY
2. Windmills powering the wells at the Lazy B. COURTESY OF THE O'CONNOR FAMILY
3. Sandra as a child. COURTESY OF THE O'CONNOR FAMILY
4. Sandra at a swimming hole near Groveland, California, outside Yosemite. COURTESY OF BEATSIE CHALLIS LAWS
5. The 1950–51 *Stanford Law Review,* including members Sandra Day (first row) and William Rehnquist (last row, on the left). STANFORD LAW SCHOOL PHOTO FROM THE O'CONNOR FAMILY COLLECTION
6. Sandra Day and William Rehnquist at Stanford. COURTESY OF BEATSIE CHALLIS LAWS
7. Harry and Ada Mae Day at Sandra's wedding to John O'Connor. COURTESY OF THE O'CONNOR FAMILY
8. Newlyweds John and Sandra O'Connor. COURTESY OF THE O'CONNOR FAMILY
9. Sandra Day O'Connor in evening wear. COURTESY OF THE O'CONNOR FAMILY
10. Sign at the strip mall law office of "Thomas F. Tobin and Sandra D. O'Connor." COURTESY OF THE O'CONNOR FAMILY
11. Interior of the O'Connors' home in Paradise Valley, Arizona. COURTESY OF THE O'CONNOR FAMILY
12. Senator O'Connor in the Arizona state senate. FROM *THE ARIZONA REPUBLIC,* JANUARY 16, 1972/EBBY HAWERLANDER/© 1972 GANNETT-COMMUNITY PUBLISHING. ALL RIGHTS RESERVED. USED BY PERMISSION AND PROTECTED BY THE COPYRIGHT LAWS OF THE UNITED STATES. THE PRINTING, COPYING, REDISTRIBUTION OR RETRANSMISSION OF THIS CONTENT WITHOUT EXPRESS WRITTEN PERMISSION IS PROHIBITED.
13. Sandra and John O'Connor with their three sons, Scott, Brian, and Jay, October 1981. DAVID HUME KENNERLY/GETTY IMAGES
14. Sandra Day O'Connor testifying at her confirmation hearings, September 10, 1981. © WALLY McNAMEE/CORBIS/GETTY IMAGES

15. Justice O'Connor and Chief Justice Warren Burger on the steps of the Supreme Court after her investiture, September 25, 1981. DAVID HUME KENNERLY/GETTY IMAGES

16. Justice O'Connor greets Justice Thurgood Marshall and his wife, Cissy Marshall. JAY MALLIN/REDUX

17. British prime minister Margaret Thatcher and Justice O'Connor at 10 Downing Street, July 1984. JOHN REDMAN/ASSOCIATED PRESS

18. Justice O'Connor with Chief Justice Rehnquist and Justices White, Scalia, Kennedy, Brennan, Blackmun, and Stevens at Justice Kennedy's investiture, February 18, 1988. PHOTOGRAPH BY KEN HEINEN, COLLECTION OF THE SUPREME COURT OF THE UNITED STATES

19. Justice O'Connor with President George H. W. Bush and Congressman Jim Symington at the 1994 Alfalfa Club dinner. COURTESY OF THE ALFALFA CLUB

20. Sandra O'Connor golfing in Scotland, 1979. COURTESY OF THE O'CONNOR FAMILY

21. Sandra O'Connor and a guide, fly-fishing in Alaska, 2008. COURTESY OF LYNDA AND BILL WEBSTER

22. Diana Holman, John O'Connor, and Kay Evans, 2000. COURTESY OF THE O'CONNOR FAMILY

23. Justice O'Connor and Justice Ginsburg in Statuary Hall at the U.S. Capitol, March 2001. DAVID HUME KENNERLY/GETTY IMAGES

24. Justice O'Connor and Chief Justice Rehnquist, December 2003. STEPHEN CROWLEY/*THE NEW YORK TIMES*/REDUX

25. Justice O'Connor's July 1, 2005, letter of resignation to President George W. Bush. COLLECTION OF THE SUPREME COURT OF THE UNITED STATES

26. Chief Justice Rehnquist's coffin passes Justice O'Connor on the steps of the U.S. Supreme Court, September 6, 2005. DOUG MILLS/*THE NEW YORK TIMES*/REDUX

27. President Barack Obama awarding Sandra O'Connor the Presidential Medal of Freedom, August 12, 2009. CHRISTY BOWE—GLOBE PHOTOS, INC.

28. Sandra O'Connor and Madeleine Albright at the New York Public Library's Stephen A. Schwarzman Building, March 2013. JORI KLEIN

29. Justice O'Connor with Justices Ginsburg, Sotomayor, and Kagan at the Newseum in Washington, D.C., April 11, 2012. MIKE THEILER/REUTERS PICTURES

INDEX

KEY TO ABBREVIATIONS:
FWOTSC = First Woman on the Supreme Court; JOC = John O'Connor;
SCOTUS = U.S. Supreme Court; SOC = Sandra Day O'Connor

Page numbers of photographs appear in italics.

abortion, 92, 230, 261–64, 389, 431n67
  Akron case, 192–95
  Ayotte case, 383–84
  Casey case, 278–81, 287, 312, 317,
    435n79
  Hodgson case, 266–67
  issues in Arizona, 90, 91, 92–93
  opponents to SOC's nomination
    and, 134–37, 144
  "partial birth abortions," 317
  pro-life factions, 91n, 92, 93, 134, 195,
    261, 266, 278, 389
  Reagan and, 122
  Roe v. Wade and, 91–92, 231
  SOC's views and voting on, xv,
    90–91, 91n, *121*, 127–28, 130–31,
    134, 136, 142, 221–24, 235n, 264,
    278–81, 317–18, 383–84, 420n68,
    431n67, 433n17, 435n79
  Stenberg case, 317–18
  Thornburgh case, 221
  Webster case, 261–64, 266, 278,
    433n17
  See also *Roe v. Wade*
"Abortion Politics" (Estrich and
    Sullivan), 278–79
Adams, Abigail, 78
Adams, John, 403
Adams, Kate, 296, 299

Adams, Mary, 270
affirmative action, 224, 226, 302, 303,
    389, 440n47
  Adarand case, 303–4
  Bakke case, 228–29, 347, 351
  Croson case, 259–61, 277
  Fullilove case, 232
  Gratz and *Grutter* cases, 261, 348–54,
    440n35
  Metro Broadcasting case, 303
  Scalia and, 226, 259, 260, 304, 361
  SOC and, xv, 233, 259–61, 346–54
  Wygant case, 229–33
Agrawal, Gail, 210
Aisen, Paul, 319–20, 323, 344–45, 366
Akers, Stan, 85, 94, 95, 420n46
Alamogordo, N.M., 23n
Albright, Madeleine, xii, 84, 399
Alito, Samuel, 384, 388–89
Alzheimer's disease, xvi, 311, 311n
  Ada Mae Day and, 152, 277
  JOC and, 306, 309–11, 311n, 319–24,
    344–45, 352, 356, 366–70, 375,
    377, 381, 382, 384n, 386–87,
    394–95, 394n, 443n14
  Percy and, 368–69
  SOC and, xvi, 399–402
American Bar Association's
    International Division, 288

American Pastoral (Roth), 26

Anabtawi, Iman, 204

Anderson, Joe, 73, 75

Anglo-American Legal Exchange, 117,
    125–26, 128

Antagonists, The (Simon), 265

Areen, Judy, 391

Argentina, 289n, 290

Arizona judiciary
    judicial elections vs. merit
        appointments, 102–3, 113
    SOC and removal of Jennings,
        105–6
    SOC as Court of Appeals judge,
        113–14, 118–19, 338
    SOC as Superior Court judge,
        102–13
    women judges, number of, 106

Arizona Republic, 57, 61, 68, 70, 84, 87,
    93–94, 108, 111, 134

Arizona State Assistant Attorney
    General, SOC as, 68–69

Arizona state senate, 72–99
    abortion bills, SOC and, 91, 92–93,
        127–28, 134, 136, 142, 420n68
    "the Dildo Bill," 73
    ERA and, 79–83, 90, 94–95
    lobbyists and, 73, 74, 75, 97
    race issues, 84–85
    Republican reform of, 74, 74n
    sexual harassment in, 72, 73–74, 74n
    SOC and judicial appointment bill,
        103
    SOC and spending cap bill, 96–97
    SOC and state's gender-biased laws,
        78–82, 94–95
    SOC as first woman leader, 72, 84
    SOC as majority leader, xiii–xiv,
        84–99
    SOC as senate parliamentarian, 74
    SOC as senator, 69–70, 69n, 72–84
    SOC entertaining lawmakers,
        86–87
    women in, 69, 72

Arizona State University
    Barry Goldwater Lecture Series, 384
    Sandra Day O'Connor College of
        Law, 272, 392, 395, 401

Armstrong, Scott, 157

Arsht, Adrienne, 292–93, 309

Arsht, Roxana Cannon, 293

Ashcroft, John, 363

Astor, Brooke, 185–86

Atlantic Monthly, 79

Babbitt, Bruce, 62, 73–74, 106, 109, 111,
    112, 113, 114, 338

Babbitt, Harriet "Hattie," 106, 112–14,
    338

Babcock, Barbara, 176

Baker, James A. "Jim," 126–27, 130, 132,
    144, 258, 339n, 387

Bakke, Allan, 228–29

Baldrige, Letitia, 295

Bales, Scott, 76, 214–15, 220

Banner, Stuart, 270, 287

Barr, Burton, 74–75, 79, 84, 96, 97, 110,
    133

Barr, Louise, 84

Barrett, Barbara, 86

Baucus, Max, 137, 143n

Bennett, Anthony, 398

Bentley, Barbara, 109

Berenson, Brad, 280

Beske, Elizabeth Earle, 297–98

Biagiotti, Carol, 290, 293, 395

Bickel, Alexander, 210

Bickwit, Len, 248

Bierschbach, Richard, 330–31

Bishop, Tim, 264

Biskupic, Joan, 318, 319

Bjerke, Eivand, 249

Black, Hugo, 77, 150, 265, 326n
    Douglas and, 156–57

Black, Jim, 8

Blackmun, Harry, 148–49, 148n, 159,
    160, 161, 167, 190, 212, 216, 221n,
    255, 256, 257, 312, 313
    Akron case and, 193–95
    Bakke case and, 228
    Brennan and, 168, 171, 209
    Casey case and, 279
    García case and, 210–11
    Hogan case and, 179
    Metro Broadcasting case and, 303
    "the Minnesota Twins" and, 149, 157
    retirement, 298

Roe v. Wade and, 145, 148, 149, 193,
   194, 223–24, 262, 279, 433n17
SOC and, xiii, 148–50, 171–73,
   188–90, 195, 207, 229, 256, 257,
   427n92
Thornburgh case and, 221
Webster case and, 263–64, 433n17
Blake, Robert, 305
Blake, Sylvia, 305
Blandford, Linda, 159
Bohemian Club, Ca., 183–84, 185n, 238,
   265, 275, 290, 310, 320, 367, 368
Boies, David, 330, 336
Bolin, Wesley, 108–9
Book of Mormon (Broadway play), 293
Bork, Robert, 122, 234, 235n, 238, 239,
   255, 381
Boskin, Michael, 368
Boston Globe, 267
Boxer, Barbara, 380
Brennan, William J., 125, 149n, 151, 153,
   211, 216n, 257, 273, 297, 312, 313,
   427n76
   affirmative action cases and, 226, 259
   Blackmun and, 168, 171, 209
   Craig case and, 180
   Engle case and, 170, 171
   Fay case and, 170
   García case and, 211
   Hogan case and, 179–80
   law clerks of, 162, 168, 169, 296
   making law and, 168, 212
   marriage to secretary, 188, 209
   Metro Broadcasting case, 303
   motto: "It takes five," 168, 209, 308
   personal problems, 168–69, 209
   Price Waterhouse case and, 257
   Rehnquist and, 218
   retirement, 271
   SOC and, 158, 169–71, 173, 173n,
      190, 195, 209, 211–12
   Warren and, 168
Brethren, The (Woodward and
   Armstrong), 157, 157n, 187, 425n33
Breyer, Joanna, 298, 298n
Breyer, Stephen, 298–99, 307, 312–13,
   326
   Apprendi case and, 313
   Bush v. Gore and, 327–28, 331–32

Davis case and, 316
   SOC and, 298–99, 307, 312–13, 324
   Stenberg case and, 317
"Bridge Builder, The" (poem), xv, 404
Brill, Steven, 105
Brister, Jim, 8, 21, 343
Brophy, Jeannette, 202, 379
Brophy, Ray, 202, 309, 379
Bryan Cave law firm, 244, 310, 333
Buchanan, Pat, 325
Buckley, William F., Jr., 60
Buffett, Warren, 125, 240, 306
Burger, Warren, xiii, 162, 167, 216–17,
   218, 221n, 238n
   appoints SOC to Anglo-American
      Legal Exchange, 117
   appoints SOC to Judicial Fellows
      Committee, 117
   black workers at the court and, 153
   colleagues' views of, 149, 149n, 157
   García case and, 210
   Hogan case and, 179
   "the Minnesota Twins" and, 149, 157
   retirement, 216–17, 235
   school prayer and, 213
   SOC and, 101, 115–17, 125–26, 132,
      157–58, 190, 195, 214–16,
      425n36
   SOC's swearing-in and, 149–50, 151
   Starr clerking for, 127
   Wallace dissent, 213, 214
   Wygant case and, 229
Burgess, Isabel, 69, 72
Burke, Edmund, 210
Burning Tree Club, 143, 424n57
Bush, Barbara, 258, 264, 272, 363
Bush, George H. W., 143, 183, 238n, 250,
   258–59, 261, 291, 363, 379, 404n,
   432n48
Bush, George W., 183, 249–50, 337n,
   363, 373, 377, 378, 384, 384n, 387
   Bush v. Gore and, 336
   inauguration, 339, 339n
   judicial appointments, 378–79, 381,
      384
   presidential race, 322, 325, 326, 333
   "War on Terror" policies, 364
Bush, John Ellis "Jeb," 331n
Bush, Laura Welch, 249, 363, 384, 384n

Bush v. Gore, 326–34, 331n, 439n66
    decision, justices for and against,
        332–33
    equal protection rationale, 332,
        336–37
    Kennedy writing the opinion, 332–33
    media circus and protests, 329, 330
    oral arguments and, 328, 329–32
    public response to, 336, 336n
    SOC and, 333–34, 338–40, 439n6
Bussel, Dan, 218, 220, 430n46, 431n7

campaign spending, 389, 390–91
    Citizens United case, 391
    SOC on judicial elections, 390–91
Campbell, Andy, 28–29, 31–33, 416n23
Campbell, Colin, 324
Camping, Trudy, 73
Cannon, Lois Driggs, 55, 116
Cannon, Mark, 116–17, 126
Carmichael, Ron, 97
Carswell, G. Harrold, 76n
Carter, Jimmy, 108, 117, 119–20, 144, 338
    judicial appointments, 113, 117, 123
Cartwright, Brian, 161–62, 163
Castro, Raul, 108
Catlett, Steve, 237
Catlin, George, 159
Central and Eastern European Law
        Institute (CEELI), 288, 289,
        289n, 338
Charlottesville, Va., JAG school, 52
Chautauqua, N.Y., 392–93
Chavez, Cesar, 85
Cheney, Dick, 362
Chertoff, Meryl, 391, 400
Chevy Chase Club, 185, 185n, 186, 200,
        201, 238n, 246, 262, 292, 328, 333,
        336, 369
Chew, Ginny, 367, 377
Chicago Tribune, 65
Christian, Winslow, 117
Civil Rights Act of 1964, 81, 99
Clark, William P., 130
Clinton, Bill, 284, 304, 308, 322–23
Closed Chambers (Lazarus), 255
Cohan, Stanley, 311, 319
Coleman, Cy, 186

Collins, Susan, 380
Colonial Williamsburg, 324, 325
Conlan, John, 80, 82–83, 88, 102
Cooley, Dan, 56
Cooley, Diane Porter, 26, 27, 31, 33, 36,
        38, 40, 49, 54, 56, 63
Coor, Elva, 60, 61–62
Corbet, Leo, 85, 86, 90, 109, 136
Cornyn, John, 373–74
Corpstein, Peter, 111
Covington & Burling, 355
Cowgirl Hall of Fame, 344
Cox, Claire, 367
Creighton, Ned, 75, 79
Creighton, Susan, 220
Cribb, Kenneth, 120, 235
Cruz, Romeo, 285, 290–91
C-SPAN video, SOC's breast cancer
        speech, 251–52
Cunningham, George, 83, 93

Dalrymple, Rawdon, 241, 278
Dalrymple, Ross, 278
Daschle, Tom, 325
Davidson, Lou and Ralph, 382, 394
Davis, Edith, 144, 424n61
Davis, LaShonda, 316
Davis, Loyal, 98, 144, 424n61
Dawson, Danni, 374–75, 377, 398–99
Day, Ada Mae "MO" (mother), 3, 6, 10,
        13–16, 18, 20, 24, 44–45, 54, 55,
        57, 66, 134, 203–4, 239, 293, 374,
        400
    Alzheimer's disease of, 152, 277
    death of, 277, 405
    SOC's suitors and, 33–35, 35n, 37
    SOC's swearing-in and, 152
    SOC's wedding to JOC and, 50
Day, Alan (brother), 3, 14, 20, 32, 54, 118,
        119, 203, 204, 248, 375
    as co-author of *Lazy B,* 24, 342
    Lazy B ranch and, 8, 10, 21, 66,
        277–78
    nephews and, 66
    on SOC's sense of destiny, 119
Day, Ann (sister), 3, 10, 20, 41, 54, 204,
        247–48
Day, Eleanor (aunt), 12

Day, Harry "DA" (father), 6, 7–16, 18, 24, 25, 32, 53–54, 66, 69, 95, 233, 370, 374
  character of, 7–9, 10, 11, 12, 14, 23, 24
  death of, 203–4
  JOC and, 41, 44–45, 48, 51, 184
  lassoing incident, 19–20, 415n48
  leasing of government land by, 12, 109
  relationship with SOC, 4, 6–10, 19–20, 24, 32, 40–41, 53–55, 57, 239
  SOC and flat tire story, 22–23, 23n
  SOC at Stanford and, 24, 25
  SOC's law school tuition and, 33
  on SOC's nomination, 134
  on SOC's run for Arizona judge, 104
  SOC's suitors and, 28–29, 34–35, 35n, 37
  SOC's swearing-in and, 152
Deahl, Josh, 396
death penalty, 122, 167, 171, 191, 230, 231, 294, 372–73, 427n92, 437n24
  "Kill Him, 4–4" (New York Times), 311
  SCOTUS "courtesy vote," 311–12
Deaver, Mike, 127, 130, 187
DeConcini, Dennis, 125, 423n11
DeGraw, Bette, 73, 84, 87, 89, 93, 97
DeGraw, Rick, 88, 89, 104
DeLay, Tom, 373
Delery, Stuart, 348–49
Dellinger, Walter, 112, 304, 388, 389
Democratic Party
  in Arizona, 60–61, 108, 109
  ERA and, 80
  judicial appointments and, 390
  presidential race, 2000, 325, 326
  "Solid South" and, 60
Denton, Jerry, 142–43
DiMarco, Diane, 162, 199, 242, 250
Dinh, Viet, 204, 294, 297
Dolan, Charlie, 393
Dole, Elizabeth, 161
Donaldson, Sam, 139
Dorf, Michael, 280
Douglas, Jean, 319, 320
Douglas, Les, 239
Douglas, William O., 153, 156–57, 163
Dowd, Maureen, 336

Draper, Bill, 186, 198
Driggs, Gail, 77, 116, 248–49, 309
Driggs, Gary, 110, 111–12, 116
Driggs, John, 110, 116, 248–49
Driver, Justin, 389, 396
Dunkelman, Brett, 129–30, 158–59
Dunnigan, Vaughn, 273–74, 296
Dupree, Maggie, 206, 270
DuVal, Fred, 114
Dwyer, John, 162

East, John, 137, 142
Eckstein, Paul, 62
Eichensehr, Kristen, 391
Eisenhower, Dwight D., 151, 183, 313
Elgarten, Cliff, 170
Eliot, Denise Dravo, 64–65
Ellijay, Ga., 92
Ellis, Mark, 288, 289, 338
El Paso, Tex., 5, 15–21, 24, 31
Ely, John Hart, 194
Emerson, Ralph Waldo, 155
Equal Rights Amendment (ERA), 79–82, 90, 94, 177, 231n
Estrada, Rafael "Rastus," 7, 21, 50
Estrich, Susan, 278
Evangelis, Theane, 369–70, 377

Fahey, Jane, 193, 401
Falwell, Jerry, 92, 136
Fannin, Paul, 60, 81, 110, 117
Farhadian, Tali, 370, 377
federalism, 315–16, 346, 382–83
  Davis case and, 316–17
Federalist Society, 255, 351, 378, 388, 437n19
Federal Judicial Center oral history, 102
Federal Sentencing Guidelines, 313
Feldman, Myer, 292, 309
Feminine Mystique (Friedan), 67, 80, 160
Fennemore Craig, 56, 57, 59, 80, 138
  first woman partner, 131, 133
  JOC at, 57, 67, 95, 131, 132
  women lawyers and, 66–67
Ferraro, Geraldine, 84, 268
Fielding, Fred, 125, 126, 130
Fink, Alan, 38

First National Bank of Arizona, 77
Folger, Julie, 66, 330
Fong, Ivan, 267, 270–71
Foreman, James, Jr., 275–77
Foreman, James, Sr., 275–76, 277
Fortas, Abe, 156
Fountainhead, The (film), 274
Fowler, Mary, 168, 188, 209
Francione, Gary, 190–91, 193, 194
Franke, Bill, 126
Frankfurt, Germany, 53–55
Frankfurter, Felix, 156, 265
Franklin, Barbara H., 78
Frantz, Carolyn, 344
Fried, Charles, 239
Friedan, Betty, 67, 80, 160
Friedersdorf, Max, 134, 137
Friedland, Michelle, 134, 343–44
Friendly, Henry, 217

Gallagher, Sean, 305
Garland, Lynn, 367–68
Garland, Merrick, 368
Gaston, Jeremy, 344
Gates, Bill, 306
gay rights, 179
    Bowers case, 354
    Lawrence case, 354–55
    SOC and, 354–55
Gee, James, 392, 400
Georgetown Law Center, 391
gerrymandering, 304–5, 347, 349
Gerster, Carolyn, 144
Gibson, Dunn & Crutcher, 124
    offers SOC a secretary job, 43, 125n,
        269
    SOC's speech at, 269–70
Gilbert, Cass, 150
Gilles, Steve, 212, 216, 221, 222
Gingrich, Newt, 259, 363
Ginsburg, Douglas, 238–39
Ginsburg, Ruth Bader, 82, 177, 182,
    284–87, *385*
    Bush v. Gore and, 327, 331, 332, 439n66
    Davis case and, 316
    Hogan case and, 182–83
    joins SCOTUS, xii, *283*
    judge on the D.C. Circuit, 182

judicial philosophy, 284
oral arguments and, 286
as SCOTUS liberal, 312
SOC and, xiv, 182, *283*, 284–87, 312,
    357, 372, 370, 378
United States v. Virginia and, 286–87
Giss, Harold, 85
Gohlson, Hunter, 178, 179
Goldberg, Arthur, 188–89
Goldwater, Barry, 59–60, 81, 98–99,
    125
    Reagan and, 125, 144
    SOC and, 59–60, 61, 81, 96, 108,
        110, 112, 117, 258, 258n, 362
    SOC's confirmation hearings and,
        140, 143, 149
    SOC's nomination and, 125, 132, 136,
        423n11
Goodman, Ellen, 267
Goodwin, Thomas, 73, 88–89, 94–95,
    96, 374
Gore, Al, 322, 323, 325, 326, 330, 333,
    439n11
Graham, Katharine, 185, 187, 207, 240,
    258
Grassley, Chuck, 142
Gray, Boyden, 271, 306
Green, Jordan, 68–69
Greenburg, Jan Crawford, 65, 284, 378
Greenhouse, Linda, 315, 343
Griffin, Lisa Kern, 295, 297
Griswold, Erwin, 117
Growden, Beth Harrelson, 30, 31
gun control, 231
Gutierrez, Alfredo, 73, 74, 75, 85, 87, 88,
    97, 401

Habicht, Hank, 123, 124, 136
Hakala, Leslie, 323, 429n13
Halaby, Najeeb, 337
Hall, Cynthia Holcomb, 374
Hamdi, Yaser, 364
Hamilton, Alexander, 231
Hamilton, Art, 85, 86, 89, 225, 420n46
Hamilton, John, 34–36, 35n, 416n23
Hamilton, Lee, 387
Hamilton, Marci, 266–67
Hand, Learned, 230–31, 340, 431n7

Hardt, Athia, 87
Harlan, John Marshall, 77, 210, 279
Harris, Katherine, 325–26, 331
Hart, Pearl, 72
Harvard Law School, 165n, 285
Hass, Pat, 371
Hassan II of Morocco, 183
Hauser, Richard, 139
Hayek, Friedrich, 37
Hays, Rory, 72, 79
Hazeltine, Sherman, 77
Helms, Cynthia, 158, 198, 202, 298n,
        306, 323, 324, 375, 376, 393, 400,
        401
Helms, Jesse, 134, 136–37, 144
Helms, Richard, 158, 200, 298n, 306
Henderson, Joe and Lucia, 367, 398–99
Henn, Emily, 351, 352, 355–56
Herstam, Chris, 97
Hidalgo, Eddie, 239
Hill, Anita, 273
Hishon, Elizabeth, 192
Ho, Allyson Newton, 351, 352, 356
Hoffstadt, Brian, 218, 295
Holman, Jim and Diana, 199–200, 201
Holmes, Oliver Wendell, Jr., 156, 165,
        222, 230
Hoopes, Ann, 185, 200, 291, 320, 337,
        439n6
Hoopes, Townsend "Tim," 185, 320, 337
Hoover, Herbert, 183
Hope, Judy, 114, 247, 292, 387
Hope, Tony, 292
Hopkins, Ann, 256, 433n5
Horwich, Ben, 382, 383–84
Houseworth, Dick, 59, 61, 62, 108, 118,
        321
Hubbard, Art, 84–85, 86, 89
Huck, Sue, 58, 386
Huffman, Robert, 217, 223
Hufstedler, Shirley, 117
Hull, Jane Dee, 322
Humphrey, Marshall, 110, 124
Hurwitz, Andy, 105, 114
Hyde, Henry, 134

iCivics, 393–94, 395, 400, 401
Ignatius, Nancy, 245–46, 247, 393

Ignatius, Paul, 245
"Indispensable Man, The" (poem), 377
Institute for the Advancement of the
        American Legal System, 391
Iraq Study Group, 387–88
Iron Springs, Ariz., 110, 131, 287, 342,
        403
Ivins, Molly, 346

Jackson, Jesse, 330
Jackson, Robert, 39, 42, 129
Jacquin, Bill, 83–84, 89, 93
Jasik, John, 397–98
Jefferson, Thomas, 30
Jeffries, John, 160
Jennings, Renz, 105–6, 112
Jiang Zemin, 398
Johnson, Lyndon Baines, 60, 156
Jones, Bill, 105
Jones, RonNell Anderson, 23, 24,
        341–42, 356, 360, 362–63, 365
Joondeph, Brad, 312, 318, 320
Jordan, Adalberto, 254, 256, 261
Joyce, Craig, 59, 325, 369, 437n24
Joyce, Flournoy (cousin), 19–20, 59, 369
Judicial Fellows Committee, 117
judicial minimalism, 341
Junior League of Phoenix, 61, 62, 63, 87
        SOC as president, 58, 62, 68, 71, 74,
        130

Kagan, Elena, 326–27n, *385*, 402–3
Kauffman, Don, 57, 62, 321, 386
Kauffman, Nancy, 185
Kay, Peter, 109
Kearse, Amalya, 123
Kelly, Kevin, 294
Kennedy, Anthony, 238, 263, 289n, 297,
        298, 315, 437n19
        affirmative action cases, 351
        Bush v. Gore and, 327, 328–29, 332, 337
        Casey case and, 279–80, 312, 317,
        328–29
        Catholicism of, 263, 280, 317, 388
        Citizens United case and, 391
        "courtesy vote" and, 312
        Davis case and, 316–17

Kennedy, Anthony (cont'd)
    Lawrence case and, 354–55
    Roe v. Wade and, 262
    Roper case and, 372–73
    SOC and, 312, 316–17, 324, 377–78,
        437n19
Kennedy, Cornelia, 123, 148
Kennedy, Edward "Ted," 137, 299, 397
Kennedy, John F., 154, 220, 239, 295,
    346, 376
Kennerly, David Hume, 139, 140
Kenyon, Bill, 139
Keynes, John Maynard, 32
King, Billie Jean, 187, 397
King, Steve, 373
Kirk, Alan, 310
Klein, Joan, 123n
Klein, Josh, 377
Knight, Richard, 38, 39, 416n23
Kolbe, John, 96, 118
Kolbert, Kathryn, 279
Koory, Fred, 74
Korean War, 52
Kourlis, Becky, 391, 400, 401
Kret, David, 83, 84–85, 87
Kruglick, Burt, 110
Kuhl, Carolyn, 138, 141–42
Kunasek, Carl, 201

Lake Owen, Wis., 242, 265
Lake Pleasant, Ariz., 309
Lake Powell, Ariz., 101, 116, 125
Landers, Ann, xiv
Lane, Charles, 380
LaSota, Jack, 106, 113
"Last Plantation, The" (Totenberg), 153
Laws, Beatrice "Beatsie" Challis, 35, 41,
    44, 45–46, 49, 58, 241
    on Rehnquist, 37–38, 158
    on SOC, 35–38, 39, 416n23
Laxalt, Paul, 241
Lazarus, Edward, 255, 263–64, 318
Lazy B (O'Connor and Day), 4–6,
    20–21, 24, 31, 66, 342–43, 348,
    383
Lazy B ranch, Ariz., 4–5, 14, 21, 23n,
    203–4, 342, 376
    Headquarters, 5, 19, 66, 278

rain and drought, 9–10, 11, 29
ranch hands, 6, 8–9, 14, 20–21, 50
Round Mountain, 4, 155, 203, 405
sale of, 277–78
SOC and, xi, xvi, 3, 4–12, 14–15,
    19–23, 23n, 33, 278, 333, 342–43,
    376, 405
SOC and flat tire story, 22–23, 23n,
    334
SOC's bobcat and other pets,
    5–6, 5n
SOC's boyfriends at, 28–29, 37
SOC's lessons from, 7, 22–23
SOC's parenting style and, 65
SOC's wedding, 47, 50
Leahy, Bill, 328, 361
Leahy, Patrick, 140, 300
Lee, Rex, 102, 193, 194
Leffall, LaSalle, 320–21
Legally Blonde (film), 362
legal profession, xii
    SOC mentoring women in, 112–13,
        133, 134, 176–77, 204–9
    SOC not hired by law firms, 25, 43,
        57–58, 66, 362
    SOC's dislike of lawyer advertising,
        297
    women in, growth in numbers, 176
    women judges, 78, 106, 117, 176
    women not hired by law firms, xii,
        66–67, 192, 285
Lehrer, Jim, 199
Leibovitz, Annie, 388
Letterman, David, 270
Levine, Noah, 313, 321, 323
Lewinsky, Monica, 322–23
Lewkovitz, Jerry, 70
Lidsky, Isaac, 429n13
Lincoln, Abraham, 170
Linowitz, Sol, 198
Lippman, Marc, 245, 246–47, 251
Locking Up Our Own (Foreman), 277
Long, Long Trailer, The (film), 302
Lord, Peggy, 196, 375, 387, 395
Lordsburg, N.M., 15, 20, 21
Los Angeles Times, 318
Lott, Trent, 325
Lubin, Stanley, 80–81
Lund, Nelson, 242

Machu Picchu, Peru, 400
Macomber, John, 291
Madison, James, 325
Maguire, Alan, 88–89
"Majority of One, A" (Rosen), 340
Malani, Anup, 344
Mandil, Daniel, 254, 264
marijuana laws, 438n28
Marriott, Bill, 249
Marshall, Cissy, 240
Marshall, John, 152, 154, 165, 356
Marshall, Thurgood, 161–62, 179, 190,
        195, 202, 216n, 225–26, 226n,
        236, 257, 276, 312, 362, 402
    affirmative action cases and, 226, 347
    Brown v. Board of Education and, 162, 225
    Croson case and, 260
    Hogan case and, 179, 182
    Metro Broadcasting case and, 303
    Rehnquist and, 167–68
    retirement, 273, 275, 275n
    SOC and, 225–26, 347
    swearing-in ceremony, 150
Mason, Blanche, 58
Matas, Raquel, 293
Matthews-Johnson, Tamarra, 329
McAward, Jennifer Mason, 346
McBride, Andrew, 254–56, 259–64
McCain, John, 258n
McCain-Feingold law, 357–58
McCall, Harry, Jr., 268–69
McCarthy, Diane, 82, 94, 96
McConnell, Robert "Bob," 110–11, 124,
        136, 138, 142, 143, 423n5
McCullough, David, 324
McGregor, Ruth, 23, 67, 113, 131, 133, 138,
        154, 155, 162, 180, 182, 198, 321,
        341, 400
McGrory, Mary, 141, 336
Meacham, John, 420n68, 432n48
Mecham, Evan, 111, 111n
media
    Bush v. Gore and, 329–30, 336
    comments on SOC's appearance, xiv
    Ginsburg and, 284
    SOC and fame, 206–7, 240
    SOC and reporters, 198–99, 315,
        340–41
    SOC's breast cancer and, 248

SOC's confirmation hearing and, xi,
        141, 142
    SOC's nomination and, 133, 139–40
    SOC's retirement and, 378
Meese, Edwin, 120, 126, 130, 217, 219,
        235, 387
Merritt, Deborah, 153, 162, 164, 172, 181,
        182
Metzenbaum, Howard, 137
Meyer, Cord, 239–40
Meyer, Linda, 267
Miers, Harriet, 381
Mikva, Mary, 162, 169
Miller & Chevalier, 184–85, 217, 222–23,
        240, 244, 248, 288
Mitford, Jessica, 276
Mohammed of Morocco, 183
Mondale, Walter, 144, 268
Moore, Powell, 137
Moore, Tab, 311
Moral Majority, 92, 134, 136
Motley, Eric, 133–34, 354, 381
Moyer, Homer, 184–85, 240, 288
Moyers, Bill, 97n
Munger, Charles, 125
Myers, Joan, 184

Nalen, Skip and Kim, 200, 308–9
Nardini, Bill, 218
National Coalition for Cancer
        Survivorship, 250, 394n
National Constitution Center, 341
National Organization for Women, 67
National Review, 60
National Right to Life Committee, 134
Neary, Linda, 306, 340, 344, 369
Nelson, Justin, 351, 352–53, 356, 363–64
NewsHour (TV show), 199, 324, 347, 363
Newsweek, SOC cover, 262, 263
New York Times, 297, 347
    Bush v. Gore and, 336
    FWOTSC and, 202
    Greenhouse Effect, 315
    "Kill Him, 4–4," 311
    review of *Lazy B,* 343
    Rosen cover story on SOC, 340
Nickles, Don, 134
Nine, The (Toobin), 317, 328

9/11 terrorist attacks, 343–44, 363–64
Nitze, Paul, 239
Nix-Hines, Crystal, 275n
Nixon, Richard, 69, 78, 99, 108, 183
    judicial appointments, 75–76, 76n,
        149, 167, 313
North, Oliver, 241
Notre Dame Law School, 148

Obama, Barack, 134, 205, 209, 397
O'Brien, Tim, 248
O'Connor, Brian (son), 58, 63–66, 95,
    140, 183, 248, 309, 322, 325, 329,
    330, 333, 339, 357, 367
O'Connor, Courtney (granddaughter),
    266
O'Connor, Heather (daughter-in-law),
    398
O'Connor, Jay (father-in-law), 49
O'Connor, Jay (son), 63–66, 91, 95, 132,
    140, 183–84, 203, 248, 322, 387
O'Connor, Joanie (daughter-in-law),
    263, 266, 270, 368, 386–87
O'Connor, John (JOC), 46n, 335
    alcohol and, 309, 311, 319
    Alibi Club and, 238, 238n, 305–6
    Alzheimer's and, 306, 309–11, 311n,
        319–24, 344–45, 352, 356,
        366–70, 375, 377, 381, 382, 384n,
        386–87, 394–95, 394n, 443n14
    appearance, 39
    background and family, 39–41, 49
    Bohemian Club and, 183–84, 185n,
        238, 265, 275, 290, 310, 320, 367,
        368
    on the Bork nomination, 235, 235n
    Brennan and, 211
    character and personality, 39–41, 61,
        62, 87, 118, 184, 186, 239, 240,
        305–6, 310, 320, 321
    costumes and amateur theatricals,
        117, 142, 319
    courtship and wedding to SOC,
        39–46, 57, 416n23
    dancing and, 40, 55, 61–62, 143, 175,
        186, 356
    death of, 396–97
    death of Harry Day and, 203–4

earnings and lifestyle, 95
fly-fishing and, 308–9
in Judge Advocate General's
    Corps, 52
Kennedy and, 238, 239
law career, 55–57, 59, 67, 80, 114, 132,
    152, 184–85, 240–41, 244, 310,
    333
lobbying for SOC, 113–14, 126–27,
    137
marriage of, 41, 55, 62, 64, 65–66, 73,
    111, 112, 118, 129, 175, 184, 186,
    320, 344–45, 356, 366–70, 375,
    377, 378, 381, 382, 386
memoir by, 39, 310, 342
Moroccan trip, 183
mother of, 46, 48–49, 57
Paradise Valley home, 58–59, 61,
    86–87, 95, 109–10
in Phoenix, Ariz., 56–70
Phoenix society and networking by,
    57, 58, 59, 61, 110, 115, 126
posting to Frankfurt, Germany,
    53–55
Powell and, 233–34, 265
presidential race, 2000, and, 322
Rehnquist's confirmation and, 75–76
Republican politics and, 59, 75–76,
    82, 108
retirement and, 323–24
Riggins and "Sandy Baby," 207
Scalia and, 236–38, 265, 300
sightseeing with SOC at SCOTUS
    building, 1952, 52–53
SOC and conflict of interest, 222–23
SOC as justice and, 153, 154, 157n,
    184–85, 187n, 189, 195–96,
    198–99, 201–2, 216–17, 216n,
    255
SOC considered for Arizona
    gubernatorial race and, 109–11,
    112
SOC's breast cancer and, 242–52
SOC's fame and, 240–41, 258
SOC's intellect and, 40, 41, 292
SOC's nomination and confirmation,
    127–29, 131–32, 134, 140, 422n3
SOC's parents and, 44–45, 48, 51
on SOC's shopping, 293

SOC's speeches and, 76, 270
Souter and, 272
at Stanford Law School, 39–40
Thomas and, 273, 275
travel with SOC, Argentina, 289n
Turkey cruise, 386
Waltz Group, 186
Washington diary, 239
Washington social life, *175,* 184–88,
    185n, 200, 238, 238n, 239–40,
    247, 258–59, 262, 323, 330
wedding and honeymoon, *47,* 48–52
women's rights and, 67
O'Connor, Sally (mother-in-law), 46,
    48–49, 51, 57
O'Connor, Sandra Day (SOC)
    Alfalfa Club president, 396–97
    ambition of, 19, 24, 31, 43, 63, 67–70,
        81, 97, 99, 109–11, 115, 129, 202,
        217
    Anglo-American Legal Exchange
        and, 117, 125–26, 128
    appearance, xi–xii, 18, *25,* 27–28, 39,
        68, 73, 79, 86, 115, 118–19, 141,
        251, 262, 293–94, 375, *406*
    Arizona gubernatorial race
        considered by, 109–11
    as Arizona state senator, xiii–xiv,
        69–70, 69n, *71,* 72–99, 97n
    "attractive" and "unattractive"
        categories for, 102, 117, 127, 298,
        305, 333, 363, 379
    awards and honors, 388, 397
    bar exams passed, 49–50, 56, 57
    birth of, 5
    board seats, 62, 65, 77, 79, 114–15,
        119, 199, 259, 289, 324, 341, 368
    bossiness, 14, 40, 62, 200, 275,
        290–91, 306, 341, 355–56, 362,
        369–70, 395
    Botswana safari, 398
    boyfriends and suitors, 25, 28–29,
        31–39, 416n23
    Bush family and, 258, 259–60, 264,
        272, 322, 339n, 363, 384, 384n,
        432n48
    character of, xiii, xvi, 28, 61–63,
        87, 93, 97, 111, 139–40, 164,
        200–201, 206, 239, 246, 247,
        254, 291–92, 296, 321, 329, 334,
        341, 365, 398–99
    at Chautauqua, N.Y., 392–93
    childhood, *xi, 3,* 4–24
    civic duty and, xv–xvi, 31, 53, 68, 69,
        111–12, 290, 390
    civics education and iCivics, 392–94,
        395, 400, 401, 403
    competitiveness, 14, 38, 112,
        199–200, 204, 254, 263, 265, 271
    constitutional law and, 36, 44, 139,
        164
    cooking by, 63, 128, 133, 139, 163, 200,
        249, 254, 345, 370
    courtship and wedding to JOC,
        39–46, 57
    dancing and, 28, 40, 55, 61–62, 143,
        160, *175,* 262, 356
    dignified image of, 151, 164, 206, 241,
        242, 296, 404
    earnings and lifestyle, 69n, 95, 199
    entertaining by, xiii–xiv, 61, 65,
        86–87, 118, 129, 223, 239, 338
    fame of, 240–41, 258, 289, 390
    father and, 4, 6–7, 8–10, 19–20, 24,
        32, 34–35, 40–41, 54–55, 57, 239
    father's death and, 203–4
    fiscal conservatism of, 95–96
    fly-fishing and, 308–9, 338, 371, 379,
        389, 399
    frugality of, xiv, 65
    funeral instructions by, 405
    in Germany (1952–56), 53–55
    Goldwater and, 59–60, 81, 98–99,
        108, 110, 112, 117, 125, 136, 140,
        258, 258n, 362, 423n11
    golf, tennis, bridge, and, 160,
        195–96, 199–200, 204, 205, 220,
        242, 243, 258, 264, 265, 266, 292,
        298n, 300, 305–6, 308, 320, 337,
        361, 363, 376, 424n57 (*see also*
        fly-fishing; skiing *below*)
    grandchildren, *227,* 266, 270
    grandmother Wilkey and, 16–20,
        35, 68
    as hardworking, inflexible, 74–75, 88,
        89–90, 105
    health of, 241–42, 324
    health of: Alzheimer's, xvi, 399–402

O'Connor, Sandra Day (SOC) (cont'd)
    health of: breast cancer, 227, 242–52,
        254, 262, 266, 270, 294, 432n44
    health of: hysterectomy, 124, 125
    horses and riding, xi, 6, 19, 20–21, 58
    household help, 64
    intellect of, xii, xiii, xiv, 36, 38, 40, 41,
        43, 129, 138, 160–61, 189
    Iraq Study Group and, 387–88
    Iron Springs camp and, 110, 131, 287,
        342, 403
    JOC's Alzheimer's and, 309, 319–24,
        344–45, 352, 356, 366–70, 375,
        377, 378, 381, 382, 386–87,
        394–95, 394n, 443n14
    JOC's death and, 396–97
    JOC's mother and, 46, 48–49
    as judge, Arizona, xiv, 102–19, 338
    on Judicial Fellows Committee, 117
    judicial philosophy, 127, 130, 140, 181,
        192, 210, 217, 222, 300–301, 304,
        313–17, 318, 332, 340, 341, 383,
        388, 391, 431n7, 437n19, 438n28
    judicial temperament, 104–5,
        118–19, 128, 195, 198–99, 267,
        340–41
    as Junior League president, 58, 61, 62,
        68, 71, 74, 130
    law balanced with the real world by,
        52, 68–69, 93, 192, 213, 222, 313,
        316, 331–32, 331n, 346, 382
    as lawyer, Arizona, 52, 57, 58, 68–69,
        418n36
    Lazy B and, xi, xvi, 3, 4–12, 14–15,
        19–23, 23n, 33, 278, 333, 342–43,
        376, 405
    legacy of, 374–75, 389, 402
    love of costumes and amateur
        theatricals, 117, 142, 201–2, 319
    love of history, 324–25
    love of the outdoors and nature, xvi,
        4–12, 30, 155, 207–8, 287–88
    at Machu Picchu, 400
    in male-dominated worlds, xiii, 21,
        38, 40, 98, 115, 283
    marriage of, 41, 55, 62, 64, 65–66, 73,
        111, 112, 118, 129, 175, 184, 186,
        320, 344–45, 356, 366–70, 375,
        377, 378, 381, 382, 386

    media and, xi, xiv, 57, 133, 139–40,
        198–99, 206–7, 315, 340–41, 378
    as mentor for women, 104n, 112–13,
        133, 134, 176–77, 204–5, 345–46,
        402
    Moroccan trip, 183
    as Most Powerful Woman in
        America, 187, 240, 241, 244, 341
    MPU (Mobile Party Unit, women's
        traveling group), 290–94, 375,
        387 (see also specific people)
    9/11 terrorist attacks and, 343–44,
        363–64
    Nixon and, 99
    parenting by, 63–66, 270
    philosophy of life, 18, 30, 384, 403–5
    in Phoenix, Ariz., 56–70, 337, 381,
        402
    poem read in speeches of, xv, 404
    as political moderate, xv, 60, 83, 98,
        363
    political skills of, xiii–xiv, xvi, 75,
        80–81, 82, 85–86, 92–94, 111,
        125, 137, 211, 332, 390, 396
    pregnancies of, 55, 57, 58
    Presidential Medal of Freedom, 397
    public speaking fears, 38, 104,
        250–51
    racial minorities and, 84–85,
        224–26, 347–48 (see also
        affirmative action)
    reaction to conflict, insults, protests,
        and provocations, xii, xiv–xv, 14,
        42–43, 71, 73–74, 74n, 83, 87–89,
        93, 172, 374, 403
    reading as pastime, 6, 11
    Reagan and, xiv, 95, 98, 99, 121,
        130–33, 143–45, 151, 152, 170n,
        186–87, 362, 404, 423n5
    Rehnquist in personal life of, 38–39,
        41–43, 42n, 45, 61, 75–77, 116,
        123–24, 125, 126, 129–30, 151, 301,
        305–6, 359, 371–72, 378, 379–80
        (see also U.S. Supreme Court)
    religion and, 30, 51, 83, 215, 248–49,
        432n44
    Republican Party and, 59–61, 68, 69,
        99, 108–11, 117, 124, 198, 258,
        259–60, 268, 322, 363

residence, Paradise Valley, Ariz., 58–59, 61, 86–87, 95, 109–10, 127, 390

residence, Phoenix, 381

residences, Washington and Chevy Chase, 162, 184–85, 199, 223, 246, 254, 290, 292, 338, 369–70, 381–82

retirement, 386–405

as role model, 86, 133–34, 202, 245, 342, 405

role models for, 17–18

schooling, El Paso and Lordsburg, 3, 15–21, 24, 31

as SCOTUS justice (see U.S. Supreme Court)

self-reliance, *xi,* xvi, 155, 206, 333, 342, 344

sense of destiny, 119, 202

sense of humor, 41, 73, 118, 186, 202, 251, 256, 269, 301, 306, 329, 363, 396–97, 398

sexism, gender discrimination, and, xii, xiii, 25, 33–34, 43–44, 53, 57–58, 66–67, 79, 129–30, 157–58, 257, 269, 362

as shopper, 293

shyness, 18–19, 27–28, 39, 62, 246

sightseeing at SCOTUS building, 52–53

skiing and, xvi, 55, 95, 199–200, 201, 294, 308, 309, 321, 324

social life, Phoenix, 58, 59, 61, 110, 115–16, 118, 337

social life, Washington, 161, *175,* 185–88, 238n, 247, 249–50, 258–59, 262, 270, 291–92, 315, 323, 330, 337, 338, 363, 393

sons of, 57, 58, 63–66, 64n, 68, 95, 104, 140, 203, 248, 266, 276, 357, 368, 397, 405

speaking style and voice of, 17, 27, 36, 40, 41, 75, 118, 141, 178, 219, 229, 279, 298

speeches by, 23, 72, 76, 78, 81, 118, 176–77, 250–52, 267–69, 287, 308, 337–38, 362–63, 384, 386, 390, 395, 400

at Stanford University and Law School, xii, 24, 25, 26–34, 36–44, 114–15

"state of the judiciary" conferences at Georgetown and, 391–92

as stay-at-home mom, 58

storytelling to teach a message, 23, 362

as tough, steely-eyed, xiii, 5, 21, 62, 73–74, 86, 88, 96, 112, 205–6, 254, 255, 274, 329, 399

travel and spreading the rule of law, 287–90, 289n, 343, 395, 397–98

Turkey cruise, 386

twitch of, 88, 142

volunteerism of, 53–54, 58, 62, 65, 248, 292

Waltz Group, 102, 186

wedding and honeymoon, 47, 48–52

women's rights and, xii, xv, 31, 78–82, 90–91, 94–95, 177–83, 192, 267–69, 286–87, 290, 362, 404

work-family life balance and, 176–77, 208–9, 266, 295, 355–56, 370

—SCOTUS cases

Adarand Constructors, Inc. v. Peña, 303–4, 348

Allegheny County v. ACLU, 215n, 312

Apprendi v. New Jersey, 313

Atwater v. Lago Vista, 346

Ayotte v. Planned Parenthood of Northern New England, 383–84

Bowers v. Hardwick, 354

Bush v. Gore, 326–34, 331n, 336, 337–39, 439n6, 439n11

City of Akron v. Akron Center for Reproductive Health, Inc., 192–95, 222, 264

City of Richmond v. J. A. Croson Company, 259–61, 276, 303

Clements v. Fashing, 169–70, 169–70n

Elk Grove Unified School District v. Newdow, 360–61

Engle v. Isaac, 170, 171

FERC v. Mississippi, 171–72

Ford Motor Company v. Equal Employment Opportunity Commission, 172

Garcia v. San Antonio Metropolitan Transit Authority, 210–11

—SCOTUS cases (cont'd)
  Gonzalez v. Raich, 438n28
  Gratz v. Bollinger and Grutter v. Bollinger,
    261, 348–54, 361
  Hamdi v. Rumsfeld, 364–66
  Hishon v. King & Spalding, 192
  Hodgson v. Minnesota, 266–67
  Kelo v. City of New London, 376
  Lawrence v. Texas, 354–55
  Lynch v. Donnelly, 215, 215n
  Maryland v. Craig, 267
  McConnell v. Federal Election Commission,
    357–58
  Mississippi University for Women v. Hogan,
    177–83, 287, 351, 428n11
  Planned Parenthood of Southeastern
    Pennsylvania v. Casey, 278–81, 287,
    312, 317, 435n79
  Plyler v. Doe, 168
  Price Waterhouse v. Hopkins, 256–57
  Roper v. Simmons, 372–73
  Shaw v. Reno, 305, 349
  Stenberg v. Carhart, 317–18
  Texas v. Johnson, 256, 433n4
  Thornburgh v. American College of
    Obstetricians & Gynecologists, 221, 264
  Troxel v. Granville, 438n28
  United States v. Virginia, 286–87
  Vacco v. Quill, 318
  Wallace v. Jaffree, 213–14, 217
  Webster v. Reproductive Health Services,
    261–64, 278, 433n17
  Wiggins v. Smith, 361–62, 441n3
  Wright v. West, 274
  Wygant v. Jackson Board of Education,
    229–33
  See also U.S. Supreme Court, Sandra
    Day O'Connor as justice
O'Connor, Scott (son), 57, 58, 63–66,
  64n, 68, 76, 95, 109, 110, 111, 118,
  248, 270, 304, 322
  first child of, 263, 266
  JOC's Alzheimer's and, 368, 386–87,
    394
  SOC's Alzheimer's and, 400–401
  SOC's confirmation hearings and,
    140, 143, 145
Odegaard, Shirley, 80, 81
Olmsted, Frederick Law, 26

Olson, Theodore, 439n66
Onassis, Jacqueline Kennedy, 292
Osberg, Sharon, 306
O'Sullivan, Julie, 206, 212, 295–96

Paepke, Owen, 375
Panetta, Leon, 387
Panikowski, Stan, 329–30
Paradise Valley, Ariz., 59, 59n, 80, 83,
  119, 376
  Country Club, 59, 63, 85, 98, 238n,
    337
  O'Connors' home, 58–59, 86–87
Peanuts comic strip, 219
Pelican Brief, The (film), 285
Peña, Lito, 87
People, 20, 145, 207
Pepys, Mary Noel, 288, 289
Percy, Charles, 115, 368–69
Percy, Lorraine, 368–69
Perry, David, 104
Perry, Mark, 297
Perry, William, 387
Phoenix, Ariz., 47, 56
  Adams Hotel, 74
  African Americans in, 85
  Democrats in, 61
  gender discrimination and, 67
  household help, 64
  Huger Mercy Living Center, 386–87,
    394
  JOC and local politics, 59, 60, 75–76
  O'Connors' clubs, 238n, 337
  O'Connors move to, 56–57
  O'Connors' social circle and, 58, 59,
    61, 110, 115–16, 118, 144
  Reagan's in-laws and, 98, 144,
    424n61
  Rehnquist in, 56
  Republicans in, 61
  Sandra Day O'Connor United States
    Courthouse, 406
  SOC and GOP in, 60, 63
  SOC and Heard Museum of Native
    Arts and Culture, 62, 65, 259
  SOC and JOC in the news, 57
  SOC as Junior League president, 58,
    61, 62, 68, 71, 74, 130

SOC retires to, 381, 402
SOC's law practice, 58, 418n36
SOC's volunteerism, 58, 62, 65
tech companies in, 56
Trunk 'n Tusk dinner, Reagan at, 95, 130
Valley Field Riding and Polo Club, 58, 238n, 337
Valley Leadership group, 118
Phoenix Gazette, 96
Phoenix magazine, 73
Plato, 156
"Portia's Progress" (SOC), 267–68
Posner, Richard, 326–27n, 337
Powell, Colin, 352
Powell, Lewis, 77, 133, 148n, 159–61, 167, 238, 238n, 243, 248, 378, 426n45
  Bakke case and, 228–29, 347, 349, 353
  "balancing tests," 388
  on Blackmun, 190
  Bowers case and, 354
  Brennan and, 171
  on Burger, 149
  "courtesy vote," 311
  Garcia case and, 210, 211
  Hogan case and, 179, 181–82, 428n11
  retirement, 233–34, 235
  Scalia and, 236
  school desegregation and, 160
  SOC and, xiv, 158, 159–60, 173–74, 182, 189–90, 195, 202, 216–17, 229–34, 265, 298, 324
  Wygant case and, 229–33
Powell, Lewis, III, 133
Pulliam, Eugene, 61

Quayle, Dan, 61
Quinn, Bug, 8, 22
Quinn, Sally, 198–99

Radford School for Girls, 17–18, 24, 41, 54–55
Rand, Ayn, 274
Rasmussen, Irene Lyons, 80, 94
Rathbun, Harry, 30–31, 33, 68
Reagan, Nancy, 127, 185, 424n61

Reagan, Ronald, 95, 96, 98, 120, 122, 127, 144, 183, 186, 259, 381
  abortion issue, 122, 130–31, 148, 193
  Arizona sources for, 144
  Bork nomination, 234, 235
  decision to appoint a woman Supreme Court justice, 120, 122, 123, 143, 144
  fiscal conservatism of, 95
  Goldwater and, 125, 144
  judicial appointments, 217, 234–35, 239
  "Morning in America" campaign, 290
  New Right and, 135–36
  Reagan Revolution, 122, 137, 170n, 209, 234
  SOC and, xiv, 95, 98, 99, 151, 152, 186–87, 362, 404
  SOC's nomination and, 121, 125, 127, 130–33, 143–45, 423n5
Reed, Thomas C., 99
Rehnquist, Nan Cornell, 45, 61, 305
Rehnquist, William, 36, 37, 129, 158, 198, 216n
  affirmative action and, 226, 260, 353
  Akron case and, 194
  Brennan and, 218
  Bush v. Gore and, 327, 328, 332
  cancer of, 370–72, 375–76, 378, 379, 380
  Casey case and, 279
  character of, 37, 217–18, 430n46
  as chief justice, 217–19, 237, 260, 285, 327, 370–72, 375–76, 379, 381
  clerking for Jackson, 39, 42, 129, 167
  Davis case and, 316
  death of, 359, 379–80
  Garcia case and, 210
  Ginsburg and, 285–86
  Gratz case and, 353
  Hamdi case and, 366
  health problems, 158, 426n40
  Hogan case, 179
  JOC and, 157n
  judicial philosophy, 167, 217, 316
  as "the Lone Ranger," 167
  Marshall and, 167–68
  in Phoenix, Ariz., 56, 61

Rehnquist, William (cont'd)
    politics of and influence of Hayek, 37
    Roe v. Wade and, 221, 235n
    school prayer and, 213
    SCOTUS nomination and
      confirmation, 75–76, 76n
    SCOTUS swearing-in, 77, 116
    SOC and JOC lobbying for, 76–77
    SOC as friend, 45, 56, 61, 75, 151, 301,
      305–6
    SOC as justice, 158–59, 168,
      169–70n, 189, 195, 254, 346,
      370–72, 378
    SOC as love interest, 37–38, 41–43,
      42n, 45, 218, 416n23
    SOC's nomination and, 123–24, 125,
      126
    at Stanford Law School, 36–37, 38
    Texas v. Johnson and, 433n4
    United States v. Virginia and, 286
    Webster case, 264
    wife, Nan Cornell, 45, 305
    Wygant case and, 229
religious freedom, xv, 388
    Engel case, 92
    Lynch case, 215, 215n
    SOC's "reindeer rule," 215n, 312
    Wallace case, 213–15
    See also school prayer
Renfrew, Barbara, 241, 293, 371–72
Renfrew, Charles, 128, 184, 241, 371–72,
    377, 378
Reno, Janet, 84
Republican Party, 61
    in Arizona, 60, 61, 74, 74n, 95, 98,
      108–11
    Christian Right and, 83, 92, 111, 135,
      136, 213
    Eisenhower Republicans, 60
    ERA and, 80
    George H. W. Bush presidency,
      258–59
    Goldwater conservatives, 83
    ideological shift of, 363
    JOC and, 60, 82
    judicial elections and, 390
    Phoenix GOP headquarters, 60
    presidential race (2000), 322, 325,
      326

Reagan and, 95, 99, 120, 136
SOC and, 59–60, 63, 68, 69, 83, 117,
    124, 198, 240–41, 258, 268, 322,
    363
Rhodes, John, 111, 124
Richardson, H. H., 26
Ride, Sally, xii
Riggins, John, 207
right-to-die issue, 318, 373
Riley, William, 113
Rivera, Geraldo, 330
Road to Serfdom, The (Hayek), 37
Roberts, John, 138, 378, 381, 384n, 388,
    402
Robinson, Jackie, 403
Rockefeller, John D. "Jay," IV, 115
Rockefeller, Sharon Percy, 114–15, 368
Rodriguez, Cristina, 351, 352, 356
Roe v. Wade, 91–92, 231
    Blackmun and, 145, 148, 149, 190,
      193, 194, 223–24, 262, 433n17
    justices voting against, 221
    opponents of, 91n, 92, 93, 134, 195,
      261, 266, 278, 290, 389
    Reagan and, 148
    SCOTUS revisiting, 192–95,
      261–64, 278–81
    SOC and, 128, 131, 136, 149, 196, 222,
      264
Romano, Lois, 188
Romilly, Constancia, 276
Roosevelt, Eleanor, 17–18
Roosevelt, Franklin Delano, 8, 11–12,
    165–66
Roosevelt, Selwa "Lucky," 381
Roosevelt, Theodore, 395
Rose, Jonathan, 123, 125, 127–29
Rosen, Jeffrey, 340–41, 342
Roth, Philip, 26
Roussel, Peter, 132–33
Rudd, Eldon, 110
Rwanda, 288

Sandra Day O'Connor Education Act,
    393
Sankar, Sam, 360–61
San Mateo County DA's office, 52, 57
Saul, Frank, 184, 198, 320, 338

Savage, Steve, 66
Sawin, Martica Ruhm, 28, 30
Scalia, Antonin "Nino," 235–38, 259,
    274, 285, 298, *335*, 388–89
  abortion cases and, 317
  Adarand case and, 304
  affirmative action cases and, 226, 259,
    260, 304, 361
  Alibi Club and, 306
  Bush v. Gore and, 327, 328, 332, 337,
    439n66
  Catholicism of, 236, 262, 263, 388
  Cheney and, 362
  considered for chief justice, 380–81
  Craig case and, 267
  Croson case and, 260, 261
  Davis case and, 316
  defense of the Fourth Amendment,
    313
  Ginsburg and, 299–300
  Grutter case and, 361
  Hamdi case and, 365
  Hodgson case and, 266–67
  incivility and personal attacks by,
    280, 299–300, 301, 315, 362, 403
  JOC and, 236–38, 265, 300
  judicial philosophy, 255, 300–301,
    304, 365
  Kennedy voting with, 280
  oral arguments and, 286
  Powell and, 236
  Roe v. Wade and, 235n, 262
  on the rule of law, 388
  SOC and, 235–38, 250, 265–67, 299,
    361–62, 378, 403
  Webster case and, 264
  Wiggins case and, 361–62
Scalia, Maureen, 240, 300, 328, 380
Schiavo, Terry, 373
Schlafly, Phyllis, 83, 131
Schmults, Ed, 130
Schneider, Phil, 310, 321
school desegregation, 153, 160, 303
  Brown v. Board of Education, 162, 231
  busing of schoolchildren, 122, 142
  Plessy v. Ferguson, 167, 228
  Warren Court and, 166
school prayer, 92
  Engel case, 212–13, 217

Schroeder, Mary, 66–67, 113, 114, 138
Schwab, Norma, 208
Schwab, Stewart, 191, 192, 208
Second Stage, The (Friedan), 160
Selin, Ivan and Nina, 236, 309
Setear, John, 207
Sharp, Susie Marshall, 123n
Shepard, Tazewell, 376
Silberman, Laurence, 315, 337, 439n66
Silverman, Barry, 106
Simmons, Patty, 58, 62
Simon, James, 91n, 97, 129, 131, 265
Simpson, Alan, 143, 310, 387–88, 396
Skelly, Tom, 93
Slaughter, Anne-Marie, 399
Smalley, Kathy, 208, 393, 401
Smith, Jean, 130
Smith, William French, *121*, 122–24,
    123n, 127, 128, 217, 269, 422n3
  SOC and, 124–25, 128, 130
  SOC's supporters and, 125
Sotomayor, Sonia, *385*, 402
Souter, David, 271–73, 312, 391–92
  Bush v. Gore and, 327, 332
  Casey case and, 279
  Davis case and, 316
  SOC and, 271–73, 279–80
Spencer, Stuart, 120
Spitzer, Marc, 82, 88
Srinivasan, Sri, 205
Stanford, Leland, 26
Stanford Alumni Association, 104n
Stanford University, 12, 26–27
  Branner Hall, 27–28, 31
  jobs for women graduates and, 33–34
  Regulations for Women Students, 27
  SOC at, *25,* 26–34
  SOC influenced by Rathburn, 30–31,
    33, 68
  SOC influenced by Stegner, 31
  SOC influenced by Western Civ,
    29–30, 289
  SOC on board of trustees, 114–15,
    368
  SOC's boyfriends at, 28–29, 31–32
  SOC's friends at, 26, 27, 28, 30, 31,
    55, 109, 119 (*see also* Cooley, Diane
    Porter; Laws, Beatrice "Beatsie"
    Challis)

Stanford University (cont'd)
    SOC's provisional acceptance, 24,
        415n60
    SOC's sons at, 109, 132, 140
    women undergraduates at, 27
    WW II veterans at, 26–27
Stanford University Law School, 36, 117
    Cubberly House, 38, 109
    gender barriers for women graduates,
        43–44
    gender discrimination at, 36
    Rehnquist at, 36–38
    SOC and constitutional law, 36, 44,
        139
    SOC at, xii, 34–44, 36n
    SOC in moot court competition, 38
    SOC in Order of the Coif, 43
    SOC's boyfriends and, 34–39, 35n
    SOC's test scores for admittance, 33
    special accelerated program at, 33
    tuition, 33
    women at, 35
Starr, Ken, 122, 127
    interviewing SOC, 125, 127–29, 136
    SOC's nomination and, 123, 124,
        422n3
    SOC's record on abortion and,
        127–28
Steel, Simon, 304, 305
Stegner, Wallace, 31, 342, 343
Steiger, Sam, 111, 112
Stern, Robert, 311n
Stevens, John Paul, xiii, 148, 161, 190,
        286, 312, 371
    Bush v. Gore and, 327–28, 332, 339,
        439n66
    Casey case and, 279
    Davis case and, 316
    Grutter case and, 353
    Hamdi case and, 365
    Hogan case and, 179–80
    Kelo case and, 375–76
    Metro Broadcasting case and, 303
    SOC and, 158, 202, 213–14, 353, 378,
        380
    on SOC and Scalia, 315
Stewart, Potter, 122, 123n, 124, 127, 148,
        149, 157, 162, 185n
    on obscenity, famous line, 153, 305

Stewart, Thomas, 200
Stoessel, Mary Ann, 323
Stone, Harlan, 212n
Stowe, Matt, 295
Strikis, Silvija, 293–94, 295
Stromseth, Jane, 254, 262, 263
Suggs, Sarah, 294
Sullivan, Brendan, 241
Sullivan, Kathleen, 278
Sumner, Molly Powell, 133, 159, 160
Sunstein, Cass, 318, 341, 440n47
Sununu, John, 271
Sun Valley, Idaho, 308–9
Supreme People's Court of China, 374
Symington, James, 200, 310
Symms, Steve, 134
Syverud, Kent, 205–6, 213, 257, 347–48,
        349–50, 353

Taft, William Howard, 326–27n
Taft, William Howard, III, 239
Taylor, Abby, 392, 393
Taylor, Ash, 244
Taylor, Betsy, 62–63, 184, 368, 387
Taylor, Susan, 63, 368
Tempe, Ariz., "O'Connor House," 390
Thatcher, Denis, 240
Thatcher, Margaret, 117, 240, 404n
Thomas, Clarence, 297, 301, 326, 335,
        388, 425n33
    affirmative action cases and, 226
    Bush v. Gore and, 327, 328, 332
    confirmation hearing and Anita Hill
        controversy, 273
    Davis case and, 316
    Hamdi case and, 365
    judicial philosophy, 274
    SOC and, 274–75, 301–2
Thomas, Ginni, 301–2
Thurmond, Nancy, 137, 141
Thurmond, Strom, 137, 139, 140, 142–43,
        149
Timberlake, Beverly, 18–19
Time, 74n, 139
    SOC on the cover, xi
Todd, Jim, 214, 389, 400
Toobin, Jeffrey, 317, 328
Totenberg, Nina, 153

Trammel, Jeff, 355
Truman, Harry, 156
Tutu, Desmond, 397

"Underneath Their Robes" (blog), 377
University of Michigan and University
    of Michigan Law School, 347–48,
    440n35
    affirmative action cases, 348–54, 361
USA Today, SOC as "go-to" justice, 318
U.S. Congress
    ERA and, 79
    partisan attack on the judiciary,
        372–73
U.S. Constitution, 403–4
    ERA and, 79–82, 177, 231n
    Fifteenth Amendment, 79–80
    First Amendment, 92, 212–13, 256,
        391
    Fourteenth Amendment (due
        process and equal protection
        clauses), 79–80, 81, 165–66, 168,
        170, 177, 179, 181, 194, 210,
        225–26, 262, 332, 336, 346, 354,
        426n68, 427n69, 428n11
    Fourth Amendment, 313
    Harlan's "Constitution is color
        blind," 228, 260
    as moral document, 223
    Nineteenth Amendment, 80
    "original intent" and originalism, 255,
        255n, 365
    right to privacy and, 279
    Sixth Amendment, 267, 361
    SOC's copy of, 403
    states' rights and, 316, 346
    supremacy clause, 93
    "textualism," 255
U.S. Court of Appeals
    D.C. Circuit, 182, 315
    Fourth Circuit, 5n, 205, 404
    Ninth Circuit, 117
    Second Circuit, 123
    Supreme Court justices chosen from,
        326–27n
U.S. Senate
    Bork confirmation and, 238
    Kennedy, Ted, and SOC, 137

large egos and eccentricities in, 139
opponents of SOC's confirmation,
    134–37, 144
Rehnquist confirmation and, 78
SOC's confirmation, final vote, 143,
    143n
SOC's confirmation hearings,
    137–45
U.S. Supreme Court
    abortion cases, xv, 190, 192–95,
        221–24, 230, 261–64, 266–67,
        317–18, 388, 389, 433n17
    affirmative action cases, xv, 224, 226,
        228–33, 259–61, 277, 302, 303,
        388, 389, 440n47
    Alito joins the bench, 384
    "balancing tests," 388–89
    basketball court, 147, 162–63
    bench memos, 163, 193, 266, 352
    black workers at, 153, 275
    Breyer joins the bench, 298
    building (the Marble Palace),
        150–51, 152–53, 155, 389, 404–5
    Burger as chief justice, 116–17, 122,
        125–26, 132, 151, 153, 162, 216–17,
        216n, 218, 221n, 303
    camaraderie often lacking, 155–56,
        157, 188, 195, 299, 301, 378
    campaign spending cases, 389,
        390–91
    cases per year, 139, 154, 218
    conferences, weekly, 149, 149n, 151,
        154, 155, 156, 157, 157, 164, 168, 173,
        179, 188, 190, 194, 201–2, 209,
        218, 225, 226n, 229, 236, 237, 257,
        258n, 259, 279–80, 285, 286, 298,
        299, 326, 327, 347, 353, 357
    conservatives on, 125, 149, 169, 217,
        226, 229, 235, 255, 257, 274, 278,
        312, 327, 328, 332, 337, 370–71,
        380, 388, 389, 391
    death penalty cases, 122, 167, 171, 191,
        230, 231, 294, 311–12, 372–73,
        427n92, 437n24
    FDR's "court packing" attempt, 166
    federalism cases, 316–17, 346,
        382–83
    flag-burning case, 256, 433n4
    formal courtroom, 151

U.S. Supreme Court (cont'd)
  gerrymandering cases, 304–5, 347,
    349
  Ginsburg joins the bench, xii, *283*
  habeas corpus doctrine and prisoner
    appeals, 170–71, 191, 206,
    365–66
  "I am not at rest" phrase, 232
  ideological drift on, 313–17, 327, 346,
    351, 389, 437n24
  judicial activism and, 122, 125, 140,
    168, 170–71, 181, 210, 211, 315
  judicial restraint and, 127, 165, 181,
    192, 315, 340
  June rush, 319
  junior justice, duties of, 154–55, 164,
    205, 236–37
  justices at State of the Union
    addresses, xiv
  Kennedy joins the bench, 238, 239
  law clerks, 148, 157, 160, 161–62, 163,
    191–92, 194, 204, 205, 211, 216,
    228, 237, 257, 296, 324, 378,
    437n19 (*see also specific clerks*)
  law clerks, African American,
    275–77
  law clerks, the Cabal, 255, 256, 264
  law clerks' networks, 296
  "level of scrutiny" question, 178–79,
    180–81, 260, 303, 348, 428n7,
    440n39
  liberals on, 125, 167, 213, 217, 220,
    226, 229, 256, 257, 278, 312, 327,
    332, 337, 380
  lunch at, xiii, 157, 274–75, 301, 402
  making vs. interpreting law, 165–67,
    165n
  marijuana laws and, 438n28
  Marshall as chief justice, 152, 154, 165,
    356
  moderate pragmatists on, xvi, 160,
    222, 230, 281, 290, 304, 327
  "Mr. Justice" changed to "Justice,"
    148, 148n
  oral arguments, 157, 163–64, 178, 179,
    366
  personal feuds on, 156–57, 167–68,
    265

  as a political institution, 166,
    198–99, 230, 313, 326n, 326–34,
    427n69, 439n6
  Powell appointment, 77
  public reaction to a woman justice,
    xii, 159, 187n
  racial discrimination cases, 257, 303,
    346
  Reagan's decision to appoint a
    woman justice, 120, 122, 123,
    123n, 143, 144
  Rehnquist appointment, 75–77, 167
  Rehnquist as chief justice, 217–19,
    237, 260, 285, 327, 370–72,
    375–76, 379, 381
  Rehnquist as "the Lone Ranger," 167
  Rehnquist clerking for Jackson, 39,
    42, 167
  religious freedom cases, xv, 92,
    213–15, 215n, 388
  "Rights Revolution," 166–67
  right-to-die cases, 318, 373
  rituals of chambers, 209
  Roberts as chief justice, 381, 389,
    402
  Scalia joins the bench, 235–38
  school prayer cases, 92, 212–14, 217
  sex discrimination cases, 177–83, 192,
    256–57, 286, 428n11
  Souter joins the bench, 271–73
  Spouses' Dining Room, 240
  stare decisis principle, 280
  strict constructionists on, 167, 211,
    255
  swearing-in ceremonies, 151–52
  term of 1988–89, 254–55, 264
  terrorist scares at, 364–65
  Thomas joins the bench, 273–75
  the Troika, 279–80
  use of footnotes by, 211–12, 212n
  Vinson as chief justice, 156
  Warren as chief justice (and Warren
    Court), 122, 125, 134, 153, 154, 166,
    168, 170, 209, 234, 271, 326–27n,
    346
  women's bathroom for, 284
  writs of certiorari, 153–54, 155,
    191–92, 311

—cases
 Adarand Constructors, Inc. v. Peña, 303–4, 348
 Allegheny County v. ACLU, 215n, 312
 Apprendi v. New Jersey, 313
 Atwater v. Lago Vista, 346
 Ayotte v. Planned Parenthood of Northern New England, 383–84
 Baker v. Carr, 74n
 Bowers v. Hardwick, 354
 Brown v. Board of Education, 162, 225, 231, 303
 Bush v. Gore, 326–34, 331n, 336–40, 391, 439n6, 439n11, 439n66
 Citizens United v. Federal Election Commission, 391
 City of Akron v. Akron Center for Reproductive Health, Inc., 192–95, 222, 264
 City of Richmond v. J. A. Croson Company, 259–61, 276, 303
 Clements v. Fashing, 169–70, 169–70n
 Craig v. Boren, 177, 180
 Davis v. Monroe County Board of Education, 316–17
 Dred Scott v. Sandford, 262
 Elk Grove Unified School District v. Newdow, 360–61
 Engel v. Vitale, 92, 212–13
 Engle v. Isaac, 170, 171
 Fay v. Noia, 170
 FERC v. Mississippi, 171–72
 Ford Motor Company v. Equal Employment Opportunity Commission, 172
 Fullilove v. Klutznick, 232
 Garcia v. San Antonio Metropolitan Transit Authority, 210–11
 Gonzalez v. Raich, 438n28
 Gratz v. Bollinger and Grutter v. Bollinger, 261, 348–54
 Hamdi v. Rumsfeld, 364–66
 Hishon v. King & Spalding, 192
 Hodgson v. Minnesota, 266–67
 Kelo v. City of New London, 375–76
 Korematsu v. United States, 364
 Lawrence v. Texas, 354–55
 Lynch v. Donnelly, 215, 215n
 Marbury v. Madison, 165

 Maryland v. Craig, 267
 McConnell v. Federal Election Commission, 357–58
 Metro Broadcasting, Inc. v. Federal Communications Commission, 303
 Mississippi University for Women v. Hogan, 177–83, 287, 351, 428n11
 National League of Cities v. Usery, 211
 Planned Parenthood of Southeastern Pennsylvania v. Casey, 278–81, 312, 317, 435n79
 Plessy v. Ferguson, 167, 228
 Plyler v. Doe, 168
 Price Waterhouse v. Hopkins, 256–57
 Regents of the University of California v. Bakke, 228–29, 347, 349, 351, 353
 Roe v. Wade, 91–92, 128, 136, 145, 148, 149, 222, 223–24, 231
 Roper v. Simmons, 372–73
 Shaw v. Reno, 305, 349
 Stenberg v. Carhart, 317–18
 Texas v. Johnson, 256, 433n4
 Thornburgh v. American College of Obstetricians & Gynecologists, 221, 264
 Troxel v. Granville, 438n28
 United States v. Carolene Products Co., 212n
 United States v. Virginia, 286–87
 Vacco v. Quill, 318
 Wallace v. Jaffree, 213–14, 217
 Webster v. Reproductive Health Services, 261–64, 266, 278, 433n17
 Wiggins v. Smith, 361–62, 441n3
 Wright v. West, 274
 Wygant v. Jackson Board of Education, 229–33
—Sandra Day O' Connor as justice, xiii, 283, 385, 426n45
 abortion cases and (see abortion; specific cases)
 affirmative action cases, xv, 233, 259–61, 346–54
 Alito and, 388–89
 amicus curiae briefs and, 352
 balancing dueling imperatives, 226
 Blackmun and, xiii, 148–50, 171–73, 188–90, 195, 207, 229, 256, 257, 427n92

—Sandra Day O' Connor as justice
    (*cont'd*)
    Brennan and, 169–71, 173, 173n, 190,
        195, 209, 211–12
    Breyer and, 298–99, *307,* 312–13, 324
    Burger and, *101,* 115–16, 117, 125–26,
        157–58, 190, 195, 214–16,
        425–26n36
    chambers for, as retired judge, 387
    "consequentialism" of, 383
    "conservative reflex" of, 168
    considered for chief justice, 216–17,
        366
    "constitutional avoidance" and,
        210–11
    as controlling vote, xv, xvi, 169–70,
        180, 262, 318–19, 341–42,
        350–51, 388
    "courtesy vote" and, 312
    death penalty and, 171, 206
    decision-making by, 191, 206, 312,
        313, 330–31, 334, 337, 340, 341–42,
        346, 351, 357–58, 382–84, 402
    establishment clause and, 214, 215
    evolving positions of, 313–17, 346,
        351, 437n24
    exercise class, *147,* 162–63, 208, 220,
        250, 284, 309, 355, 402
    first case, xiii
    first term, 148–73, 215–16
    Fourteenth Amendment and,
        165–66
    as FWOTSC, 198–226, 341, *385,* 403,
        404–5
    Ginsburg and, xiv, 182, *283,* 284–87,
        378
    Kennedy and, 280, 312, 316–17, 324,
        378, 437n19
    last case, 382–83
    law clerks, xii, xiv, xv, 17, 23, 67, 102,
        113, 133, 138, *147,* 162–64, 169n,
        172, 180–82, 186, 190–96, 201,
        204–10, 212–16, 218–20, 230,
        237, 239, 249, *253,* 287, 290, 291,
        369–70, 377, 437n19 (*see also*
        specific clerks)
    law clerks, African American,
        275–77, 275n
    law clerks, as protective of, 206, 341

    law clerks, "field trips" for, xvi,
        207–8, 270–71, 344, 370, 377
    law clerks, flat tire story and, 23
    law clerks, hiring of, 315, 315n, 324,
        351, 360, 429n13
    law clerks, influence of, 254–56,
        259–64, 315, 348–50, 360–61
    law clerks, mentoring of, 345–46,
        355–56, 360, 370
    law clerks, 9/11 and, 343–44
    law clerks, SOC's expectations of,
        294–96, 309, 321, 329, 357–58,
        360
    as legal pragmatist, 222, 281, 290,
        304, 337, 341, 363, 366, 382, 388,
        403, 404, 437n19
    legal scholarship and, 209–10
    Marshall and, 195, 202, 225–26, 347
    "Maybe in error but never in doubt"
        pillow, 340, 341–42
    on need for a woman justice, 77–78
    nomination and confirmation, xi–xii,
        121, 122–46, 149–50, 362, 422n3,
        423n5, 423n11, 424n43
    number of years on the court, xv
    office of, 153, 159, *253,* 402
    oral arguments and, 178, 180, 186,
        243, 250, 256, 263, 285, 286, 297,
        298, 366, 379
    political skills and assembling
        majorities, 297, 298, 303, 341
    Powell and, 159–61, 173–74, 182,
        189–90, 195, 202, 216–17,
        229–34, 265, 349, 426n45,
        427n92
    preparing for position, 138–39, 163
    pressures on, 191, 404–5
    private journal, 130, 155, 158, 171, 172,
        173, 182, 207, 211, 214, 219,
        235–36
    "the reindeer rule," 215n, 312
    Rehnquist and, 158–59, 168,
        169–70n, 189, 195, 198, 218–19,
        254, 301, 346, 370–72, 378–80,
        426n40
    replacement for, 378–79, 381, 382,
        384
    retirement, 323–24, 333, 339, 371–72,
        375, 376–84, 384n, 387, 388

robe, xiv, 152, *283*, 293
as "rudder of the Court," 365–66,
    372, 389–90
Scalia and, 235–38, 250, 265–67, 299,
    300, *335*, 361–62, 378, 403
second term, 176–96
"senior status" and "riding the
    circuit," 395–96
sensitivity to women and children,
    267–68, 281, 346
Souter and, 271–73, 279–80
Stevens and, 158, 202, 213–14, 353,
    378, 380
swearing-in ceremony, 130, 150–52
as "the swing vote," 308, 383
Thomas and, 274–75, 301–2, *335*
threats against, 373–74
White and, 154–55, 160, 179, 219–21
writing style, 280

Valenti, Jack, 198
Valtasaari, Jukka, 200
van Rensselaer, Nina, 27, 119
Vaughan, Sam, 342
Verrilli, Donald, 209, 366
Vinson, Fred, 156
Voting Rights Act, 347

Wallis, Frank, 394
Waltz Group, 102
Warren, Earl, 122, 125, 134, 153, 154, 163,
    166, 168, 326–27n
    "But is it fair?" question, 346
Washington, D.C.
    Alfalfa Club, 396–97
    Alibi Club, 238, 238n, 305–6
    Corcoran Gallery Ball, 188
    DeCarlo's restaurant, 393
    Gridiron Dinner, xiv
    Irish Times bar, 211
    Metropolitan Club, 238n, 239–40
    Milt Kronheim's, 169
    O'Connors as social stars, 185–88,
        238–39
    O'Connors' club memberships, 238n
    O'Connors' condo, 184–85, 199, 223
    Sulgrave Club, 238n, 247

University Club, 238n, 244
Wolf Trap Ball, 143
Washington, George, 325
Washington and Lee University, 243
Washingtonian magazine, 199
Washington Post, The, 157, 185, 229, 245,
    336, 380
    "Justice on the Party Circuit," 188
    SOC and, 131, 134, 141, 161
Washington Press Club, "Salute to
    Congress," 187
Watkinson, Jim, 40
Webster, Lynda, 271–72, 294, 308, 399
Webster, William, 222, 271–72
Weeks, Marcia, 90
West, Donna Carlson, 88
Western Savings and Loan, 110
West Virginia, 390–91
White, Byron, 154–55, 179, 190, 202,
    238, 269
    Akron case and, 194
    Hogan case and, 179
    Metro Broadcasting case and, 303
    Price Waterhouse case and, 257
    Roe v. Wade and, 221, 235n
    SOC and, 154–55, 160, 179, 219–21
    Texas v. Johnson and, 433n4
    Thornburgh case and, 221, 222
    Wygant case and, 229
White, Patricia, 285, 392, 395
"Why I Miss Sandra Day O'Connor"
    (Rosen), 340–41
Wiley, John, 160, 182
Wilkey, Evelyn, 19, 400
Wilkey, Mamie (grandmother), 3, 13, 17,
    18, 34, 35, 68, 215, 306
    SOC living with, 16–20
Wilkey, W. W., 17
Wilkinson, J. Harvie, III, 5n, 205, 404
Willey, Keven, 93–94
Williams, Jack, 103–4
Wilmer, Cutler & Pickering, 348–49
Wilson, Gayle, 62, 186
Wilson, Pete, 62, 186
Wisdom, John Minor, 210
women
    Arizona's laws and, 78–79, 94–95
    average age at marriage, 1950, 34
    "Bra Burner" and, 79

women (cont'd)
  double standards and, xiv, 73
  ERA and, 79–82
  "firsts" in government, 84
  frontier women, 72
  gender barriers and, xii, 25, 43–44,
      257, 269, 285
  income inequality and, 44, 53
  as judges, number of, 78
  lack of professional jobs for, 33–34,
      43, 57–58, 66–67, 269
  as lawyers, xii, 176
  SCOTUS and, xii, 159
  as SCOTUS law clerks, 148, 160,
      204
  Second Wave Feminism and, 67
  sex discrimination cases, 177–83,
      192
  SOC and women's rights, xii, xv, 31,
      78–82, 177–83, 192, 267–69,
      286–87, 290, 362, 404
  SOC as role model, 86, 133–34, 202,
      245, 342
  SOC as the Most Powerful Woman
      in America, 187, 240, 241, 244
  as SOC's law clerks, xiv, xv, 23,
      204–9, 210, 220, 254, 266–67,
      273–74, 275, 275n, 329, 343–44,
      346, 351, 355–56, 369–70
  SOC's mentoring of, 104n, 112–13,
      133, 134, 176–77, 204–9, 345–46
  submissive vs. smart, 40, 62
  women's movement, 79, 82, 119, 120
"Women in Power" (SOC), 269
Woodhouse, Barbara, 208–9, 214,
      215–16
Woodward, Bob, 157, 187
Woodward, Shirley, 204–5, 312, 321
Wray, Gay Firestone, 60–61, 63
Wynn, Bernie, 84

Yale Law School, 122, 165n, 273, 275, 276

Zoellner, Tom, 59n

About the Author

———

EVAN THOMAS is the author of nine books: *The Wise Men* (with Walter Isaacson), *The Man to See, The Very Best Men, Robert Kennedy, John Paul Jones, Sea of Thunder, The War Lovers, Ike's Bluff,* and *Being Nixon. John Paul Jones* and *Sea of Thunder* were *New York Times* bestsellers. Thomas was a writer, correspondent, and editor for thirty-three years at *Time* and *Newsweek,* including ten years (1986–96) as Washington bureau chief at *Newsweek,* where, at the time of his retirement in 2010, he was editor at large. He wrote more than one hundred cover stories and in 1999 won a National Magazine Award. He wrote *Newsweek*'s fifty-thousand-word election specials in 1996, 2000, 2004 (winner for *Newsweek* of a National Magazine Award), and 2008. He has appeared on many TV and radio talk shows, including *Meet the Press* and *The Colbert Report,* and was a guest on PBS's *Charlie Rose* more than forty times. The author of dozens of book reviews for *The New York Times* and *The Washington Post,* Thomas has taught writing and journalism at Harvard and at Princeton, where, from 2007 to 2014, he was Ferris Professor of Journalism.

About the Type

This book was set in Requiem, a typeface designed by the Hoefler Type Foundry. It is a modern typeface inspired by inscriptional capitals in Ludovico Vicentino degli Arrighi's 1523 writing manual, *Il modo de temperare le penne*. An original lowercase, a set of figures, and an italic in the chancery style that Arrighi (fl. 1522) helped popularize were created to make this adaptation of a classical design into a complete font family.